PERL

IN A NUTSHELL

D1306158

PERL

IN A NUTSHELL

Second Edition

Nathan Patwardhan, Ellen Siever,
and Stephen Spainhour

O'REILLY®

Beijing • Cambridge • Farnham • Köln • Paris • Sebastopol • Taipei • Tokyo

Perl in a Nutshell, Second Edition

by Nathan Patwardhan, Ellen Siever, and Stephen Spainhour

Published by O'Reilly & Associates, Inc., 1005 Gravenstein Highway North,
Sebastopol, CA 95472.

O'Reilly & Associates books may be purchased for educational, business, or sales
promotional use. Online editions are also available for most titles (*safari.oreilly.com*). For
more information contact our corporate/institutional sales department: 800-998-9938 or
corporate@oreilly.com.

Editor:	Linda Mui
Production Editor:	Matt Hutchinson
Cover Designer:	Edie Freedman
Interior Designer:	Melanie Wang

Printing History:

January 1999:	First Edition.
June 2002:	Second Edition.

Library of Congress Cataloging-in-Publication Data

Siever, Ellen.
    Perl in a nutshell: a desktop quick reference/Nathan Patwardhan, Ellen Siever, and
      Stephen Spainhour.-- 2nd ed.
      p. cm. -- (In a nutshell)
    ISBN 0-596-00241-6
    1. Perl (Computer program language). I. Patwardhan, Nate. II. Spainhour, Stephen. III.
      Title. IV. Nutshell handbook.
QA76.73.P22 S554 2002
005.13'3--dc21
                                             2002068428

[M]   [9/02]

Table of Contents

Part IV. CGI

Part IX. Perl/Tk

Part X. Win32

Preface

Perl is a programming language that is *useful*. By this, we mean that people don't learn Perl just because they think they should, they learn Perl because they want to get something done.

This book is for Perl programmers who need to get things done. It's for readers who have dabbled a little in Perl and want a single reference for all their needs. This book is part reference, part guide to the world of Perl. We cover the language itself, but also the Perl modules that are most popular—modules for CGI, database manipulation, XML processing, network programming, graphical interfaces, and Win32 integration.

In this second edition of the book, we added several new chapters, included some topics that we neglected in the first edition and new technologies that have emerged, and updated the material to Perl 5.8.

How This Book Is Organized

This book has 10 parts, as follows:

Part I, *Getting Started*
> Chapter 1, *Introduction to Perl*, gets you oriented to Perl and the Perl community.
>
> Chapter 2, *Installing Perl*, gives you some pointers on installing Perl and its modules on your machine. This chapter introduces you to the CPAN archive and discusses using the CPAN module to retrieve the latest versions of Perl modules.

Part II, *Language Basics*
> Chapter 3, *The Perl Executable*, is about using the *perl* program itself. It covers environment variables, command-line options, and the differences in executing the Unix and Win32 versions of Perl.

Chapter 4, *The Perl Language,* is the turbo-charged tutorial/reference to the Perl language. If you've never programmed before, then you might need a tutorial that goes more slowly. But if you have some experience with other programming languages, this chapter should teach you enough to start writing Perl programs.

Chapter 5, *Function Reference,* is a reference chapter for each of the built-in functions of Perl.

Chapter 6, *Debugging,* is about using the Perl debugger to help locate the rare errors in your programs.

Part III, *Modules*

Chapter 7, *Packages, Modules, and Objects,* gives a quick introduction to Perl packages, Perl modules, and object-oriented programming in Perl.

Chapter 8, *Standard Modules,* is a reference to each of the modules included in the standard Perl distribution.

Part IV, *CGI*

Chapter 9, *CGI Overview,* is a brief introduction to the concepts behind CGI programming.

Chapter 10, *The CGI.pm Module,* covers the very popular CGI.pm module, which is deemed essential by many CGI programmers.

Chapter 11, *Web Server Programming with mod_perl,* is about *mod_perl,* the Apache module that can be used to significantly improve CGI performance and allows you to embed Perl code into the Apache server itself.

Part V, *Databases*

Chapter 12, *Databases and Perl,* gives a brief introduction to DBM databases in Perl and provides a reference to DBI, the Database Independence package that gives you a consistent interface to many different database packages.

Part VI, *XML and SOAP*

Chapter 13, *XML and Perl,* covers the modules for XML processing with Perl.

Chapter 14, *SOAP,* gives an introduction to SOAP and web services in general, and to the SOAP::Lite module for SOAP programming with Perl.

Part VII, *Network Programming*

Chapter 15, *Sockets,* explains socket programming and how to use the IO:Socket module.

Chapter 16, *Email Connectivity,* covers the Net::SMTP and Net::POP3 modules for sending and reading email, and the Mail modules for manipulating email messages.

Chapter 17, *Usenet News,* explains the NNTP protocol and the Net::NNTP module for reading and posting Usenet news, and the News::Newsrc module for managing *.newsrc* files.

Chapter 18, *FTP,* explains the FTP protocol, the Net::FTP module for transferring files by FTP, and the Net::Netrc module for managing *.netrc* files.

Chapter 19, *Lightweight Directory Access with Net::LDAP*, covers the Net::LDAP module for using LDAP directory services within Perl applications.

Part VIII, *LWP*

Chapter 20, *The LWP Library*, covers the most commonly used parts of the huge LWP library of modules for HTTP transactions.

Part IX, *Perl/Tk*

Chapter 21, *Perl/Tk*, is a reference to the Tk extension to Perl, which creates graphical user interfaces from within a Perl program.

Part X, *Win32*

Chapter 22, *Win32 Modules and Extensions*, talks about the many Perl modules for working with the Win32 operating systems.

Chapter 23, *OLE Automation*, covers the Win32::OLE modules for OLE automation.

Chapter 24, *ODBC Extension for Win32*, covers the Win32::ODBC module.

Conventions in This Book

Italics

Used for filenames, program names, URLs, command-line options, email addresses, and to introduce new terms.

`Constant Width`

Used for code snippets, method and function names, text that should be typed literally, variables, constants, mail headers, and configuration directives.

`Constant Width Italic`

Used for replaceable items in code examples and syntax lines.

This icon indicates a note relating to the nearby text.

This icon indicates a warning relating to the nearby text.

How to Contact Us

We have tested and verified the information in this book to the best of our ability, but you may find that features have changed (or even that we have made mistakes!). Please let us know about any errors you find, as well as your suggestions for future editions, by writing to:

O'Reilly & Associates, Inc.
1005 Gravenstein Highway North

Sebastopol, CA 95472
(800) 998-9938 (in the United States or Canada)
(707) 829-0515 (international or local)
(707) 829-0104 (fax)

There is a web page for this book, which lists errata, examples, and any additional information. You can access this page at:

   http://www.oreilly.com/catalog/perlnut2/

To ask technical questions or comment on the book, send email to:

   bookquestions@oreilly.com

For more information about books, conferences, Resource Centers, and the O'Reilly Network, see the O'Reilly web site at:

   http://www.oreilly.com

Acknowledgments for the First Edition

Many thanks to everyone who helped out on this book. Thanks to Larry Wall, Randal Schwartz, Tom Christiansen, and Sriram Srinivasan for their excellent books on Perl. Some material in this book is adapted from theirs; for that, we are very grateful.

Thanks also to all the reviewers of this book, who include Randal Schwartz, Tom Christiansen, Graham Barr, Clinton Wong, and Erik Olson. Without their help, this book wouldn't be nearly as helpful as it is.

We'd like to thank Linda Mui, our editor, and Val Quercia, who kept us on track, for all their support.

Acknowledgments for the Second Edition

The second edition of this book was managed solely by Nathan Patwardhan. Thanks, Nate, for finishing this book under a difficult schedule and not complaining *too* much about being forced to edit files in the write-only format we call Docbook.

We'd also like to thank the technical reviewers for this edition: Jon Orwant, Brian Jepson, Sean Burke, David Blank-Edelman, Jason McIntosh, and Brand Hilton, all of whom gleefully agreed to review chapters of this book with little time and without much reward! Thanks to each of you for your help.

Finally, Nathan would like to thank the following people for their support: the Patwardhan, Kiebzak, and Powers families; Tabor Wells and Kendall Libby for making system administration more fun than a barrel of monkeys; Christopher Smith for the hilarious conversations and interest in working with tech pubs; David "Ira" Schwartz, Ph.D. for his significant contribution to my learning of C and Unix way back when; Julie Wasserman for introducing me to the metrics of customer satisfaction; and to the late Frank Willison for making a truly significant contribution to my life.

Getting Started

Introduction to Perl

Computer languages differ not so much in what they make possible, but in what they make easy. Perl is designed to make the easy jobs easy, without making the hard jobs impossible. Perl makes it easy to manipulate numbers, text, files, directories, computers, networks, and programs. It also makes it easy to develop, modify, and debug your own programs portably, on any modern operating system.

Perl is especially popular with systems programmers and web developers, but it also appeals to a much broader audience. Originally designed for text processing, it has grown into a sophisticated, general-purpose programming language with a rich software development environment complete with debuggers, profilers, cross-referencers, compilers, interpreters, libraries, syntax-directed editors, and all the rest of the trappings of a "real" programming language.

There are many reasons for Perl's success. For starters, Perl is freely available and freely redistributable. But that's not enough to explain the Perl phenomenon, since many other freeware packages fail to thrive. Perl is not just free; it's also fun. People feel like they can be creative in Perl, because they have freedom of expression.

Perl is both a very simple language and a very rich language. It's a simple language in that the types and structures are simple to use and understand, and it borrows heavily from other languages you may already be familiar with. You don't have to know everything there is to know about Perl before you can write useful programs.

However, Perl is also a rich language, and there is much to learn about it. That's the price of making hard things possible. Although it will take some time for you to absorb all that Perl can do, somewhere down the line you will be glad that you have access to the extensive capabilities of Perl.

What's Perl Good For?

Perl has the advantage of being easy to learn if you just want to write simple scripts—thus its appeal to the ever-impatient system administrator and the deadline-driven CGI developer. However, as you become more ambitious, Perl lets you act on those ambitions. Chapter 2 covers how to get and install Perl, and Chapters 3 through 6 cover the basics of the Perl language, its functions, and how to use the Perl debugger.

On top of the Perl language itself, however, are the Perl modules. You can think of modules as add-ons to the Perl language that allow you to streamline tasks by providing a consistent API. Perl itself is fun to use, but the modules lend Perl even more flexibility and enormous power. Furthermore, anyone can write and distribute a Perl module. Some modules are deemed important enough or popular enough to be distributed with Perl itself, but very few are actually written by the core Perl developers themselves. Chapter 7 introduces you to Perl modules, and Chapter 8 covers the standard modules that are distributed with Perl itself.

The most popular Perl module is CGI.pm, which gives a simple interface to developing common gateway interface (CGI) applications in Perl. While Perl itself is indispensable for many different tasks, its text-manipulation features make it perfect for CGI development on the Web. In fact, the resurgence of Perl over the past few years must be credited to its popularity as a CGI language. Chapters 10 and 11 talk about using Perl for CGI, including *mod_perl*, which merges Perl into the Apache web server.

Database interconnectivity is one of the most important functions of any programming language today, and Perl is no exception. DBI is a suite of modules that provide a consistent database-independent interface for Perl. Chapter 12 covers both DBI and DBM (the more primitive but surprisingly effective database interface built directly into Perl).

The eXtensible Markup Language (XML) is quickly becoming the de facto way to store electronic information of any kind. Chapter 13 covers the modules designed for Perl and XML processing, and Chapter 14 covers using Perl for managing web services with the XML-based protocol SOAP.

The Internet doesn't start and stop at CGI. Network programming is another of Perl's strengths, with a robust sockets interface and several modules for writing clients and servers for all sorts of Internet services—not only the Web, but also email, news, FTP, LDAP, etc. Chapters 15 through 19 cover the modules for developing fully functional Internet applications in Perl.

The World Wide Web, of course, is the "killer app" of the Internet. LWP is a library of modules devoted to web programming. Chapter 20 covers the LWP library.

Perl programs are traditionally command line–based, but the Perl/Tk extension can provide Perl programs with graphical user interfaces, for both Unix and Microsoft Windows. Chapter 21 gives a complete reference to Perl/Tk.

Finally, although Perl is primarily developed for Unix, recent releases of Perl for Windows 95 and Windows NT are gaining popularity, both for CGI and system administration tasks. Chapters 21 through 24 cover the Win32 modules for Perl.

As you may have noticed, this section entitled "What's Perl Good For?" has sneakily become a description of the contents of this book. This book aims at being a general-purpose reference to all things Perl.

Perl Development

Software doesn't grow on trees. Perl is free because of the donated efforts of several generous people who have devoted large chunks of their spare time to the development, maintenance, and evangelism of Perl.

Perl itself was created by Larry Wall, in an effort to produce reports for a bug-reporting system. Larry designed a new scripting language for this purpose and then released it to the Internet, thinking that someone else might find it useful. In the spirit of freeware, other people suggested improvements and even ways to implement them, and Perl transformed from a cute scripting language into a robust programming language.

Today, Larry does little actual development himself, but helps to guide several other selfless individuals in the continued development and design of the language. Currently, a team of porters are working (with Larry's guidance) on a complete rewrite of the language from the ground up, which is expected to yield a 21st-century version of the language in form and features. This rewrite will be released as Perl Version 6. At the time of this writing, progress on Perl 6 is steady but still a long way from completion.

This second edition of *Perl in a Nutshell* covers Perl 5.8.

Which Platforms Support Perl?

While Perl was developed on Unix and is closely entwined with Unix culture, it also has a strong following on the Windows and Macintosh platforms. Perl gives Windows 95, Windows NT, Macintosh, and even VMS users the opportunity to take advantage of the scripting power that Unix users take for granted.

Most Unix machines will have Perl already installed, since it's one of the first things a Unix system administrator will build for a new machine (and is in fact distributed with the operating system on some versions of Unix, such as Linux and FreeBSD). For Windows NT, Windows 95, and Macintosh, there are binary distributions of Perl that you can download for free. See Chapter 2 for information on installing Perl.

Although there is some history of other platforms not being treated seriously by the Perl community, Perl is becoming increasingly friendly to non-Unix platforms. The Win32 ports of Perl are quite stable, and as of Perl 5.8, are integrated wholly with core Perl.

Perl Resources

Paradoxically, the way in which Perl helps you the most has almost nothing to do with Perl itself, and everything to do with the people who use Perl. While people start using Perl because they need it, they continue using Perl because they love it.

The result is that the Perl community is one of the most helpful in the world, with CPAN—the Comprehensive Perl Archive Network—as one example. When Perl programmers aren't writing their own programs, they spend their time helping others write theirs. They discuss common problems and help devise solutions. They develop utilities and modules for Perl and give them away to the world at large.

The comp.lang.perl.* Newsgroups

The central meeting place for Perl aficionados is Usenet. If you're not familiar with Usenet, it's a collection of special-interest groups (called *newsgroups*) on the Internet. For most anyone using a modern browser, Usenet access is as simple as a selecting a menu option on the browser. Perl programmers should consider subscribing to the following newsgroups:

comp.lang.perl.announce
> A moderated newsgroup with announcements about new utilities or products related to Perl

comp.lang.perl.misc
> The general-purpose newsgroup devoted to non–CGI-related Perl programming questions

comp.lang.perl.moderated
> A moderated newsgroup intended to be a forum for more controlled, restrained discussions about Perl

comp.lang.perl.modules
> A newsgroup devoted to using and developing Perl modules

comp.lang.perl.tk
> A newsgroup concentrating on Perl/Tk, the graphical extension to Perl

comp.infosystems.www.authoring.cgi
> A newsgroup for CGI questions in general, but mostly for Perl-related questions

At some point, it seems like every Perl programmer subscribes to *comp.lang.perl. misc*. You may eventually abandon it if the discussion becomes too detailed, too belligerent, or too bizarre for your taste. But you'll likely find yourself coming back from time to time, either to ask a question or just to check out the latest buzz.

One bit of advice, however: before posting questions to *comp.lang.perl.misc* (or any newsgroup, for that matter), you should read the group for a few days and read the FAQ (Frequently Asked Questions list—see the next section). The *comp. lang.perl.** newsgroups are a wonderful resource if you have an interesting or unusual question, but no one can save you if you ask something that's covered in the FAQ.

By the way, if you're a first-time poster to *comp.lang.perl.misc*, you shouldn't be surprised if you receive an email message listing various resources on Perl that you may not know about. This is done via an "auto-faq" service, which scans all postings and sends this helpful email to anyone who hasn't posted earlier.

Frequently Asked Questions Lists (FAQs)

A FAQ is a Frequently Asked Questions list, with answers. FAQs are traditionally associated with Usenet newsgroups, but the term has since been adopted by web sites, technical support departments, and even health care pamphlets. In general, FAQs are written and maintained on a volunteer basis by dedicated (and generous) members of the community. The Perl FAQ is maintained by Tom Christiansen and Nathan Torkington.

The Perl FAQ was created to minimize traffic on the *comp.lang.perl.misc* newsgroup when it became clear that the same questions were being asked over and over again. However, the FAQ has transcended into a general-purpose starting point for learning anything about Perl.

The FAQ is distributed in several different formats, including HTML, PostScript, and plain ASCII text. The main FAQ source is located at *http://www.perl.com/pub/q/FAQs/*. You can also find it at *http://perlfaq.cpan.org/*, and the latest version of the FAQ is posted on a semi-regular basis on *comp.lang.perl.misc*.

In addition to the general Perl FAQ, there are also several niche FAQs that are Perl-related. They are:

Perl CGI Programming FAQ
    http://www.perl.com/CPAN-local/doc/FAQs/cgi/perl-cgi-faq.html

Perl/Tk FAQ
    http://w4.lns.cornell.edu/~pvhp/ptk/ptkTOC.html

Perl for Win32 FAQ
    http://www.ActiveState.com/support/faqs/win32/

Perl for the Mac FAQ
    http://www.perl.com/CPAN/doc/FAQs/mac/MacPerlFAQ.html

By no means should you consider this to be an exhaustive list. Also check out appropriate mailing lists (see the next section); you'll find that many mailing lists also maintain their own FAQs.

Mailing Lists

Several mailing lists are focused on more specialized aspects of Perl. Like Usenet newsgroups, mailing lists are discussion groups, but the discussion takes place over email. In general, mailing lists aren't as convenient as newsgroups, since a few hundred mail messages a day about Perl can become intrusive to any but the most obsessive Perl hackers. However, because mailing lists tend to have much smaller and more focused distributions, you'll find that they can sometimes be much more interesting and helpful than newsgroups.

There are tons of mailing lists for Perl users and developers alike. Some are specific to a particular module or distribution, such as the mailing lists for users of CGI.pm, LWP, DBI, or *mod_perl*. Other mailing lists discuss using Perl on non-Unix platforms such as Windows, Macintosh or VMS. Still more mailing lists are devoted to the development and advocacy of Perl in general.

For a list of Perl-related mailing lists, refer to the Perl Mailing List Database (*lists. cpan.org*) or to the list maintained by the Perl Mongers at *http://www.perl.org/ support/mailing_lists.html*.

Many of these mailing lists maintain a "digest" version, which means that instead of receiving individual email messages all day long, you receive a few "digests" of the messages on a regular basis. Digests of a mailing list might be preferable to the minute-by-minute onslaught of email throughout the day, depending on how involved you are in the discussion.

CPAN

The Comprehensive Perl Archive Network (CPAN) is a repository of Perl modules and scripts submitted by Perl programs worldwide. It is by far the most valuable resource for Perl programmers, so if you haven't browsed through CPAN, go there now, and expect to stay a while. There are many mirrored CPAN sites around the world, but the preferred entry point is *www.cpan.org*.

www.perl.com

There are countless web pages devoted to Perl, but probably the most useful entry site to Perl resources is *www.perl.com*. Formerly maintained by Tom Christiansen, *www.perl.com* is now maintained by O'Reilly & Associates (the publisher of this book). From *www.perl.com*, you can access Perl documentation, news, software, FAQs, articles, and (of course) Perl itself.

Perl Mongers (www.perl.org)

The Perl Mongers is a nonprofit Perl advocacy organization that exists to provide services to Perl user groups and to take the place of the now defunct Perl Institute. If you live in a major city (in the United States or abroad), it's likely that a Perl Mongers group exists in your area. You can find out more about the Perl Mongers by checkout out the main site at *www.perl.org* or a description of user group services at *www.pm.org*.

If you're curious about the location of a Perl Mongers group, you should take a look at *http://www.pm.org/groups.shtml*.

The Perl Journal

The *Perl Journal*, published by CMP, is a quarterly publication with articles and news about Perl.

If you're interested in reading past TPJ articles, some highlights are being collated into book form (or, more specifically, three-book form) and should be available by the time you read this paragraph: *Perl Programming: Best of The Perl Journal* (O'Reilly).

Perl Conferences

For years, Usenix has devoted tracks of its conferences to Perl. However, today there are not just one but multiple conferences that focus on Perl.

In 1997, O'Reilly & Associates began hosting The Perl Conference (TPC), typically held during the third week of July in a major California city. In recent years, The Perl Conference has merged with a more general conference for open source technologies, but the Perl track is by far the best attended. For more information, go to *http://conferences.oreilly.com/*.

In 1999, a nonprofit organization called YAS (Yet Another Society) started sponsoring a more grassroots, less corporate conference called YAPC (Yet Another Perl Conference), typically held twice a year in university settings. YAPC::America::North is held in the United States or Canada in June, and YAPC::Europe is held in a major European city in September. For more information, go to *http://www.yapc.org/*.

Books

There are many books written on Perl. In fact, the current popularity of Perl is often credited to the original publication of *Programming Perl*, also known as "The Camel" (because of the animal on its cover), by Larry Wall and Randal Schwartz.* The Camel is also published by O'Reilly & Associates. The Camel isn't the best place to start if you're just learning Perl from scratch, but it's essential if you want to really understand Perl and not just dabble in it.

Other Perl books published by O'Reilly & Associates are *Learning Perl* ("The Llama"), *Advanced Perl Programming*, *Perl Cookbook*, *Mastering Regular Expressions*, *Learning Perl on Win32 Systems*, *Mastering Perl/Tk*, *Perl for System Administration*, *Perl for Web Site Management*, *Mastering Algorithms with Perl*, *Programming the Perl DBI*, *Perl and XML*, and *CGI Programming with Perl*.

There are also books from other publishers, of course. Standouts include *Object-Oriented Perl* and *Elements of Programming with Perl*, both published by Manning Press, and *Effective Perl Programming* and *Network Programming with Perl*, published by Addison-Wesley Longman.

---

* The third and most recent edition of *Programming Perl* is written by Larry Wall, Tom Christiansen, and Jon Orwant.

2

Installing Perl

Some of the best things in life are free. So is Perl. Although bundled Perl distributions are frequently available on CD-ROM, perhaps installed as a core part of your operating system, most people download Perl from an online archive. CPAN, the Comprehensive Perl Archive Network, is the main distribution point for all things Perl. Whether you are looking for Perl itself, for a module, or for documentation about Perl, CPAN (*http://www.cpan.org/*) is the place to go. The ongoing development and enhancement of Perl is very much a cooperative effort, and CPAN is the place where the work of many individuals comes together.

The CPAN Architecture

CPAN represents the development interests of a cross-section of the Perl community. It contains Perl utilities, modules, documentation, and (of course) the Perl distribution itself. CPAN was created by Jarkko Hietaniemi and Andreas König.

The home for CPAN is *http://www.cpan.org/*, but CPAN is also mirrored on many other sites around the globe. This ensures that anyone with an Internet connection can have reliable access to CPAN's contents at any time. Since the structure of all CPAN sites is the same, a user searching for the current version of Perl can be sure that the *stable.tar.gz* file is the same on every site.

If you want to use anonymous FTP, the following machines should have the Perl source code plus a copy of the CPAN mirror list:

> *ftp.perl.com*
> *ftp.cs.colorado.edu*
> *ftp.cise.ufl.edu*
> *ftp.funet.fi*
> *ftp.cs.ruu.nl*

The location of the top directory of the CPAN mirror differs on these machines, so look around once you get there. It's often something like */pub/perl/CPAN*.

How Is CPAN Organized?

CPAN materials are grouped into categories, including Perl modules, distributions, documentation, announcements, ports, scripts, and contributing authors. Each category is linked to related categories. For example, links to a graphing module written by an author appear in both the module and the author areas.

Since CPAN provides the same offerings worldwide, the directory structure has been standardized; files are located in the same place in the directory hierarchy at all CPAN sites. All CPAN sites use *CPAN* as the root directory, from which the user can select a specific Perl item. From the *CPAN* directory, you have the following choices:

Item	Description
CPAN.html	CPAN info page; some general information about CPAN
ENDINGS	Description of the file extensions, such as *.tar*, *.gz*, and *.zip*
MIRRORED BY	A list of sites mirroring CPAN
MIRRORING.FROM	A list of sites mirrored by CPAN
README	A brief description of what you'll find on CPAN
README.html	An HTML-formatted version of the README file
RECENT	Recent additions to the CPAN site
RECENT.html	An HTML-formatted list of recent additions
ROADMAP	What you'll find on CPAN and where
ROADMAP.html	An HTML-formatted version of ROADMAP
SITES	An exhaustive list of CPAN sites
SITES.html	An HTML-formatted version of SITES
authors	A list of CPAN authors
clpa	An archive of comp.land.perl.announce
disclaimer.html	Before you call your lawyer, read these details about CPAN content
doc	Various Perl documentation, FAQs, etc.
index.html	CPAN starting point in you prefer to browse CPAN from the web instead of FTP
indices	Everything that is indexed
misc	Miscellaneous Perl stuff such as Larry Wall quotes and gifts
modules	Modules for Perl Version 5
other-archives	Other things yet uncategorized
ports	Various Perl ports
scripts	Various scripts appearing in Perl books
src	The Perl sources from various versions

While most people who want to use Perl for Win32 should use ActivePerl from *www.activestate.com*, if you want to roll your own, you can get the current Perl source kit from the *src* directory and click on *stable.tar.gz* (or *stable.zip*, if you're building under Win32). If you want to stand on the cutting edge of Perl development, you should download *devel.tar.gz* (or *devel.zip*, if you're building under Win32). For ports to other systems, click on *ports*. The *modules* link is the one you want if you're looking for a Perl module. From there, you can get a full list of the modules or access the modules directly by author, by CPAN category, or by module name. (The section "Getting and Installing Modules" later in this chapter talks about installing modules.) Click on *doc* for Perl documentation, FAQs, etc.

Installing Perl

Most likely, your system administrator is responsible for installing and upgrading Perl. But if you are the system administrator, or you want to install Perl on your own system, sooner or later you will find yourself installing a new version of Perl.

 If you run Perl and plan on upgrading to the latest distribution, be aware that pre-5.005 Perl extensions are not compatible with 5.6 and later. This means that you must rebuild and reinstall any dynamically loaded extensions you built under Perl distributions earlier than 5.005. If you're building under a Unix variant that's running Perl 5.005, choose the Configure option for 5.005 compatibility.

Specific installation instructions come in the *README* and *INSTALL* files of the Perl distribution kit. If you don't already have the Perl distribution, you can download it from CPAN—the latest Unix distribution is in *stable.tar.gz*. The information in this section is an overview of the installation process. The gory details are in the *INSTALL* file, which you should look at before starting, especially if you haven't done an installation before. Note that operating systems other than Unix may have special instructions; if so, follow those instructions instead of what's in this section or in *INSTALL*. Look for a file named *README.xxx*, in which *xxx* represents your operating-system type.

In addition to Perl itself, the standard distribution includes a set of core modules that are automatically installed with Perl. See the section "Getting and Installing Modules" later in this chapter to learn how to install modules that are not bundled with Perl; Chapter 8 describes the standard modules in some detail.

Installing on Unix

Typically, the Perl kit will be packed as either a *tar* file or a set of *shar* (shell archive) scripts; in either case, the file will be in a compressed format. If you got your version of Perl directly from CPAN, it is probably in "tar-gzipped" format; *tar* and *gzip* are popular Unix data-archiving formats. In any case, once you've downloaded the distribution, you need to uncompress and unpack it. The filename indicates the kind of compression that was used. A *.Z* extension indicates you need to *uncompress* the file first, while a *.gz* extension indicates you need to *gunzip* the file. You then unpack the file as appropriate, read the *README* and *INSTALL* files, and run a massive shell script called *Configure*, which tries to figure out everything about your system and creates the file *Config.pm* to store the information. After this is done, you do a series of "makes" to find header file dependencies, to compile Perl (and *a2p*, which translates *awk* scripts to Perl), to run regression tests, and to install Perl in your system directories.

If you opt to build your own Perl under Win32, you will find that the Perl source kit is also shipped in zip format, which you can easily extract with *pkunzip* or *Winzip* (*www.winzip.com*).

If you're building Perl under Unix, it is likely that your architecture and development environment is supported by *Configure*. You shouldn't have any problems with the build process or running the test suite. One common problem is not making sure that Perl is linked against all the libraries it needs to build correctly. Also, you should say "yes" when *Configure* asks if you want dynamic loading, if your system supports it. Otherwise, you won't be able to install modules that use XS, which provides an interface between Perl and C.

If you are running Linux, and you've installed Perl from a tarball (or rpm package), you should make sure everything is there; one way to do that is to check the *Config.pm* file. If MakeMaker is not correctly installed, you might need to build Perl yourself.

It's possible you'll get a compiled (binary) copy of Perl, rather than the source. In that case, make sure you get *suidperl*,* *a2p*, *s2p*, and the Perl library routines. Install these files in the directories that your version was compiled for. Note that binary distributions of Perl are made available because they're handy, not because you are restricted from getting the source and compiling it yourself. The people who give you the binary distribution ought to provide you with some form of access to the source, if only a pointer to where *they* got the source. See the *Copying* file in the distribution for more information.

Perl examples

The Perl source distribution comes with some sample scripts in the *eg/* subdirectory. Feel free to browse among them and use them. They are not installed automatically, however, so you need to copy them to the appropriate directory and possibly fix the #! line to point to the right interpreter.

The files in the *t/* and *lib/* subdirectories, although arcane in spots, can also serve as examples.

Patches

Since Perl is constantly being honed and improved, patches are sometimes made available through CPAN. Your distribution is likely to have had most of the patches applied already—run perl -v to check the patch level of your distribution. Patches are sent out with complete instructions on how to apply them using *patch*, which is available from the GNU project.

Installing on Win32

You need to obtain and install a copy of Perl yourself, unless you have had the good fortune of having either a system administrator install Perl on your system or access to a set of development tools to compile the Perl distribution.

---

* Be care ful with *suidperl*. Most people do not understand the complexities and pitfalls of *suidperl*. Also, it will likely be deprecated after the Perl 5.8 release.

The official precompiled Perl distribution for Win32 is *ActivePerl*, which is developed by ActiveState Tool Corporation (*www.activestate.com*). You'll find that ActivePerl is quite complete, down to the availability of such modules as *Win32* and *mod_perl*.

When Perl 5.005 was released, Perl developers could build their own Perl for Win32 from the same source kit that their Unix counterparts used. In addition, the Perl build mechanism for Win32 began to support more than just commercial development toolkits, such as Microsoft's Visual C++. A Perl developer who wanted to build the Perl source kit with a free development toolkit could build Perl with Cygwin (*www.cygnus.com*), a Unix layer on top of Win32, or Mingw32 (*www.mingw.org*) with *dmake*, a set of Win32 runtime libraries that provide a Unix emulation under native Win32.

 Unless there's something specific that you gain by building your own Perl for Win32, then you should use the Activestate build, ActivePerl.

ActivePerl

The canonical source for the ActivePerl distribution at the time of this writing is at *http://aspn.activestate.com/ASPN/Downloads/ActivePerl/*. Included in the distribution are:

Perl for Win32
Binary for the core Perl distribution

Perl for ISAPI
IIS plug-in for use with ISAPI-compliant web servers

PerlScript
ActiveX scripting engine

Perl Package Manager
Manager for Perl modules and extensions

The ActivePerl binary comes as a self-extracting executable that uses the standard Win32 InstallShield setup wizard to guide you through the installation process. By default, Perl is installed into the directory *C:\Perl\version*, in which *version* is the current version number (e.g., 5.005). (For information on customizing your installation, see the Win32 FAQ on the ActiveState web site.) The installation also associates the file extension *.pl* with Perl and adds the directory into which you installed Perl to your PATH environment variable.

If you want to install ActivePerl, you can do so by running the *MSI* archive that's shipped by ActiveState. If the *MSI* archive is not associated with the MSI application, you need to obtain *InstMsi.exe* from the downloads section at *www.microsoft.com*.

If you don't (or can't) install MSI on your system, ActiveState has made available a Perl installer that doesn't use MSI, but be aware that this installer doesn't have a corresponding de-installer.

Standard Perl distribution

The standard Perl distribution is available from CPAN, where you'll find binary and source distributions for the current version of Perl. The source distributions come as *.tar.gz* files, which you can extract using a utility that supports *gzip* files, *tar* files, and long filenames. Ports of both GNU *gzip* and *tar* are available for the various Win32 platforms, or you can use a graphical *zip* archive program such as WinZip. Make sure you preserve the directory structure when you unpack the distribution.

To install from the source, you need the Microsoft Visual C++ compiler, the Borland C++ compiler, or Mingw32 with EGCS gcc-2.95.X. If you're using Cygwin32, *do not* try to build Perl in the win32 subdirectory. Instead, you should run *Configure* in the *src* directory as you would when building under a Unix platform. You also need a *make* utility. Microsoft Visual C++ comes with *nmake*, or you can use *dmake*.* Once you have the distribution, start by reading the file *README.win32*. Next, edit the file *Makefile* in the *win32* subdirectory of the distribution and make sure that you're happy with the values for the install drive and directory. Then execute the following commands from the *win32* subdirectory of the distribution to build, test, and install the distribution. This example assumes that you have the proper environment variables (LIB, INCLUDE, etc.) set up for your compiler and that *nmake* is your make program.

```
C:\> nmake          Build all of Perl
C:\> nmake test     Test your distribution
C:\> nmake install  Install to target directory, as specified in the Makefile
```

 If you're running Mingw32, you'll use *dmake*, since *nmake* is part of commercial development suites—such as Microsoft Visual C++—and is not available separately.

Assuming everything is now built correctly, you just need to add the *bin* subdirectory of the installation target directory to your path or to your operating environment under Microsoft server platforms such as Windows NT. For example, if you installed the Perl distribution to *C:\Perl*, you'll want to add the directory containing *perl.exe* (e.g., *C:\Perl\bin*) to your path.

Finally, you should restart your machine so the environment changes take effect, and you're ready to go. This is of particular importance if you're running Perl under Windows 95, 98, or ME.

 Windows 95/98 users can expect significantly different functionality from their Perl distribution than Windows NT users. For various reasons, some of the Win32 modules don't work on Windows 95/98. The functionality required to implement them may be missing on Windows 95/98, or bugs in Windows 95 may prevent them from working correctly.

---

* See the *README.win32* file for information on obtaining Mingw32 and a Win32 *dmake* port.

Getting and Installing Modules

As you'll see when you look at the lists of modules and their authors on CPAN, many users have made their modules freely available. If you find an interesting problem and are thinking of writing a module to solve it, check the *modules* directory on CPAN first to see if there is a module there that you can use. The chances are good that there is a module that does what you need, or perhaps one that you can extend, rather than starting from scratch.*

Before you download a module, you might also check your system to see if it's already installed. The following command searches the libraries in the @INC array and prints the names of all modules it finds:

```
find `perl -e 'print "@INC"'` -name '*.pm' -print
```

Locating Modules

If you start from the *modules* directory on CPAN, you'll see that the modules are categorized into three subdirectories:

by-authors   *Modules by author's registered CPAN name*
by-category   *Modules by subject matter (see below)*
by-module   *Modules by namespace (i.e., MIME)*

If you know what module you want, you can go directly to it by clicking on the *by-module* entry. If you are looking for a module in a particular category, you can find it in the *by-category* subdirectory. If you know the author, click on *by-author*. However, if you aren't familiar with the categories and want to find a module that performs a certain task, you might want to get the file *00modlist.long.html*, also in the *modules* directory. This file is the "Perl 5 Modules List." It contains a list of all the modules, by category, with a brief description of the purpose of each module and a link to the author's CPAN directory for downloading.

Here is a list of the Perl Module categories, plus two for modules that don't fit anywhere else:

```
02_Perl_Core_Modules
03_Development_Support
04_Operating_System_Interfaces
05_Networking_Devices_IPC
06_Data_Type_Utilities
07_Database_Interface
08_User_Interfaces
09_Language_Interfaces
10_File_Names_Systems_Locking
11_String_Lang_Text_Proc
12_Opt_Arg_Param_Proc
13_Internationalization_Locale
14_Security_and_Encryption
```

---

* If you are interested in writing and contributing modules, there are several good starting points for learning to do so—see the *perlmodlib* manpage, the "Perl 5 Module List," and the "Perl Authors Upload Server" (*http://www.perl.com/CPAN/modules/04pause.html*).

```
15_World_Wide_Web_HTML_HTTP_CGI
16_Server_and_Daemon_Utilities
17_Archiving_and_Compression
18_Images_Pixmaps_Bitmaps
19_Mail_and_Usenet_News
20_Control_Flow_Utilities
21_File_Handle_Input_Output
22_Microsoft_Windows_Modules
23_Miscellaneous_Modules
24_Commercial_Software_Interfaces
99_Not_In_Modulelist
99_Not_Yet_In_Modulelist
```

If you are in the *by-categories* subdirectory and have selected an area from which you'd like to download a module, you'll find a list of the files in the directory. *tar* files have a *.tar.gz* extension, and README files have a *.readme* extension. You'll generally find a README file for each module; take a look at it before you decide to download the file.

Here's a sample directory listing from category 14, under the MD5 directory:

```
Digest-MD5-2.09.readme
Digest-MD5-2.09.tar.gz
GAAS
GARY
MD5-1.5.3.readme
MD5-1.5.3.tar.gz
MD5-1.6.readme
MD5-1.6.tar.gz
MD5-1.7.readme
MD5-1.7.tar.gz
NWINT
```

You'll notice that multiple versions are sometimes listed—for example, the MD5 module has Versions 1.5.3 through 1.7 available. Generally, this is to facilitate the transition to a new version of the module.

Select the *.readme* file of the most current archive and review its contents carefully. README files often give special instructions about building the module; they warn you about other modules needed for proper functioning and if the module can't be built under certain versions of Perl. If you're satisfied with what you read, download the file.

Module Installation

If you're running the standard distribution of Perl, on either a Unix or Win32 system, and you want to install a module, this section explains how to do it. If you are running the ActiveState Win32 port, you can follow the instructions covered in this section, unless you're running on a system without a development toolkit; if this is the case, see the next section.

Before installing modules, you should understand at least a little about *make*. *make* is a command designed to automate compilations; it guarantees that programs are compiled with the correct options and are linked to the current version of program modules and libraries. But it's not just for programmers—*make* is useful for any situation in which there are dependencies among a group of related files.

make uses a file known as a Makefile, which is a text file that describes the dependencies and contains instructions that tell *make* what to do. A Perl programmer who writes a module creates a file called *Makefile.PL* that comes with the module when you download it. *Makefile.PL* is a Perl script that uses another module, ExtUtils::MakeMaker (generally referred to as simply MakeMaker), to generate a Makefile specific to that module on your system.

Before you can actually install the module, you need to decide where it should go. Modules can be installed either globally, for everyone to use, or locally, for your own use. Most system administrators install popular software, including Perl modules, to be globally available. In that case, the modules are generally installed in a branch of the *lib* directory with the rest of the Perl libraries.

If you have root privileges or write access to the locations where Perl modules are installed on your system, you can proceed by moving the downloaded module file to the correct directory and running *gunzip* and *tar* to unpack it. Then *cd* to the module directory and check any README or INSTALL files, check the MANI-FEST file to be sure everything is there. If all is well, you can run the following to complete the installation:

```
% perl Makefile.PL
% make
% make test
% make install
```

If you're on a Win32 platform and are using Mingw32, do the following:

```
C:\modulename-version> perl Makefile.PL
C:\modulename-version> dmake
C:\modulename-version> dmake test
C:\modulename-version> dmake install
```

It's possible that you'll need to customize *Makefile.PL* before running it. If so, see the discussion of ExtUtils::MakeMaker in Chapter 8. Or, if you know the Make-Maker options that you'd like to add to *Makefile.PL*, you can add these options on the command line. A typical scenario would be on a system where you've installed a precompiled version of Perl, and the CC and LD options in *Config.pm* don't match your programming environment; thus, Perl modules won't build correctly. To solve this problem, you can do the following:

```
% perl Makefile.PL CC=gcc LD=gcc
```

If you are going to install the module locally (for example, if you don't have permission to install globally or you want to test it locally before installing it for general use), you need to pass a PREFIX argument to Perl when you run *Makefile.PL* to generate the Makefile. This argument tells MakeMaker to use the directory following PREFIX as the base directory when installing the module.

For example, to install a module in the directory */home/mydir/Perl/Modules*, the PREFIX argument would look like this:

```
% perl Makefile.PL PREFIX=/home/mydir/Perl/Modules
```

Then follow the remaining steps, as above:

```
% make
% make test
% make install
```

The module is now available, but when you write Perl code to use the module, there's another detail to take care of. Since Perl looks in system-wide directories as specified in the special array @INC, it won't find local modules unless you tell it where they are. Instead, you'll receive an error message such as the following:

```
Can't locate <ModuleName>.pm in @INC.
BEGIN failed--compilation aborted.
```

Thus, if you installed the module in */home/mydir/Perl/Modules*, you need to tell Perl to look in that location with the command use lib *'path'*:

```
#!/usr/local/bin/perl -w
use lib '/home/mydir/Perl/Modules';
use ModuleName;
```

Installing Modules with ActiveState Perl

Prior to Perl 5.005, ActiveState's Perl for Win32 did not support MakeMaker. If you are running Perl 5.004 (or earlier), you should upgrade because the absense of MakeMaker prevents you from installing and using most current Perl modules. While some modules can be installed manually, this is *not* suggested, since it's likely that something will be forgotten, and the module won't work correctly! You should follow all module documentation to determine which installation technique is the proper one, so that everything will be okay.

With 5.6 and later, you can use MakeMaker to install the modules, or you can use the Perl Package Manager that comes with ActivePerl.

Using MakeMaker

To install a module using MakeMaker, follow the procedure described earlier for installing when you are running the standard distribution, replacing *make* with *nmake* or *dmake* as appropriate.

Using the Perl Package Manager

The Perl Package Manager (PPM) provides a command-line interface for obtaining and installing Perl modules and extensions. To run PPM, connect to CPAN and type:

```
perl ppm.pl
```

The PPM prompt appears, and you can begin to enter PPM commands. The available commands are:

help [*command*]
> Prints the list of commands and what they do, or help for a particular command.

install *packages*
> Installs the specified packages.

quit
> Leaves PPM.

remove *packages*
> Removes the specified packages from the system.

search
> Searches for information about available packages.

set
> Sets or displays current options.

verify
> Verifies that your current installation is up-to-date.

Installing Modules with the CPAN Module

If you are just getting and installing one or a few modules, it's not a big problem to download the module's tarball and run through the build process manually. But if you don't want to cope with the brute-force approach when dealing with large module installations (such as LWP and the CPAN bundle), there is an easier way—you can use the CPAN module. The CPAN module (CPAN.pm) can be used interactively from the command line to locate, download, and install Perl modules and their dependencies, or to identify modules and authors. CPAN.pm was designed to automate the installation of Perl modules; it includes searching capabilities and the ability to retrieve files from one or more of the mirrored CPAN sites and unpack them in a dedicated directory.

To run the CPAN module interactively, enter:

```
% perl -MCPAN -e shell
```

The first time you use the CPAN module, it takes you through a series of setup questions and writes CPAN::Config if you run the above as root or your administrative user. If the above is run as a user who does not have administrative permissions, CPAN.pm determines who you are and writes *MyConfig.pm* in a subdirectory of your home directory (defaults to *~/.cpan/CPAN/MyConfig.pm*). After that, whenever you use the CPAN module for downloading other modules, it uses the *.cpan* directory as the general build and cache directory, saved as cpan_ home in the configuration file. If ReadLine support is available (i.e., Term::ReadKey and Term::ReadLine are installed), you can use command history and command completion as you enter commands.

When the module runs and is ready for commands to be entered, you'll see the prompt:

```
cpan>
```

You can then enter h to get a brief help message, or just start entering commands. The commands are all methods in the CPAN::Shell package. For commands that can operate on modules, bundles, authors, or distributions, CPAN.pm treats arguments containing a slash (/) as distributions, arguments beginning with Bundle:: as bundles, and everything else as modules or authors. The following is a listing of the interactive CPAN commands.

?

?

Displays brief help message. Same as h command.

!

! *perl-code*

evals a Perl command.

---

a

a [*authorlist*]

Searches for CPAN authors. Arguments can be strings that must be matched exactly or regular expressions, which must be enclosed in slashes and are matched in case-insensitive fashion. With no arguments, it returns a list of all authors, by CPAN ID. With arguments, it returns a list of authors if there is more than one that matches the criteria, or it returns additional information if a single author is returned. String and regular expression arguments can be combined in the same command.

```
cpan> a /^nv/ LWALL
Author          NVPAT (Nathan V. Patwardhan)
Author          LWALL (Larry Wall. Author of Perl. Busy
man.)
cpan> a /^nv/
Author id = NVPAT
     EMAIL      nvp@ora.com
     FULLNAME   Nathan V. Patwardhan
```

---

autobundle

autobundle [*bundlelist*]

Writes a bundle file containing a list of all modules that are both available from CPAN and currently installed within @INC. The file is written to the *Bundle* subdirectory of cpan_home with a name that contains the current date and a counter—for example, *Snapshot_1998_04_27_00.pm*. You can use this file as input to the install command to install the latest versions of all the modules on your system:

```
perl -MCPAN -e 'install Bundle::Snapshot_1998_04_27_00'
```

---

b

b [*bundlelist*]

Searches for CPAN bundles. Arguments are the same as for the a command, except they specify bundles. With a single argument, b displays details about the bundle; with multiple arguments, it displays a list.

clean

clean [*arglist*]

Does a *make clean* in the distribution file's directory. *arglist* can include one or more modules, bundles, distributions, or one of the values r or u to reinstall or uninstall.

d

d [*distriblist*]

Displays information about module distributions for the distribution(s) specified in *distriblist*. Arguments are the same as for the a command. Displays details for a single argument, or a list if the output consists of multiple distributions.

force

force *method* [*arglist*]

Takes as a first argument the method to invoke, which can be one of make, test, or install, and executes the command from scratch for each argument in *arglist*. The arguments may be modules or distributions.

Be warned that force also allows you to install modules that have failed some or all of the module tests. If installing modules that have failed their tests bothers you, then you shouldn't use force.

h

h

Displays brief help message. Same as ?.

i

i [*arglist*]

Displays information about the arguments specified in *arglist*, which can be an author, module, bundle, or distribution. Arguments and output are the same as for a.

install

install [*arglist*]

Installs the arguments specified in *arglist*, which can be modules or distributions. Implies test. For a distribution, install is run unconditionally. For a module, CPAN.pm checks to see if the module is up-to-date, and if so, prints a message to that effect and does not do the install. Otherwise, it finds and processes the distribution that contains the module.

look   look *arg*

Takes one argument, which is a module or distribution, gets and untars the distribution file if necessary, changes to the appropriate directory, and opens a subshell process in that directory.

m   m [*arglist*]

Displays information about modules. Arguments are the same as for the a command. Displays details for a single module, or a list if there is more than one in the output.

make   make [*arglist*]

Unconditionally runs a *make* on each argument in *arglist*, which can be a module or a distribution. For a module, CPAN.pm finds and processes the distribution that contains the module.

o   o *type* [*option*] [*value*]

Sets and queries options. Takes the following arguments:

type
    Type of options to set or query. The possible values are:

    debug
        Debugging options. Prints CPAN module options for debugging the package.

    conf
        Configuration options. Lists or sets values for CPAN module configuration variables kept in the hash %CPAN::Config. These configuration variables are:

Variable	Content
build_cache	Size of cache for directories to build modules
build_dir	Locally accessible directory to build modules
index_expire	Number of days before refetching index files
cpan_home	Local directory reserved for this package
gzip	Location of external program *gzip*
inactivity_timeout	Breaks an interactive *Makefile.PL* after inactivity_timeout seconds of inactivity (set to 0 to never break)
inhibit_startup_message	If true, does not print startup message
keep_source	If set, keeps source in local directory
keep_source_where	Where to keep source

Variable	Content
make	Location of external *make* program
make_arg	Arguments to always pass to *make*
make_install_arg	Same as make_arg for *make install*
makepl_arg	Arguments to always pass to *perl Makefile.PL*
pager	Location of external *more* program (or other pager)
tar	Location of external *tar* program
unzip	Location of external *unzip* program
urllist	Arrayref to nearby CPAN sites (or equivalent locations, such as CD-ROM)
cache_metadata	Uses serializer to cache metadata
prerequisites_policy	Sets behavior for handling module dependencies; options are follow, automatically, ask, and ignore
scan_cache	Controls the cache-scanning behavior; options are atstart and never
wait_list	An arrayref that contains the wait server(s) to try

option
> The CPAN module configuration option or options; used with conf. Can be one or more scalar or list options from the table above.

value
> Value to be set for a configuration option. The possibilities for o conf are:
>
> o conf *scalaropt*
> > Prints current value of scalar option
>
> o conf *scalaropt value*
> > Sets scalar option to *value*
>
> o conf *listopt*
> > Prints current value of list option in MakeMaker format
>
> o conf *listopt* [shift|pop]
> > Shifts or pops the array in *listopt* variable
>
> o conf *listopt* [unshift|push|splice] *list*
> > Works like the corresponding Perl functions to modify the array in *listopt* based on *list*
>
> o conf *commit*
> > Wites CPAN::Config with updated options

---

q   q

> Quits the CPAN module shell subroutine.

---

r

r

Recommendations for reinstallation. With no argument, lists all distributions that are out-of-date. With an argument, tells you whether that module or distribution is out-of-date.

readme

readme *arglist*

Finds and displays the README file for modules or distributions in *arglist*.

recompile

recompile

Runs full *make/test/install* cycle over all installed dynamically loadable modules with force in effect. Useful for completing a network installation on systems after the first installation, in which the CPAN module would otherwise declare the modules already up-to-date.

reload

reload *arg*

Reloads index files or re-evals CPAN.pm itself. *arg* may be:

cpan
    Re-evals CPAN.pm.

index
    Reloads index of files.

test

test

Runs the *make test* command.

u

u

Lists all uninstalled distributions.

Documentation

Perl documentation is written in a language known as *pod* (plain old documentation). Pod is a set of simple tags that can be processed to produce documentation in the style of Unix manpages. There are also several utility programs available that process pod text and generate output in different formats. Pod tags can be intermixed with Perl commands or can be saved in a separate file, which usually has a *.pod* extension. The pod tags and the utility programs that are included in the Perl distribution are described in Chapter 4.

Installing the Documentation

On Unix, the standard Perl installation procedure generates manpages for the Perl documentation from their pod format, although your system administrator might also choose to install the documentation as HTML files. You can also use this procedure to generate manpages for CPAN modules when you install them. You might need to modify your MANPATH environment variable to include the path to the Perl manpages, but then you should be able to read the documentation with the *man* command. In addition, Perl comes with its own command, *perldoc*, which formats the pod documentation and displays it. *perldoc* is particularly useful for reading module documentation, which might not be installed as manpages; you can also use it for reading the core Perl documentation.

The ActiveState Win32 port comes with documentation in HTML format; you can find it in the */docs* subdirectory of the distribution. Documentation specific to ActiveState's Perl for Win32 is installed in the */docs/Perl-Win32* subdirectory.

The Perl Manpages

Perl comes with lots of online documentation. To make life easier, the manpages are divided into separate sections so you don't have to wade through hundreds of pages of text to find what you are looking for. You can read them with either the *man* command or *perldoc*. Run man perl or perldoc perl to read the top-level page. This page in turn directs you to more specific pages. Or, if you know which page you want, you can go directly there by using:

```
% man perlvar
```

or:

```
% perldoc perlvar
```

The following table lists the sections in a logical order for reading through them:

Section	Description
perl	Overview (the top level)
perldelta	Changes since previous version
perlfaq	Frequently asked questions
perltoc	Table of contents for Perl documentation
perldata	Data structures
perlsyn	Syntax
perlop	Operators and precedence
perlre	Regular expressions
perlrun	Execution and options
perlfunc	Built-in functions
perlvar	Predefined variables
perlsub	Subroutines
perlmod	How modules work
perlmodlib	How to write and use modules
perlmodinstall	How to install modules from CPAN

Section	Description
perlform	Formats
perllocale	Locale support
perlref	References
perldsc	Data structures introduction
perllol	Data structures: lists of lists
perltoot	OO tutorial
perlobj	Objects
perltie	Objects hidden behind simple variables
perlbot	OO tricks and examples
perlipc	Interprocess communication
perldebug	Debugging
perldiag	Diagnostic messages
perlsec	Security
perltrap	Traps for the unwary
perlport	Portability guide
perlstyle	Style guide
perlpod	Plain old documentation
perlbook	Book information
perlembed	Embedding Perl in your C or C++ application
perlapio	Internal I/O abstraction interface
perlxs	XS application programming interface
perlxstut	XS tutorial
perlguts	Internal functions for those doing extensions
perlcall	Calling conventions from C
perlhist	History records
perlreftut	Perl references short introduction
perlrequick	Perl regular expressions quick start
perllexwarn	Perl warnings and their control
perldebtut	Perl debugging tutorial
perlopentut	Perl open( ) tutorial
perlretut	Perl regular expressions tutorial
perlboot	Perl OO tutorial for beginners
perltootc	Perl OO tutorial, part 2
perlfork	Perl fork( ) information
perlnumber	Perl number semantics
perlthrtut	Perl threads tutorial
perlunicode	Perl unicode support
perlebcdic	Considerations for running Perl on EBCDIC platforms
perlnewmod	Perl modules: preparing a new module for distribution
perlfaq1	General questions about Perl
perlfaq2	Obtaining and learning about Perl
perlfaq3	Programming tools

Section	Description
perlfaq4	Data manipulation
perlfaq5	Files and formats
perlfaq6	Regexes
perlfaq7	Perl language issues
perlfaq8	System interaction
perlfaq9	Networking
perlcompile	Perl compiler suite intro
perldebguts	Perl debugging guts and tips
perlclib	Internal replacements for standard C library functions
perlutil	Utilities packaged with the Perl distribution
perlfilter	Perl source filters
perldbmfilter	Perl DBM filters
perlapi	Perl API listing (autogenerated)
perlintern	Perl internal functions (autogenerated)
perltodo	Perl things to do
perlhack	Perl hackers guide
perl5005delta	Perl changes in Version 5.005
perl5004delta	Perl changes in Version 5.004
perlaix	Perl notes for AIX
perlamiga	Perl notes for Amiga
perlbs2000	Perl notes for POSIX-BC BS2000
perlcygwin	Perl notes for Cygwin
perldos	Perl notes for DOS
perlepoc	Perl notes for EPOC
perlhpux	Perl notes for HP-UX
perlmachten	Perl notes for Power MachTen
perlmacos	Perl notes for Mac OS (Classic)
perlmpeix	Perl notes for MPE/iX
perlos2	Perl notes for OS/2
perlos390	Perl notes for OS/390
perlsolaris	Perl notes for Solaris
perlvmesa	Perl notes for VM/ESA
perlvms	Perl notes for VMS
perlvos	Perl notes for Stratus VOS
perlwin32	Perl notes for Windows
perl561delta.pod	What's new in Perl v5.6.x (added in 5.8)
perl56delta.pod	What's new in Perl v5.6.0 (added in 5.8)
perl570delta.pod	What's new in Perl v5.7.0 (added in 5.8)
perl571delta.pod	What's new in Perl v5.7.1 (added in 5.8)
perl572delta.pod	What's new in Perl v5.7.2 (added in 5.8)
perlapollo.pod	Perl on Apollo DomainOS (added in 5.8)
perlbeos.pod	Perl on BeOS (added in 5.8)

Section	Description
perlce.pod	Perl on Windows CE (added in 5.8)
perldgux.pod	Perl on DG/UX (added in 5.8)
perlhurd.pod	Perl on GNU Hurd (added in 5.8)
perlintro.pod	A brief introduction and overview of Perl (added in 5.8)
perliol.pod	C API for Perl's implementation of I/O in Layers (added in 5.8)
perlmint.pod	Perl on Atari MiNT (added in 5.8)
perlmodstyle.pod	Perl module style guide (added in 5.8)
perlnetware.pod	Perl on Netware 5.x (added in 5.8)
perlothrtut.pod	Old tutorial on threads in Perl (added in 5.8)
perlpacktut.pod	Tutorial on pack and unpack
perlplan9.pod	Perl on Plan-9 (added in 5.8)
perlpodspec.pod	Plain Old Documentation; format specification and notes (added in 5.8)
perlqnx.pod	Perl on QNX (added in 5.8)
perltooc.pod	Tom's OO Tutorial for Class Data in Perl (added in 5.8)
perltru64.pod	Perl Version 5 on Tru64 systems (added in 5.8)
perluniintro.pod	Perl Unicode introduction (added in 5.8)
perluts.pod	Perl under UTS (added in 5.8)

Language Basics

3

The Perl Executable

The *perl* executable is normally installed in */usr/bin* or */usr/local/bin* on your machine. Some people often refer to *perl* as the Perl interpreter, but this isn't strictly correct, as you'll learn shortly.

Every Perl program must be passed through the Perl executable to be executed. The first line in many Perl programs is something like:

```
#!/usr/bin/perl
```

For Unix systems, this #! (hash-bang or shebang) line tells the shell to look for the */usr/bin/perl* program and pass the rest of the file to that */usr/bin/perl* for execution. Sometimes, you'll see different pathnames to the Perl executable, such as */usr/local/bin/perl*. You might see *perl5* or *perl6* instead of *perl* on sites that still depend on older versions of Perl.

Often, you'll see command-line options tacked on the end of *perl*, such as the notorious *–w* switch, which produces warning messages. But almost all Perl programs on Unix start with some variation of #!/usr/bin/perl.

If you get a mysterious "Command not found" error on a Perl program, it's often because the path to the Perl executable is wrong. When you download Perl programs off the Internet, copy them from one machine to another, or copy them out of a book (like this one!). The first thing you should do is make sure that the #! line points to the location of the Perl executable on your system. If you're on a Win32 platform, where the shebang path is used only to check for Perl switches, you should make sure that you run *pl2bat.bat* on the program so you can run it directly from the command line.

So what does the Perl executable do? It compiles the program internally into a parse tree and executes it immediately. Because the program is not compiled and executed in separate steps, Perl is commonly known as an interpreted language, but this is not quite true.[*]

So do you call something a Perl "script" or a Perl "program"? Typically, the word "program" is used to describe something that needs to be compiled into assembler or bytecode before executing, as in the C language. The word "script" is used to describe something that runs through an executable on your system, such as the Bourne shell. For Perl, you can use either phrase and only offend those Perl programmers who care about semantics more than you do.

What does all this mean for you? When you write a Perl program, you can just give it a correct #! line at the top of the script, make it executable with chmod +x, and run it. For 95% of Perl programmers in this world, that's all they care about.

Command Processing

In addition to specifying a #! line, you can specify a short script directly on the command line. Here are some of the possible ways to run Perl:

- Issue the *perl* command, writing your script line by line via *-e* switches on the command line:

  ```
  perl -e 'print "Hello, world\n"'      # Unix
  perl -e "print \"Hello, world\n\""    # Win32 or Unix
  perl -e "print qq[Hello, world\n]"    # Also Win32
  ```

- Issue the *perl* command, passing Perl the name of your script as the first parameter (after any switches):

  ```
  perl testpgm
  ```

- On Unix systems that support the #! notation, specify the Perl command on the #! line, make your script executable, and invoke it from the shell (as described above).

- Pass your script to Perl via standard input. For example, under Unix:

  ```
  echo "print 'Hello, world'" | perl -
  % perl
  print "Hello, world\n";
  ^D
  ```

- On Win32 systems, you can associate an extension (e.g., *.plx*) with a file type and double-click on the icon for a Perl script with that file type. Or, as mentioned earlier, do this:

  ```
  (open a "DOS" window)
  C:\> (edit your Perl program in your favorite editor)
  C:\> pl2bat yourprog.plx
  C:\> .\yourprog.bat
  (program output here)
  ```

---

[*] Unlike strictly compiled languages, the compiled form of a Perl program is not stored as a separate file. However, Versions 5.6 and later give you the option of using a standalone Perl compiler that creates bytecode to be executed separately. We'll say more about the compiler later in this chapter.

If you are using the ActiveState version of Win32 Perl, the installer normally prompts you to create the association.

- On Win32 systems, if you double-click on the icon for the Perl executable, you'll find yourself in a command-prompt window with a blinking cursor. You can enter your Perl commands, indicating the end of your input with Ctrl-Z, and Perl will compile and execute your script.

Perl parses the input file from the beginning, unless you've specified the *–x* switch (see the section "Command-Line Options" later in this chapter). If there is a #! line, it is always examined for switches as the line is being parsed. Thus, switches behave consistently regardless of how Perl was invoked.

After locating your script, Perl compiles the entire script into an internal form. If there are any compilation errors, execution of the script is not attempted. If the script is syntactically correct, it is executed. If the script runs off the end without hitting an exit or die operator, an implicit exit(0) is provided to indicate successful completion.

Command-Line Options

Perl expects any command-line options, also known as *switches* or *flags*, to come first on the command line. The next item is usually the name of the script, followed by any additional arguments (often filenames) to be passed into the script. Some of these additional arguments may be switches, but if so, they must be processed by the script, since Perl gives up parsing switches as soon as it sees either a non-switch item or the special -- switch that terminates switch processing.

A single-character switch with no argument may be combined (bundled) with the switch that follows it, if any. For example:

```
#!/usr/bin/perl -spi.bak
```

is the same as:

```
#!/usr/bin/perl -s -p -i.bak
```

Perl recognizes the switches listed in Table 3-1.

Table 3-1. Perl switches

Switch	Function
--	Terminates switch processing, even if the next argument starts with a minus. It has no other effect.
–0[octnum]	Specifies the record separator ($/) as an octal number. If octnum is not present, the null character is the separator. Other switches may precede or follow the octal number.
–a	Turns on autosplit mode when used with –n or –p. An implicit split of the @F array is inserted as the first command inside the implicit while loop produced by –n or –p. The default field delimiter is whitespace; a different field delimiter may be specified using –F.
–c	Causes Perl to check the syntax of the script and exit without executing it. More or less equivalent to having exit(0) as the first statement in your program.
–d	Runs the script under the Perl debugger. See Chapter 6.

Table 3-1. Perl switches (continued)

Switch	Function
—d:foo	Runs the script under the control of a debugging or tracing module installed in the Perl library as Devel::*foo*. For example, *—d:DProf* executes the script using the Devel::DProf profiler. See also the section on DProf in Chapter 6.
—Dnumber *—Dlist*	Sets debugging flags. (This works only if debugging was compiled into the version of Perl you are running.) You may specify either a number that is the sum of the bits you want, or a list of letters. To watch how Perl executes your script, for instance, use *—D14* or *—Dslt*. Another useful value is *—D1024* (*—Dx*), which lists your compiled syntax tree. And *—D512* (*—Dr*) displays compiled regular expressions. The numeric value of the flags is available internally as the special variable $^D. Here are the assigned bit values:

Bit	Letter	Meaning
1	p	Tokenizing and parsing
2	s	Stack snapshots
4	l	Label stack processing
8	t	Trace execution
16	o	Object method lookup
32	c	String/numeric conversions
64	P	Print preprocessor command for *—P*
128	m	Memory allocation
256	f	Format processing
512	r	Regular expression processing
1,024	x	Syntax tree dump
2,048	u	Tainting checks
4,096	L	Memory leaks (not supported anymore)
8,192	H	Hash dump; usurps *values*
16,384	X	Scratchpad allocation
32,768	D	Cleaning up

Switch	Function
—e commandline	May be used to enter one or more lines of script. If *—e* is used, Perl does not look for the name of a script in the argument list. Multiple *—e* commands may be given to build up a multiline script. (Make sure to use semicolons where you would in a normal program.)
—Fpattern	Specifies the pattern to split on if *—a* is also in effect. The pattern may be surrounded by //, ' ', or ""; otherwise it is put in single quotes. As of Perl 5.8, the *—F* option is recognized on the #! line.
—h	Prints a summary of Perl's command-line options.
—i[extension]	Specifies that files processed by the <> construct are to be edited in-place. Perl does this by renaming the input file, opening the output file by the original name, and selecting that output file as the default for print statements. The extension, if supplied, is added to the name of the old file to make a backup copy. If no extension is supplied, no backup is made.
—I[directory]	Directories specified by *—I* are prepended to @INC, which holds the search path for modules. If *—P* is also specified, to invoke the C preprocessor, *—I* tells the preprocessor where to search for include files. By default, it searches */usr/include* and */usr/lib/perl*.
—l[octnum]	Enables automatic line-end processing. This switch has two effects. First, when it's used with *—n* or *—p*, it causes the line terminator to be automatically chomped. Second, it sets $\ to the value of *octnum* so any print statements will have a line terminator of ASCII value *octnum* added back on. If *octnum* is omitted, $\ is set to the current value of $/, which is typically a newline. So, to trim lines to 80 columns, say this: `perl -lpe 'substr($_, 80) = ""'`

Table 3-1. Perl switches (continued)

Switch	Function
–m[-]module *–M[-]module* *–M[-]'module …'* *–[mM][-]modulearg[,arg]…* *–mmodule*	Executes use *module* before executing your script.
–Mmodule	Executes use *module* before executing your script. The command is formed by interpolation, so you can use quotes to add extra code after the module name—for example, *–M'module qw(foo bar)'*. If the first character after the *–M* or *–m* is a minus (-), then the use is replaced with no. You can also say *–m module=foo,bar* or *-Mmodule= foo,bar* as a shortcut for *–M'module qw(foo bar)'*. This avoids the need to use quotes when importing symbols. The actual code generated by *–Mmodule=foo,bar* is: `use module split(/,/, q{foo,bar})` The = form removes the distinction between *–m* and *–M*.

–n	Causes Perl to assume the following loop around your script, which makes it iterate over filename arguments:
	
	`LINE:`
	`while (<>) {`
	`    ...      # Your script goes here`
	
	By default, the lines are not printed. (See *–p* to have lines printed.) BEGIN and END blocks may be used to capture control before or after the implicit loop.

–p	Causes Perl to assume the following loop around your script, which makes it iterate over filename arguments:
	
	`LINE:`
	`while (<>) {`
	`    ...      # Your script goes here`
	`} continue {`
	`    print;`
	
	The lines are printed automatically. To suppress printing, use the *–n* switch. If both are specified, the *–p* switch overrides *–n*. BEGIN and END blocks may be used to capture control before or after the implicit loop.

–P	Causes your script to run through the C preprocessor before compilation by Perl. (Since both comments and *cpp* directives begin with the # character, you should avoid starting comments with any words recognized by the C preprocessor, such as if, else, or define.)
–s	Enables some rudimentary parsing of switches on the command line after the script name but before any filename arguments or the -- switch terminator. Any switch found there is removed from @ARGV, and a variable of the same name as the switch is set in the Perl script. No switch bundling is allowed, since multicharacter switches are allowed. As of Perl 5.8, *–s* is recognized on the # ! line.
–S	Makes Perl use the PATH environment variable to search for the script (unless the name of the script starts with a slash). Typically, this is used to emulate # ! startup on machines that don't support # !.
–t	Forces "taint" checks to be turned on, but warning will be issued instead of fatal errors. Warnings can be controlled with no warnings qw (taint). Designed for use in development only; *–T* is preferred for production code. New in 5.8.
–T	Forces "taint" checks to be turned on. Ordinarily, these checks are done only when running setuid or setgid. It's a good idea to turn them on explicitly for programs run on another user's behalf, such as CGI programs.

Table 3-1. Perl switches (continued)

Switch	Function
−u	Causes Perl to dump core after compiling your script. You can take this core dump and turn it into an executable file by using the *undump* program (not supplied). This speeds startup at the expense of some disk space (which you can minimize by stripping the executable). If you want to execute a portion of your script before dumping, use Perl's dump operator instead. Note: availability of *undump* is platform-specific; it may not be available for a specific port of Perl.
−U	Allows Perl to do unsafe operations. Currently, the only "unsafe" operations are the unlinking of directories while running as superuser and running setuid programs with fatal taint checks turned into warnings.
−v	Prints the version and patch level of your Perl executable.
−V	Prints a summary of the major Perl configuration values and the current value of @INC.
−V:name	Prints the value of the named configuration variable to STDOUT.
−w	Prints warnings about identifiers that are mentioned only once and scalar variables that are used before being set. Also warns about redefined subroutines and references to undefined filehandles or to filehandles opened as read-only that you are attempting to write on. Warns you if you use a non-number as though it was a number, if you use an array as though it was a scalar, if your subroutines recurse more than 100 levels deep, etc.
−x[directory]	Tells Perl to extract a script that is embedded in a message by looking for the first line that starts with #! and contains the string "perl". Any meaningful switches on that line after the word "perl" are applied. If a directory name is specified, Perl switches to that directory before running the script. The script must be terminated with __END__ or __DATA__ if there is trailing text to be ignored. (The script can process any or all of the trailing text via the DATA filehandle if desired.)

Environment Variables

Environment variables are used to set user preferences. Individual Perl modules or programs are always free to define their own environment variables, and there is also a set of special environment variables used in the CGI environment (see Chapter 9).

Perl uses the following environment variables:

HOME
Used if chdir has no argument.

LOGDIR
Used if chdir has no argument and HOME is not set.

PATH
Used in executing subprocesses and in finding the script if −S is used.

PATHEXT
On Win32 systems, if you want to avoid typing the extension every time you execute a Perl script, you can set the PATHEXT environment variable so that it includes Perl scripts. For example:

```
C:\> set PATHEXT=%PATHEXT%;.PLX
```

This setting lets you type:

```
C:\> myscript
```

without including the file extension. Be careful when setting PATHEXT permanently—it also includes executable file types such as *.com, .exe, .bat,* and *.cmd.* If you inadvertently lose those extensions, you'll have difficulty invoking applications and script files.

PERL5LIB

A colon-separated list of directories in which to look for Perl library files before looking in the standard library and the current directory. If PERL5LIB is not defined, PERLLIB is used. When running taint checks, neither variable is used. The script should instead say:

```
use lib "/my/directory";
```

PERL5OPT

Command-line options (switches). Switches in this variable are taken as if they were on every Perl command line. Only the *–[DIMUdmw]* switches are allowed. When running taint checks, this variable is ignored.

PERLLIB

A colon-separated list of directories in which to look for Perl library files before looking in the standard library and the current directory. If PERL5LIB is defined, PERLLIB is not used.

PERL5DB

The command used to load the debugger code. The default is:

```
BEGIN { require 'perl5db.pl' }
```

PERL5SHELL

On Win32 systems, may be set to an alternative shell for Perl to use internally to execute "backtick" commands or the system function.

PERL_DEBUG_MSTATS

Relevant only if your Perl executable was built with –DDEBUGGING_ MSTATS. If set, causes memory statistics to be dumped after execution. If set to an integer greater than 1, it also causes memory statistics to be dumped after compilation.

PERL_DESTRUCT_LEVEL

Relevant only if your Perl executable was built with –DDEBUGGING. Controls the behavior of global destruction of objects and other references.

Perl also has environment variables that control how Perl handles data specific to particular natural languages. See the *perllocale* manpage.

The Perl Compiler

Starting with Perl 5.005, the Perl compiler became part of the standard Perl distribution. You'll find that with Perl 5.6 and later, the Perl compiler has become far more stable. The compiler allows you to distribute Perl programs in binary form, which enables easy packaging of Perl-based programs without relying on the source machine to have the correct version of Perl and the correct modules installed. After the initial compilation, running a compiled program should be faster because it doesn't have to be recompiled each time it's run. However, you shouldn't expect that the compiled code itself will run faster than the original Perl source or that the executable will be smaller—in reality, the executable file is likely to be significantly bigger.

This initial release of the compiler is still considered to be a beta version. It's distributed as an extension module, B, that comes with the following backends:

Bytecode
> Translates a script into platform-independent Perl bytecode.

C
> Translates a Perl script into C code.

CC
> Translates a Perl script into optimized C code.

Deparse
> Regenerates Perl source code from a compiled program.

Lint
> Extends the Perl –*w* option. Named after the Unix Lint program-checker.

Showlex
> Shows lexical variables used in functions or files.

Xref
> Creates a cross-reference listing for a program.

Once you've generated the C code with either the C or the CC backend, you run the *cc_harness* program to compile it into an executable. There is also a *byteperl* interpreter that lets you run the code you've generated with the Bytecode backend.

Here's an example that takes a simple "Hello world" program and uses the CC backend to generate C code:

```
% perl -MO=CC,-ohi.c hi.pl
hi.pl syntax OK
% perl cc_harness -O2 -ohi hi.c
# You may have to provide the full path of where cc_harness lives
gcc -B/usr/ccs/bin/ -D_REENTRANT -DDEBUGGING -I/usr/local/include
-I/usr/local/lib/perl5/sun4-solaris-thread/5.00466/CORE -O2 -ohi hi.c
-L/usr/local/lib /usr/local/lib/perl5/sun4-solaris-thread/5.00466/CORE/
libperl.a
-lsocket -lnsl -lgdbm -ldl -lm -lposix4 -lpthread -lc -lcrypt
% hi
Hi there, world!
```

The compiler also comes with a frontend, *perlcc*. You can use it to compile code into a standalone executable or compile a module (a *.pm* file) into a shared object (an *.so* file) that can be included in a Perl program via *use*. For example:

```
% perlcc a.p        # Compiles into the executable 'a'
% perlcc A.pm       # Compiles into A.so
```

The following options can be used with *perlcc*:

–argv arguments
> Used with *–run* or *–e*. Passes the string *arguments* to the executable as @ARGV.

–C c_code_name
> Gives the name *c_code_name* to the generated C code that will be compiled. Valid only if you are compiling one file on the command line.

–e perl_line_to_execute
> Works like *perl –e* to compile "one-liners." The default is to compile and run the code. With *–o*, it saves the resulting executable.

–gen
> Creates the intermediate C code but doesn't compile the results; does an implicit *–sav*.

–I include_directories
> Adds directories inside *include_directories* to the compilation command.

–L library_directories
> Adds directories in *library_directories* to the compilation command.

–log logname
> Opens a log file (for append) for saving text from a compile command.

–mod
> Tells *perlcc* to compile the files given at the command line as modules. Usually used with module files that don't end with *.pm*.

–o executable_name
> Gives the name *executable_name* to the executable that will be compiled. Only valid if compiling one file on the command line.

–prog
> Tells *perlcc* to compile the files given at the command line as programs. Usually used with program files that don't end with a *.p*, *.pl*, or *.bat* extension.

–regex rename_regex
> Provides the rule *rename_regex* for creating executable filenames, in which *rename_regex* is a Perl regular expression.

–run
> Immediately runs the generated Perl code. Note that the rest of @ARGV is interpreted as arguments to the program being compiled.

–sav
> Tells Perl to save the intermediate C code.

–verbose verbose_level
> Compiles verbosely, setting *verbose_level* to control the degree of verbosity. *verbose_level* can be given as either a sum of bits or a list of letters. Values are listed in the following table.

Bit	Letter	Action
1	g	Code generation errors to STDERR.
2	a	Compilation errors to STDERR.
4	t	Descriptive text to STDERR.
8	f	Code generation errors to file. Requires –log.
16	c	Compilation errors to file. Requires –log.
32	d	Descriptive text to file. Requires –log.

With –log, the default level is 63; otherwise the default level is 7.

There are two environment variables that you can set for perlcc: PERL_SCRIPT_EXT and PERL_MODULE_EXT. These can be used to modify the default extensions that perlcc recognizes for programs and modules. The variables take colon-separated Perl regular expressions.

The modules that comprise the compiler are described in Chapter 8. Also see the documentation that comes with the compiler, which includes more complete information on installing and using it.

Threads

Perl 5.6 and later also include native multithreading capability, which is distributed with Perl as a set of modules. The threads modules have improved since the 5.005 release, but should still be considered an experimental feature and aren't automatically compiled in with Perl.

Pay close attention to Configure when you build Perl so that you don't include threads support if you don't want it.

You might want to build a separate version of Perl with threads enabled, if you'd like to test the threads feature under your platform.

Chapter 8 describes the individual thread modules. For information on using threads, refer to the perlthrtut manpage (included with more recent distributions of Perl).

The Perl Language

This chapter is a quick and merciless guide to the Perl language itself. If you're trying to learn Perl from scratch and would prefer to be taught rather than to have things thrown at you, then you might be better off with *Learning Perl, 3rd Edition* by Randal L. Schwartz and Tom Phoenix. However, if you already know some other programming languages and just want to learn the particulars of Perl, this chapter is for you. Sit tight, and forgive us for being terse—we have a lot of ground to cover.

If you want a more complete discussion of the Perl language and its idiosyncrasies (and we mean *complete*), see *Programming Perl, 3rd Edition* by Larry Wall, Tom Christiansen, and Jon Orwant.

Program Structure

Perl is a particularly forgiving language, as far as program layout goes. There are no rules about indentation, newlines, etc. Most lines end with semicolons, but not everything has to. Most things don't have to be declared, except for a couple of things that do. Here are the bare essentials:

Whitespace
> Whitespace is required only between items that would otherwise be confused as a single term. All types of whitespace—spaces, tabs, newlines, etc.—are equivalent in this context. A comment counts as whitespace. Different types of whitespace are distinguishable within quoted strings, formats, and certain line-oriented forms of quoting. For example, in a quoted string, a newline, a space, and a tab are interpreted as unique characters.

Semicolons
> Every simple statement must end with a semicolon. Compound statements contain brace-delimited blocks of other statements and do not require

terminating semicolons after the ending brace. A final simple statement in a block also does not require a semicolon.

Declarations

Only subroutines and report formats need to be explicitly declared. All other user-created objects are automatically created with a null or 0 value unless they are defined by some explicit operation such as assignment. The *–w* command-line switch will warn you about using undefined values.

You may force yourself to declare your variables by including the use strict pragma in your programs (see Chapter 8 for more information on pragmas and strict in particular). This causes an error if you do not explicitly declare your variables.

Comments and documentation

Comments within a program are indicated by a pound sign (#). Everything following a pound sign to the end of the line is interpreted as a comment.

Lines starting with = are interpreted as the start of a section of embedded documentation (pod), and all subsequent lines until the next =cut are ignored by the compiler. See the section "Formats" later in this chapter for more information on pod format.

Data Types and Variables

Perl has three basic data types: *scalars*, *arrays*, and *hashes*.

Scalars are essentially simple variables. They are preceded by a dollar sign ($). A scalar is either a number, a string, or a reference. (A reference is a scalar that points to another piece of data. References are discussed later in this chapter.) If you provide a string in which a number is expected or vice versa, Perl automatically converts the operand using fairly intuitive rules.

Arrays are ordered lists of scalars accessed with a numeric subscript (subscripts start at 0). They are preceded by an "at" sign (@).

Hashes are unordered sets of key/value pairs accessed with the keys as subscripts. They are preceded by a percent sign (%).

Numbers

Perl stores numbers internally as either signed integers or double-precision, floating-point values. Numeric literals are specified by any of the following floating-point or integer formats:

12345
: Integer

-54321
: Negative integer

12345.67
: Floating point

```
6.02E23
```
Scientific notation

```
0xffff
```
Hexadecimal

```
0377
```
Octal

```
4_294_967_296
```
Underline for legibility

Since Perl uses the comma as a list separator, you cannot use a comma for improving the legibility of a large number. To improve legibility, Perl allows you to use an underscore character instead. The underscore works only within literal numbers specified in your program, not in strings functioning as numbers or in data read from somewhere else. Similarly, the leading 0x for hex and 0 for octal work only for literals. The automatic conversion of a string to a number does not recognize these prefixes—you must do an explicit conversion.

Be aware that in Perl 5.8, there are many changes in how Perl deals with integers and floating-point numbers. Regardless of how your system handles numbers and conversion between characters and numbers, Perl 5.8 works around system deficiencies to force more accurate number handling. Furthermore, whereas prior to 5.8 Perl used floating-point numbers exclusively in math operations, Perl 5.8 now uses and stores integers in numeric conversions and in arithmetic operations.

String Interpolation

Strings are sequences of characters. String literals are usually delimited by either single (') or double (") quotes. Double-quoted string literals are subject to backslash and variable interpolation, and single-quoted strings are not (except for \' and \\, used to put single quotes and backslashes into single-quoted strings). You can embed newlines directly in your strings.

Table 4-1 lists all the backslashed or escape characters that can be used in double-quoted strings.

Table 4-1. Double-quoted string representations

Code	Meaning
\n	Newline
\r	Carriage return
\t	Horizontal tab
\f	Form feed
\b	Backspace
\a	Alert (bell)
\e	ESC character
\033	ESC in octal
\x7f	DEL in hexadecimal
\cC	Ctrl-C

Table 4-1. Double-quoted string representations (continued)

Code	Meaning
\\	Backslash
\"	Double quote
\u	Force next character to uppercase
\l	Force next character to lowercase
\U	Force all following characters to uppercase
\L	Force all following characters to lowercase
\Q	Backslash all following non-alphanumeric characters
\E	End \U, \L, or \Q

Table 4-2 lists alternative quoting schemes that can be used in Perl. These are useful in diminishing the number of commas and quotes you may have to type, and they allow you not to worry about escaping characters such as backslashes when there are many instances in your data. The generic forms allow you to use any non-alphanumeric, non-whitespace characters as delimiters in place of the slash (/). If the delimiters are single quotes, no variable interpolation is done on the pattern. Parentheses, brackets, braces, and angle brackets can be used as delimiters in their standard opening and closing pairs.

Table 4-2. Quoting syntax in Perl

Customary	Generic	Meaning	Interpolation
' '	q//	Literal	No
" "	qq//	Literal	Yes
` `	qx//	Command	Yes
( )	qw//	Word list	No
( )	qr//	Pattern	Yes
//	m//	Pattern match	Yes
s///	s///	Substitution	Yes
y///	tr///	Translation	No

Here Documents

A line-oriented form of quoting is based on the Unix shell "here-document" syntax. Following a <<, you specify a string to terminate the quoted material, and all lines following the current line down to the terminating string are the value of the item. This is of particular importance if you're trying to print something like HTML that would be cleaner to print as a chunk instead of as individual lines. For example:

```
#!/usr/local/bin/perl -w

my $Price = 'right';

print <<"EOF";
```

```
The price is $Price.
EOF
```

The terminating string does not have to be quoted. For example, the previous
example could have been written as:

```
#!/usr/local/bin/perl -w

my $Price = 'right';

print <<EOF;
The price is $Price.
EOF
```

You can assign here documents to a string:

```
my $assign_this_heredoc =<< "EOS";
This string is assigned to $whatever.
EOS
```

You can use a here document to execute commands:

```
#!/usr/local/bin/perl -w

print <<`CMD`;
ls -l
CMD
```

You can stack here documents:

```
#!/usr/local/bin/perl -w

print <<"joe", <<"momma"; # You can stack them
I said foo.
joe
I said bar.
momma
```

One caveat about here documents: you may have noticed in each of these examples that the quoted text is always left-justified. That's because any whitespace
used for indentation will be included in the string. For example:

```
#!/usr/local/bin/perl -w

print <<"    INDENTED";
    Same old, same old.
    INDENTED
```

Although you can use a trick of including whitespace in the terminating tag to
keep it indented (as we did here), the string itself will have the whitespace
embedded—in this case, it will be Same old, same old..

Lists

A list is an ordered group of scalar values. A literal list can be composed as a
comma-separated list of values contained in parentheses, for example:

```
(1,2,3)                # Array of three values 1, 2, and 3
("one","two","three")  # Array of three values "one", "two", and "three"
```

The generic form of list creation uses the quoting operator qw// to contain a list of values separated by whitespace:

```
qw/snap crackle pop/
```

With the quoting operators, you're not limited to // when you use one of the operators. You can use just about any character you want. The following is exactly the same as the example above:

```
qw!snap crackle pop!
```

It's important that you remember not to use any delimiters except whitespace with qw//. If you do, these delimiters will be handled as list members:

```
@foods = qw/fish, beef, lettuce, cat, apple/; # EL WRONG-O!
foreach (@foods) {
    print $_; # Prints fish and then a literal comma, etc.
}
```

Variables

A variable always begins with the character that identifies its type: $, @, or %. Most of the variable names you create can begin with a letter or underscore, followed by any combination of letters, digits, or underscores, up to 255 characters in length. Upper- and lowercase letters are distinct. Variable names that begin with a digit can contain only digits, and variable names that begin with a character other than an alphanumeric or underscore can contain only that character. The latter forms are usually predefined variables in Perl, so it is best to name your variables beginning with a letter or underscore.

Variables have the undef value before they are first assigned or when they become "empty." For scalar variables, undef evaluates to 0 when used as a number, and a zero-length, empty string ("") when used as a string.

Simple variable assignment uses the assignment operator (=) with the appropriate data. For example:

```
$age = 26;              # Assigns 26 to $age
@date = (8, 24, 70);    # Assigns the three-element list to @date
%fruit = ('apples', 3, 'oranges', 6);
  # Assigns the list elements to %fruit in key/value pairs
```

Scalar variables are always named with an initial $, even when referring to a scalar value that is part of an array or hash.

Every variable type has its own namespace. You can, without fear of conflict, use the same name for a scalar variable, an array, or a hash (or, for that matter, a filehandle, a subroutine name, or a label). This means that $foo and @foo are two different variables. It also means that $foo[1] is an element of @foo, not a part of $foo.

Arrays

An array is a variable that stores an ordered list of scalar values. Arrays are preceded by an "at" sign (@).

```
@numbers = (1,2,3);        # Set the array @numbers to (1,2,3)
```

To refer to a single element of an array, use the dollar sign ($) with the variable name (it's a scalar), followed by the index of the element in square brackets (the *subscript operator*). Array elements are numbered starting at 0. Negative indexes count backwards from the last element in the list (i.e., −1 refers to the last element of the list). For example, in this list:

```
@date = (8, 24, 70);
```

$date[2] is the value of the third element, 70.

Hashes

A hash is a set of key/value pairs. Hashes are preceded by a percent sign (%). To refer to a single element of a hash, you use the hash variable name followed by the "key" associated with the value in braces. For example, the hash:

```
%fruit = ('apples', 3, 'oranges', 6);
```

has two values (in key/value pairs). If you want to get the value associated with the key apples, you use $fruit{'apples'}.

It is often more readable to use the => operator in defining key/value pairs. The => operator is similar to a comma, but it's more visually distinctive and quotes any bare identifiers to the left of it:

```
%fruit = (
    apples  => 3,
    oranges => 6
);
```

Scalar and List Contexts

Every operation that you invoke in a Perl script is evaluated in a specific context, and how that operation behaves may depend on the context it is being called in. There are two major contexts: *scalar* and *list*. All operators know which context they are in, and some return lists in contexts wanting a list and scalars in contexts wanting a scalar. For example, the localtime function returns a nine-element list in list context:

```
($sec,$min,$hour,$mday,$mon,$year,$wday,$yday,$isdst) = localtime();
```

But in a scalar context, localtime returns the number of seconds since January 1, 1970:

```
$now = localtime();
```

Statements that look confusing are easy to evaluate by identifying the proper context. For example, assigning what is commonly a list literal to a scalar variable:

```
$a = (2, 4, 6, 8);
```

gives $a the value 8. The context forces the right side to evaluate to a scalar, and the action of the comma operator in the expression (in the scalar context) returns the value farthest to the right.

Another type of statement that might be confusing is the evaluation of an array or hash variable as a scalar. For example:

```
$b = @c;
```

When an array variable is evaluated as a scalar, the number of elements in the array is returned. This type of evaluation is useful for finding the number of elements in an array. The special $#*array* form of an array value returns the index of the last member of the list (one less than the number of elements).

If necessary, you can force a scalar context in the middle of a list by using the scalar function.

Declarations and Scope

In Perl, only subroutines and formats require explicit declaration. Variables (and similar constructs) are automatically created when they are first assigned.

Variable declaration comes into play when you need to limit the scope of a variable's use. You can do this in two ways:

Dynamic scoping
Creates temporary objects within a scope. Dynamically scoped constructs are visible globally, but take action only within their defined scopes. Dynamic scoping applies to variables declared with local.

Lexical scoping
Creates private constructs that are visible only within their scopes. The most frequently seen form of lexically scoped declaration is the declaration of my variables.

Therefore, we can say that a local variable is *dynamically scoped*, whereas a my variable is *lexically scoped*. Dynamically scoped variables are visible to functions called from within the block in which they are declared. Lexically scoped variables, on the other hand, are totally hidden from the outside world, including any called subroutines, unless they are declared within the same scope. See the section "Subroutines" later in this chapter for further discussion.

Statements

A simple statement is an expression evaluated for its side effects. Every simple statement must end in a semicolon, unless it is the final statement in a block.

A sequence of statements that defines a scope is called a *block*. Generally, a block is delimited by braces, or { }. Compound statements are built out of expressions and blocks. A conditional expression is evaluated to determine whether a statement block will be executed. Compound statements are defined in terms of blocks, not statements, which means that braces are required.

Any block can be given a label. *Labels* are identifiers that follow the variable-naming rules (i.e., they begin with a letter or underscore and can contain alphanumerics and

---

underscores). They are placed just before the block and are followed by a colon, such as SOMELABEL here:

```
SOMELABEL: {
    ...statements...
    }
```

By convention, labels are all uppercase, so as not to conflict with reserved words. Labels are used with the loop control commands next, last, and redo to alter the flow of execution in your programs.

Conditionals and Loops

The if and unless statements execute blocks of code depending on whether a condition is met. These statements take the following forms:

```
if (expression) {block} else {block}

unless (expression) {block} else {block}

if (expression1) {block}
elsif (expression2) {block}
    ...
elsif (lastexpression) {block}
else {block}
```

while loops

The while statement repeatedly executes a block as long as its conditional expression is true. For example:

```
while (<INFILE>) {
    chomp;
    print OUTFILE, "$_\n";
}
```

This loop reads each line from the file opened with the filehandle INFILE and prints them to the OUTFILE filehandle. The loop will cease when it encounters an end-of-file.

If the word while is replaced by the word until, the sense of the test is reversed. The conditional is still tested before the first iteration, though.

The while statement has an optional extra block on the end called a continue block. This block is executed before every successive iteration of the loop, even if the main while block is exited early by the loop control command next. However, the continue block is not executed if the main block is exited by a last statement. The continue block is always executed before the conditional is reevaluated.

for loops

The for loop has three semicolon-separated expressions within its parentheses. These three expressions function respectively as the initialization, the condition, and the reinitialization expressions of the loop. The for loop can be defined in terms of the corresponding while loop:

```
for ($i = 1; $i < 10; $i++) {
    ...
}
```

This is the same as:

```
$i = 1;
while ($i < 10) {
    ...
}
continue {
    $i++;
}
```

foreach loops

The foreach loop iterates over a list value and sets the control variable (*var*) to be each element of the list in turn:

```
foreach var (list) {
    ...
}
```

Like the while statement, the foreach statement can also take a continue block.

Modifiers

Any simple statement may be followed by a single modifier that gives the statement a conditional or looping mechanism. This syntax provides a simpler and often more elegant method than using the corresponding compound statements. These modifiers are:

```
statement if EXPR;
statement unless EXPR;
statement while EXPR;
statement until EXPR;
```

For example:

```
$i = $num if ($num < 50); # $i will be less than 50
$j = $cnt unless ($cnt < 100); # $j will equal 100 or greater
$lines++ while <FILE>;
print "$_\n" until /The end/;
```

The conditional is evaluated first with the while and until modifiers except when applied to a do {} statement, in which case the block executes once before the conditional is evaluated. For example:

```
do {
    $line = <STDIN>;
    ...
} until $line eq ".\n";
```

For more information on do, see Chapter 5.

Loop control

You can put a label on a loop to give it a name. The loop's label identifies the loop for the loop-control commands next, last, and redo:

```
LINE: while (<SCRIPT>) {
    print;
    next LINE if /^#/;       # Discard comments
    }
```

The syntax for the loop-control commands is:

```
last label
next label
redo label
```

If the label is omitted, the loop-control command refers to the innermost enclosing loop.

The last command is like the break statement in C (as used in loops); it immediately exits the loop in question. The continue block, if any, is not executed.

The next command is like the continue statement in C; it skips the rest of the current iteration and starts the next iteration of the loop. If there is a continue block on the loop, it is always executed just before the conditional is reevaluated.

The redo command restarts the loop block without evaluating the conditional again. The continue block, if any, is not executed.

goto

Perl supports a goto command. There are three forms: goto *label*, goto *expr*, and goto *&name*. In general, you shouldn't need to use goto, which you'll conclude if you do a search for goto in the *comp.lang.perl.misc* archives on *www.dejanews.com*.

The goto *label* form finds the statement labeled with *label* and resumes execution there. It may not be used to go inside any construct that requires initialization, such as a subroutine or a foreach loop.

The goto *expr* form expects the expression to return a label name.

The goto *&name* form substitutes a call to the named subroutine for the currently running subroutine.

Special Variables

Some variables have a predefined, special meaning in Perl. They use punctuation characters after the usual variable indicator ($, @, or %), such as $_. The explicit, long-form names are the variables' equivalents when you use the English module by including use English; at the top of your program.

Global Special Variables

The most common special variable is $_, which contains the default input and pattern-searching string. For example:

```
foreach ('hickory','dickory','doc') {
        print;
}
```

The first time the loop is executed, "hickory" is printed. The second time around, "dickory" is printed, and the third time, "doc" is printed. That's because in each iteration of the loop, the current string is placed in $_ and is used by default by print. Here are the places where Perl will assume $_, even if you don't specify it:

- Various unary functions, including functions such as ord and int, as well as the all file tests (-f, -d), except for -t, which defaults to STDIN.
- Various list functions such as print and unlink.
- The pattern-matching operations m//, s///, and tr/// when used without an =~ operator.
- The default iterator variable in a foreach loop if no other variable is supplied.
- The implicit iterator variable in the grep and map functions.
- The default place to put an input record when a line-input operation's result is tested by itself as the sole criterion of a while test (i.e., <*filehandle*>). Note that outside of a while test, this does not happen.

The following is a complete listing of global special variables:

$_
$ARG
> The default input and pattern-searching space.

$.
$INPUT_LINE_NUMBER
$NR
> The current input line number of the last filehandle that was read. An explicit close on the filehandle resets the line number.

$/
$INPUT_RECORD_SEPARATOR
$RS
> The input record separator; newline by default. If set to the null string, it treats blank lines as delimiters.

$,
$OUTPUT_FIELD_SEPARATOR
$OFS
> The output field separator for the print operator.

$\
$OUTPUT_RECORD_SEPARATOR
$ORS
> The output record separator for the print operator.

$

$LIST_SEPARATOR

> Like $, except that it applies to list values interpolated into a double-quoted string (or similar interpreted string). Default is a space.

$;

$SUBSCRIPT_SEPARATOR

$SUBSEP

> The subscript separator for multidimensional array emulation. Default is \034.

$^L

$FORMAT_FORMFEED

> What a format outputs to perform a formfeed. Default is \f.

$:

$FORMAT_LINE_BREAK_CHARACTERS

> The current set of characters after which a string may be broken to fill continuation fields (starting with ^) in a format. Default is \n".

$^A

$ACCUMULATOR

> The current value of the write accumulator for format lines.

$#

$OFMT

> Contains the output format for printed numbers (deprecated).

$?

$CHILD_ERROR

> The status returned by the last pipe close, backtick (' ') command, or system operator.

$!

$OS_ERROR

$ERRNO

> If used in a numeric context, yields the current value of the errno variable, identifying the last system call error. If used in a string context, yields the corresponding system error string.

$@

$EVAL_ERROR

> The Perl syntax error message from the last eval command.

$$

$PROCESS_ID

$PID

> The pid of the Perl process running this script.

$<

$REAL_USER_ID

$UID

> The real user ID (uid) of this process.

$>
$EFFECTIVE_USER_ID
$EUID
> The effective uid of this process.

$(
$REAL_GROUP_ID
$GID
> The real group ID (gid) of this process.

$)
$EFFECTIVE_GROUP_ID
$EGID
> The effective gid of this process.

$0
$PROGRAM_NAME
> Contains the name of the file containing the Perl script being executed.

$[
> The index of the first element in an array and of the first character in a substring. Default is 0.

$]
$PERL_VERSION
> Returns the version plus patch level divided by 1,000.

$^D
$DEBUGGING
> The current value of the debugging flags.

$^E
$EXTENDED_OS_ERROR
> Extended error message on some platforms.

$^F
$SYSTEM_FD_MAX
> The maximum system file descriptor, ordinarily 2.

$^H
> Contains internal compiler hints enabled by certain pragmatic modules.

$^I
$INPLACE_EDIT
> The current value of the inplace-edit extension. Use undef to disable inplace editing.

$^M
> The contents of $M can be used as an emergency memory pool in case Perl dies with an out-of-memory error. Use of $M requires a special compilation of Perl. See the INSTALL document for more information.

$^O
$OSNAME
> Contains the name of the operating system for which the current Perl binary was compiled.

`$^P`
`$PERLDB`
> The internal flag that the debugger clears so that it doesn't debug itself.

`$^T`
`$BASETIME`
> The time at which the script began running, in seconds since the epoch.

`$^W`
`$WARNING`
> The current value of the warning switch, either true or false.

`$^X`
`$EXECUTABLE_NAME`
> The name that the Perl binary itself was executed as. As of Perl 5.8, Perl asks the operating system instead of using C's argv[0].

`$ARGV`
> Contains the name of the current file when reading from <ARGV>.

Global Special Arrays and Hashes

`@ARGV`
> The array containing the command-line arguments intended for the script.

`@INC`
> The array containing the list of places to look for Perl scripts to be evaluated by the do, require, or use constructs.

`@F`
> The array into which the input lines are split when the *−a* command-line switch is given.

`%INC`
> The hash containing entries for the filename of each file that has been included via do or require.

`%ENV`
> The hash containing your current environment.

`%SIG`
> The hash used to set signal handlers for various signals.

Global Special Filehandles

`ARGV`
> The special filehandle that iterates over command-line filenames in @ARGV. Usually written as the null filehandle in <>.

`STDERR`
> The special filehandle for standard error in any package.

`STDIN`
> The special filehandle for standard input in any package.

STDOUT

The special filehandle for standard output in any package.

DATA

The special filehandle that refers to anything following the __END__ token in the file containing the script. Or the special filehandle for anything following the __DATA__ token in a required file, as long as you're reading data in the same package __DATA__ was found in.

_ (underscore)

The special filehandle used to cache the information from the last stat, lstat, or file test operator.

Global Special Constants

__END__

Indicates the logical end of your program. Any following text is ignored, but may be read via the DATA filehandle.

__FILE__

Represents the filename at the point in your program where it's used. Not interpolated into strings.

__LINE__

Represents the current line number. Not interpolated into strings.

__PACKAGE__

Represents the current package name at compile time, or undefined if there is no current package. Not interpolated into strings.

Regular Expression Special Variables

For more information on regular expressions, see the section "Regular Expressions" later in this chapter.

$digit

Contains the text matched by the corresponding set of parentheses in the last pattern matched. For example, $1 matches whatever was contained in the first set of parentheses in the previous regular expression.

$&
$MATCH

The string matched by the last successful pattern match.

$'
$PREMATCH

The string preceding whatever was matched by the last successful pattern match.

$'
$POSTMATCH

The string following whatever was matched by the last successful pattern match.

```
$+
```
$LAST_PAREN_MATCH

> The last bracket matched by the last search pattern. This is useful if you don't know which of a set of alternative patterns was matched. For example:

```
/Version: (.*)|Revision: (.*)/ && ($rev = $+);
```

```
$^N
```

> The string matched by the most recently closed group. This is most useful inside (?{...}) blocks for examining matched text. If you have multiple matches denoted by parentheses, $^N can be used in lieu of $1, $2, $3, etc., so you don't have to manually count the number of sets of parentheses that denote your matches. For example:

```
#!/usr/local/bin/perl -w

$words = "person|here";
$words =~ /(\w+)\|(\w+)/;
print $^N;    # Prints 'here'
```

Filehandle Special Variables

Most of these variables apply only when using formats. See the section "Unicode" later in this chapter.

```
$|
```
$OUTPUT_AUTOFLUSH

> If set to nonzero, forces an fflush(3) after every write or print on the currently selected output channel.

```
$%
```
$FORMAT_PAGE_NUMBER

> The current page number of the currently selected output channel.

```
$=
```
$FORMAT_LINES_PER_PAGE

> The current page length (printable lines) of the currently selected output channel. Default is 60.

```
$-
```
$FORMAT_LINES_LEFT

> The number of lines left on the page of the currently selected output channel.

```
$~
```
$FORMAT_NAME

> The name of the current report format for the currently selected output channel. Default is the name of the filehandle.

```
$^
```
$FORMAT_TOP_NAME

> The name of the current top-of-page format for the currently selected output channel. Default is the name of the filehandle with _TOP appended.

Operators

Table 4-3 lists all the Perl operators from highest to lowest precedence and indicates their associativity.

Table 4-3. Perl associativity and operators, listed by precedence

Associativity	Operators
Left	Terms and list operators (leftward)
Left	-> (method call, dereference)
Nonassociative	++ -- (autoincrement, autodecrement)
Right	** (exponentiation)
Right	! ~ \ and unary + and - (logical not, bit-not, reference, unary plus, unary minus)
Left	=~ !~ (matches, doesn't match)
Left	* / % x (multiply, divide, modulus, string replicate)
Left	+ - . (addition, subtraction, string concatenation)
Left	<< >> (left bit-shift, right bit-shift)
Nonassociative	Named unary operators and file-test operators
Nonassociative	< > <= >= lt gt le ge (less than, greater than, less than or equal to, greater than or equal to, and their string equivalents)
Nonassociative	== != <=> eq ne cmp (equal to, not equal to, signed comparison, and their string equivalents)
Left	& (bit-and)
Left	| ^ (bit-or, bit-xor)
Left	&& (logical AND)
Left	|| (logical OR)
Nonassociative	.. ... (range)
Right	?: (ternary conditional)
Right	= += -= *= and so on (assignment operators)
Left	, => (comma, arrow comma)
Nonassociative	List operators (rightward)
Right	not (logical not)
Left	and (logical and)
Left	or xor (logical or, xor)

You can clarify your expressions by using parentheses to group any part of an expression. Anything in parentheses will be evaluated as a single unit within a larger expression.

With very few exceptions, Perl operators act upon scalar values only, not upon list values.

Terms that take highest precedence in Perl include variables, quote and quotelike operators, any expression in parentheses, and any function with arguments in parentheses.

A list operator is a function that can take a list of values as its argument. List operators take highest precedence when considering what's to the left of them. They have considerably lower precedence when looking to their right, which is the expected result.

Also parsed as high-precedence terms are the do{} and eval{} constructs, as well as subroutine and method calls, the anonymous array and hash composers ([] and {}), and the anonymous subroutine composer sub{}.

A unary operator is a function that takes a single scalar value as its argument. Unary operators have a lower precedence than list operators because they expect and take only one value.

The Arrow Operator

The arrow operator is a dereference operator. It can be used for references to arrays, hashes, code references, or for calling methods on objects. See the discussion of references in Chapter 7.

Unary Operators

Unary ! performs logical negation, that is, "not." The not operator is a lower-precedence version of !.

Unary - performs arithmetic negation if the operand is numeric. If the operand is an identifier, then a string consisting of a minus sign concatenated with the identifier is returned. Otherwise, if the string starts with a plus or minus, a string starting with the opposite sign is returned.

Unary ~ performs bitwise negation, that is, one's complement. For example, on a 32-bit machine, ~0xFF is 0xFFFFFF00. If the argument to ~ is a string instead of a number, a string of identical length is returned, but with all the bits of the string complemented.

Unary + has no semantic effect whatsoever, even on strings. It is syntactically useful for separating a function name from a parenthesized expression that would otherwise be interpreted as the complete list of function arguments.

Unary \ creates a reference to whatever follows it (see "References and Complex Data Structures" later in this chapter). Do not confuse this behavior with the behavior of the backslash within a string. The \ operator may also be used on a parenthesized list value in a list context, in which case it returns references to each element of the list.

Arithmetic Operators

Binary ** is the exponentiation operator. Note that it binds even more tightly than unary minus, so -2**4 is -(2**4), not (-2)**4. Also note that ** has right associativity, so:

```
$e = 2 ** 3 ** 4;
```

evaluates to 2 to the 81st power, not 8 to the 4th power.

The * (multiply) and / (divide) operators work exactly as you might expect, multiplying or dividing their two operands. Division is done in floating-point mode, unless integer mode in enabled (via use integer).

The % (modulus) operator converts its operands to integers before finding the remainder according to integer division. For the same operation in floating-point mode, you may prefer to use the fmod( ) function from the POSIX module (see Chapter 8).

Comparison Operators

Comparison operators can be categorized into relational and equality operators.

Relational operators

Perl has two classes of relational operators. One class operates on numeric values, and the other operates on string values. String comparisons are based on the ASCII collating sequence. Relational operators are nonassociative, so $a < $b < $c is a syntax error.

Numeric	String	Meaning
>	gt	Greater than
>=	ge	Greater than or equal to
<	lt	Less than
<=	le	Less than or equal to

Equality operators

The equal and not-equal operators return 1 for true and "" for false (just as the relational operators do). The <=> and *cmp* operators return -1 if the left operand is less than the right operand, 0 if they are equal, and +1 if the left operand is greater than the right.

Numeric	String	Meaning
==	eq	Equal to
!=	ne	Not equal to
<=>	cmp	Comparison, with signed result

Autoincrement and Autodecrement

If placed before a variable, the ++ and -- operators increment or decrement the variable before returning the value. If placed after, they increment or decrement the variable after returning the value.

Assignment Operators

Perl recognizes the following operators for assigning a value to a variable:

```
=     **=     +=     *=     &=     <<=     &&=
-=    /=      |=     >>=    ||=    .=      %=
^=    x=
```

Each operator requires a variable on the left side and an expression on the right side. For the simple assignment operator, =, the value of the expression is stored in the designated variable. For the other operators, Perl evaluates the expression:

```
$var OP= $value
```

as if it was written:

```
$var = $var OP $value
```

except that $var is evaluated only once. For example:

```
$a += 2;    # Same as $a = $a + 2
```

Pattern Match Operators

Binary =~ binds a scalar expression to a pattern match, substitution, or translation. These operations search or modify the string $_ by default.

Binary !~ is just like =~ except the return value is negated in the logical sense. The following expressions are functionally equivalent:

```
$string !~ /pattern/
not $string =~ /pattern/
```

See the section "Regular Expressions" later in this chapter.

File Test Operators

A file test operator is a unary operator that tests a filename or a filehandle.

Operator	Meaning
-r	File is readable by effective uid/gid
-w	File is writable by effective uid/gid
-x	File is executable by effective uid/gid
-o	File is owned by effective uid
-R	File is readable by real uid/gid
-W	File is writable by real uid/gid
-X	File is executable by real uid/gid
-O	File is owned by real uid
-e	File exists
-z	File has zero size
-s	File has nonzero size (returns size)
-f	File is a plain file
-d	File is a directory

Operator	Meaning
-l	File is a symbolic link
-p	File is a named pipe (FIFO)
-S	File is a socket
-b	File is a block special file
-c	File is a character special file
-t	Filehandle is opened to a tty
-u	File has setuid bit set
-g	File has setgid bit set
-k	File has sticky bit set
-T	File is a text file
-B	File is a binary file (opposite of -T)
-M	Age of file (at startup) in days since modification
-A	Age of file (at startup) in days since last access
-C	Age of file (at startup) in days since inode change

Logical Operators

Perl provides the && (logical AND) and || (logical OR) operators. They evaluate from left to right testing the truth of the statement.

Example	Name	Result
$a && $b	And	$a if $a is false, $b otherwise
$a || $b	Or	$a if $a is true, $b otherwise

For example, an oft-appearing idiom in Perl programs is:

```
open(FILE, "somefile") || die "Cannot open somefile: $!\n";
```

In this case, Perl first evaluates the open function. If the value is true (because somefile was successfully opened), the execution of the die function is unnecessary and is skipped.

Perl also provides lower-precedence and and or operators that are more readable.

Bitwise Operators

Perl has bitwise AND, OR, and XOR (exclusive OR) operators: &, |, and ^. These operators work differently on numeric values than they do on strings. If either operand is a number, then both operands are converted to integers, and the bitwise operation is performed between the two integers. If both operands are strings, these operators do bitwise operations between corresponding bits from the two strings.

Miscellaneous Operators

The following operators don't fit into any of the previous categories.

Range operator

The .. range operator is really two different operators depending on the context. In a list context, it returns a list of values counting (by ones) from the left value to the right value.

In a scalar context, .. returns a Boolean value. It is false as long as its left operand is false. Once the left operand is true, the range operator stays true until the right operand is true, after which the range operator becomes false again. The right operand is not evaluated while the operator is in the false state, and the left operand is not evaluated while the operator is in the true state.

The alternate version of this operator, ..., does not test the right operand immediately when the operator becomes true; it waits until the next evaluation.

Conditional operator

Ternary ?: is the conditional operator. It works like an if-then-else statement but can safely be embedded within other operations and functions:

```
test_expr ? if_true_expr : if_false_expr
```

If the test_expr is true, only the if_true_expr is evaluated. Otherwise, only the if_false_expr is evaluated. Either way, the value of the evaluated expression becomes the value of the entire expression.

Comma operator

In a list context, , is the list argument separator and inserts both its arguments into the list. In scalar context, , evaluates its left argument, throws that value away, then evaluates its right argument and returns that value.

The => operator is mostly just a synonym for the comma operator. It's useful for documenting arguments that come in pairs. It also forces any identifier to the left of it to be interpreted as a string.

String operator

The concatenation operator . is used to add strings together:

```
print 'abc' . 'def';        # Prints abcdef
print $a . $b;              # Concatenates the string values of $a and $b
```

Binary x is the string repetition operator. In scalar context, it returns a concatenated string consisting of the left operand repeated the number of times specified by the right operand:

```
print '-' x 80;                          # Prints row of dashes
print "\t" x ($tab/8), ' ' x ($tab%8);   # Tabs over
```

In list context, if the left operand is a list in parentheses, the x works as a list replicator rather than a string replicator. This is useful for initializing all the elements of an array of indeterminate length to the same value:

```
@ones = (1) x 80;       # A list of 80 1s
@ones = (5) x @ones;    # Set all elements to 5
```

Regular Expressions

Regular expressions are used several ways in Perl. They're used in conditionals to determine whether a string matches a particular pattern. They're also used to find patterns in strings and replace the match with something else.

The ordinary pattern match operator looks like */pattern/*. It matches against the $_ variable by default. If the pattern is found in the string, the operator returns true (1); if there is no match, a false value ("") is returned.

The substitution operator looks like *s/pattern/replace/*. This operator searches $_ by default. If it finds the specified *pattern*, it is replaced with the string in *replace*. If *pattern* is not matched, nothing happens.

You may specify a variable other than $_ with the =~ binding operator (or the negated !~ binding operator, which returns true if the pattern is not matched). For example:

```
$text =~ /sampo/;
```

Pattern-Matching Operators

The following list defines Perl's pattern-matching operators. Some of the operators have alternative "quoting" schemes and have a set of modifiers that can be placed directly after the operators to affect the match operation in some way.

m/*pattern*/gimosxe
  Searches a string for a pattern match. Modifiers are:

Modifier	Meaning
g	Match globally, i.e., find all occurrences.
i	Do case-insensitive pattern matching.
m	Treat string as multiple lines.
o	Compile pattern only once.
s	Treat string as single line.
x	Use extended regular expressions.

If / is the delimiter, then the initial m is optional. With m, you can use any pair of non-alphanumeric, non-whitespace characters as delimiters.

?*pattern*?
  This operator is just like the m/*pattern*/ search, except it matches only once.

qr/*pattern*/imosx
  Creates a precompiled regular expression from *pattern*, which can be passed around in variables and interpolated into other regular expressions. The modifiers are the same as those for m// above.

s/*pattern*/*replacement*/egimosx
  Searches a string for *pattern* and replaces any match with the *replacement* text. Returns the number of substitutions made, which can be more than one

with the /g modifier. Otherwise, it returns false (0). If no string is specified via the =~ or !~ operator, the $_ variable is searched and modified. Modifiers are:

Modifier	Meaning
e	Evaluate the right side as an expression.
g	Replace globally, i.e., all occurrences.
cg	Continue search after g failed. No longer supported for s/// as of Perl 5.8.
i	Do case-insensitive pattern matching.
m	Treat string as multiple lines.
o	Compile pattern only once.
s	Treat string as single line.
x	Use extended regular expressions.

Any non-alphanumeric, non-whitespace delimiter may replace the slashes. If single quotes are used, no interpretation is done on the replacement string (the /e modifier overrides this, however).

tr/*pattern1*/*pattern2*/cds
y/*pattern1*/*pattern2*/cds

This operator scans a string character by character and replaces all occurrences of the characters found in *pattern1* with the corresponding character in *pattern2*. It returns the number of characters replaced or deleted. If no string is specified via the =~ or !~ operator, the $_ string is translated. Modifiers are:

Modifier	Meaning
c	Complement *pattern1*.
d	Delete found but unreplaced characters.
s	Squash duplicate replaced characters.

Regular Expression Syntax

The simplest kind of regular expression is a literal string. More complicated patterns involve the use of *metacharacters* to describe all the different choices and variations that you want to build into a pattern. Metacharacters don't match themselves, but describe something else. The metacharacters are:

Metacharacter	Meaning
\	Escapes the character(s) immediately following it
.	Matches any single character except a newline (unless /s is used)
^	Matches at the beginning of the string (or line, if /m is used)
$	Matches at the end of the string (or line, if /m is used)
*	Matches the preceding element 0 or more times
+	Matches the preceding element 1 or more times
?	Matches the preceding element 0 or 1 times
{...}	Specifies a range of occurrences for the element preceding it

Metacharacter	Meaning
[...]	Matches any one of the class of characters contained within the brackets
(...)	Groups regular expressions
|	Matches either the expression preceding or following it

The . (single dot) is a wildcard character. When used in a regular expression, it can match any single character. The exception is the newline character (\n), except when you use the /s modifier on the pattern match operator. This modifier treats the string to be matched against as a single "long" string with embedded newlines.

The ^ and $ metacharacters are used as anchors in a regular expression. The ^ matches the beginning of a line. This character should appear only at the beginning of an expression to match the beginning of the line. The exception to this is when the /m (multiline) modifier is used, in which case it will match at the beginning of the string and after every newline (except the last, if there is one). Otherwise, ^ will match itself, unescaped, anywhere in a pattern, except if it is the first character in a bracketed character class, in which case it negates the class.

Similarly, $ will match the end of a line (just before a newline character) only if it is at the end of a pattern, unless /m is used, in which case it matches just before every newline and at the end of a string. You need to escape $ to match a literal dollar sign in all cases, because if $ isn't at the end of a pattern (or placed right before a) or]), Perl will attempt to do variable interpretation. The same holds true for the @ sign, which Perl will interpret as an array variable start unless it is backslashed.

The *, +, and ? metacharacters are called *quantifiers*. They specify the number of times to match something. They act on the element immediately preceding them, which could be a single character (including the .), a grouped expression in parentheses, or a character class. The {...} construct is a generalized modifier. You can put two numbers separated by a comma within the braces to specify minimum and maximum numbers that the preceding element can match.

Parentheses are used to group characters or expressions. They also have the side effect of remembering what they matched so you can recall and reuse patterns with a special group of variables.

The | is the alternation operator in regular expressions. It matches either what's on its left side or right side. It does not affect only single characters. For example:

```
/you|me|him|her/
```

looks for any of the four words. You should use parentheses to provide boundaries for alternation:

```
/And(y|rew)/
```

This will match either "Andy" or "Andrew".

Escaped Sequences

The following table lists the backslashed representations of characters that you can use in regular expressions:

Code	Matches
\a	Alarm (beep)
\n	Newline
\r	Carriage return
\t	Tab
\f	Formfeed
\e	Escape
\038	Any octal ASCII value
\x7f	Any hexadecimal ASCII value
\x{263a}	A wide hexadecimal value
\c*x*	Control-*x*
\N{*name*}	A named character

Character Classes

The [...] construct is used to list a set of characters (a *character class*) of which *one* will match. Brackets are often used when capitalization is uncertain in a match:

```
/[tT]here/
```

A dash (-) may be used to indicate a range of characters in a character class:

```
/[a-zA-Z]/;  # Match any single letter
/[0-9]/;     # Match any single digit
```

To put a literal dash in the list you must use a backslash before it (\-).

By placing a ^ as the first element in the brackets, you create a negated character class, i.e., it matches any character not in the list. For example:

```
/[^A-Z]/;    # Matches any character other than an uppercase letter
```

Some common character classes have their own predefined escape sequences for your programming convenience:

Code	Matches
\d	A digit, same as [0-9]
\D	A nondigit, same as [^0-9]
\w	A word character (alphanumeric), same as [a-zA-Z_0-9]
\W	A non-word character, [^a-zA-Z_0-9]
\s	A whitespace character, same as [\t\n\r\f]
\S	A non-whitespace character, [^ \t\n\r\f]
\C	Match a character (byte)

Code	Matches
\pP	Match P-named (Unicode) property
\PP	Match non-P
\X	Match extended unicode sequence

While Perl implements lc( ) and uc( ), which you can use for testing the proper case of words or characters, you can do the same with escape sequences:

Code	Matches
\l	Lowercase until next character
\u	Uppercase until next character
\L	Lowercase until \E
\U	Uppercase until \E
\Q	Disable pattern metacharacters until \E
\E	End case modification

These elements match any single element in (or not in) their class. A \w matches only one character of a word. Using a modifier, you can match a whole word, for example, with \w+. The abbreviated classes may also be used within brackets as elements of other character classes.

Anchors

Anchors don't match any characters; they match places within a string. The two most common anchors are ^ and $, which match the beginning and end of a line, respectively. The following table lists the anchoring patterns used to match certain boundaries in regular expressions:

Assertion	Meaning
^	Matches at the beginning of the string (or line, if /m is used)
$	Matches at the end of the string (or line, if /m is used)
\b	Matches at word boundary (between \w and \W)
\B	Matches except at word boundary
\A	Matches at the beginning of the string
\Z	Matches at the end of the string or before a newline
\z	Matches only at the end of the string
\G	Matches where previous m//g left off
\c	Suppresses resetting of search position when used with \g. Without \c, search pattern is reset to the beginning of the string.

The $ and \Z assertions can match not only at the end of the string, but also one character earlier than that, if the last character of the string is a newline.

Quantifiers

Quantifiers are used to specify the number of instances of the previous element that can match. For instance, you could say "match any number of a's, including none" (a*), or "match between 5 and 10 instances of the word 'owie' ((owie){5,10})".

Quantifiers, by nature, are greedy. That is, the way the Perl regular expression "engine" works is that it will look for the biggest match possible (the farthest to the right) unless you tell it not to. Say you are searching a string that reads:

```
a whatever foo, b whatever foo
```

and you want to find a and foo with something in between. You might use:

```
/a.*foo/
```

A . followed by a * looks for any character, any number of times, until foo is found. But since Perl will look as far to the right as possible to find foo, the first instance of foo is swallowed up by the greedy .* expression.

Therefore, all the quantifiers have a notation that allows for minimal matching, so they are nongreedy. This notation uses a question mark immediately following the quantifier to force Perl to look for the earliest available match (farthest to the left). The following table lists the regular expression quantifiers and their nongreedy forms:

Maximal	Minimal	Allowed range
{n,m}	{n,m}?	Must occur at least n times but no more than m times
{n,}	{n,}?	Must occur at least n times
{n}	{n}?	Must match exactly n times
*	*?	0 or more times (same as {0,})
+	+?	1 or more times (same as {1,})
?	??	0 or 1 time (same as {0,1})

Pattern Match Variables

Parentheses not only group elements in a regular expression, they also remember the patterns they match. Every match from a parenthesized element is saved to a special, read-only variable indicated by a number. You can recall and reuse a match by using these variables.

Within a pattern, each parenthesized element saves its match to a numbered variable, in order starting with 1. You can recall these matches within the expression by using \1, \2, and so on.

Outside of the matching pattern, the matched variables are recalled with the usual dollar sign, i.e., $1, $2, etc. The dollar sign notation should be used in the replacement expression of a substitution and anywhere else you might want to use the variables in your program. For example, to implement "i before e, except after c":

```
s/([^c])ei/$1ie/g;
```

The backreferencing variables are:

$+ Returns the last parenthesized pattern match

$& Returns the entire matched string

$' Returns everything before the matched string

$´ Returns everything after the matched string

Backreferencing with these variables will slow down your program noticeably for all regular expressions.

Extended Regular Expressions

Perl defines an extended syntax for regular expressions. The syntax is a pair of parentheses with a question mark as the first thing within the parentheses. The character after the question mark gives the function of the extension. The extensions are:

(?#*text*)
: A comment. The text is ignored.

(?:...)
(?imsx-imsx:...)
: This groups things like (...) but doesn't make backreferences.

(?=...)
: A zero-width positive lookahead assertion. For example, /\w+(?=\t)/ matches a word followed by a tab, without including the tab in $&.

(?!...)
: A zero-width negative lookahead assertion. For example, /foo(?!bar)/ matches any occurrence of foo that isn't followed by bar.

(?<...)
: A zero-width positive lookbehind assertion. For example, /(?<bad)boy/ matches the word boy that follows bad, without including bad in $&. This works only for fixed-width lookbehind.

(?{*code*})
: An experimental regular expression feature to evaluate any embedded Perl code. This evaluation always succeeds, and *code* is not interpolated.

(?<!=...)
: A zero-width negative lookbehind assertion. For example, /(?<!=bad)boy/ matches any occurrence of boy that doesn't follow bad. This works only for fixed-width lookbehind.

(?>...)
: Matches the substring that the standalone pattern would match if anchored at the given position.

(?(*condition*)*yes-pattern*|*no-pattern*)
(?(*condition*)*yes-pattern*)
: Matches a pattern determined by a condition. *condition* should be either an integer, which is true if the pair of parentheses corresponding to the integer

has matched, or a lookahead, lookbehind, or evaluate, zero-width assertion. *no-pattern* will be used to match if the condition was not meant, but it is also optional.

(?imsx-imsx)

One or more embedded pattern-match modifiers. Modifiers are switched off if they follow a - (dash). The modifiers are defined as follows:

Modifier	Meaning
i	Do case-insensitive pattern matching.
m	Treat string as multiple lines.
s	Treat string as single line.
x	Use extended regular expressions.

Subroutines

Subroutines are declared using one of these forms:

```
sub name {block}
sub name (proto) {block}
```

Prototypes allow you to put constraints on the arguments you provide to your subroutines.

You can also create anonymous subroutines at runtime, which will be available for use through a reference:

```
$subref = sub {block};
```

Calling Subroutines

The ampersand (&) is the identifier used to call subroutines. Most of the time, however, subroutines can be used in an expression just like built-in functions. To call subroutines directly:

```
name(args);      # & is optional with parentheses
name args;       # Parens optional if predeclared/imported
&name;           # Passes current @_ to subroutine
```

To call subroutines indirectly (by name or by reference):

```
&$subref(args);  # & is not optional on indirect call
&$subref;        # Passes current @_ to subroutine
```

Passing Arguments

All arguments to a subroutine are passed as a single, flat list of scalars, and return values are returned the same way. Any arrays or hashes passed in these lists will have their values interpolated into the flattened list.

Any arguments passed to a subroutine come in as the array @_.

You may use the explicit return statement to return a value and leave the subroutine at any point.

Passing References

If you want to pass more than one array or hash into or out of a function and maintain their integrity, you should pass references as arguments. The simplest way to do this is to take your named variables and put a backslash in front of them in the argument list:

```
@returnlist = ref_conversion(\@temps1, \@temps2, \@temps3);
```

This sends references to the three arrays to the subroutine (and saves you the step of creating your own named references to send to the function). The references to the arrays are passed to the subroutine as the three-member @_ array. The subroutine will have to dereference the arguments so that the data values may be used.

Returning references is a simple matter of returning scalars that are references. This way, you can return distinct hashes and arrays.

Private and Local Variables

Any variables you use in the function that aren't declared private are global variables. In subroutines, you'll often want to use variables that won't be used anywhere else in your program, and you don't want them taking up memory when the subroutine is not being executed. You also might not want to alter variables in subroutines that might have the same name as global variables.

The my function declares variables that are *lexically scoped* within the subroutine. Lexically scoped variables are private variables that exist only within the block or subroutine in which they are declared. Outside of their scope, they are invisible and can't be altered in any way.

To scope multiple variables at once, use a list in parentheses. You can also assign a variable in a my statement:

```
my @list = (44, 55, 66);
my $cd = "orb";
```

Dynamic variables are visible to other subroutines called from within their scope, are defined with local, and are not private variables but global variables with temporary values. When a subroutine is executed, the global value is hidden away, and the local value is used. Once the scope is exited, the original global value is used. Most of the time, you will want to use my to localize parameters in a subroutine.

Prototypes

Prototypes allow you to design your subroutines to take arguments with constraints on the number of parameters and types of data. To declare a function with prototypes, use the prototype symbols in the declaration line like this:

```
sub addem ($$) {
...
}
```

In this case, the function expects two scalar arguments. The following table gives the various prototype symbols:

Symbol	Meaning
$	Scalar
@	List
%	Hash
&	Anonymous subroutine
*	Typeglob

A backslash placed before one of these symbols forces the argument to be that exact variable type. For instance, a function that requires a hash variable would be declared like this:

```
sub hashfunc (\%);
```

Unbackslashed @ or % symbols act exactly alike and will eat up all remaining arguments, forcing list context. Likewise, a $ forces scalar context on an argument, so taking an array or hash variable for that parameter would probably yield unwanted results.

A semicolon separates mandatory arguments from optional arguments. For example:

```
sub newsplit (\@$;$);
```

requires two arguments: an array variable and a scalar. The third scalar is optional. Placing a semicolon before @ and % is not necessary since lists can be null.

A typeglob prototype symbol (*) will always turn its argument into a reference to a symbol table entry. It is most often used for filehandles.

References and Complex Data Structures

A Perl reference is a fundamental data type that "points" to another piece of data or code. A reference knows the location of the information and the type of data stored there.

A reference is a scalar and can be used anywhere a scalar can be used. Any array element or hash value can contain a reference (a hash key cannot contain a reference), which is how nested data structures are built in Perl. You can construct lists containing references to other lists, which can contain references to hashes, and so on.

Creating References

You can create a reference to an existing variable or subroutine by prefixing it with a backslash:

```
$a = "fondue";
@alist = ("pitt", "hanks", "cage", "cruise");
```

```
%song = ("mother" => "crying", "brother" => "dying");
sub freaky_friday { s/mother/daughter/ }
# Create references
$ra = \$a;
$ralist = \@alist;
$rsong = \%song;
$rsub = \&freaky_friday; # '&' required for subroutine names
```

References to scalar constants are created similarly:

```
$pi = \3.14159;
$myname = \"Charlie";
```

Note that all references are prefixed by a $, even if they refer to an array or hash. All references are scalars; thus, you can copy a reference to another scalar or even reference another reference:

```
$aref = \@names;
$bref = $aref;           # Both refer to @names
$cref = \$aref;          # $cref is a reference to $aref
```

Because arrays and hashes are collections of scalars, you can create references to individual elements by prefixing their names with backslashes:

```
$star = \$alist[2];      # Refers to third element of @alist
$action = \$song{mother}; # Refers to the 'mother' value of %song
```

Referencing anonymous data

It is also possible to take references to literal data not stored in a variable. This data is called *anonymous* because it is not bound to any named variable.

To create a reference to a scalar constant, simply backslash the literal string or number.

To create a reference to an anonymous array, place the list of values in square brackets:

```
$shortbread = [ "flour", "butter", "eggs", "sugar" ];
```

This creates a reference to an array, but the array is available only through the reference $shortbread.

A reference to an anonymous hash uses braces around the list of elements:

```
$cast = { host     => "Space Ghost",
          musician => "Zorak",
          director => "Moltar" };
```

Dereferencing

Dereferencing returns the value a reference points to. The general method of dereferencing uses the reference variable substituted for the regular name part of a variable. If $r is a reference, then $$r, @$r, or %$r retrieve the value that is referred to, depending on whether $r is pointing to a scalar, array, or hash. A reference can be used in all the places where an ordinary data type can be used.

When a reference is accidentally evaluated as a plain scalar, it returns a string that indicates the type of data it points to and the memory address of the data.

If you just want to know the type of data that is being referenced, use ref, which returns one of the following strings if its argument is a reference. Otherwise, it returns false.

```
SCALAR
ARRAY
HASH
CODE
GLOB
REF
```

Arrow dereferencing

References to arrays, hashes, and subroutines can be dereferenced using the -> operator. This operator dereferences the expression to its left, which must resolve to an array or hash and accesses the element represented by the subscripted expression on its right. For example, these three statements are equivalent:

```
$$arrayref[0] = "man";
${$arrayref}[0] = "man";
$arrayref->[0] = "man";
```

The first statement dereferences $arrayref first and finds the first element of that array. The second uses braces to clarify this procedure. The third statement uses the arrow notation to do the same thing.

The arrow dereferencing notation can be used only to access a single scalar value. You cannot use arrow operators in expressions that return either slices or whole arrays or hashes.

Filehandles

A filehandle is the name for an I/O connection between your Perl process and the operating system. Filehandle names are like label names but use their own namespace. Like label names, the convention is to use all uppercase letters for file-handle names.

Every Perl program has three filehandles that are automatically opened: STDIN, STDOUT, and STDERR. By default, the print and write functions write to STDOUT. Additional filehandles are created using the open function:

```
open (DATA, "numbers.txt");
```

DATA is the new filehandle that is attached to the external file, which is now opened for reading. You can open filehandles for reading, writing, and appending to external files and devices. To open a file for writing, prefix the filename with a greater-than sign:

```
open(OUT, ">outfile");
```

To open a file for appending, prefix the filename with two greater-than signs:

```
open(LOGFILE, ">>error_log");
```

The open function returns true if the file is successfully opened, and false if it failed to open. Opening a file can fail for any number of reasons, e.g., a file does not exist, is write-protected, or you don't have permission for a file or directory. However, a filehandle that has not been successfully opened can still be read from (giving you an immediate EOF) or written to with no noticeable effects.

You should always check the result of open immediately and report an error if the operation does not succeed. The warn function can report an error to standard error if something goes wrong, and die can terminate your program and tell you what went wrong. For example:

```
open(LOGFILE, "/usr/httpd/error_log")
        || warn "Could not open /usr/httpd/error_log.\n";
open(DATA, ">/tmp/data") || die "Could not create /tmp/data\n.";
```

Once the file is opened, you can access the data using the diamond operator, *<filehandle>*. This is the line-input operator. When used on a filehandle in a scalar context, it returns a line from a filehandle as a string. Each time it is called, it returns the next line from the filehandle until it reaches the end-of-file. The operator keeps track of the line it is on in the file, unless the filehandle is closed and reopened, which resets the operator to the top-of-file.

For example, the following prints any line containing the word "secret.html" from the LOGFILE filehandle:

```
while (<LOGFILE>) {
        print "$_\n" if /secret\.html/;
}
```

In a list context, the line-input operator returns a list in which each line is an element. The empty <> operator reads from the ARGV filehandle, which reads the array of filenames from the Perl command line. If @ARGV is empty, the operator resorts to standard input.

A number of functions send output to a filehandle. The filehandle must already be opened for writing, of course. In the previous example, print wrote to the STDOUT filehandle, even though it wasn't specified. Without a filehandle, print defaults to the currently selected output filehandle, which will be STDOUT until you open and select another one in your program. See the select function (file-handle version) for more information.

If your program involves more than a couple of open filehandles, you should specify the filehandles for all of your I/O functions to be safe:

```
print LOGFILE "======= Generated report $date ======="
```

To close a filehandle, use the close function. Filehandles are also closed when the program exits.

Perl 5.8 and PerlIO

Perl 5.8 does I/O via PerlIO instead of through your system's I/O (STDIO). By implementing open( ) with PerlIO, the default behavior of open is changed to support a three-argument format. For example:

```
open($fh, '>:utf-8', $filename)
    or die("...");    # Open $filename and support utf-8
```

In this example, the filehandle is marked with utf-8 (or utf8 for EBCDIC users) to accept Perl's internal Unicode encoding.

The PerlIO layers are:

unix
> Low-level read/write

stdio
> Standard I/O

perlio
> Portable implementation of buffering

crlf
> Win32

Also in Perl 5.8, you are no longer required to name a filehandle in open( ) because Perl will handle the filehandles internally:

```
open($fh, ...) or ...
```

You can also use anonymous temporary files with the new form of open( ):

```
open($fh, ">", undef) or ...
```

Pipes can also be used with a multiple-argument form of open. The following code is roughly equivalent to the Unix command 'ls -al':

```
open($fh, "-|", 'ls -al', '/users') or ...
```

Signals

Perl supports many facilities for Interprocess Communication (IPC), including signals and sockets. Regardless of which IPC form you use with Perl, you'll almost always tangle with signals.

Signals can be generated from any source, including key sequences on your keyboard, an event on your system, or from a failed program.

For quite some time, Perl has used a simple signal handling module, in which %SIG was populated with keys that represented the signal handlers your system supported. You'd invoke one of these handlers when Perl came across $SIG{'whatever_signal_here'}. In fact, even in Perl 5.8, the %SIG interface is the same, but the behavior of signals is entirely different. More on this shortly.

For signals to be useful, they must be trapped and dealt with. However, you shouldn't try to do too much when you trap a signal. Generally, you should only generate a warning and deal with the condition that caused the error. In a way, Perl's %SIG keeps you from doing too much. %SIG works like this:

```
$SIG{I_GOT_THIS_SIGNAL} = \&now_call_this_sub_to_handle_it;
sub now_call_this_sub_to_handle it {
    ...
}
```

If you need to know which signals Perl is aware of, do a 'kill -l' on a Unix system, or use *Config.pm*:

```
#!/usr/local/bin/perl -w

use Config;

print "Perl knows about the following signals:\n";
print $Config{sig_name_init}, "\n";
```

Here's a simple snippet that lets you know if someone sent you a HUP signal:

```
$SIG{HUP} = \&hic_hup;
sub hic_hup {
    my $signal = shift;
    # Don't die for now.  Just warn us.
    warn "Somebody sent me a SIG${signal}\n";
}
```

Often, the type of signal you encounter in your Perl program will dictate how you should handle it. For example, you should assign 'IGNORE' to the 'CHLD' signal on many Unix platforms to reduce the possibility of creating zombie processes. Other signals, such as KILL and STOP, cannot and should not be ignored so easily. For this purpose, Perl lets you use a local( ) statement, which lets you temporarily ignore a signal:

```
sub kill_handler {
    local $SIG{KILL} = 'IGNORE'; # Inherited by all functions here
    i_will_settle_for_denial();
}

sub i_will_settle_for_denial {
    # KILL ignored for now.  Go in peace.
}
```

Unix allows you to kill processes with negative process IDs by sending a *signal zero*. If you have a program that starts itself and several children, use 'kill -PARENT_PID' to kill the parent and all of the children processes. But obviously, if you send a HUP to the parent, you don't want the parent to die. You can avoid this with Perl and signals:

```
sub be_nice_to_your_parents {
    local($SIG{HUP}) = 'IGNORE';
    kill('HUP', -$$);    # This pid and its kids
}
```

Naturally, you don't have to do anything fancy with signal handlers. You can simply die if the given $SIG{NAME} won't cause negative effects on your system if you mishandle it:

```
$SIG{INT} = sub {
    die "\nYou've interrupted me for one last time!\n"
};
```

Keep in mind that it's not all fun and games with Perl and signals. If you don't know how your system's C library and its signals implementation behave, or if

---

you haven't read the instructions before firing your BB gun, you'll shoot your eye out. We guarantee it!

As of Perl 5.8, you can probably be a little more confident in Perl's ability to handle even a bad system-specific signals implementation. In the old days, when men were men and eyeless men were everywhere, a bad signals implementation at both a system and Perl level, or a signal cropping up at the wrong time, could corrupt Perl's internal state. Thankfully, Perl 5.8 and later will postpone signal handling until it's safe to proceed. This means that while the signals interface doesn't change, even if your program catches a signal at a specific place, Perl 5.8 and later will finish whatever they are doing when the signal is encountered.

Finally, signals aren't limited to coping with the behaviors of processes. You can also trap alarm signals for Perl functions and system calls alike if your Perl code lives in an eval( ) block. For example, let's say you want to ping a host, your-host.your.domain, and you want the ping process to timeout in a reasonable amount of time if your-host.your.domain isn't available. You can use alarm( ) inside of eval( ), like so:

```
#!/usr/local/bin/perl -w

my $to_ping = 'your-host.your.domain';
my $a_secs = 5;

eval {
    local $SIG{ALRM} = sub { die "no dice for $to_ping" };
    alarm $a_secs;
    system("/usr/sbin/ping", $to_ping);
    alarm 0;
};

if ($@ and $@ !~ /no dice for $to_ping/) { die }
```

Note that you may have to wait for the ping command itself to timeout. While alarm occurs after $a_secs, you won't see the "no dice for…" message until system( ) (or qx( )) is complete. This is not the case for Perl functions such as flock( ), open( ), etc.

Unicode

Unicode provides a unique number for every character, regardless of the computing platform, program, or programming language. This is particularly important because without a standard such as Unicode, computers would continue to use different encoding classes for characters, many of which would conflict if character classes were used together.

Unicode support was introduced to Perl with Perl 5.6. Although it is still not completely adherent in the Unicode spec, Unicode support has matured significantly under Perl 5.8. You can now use Unicode reliably with file I/O and with regular expressions. With regular expressions, the pattern will adapt to the data and will automatically switch to the correct Unicode character scheme.

Perl's Unicode implementation falls into the following categories:

I/O

> There is currently no way in Perl to mark data that's read from or written to a file as being of type Unicode (utf8). Future versions of Perl will support such a feature.

Regular expressions

> The determination whether to match Unicode characters is made when the pattern is compiled, based on whether the pattern contains Unicode characters and not when matching happens at runtime. This will be changed to match Unicode characters at runtime.

`use utf8`

> The utf8 module is still needed to enable a few Unicode features. The `utf8` pragma, as implemented by the utf8 module, implements tables used for Unicode support. You must load the `utf8` pragma explicitly to enable recognition of UTF-8 encoded literals and identifiers in the source text.

Byte and character semantics

> As of 5.6.0, Perl uses logically wide characters to represent strings internally. This internal representation uses the UTF-8 encoding. Future versions of Perl will work with characters rather than bytes. This was a purposeful decision made so Perl 5.6 could transition from byte semantics to character semantics in programs. Perl will make the decision to switch to character semantics if it finds that the input data has characters on which it can safely operate with UTF-8. You can disable character semantics by using the `bytes` pragma, as explained in Chapter 8. Character semantics have the following effects:

> - Strings and patterns may contain characters that have an ordinal value larger than 255.
> - Identifiers within a Perl program may contain Unicode alphanumeric characters.
> - Regular expressions match characters and not bytes.
> - Character classes in regular expressions match characters and not bytes.
> - Named Unicode properties and block ranges may be used as character classes with the \p and \P constructs.
> - \X matches any extended Unicode sequence.
> - `tr//` matches characters instead of bytes.
> - Case translation operators use the Unicode case translation tables when provided character input.
> - Most operators that deal with positions or lengths in a string switch to using character positions.
> - `pack( )` and `unpack( )` do not change.
> - Bit operators work on characters.
> - `scalar reverse( )` reverses characters and not bytes.

Formats

Formats are a mechanism for generating formatted reports for outputting data and are defined with the `format` keyword. The general form looks like:

```
format name =
...template lines...
...argument line...
.
```

Most of your format names will be the same as the filehandle names for which they are used. The default format for a filehandle is the one with the same name.

The format definition is like a subroutine definition. It doesn't contain immediately executed code and can therefore be placed anywhere in the file with the rest of the program; they are commonly placed near the end of the file with subroutine definitions. To output to a format, use the `write` function instead of `print`.

The template lines contain literal text and fieldholders. Fieldholders contain symbols that describe the size and positioning of the area on the line where data is output. An argument line immediately follows a template line that contains the fields to be replaced by data. The argument line is a list of variables (or expressions), separated by commas, that fill the fields in the previous line in the order they are listed.

Here's an example of a template line with two fieldholders and the argument line that follows:

```
Hello, my name is @<<<<<<<<<< and I'm @<< years old.
$name, $age
```

The fieldholders are `@<<<<<<<<<<` and `@<<`, which specify left-justified text fields with 11 and 3 characters, respectively.

Most fieldholders start with @. The characters following @ indicate the type of field, while the number of characters (including @) indicate the field width. The following fieldholder characters determine the positioning of text fields:

`<<<<` *(left angle brackets)*
: A left-justified field; if the value is shorter than the field width, it will be padded on the right with spaces.

`>>>>` *(right angle brackets)*
: A right-justified field; if the value is too short, it will be padded on the left with spaces.

`||||` *(vertical bars)*
: A centered field; if the value is too short, it will be padded on both sides with spaces, enough on each side to center the value within the field.

Another kind of fieldholder is a *fixed-precision numeric field*. This field also begins with @, and is followed by one or more hashmarks (###) with an optional dot (indicating a decimal point). For example:

```
format MONEY =
Assets: @#####.## Liabilities: @#####.## Net: @#####.##
```

```
$assets, $liabilities, $assets-$liabilities
```

The multiline fieldholder allows you to include a value that may have many lines of information. This fieldholder is denoted by @* on a line by itself. The next line defines the value that will be substituted into the field, which in this case may be an expression that results in a value that contains many newlines.

Another kind of fieldholder is a *filled field*. This fieldholder allows you to create a filled paragraph, breaking the text into conveniently sized lines at word boundaries, wrapping the lines as needed. A filled field is denoted by replacing the @ marker in a text fieldholder with a caret (^<<<, for example). The corresponding value for a filled field (on the following line of the format) must be a scalar variable containing text, rather than an expression that returns a scalar value. When Perl is filling the filled field, it takes the value of the variable and removes as many words as will fit in the field. Subsequent calls for the variable in a filled field will continue where the last one left off.

If the variable's contents are exhausted before the number of fields, you will simply end up with blank lines. You can suppress blank lines by placing a tilde (~) on the line. Any line that contains a tilde character is not output if the line would have otherwise printed blank (i.e., just whitespace). The tilde itself always prints as a blank and can be placed anywhere a space could have been placed in the line.

If the text in the variable is longer than what can be filled in the fields, output continues only until the fields run out. The shortcut to get the string to print until it ends is to use two consecutive tildes (~~) on a line. This causes the line to repeat automatically until the result is a completely blank line (which will be suppressed).

Default values for format parameters all relate to the format of the currently selected filehandle. The currently selected filehandle starts out as STDOUT, which makes it easy to print things on the standard output. However, you can change the currently selected filehandle with the select function, which takes a single filehandle (or a scalar variable containing the name of a filehandle) as an argument. Once the currently selected filehandle is changed, it affects all future operations that depend on the currently selected filehandle.

Pod

Pod is a simple, but surprisingly capable, text formatter that uses tags to tell a translator how to format the text. The tags serve several purposes:

- They tell the formatter how to lay out text on the page.
- They provide font and cross-reference information.
- They start and stop parsing of code.

The last item is indicative of one of pod's most useful features—that it can be intermixed with Perl code. While it can be difficult to force yourself to go back and write documentation for your code after the fact, with Perl you can simply intermingle the documentation with the code, and do it all at once. It also lets you use the same text as both code documentation and user documentation.

A pod translator reads a file paragraph by paragraph, ignoring text that isn't pod, and converting it to the proper format. Paragraphs are separated by blank lines (not just by newlines). The various translators recognize three kinds of paragraphs:

Command

Commands begin with =, followed immediately by the command identifier:

```
=cut
```

They can also be followed by text:

```
=head2 Second-level head
```

A blank line signals the end of the command.

Text

A paragraph consisting of a block of text, generally filled and possibly justified, depending on the translator. For example, a command such as =head2 will probably be followed with a text paragraph:

```
=head2 Pod
```

```
Pod is a simple, but surprisingly capable, text formatter that uses
tags to tell a translator how to format the text.
```

Verbatim

A paragraph that is to be reproduced as is, with no filling or justification. To create a verbatim paragraph, indent each line of text with at least one space:

```
Don't fill this paragraph. It's supposed
to look exactly like this on the page.
There are blanks at the beginning of each line.
```

Paragraph Tags

The following paragraph tags are recognized as valid pod commands.

=back

```
=back
```

Moves left margin back to where it was before the last =over. Ends the innermost =over/=back block of indented text. If there are multiple levels of indent, one =back is needed for each level.

=begin

```
=begin format
```

Starts a block of text that will be passed directly to a particular formatter rather than being treated as pod. For example:

```
=begin html
```

A =begin/=end block is like =for except that it doesn't necessarily apply to a single paragraph.

=cut

=cut

Indicates the end of pod text. Tells the compiler that there isn't anymore pod (for now) and to start compiling again.

=end

=end

Ends a =begin block. Tells the translator to treat what follows as pod again.

=for

=for *format*

Indicates a format change, for the next paragraph only.

=head1

=head1 *text*

text following the tag is formatted as a top-level heading. Generally all uppercase.

=head2

=head2 *text*

text following the tag is formatted as a second-level heading.

=item

=item *text*

Starts a list. Lists should always be inside an over/back block. Many translators use the value of *text* on the first =item to determine the type of list:

=item *

> Bulleted list. An asterisk (*) is commonly used for the bullet, but can be replaced with any other single character. Followed by a blank line and then the text of the bulleted item:
>
>   =item *
>
>   This is the text of the bullet.

=item *n*

> Numbered list. Replace *n* with 1 on the first item, 2 on the second, and so on. Pod does not automatically generate the numbers.

=item *text*

> Definition list. Formats *text* as the term and the following paragraph as the body of the list item. For example:
>
>   =item <HTML>
>
>   Indicates the beginning of an HTML file

The exact appearance of the output depends on the translator you use, but it will look pretty much like this:

```
<HTML>
    Indicates the beginning of an HTML file
```

=over   =over *n*

Specifies the beginning of a list, in which *n* indicates the depth of the indent. For example, =over 4 will indent four spaces. Another =over before a =back creates nested lists. The =over tag should be followed by at least one =item.

=pod   =pod

Indicates the beginning of pod text. A translator starts to pay attention when it sees this tag, and the compiler ignores everything from there to the next =cut.

Interior Sequences

In addition to the paragraph tags, pod has a set of tags that apply within text, either in a paragraph or a command. These interior sequences are:

Sequence	Function
B<*text*>	Makes text bold, usually for switches and programs
C<*code*>	Literal code
E<*escape*>	Named character:
E<gt>	Literal >
E<lt>	Literal <
E<*html*>	Non-numeric HTML entity
E<*n*>	Character number *n*, usually an ASCII character
F<*file*>	Filename
I<*text*>	Italicize *text*, usually for emphasis or variables
L<*name*>	Link (cross-reference) to *name*:
L<*name*>	Manpage
L<*name/ident*>	Item in a manpage
L<*name*/"*sec*">	Section in another manpage
L<"*sec*">	Section in this manpage; quotes are optional
L</"*sec*">	Same as L<"*sec*">
S<*text*>	*text* has non-breaking spaces
X<*index*>	Index entry
Z<>	Zero-width character

Pod Utilities

As mentioned earlier, a number of utility programs have been written to convert files from pod to a variety of output formats. Some of the utilities are described here, particularly those that are part of the Perl distribution. Other programs are available on CPAN.

---

perldoc

perldoc [*options*] *docname*

Formats and displays Perl pod documentation. Extracts the documentation from pod format and displays it. For all options except –*f*, *docname* is the name of the manpage, module, or program containing pod to be displayed. For –*f*, it's the name of a built-in Perl function to be displayed.

Options

–*f function*
    Formats and displays documentation for the specified Perl function.

–*h*
    Displays help message.

–*l*
    Displays full path to the module.

–*m*
    Displays entire module, both code and pod text, without formatting the pod.

–*t*
    Displays using text formatter instead of nroff. Faster, but output is less fancy.

–*u*
    Unformatted. Finds and displays the document without formatting it.

–*v*
    Verbose. Describes search for the file, showing directories searched and where file was found.

perldoc applies switches found in the PERLDOC environment variable before those from the command line. It searches directories specified by the PERL5LIB, PERLLIB (if PERL5LIB isn't defined), and PATH environment variables.

---

pod2fm

pod2fm [*options*] *file*

Translates pod to FrameMaker format.

Options

–*book [bookname]*
    If set, creates FrameMaker book file. If not specified, *bookname* defaults to perl; filename extension is *.book* in either case.

-[no]doc
> Whether to convert a MIF-format *.doc* output file to binary FrameMaker format. Default is *-doc*.

-format type
> Which format to copy from the template document specified with the *-template* option. Type can be a comma-separated list, and *-format* can also be specified more than once. Legal types are:

Type	Description
all	All types (the default)
Character	Character formats
Paragraph	Paragraph formats
Page	Master page layouts
Reference	Reference page layouts
Table	Table formats
Variables	Variable definitions
Math	Math definitions
Cross	Cross-reference definitions
Color	Color definitions
Conditional	Conditional text definitions
Break	Preserves page breaks; controls how the other types are used
Other	Preserves other format changes; controls how the other types are used

-[no]index
> Whether to generate an index. Defaults to *-noindex*.

-[no]lock
> Whether to lock file as read-only so you can use hypertext marker feature. Defaults to *-nolock*.

-[no]mmlonly
> Whether to stop execution after generating the MML version of the file. Default is *-nommlonly*.

-[no]open
> Whether to try to open the book after creating it; requires the *-book* option.

-template document
> Specifies a template document for *pod2fm* copies a format for use in formatting the output. *document* is the path to the template document.

-[no]toc
> Whether to generate a table of contents. Defaults to *-notoc*.

pod2html　　　pod2html [*options*] *inputfile*

Translates files from pod to HTML format. Wrapper around the standard module Pod::Html; see Chapter 8 for the options, which are passed to Pod::Html as arguments.

pod2latex　　　pod2latex *inputfile*

Translates files from pod to LaTeX format. Writes output to a file with *.tex* extension.

pod2man　　　pod2man [*options*] *inputfile*

Translates pod directives in file *inputfile* to Unix manpage format. Converts pod-tagged text to nroff source that can be viewed by the *man* command, or troff for typesetting.

Options

--center=*string*
> Sets centered header to *string*. Defaults to "User Contributed Perl Documentation" unless -\-official flag is set, in which case it defaults to "Perl Programmers Reference Guide."

--date=*string*
> Sets left-hand footer string to date.

--fixed=*font*
> Specifies the fixed-width font to use for code examples.

--lax
> If set, ignores missing sections.

--official
> If set, uses default header as shown for -\-*center* above.

--release=*rel*
> Sets centered footer. Defaults to current Perl release.

--section=*manext*
> Sets manpage section for nroff .TH macro. Default is 3 (functions) if filename ends in *.pm*; otherwise 1 (user commands).

pod2text　　　pod2text < *input*

Translates pod to text and displays it. A wrapper around the Pod::Text module.

Options

--help
> Displays help information.

--htmlroot=*name*
> Sets base URL for the HTML files to *name*.

`--index`
Generates index at top of the HTML file (default).

`--infile=`*name*
Converts pod file *name*. Default is to take input from STDIN.

`--libpods=`*name*`:...:`*name*
List of page names (e.g., "perlfunc") that contain linkable
=items.

`--outfile=`*name*
Creates HTML file *name*. Default is to send output to STDOUT.

`--podroot=`*name*
Uses *name* as base directory for finding library pods.

`--podpath=`*name*`:...:`*name*
Lists *podroot* subdirectories with pod files whose HTML-
converted forms can be linked to in cross-references.

`--netscape`
Uses Netscape HTML directives when applicable.

`--noindex`
Does not generate index at top of the HTML file.

`--nonetscape`
Does not use Netscape HTML directives (default).

`--norecurse`
Does not recurse into subdirectories specified in *podpath*.

`--recurse`
Recurses into subdirectories specified in *podpath* (default).

`--title=`*title*
Specifies title for the resulting HTML file.

`--verbose`
Displays progress messages.

5

Function Reference

This chapter gives a brief description of Perl's built-in functions. Each description gives the syntax of the function, with the types and order of its arguments.

Required arguments are shown in italics, separated by commas. If an argument must be a specific variable type, that variable's identifier will be used (e.g., a percent sign for a hash, %*hash*). Optional arguments are placed in brackets. Do not use the brackets in function calls unless you really want to use an anonymous hash reference.

There are different ways to use a built-in function. For starters, any argument that requires a scalar value can be made up of any expression that returns one. For example, you can obtain the square root of the first value in an array:

```
$root = sqrt (shift @numbers);
```

shift removes the first element of @numbers and returns it to be used by sqrt.

Many functions take a list of scalars for arguments. Any array variable or other expression that returns a list can be used for all or part of the arguments. For example:

```
chmod (split /,/ FILELIST>); # An expression returns a list
chmod 0755, @executables;    # Array used for part of arguments
```

In the first line, the split expression reads a string from a filehandle and splits it into a list. The list provides proper arguments for chmod. The second line uses an array that contains a list of filenames for chmod to act upon.

Parentheses are not required around a function's arguments. However, without parentheses, functions are viewed as operators in an expression (the same is true of predeclared subroutines). If you use a function in a complex expression, you may want to use parentheses for clarity. See Chapter 4 for more about precedence in Perl expressions.

Perl Functions by Category

Here are Perl's functions and function-like keywords, arranged by category. Note that some functions appear in more than one category.

Scalar manipulation
> chomp, chop, chr, crypt, hex, index, lc, lcfirst, length, oct, ord, pack, q//, qq//, reverse, rindex, sprintf, substr, tr///, uc, ucfirst, y///

Regular expressions and pattern matching
> m//, pos, qr//, quotemeta, s///, split, study

Numeric functions
> abs, atan2, cos, exp, hex, int, log, oct, rand, sin, sqrt, srand

Array processing
> pop, push, shift, splice, unshift

List processing
> grep, join, map, qw//, reverse, sort, unpack

Hash processing
> delete, each, exists, keys, values

Input and output
> binmode, close, closedir, dbmclose, dbmopen, die, eof, fileno, flock, format, getc, print, printf, read, readdir, rewinddir, seek, seekdir, select, syscall, sysread, sysseek, syswrite, tell, telldir, truncate, warn, write

Fixed-length data and records
> pack, read, syscall, sysread, syswrite, unpack, vec

Filehandles, files, and directories
> chdir, chmod, chown, chroot, fcntl, glob, ioctl, link, lstat, mkdir, open, opendir, readlink, rename, rmdir, stat, symlink, sysopen, umask, unlink, utime

Flow of program control
> caller, continue, die, do, dump, eval, exit, goto, last, next, redo, return, sub, wantarray

Scoping
> caller, import, local, my, package, use

Miscellaneous
> defined, dump, eval, formline, local, my, prototype, reset, scalar, undef, wantarray

Processes and process groups
> alarm, exec, fork, getpgrp, getppid, getpriority, kill, pipe, qx//, setpgrp, setpriority, sleep, system, times, wait, waitpid

Library modules
> do, import, no, package, require, use

Classes and objects
> bless, dbmclose, dbmopen, package, ref, tie, tied, untie, use

Low-level socket access
accept, bind, connect, getpeername, getsockname, getsockopt, listen, recv, send, setsockopt, shutdown, socket, socketpair

System V interprocess communication
msgctl, msgget, msgrcv, msgsnd, semctl, semget, semop, shmctl, shmget, shmread, shmwrite

Fetching user and group information
endgrent, endhostent, endnetent, endpwent, getgrent, getgrgid, getgrnam, getlogin, getpwent, getpwnam, getpwuid, setgrent, setpwent

Fetching network information
endprotoent, endservent, gethostbyaddr, gethostbyname, gethostent, getnetbyaddr, getnetbyname, getnetent, getprotobyname, getprotobynumber, getprotoent, getservbyname, getservbyport, getservent, sethostent, setnetent, setprotoent, setservent

Time
gmtime, localtime, time, times

Perl Functions in Alphabetical Order

abs

abs *value*

Returns the absolute value of its argument (or $_ if omitted).

accept

accept *newsocket, genericsocket*

Readies a server process to accept socket connections from clients. Execution is suspended until a connection is made, at which time the *newsocket* filehandle is opened and attached to the newly made connection. The function returns the connected address if the call succeeds or false otherwise (and it puts the error code into $!). *genericsocket* must be a filehandle already opened via the socket function and bound to one of the server's network addresses.

alarm

alarm *n*

Sends a SIGALRM signal to the executing Perl program after *n* seconds. On some older systems, alarms go off "at the top of the second," so, for instance, an alarm 1 may go off anywhere between 0 to 1 seconds from now, depending on when in the current second it is. An alarm 2 may go off anywhere from 1 to 2 seconds from now. And so on.

Each call disables the previous timer, and an argument of 0 may be supplied to cancel the previous timer without starting a new one. The return value is the number of seconds remaining on the previous timer.

atan2

atan2 *y, x*

Returns the arctangent of *y*/*x* in the range $-\pi$ to π. A quick way to get an approximate value of π is to say:

```
$pi = atan2(1,1) * 4;
```

For the tangent operation, you may use the POSIX::tan( ) function, or use the familiar relation:

```
sub tan { sin($_[0]) / cos($_[0]) }
```

bind

bind *socket, address*

Attaches an address to an already opened socket specified by the *socket* filehandle. The function returns true for success, false otherwise (and puts the error code into $!). *address* should be a packed address of the proper type for the socket.

binmode

binmode *filehandle*

Arranges for the file to be treated in binary mode on operating systems that distinguish between binary and text files. It should be called after open but before any I/O is done on the filehandle. The only way to reset binary mode on a filehandle is to reopen the file.

binmode has no effect under Unix, Plan9, or other systems that use a single \n (newline) character as a line delimiter. On systems such as Win32 or MS-DOS, binmode is needed to prevent the translation of the line delimiter characters to and from \n.

bless

bless *$ref, [classname]*

Looks up the item pointed to by reference *ref* and tells the item that it is now an object in the *classname* package—or the current package if no class name is specified. It returns the reference for convenience, since a bless is often the last thing in a constructor function. (Always use the two-argument version if the constructor doing the blessing might be inherited by a derived class. In such cases, the class you want to bless your object into will normally be found as the first argument to the constructor in question.)

caller

caller [*n*]

Returns information about the stack of current subroutine calls. Without an argument, it returns the package name in a scalar context; in a list context, it returns the package name, filename, and line number from which the currently executing subroutine was called:

```
($package, $filename, $line) = caller;
```

With an argument it evaluates *n* as the number of stack frames to go back before the current one. It also reports some additional information that the debugger uses to print a stack trace:

```
$i = 0;
while (($pack, $file, $line, $subname, $hasargs,
        $wantarray, $evaltext, $is_require) =
caller($i++)) {
    ...
}
```

Furthermore, when called from within the DB package, caller returns more detailed information: it sets the list variable @DB::args as the argument passed in the given stack frame.

---

chdir   chdir *dirname*

Changes the working directory to *dirname*, if possible. If *dirname* is omitted, it changes to the home directory. The function returns 1 upon success, 0 otherwise (and puts the error code into $!).

---

chmod   chmod *mode, filelist*

Changes the permissions of a list of files. The first argument must be the permissions mode given in its octal number representation. The function returns the number of files successfully changed. For example:

```
$cnt = chmod 0755, 'file1', 'file2';
```

will set $cnt to 0, 1, or 2, depending on how many files got changed (in the sense that the operation succeeded, not in the sense that the bits were different afterward).

---

chomp   chomp *$var*

chomp *@list*

Removes any line-ending characters of a string in *$var*, or each string in *@list*, that correspond to the current value of $/ (not just any last character, as chop does). chomp returns the number of characters deleted. If $/ is empty (in paragraph mode), chomp removes all newlines from the selected string (or strings, if chomping a list). If no argument is given, the function chomps the $_ variable.

---

chop   chop *$var*

chop *@list*

Chops off the last character of a string contained in the variable *$var* (or strings in each element of a *@list*) and returns the character chopped. The chop operator is used primarily to remove the

---

newline from the end of an input record but is more efficient than s/\n$//. If no argument is given, the function chops the $_ variable.

chown   chown *uid, gid, files*

Changes the owner and group of a list of files. The first two arguments must be the *numerical uid* and *gid*, in that order. The function returns the number of files successfully changed.

On most systems, you are not allowed to change the ownership of the file unless you're the superuser, although you should be able to change the group to any of your secondary groups. On insecure systems, these restrictions may be relaxed, but this is not a portable assumption.

chr   chr *number*

Returns the character represented by *number* in the character set. For example, chr(65) is "A" in ASCII.

chroot   chroot *dirname*

Changes the root directory for the current process to *dirname*—the starting point for pathnames beginning with /. This directory is inherited across exec calls and by all subprocesses. There is no way to undo a chroot. Only the superuser can use this function.

close   close *filehandle*

Closes the file, socket, or pipe associated with the given filehandle. You don't have to close *filehandle* if you are immediately going to do another open on it, since the next open will close it for you. However, an explicit close on an input file resets the line counter ($.), while the implicit close done by open does not. Closing a pipe will wait for the process executing on the pipe to complete and will prevent the script from exiting before the pipeline is finished. Also, closing a pipe explicitly puts the status value of the command executing on the pipe into $?.

filehandle may be an expression with a value that gives a real filehandle name. It may also be a reference to a filehandle object returned by some of the object-oriented I/O packages.

closedir   closedir *dirhandle*

Closes a directory associated with the given directory handle opened by opendir.

connect   connect *socket, address*

Initiates a connection with another process that is waiting at an
accept on the filehandle *socket*. The function returns true for
success, false otherwise (and puts the error code into $!). *address* is
a packed network address of the proper type for *socket*.

To disconnect a socket, use either close or shutdown.

---

cos   cos *num*

Returns the cosine of *num* (expressed in radians). For the inverse
cosine operation, you may use the POSIX::acos() function, or use
this relation:

```
sub acos { atan2( sqrt(1 - $_[0] * $_[0]), $_[0] ) }
```

---

crypt   crypt *string, salt*

Used by the passwd function on Unix systems to produce a unique
13-character string (stored in the system's password file) from the
first 8 characters of the given *string* and the 2-character *salt*. The
Perl function operates the same way and returns a 13-character
string with the first 2 characters as the *salt*. crypt uses a modified
version of the Data Encryption Standard, which produces a one-
way encryption; the resulting string cannot be decrypted to determine the original string. crypt can be used to check that a
password is correct by comparing the string from the function to
the string found in */etc/passwd* (if you have permission to do this):

```
if (crypt ($guess, $pass) eq $pass) {
        # guess is correct
}
```

The variable $pass is the password string from the password file.
crypt merely uses the first two characters from this string for the
salt argument.

---

dbmclose   dbmclose *%hash*

Breaks the binding between a DBM file and a hash.

This function is actually just a call to untie with the proper arguments, but is provided for backward compatibility with older
versions of Perl.

---

dbmopen   dbmopen *%hash, dbname, mode*

Binds a DBM file (*dbname*) to a hash (*%hash*). *dbname* is the name of
the database without the *.dir* or *.pag* extension. Note that while not
deprecated, dbmopen has basically been superseded by tie(). If the
database does not exist, and a valid mode is specified, the database

---

is created with the permissions specified by *mode* (as modified by the umask). To prevent creation of the database if it doesn't exist, you may specify a *mode* of undef, and the function will return a false value if it can't find an existing database. If your system supports only the older DBM functions, you may have only one dbmopen in your program.

Values assigned to the hash prior to the dbmopen are not accessible. If you don't have write access to the DBM file, you can only read the hash variables, not set them.

This function is actually just a call to tie with the proper arguments, but is provided for backward compatibility with older versions of Perl.

---

defined
defined *expr*

Returns a Boolean value saying whether the scalar value resulting from *expr* has a real value. If no argument is given, defined checks $_.

A scalar that contains no valid string, numeric, or reference value is known as the undefined value, or undef. Many operations return the undefined value under exceptional conditions, such as end-of-file, uninitialized variable, system error, and so on. This function allows you to distinguish between an undefined null string and a defined null string when you're using operators that might return a real null string.

You can use defined to see if a subroutine exists, that is, if the subroutine definition has been successfully parsed. However, using defined on an array or a hash is not guaranteed to produce intuitive results and should be avoided.

---

delete
delete $*hash*{*key*}

delete @*hash*{@*keys*}

Deletes the specified *key* or *keys* and associated values from the specified *hash*. (It doesn't delete a file. See unlink for that.) Deleting from $ENV{} modifies the environment. Deleting from a hash that is bound to a (writable) DBM file deletes the entry from the DBM file.

For normal hashes, the delete function returns the value (not the key) that was deleted, but this behavior is not guaranteed for tied hashes, such as those bound to DBM files. To test whether a hash element has been deleted, use exists.

---

die
die *message*

Prints *message* to the standard error output and exits the Perl program with a nonzero exit status. *message* can be a list value, like the arguments to print, from which the elements are concatenated into a single string for output. If *message* does not end with a newline (\n), the current script filename, line number, and input line number (if any) are appended to the message with a newline. With no argument, the function outputs the string Died as its default.

die exits the programs with the current value of the $! variable, which contains the text describing the most recent operating system error value. This value can be used in the *message* to describe what the problem may have been.

die behaves differently inside an eval statement. It places the error message in the $@ variable and aborts the eval, which returns an undefined value. This use of die can raise runtime exceptions that can be caught at a higher level of the program.

---

do   do {*block*}

Executes the sequence of commands in the *block* and returns the value of the last expression evaluated. When modified by a loop modifier, Perl executes the *block* once before testing the loop condition. (On other statements, the loop modifiers test the conditional first.)

---

dump   dump *label*

During program execution, causes an immediate core dump after code previous to it has already been executed. Primarily, this is so that you can use the undump program to turn your core dump into an executable binary after having initialized all your variables at the beginning of the program. Please note that you shouldn't use dump( ) or undump( ) with the availability of the Perl Compiler (B modules) as part of your Perl distribution. In addition, you're unlikely to have success with dump or undump on most modern Unix systems (that support dynamic loading from libdl). dump arranges for the revived binary, when run, to begin by executing a goto label (with all the restrictions that goto suffers). Think of the operation as a goto with an intervening core dump and reincarnation. If *label* is omitted, the function arranges for the program to restart from the top. Note that any files opened at the time of the dump will no longer be open when the program is reincarnated. See also the *–u* command-line switch.

As of Perl 5.8, dump is now largely obsolete, partly because it's difficult to convert a core file into an executable, and because the real compiler backends for generating portable bytecode and compilable C code have superseded it. That's why you should now invoke it as "CORE::dump( )" if you don't want to be warned against a possible typo.

The undump program is not available on all systems and may not be compatible with specific ports of Perl.

each   each %*hash*

Returns a two-element list consisting of the key and value for the next element of a hash. With successive calls to each, you can iterate over the entire hash. Entries are returned in an indeterminate order. When the hash is entirely read, a null list is returned. The next call to each after that will start a new iteration. The iterator can be reset either by reading all the elements from the hash or by calling the keys function in scalar context. You must not add elements to the hash while iterating over it, although you are permitted to use delete. In a scalar context, each returns only the key.

There is a single iterator for each hash, shared by all each, keys, and values function calls in the program. This means that after a keys or values call, the next each call will start again from the beginning.

endgrent   endgrent

Closes the groups file (usually */etc/group* on Unix systems) if open. Not implemented on Win32 systems.

endhostent   endhostent

Closes the hosts file (usually */etc/hosts* on Unix systems) if open. Not implemented on Win32 systems.

endnetent   endnetent

Closes the networks file (usually */etc/networks* on Unix systems) if open. Not implemented on Win32 systems.

endprotoent   endprotoent

Closes the prototypes file (usually */etc/prototypes* on Unix systems) if open. Not implemented on Win32 systems.

endpwent   endpwent

Closes the password file (*/etc/passwd* or equivalent on Unix systems) if open. Not implemented on Win32 systems.

endservent   endservent

Closes the services file (usually */etc/services* on Unix systems) if open. Not implemented on Win32 systems.

eof

eof *filehandle*

eof( )

Returns true if the next read on *filehandle* will return end-of-file, or if *filehandle* is not open. *filehandle* may be an expression with a value that gives the real filehandle name. An eof without an argument returns the end-of-file status for the last file read. Empty parentheses ( ) may be used in connection with the combined files listed on the command line. That is, inside a while (<>) loop, eof( ) will detect the end of only the last of a group of files. Use eof(ARGV) or eof (without parentheses) to test each file in a while (<>) loop. For example, the following code inserts dashes just before the last line of the last file:

```
while (<>) {
    if (eof( )) {
        print "-" x 30, "\n";
    }
    print;
}
```

eval

eval *string*

eval {*block*}

Evaluates the expression or code in its argument at runtime as a separate Perl program within the context of the larger script. Any variable settings remain afterward, as do any subroutine or format definitions. The code of the eval is treated as a block, so any locally scoped variables declared within the eval last only until the eval is done. (See also local and my.) The value returned from an eval is the value of the last expression evaluated. Like subroutines, you may also use the return function to return a value and exit the eval.

With eval *string*, the contents of *string* are compiled and executed at runtime. For example:

```
$a = 3, $b = 4;
$c = '$a * $b';
print (eval "$c"); # Prints 12
```

The string form of eval is useful for executing strings produced at runtime from standard or other dynamic input sources. If the string produces an error, either from syntax or at runtime, the eval exits with the undefined value and places the error in $@. If *string* is omitted, the operator evaluates $_.

The block form of eval is used in Perl programs to handle runtime errors (exceptions). The code in *block* is compiled only once during the compilation of the main program. If there is a syntax error in the block, it will produce an error at compile time. If the code in *block* produces a runtime error (or if a die statement is encountered), the eval exits, and the error is placed in $@. For example, the following code can be used to trap a divide-by-zero error at runtime:

```
eval {
    $a = 10; $b = 0;
    $c = $a / $b;      # Causes runtime error
                       # Trapped by eval
};
print $@;              # Prints "Illegal division by 0 at
                       # try.pl line 3"
```

As with any code in a block, a final semicolon is not required.

exec

exec *command*

Terminates the currently running Perl script and executes the program named in *command*. The Perl program does not resume after the exec unless the exec cannot be run and produces an error. Unlike system, the executed *command* is not forked off into a child process. An exec completely replaces the script in its current process.

command may be a scalar containing a string with the name of the program to run and any arguments. This string is checked for shell metacharacters, and if there are any, passes the string to /bin/sh/ -c for parsing. Otherwise, the string is read as a program command, bypassing any shell processing. The first word of the string is used as the program name, with any remaining words used as arguments.

command may also be a list value in which the first element is parsed as the program name and remaining elements as arguments. For example:

```
exec 'echo', 'Your arguments are: ', @ARGV;
```

The exec function is not implemented for Perl on Win32 platforms.

exists

exists *$hash{$key}*

Returns true if the specified hash key exists, even if the corresponding value is undefined.

exit

exit *status*

Exits the current Perl process immediately with that value given by *status*. This could be the entire Perl script you are running or only a child process created by fork. Here's a fragment that lets a user exit the program by typing x or X:

```
$ans = <STDIN>;
exit 0 if $ans =~ /^[Xx]/;
```

If *status* is omitted, the function exits with 0. You shouldn't use exit to abort a subroutine if there's any chance that someone might want to trap whatever error happened. Use die instead, which can be trapped by an eval.

exp

exp *num*

Returns *e* to the power of *num*. If *num* is omitted, it gives exp($_). To do general exponentiation, use the ** operator.

fcntl

fcntl *filehandle, function, arg*

Calls the file control *function* (with the function-specific *arg*) to use on the file or device opened with *filehandle*. fcntl calls Unix's fcntl function (not available on Win32 platforms). If the function is not implemented, the program exits with a fatal error. fcntl sets file descriptors for a filehandle. This built-in command is usable when you use the Fcntl module in the standard distribution:

    use Fcntl;

This module imports the correct *function* definitions. See the description of the Fcntl module in Chapter 8.

The return value of fcntl (and ioctl) is as follows:

System call returns	Perl returns
-1	Undefined value
0	String "0 but true"
Anything else	That number

Thus Perl returns true on success and false on failure, yet you can still easily determine the actual value returned by the operating system.

fileno

fileno *filehandle*

Returns the file descriptor for a filehandle. (A file descriptor is a small integer, unlike the filehandle, which is a symbol.) It returns undef if the handle is not open. It's useful for constructing bitmaps for select and for passing to certain obscure system calls if syscall is implemented. It's also useful for double-checking that the open function gave you the file descriptor you wanted.

flock

flock *filehandle, operation*

Establishes or removes a lock on a file opened with *filehandle*. This function calls one of the Unix functions flock, lockf, or the locking capabilities of fcntl, whichever your system supports. If none of these functions exist on your system, flock will produce a fatal error.

operation is the type of locking function to perform. The number by each operation name is the argument that Perl's flock takes by default. You may also use the operation names if you explicitly import them from the Fcntl module with use Fcntl ":flock".

LOCK_SH *(1)*
> Establishes a shared lock on the file (read lock).

LOCK_EX *(2)*
> Establishes an exclusive lock on the file (write lock).

LOCK_UN *(8)*
> Removes a lock from the file.

LOCK_NB *(4)*
> Prevents flock from blocking while trying to establish a lock with LOCK_SH or LOCK_EX and instructs it to return immediately. LOCK_NB must be *or*ed with the other operation as an expression for the operation argument, i.e., (LOCK_EX | LOCK_NB).

fork

fork

Spawns a child process that executes the code immediately following the fork call until the process is terminated (usually with an exit). The child process runs parallel to the parent process and shares all the parent's variables and open filehandles. The function returns the child pid to the parent process and 0 to the child process on success. If it fails, it returns the undefined value to the parent process, and no child process is created. If you fork your child processes, you'll have to wait on their zombies when they die. (See the wait function for more information.) The fork function is unlikely to be implemented on any operating system not resembling Unix, unless it purports POSIX compliance.

formline

formline *picture, variables*

Internal function used by formats, although you may also call it. It formats a list of values (*variables*) according to the contents of *picture*, placing the output into the format output accumulator, $^A. When a write is done, the contents of $^A are written to a filehandle, but you can also read $^A yourself and set $^A back to "". Note that a format typically does one formline per line of form, but the formline function itself doesn't care how many newlines are embedded in the *picture*. This means that the ~ and ~~ tokens will treat the entire *picture* as a single line. Thus, you may need to use multiple formlines to implement a single-record format, such as the format compiler.

Be careful if you put double quotes around the picture, since an @ character may be taken to mean the beginning of an array name. formline always returns true. See Chapter 4 for more information.

getc   getc *filehandle*

Returns the next byte from the input file attached to *filehandle*. At
end-of-file, it returns a null string. If *filehandle* is omitted, the
function reads from STDIN. This operator is very slow, but is occasionally useful for single-character input from the keyboard.

getgrent   getgrent

Returns the next entry from the systems group file (usually */etc/*
group on Unix systems) starting from the top. Returns null when
end-of-file is reached. The return value from getgrent in list
context is:

    ($name, $passwd, $gid, $members)

in which $members contains a space-separated list of the login
names of the members of the group. In scalar context, getgrent
returns only the group name.

getgrgid   getgrgid *gid*

Retrieves a group file (*/etc/group*) entry by group number *gid*. The
return value in list context is:

    ($name, $passwd, $gid, $members)

in which $members contains a space-separated list of the login
names of the members of the group. If you want to do this repeatedly, consider caching the data in a hash using getgrent. In scalar
context, getgrgid returns only the group name.

getgrnam   getgrnam *name*

Retrieves a group file entry by the group name *name*. The return
value in list context is:

    ($name, $passwd, $gid, $members)

in which $members contains a space-separated list of the login
names of the members of the group. In scalar context, getgrnam
returns only the numeric group ID.

gethostbyaddr   gethostbyaddr *address*, [*addrtype*]

Retrieves the hostname (and alternate addresses) of a packed binary
network *address*. (*addrtype* indicates the type of address given.
Since gethostbyaddr is used almost solely for Internet IP addresses,
addrtype is not needed.) The return value in list context is:

    ($name, $aliases, $addrtype, $length, @addrs)

in which @addrs is a list of packed binary addresses. In the Internet domain, each address is four bytes long and can be unpacked by something like:

```
($a, $b, $c, $d) = unpack('C4', $addrs[0]);
```

In scalar context, gethostbyaddr returns only the hostname.

---

gethostbyname   gethostbyname *name*

Retrieves the address (and other names) of a network hostname. The return value in list context is:

```
($name, $aliases, $addrtype, $length, @addrs)
```

in which @addrs is a list of raw addresses. In scalar context, gethostbyname returns only the host address.

---

gethostent   gethostent

Retrieves the next entry from your system's network hosts file (usually */etc/hosts* on Unix). The return value from gethostent is:

```
($name, $aliases, $addrtype, $length, @addrs)
```

in which @addrs is a list of raw addresses. Scripts that use this function should not be considered portable.

---

getlogin   getlogin

Returns the current login from */etc/utmp* (Unix systems only), if any. If null, use getpwuid. For example:

```
$login = getlogin || getpwuid($<) || "Intruder!!";
```

---

getnetbyaddr   getnetbyaddr *address*, [*addrtype*]

Retrieves the network name or names of the given network *address*. (*addrtype* indicates the type of address. Often, this function is used for IP addresses, in which the type is not needed.) The return value in list context is:

```
($name, $aliases, $addrtype, $net)
```

In scalar context, getnetbyaddr returns only the network name.

---

getnetbyname   getnetbyname *name*

Retrieves the network address of a network *name*. The return value in list context is:

```
($name, $aliases, $addrtype, $net)
```

In scalar context, getnetbyname returns only the network address.

getnetent   getnetent

Retrieves the next line from your */etc/networks* file, or system equivalent. The return value in list context is:

    ($name, $aliases, $addrtype, $net)

In scalar context, getnetent returns only the network name.

---

getpeername   getpeername *socket*

Returns the packed socket address of the other end of the *socket*
connection. For example:

    use Socket;
    $hersockaddr = getpeername SOCK;
    ($port, $heraddr) = unpack_sockaddr_in($hersockaddr);
    $herhostname = gethostbyaddr($heraddr, AF_INET);
    $herstraddr = inet_ntoa($heraddr);

---

getpgrp   getpgrp *pid*

Returns the current process group for the specified process ID
(*pid*). Use a *pid* of 0 for the current process. Invoking getpgrp will
produce a fatal error if used on a machine that doesn't implement
the getpgrp system call. If *pid* is omitted, the function returns the
process group of the current process (the same as using a *pid* of 0).
On systems implementing this operator with the POSIX getpgrp(2)
system call, *pid* must be omitted or, if supplied, must be 0.

---

getppid   getppid

Returns the process ID of the parent process. On a typical Unix
system, if your parent process ID changes to 1, your parent process
has died, and you've been adopted by the *init* program.

---

getpriority   getpriority *type, id*

Returns the current priority for a process, a process group, or a
user. *type* indicates which of these three process types to return.
(The type identifiers are system-specific. Consult the manpage for
getpriority.) The *id* gives the specific ID of the corresponding
process type in *type*: a process ID, a process-group ID, or a user ID.
The value 0 in *who* gives the priority for the current process,
process group, or user.

The priority will be an integer value. Lower values indicate higher
priority (negative values may be returned on some systems).
Invoking getpriority will produce a fatal error if used on a
machine that doesn't implement the getpriority system call.

---

getprotobyname getprotobyname *name*

> Translates a protocol name to its corresponding number. The return value in list context is:
>
> ```
> ($name, $aliases, $protocol_number)
> ```
>
> In scalar context, getprotobyname returns only the protocol number.

getprotobynumber

> getprotobynumber *number*
>
> Translates a protocol number to its corresponding name. The return value in list context is:
>
> ```
> ($name, $aliases, $protocol_number)
> ```
>
> In scalar context, getprotobynumber returns only the protocol name.

getprotoent getprotoent

> Retrieves the next line from the */etc/protocols* file (on some Unix systems). Returns null at the end of the file. The return value from getprotoent is:
>
> ```
> ($name, $aliases, $protocol_number)
> ```
>
> In scalar context, getprotoent returns only the protocol name.

getpwent getpwent

> Retrieves the next line from the */etc/passwd* file (or its equivalent coming from another server). Returns null at the end of the file. The return value in list context is:
>
> ```
> ($name,$passwd,$uid,$gid,$quota,$comment,$gcos,$dir,$shell)
> ```
>
> Some machines may use the quota and comment fields for other purposes, but the remaining fields will always be the same. To set up a hash for translating login names to uids, do this:
>
> ```
> while (($name, $passwd, $uid) = getpwent) {
>     $uid{$name} = $uid;
> }
> ```
>
> In scalar context, getpwent returns only the username.

getpwnam getpwnam *name*

> Retrieves the *passwd* file entry of a user *name*. The return value in list context is:
>
> ```
> ($name,$passwd,$uid,$gid,$quota,$comment,$gcos,$dir,$shell)
> ```
>
> If you want to do this repeatedly, consider caching the data in a hash using getpwent.
>
> In scalar context, getpwnam returns only the numeric user ID.

getpwuid

getpwuid *uid*

Retrieves the *passwd* file entry with the user ID *uid*. The return value in list context is:

    ($name,$passwd,$uid,$gid,$quota,$comment,$gcos,$dir,$shell)

If you want to do this repeatedly, consider slurping the data into a hash using getpwent.

In scalar context, getpwuid returns the username.

getservbyname

getservbyname *name, proto*

Translates a service (port) name to its corresponding port number. *proto* is a protocol name such as tcp. The return value in list context is:

    ($name, $aliases, $port_number, $protocol_name)

In scalar context, getservbyname returns only the service port number.

getservbyport

getservbyport *port, proto*

Translates a service (port) number to its corresponding names. *proto* is a protocol name such as tcp. The return value in list context is:

    ($name, $aliases, $port_number, $protocol_name)

In scalar context, getservbyport returns only the service port name.

getservent

getservent

Retrieves the next listing from the */etc/services* file or its equivalent. Returns null at the end of the file. The return value in list context is:

    ($name, $aliases, $port_number, $protocol_name)

In scalar context, getservent returns only the service port name.

getsockname

getsockname *socket*

Returns the packed socket address of this end of the *socket* connection.

getsockopt

getsockopt *socket, level, optname*

Returns the value of the socket option *optname*, or the undefined value if there is an error. *level* identifies the protocol level used by *socket*. Options vary for different protocols. See also setsockopt.

glob

glob *expr*

Performs filename expansion (globbing) on *expr*, returning the next successive name on each call. If *expr* is omitted, $_ is globbed instead. This is the internal function implementing the <*> operator, except that it may be easier to type this way.

The glob function is not related to the Perl notion of typeglobs, other than that they both use a * to represent multiple items.

gmtime

gmtime *expr*

Converts a time string as returned by the time function to a nine-element list with the time correct for Greenwich Mean Time zone (a.k.a. GMT, UTC, etc.). Typically used as follows:

```
($sec,$min,$hour,$mday,$mon,$year,$wday,$yday,$isdst) =
    gmtime(time);
```

All list elements are numeric and come straight out of a C language struct tm. In particular, this means that $mon has the range 0..11, $wday has the range 0..6, and the year has had 1,900 subtracted from it. (You can remember which elements are 0-based because you're always using these as subscripts into 0-based arrays containing month and day names.) If *expr* is omitted, it does gmtime(time). For example, to print the current month in London:

```
$london_month = (qw(Jan Feb Mar Apr May Jun
        Jul Aug Sep Oct Nov Dec))[(gmtime)[4]];
```

The Perl library module Time::Local contains a subroutine, timegm( ), that can convert in the opposite direction.

In scalar context, gmtime returns a ctime(3)-like string based on the GMT time value.

goto

goto *label*

goto &*name*

Finds the statement labeled with *label* (or an expression that evaluates to a label) and resumes execution there. It may not be used to go into any construct that requires initialization, such as a subroutine or a foreach loop. It also can't be used to go into a construct that is optimized away. It can be used to go almost anywhere else within the dynamic scope, including out of subroutines, but for that purpose, it's usually better to use another construct, such as last or die.

goto &*name* substitutes a call to the named subroutine for the currently running subroutine. This is used by AUTOLOAD subroutines that wish to load another subroutine and pretend that this subroutine—and not the original one—had been called in the first place (except that any modifications to @_ in the original subroutine are propagated to the replacement subroutine). After the goto, not even caller will be able to tell that the original routine was called first.

grep

```
grep expr, list
```

```
grep {block} list
```

Evaluates *expr* or *block* in a Boolean context for each element of *list*, temporarily setting $_ to each element in turn. In list context, it returns a list of those elements for which the expression is true. Mostly used like Unix *grep*, in which *expr* is a search pattern, and list elements that match are returned. In scalar context, grep returns the number of times the expression was true.

For example, presuming @all_lines contains lines of code, this example weeds out comment lines:

```
@code_lines = grep !/^#/, @all_lines;
```

hex

```
hex hexnum
```

Converts a hexadecimal string *hexnum* into its equivalent decimal value. If *hexnum* is omitted, it interprets $_. The following code sets $number to 4,294,906,560:

```
$number = hex("ffff12c0");
```

To do the inverse function, use:

```
sprintf "%lx", $number;   # That's a letter 'l', not a one
```

index

```
index string, substr, [start]
```

Returns the position of the first occurrence of *substr* in *string*. The *start*, if specified, specifies the position to start looking in the string. Positions are integer numbers based at 0. If the substring is not found, the index function returns -1.

int

```
int num
```

Returns the integer portion of *num*. If *num* is omitted, the function uses $_.

ioctl

```
ioctl filehandle, function, arg
```

Calls the ioctl Unix system call to perform *function* (with the function-specific *arg*) on the file or device opened with *filehandle*. See fcntl for a description of return values.

join

join *char, list*

Joins the separate strings of *list* into a single string with fields separated by the value of *char* and returns the string. For example:

```
$_ = join ':',
$login,$passwd,$uid,$gid,$gcos,$home,$shell;
```

To do the opposite, see split. To join things together into fixed-position fields, see pack.

keys

keys *%hash*

Returns a list consisting of all the keys of the named hash. The keys are returned in an apparently random order, but it is the same order that either the values or each function produces (assuming that the hash has not been modified between calls).

In scalar context, keys returns the number of elements of the hash (and resets the each iterator).

keys can be used as an lvalue to increase the number of hash buckets allocated for the hash:

```
keys %hash = 200;
```

kill

kill *sig, processes*

Sends a signal, *sig*, to a list of *processes*. You may use a signal name in quotes (without a SIG on the front). This function returns the number of processes successfully signaled. If the signal is negative, the function kills process groups instead of processes.

last

last *label*

Immediately exits the loop identified by *label*. If *label* is omitted, the command refers to the innermost enclosing loop.

lc

lc *string*

Returns a lowercase version of *string* (or $_, if omitted). This is the internal function implementing the \L escape in double-quoted strings.

lcfirst

lcfirst *string*

Returns a version of *string* (or $_, if omitted) with the first character lowercased. This is the internal function implementing the \l escape in double-quoted strings.

length

length *val*

Returns the length in bytes of the scalar value *val*. If *val* is omitted, the function returns the length of $_.

Do not try to use length to find the size of an array or hash. Use scalar *@array* for the size of an array, and scalar keys *%hash* for the size of a hash.

link

link *oldfile, newfile*

Creates a Unix hard link from a new filename, *newfile*, to an existing file, *oldfile*, on the same filesystem. The function returns 1 for success, 0 otherwise (and puts the error code into $!). This function is unlikely to be implemented on non-Unix systems. See also symlink.

listen

listen *socket, queuesize*

Tells the operating system that you are ready to accept connections on *socket* and sets the number of waiting connections to *queuesize*. If the queue is full, clients trying to connect to the socket will be refused connection.

local

local *vars*

Declares one or more global variables *vars* to have temporary values within the innermost enclosing block, subroutine, eval, or file. The new value is initially undef for scalars and ( ) for arrays and hashes. If more than one variable is listed, the list must be placed in parentheses, because the operator binds more tightly than a comma. All the listed variables must be legal lvalues, that is, something you can assign to. This operator works by saving the current values of those variables on a hidden stack and restoring them upon exiting the block, subroutine, eval, or file.

Subroutines called within the scope of a local variable will see the localized inner value of the variable. The technical term for this process is "dynamic scoping." Use my for true private variables.

localtime

localtime *val*

Converts the value returned by time to a nine-element list with the time corrected for the local time zone. It's typically used as follows:

```
($sec,$min,$hour,$mday,$mon,$year,$wday,$yday,$isdst) =
    localtime(time);
```

All list elements are numeric. The element $mon (month) has the range 0..11, and $wday (weekday) has the range 0..6. The year has had 1,900 subtracted from it. (You can remember which elements are 0-based because you're always using them as subscripts into 0-based arrays containing month and day names.) If *val* is omitted, it does localtime(time). For example, to get the name of the current day of the week:

```
$thisday = (Sun,Mon,Tue,Wed,Thu,Fri,Sat)[(localtime)[6]];
```

The Perl library module Time::Local contains a subroutine, timelocal( ), that can convert in the opposite direction.

In scalar context, localtime returns a ctime(3)-like string based on the localtime value.

log

```
log num
```

Returns logarithm (base *e*) of *num*. If *num* is omitted, the function uses $_.

lstat

```
lstat file
```

Like stat, returns information on *file*, except that if *file* is a symbolic link, lstat returns information about the link; stat returns information about the file pointed to by the link. (If symbolic links are unimplemented on your system, a normal stat is done instead.)

map

```
map {block} list
```

```
map expr, list
```

Evaluates the *block* or *expr* for each element of *list* (locally setting $_ to each element) and returns the list value composed of the results of each evaluation. It evaluates *block* or *expr* in a list context, so each element of *list* may produce zero, one, or more elements in the returned value. These are all flattened into one list. For instance:

```
@words = map { split ' ' } @lines;
```

splits a list of lines into a list of words. Often, though, there is a one-to-one mapping between input values and output values:

```
@chars = map chr, @nums;
```

This statement translates a list of numbers to the corresponding characters.

mkdir

```
mkdir filename, mode
```

Creates the directory specified by *filename*, with permissions specified by the numeric *mode* (as modified by the current umask). If it succeeds, it returns 1; otherwise, it returns 0 and sets $! (from the value of errno).

msgctl   msgctl *id, cmd, arg*

Calls the msgctl system call, which is used to perform different control operations on IPC message queues. (See the msgctl documentation on your system for details.) If *cmd* is &IPC_STAT, then *arg* must be a variable that will hold the returned msqid_ds structure. The return values work like those of fnctl: the undefined value for error, 0 but true for zero, or the actual return value otherwise. On error, it puts the error code into $!. Before calling, you should say:

```
require "ipc.ph";
require "msg.ph";
```

This function is available only on machines supporting System V IPC.

msgget   msgget *key, flags*

Calls the System V IPC msgget system call. See the msgget documentation on your system for details. The function returns the message queue ID, or the undefined value if there is an error. On error, it puts the error code into $!. Before calling, you should say:

```
require "ipc.ph";
require "msg.ph";
```

This function is available only on machines supporting System V IPC.

msgrcv   msgrcv *id, var, size, type, flags*

Calls the System V IPC msgrcv system call to receive a message from message queue *id* into variable *var* with a maximum message size of *size*. When a message is received, the message type will be the first thing in *var*, and the maximum length of *var* is *size* plus the size of the message type. The function returns true if successful, or false if there is an error. On error, it puts the error code into $!. Before calling, you should say:

```
require "ipc.ph";
require "msg.ph";
```

This function is available only on machines supporting System V IPC.

msgsnd   msgsnd *id, msg, flags*

Calls the System V IPC msgsnd system call to send the message *msg* to the message queue *id*. *msg* must begin with the long integer message type. You can create a message like this:

```
$msg = pack "L a*", $type, $text_of_message;
```

The function returns true if successful, or false if there is an error. On error, it puts the error code into $!. Before calling, you should say:

```
require "ipc.ph";
require "msg.ph";
```

This function is available only on machines supporting System V IPC.

my   my *vars*

Declares one or more private variables to exist only within the innermost enclosing block, subroutine, eval, or file. The new value is initially undef for scalars and ( ) for arrays and hashes. If more than one variable is listed, the list must be placed in parentheses, because the operator binds more tightly than a comma. Only simple scalars or complete arrays and hashes may be declared this way. The variable name may not be package-qualified, because package variables are all global, and private variables are not related to any package.

Unlike local, this operator has nothing to do with global variables, other than hiding any other variable of the same name from view within its scope. (A global variable can always be accessed through its package-qualified form or a symbolic reference, however.) A private variable is not visible until the statement after its declaration. Subroutines called from within the scope of such a private variable cannot see the private variable unless the subroutine is also textually declared within the scope of the variable.

next   next *label*

Immediately jumps to the next iteration of the loop identified by *label* or the innermost enclosing loop, if there is no argument. If there is a continue block, it will be executed immediately after the next, before the loop is reiterated.

no   no *Module list*

Effectively "undoes" the use function. Used to deactivate pragmas (compiler directives) for sections of your program. For instance:

```
no strict 'refs'
```

allows soft references to the end of the block scope if:

```
use strict 'refs'
```

was previously invoked.

oct   oct *ostring*

Interprets *ostring* as an octal string and returns the equivalent decimal value. (If *ostring* happens to start with 0x, it is interpreted as a hex string instead.) The following will handle decimal, octal, and hex in the standard notation:

```
$val = oct $val if $val =~ /^0/;
```

If *ostring* is omitted, the function interprets $_. To perform the inverse function on octal numbers, use:

```
$oct_string = sprintf "%lo", $number;
```

---

open

open *filehandle, filename*

open *filehandle, mode, filename*

open *filehandle, mode, expr, list* (new in 5.8)

open *filehandle, mode, reference* (new in 5.8)

Opens the file given by *filename* and associates it with *filehandle*. If *filehandle* is omitted, the scalar variable of the same name as the *filehandle* must contain the filename. (And you must also be careful to use or die after the statement rather than || die, because the precedence of || is higher than list operators such as open.)

If *filename* is preceded by either < or nothing, the file is opened for input (read-only). If *filename* is preceded by >, the file is opened for output. If the file doesn't exist, it will be created; if the file exists, it will be overwritten with output using >. Preceding the filename with >> opens an output file for appending. For both read and write access, use a + before < or >.

If you choose to use the three-or-more-arguments form of open, you can use separate *mode* and *filename* arguments, such as open($fh, $mode, $filename), in which $mode represents an open mode or pipe. For example:

```
my $mode = '+<';
my $filename = 'whatever.txt';
open(FH, $mode, $filename)
    or die("can't open $filename: $!");
```

As covered in Chapter 4, you can build Perl 5.8 and newer with PerlIO support, which offers additional features for your system's I/O (STDIO). This allows you to do neat things, such as specify utf-8 as your default encoding for all of your I/O, or set your default line endings with 'crlf'. In addition, you can select piping to or extracting information from an external program with '|-' and '-|', respectively. For example:

```
my $prog = "webster overworked";
open($fh, '-|', $prog)
    or die("can't open pipe to '$prog': $!");
```

or, similarly:

```
my @prog_info = qw(/usr/contrib/bin/webster overworked);
open($fh, '-|', @prog_info)
    or die(...);
```

A filehandle may also be attached to a process by using a piped command. If the filename begins with |, the filename is interpreted as a command to which output is to be piped. If the filename ends with a |, the filename is interpreted as a command that pipes input to you. You may not have an open command that pipes both in and out.

Any pipe command containing shell metacharacters is passed to the shell for execution; otherwise, it is executed directly by Perl. The filename - refers to STDIN, and > refers to STDOUT. open returns nonzero upon success, the undefined value otherwise. If the open involved a pipe, the return value happens to be the process ID of the subprocess.

opendir

opendir *dirhandle, directory*

Opens a *directory* for processing by readdir, telldir, seekdir, rewinddir, and closedir. The function returns true if successful. Directory handles have their own namespace separate from filehandles.

---

ord

ord *expr*

Returns the numeric ASCII value of the first character of *expr*. If *expr* is omitted, it uses $_. The return value is always unsigned. If you want a signed value, use unpack('c', *expr*). If you want all the characters of the string converted to a list of numbers, use unpack('C*', *expr*) instead.

---

our

our *vars*

Declares the listed variables to be valid globals within the enclosing block, file, or eval. *vars* must be in parentheses if more than one value is used. our( ) has the same scoping rules as a "my" declaration but does not create a local variable. Variables that you create with our( ) will be visible across its lexical scope and may cross package boundaries. Unlike use *vars*, our( ) is not package scoped; the package in which the variable is entered is determined at the point of declaration, not at the time of use. This means the following behavior holds:

```
package Foo;
            our $bar;              # Declares $Foo::bar
    for rest of lexical scope
            $bar = 20;

            package Bar;
            print $bar;            # Prints 20
```

You my use multiple our declarations in the same lexical scope if they are in different packages. If they are in the same package, Perl will emit warnings if you have asked for them:

```
use warnings;
            package Foo;
            our $bar;            # Declares $Foo::bar
  for rest of lexical scope
            $bar = 20;

            package Bar;
            our $bar = 30;       # Declares $Bar::bar
  for rest of lexical scope
            print $bar;          # Prints 30
            our $bar;            # Emits warning
```

---

pack

pack *template*, *list*

Takes a list of values and packs it into a binary structure, returning the string containing the structure. *template* is a sequence of characters that give the order and type of values, as follows:

Character	Meaning
@	Null-fill to absolute position.
(	Start of a ( ) group.
a	An ASCII string, will be null padded.
A	An ASCII string, will be space padded.
b	A bit string, low-to-high order (such as vec( )).
B	A bit string, high-to-low order.
c	A signed char value.
C	An unsigned char value.
d	A double-precision float in the native format.
D	A long double-precision float in the native format. Long doubles are avai able only if your system supports long double values and if Perl has been compiled to support these values. Causes a fatal error otherwise. New in 5.8.
f	A single-precision float in the native format.
F	A floating-point value in the native format, i.e., a Perl internal floating-point value (NV). New in 5.8.
h	A hexadecimal string, low nybble first.
H	A hexadecimal string, high nybble first.
i	A signed integer value.
I	An unsigned integer value.
l	A signed long value.
j	A signed integer value, i.e., a Perl internal integer (IV). New in 5.8.
J	An unsigned integer value, i.e., a Perl internal unsigned integer (UV). New in 5.8.
L	An unsigned long value.
n	A short in "network" (big-endian) order.

Character	Meaning
N	A long in "network" (big-endian) order.
p	A pointer to a string.
P	A pointer to a structure (fixed-length string).
q	A signed quad (64-bit) value. New in 5.8.
Q	An unsigned quad value. Quads are available only if your system supports 64-bit integer values and if Perl has been compiled to support these values. Causes a fatal error otherwise. New in 5.8.
s	A signed short value.
S	An unsigned short value.
v	A short in "VAX" (little-endian) order.
V	A long in "VAX" (little-endian) order.
u	A uuencoded string.
U	A Unicode character number. Encodes to UTF-8 internally (or UTF-EBCDIC in EBCDIC platforms). New in 5.8.
w	A BER compressed integer.
x	A null byte.
X	Back up a byte.
Z	A null terminated (ASCII) string. Will be null padded. New in 5.8.

Each character may optionally be followed by a number that gives a repeat count. Together the character and the repeat count make a field specifier. Field specifiers may be separated by whitespace, which will be ignored. With all types except a and A, the pack function will gobble up that many values from the *list*. Specifying * for the repeat count means to use however many items are left. The a and A types gobble just one value, but pack it as a string of length *count*, padding with nulls or spaces as necessary. (When unpacking, A strips trailing spaces and nulls, but a does not.) Real numbers (floats and doubles) are in the native machine format only; due to the multiplicity of floating formats, and the lack of a standard network representation, no facility for interchange has been made.

Generally, the same template may also be used in the unpack function. If you want to join variable length fields with a delimiter, use the join function.

---

package   package *namespace*

Declares that the rest of the innermost enclosing block, subroutine, eval, or file belongs to the indicated *namespace*. (The scope of a package declaration is thus the same as the scope of a local or my declaration.) All subsequent references to unqualified global identifiers will be resolved by looking them up in the declared packages symbol table. A package declaration affects only global variables—including those you've used local on—but not lexical variables created with my.

Using package without an argument is possible, but since its semantics are unclear, package; has been deprecated in Perl 5.8. If you intend to disallow variables that aren't fully qualified, use strict; instead.

Typically, you put a package declaration as the first thing in a file that will be included by the require or use operator, but you can put one anywhere that a statement would be legal. When defining a class or a module file, it is customary to name the package the same name as the file, to avoid confusion. (It's also customary to name such packages beginning with a capital letter, because lowercase modules are, by convention, interpreted as pragmas.)

pipe　　　pipe *readhandle, writehandle*

Opens a pair of connected pipes. This call is almost always used right before a fork, after which the pipes reader should close *writehandle*, and the writer should close *readhandle*. (Otherwise, the pipe won't indicate end-of-file to the reader when the writer closes it.) Note that if you set up a loop of piped processes, deadlock can occur unless you are very careful. In addition, note that Perl's pipes use standard I/O buffering, so you may need to set $| on your *writehandle* to flush after each output command, depending on the application. See select *filehandle*.

pop　　　pop *@array*

Treats an array like a stack, popping and returning the last value of the array and shortening the array by one element. If *array* is omitted, the function pops @ARGV (in the main program) or @_ (in subroutines).

If there are no elements in the array, pop returns the undefined value. See also push and shift. If you want to pop more than one element, use splice.

pos　　　pos *$scalar*

Returns the location in *scalar* where the last m//g search over *scalar* left off. It returns the offset of the character after the last one matched. This is the offset where the next m//g search on that string will start. Remember that the offset of the beginning of the string is 0. For example:

```
$grafitto = "fee fie foe foo";
while ($grafitto =~ m/e/g) {
    print pos $grafitto, "\n";
}
```

prints 2, 3, 7, and 11, the offsets of each of the characters following an "e". The pos function may be assigned a value to tell the next m//g where to start.

print

print [*filehandle*] *list*

Prints a string or a comma-separated list of strings to the specified *filehandle*. If no filehandle is given, the function prints to the currently open filehandle (STDOUT initially). The function returns 1 if successful, 0 otherwise. *filehandle* may be a scalar variable name (unsubscripted), in which case the variable contains either the name of the actual filehandle or a reference to a filehandle object from one of the object-oriented filehandle packages. *filehandle* may also be a block that returns either kind of value:

```
print { $OK ? "STDOUT" : "STDERR" } "stuff\n";
print { $iohandle[$i] } "stuff\n";
```

If *list* is also omitted, $_ is printed. Note that because print takes a list, anything in the *list* is evaluated in list context.

printf

printf [*filehandle*] *format, list*

Prints a formatted string of the elements in *list* to *filehandle* or, if omitted, the currently selected output filehandle. This is similar to the C library's printf and fprintf functions, except that the * field width specifier is not supported. The function is exactly equivalent to:

```
print filehandle sprintf(format, list);
```

printf and sprintf use the same format syntax, but sprintf returns only a string; it doesn't print to a filehandle. The *format* string contains text with embedded field specifiers into which the elements of *list* are substituted in order, one per field. Field specifiers follow the form:

%*m.nx*

A percent sign begins each field, and *x* is the type of field. The optional *m* gives the minimum field width for appropriate field types (negative *m* left-justifies). The *.n* gives the precision for a specific field type, such as the number of digits after a decimal point for floating-point numbers, the maximum length for a string, and the minimum length for an integer.

Field specifiers (*x*) may be the following:

Code	Meaning
%	Percent sign
c	Character
d	Decimal integer
e	Exponential format floating-point number
E	Exponential format floating-point number with uppercase E
f	Fixed-point format floating-point number
g	Floating-point number, in either exponential or fixed decimal notation
G	Like g with uppercase E (if applicable)
ld	Long decimal integer

Code	Meaning
lo	Long octal integer
lu	Long unsigned decimal integer
lx	Long hexadecimal integer
o	Octal integer
s	String
u	Unsigned decimal integer
x	Hexadecimal integer
X	Hexadecimal integer with uppercase letters
p	The Perl value's address in hexadecimal
n	Special value that stores the number of characters output so far into the next variable in the parameter list

prototype

prototype *function*

Returns the prototype of a function as a string, or undef if the function has no prototype. *function* is the name of the function or a reference to it.

push

push @*array*, *list*

Pushes the elements of *list* onto the end of *array*. The length of *array* increases by the length of *list*. The function returns this new length. See also pop and unshift.

q/*string*/

q/*string*/

qq/*string*/

qx/*string*/

qw/*strings*/

Generalized forms of quoting. q// is equivalent to using single quotes (literal, no variable interpolation). qq// is equivalent to double quotes (literal, interpolated). qx// is equivalent to using backticks for commands (interpolated). And qw// is equivalent to splitting a single-quoted string on whitespace.

quotemeta

quotemeta *expr*

Returns the value of *expr* (or $_ if not specified) with all non-alphanumeric characters backslashed. This is the internal function implementing the \Q escape in interpolative contexts (including double-quoted strings, backticks, and patterns).

rand

rand *num*

Returns a random fractional number between 0 and the value of *num*. (*num* should be positive.) If *num* is omitted, the function returns a value between 0 and 1 (including 0, but excluding 1). See also srand.

To get an integral value, combine this with int, as in:

```
$roll = int(rand 6) + 1;        # $roll is now an integer
between 1 and 6
```

read

read *filehandle, $var, length, [offset]*

Attempts to read *length* bytes of data into variable *var* from the specified *filehandle*. The function returns the number of bytes actually read, or 0 at end-of-file. It returns the undefined value on error. *var* will grow or shrink to the length actually read. The *offset*, if specified, says where in the variable to start putting bytes, so that you can do a read into the middle of a string.

To copy data from the filehandle FROM into the filehandle TO, you could say:

```
while (read FROM, $buf, 16384) {
    print TO $buf;
}
```

Note that the opposite of read is simply print, which already knows the length of the string you want to write and can write a string of any length.

Perl's read function is actually implemented in terms of standard I/O's fread function, so the actual read system call may read more than *length* bytes to fill the input buffer, and fread may do more than one system read to fill the buffer. To gain greater control, specify the real system call using sysread.

readdir

readdir *dirhandle*

Reads directory entries from a directory handle opened by opendir. In scalar context, this function returns the next directory entry, if any; otherwise, it returns an undefined value. In list context, it returns all the rest of the entries in the directory, which will of course be a null list if there are none.

readline

readline **filehandle*

Reads a line or lines from the specified *filehandle*. (A typeglob of the filehandle name should be supplied.) Returns one line per call in a scalar context. Returns a list of all lines until the end-of-file in list context.

readlink   readlink *name*

Returns the name of a file pointed to by the symbolic link *name*. *name* should evaluate to a filename, the last component of which is a symbolic link. If it is not a symbolic link, or if symbolic links are not implemented, or if a system error occurs, the undefined value is returned, and you should check the error code in $!. If *name* is omitted, the function uses $_.

readpipe   readpipe *cmd*

Executes *cmd* as a system command and returns the collected standard output of the command. In a scalar context, the output is returned as a single, possibly multiline, string. In list context, a list of output lines is returned.

recv   recv *socket*, $*var*, *len*, *flags*

Receives a message on a socket. It attempts to receive *len* bytes of data into variable *var* from the specified *socket* filehandle. The function returns the address of the sender, or the undefined value if there's an error. *var* will grow or shrink to the length actually read. The function takes the same flags as the recv(2) system call.

redo   redo [*label*]

Restarts a loop block identified by *label* without reevaluating the conditional. The continue block, if any, is not executed. If the *label* is omitted, the command refers to the innermost enclosing loop.

ref   ref $*var*

Returns a string indicating the type of the object referenced if *var* is a reference; returns the null string otherwise. Built-in types include:

REF
SCALAR
ARRAY
HASH
CODE
GLOB

If the referenced object has been blessed into a package, that package name is returned instead. You can think of ref as a "typeof" operator.

rename   rename *oldname*, *newname*

Changes the name of a file from *oldname* to *newname*. It returns 1 for success, 0 otherwise (and puts the error code into $!). It will not work across filesystem boundaries. If there is already a file named *newname*, it will be destroyed.

---

require

require *filename*

require *num*

require *package*

Language
Basics

Asserts a dependency of some kind depending on its argument. (If an argument is not supplied, $_ is used.)

If the argument is a string *filename*, this function includes and executes the Perl code found in the separate file of that name. This is similar to performing an eval on the contents of the file, except that require checks to see that the library file has not been included already. The function also knows how to search the include path stored in the @INC array.

If requires argument is a number *num*, the version number of the currently executing Perl binary (as known by $]) is compared to *num*. If it is smaller, execution is immediately aborted. Thus, a script that requires Perl version 5.003 can have as its first line:

    require 5.003;

and earlier versions of Perl will abort.

If require's argument is a package name, require assumes an automatic *.pm* suffix, making it easy to load standard modules. This is like use, except that it happens at runtime, not compile time, and the import routine is not called.

---

reset

reset *expr*

Used at the top of a loop or in a continue block at the end of a loop to clear global variables or reset ?? searches so they work again. *expr* is a list of single characters (hyphens are allowed for ranges). All scalar variables, arrays, and hashes beginning with one of those letters are reset to their pristine state. If *expr* is omitted, one-match searches (?PATTERN?) are reset to match again. The function resets variables or searches for the current package only. It always returns 1.

Lexical variables (created by my) are not affected. Use of reset is vaguely deprecated.

---

return

return *expr*

Returns from a subroutine (or eval) with the value of *expr*. (In the absence of an explicit return, the value of the last expression evaluated is returned.) Use of return outside of a subroutine or eval will result in a fatal error.

The supplied expression will be evaluated in the context of the subroutine invocation. That is, if the subroutine was called in a scalar context, *expr* is also evaluated in scalar context. If the subroutine was invoked in a list context, then *expr* is also evaluated in list context and can return a list value. A return with no argument returns the undefined value in scalar context and a null list in list context. The context of the subroutine call can be determined from within the subroutine by using the (misnamed) wantarray function.

reverse   reverse *list*

Returns a list value consisting of the elements of *list* in the opposite order. This is fairly efficient because it just swaps the pointers around. In scalar context, the function concatenates all the elements of *list* together and returns the reverse of this character by character.

rewinddir   rewinddir *dirhandle*

Sets the current position to the beginning of the directory for the readdir routine on *dirhandle*. The function may not be available on all machines that support readdir.

rindex   rindex *str, substr, [position]*

Works just like index except that it returns the position of the last occurrence of *substr* in *str* (a reverse index). The function returns -1 if not found. *position*, if specified, is the rightmost position that may be returned, i.e., how far in the string the function can search.

rmdir   rmdir *name*

Deletes the directory specified by *name* if it is empty. If it succeeds, it returns 1; otherwise, it returns 0 and puts the error code into $!. If *name* is omitted, the function uses $_.

scalar   scalar *expr*

Forces an expression *expr* to be evaluated in scalar context.

seek   seek *filehandle, offset, whence*

Positions the file pointer for *filehandle*, just like the fseek(3) call of standard I/O. The first position in a file is at offset 0, not offset 1, and offsets refer to byte positions, not line numbers. The function returns 1 upon success, 0 otherwise. For handiness, the function can calculate offsets from various file positions for you. The value of *whence* specifies which of three file positions your *offset* is relative to: 0, the beginning of the file; 1, the current position in the file; or 2, the end of the file. *offset* may be negative for a *whence* of 1 or 2.

seekdir

seekdir *dirhandle, pos*

Sets the current position for the readdir routine on *dirhandle*. *pos* must be a value returned by telldir. This function has the same caveats about possible directory compaction as the corresponding system library routine.

select

select *filehandle*

Returns the currently selected output filehandle, and if *filehandle* is supplied, sets that as the current default filehandle for output. This has two effects. First, a write or a print without a filehandle argument will default to this *filehandle*. Second, special variables related to output will refer to this output filehandle.

select

select *rbits, wbits, ebits, timeout*

The four-argument select operator is totally unrelated to the previously described select operator. This operator is for discovering which (if any) of your file descriptors are ready to do input or output, or to report an exceptional condition. It calls the select(2) system call with the bitmasks you've specified, which you can construct using fileno and vec, like this:

```
$rbits = $wbits = $ebits = "";
vec($rbits, fileno(STDIN), 1) = 1;
vec($wbits, fileno(STDOUT), 1) = 1;
$ein = $rin | $win;
```

The select call blocks until one or more file descriptors is ready for reading, writing, or reporting an error condition. *timeout* is given in seconds and tells select how long to wait.

semctl

semctl *id, semnum, cmd, arg*

Calls the System V IPC system call semctl(2). If *cmd* is &IPC_STAT or &GETALL, then *arg* must be a variable which will hold the returned semid_ds structure or semaphore value array. The function returns like ioctl: the undefined value for error, 0 but true for zero, or the actual return value otherwise. On error, it puts the error code into $!. Before calling, you should say:

```
require "ipc.ph";
require "sem.ph";
```

This function is available only on machines supporting System V IPC.

semget   semget *key, nsems, size, flags*

Calls the System V IPC system call semget(2). The function returns the semaphore ID, or the undefined value if there is an error. On error, it puts the error code into $!. Before calling, you should say:

```
require "ipc.ph";
require "sem.ph";
```

This function is available only on machines supporting System V IPC.

semop   semop *key, opstring*

Calls the System V IPC system call semop(2) to perform semaphore operations such as signaling and waiting. *opstring* must be a packed array of semop structures. You can make each semop structure by saying pack('s*', $semnum, $semop, $semflag). The number of semaphore operations is implied by the length of *opstring*. The function returns true if successful or false if there is an error. On error, it puts the error code into $!. Before calling, you should say:

```
require "ipc.ph";
require "sem.ph";
```

This function is available only on machines supporting System V IPC.

send   send *socket, msg, flags, [dest]*

Sends a message *msg* on a socket. It takes the same flags as the system call of the same name (see send(2)). On unconnected sockets, you must specify a destination *dest* to send to, in which case send works like sendto(2). The function returns the number of bytes sent, or the undefined value if there is an error. On error, it puts the error code into $!.

Some non-Unix systems improperly treat sockets as different objects than ordinary file descriptors, which means that you must always use send and recv on sockets rather than the standard I/O operators.

sethostent   sethostent *stayopen*

Opens the hosts file (usually */etc/hosts* on Unix systems) and resets the "current" selection to the top of the file. *stayopen*, if nonzero, keeps the file open across calls to other functions. Not implemented on Win32 systems.

setgrent

setgrent

Opens the groups file (usually */etc/group* on Unix systems) and resets the top of the file as the starting point for any read and/or write functions on the file (with the proper permissions). This function will reset the getgrent function back to retrieve group entries from the start of the group file. Not implemented on Win32 systems.

setnetent

setnetent *stayopen*

Opens the networks file (usually */etc/group*) and resets the "current" selection to the top of the file. *stayopen*, if nonzero, keeps the file open across calls to other functions. Not implemented on Win32 systems.

setpgrp

setpgrp *pid, pgrp*

Sets the current process group *pgrp* for the specified *pid* (use a *pid* of 0 for the current process). Invoking setpgrp will produce a fatal error if used on a machine that doesn't implement setpgrp(2). Some systems will ignore the arguments you provide and always do setpgrp(0, $$). Fortunately, those are the arguments you usually provide. (For better portability, use the setpgid( ) function in the POSIX module, or if you're really just trying to daemonize your script, consider the POSIX::setsid( ) function as well.)

setpriority

setpriority *which, who, priority*

Sets the current *priority* for a process, a process group, or a user. *which* must indicate one of these types: PRIO_PROCESS, PRIO_PGRP, or PRIO_USER. *who*, therefore, identifies the specific process, process group, or user with its ID. *priority* is an integer number that will be added to or subtracted from the current priority; the lower the number, the higher the priority. The interpretation of a given priority may vary from one operating system to the next. See setpriority on your system. Invoking setpriority will produce a fatal error if used on a machine that doesn't implement setpriority.

setprotoent

setprotoent *stayopen*

Opens the prototypes file (usually */etc/prototypes*) and resets the "current" selection to the top of the file. *stayopen*, if nonzero, keeps the file open across calls to other functions. Not implemented on Win32 systems.

setpwent

setpwent

Opens the password file (usually */etc/passwd*) and resets the top of the file as the starting point for any read and/or write functions on the file (with the proper permissions). This function will reset the getpwent function back to retrieve group entries from the start of the group file. Not implemented on Win32 systems.

setservent

setservent *stayopen*

Opens the services file (usually */etc/services*) and resets the "current" selection to the top of the file. *stayopen*, if nonzero, keeps the file open across calls to other functions. Not implemented on Win32 systems.

setsockopt

setsockopt *socket, level, optname, optval*

Sets the socket option requested (*optname*) to the value *optval*. The function returns undefined if there is an error. *optval* may be specified as undef if you don't want to pass an argument. *level* specifies the protocol type used on the socket.

shift

shift *@array*

Removes the first value of *@array* and returns it, shortening the array by 1 and moving everything down. If there are no elements in the array, the function returns the undefined value. If *@array* is omitted, the function shifts @ARGV (in the main program), or @_ (in subroutines). See also unshift, push, pop, and splice. The shift and unshift functions do the same thing to the left end of an array that pop and push do to the right end.

shmctl

shmctl *id, cmd, arg*

Calls the System V IPC system call, shmctl(2), for performing operations on shared memory segments. If *cmd* is &IPC_STAT, then *arg* must be a variable that will hold the returned shmid_ds structure. The function returns like ioctl: the undefined value for error, "0 but true" for 0, or the actual return value otherwise. On error, it puts the error code into $!. Before calling, you should say:

    require "ipc.ph";
    require "shm.ph";

This function is available only on machines supporting System V IPC.

shmget

shmget *key, size, flags*

Calls the System V IPC system call, shmget(2). The function returns the shared memory segment ID, or the undefined value if there is an error. On error, it puts the error code into $!. Before calling, you should say:

```
require "ipc.ph";
require "shm.ph";
```

This function is available only on machines supporting System V IPC.

shmread
   shmread *id, var, pos, size*

Reads from the shared memory segment *id* starting at position *pos* for size *size* (by attaching to it, copying out, and detaching from it). *var* must be a variable that will hold the data read. The function returns true if successful or false if there is an error. On error, it puts the error code into $!. This function is available only on machines supporting System V IPC.

shmwrite
   shmwrite *id, string, pos, size*

Writes to the shared memory segment ID starting at position *pos* for size *size* (by attaching to it, copying in, and detaching from it). If *string* is too long, only *size* bytes are used; if *string* is too short, nulls are written to fill out *size* bytes. The function returns true if successful or false if there is an error. On error, it puts the error code into $!. This function is available only on machines supporting System V IPC.

shutdown
   shutdown *socket, how*

Shuts down a socket connection in the manner indicated by *how*. If *how* is 0, further receives are disallowed. If *how* is 1, further sends are disallowed. If *how* is 2, everything is disallowed.

This function will not shut down your system; you'll have to execute an external program to do that. See system.

sin
   sin *num*

Returns the sine of *num* (expressed in radians). If *num* is omitted, it returns the sine of $_.

sleep
   sleep *n*

Causes the script to sleep for *n* seconds, or forever if no argument is given. It may be interrupted by sending the process a SIGALRM. The function returns the number of seconds actually slept. On some systems, the function sleeps till the "top of the second." So, for instance, a sleep 1 may sleep anywhere from 0 to 1 second, depending on when in the current second you started sleeping.

socket

socket *socket, domain, type, protocol*

Opens a socket of the specified kind and attaches it to filehandle *socket*. *domain*, *type*, and *protocol* are specified the same as for socket(2). Before using this function, your program should contain the line:

    use Socket;

This setting gives you the proper constants. The function returns true if successful.

socketpair

socketpair *sock1, sock2, domain, type, prtcl*

Creates an unnamed pair of sockets in the specified *domain* and of the specified *type*. *domain*, *type*, and *protocol* are specified the same as for socketpair(2). If socketpair is unimplemented, invoking this function yields a fatal error. The function returns true if successful.

This function is typically used just before a fork. One of the resulting processes should close *sock1*, and the other should close *sock2*. You can use these sockets bidirectionally, unlike the filehandles created by the pipe function.

sort

sort [*code*] *list*

Sorts a *list* and returns the sorted list value. By default (without a *code* argument), it sorts in standard string comparison order (undefined values sorting before defined null strings, which sort before everything else). *code*, if given, may be the name of a subroutine or a code block (anonymous subroutine) that defines its own comparison mechanism for sorting elements of *list*. The routine must return to the sort function an integer less than, equal to, or greater than 0, depending on how the elements of the list will be ordered. (The handy <=> and cmp operators can be used to perform three-way numeric and string comparisons.)

The normal calling code for subroutines is bypassed, with the following effects: the subroutine may not be a recursive subroutine, and the two elements to be compared are passed into the subroutine as $a and $b, not via @_. The variables $a and $b are passed by reference, so don't modify them in the subroutine.

Do not declare $a and $b as lexical variables (with my). They are package globals (though they're exempt from the usual restrictions on globals when you're using use strict). However, you do need to make sure your sort routine is in the same package, or else you must qualify $a and $b with the package name of the caller.

In versions preceding 5.005, Perl's sort is implemented in terms of C's qsort(3) function. Some qsort(3) versions will dump core if your sort subroutine provides inconsistent ordering of values. As of 5.005, however, this is no longer true.

splice

splice @*array*, *pos*, [*n*], [*list*]

Removes *n* number of elements from @*array* starting at position *pos*, replacing them with the elements of *list*, if provided. The function returns the elements removed from the array. The array grows or shrinks as necessary. If *n* is omitted, the function removes everything from *pos* onward.

split

split /*pattern*/, *string*, [*limit*]

Scans a *string* for delimiters that match *pattern* and splits the string into a list of substrings, returning the resulting list value in list context, or the count of substrings in scalar context. The delimiters are determined by repeated pattern matching, using the regular expression given in *pattern*, so the delimiters may be of any size and need not be the same string on every match. If the *pattern* doesn't match at all, split returns the original string as a single substring. If it matches once, you get two substrings, and so on.

If *limit* is specified and is not negative, the function splits into no more than that many fields. If *limit* is negative, it is treated as if an arbitrarily large *limit* has been specified. If *limit* is omitted, trailing null fields are stripped from the result (which potential users of pop would do well to remember). If *string* is omitted, the function splits the $_ string. If *pattern* is also omitted, the function splits on whitespace, /\s+/, after skipping any leading whitespace.

If the *pattern* contains parentheses, then the substring matched by each pair of parentheses is included in the resulting list, interspersed with the fields that are ordinarily returned. Here's a simple case:

    split /([-,])/, "1-10,20";

This produces the list value:

    (1, '-', 10, ',', 20)

sprintf

sprintf *format*, *list*

Returns a string formatted by the printf conventions. The *format* string contains text with embedded field specifiers into which the elements of *list* are substituted, one per field. Field specifiers are roughly of the form:

    %*m*.*nx*

in which *m* and *n* are optional sizes with interpretation that depends on the type of field, and *x* is one of the following:

Code	Meaning
%	Percent sign
c	Character
d	Decimal integer

Code	Meaning
e	Exponential format floating-point number
E	Exponential format floating-point number with uppercase E
f	Fixed-point format floating-point number
g	Floating-point number, in either exponential or fixed decimal notation
G	Like g with uppercase E (if applicable)
ld	Long decimal integer
lo	Long octal integer
lu	Long unsigned decimal integer
lx	Long hexadecimal integer
o	Octal integer
s	String
u	Unsigned decimal integer
x	Hexadecimal integer
X	Hexadecimal integer with uppercase letters
p	The Perl value's address in hexadecimal
n	Special value that stores the number of characters output so far into the next variable in the parameter list.

m is typically the minimum length of the field (negative for left-justified), and *n* is precision for exponential formats and the maximum length for other formats. Padding is typically done with spaces for strings and zeroes for numbers. The * character as a length specifier is not supported.

sqrt

sqrt *num*

Returns the square root of *num*, or $_ if omitted. For other roots such as cube roots, you can use the ** operator to raise something to a fractional power.

srand

srand *expr*

Sets the random number seed for the rand operator so that rand can produce a different sequence each time you run your program. If *expr* is omitted, a default seed is used that is a mix of difficult-to-predict, system-dependent values. If you call rand and haven't called srand, rand calls srand with the default seed.

stat

stat *file*

Returns a 13-element list giving the statistics for a *file*, indicated by either a filehandle or an expression that gives its name. It's typically used as follows:

```
($dev,$ino,$mode,$nlink,$uid,$gid,$rdev,$size,
    $atime,$mtime,$ctime,$blksize,$blocks)
        = stat $filename;
```

Not all fields are supported on all filesystem types. Here are the meanings of the fields:

Field	Meaning
dev	Device number of filesystem
ino	Inode number
mode	File mode (type and permissions)
nlink	Number of (hard) links to the file
uid	Numeric user ID of file's owner
gid	Numeric group ID of file's owner
rdev	The device identifier (special files only)
size	Total size of file, in bytes
atime	Last access time since the epoch
mtime	Last modification time since the epoch
ctime	Inode change time (not creation time!) since the epoch
blksize	Preferred blocksize for file system I/O
blocks	Actual number of blocks allocated

$dev and $ino, taken together, uniquely identify a file. The $blksize and $blocks are likely defined only on BSD-derived filesystems. The $blocks field (if defined) is reported in 512-byte blocks. Note that $blocks*512 can differ greatly from $size for files containing unallocated blocks, or "holes," which aren't counted in $blocks.

If stat is passed the special filehandle consisting of an underline, no actual stat is done, but the current contents of the stat structure from the last stat or stat-based file test (the -x operators) is returned.

study

study *scalar*

This function takes extra time to study *scalar* ($_ if unspecified) in anticipation of doing many pattern matches on the string before it is next modified. You may have only one study active at a time—if you study a different scalar, the first is "unstudied."

sub

sub *name* [*proto*] {*block*}

sub [*proto*] *name*

Declares and defines a subroutine. *name* is the name given to the subroutine; *block* is the code that will be executed when the subroutine is called. Without *block*, this statement declares only a subroutine, which must be defined at a later point in your program. *proto* is a sequence of symbols that places constraints on the arguments that the subroutine will receive. See Chapter 4.

substr   substr *string, pos,* [*n, replacement*]

Extracts and returns a substring *n* characters long, starting at character position *pos*, from a given *string*. If *pos* is negative, the
substring starts that far from the end of the string instead. If *n* is
omitted, everything to the end of the string is returned. If *n* is negative, the length is calculated to leave that many characters off the
end of the string.

You can use substr( ) as an lvalue—replacing the delimited
substring with a new string—if *string* is given as an lvalue. You
can also specify a *replacement* string in the fourth parameter to
replace the substring. The original extracted substring is still
returned.

symlink   symlink *oldfile, newfile*

Creates a new filename symbolically linked to the old filename.
The function returns 1 for success, 0 otherwise. On systems that
don't support symbolic links, it produces a fatal error at runtime.
Be careful if you supply a relative symbolic link, since it will be
interpreted relative to the location of the symbolic link itself, not
your current working directory. See also link and readlink.

syscall   syscall *list*

Calls the system call specified as the first element of the list,
passing the remaining elements as arguments to the system call.
The function produces a fatal error if syscall(2) is unimplemented. The arguments are interpreted as follows: if a given
argument is numeric, the argument is passed as a C integer. If not,
a pointer to the string value is passed.

sysopen   sysopen *filehandle, filename, mode,* [*perms*]

Opens the file given by *filename* and associates it with *filehandle*.
This function calls open(2) with the parameters *filename*, *mode*, and
perms.

The possible values and flag bits of the *mode* parameter are system-
dependent; they are available via the Fcntl library module.
However, for historical reasons, some values are universal: 0 means
read-only, 1 means write-only, and 2 means read/write.

If the file named by *filename* does not exist, and sysopen creates it
(typically because *mode* includes the O_CREAT flag), then the value of
perms specifies the permissions of the newly created file. If *perms* is
omitted, the default value is 0666, which allows read and write for
all. This default is reasonable. See umask.

The FileHandle module provides a more object-oriented approach
to sysopen. See also open.

sysread

sysread *filehandle, scalar, length, [offset]*

Reads *length* bytes of data into variable *scalar* from the specified *filehandle*. The function returns the number of bytes actually read, or 0 at end-of-file. It returns the undefined value on error. *scalar* will grow or shrink to the length actually read. The *offset*, if specified, says where in the string to start putting the bytes so you can read into the middle of a string that's being used as a buffer. You should be prepared to handle the problems (such as interrupted system calls) that standard I/O normally handles for you.

sysseek

sysseek *filehandle, offset, whence*

A variant of seek( ) that sets and gets the file's system read/write position using the lseek(2) system call. It's the only reliable way to seek before a sysread( ) or syswrite( ). Returns the new position, or undef on failure. Arguments are the same as for seek.

system

system *list*

Executes any program on the system for you. It does exactly the same thing as exec *list* except that it does a fork first, and then, after the exec, it waits for the execed program to complete. That is, it runs the program for you and returns when it's done, unlike exec, which never returns (if it succeeds). Note that argument processing varies depending on the number of arguments, as described for exec. The return value is the exit status of the program as returned by the wait(2) call. To get the actual exit value, divide by 256. (The lower eight bits are set if the process died from a signal.) See exec.

syswrite

syswrite *filehandle, scalar, length, [offset]*

Writes *length* bytes of data from variable *scalar* to the specified *filehandle*. The function returns the number of bytes actually written, or the undefined value on error. You should be prepared to handle the problems that standard I/O normally handles for you, such as partial writes. The *offset*, if specified, says where in the string to start writing from, in case you're using the string as a buffer, for instance, or need to recover from a partial write.

Do not mix calls to print (or write) and syswrite on the same filehandle unless you really know what you're doing.

tell

tell *filehandle*

Returns the current file position (in bytes, 0-based) for *filehandle*. This value is typically fed to the seek function at a future time to get back to the current position. If *filehandle* is omitted, the function returns the position of the last file read. File positions are only meaningful on regular files. Devices, pipes, and sockets have no file position.

telldir

telldir *dirhandle*

Returns the current position of the readdir routines on a directory handle (*dirhandle*). This value may be given to seekdir to access a particular location in a directory. The function has the same caveats about possible directory compaction as the corresponding system library routine. This function may not be implemented everywhere that readdir is. Even if it is, no calculation may be done with the return value. It's just an opaque value, meaningful only to seekdir.

tie

tie *variable, classname, list*

Binds a *variable* to a package class, *classname*, that will provide the implementation for the variable. Any additional arguments (*list*) are passed to the "new" method of the class (meaning TIESCALAR, TIEARRAY, or TIEHASH). Typically, these are arguments that might be passed to the dbm_open(3) function of C, but this is package-dependent. The object returned by the "new" method is also returned by the tie function, which can be useful if you want to access other methods in *classname*. (The object can also be accessed through the tied function.)

A class implementing a hash should provide the following methods:

```
TIEHASH $class, LIST
DESTROY $self
FETCH $self, $key
STORE $self, $key, $value
DELETE $self, $key
EXISTS $self, $key
FIRSTKEY $self
NEXTKEY $self, $lastkey
```

A class implementing an ordinary array should provide the following methods:

```
TIEARRAY $classname, LIST
DESTROY $self
FETCH $self, $subscript
STORE $self, $subscript, $value
```

A class implementing a scalar should provide the following methods:

```
TIESCALAR $classname, LIST
DESTROY $self
FETCH $self,
STORE $self, $value
```

Unlike dbmopen, the tie function will not use or require a module for you—you need to do that explicitly yourself.

tied   tied *variable*

Returns a reference to the object underlying *variable* (the same value that was originally returned by the tie call that bound the variable to a package). It returns the undefined value if *variable* isn't tied to a package. So, for example, you can use:

    ref tied %hash

to find out which package your hash is currently tied to.

time   time

Returns the number of non-leap seconds since January 1, 1970, UTC. The returned value is suitable for feeding to gmtime and localtime, for comparison with file modification and access times returned by stat, and for feeding to utime.

times   times

Returns a four-element list giving the user and system CPU times, in seconds (possibly fractional), for this process and for the children of this process:

    ($user, $system, $cuser, $csystem) = times;

For example, to time the execution speed of a section of Perl code:

    $start = (times)[0];
    ...
    $end = (times)[0];
    printf "that took %.2f CPU seconds\n", $end - $start;

truncate   truncate *file, length*

Truncates a *file* (given as a filehandle or by name) to the specified length. The function produces a fatal error if truncate(2) or an equivalent isn't implemented on your system.

uc   uc *string*

Returns an uppercased version of *string* (or $_ if *string* is omitted). This is the internal function implementing the \U escape in double-quoted strings. POSIX setlocale(3) settings are respected.

ucfirst   ucfirst *string*

Returns a version of *string* (or $_ if *string* is omitted) with the first character uppercased. This is the internal function that implements the \u escape in double-quoted strings. POSIX setlocale(3) settings are respected.

umask

umask *expr*

Sets the umask for the process to *expr* and returns the old one. (The umask tells Unix which permission bits to disallow when creating a file.) If *expr* is omitted, the function merely returns the current umask. For example, to ensure that the "other" bits are turned on and that the "user" bits are turned off, try something like:

```
umask((umask( ) & 077) | 7);
```

undef

undef *expr*

Undefines the value of *expr*, which must be an lvalue. Use only on a scalar value, an entire array or hash, or a subroutine name (using the & prefix). Any storage associated with the object will be recovered for reuse (though not returned to the system, for most versions of Unix). The undef function will probably not do what you expect on most special variables. The function always returns the undefined value. This is useful because you can omit the *expr*, in which case nothing gets undefined, but you still get an undefined value that you could, for instance, return from a subroutine to indicate an error.

You may use undef as a placeholder on the left side of a list assignment, in which case the corresponding value from the right side is simply discarded. Apart from that, you may not use undef as an lvalue.

unlink

unlink *list*

Deletes a list of files. (Under Unix, it will remove a link to a file, but the file may still exist if another link references it.) If *list* is omitted, it unlinks the file given in $_. The function returns the number of files successfully deleted. Note that unlink will not delete directories unless you are the superuser and the –U flag is supplied to Perl. Even if these conditions are met, be warned that unlinking a directory can inflict serious damage on your filesystem. Use rmdir instead.

unpack

unpack *template, string*

Takes a string (*string*) representing a data structure and expands it into a list value, returning the list value. (unpack does the reverse of pack.) In a scalar context, it can be used to unpack a single value. The *template* has much the same format as the pack function—it specifies the order and type of the values to be unpacked. See pack for a more detailed description of *template*.

unshift	unshift *@array, list*
	Prepends the elements of *list* to the front of the array and returns the new number of elements in the array.

untie	untie *variable*
	Breaks the binding between a variable and a package. See tie.

use	use *Module list*
	use *version*
	use *Module version list*

If the first argument is a number, it is treated as a version number. If the version of Perl is less than *version*, an error message is printed and Perl exits. This provides a way to check the Perl version at compilation time instead of waiting for runtime.

If *version* appears between *Module* and *list*, then use calls the version method in class *Module* with *version* as an argument.

Otherwise, use imports some semantics into the current package from the named *Module*, generally by aliasing certain subroutine or variable names into your package. It is exactly equivalent to the following:

```
BEGIN { require Module; import Module list; }
```

The BEGIN forces the require and import to happen at compile time. The require makes sure that the module is loaded into memory if it hasn't been yet. The import is not a built-in function—it's just an ordinary static method call into the package named by *Module* that tells the module to import the list of features back into the current package. The module can implement its import method any way it likes, though most modules just choose to derive their import method via inheritance from the Exporter class defined in the Exporter module.

If you don't want your namespace altered, explicitly supply an empty list:

```
use Module ( );
```

This is exactly equivalent to the following:

```
BEGIN { require Module; }
```

Because this is a wide-open interface, pragmas (compiler directives) are also implemented this way. (See Chapter 8 for descriptions of the currently implemented pragmas.) These pseudomodules typically import semantics into the current block scope, unlike ordinary modules, which import symbols into the current package. (The latter are effective through the end of the file.)

There's a corresponding declaration, no, that "unimports" any meanings originally imported by use but have since become less important:

```
no integer;
no strict 'refs';
```

utime

utime *atime, mtime, files*

Changes the access time (*atime*) and modification time (*mtime*) on each file in a list of *files*. The first two elements must be the *numerical* access and modification times, in that order. The function returns the number of files successfully changed. The inode change time of each file is set to the current time. Here's an example of a utime command:

```
#!/usr/bin/perl
$now = time;
utime $now, $now, @ARGV;
```

To read the times from existing files, use stat.

values

values *%hash*

Returns a list consisting of all the values of the named hash. The values are returned in an apparently random order, but it is the same order that the keys or each function would produce on the same hash. To sort the hash by its values, see the example under keys. Note that using values on a hash bound to a very large DBM file will produce a very large list, causing you to have a very large process, and leaving you in a bind. You might prefer to use the each function, which will iterate over the hash entries one by one without reading them all into a single list.

vec

vec *string, offset, bits*

Treats a *string* as a vector of unsigned integers and returns the value of the element specified by *offset* and *bits*. The function may also be assigned to, which causes the element to be modified. The purpose of the function is to provide compact storage of lists of small integers. The integers may be very small—vectors can hold numbers that are as small as one bit, resulting in a bitstring.

The *offset* specifies the number of elements to skip over to find the one you want. *bits* is the number of bits per element in the vector, so each element can contain an unsigned integer in the range 0..(2**bits)-1. bits must be one of 1, 2, 4, 8, 16, or 32. As many elements as possible are packed into each byte, and the ordering is such that vec($vectorstring,0,1) is guaranteed to go into the lowest bit of the first byte of the string. To find the position of the byte in which an element will be placed, you have to multiply the *offset* by the number of elements per byte. When *bits* is 1, there are eight elements per byte. When *bits* is 2, there are four elements per byte. When *bits* is 4, there are two elements (called nybbles) per byte. And so on.

Regardless of whether your system is big-endian or little-endian, vec($foo, 0, 8) always refers to the first byte of string $foo. See select for examples of bitmaps generated with vec.

Vectors created with vec can also be manipulated with the logical operators |, &, ^, and ~, which will assume a bit vector operation is desired when the operands are strings. A bit vector (*bits* == 1) can be translated to or from a string of 1s and 0s by supplying a b* template to unpack or pack. Similarly, a vector of nybbles (*bits* == 4) can be translated with an h* template.

---

wait

wait

Waits for a child process to terminate and returns the pid of the deceased process, or -1 if there are no child processes. The status is returned in $?. If you get zombie child processes, you are probably calling either this function or waitpid. A common strategy to avoid such zombies is:

```
$SIG{CHLD} = sub { wait };
```

If you expected a child and didn't find it, you probably had a call to system, a close on a pipe, or backticks between the fork and the wait. These constructs also do a wait(2) and may have harvested your child process. Use waitpid to avoid this problem.

---

waitpid

waitpid *pid, flags*

Waits for a particular child process *pid* to terminate and returns the pid when the process is dead, or -1 if there are no child processes or if the *flags* specify nonblocking and the process isn't dead yet. The status of the dead process is returned in $?. To get valid flag values, do the following:

```
use POSIX "sys_wait_h";
```

On systems that implement neither the waitpid(2) nor the wait4(2) system call, *flags* may be specified only as 0. In other words, you can wait for a specific *pid*, but you can't do it in nonblocking mode.

---

wantarray

wantarray

Returns true if the context of the currently executing subroutine is looking for a list value. The function returns false if the context is looking for a scalar. May also return undef if a subroutine's return value will not be used at all.

warn   warn *msg*

Produces a message on STDERR just like die, but doesn't try to exit or throw an exception. For example:

    warn "Debug enabled" if $debug;

If the message supplied is null, the message "Something's wrong" is used. As with die, a message not ending with a newline will have file and line number information automatically appended. The warn operator is unrelated to the *–w* switch.

write   write *filehandle*

Writes a formatted record (possibly multiline) to the specified *filehandle*, using the format associated with that filehandle (see Chapter 4). By default, the format for a filehandle is the one having the same name as the filehandle.

If *filehandle* is unspecified, output goes to the current default output filehandle, which starts as STDOUT but may be changed by the select operator. If the *filehandle* is an expression, then the expression is evaluated to determine the actual *filehandle* at runtime.

Note that write is not the opposite of read. Use print for simple string output. If you want to bypass standard I/O, see syswrite.

6

Debugging

Of course everyone writes perfect code on the first try, but on those rare occasions when something goes wrong, and you're having trouble with your Perl script, there are several things you can do:

- Run the script with the *–w* switch, which prints warnings about possible problems in your code.
- Use the Perl debugger.
- Use another debugger, or a profiler such as the Devel::DProf module.

The major focus of this chapter is the Perl debugger, which provides an interactive Perl environment. The chapter also describes the DProf module and the *dprofpp* program that comes with it; together they can provide you with a profile of your Perl script. If you've ever used any debugger, and you understand concepts such as breakpoints and backtraces, you'll have no trouble learning to use the Perl debugger. Even if you haven't used another debugger, the command descriptions and some experimenting should get you going.

The Perl Debugger

To run your script under the Perl source debugger, invoke Perl with the *–d* switch:

```
perl -d myprogram
```

This works like an interactive Perl environment, prompting for debugger commands that let you examine source code, set breakpoints, get stack backtraces, change the values of variables, etc. If your program takes any switches or arguments, you must include them in the command:

```
perl -d myprogram myinput
```

In Perl, the debugger is not a separate program as it is in the typical compiled environment. Instead, the *–d* flag tells the compiler to insert source information into the parse trees it's about to hand off to the interpreter. This means your code must compile correctly for the debugger to work on it—the debugger won't run until you have fixed all compiler errors.

After your code has compiled, and the debugger has started up, the program halts right before the first runtime executable statement (see the section "Using the Debugger" regarding compile time statements) and waits for you to enter a debugger command. Whenever the debugger halts and shows you a line of code, it always displays the line it's about to execute, rather than the one it has just executed.

Any command not recognized by the debugger is directly executed as Perl code in the current package. To be recognized by the debugger, the command must start at the beginning of the line; otherwise, the debugger assumes it's for Perl.

Debugger Commands

The debugger understands the following commands.

-   -

Lists the previous few lines.

.   .

Returns debugger pointer to the last-executed line and prints it out.

/pattern/   /pattern/

Searches forward for *pattern*; final / is optional.

?pattern?   ?pattern?

Searches backward for *pattern*; final ? is optional.

<   < [command]

Sets a Perl command to run before every debugger prompt. A multiline *command* may be entered by backslashing the newlines. With no *command*, the list of actions is reset.

<<   << [command]

Adds to the list of Perl commands to run before each debugger prompt.

\<CR\>	\<CR\> Repeats last n or s command.
\>	\> [*command*] Sets a Perl command to run after the prompt when you've just given a command to return to executing the script. A multiline *command* may be entered by backslashing the newlines.
\>\>	\>\> [*command*] Adds to the list of Perl commands to run after each debugger prompt.
{	{ [*commandline*] Sets a debugger command to run before each prompt.
{{	{{ [*commandline*] Adds to the list of debugger commands to run before each prompt.
!	! [*number*] Reruns a previous command (defaults to the last command executed).
!	! -*number* Reruns *number*th-to-last command.
!	! *pattern* Reruns last command that started with *pattern*. See 0 recallCommand.
!!	!! *cmd* Runs *cmd* in a subprocess (which reads from DB::IN and writes to DB::OUT). See 0 shellBang.
|	| *dbcmd* Runs specified debugger command, piping DB::OUT to $ENV{PAGER}.

| || | || *dbcmd* |

Same as |*dbcmd*, but DB::OUT is temporarily selected as well. Often used with commands that would otherwise produce long output, such as:

```
|V main
```

| = | = [*alias value*] |

Defines a command alias. If *alias* and *value* are omitted, lists all current aliases.

| **A** | A |

Deletes all installed actions.

| **a** | a [*line*] *command* |

Sets an action to be done before the *line* is executed. The following steps are taken:

- Checks for a breakpoint at this line
- Prints the line if necessary
- Performs any actions associated with the line
- Prompts the user if at a breakpoint or in single-step mode
- Evaluates the line

For example, the following prints the value of $foo (and DB FOUND) every time line 53 is passed:

```
a 53 print "DB FOUND $foo\n"
```

| **b** | b [*line*] [*condition*] |

Sets a breakpoint at *line*, which must begin an executable statement. If *line* is omitted, sets a breakpoint on the line that is about to be executed. *condition*, if given, is evaluated each time the statement is reached, and a breakpoint is taken if *condition* is true:

```
b 237 $x > 30
b 33 /pattern/i
```

| **b** | b *subname* [*condition*] |

Sets a (possibly conditional) breakpoint at the first line of the named subroutine.

| **b** | b load *filename* |

Sets a breakpoint on requireing the given file.

b	`b postpone subname [condition]`
	Sets a (possibly conditional) breakpoint at the first line of subroutine *subname* after it has been compiled.

b	`b compile subname`
	Stops after the subroutine has been compiled.

c	`c [line	sub]`
	Continues, optionally inserting a one-time-only breakpoint at the specified line or subroutine.

command	*command*
	Executes *command* as a Perl statement. A semicolon is not needed at the end.

D	`D`
	Deletes all installed breakpoints

d	`d [line]`
	Deletes the breakpoint at the specified *line*. If *line* is omitted, deletes the breakpoint on the line that is about to be executed..

f	`f filename`
	Switches to viewing a different file.

H	`H [-number]`
	Displays last *number* commands. If *number* is omitted, it lists all previous commands. Only commands longer than one character are listed.

h	`h [command]`
	Prints a help message, listing the available debugger commands.
	If you supply another debugger command as an argument to the h command, it prints out the description for just that command. The command h h produces a more compact help listing designed to fit on one screen.

L

L

Lists all breakpoints and actions for the current file.

l

l [*linespec*]

If *linespec* is omitted, lists the next few lines. Otherwise, lists the lines specified by *linespec*, which can be one of the following:

line
Lists the single line *line*

min+incr
Lists *incr*+1 lines starting at *min*

min-max
Lists lines *min* through *max*

subname
Lists the first few lines from subroutine *subname*.

Also see the w and - commands.

m

m *expr*

evals the expression in array context and prints methods callable on the first element of the result.

m

m *class*

Prints methods callable via the given class.

n

n

Next. Passes over subroutine calls and executes the next statement at this level.

0

O [*opt*[="*val*"]] [*opt*'val'] [*opt*?]

Sets or queries option values. If omitted, *val* defaults to 1. *opt*? displays the value of option *opt*. *opt* can be abbreviated to the shortest unique string, and multiple options can be specified. The possible options are:

AutoTrace
Affects printing of messages at every possible breaking point.

frame
Enables printing of messages on entry and exit from subroutines.

inhibit_exit
Enables stepping off the end of the script.

maxTraceLen

> Gives the maximum length of evals/args listed in the stack trace.

ornaments

> Affects the appearance of the command line on the screen.

pager

> Specifies the program to use for output of pager-piped commands (those beginning with a | character). Default value is $ENV{PAGER}.

PrintRet

> Enables printing of return value after r command.

recallCommand, ShellBang

> Specifies the characters used to recall previous commands or spawn a shell. By default, these are both set to !.

The following options affect what happens with the V, X, and x commands:

arrayDepth, hashDepth

> Prints only to depth n ("" for all).

compactDump, veryCompact

> Changes style of array and hash dumps.

DumpDBFiles

> Dumps arrays holding debugged files.

DumpPackages

> Dumps symbol tables of packages.

globPrint

> Specifies whether to print contents of globs.

quote, HighBit, undefPrint

> Changes style of string dump.

signalLevel, warnLevel, dieLevel

> Specifies level of verbosity.

tkRunning

> Runs Tk while prompting (with ReadLine).

During startup, debugger options are initialized from $ENV{PERLDB_OPTS}. You can set the additional initialization options TTY, noTTY, ReadLine, and NonStop there. See the section "Customizing the Debugger" later in this chapter for more information.

---

p
      p expr

> Same as print DB::OUT *expr* in the current package. In particular, does not dump nested data structures and objects, unlike the x command. The DB::OUT handle is opened to */dev/tty* (or perhaps an editor window) no matter where standard output may have been redirected to.

q

q or ^D

Quits the debugger.

R

R

Restarts the debugger. As much of your history is maintained across the sessions as possible, but some internal settings and command-line options may be lost.

r

r

Returns from current subroutine.

S

S [[!]*pattern*]

Lists subroutine names matching (or, if ! is specified, not matching) *pattern*. If *pattern* is omitted, lists all subroutines.

s

s [*expr*]

Single steps. Executes until it reaches the beginning of another statement, descending into subroutine calls. If an expression is supplied that includes a function call, the function is also single-stepped.

T

T

Produces a stack backtrace. For example:

```
DB<2> T
$ = main::infested called from file 'Ambulation.pm' line
10
@ = Ambulation::legs(1, 2, 3, 4) called from file
'camel_flea' line 7
$ = main::pests('bactrian', 4) called from file
'camel_flea' line 4
```

The lefthand character ($ or @) tells whether the function was called in a scalar or list context. The example shows three lines because it was three functions deep when the stack backtrace ran.

t

t

Toggles trace mode.

t

t *expr*

Traces through execution of *expr*.

v

v

Shows versions of loaded modules.

V

V [*pkg* [*vars*]]

Displays all (or some) variables in package *pkg* using a data pretty-printer (which displays keys and their values for hashes, makes control characters printable, prints nested data structures in a legible fashion, and so on). *pkg* defaults to the main package. Make sure you enter the identifiers without a type specifier such as $ or @, like this:

    V DB filename line

In place of a variable name, you can use ~*pattern* or !*pattern* to print existing variables with names that either match or don't match the specified regular expression.

w

w [*line*]

Lists a window of a few lines around the given *line*, or lists the current line if *line* is omitted.

X

X [*vars*]

Same as V *currentpackage* [*vars*].

x

x *expr*

evals the expression in a list context and dumps out the result in a pretty-printed fashion. Unlike the print command above, prints nested data structures recursively.

Using the Debugger

If you have any compile time executable statements (code within a BEGIN block or a use statement), they are not stopped by the debugger, although requires are.

The debugger prompt is something like this:

    DB<8>

or even this:

    DB<<17>>

The number in angle brackets is the command number. A *csh*-like history mechanism lets you access previous commands by number. For example, !17 repeats command number 17. The number of angle brackets indicates the depth of the debugger. You get more than one set of brackets, for example, if you're already at a breakpoint and print out the result of a function call that itself also has a breakpoint.

If you want to enter a multiline command, such as a subroutine definition with several statements, you can use a backslash to escape the newline that would normally end the debugger command:

```
DB<1> sub foo { \
cont:   print "fooline\n"; \
cont: }
DB<2> foo
fooline
```

You can maintain limited control over the Perl debugger from within your Perl script. You might do this, for example, to set an automatic breakpoint at a certain subroutine whenever a particular program is run under the debugger. Setting $DB::single to 1 causes execution to stop at the next statement, as though you'd used the debugger's s command. Setting $DB::single to 2 is equivalent to typing the n command, and the $DB::trace variable can be set to 1 to simulate the t command.

Once you are in the debugger, you can terminate the session by entering q or Ctrl-D at the prompt. You can also restart the debugger with R.

Customizing the Debugger

You can do some customizing by setting up a *.perldb* file with initialization code. When it starts up, the debugger reads and processes this file. For instance, you can set up aliases such as these:

```
$DB::alias{'len'}  = 's/^len(.*)/p length($1)/';
$DB::alias{'stop'} = 's/^stop (at|in)/b/';
$DB::alias{'ps'}   = 's/^ps\b/p scalar /';
$DB::alias{'quit'} = 's/^quit\b.*/exit/';
```

You can also use this file to set options and define a subroutine, &afterinit, to be executed after the debugger is initialized.

After the configuration file has been processed, the debugger consults the environment variable PERLDB_OPTS and parses its contents as arguments to the O opt=val debugger command.

While any options can be set in PERLDB_OPTS, the following options can *only* be specified at startup. If you want to set them in your configuration file, call &parse_options("opt=val").

TTY
> The TTY to use for debugging I/O.

noTTY
> If set, goes in NonStop mode. On an interrupt, if TTY is not set, it uses the value of noTTY or */tmp/perldbtty$$* to find the TTY using Term::Rendezvous. The current variant is to have the name of the TTY in this file.

ReadLine

> If false, a dummy ReadLine is used so you can debug ReadLine applications.

NonStop

> If true, no interaction is performed until an interrupt.

LineInfo

> File or pipe to print line number information to. If it's a pipe, then a short,
> *emacs*-like message is used.

For example, if you create the following *.perldb* file:

```
&parse_options("NonStop=1 LineInfo=db.out");
sub afterinit { $trace = 1; }
```

your script will run without human intervention, putting trace information into
the file *db.out*.

The Perl Profiler

You can supply an alternative debugger for Perl to run by invoking your script
with the *–d:module* switch. One of the most popular alternative debuggers for Perl
is DProf, the Perl profiler. As of this writing, DProf is not included with the standard Perl distribution, but it is expected to be included soon.

Meanwhile, you can fetch the Devel::DProf module from CPAN. Once it has been
properly installed on your system, you can use it to profile the Perl program in
testpgm by typing:

```
perl -d:DProf testpgm
```

As your script runs, DProf gathers profile information. When the script terminates, the profiler dumps the gathered information to a file called *tmon.out*. A tool
such as *dprofpp*, which is supplied with the Devel::DProf package, can be run to
interpret the profile. If you run *dprofpp* against the *tmon.out* file created by DProf
in the example above, you'll see something like the following:

```
% dprofpp tmon.out
Total Elapsed Time =    0.15 Seconds
   User+System Time =    0.1 Seconds
Exclusive Times
%Time Seconds      # Calls sec/call Name
 30.0  0.030          1   0.0300 Text::Wrap::CODE(0x175f08)
 20.0  0.020          1   0.0200 main::CODE(0xc7880)
 20.0  0.020          1   0.0200 main::CODE(0xfe480)
 10.0  0.010          1   0.0100 Text::Wrap::CODE(0x17151c)
 10.0  0.010         10   0.0010 Text::Tabs::expand
 0.00  0.000          1   0.0000 lib::CODE(0xfe5b8)
 0.00  0.000          3   0.0000 Exporter::export
 0.00  0.000          1   0.0000 Config::FETCH
 0.00  0.000          1   0.0000 lib::import
 0.00  0.000          1   0.0000 Text::Wrap::CODE(0x171438)
 0.00  0.000          3   0.0000 vars::import
 0.00  0.000          3   0.0000 Exporter::import
 0.00  0.000          2   0.0000 strict::import
```

```
0.00    0.000       1    0.0000 Text::Wrap::CODE(0x171684)
0.00    0.000       1    0.0000 lib::CODE(0xfe4d4)
```

The output shows the 15 subroutines that use the most time; you can then focus your efforts on those subroutines where tuning the code will have the greatest effect. This output is an example of running the *dprofpp* command with the default option set. The following are the options that are available:

–a

Sorts output alphabetically by subroutine name.

–E

Default. Displays all subroutine times exclusive of child subroutine times.

–F

Forces generation of fake exit timestamps if *dprofpp* reports that the profile is garbled. Useful only if *dprofpp* determines that the profile is garbled due to missing exit timestamps.

–I

Displays all subroutine times inclusive of child subroutine times.

–l

Sorts by number of calls to the subroutines.

–O cnt

Shows only *cnt* subroutines. The default is 15.

–p script

Profiles the given script and interprets its profile data, combining the usual two steps into one.

–Q

Used with *–p*, profiles the script and quits without interpreting the data.

–q

Does not display column headers.

–r

Displays elapsed real times.

–s

Displays system times only.

–T

Displays subroutine calls, but not subroutine statistics.

–t

Displays subroutine call tree, but not subroutine statistics. A subroutine called multiple times is shown only once, with a repeat count.

–U

Displays unsorted output.

–u

Displays user times only.

–V

Prints the *dprofpp* version number.

−*v*

> Sorts by average time spent in subroutines during each call.

−*z*

> Default. Sorts by amount of user and system time used, so that the first few lines should show which subroutines are using the most time.

The perlbug Program

As you develop and debug your own code, it's possible that you'll run into a bug in Perl itself. If you do, the best way to report it is with the *perlbug* program. *perlbug* is a Perl program designed to automate the process of reporting bugs in the Perl standard distribution and the standard modules. It works interactively, prompting you for the information needed and generating an email message addressed to *perlbug@perl.com*. (If the bug you found is in one of the nonstandard Perl ports, see the documentation for that port to find out how to report bugs.) When you run *perlbug*, it prompts you to include all relevant information, making it easier for the Perl developers to reproduce and track down the bug. If you come up with a patch to resolve the problem, include that too.

Don't use *perlbug* to get help debugging your code (for that, see the list of news-groups and other resources in Chapter 1). But if you believe you've found a bug in Perl itself, *perlbug* is the way to report it.

To run *perlbug*, simply enter the command with any options you want to include. For example:

```
% perlbug -t
```

The possible options are:

−*a address*
> Email address to send report to. Default is *perlbug@perl.com*.

−*b body*
> Body of report. If not included on the command line or in a file, you are given a chance to edit it.

−*C*
> Don't send a copy to your Perl administrator.

−*c address*
> Email address where copy should be sent. Default is your Perl administrator.

−*d*
> Data mode. (The default if you redirect or pipe input.) Prints your configuration data, without mailing anything. Use with −*v* to get more complete data.

−*e editor*
> Editor to use. Defaults to your default editor or to *vi*.

−*f file*
> File containing prepared body of report.

−*h*
> Prints help message.

–ok

> Reports successful build on this system to Perl porters. Forces *–S* and *–C*; forces and supplies values for *–s* and *–b*. Use with *–v* to get more complete data. Only reports if this system is less than 60 days old.

–okay

> Like *–ok* but will report on systems older than 60 days.

–r address

> Return address. If not specified on the command line, *perlbug* prompts for it.

–S

> Send without asking for confirmation.

–s subject

> Subject to include. If not specified on command line, *perlbug* prompts for it.

–t

> Test mode. Target address defaults to *perlbug-test@perl.com*.

–v

> Verbose. Includes verbose configuration data in report.

Modules

7

Packages, Modules, and Objects

Over the years, Perl has evolved from a utilitarian scripting tool into a sophisticated object-oriented programming language. Many people continue to use Perl just for simple scripts, and Perl will continue to make simple tasks easy. However, Perl can also make difficult tasks possible by writing reusable code and using object-oriented programming techniques.

This chapter explains what Perl modules are and how to use them in your programs. Modules are written to accomplish tasks that either aren't implemented by Perl's built-in functions, or that could be done better. We say modules are "reusable" because anyone who needs to accomplish the same task can use that module instead of writing the code from scratch. As you write more and more Perl code, you'll undoubtedly find yourself using many of the modules other Perl programmers have provided. You may also find yourself writing modules and making them available for others to use.

The remainder of this book describes a significant portion of the functionality that's present in publicly available Perl modules. You'll find that a number of *standard* or *core* modules are distributed with Perl; many of these modules are discussed in Chapter 8. Scores of other modules are available on CPAN, and virtually any task you'd like to accomplish in Perl is implemented in a module found there. For unbundled modules, you'll need to install the module on your system and integrate it into your program with the use function.

The use function is often the key to working with modules. For example, to bring the functionality of the popular CGI module into your program, you need to install the *CGI.pm* module (the *.pm* stands for Perl module) and put this line near the top of your program:

```
use CGI;
```

Now your program can use the many functions and variables made available by the CGI module.

Packages (from which modules are built) are also a mechanism by which Perl's object-oriented features are implemented. But object-oriented programming isn't for everyone, and there's nothing in packages that forces the programmer to work with the object-oriented paradigm.

Namespaces and Packages

A namespace does what it says: it stores names (or identifiers), including names of variables, subroutines, filehandles, and formats. Each namespace has its own *symbol table*, which is basically a hash with a key for each identifier.

The default namespace for programs is main, but you can define other namespaces and variables and use them in your program. Variables in different namespaces can even have the same name, but they are completely distinct from one another.

In Perl, a namespace is held in a *package*. By convention, package names start with a capital letter, and you should follow that convention when you create your own packages.

Each package starts with a package declaration. The package call takes one argument: the name of the package. Within the scope of a package declaration, all regular identifiers are created within that package (except for my variables).

From inside one package, you can refer to variables from another package by "qualifying" them with the package name. To do this, place the name of the package followed by two colons (::) before the identifier's name, e.g., $Package::varname.

If the package name is null, the main package is assumed. For example, $var and $::var are the same as $main::var.

Packages may be nested inside other packages. However, the package name must still be fully qualified. For example, if the package Province is declared inside the package Nation, a variable in the Province package is called as $Nation::Province::var. You cannot use a "relative" package name such as $Province::var within the Nation package for the same thing.

The default main namespace contains all other packages within it.

Modules

A *module* is a package defined in a file with a name that is the same as the package's. Perl locates modules by searching the @INC array, which contains a list of library directories. Perl's use of @INC is roughly comparable to the Unix shell's use of the PATH environment variable to locate executable programs. @INC is defined when Perl is built and can be supplemented with the *–I* command-line option to Perl or with use lib within a program.

When you refer to ModuleName in your program, Perl searches in the directories listed in @INC for the module file *ModuleName.pm* and uses the first one it finds. When you refer to a module embedded in another package, such as ParentPackage::ModuleName,

Perl looks for a *ParentPackage/* subdirectory in the @INC path, and for a *Module-Name.pm* file in that subdirectory.

Every Perl installation includes a central *lib* directory. The actual pathname of this directory varies from system to system, but it's commonly */usr/lib/perl* or */usr/local/lib/perl*. Looking at the central *lib* directory for your Perl distribution, you'll see something like this:

```
% ls -aF /usr/local/lib/perl
./                 I18N/           bigfloat.pl      less.pm
../                IO/             bigint.pl        lib.pm
AnyDBM_File.pm     IPC/            bigrat.pl        locale.pm
AutoLoader.pm      Math/           blib.pm          look.pl
AutoSplit.pm       Net/            cacheout.pl      man/
Benchmark.pm       Pod/            chat2.pl         newgetopt.pl
Bundle/            Search/         complete.pl      open2.pl
CGI/               SelectSaver.pm  constant.pm      open3.pl
CGI.pm             SelfLoader.pm   ctime.pl         perl5db.pl
CPAN/              Shell.pm        diagnostics.pm   pod/
CPAN.pm            Symbol.pm       dotsh.pl         pwd.pl
Carp.pm            Sys/            dumpvar.pl       shellwords.pl
      ...
```

When you request the AnyDBM_File module, it uses *AnyDBM_File.pm*. When you request the Math::Complex module, it looks for *Math/Complex.pm*.

A module can be included in your program with use or require. Both use and require read in a module file for use with your program.

```
require Module;
```

or:

```
use Module;
```

use can also take a list of strings naming entities that you want to import from the module. The list only has to include entities that are not automatically exported by the module. You don't have to provide this list if the module automatically exports all the entities you need.

```
use Module qw(const1 const2 func1 func2 func3);
```

The difference between use and require is that use pulls in the module at compile time. This means that functions such as *func1* or *func2* can be used as predeclared list operators throughout the file. The require call does not necessarily load the module during compilation, so you must explicitly qualify its routines with the package name.

Object-Oriented Perl

In Perl circles, modules and object-oriented programming are often spoken of in the same breath, but the connection is misleading. The implementation of modules in Perl is object-oriented, but that doesn't mean that the actual modules are objectified. Perl modules don't necessarily involve objects just because the Perl programmer has encapsulated their code in a module.

Generally, an object is an instance of a class. So in Perl terms, the object is created by calling a constructor, and will be used to create a new object and a reference to it. (Often, the constructor is named new, but Create is also used in Win32 classes.) This reference is a regular scalar variable, except that it refers to an underlying object that knows which class it belongs to. In your programs, you will use the reference to manipulate the object.

Methods are subroutines that expect an object reference as a first argument, such as:

```
sub in_class {
    my $class = shift; # object reference
    my ($this, $that) = @_; # params
}
```

Methods may be invoked like this:

```
PackageName->constructor(args)->method_name(args);
```

or:

```
$object = PackageName->constructor(args);
$object->method_name(args);
```

Objects have a specific set of available methods within their class, but they also inherit methods from their parent class, if they have one.

Objects are destroyed when the last reference to them goes away. You can control this capture before the object is destroyed with the DESTROY method. The DESTROY method should be defined somewhere in the class. You do not call DESTROY explicitly; it will be called at an appropriate time. Object references contained in the current object will be freed when the current object is freed. Most of the time, you won't need to explicitly destroy an object, but there are occasions when you should, such as when you are done with a socket object.

Object Syntax

Perl uses two forms of syntax for invoking methods on objects. For both types of syntax, the object reference or class name is given as the first argument. A method that takes a class name is called a *class method*, and one that takes an object reference is called an *instance method*.

Class methods provide functionality for the entire class, not just for a single object that belongs to the class. Class methods expect a class name as their first argument. Following this explanation, a constructor is an example of a class method:

```
sub new {
    my $self = {};
    bless $self;
    return $self;
}
```

On the other hand, an instance method expects an object reference as its first argument. An instance method will shift the first argument and use this argument as a reference:

```
sub instance_method {
    my $self = shift;
    my($one, $two, $three) = @_;
    # do stuff
}
```

Here is an example of a constructor creating a new object and returning a reference:

```
$tri = Triangle::Right->new(side1 => 3, side2 => 4);
```

This example creates a new right-triangle object and references it with $tri. The parameters are given as a hash-style list. This is common for constructors, since they set initial parameters for an object that is probably just a hash. Now that we have an object, we can invoke a method on it. Suppose Triangle::Right defines a method, hypot, that returns the length of the hypotenuse for a given right-triangle object. It would be used like this:

```
$h = $tri->hypot;
print "The hypotenuse is: $h.\n";
```

In this particular example, there happens to be no additional arguments to the hypot method, but there could have been.

With the arrow (->) notation, the left side of the arrow must be an object reference or a class name, while the right side of the arrow must be a method defined for that object. Any arguments must follow the method inside of parentheses. For example:

```
$obj->method(args)
CLASS->method(args)
```

You have to use parentheses because this form can't be used as a list operator, although the first type of method syntax can.

The examples given above would look like this using the arrow syntax:

```
$tri = Triangle::Right->new(side1 => 3, side2 => 4);
$h = $tri->hypot();
print "The hypotenuse is: $h.\n";
```

The arrow syntax provides a helpful visual relationship between the object and its method, but both forms of syntax do the same thing. Precedence for the arrow syntax is left-to-right, exactly the same as for the dereferencing operator. This allows you to chain together objects and methods if you want to simplify things. You just have to make sure you have an object to the left of the arrow and a method to the right:

```
%sides = (side1 => 3, side2 => 4);
$h = Triangle::Right->new(%sides)->hypot();
print "The hypotenuse is: $h.\n";
```

In this example, you never assign a variable name to the right-triangle object; the reference is passed directly to the hypot method.

8

Standard Modules

We've talked about the extent to which Perl benefits from user contributions. In fact, many contributed modules are so generally useful that they are now distributed with Perl itself. This chapter describes these "standard modules"; if you are running Perl 5.005, all these modules are already available to you. If you are running an earlier version of Perl, and you find that a module you want isn't on your system, or if you simply don't find what you need among the modules in this chapter, check CPAN for one that does what you want.

While this chapter primarily covers standard Perl modules called at execution time from your program, it also covers the "pragmatic" modules that affect the compilation phase. (A pragma is a compiler directive that provides hints to the compiler.) By convention, the names of the pragmatic modules are all lowercase, while the names of other modules begin with an uppercase letter and are of mixed case.

The Win32-specific modules are not included in this chapter, but are described in Chapter 19.

The following table provides a quick look at the standard modules and what they do:

Module	Function
AnyDBM_File	Provides framework for multiple DBMs
Attribute::Handlers	Simpler definition of attribute handlers (new in 5.8)
attributes	Sets or gets attributes of a subroutine
attrs	Sets or gets attributes of a subroutine (deprecated)
AutoLoader	Loads functions only on demand
AutoSplit	Splits a module for autoloading
autouse	Postpones loading modules until a function is used
B	Perl compiler and tools
base	Establishes IS-A relationship with base class at compile time

Module	Function
Benchmark	Checks and compares running times of code
bigint	Transparent big integer support for Perl (new in 5.8)
bignum	Transparent BigNumber support for Perl (new in 5.8)
bigrat	Transparent BigNumber/BigRational support for Perl (new in 5.8)
blib	Uses MakeMaker's uninstalled version of a package
bytes	Perl pragma to force byte semantics rather than character semantics
ByteLoader	Loads byte-compiled Perl code
Carp	Generates error messages
CGI	Simple Common Gateway Interface class
CGI::Apache	Sets up environment to use CGI with Perl-Apache API
CGI::Carp	CGI routines for writing to HTTPD (or other) error log
CGI::Cookie	CGI interface to Netscape (HTTP/1.1) cookies
CGI::Fast	CGI interface for FastCGI
CGI::Pretty	Module to produce nicely formatted HTML code
CGI::Push	Interface for server push operations
CGI::Switch	Tries multiple constructors and returns the first available CGI object
charnames	Defines character names for \N{named} string literal escape
Class::ISA	Reports the search path for a class's ISA tree (new in 5.8)
Class::Struct	Declares struct-like datatypes as Perl classes
Config	Accesses Perl configuration information
constant	Perl pragma to declare constants
CPAN	Queries, downloads, and builds Perl modules from CPAN sites
CPAN::FirstTime	Utility for CPAN::Config file initialization
CPAN::Nox	Wrapper around CPAN.pm without using any XS module
Cwd	Gets pathname of current working directory
Data::Dumper	Returns Perl data structures as strings
DB	Programmatic interface to the Perl debugging API
DB_File	Accesses Berkeley DB
Devel::DProf	Perl Code Profiler
Devel::PPPort	Module that assists with module porting between Perl versions
Devel::SelfStubber	Generates stubs for a self-loading module
diagnostics	Forces verbose warning diagnostics
Digest	Modules that calculate message digests (new in 5.8)
Digest::MD5	Perl interface to the MD5 Algorithm (new in 5.8)
DirHandle	Supplies object methods for directory handles
Dumpvalue	Provides a screen dump of Perl data
DynaLoader	Automatic dynamic loading of Perl modules
encoding	Allows you to write your script in nonasii or nonutf8 (new in 5.8)
English	Uses English or *awk* names for punctuation variables
Env	Imports environment variables
Errno	System errno constants from *errno.h* include file
Exporter	Default import method for modules

Module	Function
ExtUtils::Command	Utilities to replace common Unix commands
ExtUtils::Command::MM	Commands that the MM's can use in Makefiles (new in 5.8)
ExtUtils::Constant	Generates XS code to import C header constants (new in 5.8)
ExtUtils::Embed	Utilities for embedding Perl in C/C++ applications
ExtUtils::Install	Installs files from here to there
ExtUtils::Installed	Inventory management of installed modules
ExtUtils::Liblist	Determines libraries to use and how to use them
ExtUtils::MakeMaker	Creates a Makefile for a Perl extension
ExtUtils::Manifest	Utilities to write and check a MANIFEST file
ExtUtils::Miniperl	Writes the C code for *perlmain.c*
ExtUtils::Mkbootstrap	Makes a bootstrap file for use by DynaLoader
ExtUtils::Mksymlists	Writes linker option files for dynamic extension
ExtUtils::MM	Operating system–adjusted ExtUtils::MakeMaker subclass (new in 5.8)
ExtUtils::MM_Any	Platform-agnostic MM methods (new in 5.8)
ExtUtils::MM_BeOS	Methods that override UN*X behavior in ExtUtils::MakeMaker (new in 5.8)
ExtUtils::MM_DOS	DOS-specific subclass of ExtUtils::MM_Unix (new in 5.8)
ExtUtils::MM_NW5	Methods that override UN*X behavior in ExtUtils::MakeMaker (new in 5.8)
ExtUtils::MM_OS2	Methods to override Unix behavior in ExtUtils::MakeMaker
ExtUtils::MM_Unix	Methods used by ExtUtils::MakeMaker
ExtUtils::MM_UWIN	U/WIN-specific subclass of ExtUtils::MM_Unix (new in 5.8)
ExtUtils::MM_VMS	Methods to override Unix behavior in ExtUtils::MakeMaker
ExtUtils::MM_Win32	Methods to override Unix behavior in ExtUtils::MakeMaker
ExtUtils::MY	ExtUtils::MakeMaker subclass for customization (new in 5.8)
ExtUtils::Packlist	Manages *.packlist* files
ExtUtils::testlib	Adds *blib/** directories to @INC
Fatal	Replaces functions with equivalents that succeed or die
Fcntl	Loads the C *fcntl.h* defines
fields	Perl pragma to provide compile time–verified class fields
File::Basename	Parses file specifications
File::CheckTree	Runs many tests on a collection of files
File::Compare	Compares files or filehandles
File::Copy	Copies files or filehandles
File::DosGlob	DOS-like globbing with enhancements
File::Find	Traverses a file tree
File::Path	Creates or removes a series of directories
File::Spec	Portably performs operations on filenames
File::Spec::Cygwin	Methods for Cygwin file specs (new in 5.8)
File::stat	By-name interface to Perl's built-in stat functions
File::Temp	Returns the name and handle of a temporary file safely
FileCache	Keeps more files open than the system permits
FileHandle	Supplies object methods for filehandles
Filter::Simple	Simplified source filtering (new in 5.8)

Module	Function
Filter::Util::Call	Perl Source Filter Utility Module (new in 5.8)
FindBin	Locates directory of original Perl script
GDBM_File	Tied access to GDBM library
Getopt::Long	Extended processing of command-line options
Getopt::Std	Processes single-character options with option clustering
Hash::Util	A selection of general utility hash subroutines (new in 5.8)
I18N::Collate	Compares 8-bit scalar data according to the current locale
I18N::Langinfo	Queries locale information (new in 5.8)
I18N::LangTags	Functions for dealing with RFC3066-style language tags (new in 5.8)
I18N::LangTags::List	Tags and names for human languages (new in 5.8)
if	Uses a Perl module if a condition holds (new in 5.8)
integer	Does arithmetic in integer instead of double
IO	Loads various I/O modules
IO::File	Supplies object methods for filehandles
IO::Handle	Supplies object methods for I/O handles
IO::Pipe	Supplies object methods for pipes
IO::Seekable	Supplies seek-based methods for I/O objects
IO::Select	Object-oriented interface to the select system call
IO::Socket	Object interface to socket communications
IPC::Msg	System V Msg IPC object class
IPC::Open2	Opens a process for both reading and writing
IPC::Open3	Opens a process for reading, writing, and error handling
IPC::Semaphore	System V Semaphore IPC object class
IPC::SysV	System V IPC constants
less	Perl pragma to request less of something from the compiler
lib	Manipulates @INC at compile time
List::Util	A selection of general utility list subroutines (new in 5.8)
locale	Perl pragma to use and avoid POSIX locales for built-in operations
Math::BigFloat	Arbitrary-length floating-point math package
Math::BigInt	Arbitrary-length integer math package
Math::BigInt::Calc	Pure Perl module to support Math::BigInt (new in 5.8)
Math::BigRat	Arbitrarily big rationals (new in 5.8)
Math::Complex	Complex numbers package
Math::Trig	Trigonometric functions
MIME::Base64	Encoding and decoding of base64 strings (new in 5.8)
MIME::QuotedPrint	Encoding and decoding of quoted, printable strings (new in 5.8)
NDBM_File	Tied access to NDBM files
Net::Cmd	Network Command class (new in 5.8)
Net::Config	Local configuration data for libnet (new in 5.8)
Net::Domain	Attempts to evaluate the current host's Internet name and domain (new in 5.8)
Net::FTP	FTP Client class (new in 5.8)
Net::hostent	By-name interface to Perl's built-in gethost* functions

Module	Function
Net::netent	By-name interface to Perl's built-in getnet* functions
Net::Netrc	OO interface to user's netrc file (new in 5.8)
Net::NNTP	NNTP Client class (new in 5.8)
Net::Ping	Checks whether a host is online
Net::POP3	Post Office Protocol 3 Client class (new in 5.8)
Net::protoent	By-name interface to Perl's built-in getproto* functions
Net::servent	By-name interface to Perl's built-in getserv* functions
Net::SMTP	Simple Mail Transfer Protocol Client class (new in 5.8)
Net::Time	Time and daytime network client interface (new in 5.8)
ODBM_File	Tied access to ODBM files
Opcode	Disables named opcodes when compiling Perl code
ops	Restricts unsafe operations when compiling
overload	Overloads Perl's mathematical operations
PerlIO	On-demand loader for PerlIO layers and root of PerlIO::* namespace (added in 5.8)
PerlIO::Scalar	Support module for in-memory I/O (new in 5.8)
PerlIO::Via	Helper class for PerlIO layers implemented in Perl (new in 5.8)
Pod::Functions	Used in converting from pod to HTML
Pod::Html	Module to convert pod files to HTML
Pod::ParseLink	Parses link-formatting code in POD documents (new in 5.8)
Pod::Text	Converts pod data to formatted ASCII text
POSIX	Perl interface to IEEE Std 1003.1
re	Perl pragma to alter regular expression behavior
Safe	Creates safe namespaces for evaluating Perl code
Scalar::Util	A selection of general-utility scalar subroutines (new in 5.8)
SDBM_File	Tied access to SDBM files
Search::Dict	Searches for key in dictionary file
SelectSaver	Saves and restores selected filehandle
SelfLoader	Loads functions only on demand
Shell	Runs shell commands transparently within Perl
sigtrap	Enables stack backtrace on unexpected signals
Socket	Loads the C *socket.h* defines and structure manipulators
sort	Perl pragma that controls sort behavior (new in 5.8)
Storable	Persistence for Perl data structures (new in 5.8)
strict	Restricts unsafe constructs
subs	Predeclares subroutine names
Switch	A switch statement for Perl (new in 5.8)
Symbol	Generates anonymous globs; qualifies variable names
Sys::Hostname	Tries every conceivable way to get hostname
Sys::Syslog	Perl interface to Unix syslog(3) calls
Term::Cap	Terminal capabilities interface
Term::Complete	Word completion module
Term::ReadLine	Interface to various ReadLine packages

Module	Function
Test	Framework for writing test scripts
Test::Builder	Backend for building text libraries (new in 5.8)
Test::Harness	Runs Perl standard test scripts with statistics
Test::More	Yet another framework for writing test scripts (new in 5.8)
Test::Simple	Basic utilities for writing tests (new in 5.8)
Text::Abbrev	Creates an abbreviation table from a list
Text::Balanced	Extracts delimited text sequences from strings (new in 5.8)
Text::ParseWords	Parses text into a list of tokens
Text::Soundex	The soundex algorithm described by Knuth
Text::Tabs	Expands and unexpands tabs
Text::Wrap	Wraps text into a paragraph
Thread	Multithreading support
Thread::Queue	Thread-safe queues
Thread::Semaphore	Thread-safe semaphores
Thread::Signal	Starts a thread that runs signal handlers reliably
Thread::Specific	Thread-specific keys
Tie::Array	Base class definitions for tied arrays
Tie::File	Accesses the lines of a disk file via a Perl array (new in 5.8)
Tie::Handle	Base class definitions for tied handles
Tie::Hash	Base class definitions for tied hashes
Tie::Memorize	Adds data to a hash when needed (new in 5.8)
Tie::RefHash	Uses references as hash keys
Tie::Scalar	Base class definitions for tied scalars
Tie::SubstrHash	Fixed table size, fixed key length hashing
Time::gmtime	By-name interface to Perl's built-in `gmtime` function
Time::HiRes	High-resolution alarm, sleep, gettimeofday, interval timers (new in 5.8)
Time::Local	Computes time from local and GMT time
Time::localtime	By-name interface to Perl's built-in `localtime` function
Time::tm	Internal object used by Time::gmtime and Time::localtime
UNIVERSAL	Base class for all classes (blessed references)
User::grent	By-name interface to Perl's built-in `getgr*` functions
User::pwent	By-name interface to Perl's built-in `getpw*` functions
utf8	Perl pragma to enable/disable UTF-8 in source code
vars	Predeclares global variable names
vmsish	Perl pragma that controls VMS-specific language features (new in 5.8)
XS::Typemap	Module that tests the XS typemaps distributed with Perl (new in 5.8)

In the remainder of this chapter, the modules are arranged in alphabetical order for easy reference. For more detail about a module, use the *perldoc* command to read the manpage for that module (see Chapter 4, for information on *perldoc*).

AnyDBM_File

Provides a single Database Manager (DBM) interface regardless of the DBM implementation you use. The module inherits from the various DBM packages; by default, it inherits from NDBM_File. If it doesn't find NDBM_File, the default search order is: DB_File, GDBM_File, SDBM_File (which comes with Perl), and finally, ODBM_File. You can override this default order by redefining @ISA:

```
@AnyDBM_File::ISA = qw(DB_File GDBM_File NDBM_File);
```

However, an explicit use takes priority over the @ISA ordering.

Perl's dbmopen function simply calls tie to bind a hash to AnyDBM_File. The effect is to bind the hash to one of the specific DBM classes that AnyDBM_File inherits from.

Attribute::Handlers

Implements a simpler definition of attribute handlers. When inherited by a package, Attribute::Handlers allows that package's class to define handler subroutines for specific attributes. When inherited by a package, these handlers will be called by the same names as the original attribute-handling subroutines. Attribute handlers will be called at one of the following compilation phases: BEGIN, CHECK, INIT, or END blocks. Note that Attribute::Handlers is shipped with the Perl source kit as of Version 5.8.

Handlers are defined as subroutines and named as the desired attribute. In the following example, the attribute is :ATTR, which lives in a subroutine that's called Nate1() in the HandlerBing class:

```
package HandlerBing;
use Attribute::Handlers;
sub Nate1 :ATTR {
    my(@attrs) = @_; # We simply want to test by dumping the attributes
    print "attributes: \n",
        join("\n", @attrs), "\n";
}
 # true.
1;
```

This stub for the HandlerBing class creates a handler for the attribute :Nate1. When you want to use this handler while within HandlerBing, you can do the following:

```
sub Nate2 :Nate1 {
    my (@stuff) = @_;
        print STDERR "in Nate2 ", join("\n", @stuff), "\n";
}
```

When you call Nate2, it invokes the Nate1 handler and passes the following elements into the @_ array:

0   The name of the package in which the handler was declared

1   A reference to the symbol table entry (a typeglob) that contains the subroutine

2   A reference to the subroutine

3   The name of the attribute itself

4   Any data associated with that attribute

5   The name of the compilation phase in which the handler was invoked

The same holds true for declaring any variables with the :Nate1 attribute within HandlerBing:

```
my $monica :Nate1;
my $phoebe :Nate1;
```

Attribute::Handlers also supports typed lexicals. This is a nice feature, since you can invoke a handler from a package that defines another one from whatever package you're in (or writing!). For example:

```
package MustNotSeeTV;
my HandlerBring $whatever : Nate1;
# true
1;
```

You can apply handlers only by type, if you wish. You can do this by passing a built-in type to :ATTR:

```
package ReRun;
sub Tiresome :ATTR(HASH) { print "your reruns have become tiresome\n"; }
# true
1;
```

In the above code, Tiresome is an attribute handler that applies only to HASHes. And certainly, you can declare separate handlers (of the same names) for the other types.

If you have problems passing certain data to a handler, such as now..later or laugh@you, you can use the RAWDATA type to pass this data cleanly:

```
sub RawLikeSushi : ATTR(RAWDATA) { ... do something ... }
```

Attribute::Handlers implements the following diagnostics (from the Attribute::Handlers manpage):

Bad attribute type: ATTR(%s)
> An attribute handler was specified with an :ATTR(*ref_type*), but the type of referent it was defined to handle wasn't one of the five permitted: SCALAR, ARRAY, HASH, CODE, or ANY.

Attribute handler %s *doesn't handle* %s *attributes*
> A handler for attributes of the specified name was defined, but not for the specified type of declaration. Typically encountered when trying to apply a VAR attribute handler to a subroutine, or a SCALAR attribute handler to another type of variable.

Declaration of %s *attribute in* %s *package may clash with future reserved word*
> A handler for an attribute with an all-lowercase name was declared. An attribute with an all-lowercase name might mean something to Perl itself someday, even though most don't yet. Use a mixed-case attribute name instead.

Can't have two ATTR *specifiers on one subroutine*

You just can't, okay? Instead, put all the specifications together, separated by commas in a single ATTR(*specifications*).

Can't autotie a %s

You can declare autoties only for types SCALAR, ARRAY, and HASH. They're the only things (apart from typeglobs, which are not declarable) that Perl can tie.

Internal error: %s *symbol went missing*

Something is rotten in the state of the program. An attributed subroutine ceased to exist between the point where it was declared and the point where its attribute handler(s) would have been called.

Won't be able to apply an END *handler*

You tried to define an END handler for an attribute that is applied to a lexical variable. Since the variable may not be available during END, this will fail.

attributes

Replacement for *attrs.pm* that sets or gets the attributes of subroutines. Attributes are set at compile time. If an attribute is unrecognized, it will result in a fatal error. While the error is trappable, it will stop the compilation within an eval. You must be careful about naming your attributes; an attribute that's all lowercase and not a built-in attribute will result in a warning (unless you use warnings "reserved"). An example of *attributes* is:

```
sub foo : method ;
    use attributes ();   # Optional, to get subroutine declarations
    my @attrlist = attributes::get(\&foo);
```

The built-in attributes are:

locked

Setting this attribute is meaningful only when the subroutine or method will be called by multiple threads. When set on a method subroutine (i.e., one marked with the method attribute), Perl ensures that any invocation of it implicitly locks its first argument before execution. When set on a non-method subroutine, Perl ensures that a lock is taken on the subroutine itself before execution. The semantics of the lock are exactly those of one explicitly taken with the "lock" operator immediately after the subroutine is entered.

method

Indicates that the referenced subroutine is a method. This has a meaning when taken together with the locked attribute. It also means that a subroutine so marked will not trigger the "Ambiguous call resolved as CORE::%s" warning.

lvalue

Indicates that the referenced subroutine is a valid lvalue and can be assigned to. The subroutine must return a modifiable value such as a scalar variable, as described in the perlsub manpage.

There are no built-in attributes for anything other than subroutines.

attrs

Sets or gets the attributes of subroutines. Attributes are set for a subroutine at compile time; therefore, setting an invalid attribute results in a compile-time error. Note that *attrs* has been deprecated. You should use the *attributes* form instead. During execution, when you call `attrs::get` on a subroutine reference or name, it returns the list of attributes that are set. Note that `attrs::get` is not exported. The old usage of *attrs* is as follows:

```
sub test {
    use attrs qw(locked method);
    ...
}
@a = attrs::get(\test);
```

You should use a form like the following instead:

```
sub test : locked method { }
```

You can read more about *attributes* in the next section.

The valid attributes are:

locked
> Meaningful only when the subroutine or method will be called by multiple threads. When set on a subroutine that also has the method attribute set, invoking that subroutine implicitly locks its first argument before execution. On a non-method subroutine, a lock is taken on the subroutine itself before execution. The lock semantics are identical to one taken explicitly with the lock operator immediately after entering the subroutine.

method
> The invoking subroutine is a method.

AutoLoader

Delays the loading of functions until they are used. Each function is placed in a file that has the same name as the function, with an *.al* extension. The files are stored in a subdirectory of the *auto/* directory that is named after the package. For example, the function `GoodStuff::whatever` is loaded from the file *auto/GoodStuff/whatever.al*. Should always be used and not required.

A module using the AutoLoader has the special marker, `__END__` prior to the declarations for the subroutine to be autoloaded. Any code before this marker is loaded and compiled when the module is used, but at the marker, Perl stops parsing the file.

Later, during execution, when a subroutine that isn't yet in memory is called, the `AUTOLOAD` function attempts to find it in a directory relative to the location of the module file. For example, if *POSIX.pm* is in the directory */usr/local/lib/perl5*, then AutoLoader looks for POSIX subroutines in */usr/local/lib/perl5/auto/POSIX/*.al*.

AutoSplit

Splits a program or module into files that the AutoLoader can handle. It can be called from a program or from the command line:

```
# From a program
use AutoSplit;
autosplit_modules(@ARGV)

# From the command line
perl -MAutoSplit -e 'autosplit(FILE, DIR, KEEP, CHECK, MODTIME)' ...

# Another interface
perl -MAutoSplit -e 'autosplit_lib_modules(@ARGV)' ...
```

AutoSplit is used by MakeMaker as well as by the standard Perl libraries. It operates on a file, splitting off subroutines that come after the _ _END_ _ marker and storing them as described above for AutoLoader, creating any necessary directories along the way. AutoSplit has two functions.

autosplit

autosplit (*file, dir, keep, check, modtime*)

Splits the module into files. Each file is given the name of the subroutine it contains, with *.al* appended. autosplit also creates the file *autosplit.ix*, which serves as both a forward declaration of all package routines and as a timestamp showing when the hierarchy was last updated. Takes the following arguments:

file
  Filename of program or module to be split.

dir
  Name of directory hierarchy in which to store the split files.

keep
  If false, preexisting *.al* files in the *auto* directory that are no longer part of the module are deleted.

check
  If true, checks to be sure the module being split includes a use AutoLoader statement. If the statement is missing, autosplit doesn't process the module.

modtime
  If true, splits the module only if it is newer than *autosplit.ix*.

autosplit_lib_modules

autosplit_lib_modules (*@ARGV*)

Takes a list of modules that are assumed to be in a *lib* subdirectory of the current directory, processes them as described above for autosplit, and stores the resulting file in the directory *lib/auto*. Used in building Perl.

autouse

Pragma for postponing the loading of a module from compile time to execution time. The module isn't loaded until one of its subroutines is used; the subroutines all have to be exported by the module:

```
use autouse module => qw(sub1 [sub2 ...])
```

Use with care, since problems that might otherwise be found during compilation won't crop up until your program is already executing.

B

The Perl compiler. To use the compiler, you don't need to use this module. See the O module, which is the user frontend to the compiler; see also the compiler section of Chapter 3. The B module provides the classes for implementing backends for the compiler. If you plan to write a new backend, read the B manpage for the details of the module.

B::Asmdata

Contains autogenerated data about Perl ops; used to generate bytecode. Any changes made to this file will be lost.

B::Assembler

Assembles Perl bytecode.

B::Bblock

Walks the basic blocks of a program. Invoked as:

```
perl -MO=Bblock[,options] filename
```

B::Bytecode

The bytecode backend for the Perl compiler. Takes Perl source code and generates platform-independent bytecode that can be run with the *byteperl* executable or can be loaded via the byteload_fh function in the B module. Compiling with the bytecode backend won't speed up execution of your program, but it may improve start-up time. Invoke as:

```
perl -MO=Bytecode[,options] program
```

in which *program* is the name of the Perl script to compile. Any non-option arguments are treated as the names of objects to be saved; the main program is assumed if there are no extra arguments. Possible options are:

--

   Forces end of options.

−*Dopts*

   Debug options, which can be concatenated or specified separately. Possible options are:

   a   Tells the bytecode assembler to include assembler source in its output as bytecode comments

   b   Prints debugging information about bytecompiler progress

   C   Prints each CV from the final walk through the symbol tree

   o   Prints each OP as it's processed

−*fopt*

   Forces individual optimizations on or off. Preceding an optimization with no- turns that option off (e.g., no-compress-nullops). Possible values of *opt* are:

   bypass-nullops

      If op->op_next ever points to a NULLOP, replaces the op_next field with the first non-NULLOP in the path of execution.

   compress-nullops

      Fills in only the necessary fields of ops that have been optimized away by Perl's internal compiler.

   omit-sequence-numbers

      Leaves out the code to fill in the op_seq field for all ops that are used only by Perl's internal compiler.

   strip-syntax-tree

      Leaves out the code to fill in the internal syntax tree pointers. Use of this option breaks any goto *label* statements and prevents later recompiling or disassembling of the resulting program.

−*m*

   Compiles as a module rather than as a standalone program.

−*ofilename*

   Sends output to *filename* instead of STDOUT.

−*O[n]*

   Sets the optimization level to *n*, in in which *n* is an integer. *n* defaults to 1. -O1 sets -fcompress-nullops -fomit-sequence-numbers, and -O6 adds -fstrip-syntax-tree.

−*S*

   Outputs bytecode assembler source instead of assembling it into bytecode.

B::C

The C backend for the Perl compiler. Generates C source code from Perl source; the generated code corresponds to Perl's internal structures for running the program. Compiling with the C backend won't speed up execution of your program, but it may improve start-up time. Invoke as:

```
perl -MO=C[,options] program
```

in which *program* is the name of the Perl script to compile. Any non-option arguments are treated as the names of objects to be saved; the main program is assumed if there are no extra arguments. Possible options are:

--

> Forces end of options.

–*Dopts*
> Debug options, which can be concatenated or specified separately. Possible options are:
>
> A   Prints AV information on saving
>
> c   Prints COPs as they are processed, including file and line number
>
> C   Prints CV information on saving
>
> M   Prints MAGIC information on saving
>
> o   Prints each OP as it's processed

–*fopt*
> Forces individual optimizations on or off. Possible values of *opt* are:
>
> cog
> > Copy-on-grow. PVs are declared and initialized statically.
>
> no-cog
> > No copy-on-grow.

–*ofilename*
> Sends output to *filename* instead of to STDOUT.

–*O[n]*
> Sets optimization level, in which *n* is an integer. *n* defaults to 1. Currently, values of 1 and higher set cog.

–*uPackname*
> Forces apparently unused subroutines from package *Packname* to be compiled, letting programs use eval "foo( )" even if subroutine foo isn't seen to be used at compile time. You can specify multiple –*u* options.

–*v*
> Compiles verbosely.

B::CC

The CC backend for the Perl compiler. Generates optimized C source code that corresponds to your program's flow. The initial version included in Perl 5.005

actually includes few optimizations, but this will change. Programs compiled with this backend may start up and execute slightly faster. Invoke as:

```
perl -MO=C[,options] program
```

program is the name of the Perl script to compile. Any non-option arguments are treated as the names of objects to be saved; the main program is assumed if there are no extra arguments. Possible options are:

--

Forces end of options.

–Dopts

Debug options, which can be concatenated or specified separately. Possible options are:

l   Outputs the filename and line number of each original line of Perl code as it is processed

O   Outputs each OP as it is compiled

p   Outputs the contents of the shadow pad of lexicals as it is loaded for each sub or for the main program

q   Outputs the name of each fake PP function in the queue as it's about to be processed

r   Writes debugging output to STDERR instead of as comments in the C output

s   Outputs the contents of the shadow stack at each OP

t   Outputs timing information of the stages of compilation

–fopt

Forces individual optimizations on or off. Possible values of *opt* are:

freetmps-each-bblock
    Runs FREETMPS at the end of each basic block instead of at the end of each statement. freetmps-each-loop and freetmps-each-bblock are mutually exclusive.

freetmps-each-loop
    Runs FREETMPS at the end of each loop instead of at the end of each statement. freetmps-each-loop and freetmps-each-bblock are mutually exclusive.

omit-taint
    Doesn't generate code for handling Perl's tainting mechanism.

–mModulename

Generates source for an XSUB module instead of for an executable.

–ofilename

Sends output to *filename* instead of to STDOUT.

–O[n]

Sets optimization level, in which *n* is an integer. *n* defaults to 1. Currently, -O1 sets -ffreetmps-each-bblock, and -O2 sets -ffreetmps-each-loop.

−uPackname

> Forces apparently unused subroutines from package *Packname* to be compiled, permitting programs to use eval "foo( )" even if subroutine foo isn't seen to be used at compile time. You can specify multiple *−u* options.

−v

> Compiles verbosely.

B::Concise

A module that walks the Perl syntax tree, printing concise info about the internal OPs of a Perl program's syntax tree. The format of the information displayed is customizable. Its function is similar to that of Perl's *−Dx* debugging flag or the B::Terse module, but it is more sophisticated and flexible. Invoke as:

```
perl -MO=Concise[,options] program
```

program is the name of the Perl script to compile. Any non-option arguments are treated as the names of objects to be saved; the main program is assumed if there are no extra arguments. Possible options are:

−basic

> Prints OPs in the order they appear in the OP tree (a preorder traversal, starting at the root). Default.

−exec

> Prints OPs in the order they would normally execute. For the majority of constructs, this is a postorder traversal of the tree, ending at the root.

−tree

> Prints OPs in a text approximation of a tree, with the root of the tree at the left and "left-to-right" order of children transformed into "top-to-bottom". Unsuitable for large programs.

−compact

> Uses a tree format in which the minimum amount of space is used for the lines connecting nodes (one character in most cases).

−loose

> Uses a tree format that uses longer edges to separate OP nodes. Default.

−vt

> Uses tree-connecting characters drawn from the VT100 line-drawing set.

−ascii

> Draws the tree with standard ASCII characters such as + and |. Default.

−main

> Includes the main program in the output, even if subroutines were also specified.

−basen

> Prints OP sequence numbers in base n, with n <= 62. The default is 36.

−bigendian

> Prints sequence numbers with the most significant digit first. Default.

–littleendian
>   Prints sequence numbers with the least significant digit first.

–concise
>   Uses the author's favorite set of formatting conventions. Default.

–terse
>   Uses formatting conventions that emulate the output of B::Terse.

–linenoise
>   Uses formatting conventions in which the name of each OP, rather than written out in full, is represented by a one- or two-character abbreviation.

–debug
>   Uses formatting conventions reminiscient of B::Debug.

–env
>   Uses formatting conventions read from the environment variables B_ CONCISE_FORMAT, B_CONCISE_GOTO_FORMAT, and B_CONCISE_ TREE_FORMAT.

B::Debug

Walks the Perl syntax tree, printing debug information about ops. Invoke as:

```
perl -MO=Debug[,exec] filename
```

If exec is specified, walks in execution order rather than in syntax order.

B::Deparse

Perl compiler backend that generates Perl source code from the internal compiled structure of a program. The output won't be exactly the same as the original program, but it will be close. Invoke as:

```
perl -MO=Deparse[,options] program
```

program is the name of the program that will be deparsed. The options are comma-separated and follow normal backend option conventions. The possible options are:

–l
>   Adds #line declarations to the output based on line and file locations of the original code.

–p
>   Prints parentheses wherever they are legal, not just where they are required. Useful for seeing how Perl is parsing your expressions.

–sletters
>   Provides style options for the output. In this initial release, the only style option provided is C, which "cuddles" else, elsif, and continue blocks so that, for example, you would get:
>
>   ```
>   } else {
>   ```

instead of:

```
    }
      else {
```

The default is to not cuddle.

–uPackage

> Deparses subroutines in package *Package* as well as the main program, subroutines called by the main program, and subroutines in the main program. Multiple *–u* arguments can be given, separated by commas.

B::Disassembler

Disassembles Perl bytecode.

B::Lint

Provides program checking for Perl programs. Equivalent to running Perl with the *–w* option. Named after the Unix *lint* program for checking C programs. Invoked as:

```
perl -MO=Lint[,options] program
```

program is the name of the Perl program that will be checked. The options are separated by commas and follow normal backend option conventions. Most of the options are *lint*-check options, in which each option is a word specifying one *lint* check. Preceding an option with *no-* turns off that option. Options specified later override earlier options. There is also one non–lint-check option, *–u*. Here is the list of available options:

all

> Turns all warnings on.

context

> Warns whenever an array is used in implicit scalar context.

dollar-underscore

> Warns whenever $_ is explicitly used anywhere or whenever it is used as the implicit argument of a print statement.

implicit-read

> Warns whenever an operation implicitly reads a Perl special variable.

implicit-write

> Warns whenever an operation implicitly writes to a Perl special variable.

none

> Turns off all warnings.

private-names

> Warns whenever any variable, subroutine, or method name lives in a non-current package but begins with an underscore (_). Doesn't warn about an underscore as a single-character name, e.g., $_.

regexp-variables
> Warns whenever one of the regular expression variables $´, $&, or $' is used.

–u Package
> Normally checks only the main program code and all subroutines defined in package main. *–u* lets you specify other packages to be checked.

undefined-subs
> Warns whenever an undefined subroutine is invoked.

B::Showlex

Shows lexical variables used in functions or files. Invoke as:

```
perl -MO=Showlex[,sub] filename
```

If *sub* is provided and is the name of a subroutine in file *filename*, B::Showlex prints the lexical variables used in that subroutine. Otherwise, it prints the file-scope lexicals in *filename*.

B::Stackobj

Serves as a helper module for the CC backend.

B::Terse

Walks the Perl syntax tree, printing terse information about the ops. Invoke as:

```
perl -MO=Terse[,exec] filename
```

If exec is specified, walks the tree in execution order instead of syntax order.

B::Xref

Perl compiler backend that generates a cross-reference listing of variables, subroutines, and formats in a Perl program. Results are grouped by file, then subroutine, then package, then objects within the package with line numbers. The line numbers are given as a comma-separated list. A line number may be preceded by one of the following code letters:

Code	Meaning
%	Subroutine or method call
f	Format definition
i	Introduction, e.g., a lexical defined with my
s	Subroutine definition

Invoke B::Xref like this:

```
perl -MO=Xref[,options] program
```

program is the Perl program whose cross-reference you want. Options are separated by commas and follow normal backend option conventions. The possible options are:

–*D*

Specifies internal debug options. Most useful if specified with –*r* option. Debug options are:

0   Prints each operator as it's being processed, in the execution order of the program

t   Prints the object on the top of the stack as it is being tracked

–*ofilename*
Sends output to *filename* instead of to STDOUT.

–*r*

Produces raw output in machine-readable form for each definition or use of a variable, subroutine, or format.

Modules

base

Provides a shortcut for setting up @ISA. You can say:

```
use base qw(A B);
```

instead of:

```
BEGIN {
    require Foo;
    require Bar;
    push @ISA, qw(Foo Bar);
}
```

Benchmark

Provides routines for timing the execution of your code and formatting the results. Inherits only from the Exporter class. It has the following functions.

new	new *Benchmark*
	Returns the current time. By getting the current time before and after running the code, you can calculate the time it takes the code to run.
clearallcache	clearallcache
	Clears the entire cache. Exported on request.
clearcache	clearcache (*count*)
	Clears the cached time for *count* rounds of the null loop. Exported on request.

debug Benchmark->debug(*flag*)

Enables or disables debugging by setting the $Benchmark::Debug flag.

disablecache disablecache

Disables use of the cache. Exported on request.

enablecache enablecache

Resumes caching. Exported on request.

timediff timediff (*t1*, *t2*)

Calculates the difference between two times and returns the difference as a Benchmark object suitable for passing to timestr. Always exported.

timeit timeit (*count*, *code*)

Runs *code* and reports the time it took. Always exported. Takes the following arguments:

count
    The number of times to run the loop

code
    The code to run, specified as either a code reference or a string

timestr timestr (*timediff*[, *style*[, *format*]])

Converts times to printable strings. Always exported. Takes the following arguments:

timediff
    The object containing the times to be formatted.

style
    The output format. The possible values of style are:

    all
        Shows all of the following times: wallclock, user, system, user time of children, and system time of children

    auto
        Like all, except that if the children times are both 0, it acts like noc

    noc
        Shows all except the two children times

    nop
        Shows only wallclock and the two children times

Indicates the printf(3)-style format specifier (without the leading %) to use for printing the times. The default is 5.2f.

timethese

timethese (*count*, \%*codehashref*[, *style*])

Times each of several pieces of code and reports the results separately. Always exported. Takes the following arguments:

count
The number of times to run the loop.

\%*codehashref*
Reference to a hash in which the keys are names and the values are either strings or code references; each key/value pair specifies a piece of code to run.

style
Determines the format of the output. See timestr for the possible values of *style*.

timethis

timethis (*count*, *code*[, *title*[, *style*]])

Runs a chunk of code several times. Always exported. Takes the following arguments:

count
The number of times to run the loop.

code
The code to run, specified as either a code reference or a string.

title
The title of the result; default is "timethis COUNT".

style
Determines the format of the output. See timestr for the possible values of *style*.

bigint

Provides big-integer support for Perl. Prior to 5.8, and for 32-bit architectures, Perl supported whatever numbers your platform supported. This wasn't always the best solution when dealing with large numbers. Thus, the integer-related math modules were born, including Math::BigInt and bigint. Math::BigInt and bigint override all of the core Perl math functions and still support large integers. As of Perl 5.8, *bigint.pm* is shipped with the Perl source kit.

For example:

```
#!/usr/local/bin/perl -w
use bigint;
```

```
my $num1 = 4;
my $num2 = 1024;
 print $num1 ** $num2, "\n";  # Prints a very large number
```

bignum

Supports whatever big numbers you give it, including large integers and floats. In addition, bignum lets you specify options for the accuracy and precision of numbers that you'll calculate with it.

For example:

```
#!/usr/local/bin/perl -w
use bignum;

my $num1 = 4;
my $num2 = 5;
my $mult = $num1 * $num2;

print sqrt($mult),"\n"; # Yup
```

For a number that would be large, you can use bignum's accuracy option, a, to set the number of places after the decimal:

```
perl -Mbignum=a,50 -le 'print sqrt(20), "\n";'
```

If you wish to use rounding with bignum, you can use the precision option, p, with a 0 or 1 value to round up a value:

```
perl -Mbignum=p,0 -le 'print sqrt(24), "\n";' # Gives 5
```

To enable tracing for bignum, use the t or trace options:

```
/usr/local/perl5.8-prerc1/bin/perl5.7.3 -Mbignum=p,0,t -le 'print sqrt(24)'
MBI import Math::BigInt::Trace :constant upgrade Math::BigFloat::Trace lib
Calc
MBF import Math::BigFloat::Trace :constant downgrade Math::BigInt::Trace
MBI new '24' => '24' (Math::BigInt::Trace)
MBF new '24' => '24' (Math::BigFloat)
MBF new '4' => '4' (Math::BigFloat)
MBF new '1E-4' => '0' (Math::BigFloat)
MBI new '2' => '2' (Math::BigInt::Trace)
MBF new '2' => '2' (Math::BigInt::Trace)
MBI new '38' => '38' (Math::BigInt::Trace)
MBI new '38' => '38' (Math::BigInt::Trace)
```

The l, or lib, option lets you specify a different math library:

```
perl -Mbignum=l,new_math_lib -e 'print $this ** $that'
```

The v, or version, option shows you the version of all modules used by bignum and then exits.

bigrat

Implements big rational support for Perl. For example, if you want to add the fractions 1/2 + 3/8, you can use bigrat to calculate the result and display it in fractional form: 7/8. Or in Perl terms:

```
#!/usr/local/bin/perl -w
use bigrat;

my $frac1 = 1/2;
my $frac2 = 3/8;
print $frac1 + $frac2, "\n"; # Prints 7/8
```

As of Perl 5.8, bigrat is shipped with the Perl source kit.

blib

Pragma for testing programs against a package before the package has been installed. Given a directory path, blib starts looking for a blib directory structure in that directory; if it doesn't find one there, it works its way back up five levels. If no path is specified, it starts looking in the current directory.

blib is meant to be used from the command line:

```
perl -Mblib script [args...]
perl -Mblib=dir script [args...]
```

However, you can also call it from a Perl program:

```
use blib;
use blib 'dir';
```

bytes

The use bytes pragma disables character semantics for the rest of the lexical scope in which it appears. no bytes can reverse the effect of use bytes within the current lexical scope. Perl normally assumes character semantics in the presence of character data (i.e., data from a source marked as being of a particular character encoding). When use bytes is in effect, the encoding is temporarily ignored, and each string is treated as a series of bytes.

bytes is used as follows:

```
$x = chr(400);
    print "Length is ", length $x, "\n";      # "Length is 1"
    printf "Contents are %vd\n", $x;           # "Contents are 400"
    {
        use bytes;
        print "Length is ", length $x, "\n"; # "Length is 2"
        printf "Contents are %vd\n", $x;      # "Contents are 198.144"
    }
```

ByteLoader

ByteLoader is used to load byte-compiled Perl code. It uses the source filter mechanism to read the bytecode and insert it into the compiled code at the appropriate point. You will probably never interact with ByteLoader programatically.

Carp

Provides routines for generating error messages. Its subroutines generally report errors from the perspective of the calling program. It has the following functions.

carp	carp *msg*
	Warns of an error; reports the error as having occurred in the calling routine, not in the routine that contains the carp.
	`Use Carp;` `carp "text of error message";`
cluck	cluck *msg*
	Warns of errors and prints a stack backtrace; reports the error as having occurred in the calling routine. Not exported by default.
	`use Carp qw(cluck);` `cluck "text of error message";`
confess	confess *msg*
	Dies and prints a stack backtrace. Reports the error as having occurred at the point where confess was called.
croak	croak *msg*
	Dies and reports error as having occurred in the calling routine.

CGI

The Common Gateway Interface (CGI) library permits object-oriented web form creation and processing. The CGI.pm module contains the bulk of functionality for CGI programming. Four subclasses provide interfaces to various server environments and additional features. They are described below. For complete information on how CGI works and a description of CGI.pm, see Chapters 9 and 10.

CGI::Apache

Sets up the environment for using CGI.pm with the Perl-Apache API. The new constructor for this class creates an Apache::CGI class object that interfaces to the API.

CGI::Carp

Creates Carp-like CGI routines for writing error messages to the HTTPD or other error log. Exports functions for warn, die, carp, confess, and croak. The functions write timestamped error messages to your server log or other output that you specify. See the section "Carp" for details on the Carp functions.

Two other functions are provided by this module. Neither are automatically exported, so you must explicitly import them in use:

```
use CGI::Carp qw(carpout fatalsToBrowser);
```

---

carpout carpout *fh

Sends error messages to the filehandle fh. You should provide a reference to the filehandle glob, although you can also just use the filehandle's name for this function.

---

fatalsToBrowser fatalsToBrowser

When this routine is imported via use, fatal errors, such as those produced by die and confess, send error messages to the browser as well as the error log. A simple HTTP response is created with the error message, followed by a request to send mail to the web administrator.

CGI::Cookie

Provides an interface to Netscape (HTTP/1.1) cookies that can be used in conjunction with CGI.pm or independently. To use CGI::Cookie, create a new cookie object with the constructor new. You can then send the cookie to the browser in one of the following ways:

- From a CGI script, create a Set-Cookie field in the HTTP header for each cookie you want to send ($c is the cookie object):

```
print "Set-Cookie: $c0";
```

- With CGI.pm (see Chapter 10), use the header method with a -cookie argument:

```
print header(-cookie=>$c);
```

- Using *mod_perl* (see Chapter 11), use the request object's header_out method:

      $r->header_out('Set-Cookie',$c);

The following methods are provided for CGI::Cookie.

---

new $c = new CGI::Cookie(*attribs*)

Constructor. Creates a new cookie. Attributes are:

-domain = *domain_name*
> Optional. Points to domain name or fully qualified hostname to which cookie will be returned. If missing, browser will return cookie only to the server that set it.

-expires = *date*
> Optional expiration date in any of the date formats recognized by CGI.pm. If missing, cookie expires at the end of this browser session.

-name = *name*
> Required. Scalar value with the cookie name.

-path = *path*
> Optional. Points to a partial URL on the current server; cookies will be returned to any URL beginning with this path. Defaults to /.

-secure = *boolean*
> Optional. If true, browser will return cookie only if a cryptographic protocol is in use.

-value = *value*
> Required. The value of the cookie; can be a scalar, an array reference, or a hash reference.

---

as_string $c->as_string

Turns internal representation of cookie into RFC-compliant text. Called internally by overloading the "" operator, or can be called directly.

---

domain $c->domain(*val*)

Gets or sets the cookie's domain. With no parameter, gets the current value; otherwise, sets the new value.

---

expires $c->expires(*val*)

Gets or sets the cookie's expiration date. With no parameter, gets the current expiration date; otherwise, sets the new value.

fetch	%*cookies* = fetch CGI::Cookie
	Returns a hash containing cookies returned by the browser, in which the keys are the cookie names and the values are the cookie values. In a scalar context, fetch returns a hash reference.
name	$*c*->name(*val*)
	Gets or sets the cookie's name. With no parameter, returns the current name; otherwise, sets the new value.
parse	%*cookies* = parse CGI::Cookie(*stored_cookies*)
	Retrieves cookies stored in an external form.
path	$*c*->path(*val*)
	Gets or sets the cookie's path. With no parameter, returns the current path; otherwise, sets the new value.
raw_fetch	%*cookies* = raw_fetch CGI::Cookie
	Like fetch, but does no unescaping of reserved characters; useful for retrieving cookies set by a foreign server.
value	$*c*->value(*val*)
	Gets or sets the cookie's value. With no parameter, returns the current value; otherwise, sets the new value. In array context, returns the current value as an array. In scalar context, returns the first value of a multivalued cookie.

CGI::Fast

CGI interface for FastCGI. FastCGI is a type of gateway for web servers that improves performance by loading scripts as persistently running processes. CGI::Fast provides a new constructor to create a CGI object that runs in this environment. FastCGI requires both a server and a version of Perl that are FastCGI-enabled. See *www.fastcgi.com* for more information.

CGI::Pretty

Allows users of CGI to output nicely formatted HTML code by adding carriage returns and indentations to HTML markup for easy readability. For example, the following code:

```
#!/usr/local/bin/perl -w

use CGI qw(:all);

my $query = CGI->new();

print $query->start_html();
print $query->table( TR( td( "foo" ) ) );
print $query->end_html();
```

outputs the following HTML:

```
<?xml version="1.0" encoding="utf-8"?>
<!DOCTYPE html
        PUBLIC "-//W3C//DTD XHTML Basic 1.0//EN"
        "http://www.w3.org/TR/xhtml-basic/xhtml-basic10.dtd">
<html xmlns="http://www.w3.org/1999/xhtml" lang="en-US"><head><title>
Untitled Document</title>
</head><body><table><tr><td>foo</td></tr></table></body></html>
```

which is ugly. You can make it prettier with CGI::Pretty:

```
#!/usr/local/bin/perl -w

use CGI::Pretty qw( :html3 );

my $query = CGI->new();

print $query->start_html();

# Print a table with a single data element
print $query->table( TR( td( "foo" ) ) );

print $query->end_html();
```

CGI::Push

Provides an interface to do server push operations, letting you rewrite pages with content that changes regularly. A server push operation automatically sends updates to a page on a push-capable browser. CGI::Push exports the function do_push to implement page redraws. This method can be used on a CGI::Push object or on its own:

```
$q = new CGI::Push;
$q->do_push(-next_page => \&sub);
```

or:

```
do_push (-next_page => \&sub);
```

do_push requires one argument: a reference to a subroutine that will draw the next page. You may optionally specify a subroutine that draws the last page and the interval between page updates. Additional parameters to do_push are those that can be used with a CGI::headers object.

do_push	do_push (*params*)
	Implements a server push operation, which updates a page at specific intervals. Parameters are:
	-delay => *n*
	Specifies the number of seconds, *n*, to wait before the next call to the page-drawing subroutine.
	-last_page => \&*sublast*
	Runs the subroutine *sublast* to draw the last page update of a server push operation. The -last_page routine is invoked when the -next_page routine returns false. A reference to a subroutine glob should be provided for this parameter, but the name of the subroutine is also acceptable.
	-next_page => \&*sub*
	sub is the name of the subroutine responsible for redrawing the page and counting the number of iterations (if you want repeated updating). The do_push routine ends when *sub* returns false (or when the -last_page subroutine is invoked). A reference to a subroutine glob should be provided for this parameter, but the name of the subroutine is also acceptable.
	-type = *string*
	Specifies the content type of the pushed data. The default value is text/html.

CGI::Switch

Provides a new method that tries to call new in each of the Apache::CGI, CGI::XA, and CGI classes, returning the first CGI object that it successfully gets.

charnames

Pragma to provide support for \N{*charname*} escapes. Options are:

:full
    Searches for *charnames* in the list of standard Unicode character names

:short
    Searches for *charnames* in the specified script, with the \N escape expected to be of the form \N{*script:charname*}

scriptname
    Searches for all *charnames* in script *scriptname*

For example:

```
#!/usr/local/bin/perl -w

use charnames ':short';
print "\N{greek:Sigma} is an upper-case sigma.\n";
```

Class::ISA

Allows you to scan @ISA—in order and without duplicates—for names of classes that Perl would scan to find a method. This is important when using classes that are derived from other classes, which are themselves derived from other classes, and so forth. Class::ISA is bundled with the Perl 5.8 source kit.

Let's say that you called SomeClass->method(). Perl searches for method() first in SomeClass, but will search its superclasses for method() if it doesn't find it in SomeClass. For example:

```
@SomeClass::ISA = qw(SomeOther SomeOtherOther SomeOtherOtherOther);
 use Class::ISA;
print "SomeClass::ISA path is:\n ",
join(", ", Class::ISA::super_path('SomeClass')), "\n";
```

This prints:

```
SomeOther, SomeOtherOther, SomeOtherOtherOther
```

Class::ISA doesn't export anything. If classes erroneously inherit from each other; i.e., if there's a loop (or cycle) between what's inherited between classes, Perl throws an error, and Class::ISA itself will ignore the loop. If Perl can't find the method in the @ISA tree, it looks in UNIVERSAL, but Class::ISA does not. You may do something like the following to search in UNIVERSAL as well:

```
@supers = (Class::Tree::super_path($CLASS), 'UNIVERSAL');
```

Here are the Class::ISA methods.

self_and_super_path

> Class::ISA::self_and_super_path($CLASS)
>
> Identical to super_path, except that $CLASS is included as the first element.

self_and_super_versions

> Class::ISA::self_and_super_versions($CLASS)
>
> Returns a hash with keys that are $CLASS (and its superclasses) and values that are the contents of the $VERSION of each class. If $VERSION does not exist, sel_and_super_versions returns undef.

Class::ISA::super_path(*class*)

Returns an ordered list of names of classes that Perl would search through to find a method. Note that no duplicates will be allowed in the list; nor will *class* be included in the list. UNIVERSAL is not included in the list, but if you need it, you should add it to the end of the list.

Class::Struct

Formerly named Class::Template; exports a single function, struct. struct takes a list of element names and types, and optionally a class name, and creates a Perl class that implements a struct-like data structure. It also creates a constructor method, new, for creating objects of the class (so a class created this way must not itself define a new method).

Each element in the struct data has an accessor method, which is used to assign to the element and to fetch its value. The default accessor can be overridden by declaring a sub of the same name in the package. Each element's type can be scalar, array, hash, or class.

struct

struct (*paramlist*)

Creates a class, with object methods for each element of the class. The parameter list *paramlist* can take one of three forms:

```
struct( CLASS_NAME => [ ELEMENT_LIST ]);
# Object is array-based
struct( CLASS_NAME => { ELEMENT_LIST });
# Object is hash-based
struct( ELEMENT_LIST );      # Class name is current, and
package name                  # object is array-based
```

The array-based element lists are faster and smaller, but the hash-based list is more flexible. The class that is created can be a subclass of the UNIVERSAL class, but not of any other class.

Element list

The items in the ELEMENT_LIST are of the form:

```
NAME => TYPE, ...
```

in which each NAME=>TYPE pair declares one element of the struct. Each element name is defined as an accessor method, unless a method is explicitly defined with that name. (In that case, a warning is issued if the –*w* flag is set.)

Element types and accessor methods

There are four possible element types, each represented by a string. Each string may start with an asterisk (*), indicating that a reference to the element will be returned. The type of an element determines the accessor method provided. The following list shows the element types, the strings that represent them, and the accessor:

array (@ or *@)
> The element is an array, initialized to ( ). With no argument, the accessor returns a reference to the element's whole array. With one or two arguments, the first argument is an index specifying one element of the array; the second argument, if present, is the value that will be assigned to that array element.

class (Class_Name or *Class_Name)
> The element's value must be a reference blessed to the named class or to one of its subclasses. The element is initialized to the result of calling the new constructor of the named class. The accessor's argument, if any, is the value that will be assigned to the element. The accessor croaks if it's not an appropriate object reference.

hash (% or *%)
> The element is a hash, initialized to ( ). With no argument, the accessor returns a reference to the element's whole hash. With one or two arguments, the first argument is a key specifying one element of the hash; the second argument, if present, is the value to be assigned to that hash element.

scalar ($ or *$)
> The element is a scalar, initialized to undef. The accessor's argument, if any, is assigned to the element.

Config

Used to access configuration information. When Perl is built, the Configure script obtains and saves this information in a hash, %Config, in *Config.pm* itself. Config checks to be sure it's running with the same Perl version as the one that created the hash.

The index into the hash is the shell variable name. %Config is always exported; the following three functions are exported on request.

---

config_sh　　　config_sh

Returns all Perl configuration information.

```
use Config(qw(config_sh));
print config_sh();
```

returns:

```
archlibexp='sun4-solaris'
cc='cc'
```

```
ccflags='-I/usr/local/include/sfio -I/usr/local/include'
...
```

---

config_vars

config_vars (*names*)

Returns the name/value pairs for the requested configuration variables. Prints the results to STDOUT.

```
use Config(qw(config_vars));
print config_vars(qw(osname ccflags));
```

returns:

```
osname='solaris'
ccflags='-I/usr/local/include/sfio -I/usr/local/include'
```

---

myconfig

myconfig

Returns a summary of the major Perl configuration values.

---

constant

A Perl pragma that declares compile-time constants with a given scalar or list value. By default, the value is evaluated in list context, but you can override the default by specifying scalar:

```
use constant NAME1 => value1;
use constant NAME2 => scalar value2;
```

CPAN

Lets you access CPAN; search for a module, a bundle, an author, or a distribution; download a module or distribution; install it; and make it. The CPAN module can be used either interactively from the command line or programmatically:

```
perl -MCPAN -eshell;          # Run from the command line
```

or:

```
use CPAN;

my $obj = CPAN::Shell->install('ExtUtils::MakeMaker');
```

This section describes the use of the CPAN module from a program. See Chapter 2 for information on using it interactively and for details of the available commands. These commands, available interactively from the shell, are methods of the class CPAN::Shell. From a program, they are available both as methods (e. g., CPAN::Shell->install(...)) and as functions in the calling package (e.g., install(...)).

Each of the commands that produce listings of modules (r, autobundle, and u) returns a list of the IDs of all modules within the list. The IDs of all objects available

---

within a program are strings that can be expanded to the corresponding real objects with the CPAN::Shell->expand("Module",@things) method. expand returns a list of CPAN::Module objects according to the @things arguments. In scalar context, it returns only the first element of the list.

Session and Cache Managers

The CPAN module contains a session manager, which keeps track of objects that have been fetched, built, and installed in the current session. No status is retained between sessions.

There is also a cache manager, which keeps track of disk space used and deletes extra space. The cache manager keeps track of the build directory, $CPAN::Config->{build_dir}, and uses a simple FIFO mechanism to delete directories below build_dir when they grow bigger than $CPAN::Config->{build_cache}.

The original distribution files are kept in the directory $CPAN::Config->{keep_source_where}. This directory is not covered by the cache manager but must be controlled by the user. If the same directory is used as both build_dir and keep_source_where, your sources are deleted with the same FIFO mechanism.

Bundles

The CPAN module recognizes a bundle as a Perl module in the namespace Bundle:: that does not define any functions or methods and usually contains only pod documentation. It starts like a Perl module with a package declaration and a $VERSION variable. After that, the pod section looks like any other pod except that it contains a special section that begins with:

```
=head1 CONTENTS
```

This section consists of lines such as:

```
Module_Name [Version_String] [- optional text]
```

in which Module_Name is the name of a module (for example, Term::ReadLine), not the name of a distribution file, and the version and text are optional. If there is text, it is preceded by a -. The distribution of a bundle should follow the same convention as other distributions.

Bundles are treated specially in the CPAN package. When you tell CPAN to install a bundle, it installs all the modules in the CONTENTS section of the pod. You can install your own bundles locally by placing a conforming bundle file somewhere in your @INC path. The autobundle command available in the shell interface does that for you by including all currently installed modules in a snapshot bundle file (see Chapter 2).

Configuration

When the CPAN module is installed, a site-wide configuration file is created: *CPAN/Config.pm*. The default values defined there can be overridden locally in the file *CPAN/MyConfig.pm*. You can store this file in *$HOME/.cpan/CPAN/MyConfig.pm*, because *$HOME/.cpan* is added to the search path of the CPAN

---

module before the use or require statements. Chapter 2 lists the keys defined in the hash reference $CPAN::Config and how to set and query them.

CD-ROM Support

The *urllist* parameter in the configuration table contains a list of URLs that will be used for downloading. If the list contains any *file* URLs, CPAN looks there first for files (except index files). So if you are using a CD-ROM containing the CPAN contents, include the CD-ROM as a *file* URL at the end of *urllist* since it is likely to be out-of-date. You can do this with:

```
o conf urllist push file://localhost/CDROM/CPAN
```

CPAN::FirstTime

The CPAN::FirstTime module has one function, init, which is an initialization routine called automatically the first time a user uses the CPAN module. It asks the user a series of questions and writes the answers into a CPAN::Config file.

CPAN::Nox

A wrapper for CPAN.pm that prevents the use of any compiled extensions while it's executing. Run it in interactive mode if you have upgraded Perl but your extensions aren't working:

```
perl -MCPAN::Nox -eshell;
```

Cwd

The Cwd module provides three functions that get the pathname of the current working directory. Using these functions instead of the *pwd* command will make your code more portable, because not all systems have *pwd*.

---

cwd   cwd

Gets the current working directory. This is the safest way to get it.

---

fastcwd   fastcwd

A faster way to get the directory, but somewhat more dangerous because of the way it works internally.

---

getcwd   getcwd

Does the same thing as cwd by reimplementing the C library functions getcwd(3) or getwd(3) in Perl.

Data::Dumper

Converts Perl data structures into strings that can be printed or used with eval to reconstruct the original structures. Takes a list of scalars or reference variables and writes out their contents in Perl syntax. Several interfaces to Data::Dumper are provided:

- Simple procedural interface:

      print Dumper($foo, $bar);

- Extended usage with names:

      print Data::Dumper->Dump([$foo, $bar], [qw(foo *ary)]);

- Object-oriented interface:

      $d = Data::Dumper->new([$foo, $bar], [qw(foo *ary)]);
      ...
      print $d->Dump;

By default, references are identified as $VARn, in which n is a numeric suffix. References to substructures within $VARn are labeled using arrow notation. In the extended usage form, references can be given user-specified names. See the Data::Dumper manpage for examples of the module's use.

Several configuration variables can be used to control the output generated using the procedural interface. These variables control the default state of the object created by the new method. Each variable has a corresponding method that can be used later to query or modify the object. In the following list, each variable is followed by the corresponding method:

$Data::Dumper::Bless
$obj->Bless([newval])
> Can be set to a string that specifies an alternative to the bless built-in operator used to create objects. A function with the specified name should exist and should accept the same arguments as the built-in. Default is bless.

$Data::Dumper::Deepcopy
$obj->Deepcopy([newval])
> If set to a Boolean value, enables deep copies of structures; cross-referencing is then done only when absolutely essential. Default is 0.

$Data::Dumper::Indent
$obj->Indent([newval])
> Controls the style of indentation for the output. Can be set to:

> 0   No newlines, indentation, or spaces between list items

> 1   Newlines, but each level in the structure is indented a fixed amount

> 2   Default. Takes into account the length of hash keys so the hash values line up.

> 3   Like 2, but also annotates array elements with their index, with each annotation on its own line

`$Data::Dumper::Freezer`
`$obj->Freezer([`*`newval`*`])`

If set to a method name, Data::Dumper invokes that method via the object before attempting to turn it into a string. Set to an empty string to disable. Default is empty string.

`$Data::Dumper::Pad`
`$obj->Pad([`*`newval`*`])`

Specifies the string prefixed to every output line. Default is an empty string.

`$Data::Dumper::Purity`
`$obj->Purity([`*`newval`*`])`

Controls degree to which eval can recreate the original reference structures. Setting the value to 1 outputs additional Perl statements to correctly recreate nested references. Default is 0.

`$Data::Dumper::Quotekeys`
`$obj->Quotekeys([`*`newval`*`])`

If set to a Boolean value, controls whether hash keys are quoted. If false, avoids quoting hash keys that look like a simple string. Default is 1, which always quotes hash keys.

`$Data::Dumper::Terse`
`$obj->Terse([`*`newval`*`])`

When set, Data::Dumper outputs single, non–self-referential values as atoms or terms rather than as statements. $VAR*n* names are avoided as much as possible. Such output may not be parsable by eval.

`$Data::Dumper::Toaster`
`$obj->Toaster([`*`newval`*`])`

If set to a method name, Data::Dumper issues a method call for any objects that will be dumped using the syntax bless(data, class)->method( ). Set to an empty string to disable. Default is empty string.

`$Data::Dumper::Useqq`
`$obj->Useqq([`*`newval`*`])`

When set, enables the use of double quotes to represent string values. In addition, \n, \t, and \r are used to represent non-space whitespace; "unsafe" characters are backslashed; and unprintable characters are output as quoted octal integers. Default is 0. Currently, the Dumpxs method does not honor this flag.

`$Data::Dumper::Varnam`
`$obj->Varname([`*`newval`*`])`

Specifies the prefix to use for tagging variable names in the output. Default is VAR.

The following methods and functions are provided.

---

new   `$obj = Data::Dumper->new(`*`arrayref`*`[, `*`arrayref`*`])`

Constructor. Creates a new Data::Dumper object. The first argument is an anonymous array of values to be dumped. The optional

---

second argument is an anonymous array of names for the values. The names don't need a leading $ and must be comprised of alphanumeric characters. You can begin a name with a * to specify that the dereferenced type must be dumped instead of the reference itself for array and hash references.

Dump $obj->Dump

Data::Dumper->Dump(*arrayref*[, *arrayref*])

Returns stringified form of values stored in the object with their order preserved, subject to the configuration options. In array context, returns a list of strings corresponding to the supplied values.

Dumper   Dumper (*list*)

Function that returns the stringified form of the values in the list, subject to the configuration options. The values are named $VAR*n* in the output. Returns a list of strings in array context.

DumperX   DumperX (*list*)

Identical to Dumper, except that it calls the xsub implementation. Available only if the xsub extension to Data::Dumper is installed.

Dumpxs $obj->Dumpxs

Data::Dumper->Dumpxs(*arrayref*[, *arrayref*])

Identical to Dump, but written in C and therefore much faster. Available only if the xsub extension to Data::Dumper is installed.

Reset $obj->Reset

Clears the internal table of "seen" references, returning the object itself.

Seen $obj->Seen([*hashref*])

Queries or adds to the internal table of references that have been encountered. The references aren't dumped, but their names are inserted when they are encountered subsequently. With no argument, returns the "seen" list of name => value pairs, in array context. Otherwise, returns the object itself.

Values $obj->Values([arrayref])

Queries or replaces the internal array of values to be dumped. With no arguments, returns the names. Otherwise, returns the object itself.

DB

The DB module abstracts and provides all of the hooks into Perl internal debugging functionality, so that various implementations of Perl debuggers (or packages that want simply to get at the "privileged" debugging data) can all benefit from the development of this common code. The following "public" global names can be read by clients of this API, but should be considered read-only:

$DB_HASH
  Stores key/data pairs in data files; equivalent to other hashing packages such as DBM, NDBM, ODBM, GDBM, and SDBM.

$DB::sub
  Name of current executing subroutine.

%DB::sub
  The keys of this hash are the names of all the known subroutines. Each value is an encoded string that has the sprintf format ("%s:%d-%d", filename, fromline, toline).

$DB::single
  Single-step flag. Will be true if the API will stop at the next statement.

$DB::signal
  Signal flag. Will be true if a signal was caught.

$DB::trace
  This flag is set to true if the API is tracing through subroutine calls.

@DB::args
  Contains the arguments of current subroutine, or the @ARGV array if in the toplevel context.

@DB::dbline
  List of lines in currently loaded file.

%DB::dbline
  Actions in current file (keys are line numbers). The values are strings that have the sprintf format ("%s\000%s", breakcondition, actioncode).

$DB::package
  Package namespace of currently executing code.

$DB::filename
  Currently loaded filename.

`$DB::subname`
> Fully qualified name of currently executing subroutine.

`$DB::lineno`
> Line number that will be executed next.

API Methods

The following are methods in the DB base class. A client must access these methods by inheritance, since the API keeps track of clients through the inheritance mechanism.

`CLIENT->register( )`
> Registers a client object/package

`CLIENT->evalcode(STRING)`
> evals *STRING* in executing code context

`CLIENT->skippkg('Skip::Me')`
> Asks DB not to stop in these packages

`CLIENT->run( )`
> Runs some more (until a breakpt is reached)

`CLIENT->step( )`
> Single step

`CLIENT->next( )`
> Steps over

`CLIENT->done( )`
> Deregisters from the debugging API

Client Callback Methods

The following "virtual" methods are called by the API at appropriate points. The API provides only empty versions of these methods by default, but they can be defined by the client as needed.

`CLIENT->init( )`
> Called after debug API initializes itself.

`CLIENT->prestop([STRING])`
> Usually inherited from DB package. If no arguments are passed, returns the prestop action string.

`CLIENT->stop( )`
> Called when execution stops, with the filename and line number as arguments.

`CLIENT->idle( )`
> Called while stopped, e.g., in a client event loop.

`CLIENT->poststop([STRING])`
> Usually inherited from DB package. If no arguments are passed, returns the poststop action string.

CLIENT->evalcode(*STRING*)

Usually inherited from DB package. Asks for a *STRING* to be evaled in executing code context.

CLIENT->cleanup( )

Called just before exit.

CLIENT->output(*LIST*)

Called when API must show a message (warnings, errors etc.).

DB_File

Ties a Perl hash to one of the Berkeley DB database types and lets you use functions provided in the DB API:

```
[$X =] tie %hash,  "DB_File", $filename [, $flags, $mode, $DB_HASH];
[$X =] tie %hash,  "DB_File", $filename, $flags, $mode, $DB_BTREE;
[$X =] tie @array, "DB_File", $filename, $flags, $mode, $DB_RECNO;
```

The types are:

$DB_HASH

Stores key/data pairs in data files. Equivalent to other hashing packages such as DBM, NDBM, ODBM, GDBM, and SDBM.

$DB_BTREE

Stores key/data pairs in a binary tree.

$DB_RECNO

Uses a record (line) number to access fixed-length and variable-length flat text files through the same key/value-pair interface as in $DB_HASH and $DB_BTREE.

After you've tied a hash to a database:

```
$db = tie %hash, "DB_File", "filename";
```

you can access the Berkeley DB API functions:

```
$db->put($key, $value, R_NOOVERWRITE);  # Invoke the DB "put" function
```

All the functions defined in the *dbopen(3)* manpage are available except close and dbopen itself. The constants defined in the *dbopen* manpage are also available.

The following are the functions available (the comments note only the differences from the equivalent C function).

---

del $X->del(*key*[, *flags*])

Removes key/value pairs from the database. *flags* is optional.

---

fd $X->fd

Returns a file descriptor that represents the underlying database. No difference from the equivalent C function.

---

get $X->get(key, value[, flags])

Retrieves data from the database by key. *flags* is optional. The value associated with *key* is returned in *value*.

put $X->put(key, value[, flags])

Stores a key/value pair in the database. *flags* is optional. If R_IAFTER or R_IBEFORE is set, then *key* is set to the record number of the inserted key/value pair.

seq $X->seq(key, value[, flags])

Returns the next sequential key/value pair from the database. *flags* is optional. Both *key* and *value* are set.

sync $X->sync([flags])

Synchronizes the database by flushing any cached data to disk. *flags* is optional.

Devel::DProf

Devel::DProf is a Perl code profiler. It collects information on the execution time of a Perl script and of the subroutines in that script. To profile a Perl script, run *perl* with the *–d* debugging switch:

```
perl -d:DProf test.pl
```

When the script terminates (or when the output buffer is filled) the profiler will dump the profile information to a file called *tmon.out*. A tool such as *dprofpp* can be used to interpret the information. The following command will print the top 15 subroutines that used the most time:

```
dprofpp
```

To print an execution graph of the subroutines in the script, use the following command:

```
dprofpp -T
```

Devel::PPPort

Allows you to write Perl code that's as compatible as possible with the widest range of Perl interpreters. Devel::PPPort ships with *pport.h*, with which you can incorporate some of the newest features of Perl with your older Perl releases. Devel::PPPort is important for developing modules, since newer Perl versions do not have as many issues with namespace pollution that older Perl versions had.

To use Devel::PPPort, copy *ppport.h* to wherever you're doing your development work, and use the WriteFile() method when you're ready to generate the necessary code. WriteFile() is used to write a C header file for XS modules. *ppport.h* contains a series of macros that allow XS to be built under older versions of Perl. For example:

```
my $port_file = '/users1/nvp/Perl/XS/Projects/ppport.h';
Devel::PPPort::WriteFile($port_file);
```

This generates *ppport.h* in */users1/nvp/Perl/XS/Projects*.

WriteFile() takes an optional parameter representing the filename of the *ppport* header file. If empty, *ppport.h* is generated in the current directory. WriteFile() returns true if the write was successful, and false otherwise.

ppport.h provides access to the Perl API.

Devel::SelfStubber

Generates stubs in a module that uses the SelfLoader, either printing the necessary stubs or generating the whole module with the stubs inserted in the correct location before the __DATA__ token. The default is to simply print the stubs.

stub	stub (*module*[, *dir*])

Generates the stubs. Takes the following arguments:

module
> Name of the module, in the form Devel::SelfStubber (with no .*pm* at the end).

dir
> Library directory that contains the module. Defaults to the current directory.

To simply print the stubs:

```
use Devel::SelfStubber;
Devel::SelfStubber->stub(module, dir);
```

To generate the whole module, with the stubs inserted correctly, set the variable $Devel::SelfStubber::JUST_STUBS to 0:

```
use Devel::SelfStubber;
$Devel::SelfStubber::JUST_STUBS = 0;
Devel::SelfStubber->stub(module, dir);
```

diagnostics

Provides more descriptive diagnostics than those generated by the Perl compiler and interpreter. Uses the longer, more explanatory error messages found in the *perldiag* manpage. Can be used as a pragma or as a standalone program, *splain*. When used as a pragma, diagnostics affects the compilation phase of your program as well as the execution phase. As a standalone module, it is used to post-process errors after execution has completed.

The *splain* program links to *diagnostics.pm* to act on the standard error output of a Perl program. The program's output can be sent to a file, which is then used as input to *splain*, or it can be piped directly to *splain*. Output from *splain* is directed to STDOUT.

Options

-p   Sets the variable $diagnostics::PRETTY to true

-v   Prints the *perldiag* manpage introduction, then any diagnostic messages

As a pragma:

```
use diagnostics [-verbose]
```

enables the use of diagnostics in your program (and enables Perl's *-w* flag). Compilation is then subject to the enhanced diagnostics, which are issued to STDERR. Set the diagnostics::PRETTY variable in a BEGIN block to provide nicer escape sequences for pagers, so your output looks better. The -verbose option prints the *perldiag* manpage introduction, then any diagnostic messages. Functions are:

enable
    Turns diagnostics on at runtime

disable
    Turns diagnostics off at runtime

Digest

The Digest modules (Digest::MD2, Digest::MD5, Digest::SHA1, and Digest::-HMAC) calculate a digest of data that they encounter. These digests are often referred to as "fingerprints," "hashes," or "sums." The Digest modules return a small, fixed-length string, depending on how you've requested your data. If you change your data and regenerate the digest, the digest will be different each time the data itself changes. As of Perl 5.8, the Digest modules are bundled with the Perl source kit.

The Digest modules both a functional interface and an object-oriented interface. If you use the object-oriented inteface, you have the benefit of being able to send data of arbitrary length. You can also tell the Digest module to read files directly.

Digest delivers the hashed data in one of three formats: binary, hex, or base64. The following example uses Digest and calculates an MD5 sum of a string, $text, that represents the data. The data is output in hexadecimal form.

```perl
#!/usr/local/bin/perl -w
use Digest;
my $text = 'Be the ball, Danny!';
my $md5 = Digest->MD5;

$md5->add($text);
```

```
my $hashed = $md5->hexdigest;

print "The sum of \$text is [$hashed].\n";
```

This gives you:

```
The sum of $text is [6eec91414372ad157fc9d3d15b496d93].
```

Digest implements the following functions for the object-oriented interface. These functions are available to all of the Digest modules.

reset	reset()
	Alias for new.
add	add(*data*, ...)
	Appends *data* to the message for which you calculate the digest. add returns the Digest object itself.
addfile	addfile(*io_handle*)
	Reads *io_handle* until end-of-file and, like add, appends the content to the message for which you calculate the digest. addfile returns the Digest object itself.
b64digest	b64digest()
	Same as digest, but returns the digest in base64-encoded form.
digest	digest()
	Returns the binary digest for the message. Note that digest is a destructive operation, in that the Digest object is reset so it can be used to create another value.
hexdigest	hexdigest()
	Same as digest, but returns digest in hexadecimal form.

Digest::MD5

The Digest::MD5 module allows simpler creation of MD5 hashes. MD5 takes as input a message of arbitrary length and creates a 128-bit fingerprint, or digest, of the input. Like the Digest module, Digest::MD5 implements both a functional and object-oriented interface, which offer the same benefits. Digest::MD5 also outputs binary (16 bytes long), hexadecimal (32 characters long), and base64 (22 characters long) data.

To rewrite the example in the "Digest" section:

```
#!/usr/local/bin/perl -w
# Yes, functional interface
use Digest::MD5 qw(md5_hex);

my $text = 'Be the ball, Danny!';
my $hexed = md5_hex($text);

print "The sum of \$text is [$hexed].\n";
```

You can use the object-oriented interface like so:

```
#!/usr/local/bin/perl -w

use Digest::MD5;

my $text = 'Be the ball, Danny!';
my $md5 = Digest::MD5->new();

$md5->add($text);

my $sum = $md5->hexdigest;
print "The sum of \$text is [$sum].\n";
```

Digest::MD5 implements (and exports) the following functions.

---

new   new()

Constructor. Returns a new Digest::MD5 object. You can add data to $object and retrieve the digest itself. If you can new more than once, it will reset the existing digest and create a new Digest::MD5 object.

---

reset   reset()

An alias for new.

---

add   add(*data*, ...)

Appends *data* to the message for which you calculate the digest. add returns the Digest object itself. For example:

```
open(FILE, ...) or ...
while (<FILE>) {
    $md5->add($_);
} close(FILE);
```

addfile	`addfile(io_handle)`

Reads *io_handle* until end-of-file and appends the content to the message for which you calculate the digest. `addfile` returns the Digest object itself. For example:

```
open(FILE, $file) or ...
print Digest::MD5->new->addfile(*FILE)->hexdigest, "
$file\n";
close(FILE);
```

b64digest	`b64digest()`

Same as `digest`, but returns the digest in base64-encoded form.

digest	`digest()`

Returns the binary digest for the message. Note that `digest` is a destructive operation, in that the Digest object is reset so it can be used to create another value.

hexdigest	`hexdigest()`

Same as `digest`, but returns digest in hexadecimal form.

The following functions are implemented by the functional interface.

md5	`md5(data, ...)`

Calculates the MD5 digest of *data* and returns it in binary form.

md5_base64	`md5_base64(data,...)`

Same as `md5`, but returns the digest as a base64-encoded string.

md5_hex	`md5_hex(data,...)`

Same as `md5`, but returns the digest in hexadecimal form.

DirHandle

Provides methods for accessing Perl's directory functions, avoiding namespace pollution. Creates anonymous glob to hold a directory handle and closes the dirhandle automatically when the last reference goes out of scope. The following methods are provided.

---

new dh = new DirHandle [*dirname*]

Constructor. Creates a new directory handle. The optional directory name, *dirname*, defaults to the current directory.

---

close $dh->close( )

Closes a directory handle; equivalent to the closedir function.

---

open $dh->open(*dirname*)

Opens directory *dirname*; equivalent to the opendir function.

---

read $dh->read( )

Reads directory entries. Equivalent to the readdir function. In scalar context, reads the next directory entry; in list context, reads all entries.

---

rewind $dh->rewind( )

Sets current position to beginning of directory; equivalent to the rewinddir function.

Dumpvalue

The Dumpvalue module is used to provide a screen dump of Perl data. Whether you're trying to look at global variables or you'd like to dump the symbol table so that you can examine it, Dumpvalue will prove useful to you. Here's an example that dumps the symbol table of CGI.pm:

```
#!/usr/local/bin/perl -w

use Dumpvalue;
use CGI qw(:all);

my $dumper = Dumpvalue->new('DumpPackages' => 1);

$dumper->dumpvars('CGI');
```

DynaLoader

The standard Perl interface to the dynamic linking mechanisms available on many platforms.

Using DynaLoader

Use DynaLoader like this:

```
package Module;
require DynaLoader;
@ISA = qw(... DynaLoader ...);

bootstrap Module;
```

The `bootstrap` method calls your module's bootstrap routine directly if the module is statically linked into Perl. Otherwise, the module inherits the `bootstrap` method from DynaLoader, which loads in your module and calls its `bootstrap` method.

Extending to New Architectures

If you want to extend DynaLoader to a new architecture, you need to know about its internal interface. The variables it uses are:

`$dl_debug`
> Enables internal debugging messages on the Perl side of the DynaLoader; by default, is set to `$ENV{'PERL_DL_DEBUG'}` if that is defined. A similar debugging variable is added to the C code (see *dlutils.c*) and enabled if Perl was built with the *–DDEBUGGING* flag, or it can be set via the PERL_DL_DEBUG environment variable. Set to 1 for minimal information or higher for more detail.

`@dl_library_path`
> Default list of directories to search for libraries; initialized to hold the list of directories in `$Config{'libpth'}`. Should also be initialized with other directories that can be determined from the environment at runtime.

`@dl_resolve_using`
> List of additional libraries or other shared objects for resolving undefined symbols. Required only on platforms without automatic handling for dependent libraries.

`@dl_require_symbols`
> List of one or more symbol names in the library/object file to be dynamically loaded. Only required on some platforms.

Of the following subroutines, `bootstrap` and `dl_findfile` are standard across all platforms and are defined in *DynaLoader.pm*. The others are defined in the *.xs* file that supplies the implementation for the platform.

bootstrap	bootstrap (*modulename*)
	Normal entry point for automatic dynamic loading in Perl.

dl_error	dl_error
	Gets error message text from the last failed DynaLoader function: $message = dl_error( );

dl_expandspec	dl_expandspec (*spec*)
	Used for systems that require special filename handling to deal with symbolic names for files. *spec* specifies the filenames that need the special handling.

dl_findfile	dl_findfile (*names*)
	Determines the full paths to one or more loadable files, given their generic names and optionally one or more directories. Searches directories in @dl_library_path by default and returns an empty list if no files are found.

dl_find_symbol	dl_find_symbol (*libref*, *symbol*)
	Looks in *libref* for the address of symbol *symbol*. Returns the address, or undef if not found.

dl_install_xsub	dl_install_xsub (*perl_name*, *symref*[, *filename*])

	Creates a new Perl external subroutine. Takes the following arguments:
	perl_name
	    Name of the new subroutine.
	symref
	    Pointer to the function that implements the routine.
	filename
	    The source file for the function. If not defined, DynaLoader is used.

dl_load_file	dl_load_file (*filename*)
	Dynamically loads *filename*, which must be the path to a shared object or library; returns undef on error.

dl_undef_symbols

```
dl_undef_symbols
```

Returns list of symbol names that remain undefined after dl_load_ file, or ( ) if the names are unknown.

encoding

Although Perl 5.6.0 introduced Unicode support, it was not complete until Perl 5. 8. With *encoding.pm*, you can write any Perl script with whatever encoding type you want. If you're a show off and worship anime movies, and want to write your Perl program in Kanji, use encoding, and be our guest:

```perl
# Cute example, slightly modified from the encoding.pm doc
#!/usr/local/bin/perl -w

use encoding 'euc-jp'; # Note that we support only one encoding

my $book = 'Camel';
my $Rakuda = "\xF1\xD1\xF1\xCC"; # Camel in Kanji
$book =~ s/\bCamel\b/$Rakuda/;
```

English

Provides aliases for the Perl built-in special variables. Everything else about the variables and their use remains the same. Be aware, though, that using the English module significantly slows down a program for regular expressions.

Some of the Perl variables match some *awk* built-in variables. For those cases, you'll find two English names: a short version (which is the *awk* name) and a longer version. For example, you can use either $ERRNO (the *awk* name) or $OS_ ERROR to refer to the Perl variable $!.

Here is the list of variables and their English alternatives:

Perl	English	Perl	English
@_	@ARG	$?	$CHILD_ERROR
$_	$ARG	$!	$OS_ERROR
$%	$MATCH	$!	$ERRNO
$'	$PREMATCH	$@	$EVAL_ERROR
$'	$POSTMATCH	$$	$PROCESS_ID
$+	$LAST_PAREN_MATCH	$$	$PID
$.	$INPUT_LINE_NUMBER	$<	$REAL_USER_ID
$.	$NR	$<	$UID
$/	$INPUT_RECORD_SEPARATOR	$>	$EFFECTIVE_USER_ID
$/	$RS	$>	$EUID

Perl	English	Perl	English
$|	$OUTPUT_AUTOFLUSH	$(	$REAL_GROUP_ID
$,	$OUTPUT_FIELD_SEPARATOR	$(	$GID
$,	$OFS	$)	$EFFECTIVE_GROUP_ID
$\	$OUTPUT_RECORD_SEPARATOR	$)	$EGID
$\	$ORS	$0	$PROGRAM_NAME
$"	$LIST_SEPARATOR	$]	$PERL_VERSION
$;	$SUBSCRIPT_SEPARATOR	$^A	$ACCUMULATOR
$;	$SUBSEP	$^D	$DEBUGGING
$%	$FORMAT_PAGE_NUMBER	$^F	$SYSTEM_FD_MAX
$=	$FORMAT_LINES_PER_PAGE	$^I	$INPLACE_EDIT
$-	$FORMAT_LINES_LEFT	$^P	$PERLDB
$~	$FORMAT_NAME	$^T	$BASETIME
$^	$FORMAT_TOP_NAME	$^W	$WARNING
$:	$FORMAT_LINE_BREAK_CHARACTERS	$^X	$EXECUTABLE_NAME
$^L	$FORMAT_LINEFEED	$^O	$OSNAME

Env

Lets your program treat environment variables as simple variables instead of having to access them from the %ENV pseudo-hash where they are kept. (Note that pseudo-hashes will disappear as of Perl 6.)

```
use Env;
```

```
use Env qw(var1 var2 ...);
```

Internally, Env uses an import function that ties suitably named environment variables to global Perl variables with the same names. By default, it ties all variables yielded by keys %ENV. A "suitable" environment has a name that begins with an alphabetic character and contains only alphanumeric characters or underscores.

When use Env is invoked with arguments, the arguments are interpreted as a list of environment variables to tie, but the variables don't have to exist yet. After a variable has been tied, you can use it like a normal variable, accessing or changing its value.

You untie a variable by setting its value to undef.

Errno

Provides system errno constants from *errno.h* include file. Defines and conditionally exports all the error constants defined in *errno.h*. There is one export tag, :POSIX, which exports all POSIX-defined error numbers.

The file *Errno.pm* is automatically generated and shouldn't be updated. Any changes made to the file will be lost.

Exporter

Implements a default import method for other modules to inherit if they don't want to define their own. If you are writing a module, you can do the following:

```
package Module;
use Exporter ();
@ISA = qw(Exporter);

@EXPORT = qw(...);
@EXPORT_OK = qw(...);
%EXPORT_TAGS = (tag => [...]);
```

in which @EXPORT is a list of symbols to export by default, @EXPORT_OK is a list of symbols to export on request, and %EXPORT_TAGS is a hash that defines names for sets of symbols. Names in %EXPORT_TAGS must also appear in @EXPORT or @EXPORT_OK.

Then Perl programs that want to use your module just say:

```
use Module;              # Import default symbols
use Module qw(...);      # Import listed symbols
use Module ();           # Do not import any symbols
```

The Exporter can handle specialized import lists. An import list is the list of arguments passed to the import method. If the first entry begins with !, :, or /, the list is treated as a series of specifications that add to or delete from the list. A leading ! means delete, rather than add.

Symbol	Meaning
[!]name	This name only
[!]:DEFAULT	All names in @EXPORT
[!]:tag	All names in $EXPORT_TAGS{tag} anonymous list
[!]/pattern/	All names in @EXPORT and @EXPORT_OK that match pattern

Exporter's methods are the following.

---

export_fail   module_name->export_fail(failed_symbols)

Returns a list of symbols that couldn't be imported. The default method provided by Exporter returns the list unchanged.

---

export_ok_tags   export_ok_tags(taglist)

Adds tagged sets of symbols to @EXPORT_OK.

---

export_tags   export_tags(taglist)

Adds tagged sets of symbols to @EXPORT.

export_to_level   *package*->export_to_level(*n, what_to_export*)

Used when you can't use Exporter's import method directly. Takes the following arguments:

n
> An integer specifying how far up the calling stack to export your symbols

what_to_export
> Array of symbols to export, usually @_

import   import

The default import method.

require_version   *module_name*->require_version(*value*)

Validates the version of module *module_name*, checking that it is at least *value*.

ExtUtils::Command

Provided with the standard Win32 port to replace common Unix commands in MakeFiles. Includes subroutines for the following commands.

cat   cat *file...* [> *destination*]

Concatenates all specified files into *destination* file or to STDOUT.

chmod   chmod *mode files...*

Sets Unix-like permissions on all files specified. *mode* gives the permissions to set.

cp   cp *source... destination*

Copies a single source file *source* to *destination*. Multiple source files can be specified if *destination* is an existing directory.

eqtime   eqtime *source destination*

Sets the "modified time" of *destination* to that of *source*.

| **mkpath** | mkpath *directory...* |
| | Creates *directory*, including any parent directories. |

| **mv** | mv *source... destination* |
| | Moves sourcefile *source* to *destination*. Multiple sourcefiles are allowed if *destination* is an existing directory. |

| **rm_f** | rm_f *files....* |
| | Removes *files*, even if they are read-only. |

| **rm_rf** | rm_rf *directories....* |
| | Removes *directories* recursively, even if they are read-only. |

| **test_f** | test_f *file* |
| | Tests for the existence of *file*. |

| **touch** | touch *file....* |
| | Makes sure *file* exists and sets the current timestamp. |

Modules

ExtUtils::Command::MM

Sets commands for MakeMaker to use in Makefiles. ExtUtils::Command::MM encapsulates code that would otherwise have to be done with large one-liners. This module is shipped with the Perl 5.8 source kit.

Everything is read from @ARGV, unless otherwise noted. For example:

```
test_harness($verbose, @test_libs);
```

runs the tests on @ARGV via Test::Harness passing through the $verbose flag. Any @test_libs will be unshifted onto the test's @INC.

ExtUtils::Constant

Generates XS code to import C header constants, allowing Perl modules to AUTOLOAD constants defined in C library header files. Generally, you should not touch ExtUtils::Constant functions, since they are already implemented by *h2xs*.

For example:

```
use ExtUtils::Constant qw (WriteConstants);
WriteConstants(
    NAME => 'Nate',
    NAMES => [qw(Nate Nathan Nathaniel)], # not Nat
);
# Generates wrapper code to make the values of the constants
# Nate Nathan Nathaniel available to perl
```

Currently, this module understands the following types, although *h2xs* may only know a subset. The sizes of the numeric types are chosen by the *Configure* script at compile time.

IV

Signed integer. At least 32 bits.

UV

Unsigned integer. The same size as IV.

NV

Floating-point type. Probably double. Possibly long double.

PV NUL[L]

Terminated string. Length will be determined with strlen.

PVN

A fixed-length thing, given as a pointer, length pair. If you know the length of a string at compile time, you can use this instead of PV.

SV

A mortal SV.

YES

Truth (PL_sv_yes). The value is not needed (and is ignored).

NO

Defined falsehood (PL_sv_no). The value is not needed (and is ignored).

UNDEF

The value of the macro is not needed.

ExtUtils::Constant implements the following functions.

---

assign   assign *indent, type, pre, post, value* ...

Returns a suitable assignment clause. If *type* is aggregate (e.g., PVN expects both pointer and length), then there should be multiple *value*s for the components. *pre* and *post*, if defined, give snippets of C code to proceed and follow the assignment. *pre* is at the start of a block, so variables may be defined in it.

---

autoload   autoload *package, version, autoloader*

Generates the AUTOLOAD subroutine for the module *package*. *version* is the Perl version with which the code should be backwards-

compatible. It defaults to the version of Perl running the subroutine. If *autoloader* is true, the AUTOLOAD subroutine falls back on
AutoLoader::AUTOLOAD for all names that the constant() routine
doesn't recognize.

C_constant

C_constant *package, subname, default_type, types, indent,*
breakout, item ...

Returns a list of C subroutine definitions that return the value and
type of constants when passed the name by the XS wrapper. *item...*
gives a list of constant names. These can be strings, which are taken
as a C macro name, or references to a hash with the following keys:

name
> The name of the constant, as seen by the Perl code.

type
> The type of the constant (IV, NV, etc.).

value
> A C expression for the value of the constant, or a list of C
> expressions if the type is aggregate. Defaults to name if not
> given.

macro
> The C preprocessor macro to use in the #ifdef. Defaults to
> name and is primarily used if value is an enum. If a reference or
> an array is passed, then the first element is used in place of the
> #ifdef line, and the second element is used in place of the
> #endif. This allows preprocessor constructions such as:
>
> ```
> #if defined (foo)
> #if !defined (bar)
> ...
> #endif
> #endif
> ```
>
> which are used to determine if a constant will be defined.
>
> A macro of 1 signals that the constant is always defined, so the
> #if/#endif test is omitted.

default
> Default value to use (instead of croaking with "your vendor
> has not defined...) if the macro isn't defined. Specifies a refer-
> ence to an array with type followed by value(s).

pre
> C code to use before the assignment of the value of the
> constant. This allows you to use temporary variables to extract
> a value from part of a struct and return this as value. This C
> code is placed at the start of a block, so you can declare vari-
> ables in it.

post
> C code to place between the assignment of value (temporary) and the return from the function. This allows you to clear up anything in pre. Rarely needed.

def_pre
def_post
> Equivalents of pre and post for the default value.

utf8
> Generated internally. Is 0 or undefined if name is 7-bit ASCII, no if the name is 8-bit (and so should match only if SvUTF8() is false), and yes if the name is utf8-encoded.

---

constant_types   constant_types

Returns a single scalar with #define definitions for the constants used internally between the generated C and XS functions.

C_stringify   C_stringify *name*

Returns a 7-bit ASCII correctly \-escaped version of the string passed. Suitable for C "" or ''. It will die if passed Unicode characters.

---

dump_names   dump_names *default_type, types, indent, options, item* ...

An internal function to generate the embedded Perl code to regenerate the constant subroutines. *default_type*, *types*, and *items* are the same as for C_constant. *indent* is the number of spaces to indent. *options* is a hashref of options; currently, only declare_types is recognized. If the value is true, a *types* is always declared in the generated Perl code; if defined and false, one is never declared; and if undefined, *types* is declared only if the values in *types* as passed in cannot be inferred from *default_types* and the *items*.

---

memEQ_clause   memEQ_clause *name, checked_at, indent*

Returns a suitable C if statement to check whether *name* is equal to the C variable *name*. If *checked_at* is defined, then it is used to avoid memEQ for short names.

---

params   params *what*

An internal function. *what* should be a hashref of types the constant function will return. params returns a hashref keyed IV NV PV SV to show which combination of pointers will be needed in the C argument list.

---

perl_stringify	`perl_stringify` *name*
	Returns a 7-bit ASCII correctly \\-escaped version of the string passed. Suitable for a Perl "" string.
return_clause	`return_clause` *item, indent*
	Returns a suitable #ifdef clause. *item* is a hashref passed to `C_constant` and `match_clause`. *indent* is the number of spaces to indent; defaulting is 6.
switch_clause	`switch_clause` *indent, namelen, itemhash, item ...*
	An internal function to generate a suitable `switch` clause, called by `C_constant`. *items* are in the hashref format as given in the description of `C_constant` and must all have names of the same length, given by *namelen*. *itemhash* is a reference to a hash, keyed by name, with values as the hashrefs in the *item* list.
XS_constant	`XS_constant` *package, types, subname, c_subname*
	Generates the XS code to implement the Perl subroutine *package*::constant used by *package*::AUTOLOAD to load constants. This XS code is a wrapper around a C subroutine usually generated by `C_constant` and usually named `constant`
	types should be given either as a comma-separated list of types that the C subroutine constant will generate or as a reference to a hash. It should be the same list of types that `C_constant` was given. Otherwise, `XS_constant` and `C_constant` may have different ideas about the number of parameters passed to the C function constant.
	You can call the Perl visible subroutine something other than "constant" if you give the parameter *subname*. The C subroutine it calls defaults to the name of the Perl visible subroutine, unless you give the parameter *c_subname*.

ExtUtils::Embed

Generally called from the Makefile that builds your application to provide initialization functions for embedding Perl code in C or C++ applications. For example:

```
perl -MExtUtils::Embed -e xsinit
perl -MExtUtils::Embed -e ldopts
```

Uses the configuration information kept in *Config.pm* (see the Config module above). Exports the following functions.

ccdlflags	ccdlflags
	Prints $Config{ccdlflags}.
ccflags	ccflags
	Prints $Config{ccflags}.
ccopts	ccopts
	Combines perl_inc, ccflags, and ccdlflags.
ldopts	ldopts

Outputs arguments for linking the Perl library and extensions to your application. When invoked as:

```
perl -MExtUtils::Embed -e ldopts -
```

the following options are recognized:

–std

Outputs arguments for linking the Perl library and any extensions linked with the current Perl.

–I <path1:path2>

Search path for *ModuleName.a* archives. Default is @INC.

-- <list of linker args>

Additional linker arguments to be considered.

Any additional arguments found before the -- token are taken as the names of modules to generate code for. Can also be called with parameters:

```
'ldopts($std,[@modules],[@link_args],$path)'
```

When called this way, returns the argument string rather than printing it to STDOUT. The optional parameters are:

$std

Boolean, equivalent to the *–std* option.

[@modules]

Array reference. Equivalent to adding module names before the -- token.

[@link_args]

Array reference. Equivalent to adding linker arguments after the -- token.

$path

Equivalent to the *–I* option.

perl_inc

perl_inc

For including Perl header files. For example, if you say:

    perl -MExtUtils::Embed -eperl_inc

the module prints the following:

    -I$Config{archlibexp}/CORE

xsi_body

xsi_body (*modules*)

Returns string of calls to newXS that glue the module bootstrap function to boot_ModuleName for each module in *modules*.

xsi_header

xsi_header

Returns a string defining the same EXTERN_C macro as *perlmain. c*; also #includes *perl.h* and *EXTERN.h*.

xsinit

xsinit

Generates C/C++ code for the XS initializer function. When invoked as:

    perl -MExtUtils::Embed -e xsinit -

the following options are recognized:

−o [*filename*]
: Prints to the filename specified. Defaults to *perlxsi.c*. If *filename* is STDOUT, prints to standard output.

−std
: Writes code for extensions that are linked with the current Perl.

Any additional arguments are expected to be names of modules to generate code for. Can also be called with parameters:

    'xsinit($filename,$std,[@modules])'

When called this way, the following optional parameters are accepted:

$*filename*
: Equivalent to the *−o* option.

$std
: Boolean. Equivalent to the *−std* option.

[@*modules*]
: An array reference. Equivalent to adding module names after the -- token.

xsi_protos   xsi_protos (*modules*)

Returns string of boot_$ModuleName prototypes for each module in
modules.

ExtUtils::Install

Used by MakeMaker for handling the platform-dependent installation and dein-
stallation of modules; not meant to provide general-purpose tools. Exports the
following functions.

install   install (*hashref, verbose, nonono*)

Installs files. Takes the following arguments:

\\hashref
> Reference to a hash, in which each key is a directory to copy
> from and the value is the directory to copy into. The whole
> tree below the "from" directory is copied, with timestamps
> and permissions preserved.
>
> The hash has two additional keys: read and write. After
> copying everything, install writes the list of target files to the
> file named by $hashref->{write}. If there is another file named
> by $hashref->{read}, its contents are merged into the written
> file.

verbose
> Verbose switch.

nonono
> Don't-really-do-it switch.

install_default   install_default ([*fullext*])

Calls install with the same arguments as the MakeMaker defaults.
Takes zero or one argument. With no argument, it treats $ARGV[0]
as the argument. If present, the argument contains the value of
MakeMaker's FULLEXT key.

pm_to_blib   pm_to_blib (*hashref*[, *dir*])

Takes a hash reference as the first argument and copies all the keys
of the hash to the corresponding values. Filenames with the *.pm*
extension are autosplit. The optional second argument is the
autosplit directory.

uninstall   uninstall *(packlistfile, verbose, nonono)*

Uninstalls files. Takes the following arguments:

packlistfile
    Name of file containing filenames to be unlinked

verbose
    Verbose switch

nonono
    No-don't-really-do-it-now switch

ExtUtils::Installed

Provides inventory management for installed modules, based on the contents of the *.packlist* files that are created during installation. It also permits classifying the installed files and extracting directory information from the *.packlist* files.

new   *$inst* = ExtUtils::Installed->new( )

Searches for all installed *.packlists* on the system and stores their contents. Takes no parameters; uses ExtUtils::Packlist to read the *.packlist* files.

directories   *$inst*->directories(*module*[, *string*[, *dir*[,...]]])

Returns list of directories. Returns only directories that contain files from the specified module. Parameters are:

module
    Required. The name of a module; returns a list of all directories in the package.

string
    Optional. Possible values are prog, man, or all to return program directories, manual directories, or all directories, respectively.

dir
    Optional. One or more directories. If specified, only directories under the specified directories are returned.

directory_tree   *$inst*->directory_tree(*module*[, *string*[, *dir*[,...]]])

Like directories, but includes all intermediate directories.

files $inst->files(module[, string[, dir[,...]]])

Returns list of filenames. Parameters are:

module
> Required. The name of a module; returns a list of all file-names in the package. For a list of core files, use the special module name Perl.

string
> Optional. Possible values are prog, man, or all to return program files, manual files, or all files, respectively.

dir
> Optional. One or more directories. If specified, only filenames under the specified directories are returned.

---

modules $inst->modules()

Returns list of names of all the installed modules. Calls the Perl "core" by the special name Perl.

---

packlist $inst->packlist(module)

Returns the ExtUtils::Packlist object for the specified module.

---

validate $inst->validate(module[, arg])

Takes the name of a module as a required parameter and validates that all files listed in the packlist for the module actually exist. Returns list of any missing files. With an optional second argument that evaluates to true, removes missing files from *.packlist*.

---

version $inst->version(module)

Returns the version number of the specified module.

ExtUtils::Liblist

Used for building a Makefile for a Perl module. Takes a list of libraries and returns platform-appropriate lines that can be included in the Makefile.

```
require ExtUtils::Liblist;
ExtUtils::Liblist::ext($potential_libs[, $verbose]);
```

The input list $*potential_libs* is in the form *–llib1 –llib2 –llib3*. Additional library paths may be included in the form *–L/another/path*, which affects searches for all subsequent libraries. If the Boolean $verbose is specified, verbose output messages are provided. Returns a list of four scalar values:

EXTRALIBS
> List of libraries that need to be linked with *ld* when linking a Perl binary that includes a static extension

LDLOADLIBS
> List of static or dynamic libraries that can or must be linked when creating a shared library using *ld*

LD_RUN_PATH
> Colon-separated list of the directories in LDLOADLIBS

BSLOADLIBS
> List of libraries that are needed but can be linked in dynamically with the DynaLoader at runtime

The Win32 version (in the standard Perl distribution) is different from the Unix-OS/2 version in several ways:

- *−l* and *−L* are not required on the library and path specifications.
- Entries must be libraries, not plain object files.
- If $potential_libs is empty, the return value is also empty.
- The specified libraries can include both static and import libraries.
- LDLOADLIBS and EXTRALIBS are always identical; BSLOADLIBS and LD_ RUN_PATH are always empty.

ExtUtils::MakeMaker

Writes a Makefile for module installation. Provides a function, `WriteMakefile`, which creates an object with attributes that are set from various sources and that actually write the Makefile. See Chapter 2 for information about the using the Makefile and MakeMaker during module installation. This section explains the details of actually creating the Makefile with MakeMaker. It assumes an under-standing of *make* and Makefiles.

If you are a Perl programmer writing a module, you should run *h2xs* to generate the template for your module. Among other things, *h2xs* creates a file called *Makefile.PL*, and it's *Makefile.PL* that runs MakeMaker. On the other hand, if you are installing a module, you can usually just run the *Makefile.PL* that came with the module, perhaps adding a PREFIX argument if you are installing the module locally (see Chapter 2). In either case, you shouldn't need to run ExtUtils::Make-Maker directly unless you have special requirements.

A typical call to MakeMaker might look like this example from the CGI distribution:

```
use ExtUtils::MakeMaker;
WriteMakefile(
        NAME => "CGI",
        DISTNAME => "CGI-modules",
        VERSION => "2.76",
```

```
          linkext => { LINKTYPE => '' },
          dist => {COMPRESS=>'gzip -9f', SUFFIX => 'gz'},
);
```

MakeMaker attributes can be passed as arguments to WriteMakefile, as in the example, or they can be passed as *name=value* pairs on the command line:

```
perl Makefile.PL PREFIX=/home/mydir/Perl/Modules
```

To see what MakeMaker is doing, you can say:

```
perl Makefile.PL verbose
```

The following attributes can be specified:

C

Reference to array of *.c* filenames. Initialized from a directory scan and the values portion of the XS attribute hash. Not currently used by MakeMaker but may be handy in *Makefile.PLs*.

CCFLAGS

String to be included in the compiler call command line between the INC and OPTIMIZE arguments.

CONFIG

An array reference containing a list of attributes to get from %Config. The following values are always added to CONFIG:

```
ar        cc          cccdlflags   ccdlflags
dlext     dlsrc       ld           lddlflags
ldflags   libc        lib_ext      obj_ext
ranlib    sitelibexp  sitearchexp  so
```

CONFIGURE

Reference to a subroutine that should return a hash reference. The hash may contain further attributes that need to be determined by some evaluation method.

DEFINE

An attribute containing additional defines.

DIR

Reference to array of subdirectories containing *Makefile.PL* files.

DISTNAME

Your name for distributing the package (by *tar* file). Defaults to NAME, which is described below.

DL_FUNCS

Reference to a hash of symbol names for routines to be made available as universal symbols. Each key/value pair consists of the package name and an array of routine names in that package. Used only under AIX (export lists) and VMS (linker options) at present. Defaults to "$PKG" => ["boot_$PKG"].

DL_VARS

Array of symbol names for variables to be made available as universal symbols. Used only under AIX (export lists) and VMS (linker options) at present. Defaults to [].

EXCLUDE_EXT

Array of module names to exclude when doing a static build. Ignored if INCLUDE_EXT is present.

EXE_FILES

Reference to array of executable files to be copied to the INST_SCRIPT directory. *make realclean* deletes them from there.

NO_VC

If set, the Makefile does not check the current version of MakeMaker against the version the Makefile was built under. Should be used interactively, not written into your *Makefile.PL* file.

FIRST_MAKEFILE

Name of the Makefile to be produced. Defaults to the contents of MAKE-FILE, but can be overridden.

FULLPERL

Perl binary that can run this module.

H

Reference to array of *.h* filenames. Similar to C attribute.

IMPORTS

Used only on OS/2.

INC

Directories containing include files, in *–I* form. For example:

```
INC => "-I/usr/5include -I/path/to/inc"
```

INCLUDE_EXT

Array of module names to be included when doing a static build. If present, only those modules that are explicitly mentioned are used for the build (instead of all installed extensions). It is not necessary to mention Dyna-Loader or the current module when filling in INCLUDE_EXT—they are always included.

INSTALLARCHLIB

Used by *make install*, which copies files from INST_ARCHLIB to this directory if INSTALLDIRS is set to *perl*.

INSTALLBIN

Directory to install binary files into.

INSTALLDIRS

Determines which of the two sets of installation directories to choose. There are two possible values:

perl

Uses INSTALLLPRIVLIB and INSTALLARCHLIB directories.

site

The default. Uses INSTALLSITELIB and INSTALLSITEARCH directories.

INSTALLMAN1DIR

Directory where command manpages are put during *make install*. Defaults to $Config{installman1dir}.

INSTALLMAN3DIR

Directory where library manpages are put during *make install*. Defaults to $Config{installman3dir}.

INSTALLPRIVLIB

Used by *make install*, which copies files from INST_LIB to this directory if INSTALLDIRS is set to perl.

INSTALLSCRIPT

Used by *make install*, which copies files from INST_SCRIPT to this directory.

INSTALLSITELIB

Used by *make install*, which copies files from INST_LIB to this directory if INSTALLDIRS is set to site (the default).

INSTALLSITEARCH

Used by *make install*, which copies files from INST_ARCHLIB to this directory if INSTALLDIRS is set to site (the default).

INST_ARCHLIB

Same as INST_LIB for architecture-dependent files.

INST_BIN

Directory where real binary files are put during *make*, for later copying to INSTALLBIN during *make install*.

INST_EXE

Deprecated. Old name for INST_SCRIPT, which you should use instead.

INST_LIB

Directory to hold library files for this module while it is being built.

INST_MAN1DIR

Directory to hold the command manpages at *make* time.

INST_MAN3DIR

Directory to hold the library manpages at *make* time.

INST_SCRIPT

Directory where executable files should be installed during *make*. Defaults to *./blib/bin*, to have a dummy location during testing. *make install* copies the files in INST_SCRIPT to INSTALLSCRIPT.

LDFROM

Used by the *ld* command to specify the files to link/load from. Defaults to $(OBJECT).

LIBPERL_A

Filename of the Perl library that will be used with this module. Defaults to *libperl.a*.

LIB

> Can be set only when *Makefile.PL* is run; both INSTALLPRIVLIB and INSTALLSITELIB are set to the value of LIB.

LIBS

> Anonymous array of alternative library specifications to be searched for (in order) until at least one library is found. Note that any element of the array contains a complete set of arguments for the *ld* command.

LINKTYPE

> Should be used only to force static linking (see the *linkext* attribute below). Possible values are static or dynamic. Default is dynamic unless usedl=undef in *config.sh*.

MAKEAPERL

> Boolean. Tells MakeMaker to include the rules for making a Perl binary. Normally handled automatically by MakeMaker and not needed by the user.

MAKEFILE

> Name of the Makefile to be produced.

MAN1PODS

> Reference to a hash of pod-containing files to be converted to manpages and installed as requested at configure time. Default is all EXE_FILES files that include pod directives.

MAN3PODS

> Reference to a hash of *.pm* and *.pod* files to be converted to manpages and installed as requested at configure time. Default is all *.pod* and any *.pm* files that include pod directives.

MAP_TARGET

> Name for new Perl binary if one will be produced. Default is perl.

MYEXTLIB

> Name of library that the module builds and links to.

NAME

> Perl module name for this module (e.g., DBD::Oracle). Defaults to the directory name but should be explicitly defined in the *Makefile.PL*.

NEEDS_LINKING

> Boolean. Can be set to speed up MakeMaker processing a little bit, but not needed since MakeMaker will figure out if linking is needed.

NOECHO

> Controls *make*'s echo (@) feature. Defaults to @. By setting it to an empty string, you can generate a Makefile that echos all commands. Used mainly in debugging MakeMaker itself.

NORECURS

> Boolean. If set, inhibits descending into subdirectories.

OBJECT

> List of object files. Defaults to $(BASEEXT)$(OBJ_EXT); can be set to a long string containing all object files.

OPTIMIZE

If set to -g, turns debugging on. Defaults to -0. Passed to subdirectory *makes*.

PERL

Perl binary for tasks that can be done by miniperl.

PERLMAINCC

The call to the program that can compile *perlmain.c*. Defaults to $(CC).

PERL_LIB

Directory containing the Perl library to use.

PERL_ARCHLIB

Same as PERL_LIB for architecture-dependent files.

PERL_SRC

Directory containing the Perl source code. Avoid using this attribute, since it may be undefined.

PL_FILES

Reference to hash of files to be processed as Perl programs. By default, Make-Maker turns any *.PL* file it finds (except the *Makefile.PL*) into a key and the basename of the file into the value. The *.PL* files are expected to produce output to the target files themselves.

PM

Reference to hash of *.pm* and *.pl* files to be installed.

PMLIBDIRS

Reference to array of subdirectories containing library files. Defaults to ['lib', $(BASEEXT)]. The directories are scanned, and any files they contain are installed in the corresponding location in the library. A libscan method can be used to alter the behavior. Defining PM in the *Makefile.PL* overrides PMLIBDIRS.

PREFIX

Can be used to set the three INSTALL* attributes at once so they have PREFIX as a common directory node.

PREREQ_PM

Reference to a hash of modules that need to be available to run this module (e.g., Fcntl for SDBM_File). The name of each required module is the key, and the desired version is the value. If the required version is 0, MakeMaker just checks to see if any version is installed.

SKIP

Reference to an array specifying sections of the Makefile that shouldn't be written. Do not use the SKIP attribute for the negligible speedup, which may seriously damage the resulting Makefile.

TYPEMAPS

Reference to array of typemap filenames. Use when the typemaps are in a directory other than the current directory or when they are not named typemap. The last typemap in the list takes precedence, but a typemap in the current directory has highest precedence even if it isn't listed in TYPEMAPS. The default system typemap has lowest precedence.

VERSION

Your version number for the package. Defaults to `0.1`.

VERSION_FROM

Names a file for MakeMaker to parse to find the version number for the package, so you don't need to specify VERSION. The file must contain a single line to compute the version number. The first line in the file that contains the regular expression:

```
/([\$*])(([\w:\']*)\bVERSION)\b.*\=/
```

is evaluated with eval and the result assigned to VERSION.

XS

Reference to a hash of *.xs* files. MakeMaker defaults this. For example:

```
{'name_of_file.xs' => 'name_of_file.c'}
```

The *.c* files are automatically deleted by a *make clean*.

XSOPT

String of options to pass to *xsubpp*, which might include -C++ or -extern but not typemaps, which go in TYPEMAPS.

XSPROTOARG

May be set to an empty string, which is identical to -prototypes or -noprototypes. Defaults to the empty string.

XS_VERSION

Your version number for the package's *.xs* file. Defaults to the value of VERSION.

The following lowercase attributes can be used to pass parameters to the methods that implement the corresponding part of the Makefile:

clean

Extra files to clean.

depend

Extra dependencies.

dist

Distribution options.

dynamic_lib

Options for dynamic library support.

installpm

Installation options related to AutoSplit. Deprecated as of MakeMaker 5.23. See the *pm_to_blib* entry for ExtUtils::Install.

linkext

Linking style.

macro

Extra macros to define.

Modules

realclean
> Extra files to *make realclean*.

tool_autosplit
> Attributes for the tool_autosplit method.

If specifying attributes isn't sufficient to accomplish what you want, you can define your own subroutines in the *Makefile.PL* that return the text to be written to the Makefile. You can also override MakeMaker's subroutines (described in the section "ExtUtils::MM_Unix") this way.

ExtUtils::Manifest

Provides utilities for maintaining and using a MANIFEST file. The MANIFEST file is essentially a packing list, included with a module, so the user who installs the module can be sure that all the files are actually present. The file created by ExtUtils::Manifest is a list of filenames, one per line, with an optional comment on each line.

ExtUtils::Manifest optionally uses a file called MANIFEST.SKIP, which contains regular expressions specifying files that are not to be included in MANIFEST. Manifest also defines two global variables that are used by several of the functions:

$ExtUtils::Manifest::MANIFEST
> The name of the MANIFEST file. Changing the value results in different MANIFEST and different MANIFEST.SKIP files. Default is MANIFEST.

$ExtUtils::Manifest::Quiet
> If true, the functions work silently. Default is 0.

Provides six functions, which are exportable on request.

---

filecheck   filecheck

> Finds files below the current directory that are not mentioned in the MANIFEST file. Consults MANIFEST.SKIP for files that shouldn't be included.

---

fullcheck   fullcheck

> Does both manicheck and filecheck.

---

manicheck   manicheck

> Checks whether all files in current directory's MANIFEST file really exist.

manicopy   manicopy *(read, target, how)*

Copies files to a target directory. Takes the following arguments:

read
> Hash with keys that are the names of the files to be copied. Typically returned by maniread.

target
> Target directory into which files are to be copied.

how
> Can be used to specify a different method of "copying." Values are:
>
> cp
>> Copy the files.
>
> ln
>> Create hard links.
>
> best
>> Link the files, but copy any symbolic link to make a tree with no symbolic links (the default).

manifind   manifind

Returns a hash reference whose keys are the files found below the current directory. The values are null strings, representing the MANIFEST comments that aren't there.

maniread   maniread *([file])*

Reads the MANIFEST file specified in $*file* (the default is MANIFEST). Returns a hash reference whose keys are the filenames and whose values are the comments. Discards blank lines and lines starting with #.

mkmanifest   mkmanifest

Writes the names of all files in and below the current directory to the file in the current directory named in the $ExtUtils::Manifest::MANIFEST variable. Skips files in MANIFEST.SKIP.

skipcheck   skipcheck

Lists files that were skipped because they were found in MANIFEST.SKIP.

ExtUtils::Miniperl

Generates a file, *perlmain.c*, that contains the bootstrap code to make the modules associated with the libraries available from within Perl. ExtUtils::Miniperl itself is generated automatically from a script called *minimod.PL* when Perl is built; typically, it is used from within a Makefile generated by ExtUtils::MakeMaker rather than being called directly. The module exports one subroutine.

writemain	writemain (*dirs*)
	Takes an argument list of directories that contain archive libraries needed by Perl modules and writes the file to be compiled as *perlmain.c* to STDOUT.

ExtUtils::Mkbootstrap

Typically called from a module's Makefile. It writes a **.bs* file that is needed by some architectures to do dynamic loading.

```
use ExtUtils::Mkbootstrap;
mkbootstrap();
```

ExtUtils::Mksymlists

Produces option files used by some operating systems' linkers during creation of shared libraries for dynamic extensions. Normally called from a Makefile when a module is built; it exports one function.

Mksymlists	Mksymlists (*varlist*)
	Creates the linker option file. The *varlist* argument is a list of key/value pairs. For example:

```
use ExtUtils::Mksymlists;
Mksymlists({ NAME    => $name,
             DL_VARS => [$var1, $var2, $var3],
             DL_FUNCS => [$pkg1 => [$func1, $func2],
                          $pkg2 => [$func3]]});
```

Valid keys are:

DLBASE
> The name by which the linker knows the module. If not specified, it is derived from the NAME attribute. Currently used only by OS/2.

DL_FUNCS
> Identical to the MakeMaker DL_FUNCS attribute and usually taken from it. Its value is a reference to a hash, in which each

key is a package name, and each value is a reference to an array of function names to be exported by the module.

DL_VARS

Identical to the MakeMaker DL_VARS attribute, and usually taken from it. Its value is a reference to an array of variable names to be exported by the extension.

FILE

The name of the linker option file (minus the OS-specific extension) if you don't want to use the default value (the last word of the NAME attribute).

FUNCLIST

An alternate way of specifying function names to be exported from the module. Its value is a reference to an array of function names to be exported, which are passed unaltered to the linker options file.

NAME

The name of the module for which the linker option file is to be produced. Should always be specified.

ExtUtils::MM

ExtUtils::MM is an OS-adjusted ExtUtils::MakeMaker subclass. For internal use only. For example:

```
require ExtUtils::MM;
my $mm = MM->new(...);
```

ExtUtils::MM_Any

Performs platform-agnostic MM methods. ExtUtils::MM_Any is a superclass for the ExtUtils::MM_ set of modules. For internal use only.

ExtUtils::MM_BeOS

Provides methods to override Unix behavior in ExtUtils::MakeMaker. Essentially, this module works the same way as ExtUtils::MM_Unix, but allows override for BeOS. For internal use only.

ExtUtils::MM_DOS

Provides methods to override Unix behavior in ExtUtils::MakeMaker. Essentially, this module works the same way as ExtUtils::MM_Unix, but allows override for MS-DOS. For internal use only.

ExtUtils::MM_NW5

Provides methods to override Unix behavior in ExtUtils::MakeMaker. Essentially, this module works in the same way as ExtUtils::MM_Unix, but allows override for Netware 5. For internal use only.

ExtUtils::MM_OS2

Provides methods for use with MakeMaker for OS2 systems. Used internally by MakeMaker if needed. (See ExtUtils::MM_Unix for documentation of the methods provided there.) Overrides the implementation of the methods, not the interface.

ExtUtils::MM_Unix

Provides methods for MakeMaker to handle portability issues. You never need to require this module, but you might want to if you are working on improving MakeMaker's portability

Provides methods for both Unix and non-Unix systems; on non-Unix systems, they can be overridden by methods defined in other MM_* modules. The methods are the following.

---

catdir   catdir *list*

Concatenates a list of directory names to form a complete path ending with a directory. On Unix, joins the names with /.

---

catfile   catfile *list*

Concatenates one or more directory names and a filename to form a complete path ending with a filename. On Unix, joins the names with /.

---

dir_target   dir_target *array*

Takes an array of required directory names and returns a *Makefile* entry to create an *.exists* file in the directories. Returns nothing if the entry has already been processed.

---

file_name_is_absolute

file_name_is_absolute *filename*

Takes a path as argument and returns true if it is an absolute path.

---

find_perl	find_perl *version*, *names*, *dirs*, *trace*
	Searches for an executable Perl. Takes the following arguments:
	version The executable must be at least the version given by *version*.

	names
	    Array reference. The name of the executable must be an entry
	    in the array.

	dirs
	    Array reference. The executable must be in a directory that is
	    one of the entries in the array.

	trace If true, prints debugging information.

Modules

guess_name	guess_name
	Guesses the name of the package based on the working directory's name. Called only if the NAME attribute is missing.

has_link_code	has_link_code
	Returns true if there are C, XS, MYEXTLIB, or similar objects in this object that need a compiler. Does not descend into subdirectories.

libscan	libscan *filename*
	Uses init_dirscan to find a file; returns false if the file should not be included in the library. Used primarily to keep revision-control directories from being installed.

lsdir	lsdir *dir*, *regexp*
	Returns all entries in the specified directory that match the regular expression. Takes the following arguments:
	dir Name of the directory
	regexp Regular expression to match the entries against

maybe_command

maybe_command *filename*

Returns true if *filename* is likely to be a command.

maybe_command_in_dirs

maybe_command_in_dirs

For future use.

needs_linking

needs_linking

Returns true if the module needs linking. Searches subdirectories.

nicetext

nicetext *target*

The MM_Unix version returns the argument with no processing.

path

path

Returns PATH environment variable as an array.

perl_script

perl_script *filename*

Returns true if *filename* is likely to be a Perl script. With MM_ Unix, this is true for any ordinary, readable file.

prefixify

prefixify *attrname, oldprefix, newprefix*

Processes a path attribute in $self->{ *attrname* }. Looks up the attribute in %Config if it doesn't have a value. Takes the following arguments:

attrname
: Name of the attribute to be processed

oldprefix
: Prefix to be replaced

newprefix
: New prefix, replaced in-place

replace_manpage_separator

replace_manpage_separator *filename*

Takes the filename of a package and replaces the subdirectory delimiter (/ in Unix) with ::. Returns the altered name.

Methods to Produce the Makefile

ExtUtils::MM_Unix has some additional methods that are called in sequence to produce a Makefile. The list of methods is specified in the array

@ExtUtils::MakeMaker::MM_Sections, one method per section. The routines are all called the same way and so are just listed here. Each method returns the string to be put into its section of the *Makefile*.

The methods are called in the order that they are listed in the following table, reading down the columns:

post_initialize	top_targets	realclean
const_config	linkext	dist_basics
constants	dlsyms	dist_core
const_loadlibs	dynamic	dist_dir
const_cccmd	dynamic_bs	dist_test
tool_autosplit	dynamic_lib	dist_ci
tool_xsubpp	static	install
tools_other	static_lib	force
dist	installpm	perldepend
macro	installpm_x	makefile
depend	manifypods	staticmake
post_constants	processPL	test
pasthru	installbin	test_via_harness
c_o	subdirs	test_via_script
xs_c	subdir_x	postamble
xs_o	clean	

Finally, there are two special methods: post_initialize and postamble. They each return an empty string by default and can be defined in *Makefile.PL* to insert customized text near the beginning or end of the *Makefile*.

ExtUtils::MM_UWIN

Provides methods to override Unix behavior in ExtUtils::MakeMaker. Essentially, this module works the same way as ExtUtils::MM_Unix, but allows override for the U/WIN emulator. For internal use only.

ExtUtils::MM_VMS

Provides methods for use with MakeMaker for VMS systems. Used internally by MakeMaker if needed. (See ExtUtils::MM_Unix for documentation of the methods provided there.) Overrides the implementation of the methods, not the interface.

ExtUtils::MM_Win32

Provides methods for use with MakeMaker for Win32 systems. Used internally by MakeMaker in the standard Win32 Perl distribution if needed. (See ExtUtils::MM_Unix for a documentation of the methods provided there.) Overrides the implementation of these methods, not the interface.

catfile	catfile
	Concatenates one or more directory names and a filename to form a complete path, ending with a filename.

constants	constants
	Initializes constants, .SUFFIXES, and .PHONY.

dynamic_bs	dynamic_bs
	Defines targets for bootstrap files.

dynamic_lib	dynamic_lib
	Defines how to produce the *.so (or equivalent) files.

canonpath	canonpath
	Performs a logical cleanup of a path.

dist_ci	dist_ci
	Changes command-line quoting (same as MM_Unix version).

dist_core	dist_core
	Changes command-line quoting (same as MM_Unix version).

manifypods	manifypods
	Disables manpage process.

pasthru	pasthru
	Defines the string that is passed to recursive *make* calls in subdirectories.

perl_script	perl_script *filename*
	Takes one argument, a filename, and returns the filename if the argument is likely to be a Perl script.

pm_to_blib	pm_to_blib
	Defines a target that copies all files in the hash PM to their destination and autosplits them. See ExtUtils::Install.

static_lib	static_lib
	Defines how to produce the *.a* (or equivalent) files.

test_via_harness	test_via_harness
	Helper method to write the test targets.

tool_autosplit	tool_autosplit
	Use Win32-style quoting on command line.

tools_other	tools_other
	Win32 overrides. Defines SHELL, LD, TOUCH, CP, MV, RM_F, RM_RF, CHMOD, and UMASK_NULL in the Makefile. Also defines the Perl programs MKPATH, WARN_IF_OLD_PACK-LIST, MOD_INSTALL, DOC_INSTALL, and UNINSTALL.

top_targets	top_targets
	Defines the targets all, subdirs, config, and O_FILES.

xs_o	xs_o
	Defines suffix rules to go from XS to object files directly.

ExtUtils::MY

Allows ExtUtils::MakeMaker subclass for customization. For internal use only.

ExtUtils::Packlist

Manages *.packlist* files. Supports an extended *.packlist* format. The original format is a list of absolute pathnames, one pathname per line. In the extended format, each line can also contain a list of attributes as key/value pairs, which are used by the *installperl* script. For example:

```
/usr/local/bin/perl from=/usr/local/pbeta/bin/perl5.005 type=link
/usr/local/bin/perl5.005 type=file
/usr/local/lib/perl5/5.005/AnyDBM_File.pm type=file
```

Also see ExtUtils::Installed.

new $pl = ExtUtils::Packlist->new([*plfile*])

Constructor. Takes the name of a *.packlist* as the optional parameter and returns a reference to a hash that has an entry for each line
in the *.packlist*. The value associated with each key is undef for
oldstyle *.packlists*. For files in the extended format, the value for
each key is a hash containing the key/value pairs on the line associated with that key.

packlist_file $pl->packlist_file( )

Returns the name of the associated *.packlist* file.

read $pl->read([*plfile*])

Reads the *.packlist* specified by the *plfile* parameter if given;
otherwise, reads the file associated with $pl. Calls Carp::croak if
the file doesn't exist.

validate $pl->validate([*arg*])

Checks that each file in the *.packlist* exists. An optional argument
can be specified; if the argument is present and evaluates to true,
missing files are removed from the internal hash. Returns a list of
missing files, or an empty list if the files all exist.

write $pl->write([*plfile*])

Writes to a *.packlist*. Optionally takes the name of the *.packlist* to
be written; otherwise, overwrites the *.packlist* associated with $pl.
If the value associated with a hash key is a scalar, the entry written
to the *.packlist* is a simple filename. If the value is a hash, the entry
written is the filename followed by the key/value pairs from the
hash.

ExtUtils::testlib

Used for testing a module after it's been built and before it's been installed, when
you don't want to (or can't) run *make test*. Adding:

```
use ExtUtils::testlib;
```

to your test program causes the intermediate directories used by *make* to be added
to @INC, allowing you to run the test.

Fatal

Provides a way to replace functions that return false on failure with equivalents that die instead, so you can use the functions without having to test the return values explicitly. Fatal reports errors via die; you can trap them with $SIG{__DIE__} if you want to take action before the program exits. You can use Fatal for both user-defined functions and Perl core operators except exec and system.

import	import Fatal *function*
	Wraps *function* in an equivalent function that will die on failure.

Fcntl

A translation of the C *fcntl.h* program that uses *h2xs* (which builds a Perl extension from a C header file) and the C compiler to translate #define symbols and make them available as functions. Exports the following routines by default; each routine returns the value of the #define that is the same as the routine name:

FD_CLOEXEC	F_DUPFD	F_GETFD	F_GETFL	F_GETLK
F_RDLCK	F_SETFD	F_SETFL	F_SETLK	F_SETLKW
F_UNLCK	F_WRLCK	O_APPEND	O_CREAT	O_EXCL
O_NDELAY	O_NOCTTY	O_NONBLOCK	O_RDONLY	O_RDWR
O_TRUNC	O_WRONLY			

fields

Pragma that provides the ability to define class fields at compile time by updating the %FIELDS hash in the calling package. The %FIELDS hash is set up at compile time as well; use the base pragma to copy fields from base classes, and then fields to add new fields. Lets you have objects with named fields that are as compact and fast as arrays to access. For more details, see the *fields* manpage and the pseudo-hash section of the *perlref* manpage.

File::Basename

Parses a file's path, returning its three component pieces: the path to the file, the file's basename, and the file's extension. For example, for:

    /usr/local/lib/perl5/SelectSaver.pm

the path is */usr/local/lib/perl5*, the basename is *SelectSaver*, and the extension is .*pm*. File::Basename exports the following functions.

basename	basename (*fullname*[, *suffixlist*])

Returns the first element of the list that would be produced if you called fileparse with the same arguments. Provides compatibility with the Unix *basename* command. Takes the following arguments:

fullname
> Input file specification

suffixlist
> Optional list containing patterns to be matched against the end of *fullname* to find the suffix

dirname	dirname (*fullname*)

Returns the directory portion of the input file specification. *fullname* is the input file specification.

fileparse	fileparse (*fullname*[, *suffixlist*])

Divides a file specification into its three parts, returning them in this order: filename, path, suffix.

```
($name, $path, $suffix) = fileparse($fullname,
@suffixlist)
```

The arguments are the same as for basename.

fileparse_set_fstype

fileparse_set_fstype (*os-string*)

Called before the other routines to select the appropriate file specification syntax for your operating system, to be used in future File::Basename calls. Currently valid values for *os-string* (the operating system) are VMS, MSWin32, MSDOS, AmigaOS, os2, RISCOS, and MacOS. Uses Unix syntax by default.

File::CheckTree

Runs file tests on a set of files. Exports one function, validate, which takes a single multiline string as input. Each line of the string contains a filename plus a test to run on the file. The test can be followed with || die to make it a fatal error if it fails. The default is || warn. Prepending ! to the test reverses the sense of the test. You can group tests (e.g., -rwx); only the first failed test of the group produces a warning. For example:

```
use File::CheckTree;
$warnings += validate( q{
    /vmunix             -e || die
```

```
    /bin            cd
        csh         !-ug
        sh          -ex
    /usr            -d || warn "What happened to $file?\n"
});
```

Available tests include all the standard Perl file-test operators except *–t*, *–M*, *–A*, and *–C*. Unless it dies, validate returns the number of warnings issued.

File::Compare

Compares the contents of two sources, each of which can be a file or a filehandle. Returns 0 if the sources are equal, 1 if they are unequal, and -1 on error. File::Compare provides two functions.

---

cmp   cmp (*file1*, *file2*[, *buffsize*])

                           cmp is a synonym for compare. Exported on request.

---

compare   compare (*file1*, *file2*[, *buffsize*])

                           Compares *file1* to *file2*. Exported by default. If present, *buffsize* specifies the size of the buffer to use for the comparison.

File::Copy

Copies or moves files or filehandles from one location to another. Returns 1 on success, 0 on failure, or sets $! on error.

---

copy   copy (*source*, *dest*[, *buffsize*])

                           Copies *source* to *dest*. Takes the following arguments:

                           source
                               The source string, FileHandle reference, or FileHandle glob. If *source* is a filehandle, it is read from; if it's a filename, the filehandle is opened for reading.

                           dest
                               The destination string, FileHandle reference, or FileHandle glob. *dest* is created if necessary and written to.

                           buffsize
                               Specifies the size of the buffer to be used for copying. Optional.

cp	cp (*source, dest*[, *buffsize*])
	Like copy, but exported only on request: use File::Copy "cp"
move	move (*source, dest*)
	Moves *source* to *dest*. If the destination exists and is a directory, and the source is not a directory, then the source file is renamed into the directory specified by *dest*. Return values are the same as for copy.
mv	mv (*source, dest*)
	Like move, but exported only on request: use File::Copy "mv"

File::DosGlob

Provides a portable enhanced DOS-like globbing for the standard Perl distribution. DosGlob lets you use wildcards in directory paths, is case-insensitive, and accepts both backslashes and forward slashes (although you may have to double the backslashes). Can be run three ways:

- From a Perl script:

```
require 5.004
use File::DosGlob 'glob';

@perlfiles = glob  "..\pe?l/*.p?";
print <..\pe?l/*.p?>;
```

- With the *perl* command, on the command line:

```
# From the command line (overrides only in main::)
% perl -MFile::DosGlob=glob -e "print <../pe*/*p?>"
```

- With the *perlglob.bat* program on the DOS command line:

```
% perlglob ../pe*/*p?
```

When invoked as a program from the command line, File::DosGlob prints null-separated filenames to STDOUT.

File::Find

Looks for files that match a particular expression. Exports two functions.

find
find (\&wanted, dir1[, dir2 ...])

Works like the Unix *find* command; traverses the specified directories, looking for files that match the expressions or actions you specify in a subroutine called wanted, which you must define. For example, to print out the names of all executable files, you could define wanted this way:

```
sub wanted {
    print "$File::Find::name\n" if -x;
}
```

Provides the following variables:

$File::Find::dir
> Current directory name ($_ has the current filename in that directory).

$File::Find::name
> Contains $File::Find::dir/$_. You are *chdir*ed to $File::Find::dir when find is called.

$File::Find::prune
> If true, find does not descend into any directories.

$File::Find::dont_use_nlink
> Set this variable if you're using the Andrew File System (AFS).

finddepth
finddepth (\wanted, dir1[, dir2...])

Like find, but does a depth-first search.

The standard Perl distribution comes with a Perl script, *find2perl*, which takes a Unix *find* command and turns it into a wanted subroutine.

File::Path

Creates and deletes multiple directories with specified permissions. Exports two methods.

mkpath
mkpath (*path, bool, perm*)

Creates a directory path and returns a list of all directories created. Takes the following arguments:

path
> Name of the path or reference to a list of paths to create.

bool
> Boolean. If true, mkpath prints the name of each directory as it is created. Default is false.

perm	
	Numeric mode indicating the permissions to use when creating the directories. Default is 0777.

rmtree	rmtree (*root, prt, skip*)
	Deletes subtrees from the directory structure, returning the number of files successfully deleted. Symbolic links are treated as ordinary files. Takes the following arguments:

root

Root of the subtree to delete or reference to a list of roots. The roots, and all files and directories below each root, are deleted.

prt

Boolean. If true, rmtree prints a message for each file, with the name of the file and whether it's using rmdir or unlink to remove it (or if it's skipping the file). Default is false.

skip

Boolean. If true, rmtree skips any files to which you do not have delete access (under VMS) or write access (under other operating systems). Default is false.

File::Spec

Performs common operations on file specifications in a portable way. To do this, it automatically loads the appropriate operating system–specific module, which is one of File::Spec::Mac, File::Spec::OS2, File::Spec::Unix, File::Spec::VMS, or File::Spec::Win32. The complete reference of available functions is given in File::Spec::Unix; the functions are inherited by the other modules and overridden as necessary. Subroutines should be called as class methods, rather than directly.

File::Spec::Cygwin

Implements methods for Cygwin file specs. You do not need to call this module. It is called internally by File::Spec.

File::Spec::Mac

File::Spec for MacOS.

canonpath	File::Spec->canonpath
	Nothing to do; returns what it's given.

catdir	`File::Spec->catdir(dir[, dir...])`
	Concatenates two or more directory names to form a complete path. Ends with a directory name and appends a trailing : if there isn't one. You can get a relative path by either beginning the first argument with : or putting "" as the first argument.

catfile	`File::Spec->catfile(dir[, dir...], file)`
	Concatenates one or more directory names and a filename to form a complete path that ends with a filename. Uses `catdir`.

curdir	`File::Spec->curdir`
	Returns string representing the current directory.

file_name_is_absolute	
	`File::Spec->file_name_is_absolute(path)`
	Takes a path as argument and returns true if it is an absolute path.

path	`File::Spec->path`
	Returns null list for MacPerl applications, or `$ENV{Commands}`, suitably split, for the MacPerl tool under MPW.

rootdir	`File::Spec->rootdir`
	Returns string representing the root directory. Under MacPerl, returns the name of the startup volume.

updir	`File::Spec->updir`
	Returns string representing the parent directory.

File::Spec::OS2

File::Spec for OS/2. Overrides the implementation of the File::Spec::Unix methods, but not the interface.

File::Spec::Unix

File::Spec for Unix. Provides methods for File::Spec to use in manipulating file specifications.

canonpath	`File::Spec->canonpath`
	Does logical cleanup of path.

catdir	`File::Spec->catdir(`*`dir`*`[, `*`dir`*`...])`
	Concatenates two or more directory names to form a complete path. Ends with a directory name.

catfile	`File::Spec->catfile(`*`dir`*`[, `*`dir`*`...], file)`
	Concatenates one or more directory names and a filename to form a complete path that ends with a filename.

curdir	`File::Spec->curdir`
	Returns ., representing the current directory.

file_name_is_absolute	
	`File::Spec->file_name_is_absolute(`*`path`*`)`
	Takes a path as argument and returns true if it is an absolute path.

join	`File::Spec->join(`*`dir`*`[, `*`dir`*`...], `*`file`*`)`
	Same as `catfile`.

no_upwards	`File::Spec->no_upwards(`*`files`*`)`
	Strips names of files referring to a parent directory from a list of filenames. Doesn't strip symbolic links.

path	`File::Spec->path`
	Returns the PATH environment variable as an array.

rootdir	`File::Spec->rootdir`
	Returns /, representing the root directory.

updir	`File::Spec->updir`
	Returns .., representing the parent directory.

File::Spec::VMS

File::Spec for VMS. Overrides the implementation of the File::Spec::Unix methods, but not the interface.

---

catdir   `File::Spec->catdir(dirspecs)`

Concatenates a list of directories and returns the result as a VMS-syntax directory specification.

---

catfile   `File::Spec->catfile(filespecs)`

Concatenates a list of file specifications and returns the result as a path.

---

curdir   `File::Spec->curdir`

Returns string representing the current directory.

---

file_name_is_absolute

`File::Spec->file_name_is_absolute(path)`

Takes a path as argument and returns true if it is an absolute path. Checks for VMS directory specification as well as Unix separators.

---

path   `File::Spec->path`

Translates the logical name DCL$PATH as a searchlist.

---

rootdir   `File::Spec->rootdir`

Returns string representing the root directory.

---

updir   `File::Spec->updir`

Returns string representing the parent directory.

File::Spec::Win32

File::Spec for Win32. Overrides the implementation of the File::Spec::Unix methods, but not the interface.

canonpath	`File::Spec->canonpath`
	Performs logical cleanup of a path; doesn't physically check the filesystem.

catfile	`File::Spec->catfile(dir[, dir...], file)`
	Concatenates one or more directory names and a filename to form a complete path that ends with a filename.

File::stat

Provides the same file status information as the Perl functions stat and lstat. Exports two functions that return File::stat objects. The objects have methods that return the equivalent fields from the Unix *stat(2)* call:

Field	Meaning
dev	Device number of filesystem
ino	Inode number
mode	File mode
nlink	Number of links to the file
uid	Numeric user ID of owner
gid	Numeric group ID of owner
rdev	Device identifier
size	Size of file, in bytes
atime	Last access time
mtime	Last modified time
ctime	Inode change time
blksize	Preferred blocksize for filesystem I/O
blocks	Number of blocks allocated

You can access the status fields either with the methods or by importing the fields into your namespace with the :FIELDS import tag and then accessing them by prepending st_ to the field name (e.g., $st_mode). Here are examples of doing it both ways:

```
use File::stat;

$stats = stat($file);
print $stats->uid;
print $st_uid;
```

| **lstat** | lstat (*file*) |
| | Returns the same information as stat, but if *file* is a symbolic link, returns the status information for the link. |

| **stat** | stat (*file*) |
| | Returns status information for the file or filehandle pointed to by *file*. If *file* is a symbolic link, returns the information for the file that the link points to. |

File::Temp

File::Temp can be used to create and open temporary files safely. The tempfile( ) function returns the name and the open filehandle of a temporary file. The tempdir( ) function creates a temporary directory. File::Temp guarantees that race conditions cannot occur since it returns both a filehandle and filename. In addition, File::Temp checks for safe file and directory permissions, so the sticky bits are checked for group-writable directories. To write a temp file into */tmp* (default), you would do something like the following:

```
#!/usr/local/bin/perl -w

use File::Temp qw(tempfile);

my($fh, $filename) = tempfile( );

print "opening $filename for writing...\n";
print $fh "some data ...\n";
```

FileCache

Closes and reopens files as necessary so you can always write to a file even if you already have the maximum number of files open. Exports one function.

| **cacheout** | cacheout (*path*) |
| | Makes sure the file at *path* is created and accessible through the filehandle also named *path*. You don't need to invoke cacheout between successive accesses to the same file. |

FileHandle

Provides object methods for working with filehandles. Provides the following methods.

---

new $fh = new FileHandle [filename[, mode]]

Constructor. Creates a FileHandle, which is a reference to a newly created symbol. The optional parameters, filename and mode, are passed to open. The FileHandle object is returned if the open succeeds; otherwise, it is destroyed.

---

new_from_fd $fh = new_from_fd FileHandle fd, mode

Constructor. Creates a FileHandle, but it takes the file descriptor, fd, instead of filename as a parameter, along with mode; the parameters are required.

---

fdopen $fh->fdopen fdname [openmode]

Like open, except that its first parameter is not a filename but a filehandle name, a FileHandle object, or a file descriptor number.

---

getpos $pos = $fh->getpos

If the C functions fgetpos(3) and fsetpos(3) are available, getpos returns the current position, $pos, of the FileHandle.

---

open $fh->open filename [openmode]

Takes filename and, optionally, the open mode, and opens a file. If the mode is present, it can be in Perl form (e.g., >, +<) or in POSIX form (e.g., w, r+).

---

setpos $fh->setpos pos

Uses the value (pos) returned by getpos to restore a previous position of the FileHandle.

---

setvbuf $fh->setvbuf(params)

Takes the same parameters as the C function setvbuf(3) and uses the C function to set the buffering policy for the FileHandle.

The following additional FileHandle methods act as front-ends for the corresponding built-in Perl functions (see the O'Reilly book *Programming Perl* or the *perlfunc* manpage for more details):

clearerr	getc
close	gets
eof	seek
fileno	tell

The next group of FileHandle methods correspond to Perl special variables (see *Programming Perl* or the *perlvar* manpage):

autoflush	format_page_number
format_formfeed	format_top_name
format_line_break_characters	input_line_number
format_lines_left	input_record_separator
format_lines_per_page	output_field_separator
format_name	output_record_separator

Finally, the following methods are useful:

$*fh*->print
> See Perl's built-in print function.

$*fh*->printf
> See Perl's built-in printf function.

$*fh*->getline
> Works like Perl's <FILEHANDLE> construct, except that it can be safely called in an array context (but it still returns just one line).

$*fh*->getlines
> Works like Perl's <FILEHANDLE> construct when called in an array context to read all remaining lines in a file.

Filter::Simple

Source filtering is a nice feature of newer versions of Perl (5.6 and later) because it allows the programmer to write extensions to the Perl language without tampering with the Perl source code itself. That is, you can create a macro language out of Perl.

Filter::Simple is based on Filter:Util::Call, but simplifies the means by which you can begin doing your own source filtering with Perl. Filter::Simple ships with the Perl 5.8 source kit.

Using Filter::Simple is, well, easy. Basically, Filter::Simple implements FILTER { ... }, which you can use to handle many of your simple source-filtering needs. Let's say that you want a good glass of ale, and you decide that you don't want

Perl to print, but pint instead. You can implement something like the following with Filter::Simple. First, create a module called Print_to_Pint:

```
package Print_to_Pint;

use Filter::Simple;
FILTER { s/pint/print/g; }

# true
1;
```

Now, use Print_to_Pint to do something with pint:

```
#!/usr/local/bin/perl -w

use Print_to_Pint;

my $bottles = 99;
my $last = 1;

foreach my $bottle (reverse($last .. $bottles)) {
    pint "$bottle -> burp\n";
}
```

By default, Filter::Simple ignores no behavior, i.e., it stops filtering after a no Module is encountered. You can alter this behavior by passing another argument to use Filter::Simple or to FILTER { ... }. For example:

```
package Print_to_Pint;
use Filter::Simple;
    FILTER {
        s/pint/print/g;
}
"";
```

Filter::Simple also supports FILTER_ONLY, which allows you to support multiple filters to handle different parts of your source code. FILTER_ONLY takes several subroutines as options: code, executable, string, regex, quotelike, and all. code or executable filters all Perl code, except Pod or __DATA__ types. quotelike filters other Perl quotelike stuff, including here documents. string filters all string-related parts. regex filters all pattern-literal parts of quotelike.

For example, the following module will skip all incidences of Pod in the PodSucks module:

```
package PodSucks;

use Filter::Simple;

FILTER_ONLY
    executable => sub { s/x/X/g },
    executable => sub { print }

# True. True.
1;
```

The above code might not make that much sense, but take a look at the test program now, and it should become clear:

```perl
#!/usr/local/bin/perl -w

use PodSucks;

print "Flocks of Red Sox cause shocks to the Bronx.\n";

=pod
You will fear the wrath of Pod! Fear my wrath!
=cut
```

This prints:

```
Flocks of Red SoX cause shocks to the BronX.
```

Filter::Util::Call

Provides a framework for implementing source filters in Perl code. While you may use Filter::Util::Call directly, we suggest you use Filter::Simple instead.

For example:

```perl
package Milter; # Could just as well be called 'OldJoke'

use Filter::Util::Call ;

sub import {
    my($type) = @_ ;
    filter_add(bless []) ;
}

sub filter {
    my($self) = @_;
    my($status);

    s/Shut-Up/Trouble/g

    if ($status = filter_read()) > 0;
    $status ;
}
1;
```

You'd use the above in your code like so:

```perl
#!/usr/local/bin/perl -w
use Milter;
print "Are you looking for Shut-Up?\n" ;
```

This prints:

```
Are you looking for Trouble?
```

Filter::Util::Call implements the following methods.

filter   filter()

Performs the main processing for the filter. Used with closure filters; that is, a closure filter handles the lexical variables that are maintained by the closure. The finished source, as processed by filter, will be returned in $_.

filter returns a status, as follows:

< 0

An error has been encountered.

EOF

End-of-file has been reached unexpectedly.

> 0

Everything is OK.

---

filter_add   filter_add(*ref*)

Installs the filter. filter_add takes one parameter, a reference, and depending on the kind of reference used, dictates which of the two filter types is used. CODE references result in a closure filter; otherwise, method filters are assumed.

---

filter_del   filter_del()

Disables the current filter. It doesn't destroy any filters, just tells Perl to stop using them.

---

filter_read   filter_read(*n*)

Obtains a line or block from the next filter in the chain. If there are no other filters, then the actual source file is obtained. For example:

```
$status = filter_read();      # Requests a line
$status = filter_read($size); # Requests a block of $size
```

---

filter_read_exact

filter_read_exact()

Obtains a line or block from the next filter in the chain. If there are no other filters, then the actual source file is obtained.

---

import   import()

Creates an instance of the filter. Perl calls import indirectly when it encounters use Milter in your Perl program. import will always have one parameter passed by Perl, which corresponds to the name of your package—in this case, Milter.

So, if you do this:

```
use Milter qw(pinta nina santa-maria);
```

You get in @_:

```
@_[0] => "Milter"
@_[1] => "pinta"
@_[2] => "nina"
@_[3] => "santa-maria"
```

import then calls filter_add before finishing.

FindBin

Finds the full path to a script's *bin* directory, letting you use relative paths to that directory without needing to know the actual location:

```
use FindBin;
use lib "$FindBin::Bin/../lib";
```

or:

```
use FindBin qw($Bin);
use lib "$Bin/../lib";
```

FindBin exports the following variables:

$Bin
    Path to *bin* directory from which script was invoked

$Script
    Basename of script from which Perl was invoked

$RealBin
    $Bin with all links resolved

$RealScript
    $Script with all links resolved

If you invoke Perl with the *–e* option or read the Perl script from STDIN, then FindBin sets both $Bin and $RealBin to the current directory.

GDBM_File

Allows Perl programs to make use of the facilities provided by the GNU gdbm library. Most of the *libgdbm.a* functions are available as methods of the GDBM_File interface. (See the *gdbm(3)* manpage and the description of DB_File in this chapter.) The following is an example of the use of GDBM_File:

```
use GDBM_File;

tie %hash, "GDBM_File", $filename, &GDBM_WRCREAT, 0644);
# Read/writes of %hash are now read/writes of $filename
untie %hash;
```

Getopt::Long

Lets your program accept command-line options with long names, introduced by --. Standard single-character options are also accepted. Options that start with -- may have an argument appended, following a space or an equals sign (=):

    --foo=bar
    --foo bar

Provides two functions: GetOptions and config.

config	Getopt::Long::config(*optionlist*)

Sets the variables in *optionlist* to change the default behavior of GetOptions. The following options are available:

$Getopt::Long::autoabbrev
: If true, option names can be invoked with unique abbreviations. Default is 1 (true) unless the environment variable POSIXLY_CORRECT has been set.

$Getopt::Long::getopt_compat
: If true, options can start with +. Default is 1 unless the environment variable POSIXLY_CORRECT has been set.

$Getopt::Long::order
: Value indicates whether options and non-options may be mixed on the command line:

$PERMUTE
: Non-options may be mixed with options. The default if POSIXLY_CORRECT is not set.

$REQUIRE_ORDER
: Mixing is not allowed. The default if POSIXLY_CORRECT is set.

$Getopt::Long::ignorecase
: If true, ignore case when matching options. Default is 1.

$Getopt::Long::VERSION
: The version number of this Getopt::Long implementation in the format *major.minor*.

$Getopt::Long::error
: Internal error flag. May be incremented from a callback routine to cause options-parsing to fail.

$Getopt::Long::debug
: If true, enables debugging output. Default is 0 (false).

GetOptions	*$result* = GetOptions(*option-descriptions*)

Uses descriptions from *option-descriptions* to retrieve and process the command-line options with which your Perl program was invoked. The options are taken from @ARGV. After GetOptions has processed the options, @ARGV contains only command-line arguments that were not options. Returns 0 if errors are detected. Each option description consists of two elements:

Option specifier
>Defines the option name and optionally a value as an argument specifier.

Option linkage
>A reference to a variable that is set when the option is present.

GetOptions can also take as a first argument a reference to a hash that describes the linkage for the options. The linkage specified in the argument list takes precedence over the one specified in the hash. Thus, the following are equivalent:

```
%optctl = (size => \$offset);
&GetOptions(\%optctl, "size=i");
```

and:

```
&GetOptions("size=i" => \$offset);
```

Option specifiers

Each option specifier consists of an option name and possibly an argument specifier. The name can be a name, or a list of names separated by |; the first name in the list is the true name of the option, and the others are treated as aliases. Option names may be invoked with the shortest unique abbreviation. Values for argument specifiers are:

<none>
>Option takes no argument. The option variable is set to 1.

!
>Option does not take an argument and may be negated, that is, prefixed by no.

=s
>Option takes a mandatory argument that is a string that will be assigned to the option variable. Even if the argument starts with - or --, it is assigned to the option variable rather than treated as another option.

:s
>Option takes an optional string argument. If the option is invoked with no argument, an empty string ("") is assigned to the option variable. If the argument starts with - or --, it is treated as another option rather than assigned to the option variable.

=i
>Option takes a mandatory integer argument, which may start with - to indicate a negative value.

:i

Option takes an optional integer argument that may start with - to indicate a negative value. With no argument, the value 0 is assigned to the option variable.

=f

Option takes a mandatory floating-point argument that may start with - to indicate a negative value.

:f

Option takes an optional floating-point argument that may start with - to indicate a negative value. With no argument, the value 0 is assigned to the option variable.

A hyphen (-) by itself is considered an option whose name is the empty string. A double hyphen (--) by itself terminates option processing. Any options following the double hyphen remain in @ARGV when GetOptions returns. If an argument specifier ends with @ (e.g., =s@), then the option is treated as an array.

The special option specifier <> can be used to designate a subroutine to handle non-option arguments. For this specifier to be used, the variable $Getopt::Long::order must have the value of the predefined and exported variable, $PERMUTE. See the description of Getopt::Long::config below.

Linkage specification

The linkage specifier can be a reference to any of the following:

Scalar

The new value is stored in the referenced variable. If the option occurs more than once, the previous value is overwritten.

Array

The new value is appended (pushed) onto the referenced array.

Subroutine

The referenced subroutine is called with two arguments: the option name, which is always the true name, and the option value.

If no linkage is explicitly specified, but a hash reference is passed, GetOptions puts the value in the hash. For array options, a reference to an anonymous array is generated.

If no linkage is explicitly specified, and no hash reference is passed, GetOptions puts the value into a global variable named after the option, prefixed by opt_. Characters that are not part of the variable syntax are translated to underscores. For example, --fpp-struct-return sets the variable $opt_fpp_struct_return.

Getopt::Std

Processes single-character, command-line options with option clustering. Exports two functions, which analyze @ARGV, extract information about the options, and return this information to your program in a set of variables. Processing of @ARGV stops when an argument without a leading - is encountered, if that argument is not associated with a preceding option. Otherwise, @ARGV is processed to the end and left empty.

getopt

getopt ('*switches*'[, \\%*opts*])

switches is a string of the command-line options that take arguments. For each option, getopt sets $opt_x (in which *x* is the switch) to the value entered as an argument. If \\%*opts* is specified, it is a reference to a hash in which getopt sets the key to the name of the switch and the value to the argument (and the $opt_ variables are not set).

getopts

getopts ('*switches*'[, \\%*opts*])

Like getopt, except that all valid options are included in *switches*, and options that take an argument are followed by a colon (:). For example:

```
getopt('oDI')      # -o, -D, & -I take arguments; there may
                   # be other options
getopts('o:DI')    # -o, -D, and -I are the only valid
                   # options; only -o takes an argument
```

\\%*opts* means the same as with getopt.

Hash::Util

Offers a selection of general-utility hash subroutines. Starting with Perl 5.8, hashes allow you to restrict access to the data that's stored in the hash. Individual keys can be locked so they cannot be deleted, nor can their values be changed. Hash::Util is largely intended to replace the deprecated pseudo-hashes.

For example:

```
#!/usr/local/bin/perl -w

%hash = (foo => 42, bar => 23);
lock_keys(%hash);
```

```
# Now, try to set %hash{'something'}
while(my($key, $value) = each %hash) {
    print "$key -> $value\n";
}

unlock_keys(%hash);
```

You can lock specific values as follows:

```
#!/usr/local/bin/perl -w

%hash = (foo => 42, bar => 23);
lock_key(%hash, 'foo');

# Now, try to set 'foo' and see what happens

unlock_keys(%hash, 'foo');
```

I18N::Collate

The use of I18N::Collate is now deprecated, although it is still provided for compatibility with older programs. Don't use it in new programs, because its functionality was integrated into the core Perl in Perl 5.004. See the locale pragma.

I18N::Langinfo

Provides locale-specific information for constants supported in *langinfo.h*. I18N::Langinfo implements just one function, langinfo.

---

langinfo   langinfo(*constant*)

Returns the locale-specific data associated with the specified *constant*. For example, the following prints the date and time in the format for the current locale:

```
print langinfo(D_T_FMT);
```

I18N::LangTags

Implements language tags per RFC 3066. Language tags let you specify a certain language that you'll use in a segment of text or code. I18N::LangTags lets you perform a number of common tasks with language tasks that you might come across when dealing with different protocols and applications.

I18N::LangTags is shipped with the Perl 5.8 source kit. It implements the following methods.

alternate_language_tags

```
alternate_language_tags(language)
```

Returns all language tags that are alternate forms of *language*:

```
alternate_language_tags('en'); # Returns ()
alternate_language_tags('he'); # Returns ('iw')
alternate_language_tags('iw'); # Returns ('he')
```

encode_language_tag

```
encode_language_tag(language)
```

Returns the encoding of a language tag. Returns undef if *language* is invalid.

extract_language_tags

```
extract_language_tags(source)
```

Returns a list of what is perceived as valid language tags from source. For example:

```
my $chewbacca_dialect = 'growl, growl, fr, growl, growl!';
extract_language_tags($chewbacca_dialect);
# Returns 'fr'  Chewbacca is French?!  Say it isn't so!
```

is_dialect_of

```
is_dialect_of(lang1, lang2)
```

Returns true if *lang1* represents a form of *lang2*. It doesn't go both ways, so make sure that *lang1* comes first.

```
is_dialect_of('en-US', 'en'); # true
is_dialect_of('en', 'en-US'); # false
```

is_language_tag

```
is_language_tag(language)
```

Returns true if language is a valid language tag. For example:

```
my $gutteral = 'Chewbacca';
is_language_tag($gutteral);  # false

my $pourquois = 'fr';
is_language_tag($pourquois); # true
```

locale2language_tag

locale2language_tag(*locale*)

Takes a locale name and maps it to a language tag. Certain tags aren't mappable, such as C or POSIX, in which case local2language_tag will return an empty list.

```
locale2language_tag('en');     # Returns 'en'
locale2language_tag('POSIX'); # Returns undef or ()
```

same_language_tag

same_language_tag(*lang1*, *lang2*)

Returns true if *lang1* and *lang2* both represent the same language form. For example:

```
same_language_tag('en', 'en-US'); # Returns false
en != en-US
```

similarity_language_tag

similarity_language_tag(*lang1*, *lang2*)

Returns an integer that represents the degree of similarity between *lang1* and *lang2*:

```
similarity_language_tag('fr', 'fr-ca'); # 1
similarity_language_tag('fr', 'en-US'); # 0
```

super_languages

super_languages(*language*)

Returns a list of language tags that are superordinate to *language*:

```
super_languages('en-US'); # Gets 'en'
super_languages('en');    # Gets an empty list
```

I18N::LangTags::List

Provides a lengthy and nearly comprehensive list of any language tags that you might need, from ab to zn. You should refer to the I18N::LangTags::List documentation for the list of these tags and what they represent.

I18N::LangTags::List implements the name() function that takes a language tag and returns its best attempt at an English name for it. If name() doesn't understand the language tag, it returns undef.

For example:

```
#!/usr/local/bin/perl -w
use I18N::LangTags::List;

my $tag = 'en-CA';
print "What is this tag aboot? ",
        I18N::LangTags::List::name($tag),

"\n";
```

if

The if pragma "uses" a Perl module if a condition exists. For example:

```
use if CONDITION, MODULE => ARGUMENTS;
```

integer

Pragma that tells the compiler to use integer operations from here to the end of the enclosing block. Improves processing time on systems without floating-point hardware support.

```
use integer;

$x = 10/3;    # $x is now 3, not 3.33333333333333333
```

Use the no integer directive to turn off integer inside an inner block.

IO

Loads all of the following IO modules with a single use statement: IO::Handle, IO::Seekable, IO::File, IO::Pipe, and IO::Socket.

IO::File

Inherits from IO::Handle and IO::Seekable, extending them with methods specific to filehandles. Provides three such methods.

new	$*fh* = new ([*params*])
	Constructor. Creates an IO::File object, passing any parameters to the method open. If the open fails, the object is destroyed. Otherwise, it is returned to the caller.

new_tmpfile	$*fh* = new_tmpfile
	Constructor. Creates an IO::File object opened for read/write on a newly created temporary file. If the system permits, the temporary file is anonymous; if the temporary file cannot be created or

opened, the object is destroyed. Otherwise, it is returned to the caller.

open $fh->open(*filename*[, *mode*[, *perms*]])

Opens the newly created filehandle. Accepts one, two, or three parameters. With one parameter, it acts as a frontend for Perl's built-in open function. With two parameters, the first parameter is a filename, and the second is the open mode, optionally followed by a third parameter, the file permission value.

IO::Handle

The base class for all other IO handle classes. Its main purpose is for the other IO classes to inherit from it; programs should not create IO::Handle objects directly. Provides the following methods.

new   new

Constructor. Creates a new IO::Handle object.

new_from_fd   new_from_fd (*fd*, *mode*)

Constructor. Like new, creates an IO::Handle object. It requires two parameters, which are passed to the method fdopen; if fdopen fails, the object is destroyed. Otherwise, it is returned to the caller.

clearerr $fh->clearerr

Clears the given handle's error indicator.

error $fh->error

Returns true if the given handle has experienced any errors since it was opened or since the last call to clearerr.

fdopen $fh->fdopen (*fd*, *mode*)

Like an ordinary open except that the first parameter is a filehandle name, an IO::Handle object, or a file descriptor number.

| **flush** | `$fh->flush` |
| | Flushes the given handle's buffer. |

| **getline** | `$fh->getline` |
| | Works like <`$fh`>, described in the section on "I/O Operators" in the *perlop* manpage, but is more readable and can be safely called in an array context, while still returning one line. |

| **getlines** | `$fh->getlines` |
| | Works like <`$fh`> when called in an array context to read all the remaining lines in a file, but is more readable. croaks if called in scalar context. |

| **opened** | `$fh->opened` |
| | Returns true if the object is currently a valid file descriptor. |

| **ungetc** | `$fh->ungetc (ord)` |
| | Pushes a character with the ordinal value *ord* back onto the given handle's input stream. |

| **untaint** | `$fh->untaint` |
| | Special method for working under –*T* and setuid/gid scripts. Marks the object as taint-clean, and as such, data read from it is also considered taint-clean. |

write	`$fh->write (buf, len[, offset])`
	Like write found in C; that is, the opposite of read. The wrapper for the Perl write function is `format_write`.
	IO::Handle also provides the following methods, which are not described in detail here because they are simply frontends for the corresponding built-in functions. See Chapter 5 for more information.

Method	Description
close	Closes file or pipe
eof	Returns 1 if next read will return end-of-file
fileno	Returns file descriptor for a filehandle

Method	Description
getc	Returns next character from input file
print	Prints a string or comma-separated list of strings
printf	Prints a formatted string
read	Reads data from a filehandle
stat	Returns an array of status information for a file
sysread	Reads data from a filehandle with system call read(2)
syswrite	Writes data to a filehandle with system call write(2)
truncate	Truncates a file to a specified length

Finally, the following methods act on the equivalent Perl variables. See Chapter 4 for more information.

Method	Description
autoflush	If nonzero, forces a flush now and after each write or print (default 0)
format_page_number	Current page number
format_lines_per_page	Current page length (default 60)
format_lines_left	Number of lines left on page
format_name	Name of current report format
format_top_name	Name of current top-of-page format
format_line_break_characters	Current set of linebreak chars for a format
format_formfeed	Formfeed char used by formats (default \f)
format_write	Wrapper for write function
input_record_separator	Input record separator (default newline)
input_line_number	Current input line number for last filehandle accessed
output_field_separator	Output field separator for print
output_record_separator	Output record separator for print

IO::Pipe

Provides an interface for creating pipes between processes.

new $pipe = new IO::Pipe([readfh, writefh])

Constructor. Creates an IO::Pipe object, which is a reference to a newly created symbol. The two optional arguments should be objects blessed into IO::Handle or one of its subclasses. These objects are used for the system call to pipe. With no arguments, the method handles is called on the new IO::Pipe object.

handles $pipe->handles( )

Called during construction by IO::Pipe::new on the newly created IO::Pipe object. Returns an array of two objects blessed into IO::Pipe::End, or a subclass.

reader $pipe->reader([args])

Object is reblessed into a subclass of IO::Handle and becomes a handle at the reading end of the pipe. If there are any args, then fork is called, and the arguments are passed to exec.

writer $pipe->writer([args])

The object is reblessed into a subclass of IO::Handle and becomes a handle at the writing end of the pipe. If there are any args, then fork is called, and the arguments are passed to exec.

IO::Seekable

Intended to be inherited by other IO::Handle-based objects to provide methods that allow you to seek the file descriptors. Has no constructor.

```
use IO::Seekable;
package IO::XXX;
@ISA = qw(IO::Seekable);
```

Provides two methods.

seek $fh->seek(offset, whence)

Frontend for the corresponding built-in seek function, which sets a filehandle's position in the file. Takes the following arguments:

offset
    The offset where you want to set the position.

whence
    The position in the file that the offset is relative to. Possible values are: 0 for the beginning of the file, 1 for the current position, or 2 for end of file. May also be expressed as the following constants, which are exported:

SEEK_SET
    Beginning of file

SEEK_CUR
    Current position

SEEK_END
    End of file

tell	`$fh->tell()`
	Frontend for the corresponding built-in `tell` function, which returns the current file position in bytes (starting from 0).

IO::Select

Implements an object-oriented approach to the system `select` function call. Allows the user to see which I/O handles are ready for reading, writing, or have an error condition pending.

new	`new $s = IO::Select->new([handles])`
	Constructor. Creates a new object and optionally initializes it with a set of handles.

add	`$s->add(handles)`
	Adds list of handles to the IO::Select object, to be returned when an event occurs. IO::Select keeps the list of handles in a cache, which is indexed by the handle's file number. Each handle can be an IO::Handle object, an integer, or a reference to an array, in which the first element is an IO::Handle object or an integer.

bits	`$s->bits()`
	Returns the bit string that is suitable for use as an argument to the core select call.

can_read	`$s->can_read([timeout])`
	Returns array of handles that are ready for reading. *timeout* is the maximum amount of time to wait before returning an empty list. If *timeout* is not given, and any handles are registered, then the call blocks.

can_write	`$s->can_write([timeout])`
	Same as can_read, but checks for handles that can be written to.

count	`$s->count( )`
	Returns the number of handles that the object checks for when one of the can_ methods is called or the object is passed to the select static method.
exists	`$s->exists(handle)`
	Returns the handle if it is present; otherwise, returns undef.
handles	`$s->handles`
	Returns an array of all registered handles.
has_error	`$s->has_error([timeout])`
	Same as can_read, but checks for handles that have an error condition.
remove	`$s->remove(handles)`
	Removes all the given handles from the object, locating them by file number.
select	`$s->select(read, write, error[, timeout])`
	Static method. Call it with the package name as with new. read, write, and error are either undef or IO::Select objects. The optional argument *timeout* has the same effect as for the core select call.
	Returns an array of three elements, each a reference to an array or an empty array on error. The arrays hold the handles that are ready for reading, ready for writing, and have error conditions, respectively.

IO::Socket

Provides an object interface to creating and using sockets. It is built on the IO::Handle interface and inherits all the methods defined by IO::Handle.

IO::Socket defines methods for only those operations that are common to all types of socket. IO::Socket exports all functions (and constants) defined by Socket. See Chapter 13, for detailed information.

IPC::Msg

System V Msg IPC object class. Uses constants defined in IPC::SysV.

---

new

$msg = new IPC::Msg(key, flags)

Creates a new message queue associated with key and uses flags to set the permissions. Creates the new message queue if the following are true:

- key is equal to IPC_PRIVATE.
- key doesn't already have an associated message queue, and FLAGS & IPC_CREAT is true.

---

id

$msg->id

Returns the system identifier for the message queue.

---

rcv

$msg->rcv(buf, len[, type[, flags]])

Reads a message from the queue, returning the type of the message.

---

remove

$msg->remove

Removes and destroys the message queue.

---

set

$msg->set(stat)

$msg->set(name=>value[,name=>value...])

Accepts either a stat object as returned by the stat method or a list of name/value pairs and sets the following values of the stat structure associated with the message queue:

```
uid
gid
mode (the permission bits)
qbytes
```

---

snd

$msg->snd(type, msg[, flags])

Puts a message of type type on the queue with the data from msg. See the msgsnd function.

---

stat

$ds = $msg->stat

Returns an object of type IPC::Msg::stat (which is a subclass of Class::Struct) that provides the following fields:

```
uid    gid    cuid   cgid
mode   qnum   qbytes lspid
lrpid  stime  rtime  ctime
```

See the stat function and your system documentation for more information.

IPC::Open2

Opens a child process that allows two-way communication between your program and the child. Returns the process ID of the child process or reports a fatal error on failure. Exports one function.

open2	open2 (*rdr, *wtr, cmd_with_args)

Forks a child process to execute the specified command. Takes the following arguments:

*rdr
> Represents a read filehandle that your program can use to read from the command $cmd's standard output. Can be a filehandle object or a reference to a typeglob.

*wtr
> Represents a write filehandle that your program can use to write to the command $cmd's standard input. Can be a filehandle object or a reference to a typeglob.

cmd_with_args
> The command to be executed by the child process and its arguments. Can be specified two ways:
> ```
> $cmd_with_args
> $cmd, "arg1", "arg2", ...
> ```

IPC::Open3

IPC::Open3 works like IPC::Open2.

```
use IPC::Open3;

$pid = open3($wtr, $rdr, $err, $cmd_with_args);
$pid = open3($wtr, $rdr, $err, $cmd, "arg1", "arg2", ...);
```

The following differences apply:

- The first two arguments ($wtr and $rdr) are passed in the opposite order.
- A third filehandle can be passed, for standard error. If this argument is given as "", then STDERR and STDOUT for $cmd are on the same filehandle.

- If $wtr begins with <, then the leading < is stripped from the name, and the remainder is assumed to be a regular filehandle for an open file, rather than a reference to a typeglob. open3 opens this file as STDIN for $cmd and closes it in the parent. Likewise, if $rdr or $err begins with >, then $cmd directs STD-OUT or STDERR directly to that file rather than to the parent.

IPC::Semaphore

System V Semaphore IPC object class. Uses constants defined in IPC::SysV.

new	`$sem = new IPC::Semaphore(key, nsems, flags)`
	Creates a new semaphore set associated with *key* and containing *nsems* semaphores. Uses *flags* to set the permissions. Creates the new set if the following are true:
	• *key* is equal to IPC_PRIVATE.
	• *key* doesn't already have an associated semaphore identifier, and FLAGS & IPC_CREAT is true.
getall	`$sem->getall`
	Returns the values of the semaphore set as an array.
getncnt	`$sem->getncnt(sem)`
	Returns the number of processes waiting for the semaphore *sem* to become greater than its current value.
getpid	`$sem->getpid(sem)`
	Returns the process ID of the last process that operated on semaphore *sem*.
getval	`$sem->getval(sem)`
	Returns the current value of semaphore *sem*.
getzcnt	`$sem->getzcnt(sem)`
	Returns the number of processes waiting for the semaphore *sem* to become 0.
id	`$sem->id`
	Returns the system identifier for the semaphore set.

op $sem->op(oplist)

Passes a list of operations to the semop function. oplist is the list of operations, consisting of a concatenation of smaller lists. Each of the smaller lists has three values: the semaphore number, the operation, and a flag. See the semop function in Chapter 5 for more information.

---

remove $sem->remove

Removes and destroys the semaphore set.

---

set $sem->set(stat

                      $sem->set(name=>value[, name=>value...])

Accepts either a stat object as returned by the stat method or a list of name/value pairs and sets the following values of the stat structure associated with the semaphore set:

    uid
    gid
    mode (the permission bits)

---

setall $sem->setall(values)

Sets the values of all the semaphores in the set to those given by the values list. The number of values on the list must match the number of semaphores in the set.

---

setval $sem->setval(n, value)

Sets the nth value in the semaphore set to value.

---

stat $ds = $sem->stat

Returns an object of type IPC::Semaphore::stat (which is a subclass of Class::Struct) that provides the following fields:

    uid   gid   cuid   cgid
    mode   ctime otime   nsems

IPC::SysV

Defines and conditionally exports all the constants defined in your system include files that are needed by the System V IPC calls.

ftok	ftok (*path, id*)

Returns a key based on *path* and *id* for use by msgget, semget, and shmget.

---

less

Pragma, currently unimplemented, that may someday be a compiler directive to make certain trade-offs, such as:

```
use less 'memory';
```

lib

Permits adding additional directories to Perl's default search path at compile time. The directories are added at the front of the search path.

```
use lib list;
```

adds the directories specified in *list* to @INC.

For each directory *$dir* in *list*, lib looks for an architecture-specific subdirectory that has an *auto* subdirectory under it—that is, it looks for *$dir/$archname/auto*. If it finds that directory, then *$dir/$archname* is also added to the front of @INC, preceding *$dir*.

Normally, you should only add directories to @INC. However, you can also delete directories. The statement:

```
no lib list
```

deletes the first instance of each named directory from @INC. To delete all instances of all the specified names from @INC, specify :ALL as the first parameter of *list*.

As with adding directories, lib checks for a directory called *$dir/$archname/auto* and deletes the *$dir/$archname* directory from @INC. You can restore @INC to its original value with:

```
@INC = @lib::ORIG_INC;
```

List::Util

A collection of list-related subroutines. As of Perl 5.8, List::Util is included with the Perl source kit.

You can get the first item of a list (that matches the condition in BLOCK) like so:

```
#!/usr/local/bin/perl -w
use List::Util qw(first);

my @ll = qw(one two three);
```

```
my $fir = first { defined($_) } @ll;
print "$fir\n"; # Prints 'one'
```

List::Util implements (but does not export) the following methods.

---

first   first { *BLOCK* } @*list*

Evaluates a block of Perl code and sets $_ to each element of the list in turn. If *BLOCK* is true, first returns the first element. If *BLOCK* never returns true, or @*list* has no items, then first returns undef. Note that first doesn't necessarily return the first item in a list. Consider the following:

```
my @ll = qw(1 2 3);
my $fir = first { $_ > 1 } @ll;
print "$fir\n"; # Prints '2', since as 2 is the first item
                # in BLOCK that's > 1
```

---

max   max @*list*

Returns the entry in the list with the highest numerical value. If the list is empty, max returns undef:

```
my @ll = qw(100 294 2 4 95 73);
my $max_num = max @ll;
print "$max_num\n"; # Prints '294'
```

---

maxstr   maxstr @*list*

Similar to max, except that maxstr treats all list items as strings. maxstr will return the "highest string" as determined by the gt operator. As always, if list is empty, maxstr returns undef.

```
my @ll = qw(1 3 5 nate Person pizza man carl_everett
dinosaur);
my $max_s = maxstr(@ll);
print "$max_s\n"; # Prints 'pizza'
```

---

min   min @*list*

Returns the lowest numerical value. If the list is empty, min returns undef.

---

minstr   minstr @*list*

Treats all list items as strings, but returns the "lowest string" as determined by the lt operator. If the list is empty, minstr returns undef.

reduce	reduce { *BLOCK* } *@list*

Literally "reduces" *@list* by calling *BLOCK* until there are no more items to operate on in *@list*. reduce sets $a and $b for each operation in *BLOCK* and returns the reduced list as a scalar. If *@list* is 0, *BLOCK* is not executed, and $*list*[0] is returned. If *@list* is empty, then reduce returns undef.

You can sum and concatenate a list using reduce like so:

```
my $sum_of_list = reduce { $a + $b } @ll; # sum
my $concat_list = reduce { $a . $b } @ll; # concat
```

shuffle	shuffle @LIST

Returns list items in random order.

sum	sum @LIST

Returns the sum of all items in the list. Note that sum deals only with numerical list items and will ignore any other list items. For example:

```
my @ll = qw(1 3 5 nate Person pizza man carl_everett
dinosaur 6.54);
my $sum_of_list = sum(@ll);
print "$sum_of_list\n"; # Prints '15.54'
```

locale

Pragma that tells the compiler to disable (or enable) the use of POSIX locales for built-in operations (LC_CTYPE for regular expressions and LC_COLLATE for string comparison). Each no locale or use locale affects statements to the end of the enclosing block.

Math::BigFloat

Provides methods that permit use of floating-point numbers of arbitrary length. The following apply to all methods, except as noted:

- The object $f remains unchanged.
- All methods except fcmp return a number string (*nstr*) of the form /[+-]\ d+E[+-]\d+/, with embedded whitespace ignored.
- A return value of NaN indicates that either an input parameter was "Not a Number" or that an illegal operation was attempted.
- A similar default scale value is computed for square roots.

new $f = Math::BigFloat->new(*string*)

Creates a new object, $f.

---

fabs $f->fabs( )

Returns absolute value of $f.

---

fadd $f->fadd(*nstr*)

Returns sum of *nstr* and $f.

---

fcmp $f->fcmp(*nstr*)

Compares $f to *nstr*. Returns -1, 0, or 1 depending on whether $f
is less than, equal to, or greater than *nstr*, or undef if *nstr* is not a
number.

---

fdiv $f->fdiv(*nstr*[,*n*])

Returns $f divided by *nstr* to *n* places. If *scale* (the number of
digits) is unspecified, division is computed to the number of digits
given by:

```
max($div_scale, length(dividend)+length(divisor))
```

---

ffround $f->ffround(*n*)

Returns $f rounded at *n*th place.

---

fmul $f->*fmul*(*nstr*)

Returns $f multiplied by *nstr*.

---

fneg $f->fneg( )

Returns negative of $f.

---

fnorm $f->fnorm( )

Returns normalization of $f.

---

fround $f->fround(*n*)

Returns value of $f rounded to *n* digits.

fsqrt $f->fsqrt([n])

Returns square root of $f to *n* places.

fsub $f->fsub(*nstr*)

Returns $f minus *nstr*.

Math::BigInt

Allows use of arbitrary length integers, in which the following apply to all methods, except as noted:

- The object $i remains unchanged.
- Big integer strings (*bints*) have the form /^\s*[+-]?[\d\s]+$/.
- All methods except bcmp return a big integer string or strings.
- Embedded whitespace is ignored.
- Output values are always in the canonical form: /^[+-]\d+$/.
- The return value NaN results when an input argument is not a number, or when a divide by zero is attempted.

new $i = Math::BigInt->new(*string*)

Creates a new object, $i.

babs $i->babs

Returns absolute value of $i.

badd $i->badd(*bint*)

Returns sum of *bint* and $i.

bcmp $i->bcmp(*bint*)

Compares $i to *bint*. The bcmp method returns -1, 0, or 1 depending on whether $f is less than, equal to, or greater than the number string given as an argument. If the number string is undefined or null, undef is returned.

bdiv	`$i->bdiv(bint)`
	Returns `$i` divided by `bint`. In list context, returns a two-element array containing the quotient of the division and the remainder; in scalar context, returns only the quotient.
bgcd	`$i->bgcd(bint)`
	Returns greatest common divisor of `$i` and `bint`.
bmod	`$i->bmod(bint)`
	Returns `$i` modulus `bint`.
bmul	`$i->bmul(bint)`
	Returns `$i` multiplied by `bint`.
bneg	`$i->bneg`
	Returns negative of `$i`.
bnorm	`$i->bnorm`
	Returns normalization of `$i`.
bsub	`$i->bsub(bint)`
	Returns `$i` minus `bint`.

Math::BigInt::Calc

Supports big integer calculations. Math::BigInt::Calc allows you to use library modules for core math routines. This module is shipped with the Perl 5.8 source kit.

If you've written a module that uses the same API as Math::BigInt, you can use Math::BigInt::Calc as follows:

```
use Math::BigInt lib => 'yourlibname';
use Math::BigInt lib => 'Math::BigInt::yourlibname';
```

Math::BigInt exports the following functions, which must be defined in your module so Math::BigInt can support it:

_new(*string*)
> Returns a reference to new object from reference to decimal string.

_zero()
> Returns a new object with value 0.

_one()
> Returns a new object with value 1.

_str(*obj*)
> Returns a reference to a string representing the object.

_num(*obj*)
> Returns a Perl integer or floating-point number. This may not necessarily be accurate, depending on machine-dependent, floating-point size limitations.

_add(*obj, obj*)
> Allows simple addition of two objects.

_mul(*obj, obj*)
> Allows multiplication of two objects.

_div(*obj, obj*)
> Implements division of the first object by the second. In a list context, div() returns *result, remainder*.

_sub(*obj, obj*)
> Implements simple subtraction of one object from another. A third, optional parameter indicates that the parameters are swapped.

_dec(*obj*)
> Decrements object by one.

_inc(*obj*)
> Increments object by one.

_acmp(*obj, obj*)
> The <=> operator for objects, which returns -1, 0, or 1.

_len(*obj*)
> Returns count of the decimal digits of the object.

_digit(*obj, n*)
> Returns the *n*th decimal digit of object.

_is_one(*obj*)
> Returns true if argument is 1.

_is_zero(*obj*)
> Returns true if the argument is 0.

_is_even(*obj*)
> Returns true if argument is even.

_is_odd(*obj*)
> Returns true if argument is odd.

_copy()
> Returns a reference to a true copy of the object.

_check(*obj*)
> Checks whether the internal representation is still intact. Returns 0 for OK or an error message as a string.

The following functions are optional and can be defined if the underlying library can do them quickly. If undefined, Math::BigInt will use pure Perl fallback routines to emulate these. Note that falling back to Perl's routines will cause a performance hit.

_from_hex(*string*)
> Returns a reference to a new object from a reference to a hexadecimal string.

_from_bin(*string*)
> Returns a reference to a new object from a reference to a binary string.

_as_hex(*string*)
> Returns a reference to a scalar string containing the value as an unsigned hex string. _as_hex() prepends the 0x, although you must strip all leading zeros.

_as_bin(*string*)
> Similar to _as_hex(), except that it takes a binary string that contains only zeros and ones.

_rsft(*obj*, *n*, *b*)
> Shifts object (right) in base B by n digits. Returns undef on failure.

_lsft(*obj*, *n*, *b*)
> Shifts object in base b by n digits. Returns undef on failure.

_xor(*obj1*, *obj2*)
> Does an XOR of object 1 with object 2.

_and(*obj1*, *obj2*)
> Does an AND of object 1 with object 2.

_or(*obj1*, *obj2*)
> Does an OR of object 1 with object 2.

_mod(*obj1*, *obj2*)
> Returns remainder of division of the first object by the second object.

_sqrt(*obj*)
> Returns the square root of the object.

_fac(*obj*)
> Returns. factorial of object.

_pow(*obj1*, *obj2*)
> Returns object 1 to the power of object 2.

_gcd(*obj1*, *obj2*)
> Returns the greatest common divisor of two objects.

_zeros(*obj*)
> Returns the number of trailing decimal zeros.

Math::BigRat

Allows you to use arbitrarily big rationals. Math::BigRat is shipped with the Perl 5.8 source kit.

For example:

```
#!/usr/local/bin/perl -w
use Math::BigRat;
my $rat = Math::BigRat->new('2/7');

print $rat->bstr(), "\n";
```

Math::BigRat implements the following methods.

---

new   new(*value*)

Creates a new Math::BigRat object. You can use all types of input for new(): '3/5', '2/33', '6/9', etc.

---

denominator   denominator()

Returns a copy of the denominator as a positive BigInt:

```
my $rat = Math::BigRat->new('2/7')
print $rat->denominator(), "\n"; # Prints 7
```

---

numerator   numerator()

Returns a copy of the numerator as a signed BigInt:

```
my $rat = Math::BigRat->new('2/7');
print $rat->numerator(), "\n"; # Prints 2
```

---

parts   parts()

Returns a list consisting of a signed numerator and unsigned denominator. Both are BigInts.

```
my($n, $d) = $rat->parts(); ### Ewwww, rat parts!
print "numerator: $n\n";
print "denominator: $d\n";
```

Math::Complex

Provides support for complex numbers, including a full set of mathematical functions; permits creation and manipulation of complex numbers. Numerous overload and other operations are provided for working with complex numbers.

See the documentation for the module for the complete list and also for a discussion of complex numbers. The following methods are provided.

---

emake
    `$z = Math::Complex->emake(`*`args`*`)`

    `cplxe $z = cplxe(`*`args`*`)`

    Creates a complex number using the polar form.

---

display_format
    `display_format ([`*`format`*`])`

    When called as a method, sets display format for current object. If *format* is not specified, returns the current setting. Possible settings are:

    c   Cartesian format

    p   Polar format

    When called as a function, overrides the default display format, which is Cartesian.

---

make
    `$z = Math::Complex->make(`*`args`*`)`

    `cplx $z = cplx(`*`args`*`)`

    Creates a complex number using the Cartesian form.

Math::Trig

Defines many trigonometric functions not defined by the core Perl, plus the constant pi and some additional functions for converting angles. For example:

```
use Math::Trig;

$x = tan(0.9);
$halfpi = pi/2;
```

The following functions are defined. A slash (/) between two functions means the values are aliases.

acsc/acosec, asec, acot/acotan
    Arcus cofunctions of sine, cosine, and tangent

acsch/acosech, asech, acoth/acotanh
    Arcus cofunctions of hyperbolic sine, cosine, and tangent

asin, acos, atan
    Arcus (inverse) functions of sine, cosine, and tangent

asinh, acosh, atanh
    Arcus functions of hyperbolic sine, cosine, and tangent

atan2(y, x)
: Principal value of arc tangent of y/x

csc/cosec, sec, cot/cotan
: Cofunctions of sine, cosine, and tangent

csch/cosech, sech, coth/cotanh
: Cofunctions of hyperbolic sine, cosine, and tangent

deg2rad
: Degrees to radians

deg2grad
: Degrees to gradians

grad2deg
: Gradians to degrees

grad2rad
: Gradians to radians

pi
: The trigonometric constant π

rad2deg
: Radians to degrees

rad2grad
: Radians to gradians

sinh, cosh, tanh
: Hyperbolic sine, cosine, and tangent

tan
: Tangent

MIME::Base64

Provides functions to encode and decode strings into the Base64 encoding scheme as specified in RFC 2045 (dealing with MIME, or Multipurpose Internet Mail Extensions). Base64 encoding was designed to represent data in octets in an encoded form; all data is encoded using a 65-character subset, which is comprised of A-Z, a-z, 0-9+, /, and =. MIME::Base64 ships with the Perl source kit as of 5.8.

For example:

```
#!/usr/local/bin/perl -w
use MIME::Base64;
my $stone = 'purplebarneystone';
my $b64 = encode_base64($stone);
print "$b64\n";
```

MIME::Base64 implements the following functions, both of which are exported.

decode_base64   decode_base64(*string*)

> Unpacks the base64-encoded *string* and returns the decoded data. In addition, decode_base64 ignores any character that's not part of the recognized 65-character base64 subset.

encode_base64   encode_base64(*string*, [*end_of_line*])

> Base64-encodes *string* with the optional *end_of_line* argument. To base64-encode a JPEG image that lives in a file, you should specify *end_of_line*, since encode_base64 returns base64-encoded content that's broken down into 76 characters per line. If you do not want the 76-character breaks to be imposed on you, set *end_of_line* to an empty string ("").

MIME::QuotedPrint

Provides functions to encode and decode strings into the quoted-printable encoding as specified in RFC 2045 (MIME). Quoted-printable encoding is used to represent data that's comprised of data that corresponds to ASCII characters. Nonprintable characters are represented by a triplet consisting of the = character followed by two hexadecimal digits. MIME::QuotedPrint ships with the Perl source kit as of 5.8.

MIME::QuotedPrint implements and exports the following functions.

decode_qp   decode_qp(*string*)

> Returns the plain-text version of *string*, which is quoted-printable–encoded.

encode_qp   encode_qp(*string*)

> Returns a quoted-printable–encoded version of *string*. The returned version of *string* will not be CRLF-terminated.

NDBM_File

Provides Perl programs with tied access to NDBM database files. See Perl's built-in tie function and the DB_File module.

Net::Cmd

The network command class, which is required by all of the modules under the libnet umbrella: Net::FTP, Net::SMTP, Net::POP3, etc. In addition, Net::Cmd can be inherited by a subclass of IO::Handle. Unless you are writing a new module that will become a part of libnet, Net::Cmd probably doesn't have any servicable parts that you'd be interested in, since these parts are already implemented in the underlying modules. This module is part of the core Perl distribution starting with Perl 5.8.

Net::Cmd implements the following methods, which provide an interface to the Net::Cmd object.

---

code   code()

Returns the three-digit code from the last command. If the last command is still pending, code returns 0.

---

dataend   dataend()

Stops sending data to the remote server and ensures that a final CRLF has been sent.

---

datasend   datasend(*data*)

Sends data to the remote server, converting LF to CRLF. *data* can be an array or reference to an array.

---

debug   debug(*level*)

Sets the debug level for the object. If you do not specify a value, then no debugging information will be provided. If you specify undef as the value, then the debug level will be determined by the debug level of the class.

---

message   message()

Returns a text message from the last command.

---

ok   ok()

Returns nonzero if the last code value was greater than 0 and less than 400.

---

status   status()

Returns the current status code and, if pending, returns CMD_
PENDING.

Net::Cmd implements the following class methods, which you should probably
never touch at a user level.

command   command(*command*, [, *args*, ...])

Sends a command to the remote server. Returns undef on failure.

debug_print   debug_print(*dir*, *text*)

Outputs debugging information. *dir* represents data sent to the
server, and *text* is the text that is sent.

debug_text   debug_text(*text*)

Prints debugging information.

getline   getline()

Retrieves one line, delimited by CRLF, from the remote server.
Returns undef on failure.

parse_response   parse_response(*text*)

Returns an array of two values: the three-digit status code and a
flag that is true when this is part of a multiline response. Called by
response as a method with one argument.

read_until_dot   read_until_dot()

Reads data from the remote server until a line consisting of a single
. is encountered. If the line matches .., one of the dots will be
removed. Returns a reference to a list containing the lines or undef
on failure.

response   response()

Obtains a response from the server. On success, it returns the
status code, or undef on failure.

tied_fh   tied_fh()

Returns a filehandle tied to the Net::Cmd object. After you send a command, you can read from this filehandle with read() or from <>. Returns end-of-file when the final dot is encountered.

ungetline   ungetline(*text*)

Pushes back a line of text from the server.

unsupported   unsupported()

Sets the status code to 580 and the response to Unsupported command. Returns 0.

Net::Cmd exports CMD_INFO, CMD_OK, CMD_MORE, CMD_REJECT, CMD_ERROR, and CMD_PENDING.

Net::Config

Holds configuration data for the modules in the libnet distribution. Net::Config builds this configuration interactively at install time of libnet, and the Net::Config file is further queried when you use modules such as Net::FTP. This module is part of the core Perl distribution starting with Perl 5.8.

Net::Config stores the following values (which can be undef): nntp_hosts, snpp_hosts, pop3_hosts, smtp_hosts, ph_hosts, daytime_hosts, and time_hosts. Each is a reference to an array of hostnames (in order of preference), which should be used for the given protocol. You can override any of the Net::Config values when you use any of the modules that live under the libnet umbrella. In addition, you can maintain your own *.libnetrc* to hold your custom values all the time. A sample *.libnetrc* follows:

```
$ cat .libnetrc
# .libnetrc
{
    nntp_hosts => [ "news.my.host", "news.their.host" ]
}
__END__
```

In addition to the options listed previously, the following options can be specified:

inet_domain
    Your Internet domain name.

ftp_firewall
    If you have an FTP proxy firewall (not an HTTP or SOCKS firewall), then this value should be set to the firewall hostname. If your firewall does not

listen on port 21, then this value should be set to `hostname:port` (e.g., `hostname:99`).

`ftp_firewall_type`

An integer from 1 to 7 signifying the sequence of commands that Net::FTP will use to traverse a firewall, as follows:

*   There is no firewall (default).

1   `USER user@remote.host`
    `PASS password`

2   `USER firewall_username`
    `PASS firewall_password`
    `USER user@remote.host`
    `PASS pass`

3   `USER firewall_username`
    `PASS firewall_password`
    `SITE remote.site`
    `USER user`
    `PASS pass`

4   `USER firewall_username`
    `PASS firewall_password`
    `OPEN remote.site`
    `USER user`
    `PASS pass`

5   `USER user@firewall_username@remote.site`
    `PASS pass@firewall_password`

6   `USER firewall_username@remote.site`
    `PASS firewall_password`
    `USER user`
    `PASS pass`

7   `USER user@remote.host`
    `PASS pass`
    `AUTH firewall_username`
    `RESP firewall_password`

`ftp_ext_passive`
`ftp_int_passive`

FTP servers normally work in a nonpassive mode: when you want to transfer data, you have to tell the server the address and port to connect to. This becomes a problem because some servers cannot connect to your machine through the second port because it's being used by the FTP connection. In this case, set `ftp_ext_passive` to true.

If your server is configured to only work in passive mode, you can force Net::FTP to always transfer in passive mode when not going via a firewall by setting ftp_int_passive to true.

`local_netmask`

A reference to a list of netmask strings. To be used by the `requires_firewall` function to determine if a given host is inside or outside your firewall.

The following method is supported by Net::Config.

requires_firewall

> requires_firewall(*host*)
>
> Determines if *host* is outside of your firewall. Possible return values are:
>
> -1   Cannot look up hostname
>
> 0   Host is inside firewall (or there is no FTP_firewall entry)
>
> 1   Host is outside the firewall

Net::Domain

Attempts to evaluate the current host's Internet name and domain using several methods. This module is part of the core Perl distribution starting with Perl 5.8.

For example, each of the following Net::Domain functions will return undef if the FQDN cannot be determined.

hostdomain

> hostdomain()
>
> Returns the remainder of the FQDN after the hostname has been removed.

hostfqdn

> hostfqdn()
>
> Identifies and returns the FQDN of the current host.

hostname

> hostname()
>
> Returns the smallest part of the FQDN that can be used to identify the host.

Net::FTP

Implements a simple FTP client in Perl (see Chapter 16). This module is part of the core Perl distribution starting with Perl 5.8.

Net::hostent

Overrides the core gethostbyname and gethostbyaddr functions with object-oriented versions that return Net::hostent objects. The objects have methods that return the fields of the same name from the *hostent* structure in *netdb.h*:

Field	Description
addr	Address of host, for backward compatibility
addr_list	List of addresses returned from name server
addrtype	Host address type
aliases	List of aliases
length	Length of address
name	Name of host

You can access the structure fields with the methods or by importing the fields into your namespace with the :FIELDS import tag and accessing them by prepending h_ to the field name:

```
$host_obj->name( )
$h_name
```

Net::hostent exports the following.

gethost   gethost (*host*)

Frontend for gethostbyaddr and gethostbyname. If *host* is numeric, calls gethostbyaddr; otherwise, calls gethostbyname.

gethostbyaddr   gethostbyaddr (*addr, addrtype*)

Returns information about the host with address *addr* of type *addrtype*.

gethostbyname   gethostbyname (*hostname*)

Returns information about the host with name *hostname*.

Net::netent

Returns information for a network. Overrides the core getnetbyname and getnetbyaddr functions with object-oriented versions that return Net::netent objects. The objects have methods that return the fields of the same name from the *netent* structure in *netdb.h*:

Field	Description
addrtype	Net address type
aliases	Array of aliases
name	Name of net
net	Network number

You can access the structure fields with the methods or by importing the fields into your namespace with the :FIELDS import tag and accessing them by prepending n_ to the field name:

```
$net_obj->name( )
$n_name
```

Net::netent exports the following.

---

getnet

getnet (*net*)

Frontend for getnetbyaddr and getnetbyname. If *net* is numeric, calls getnetbyaddr; otherwise, calls getnetbyname.

---

getnetbyaddr

getnetbyaddr (*addr, addrtype*)

Returns information about the net with address *addr* of type *addrtype*.

---

getnetbyname

getnetbyname (*netname*)

Returns information about the net with name *netname*.

Net::Netrc

Implements a simple interface to *.netrc* in Perl (see Chapter 16). This module is part of the core Perl distribution starting with Perl 5.8.

Net::NNTP

Implements a simple NNTP client in Perl (see Chapter 17). This module is part of the core Perl distribution starting with Perl 5.8.

Net::Ping

Provides methods to create ping objects and test the reachability of remote hosts on the network. After the object has been created, a variable number of hosts can be pinged multiple times before closing the connection. The methods are the following.

---

new

$p = Net::Ping->new([*proto*[, *def_timeout*[, *bytes*]]])

Creates a new ping object. All arguments are optional. Takes the following arguments:

---

proto

The protocol to use when doing a ping. Default is udp. The possible protocols are:

icmp

Sends an icmp echo message to the remote host. If the echoed message is received back correctly from the remote host, that host is considered reachable. Requires the program to be run as root or setuid to root.

tcp

Attempts to establish connection to remote host's echo port. If successful, remote host is considered reachable. No data is actually echoed. No special privileges are required, but overhead is higher than for the others.

udp

Sends a udp packet to remote host's echo port. If the echoed packet is received back from the remote host and contains the same data that was sent, the remote host is considered reachable. Requires no special privileges.

def_timeout

Default timeout in seconds to be used if timeout not passed to the ping method. Must be greater than zero; defaults to five seconds.

bytes

Number of bytes included in the ping packet sent to the remote host. Ignored if protocol is tcp. Default is 1 if protocol is udp, otherwise 0. These are also the minimum number of bytes; the maximum is 1,024.

---

close

$p->close( )

Closes network connection for this ping object. The connection can also be closed by undef $p and is automatically closed if the ping object goes out of scope.

---

ping

$p->ping(host[, timeout])

Pings remote host and waits for a response. Takes the following arguments:

host

Specified as either the hostname or the IP number of the remote host.

timeout

Optional, must be greater than 0 seconds if specified. Defaults to whatever was specified when the ping object was created.

If *host* cannot be found, or if there is a problem with the IP number, returns undef. Otherwise, returns 1 if the host is reachable and 0 if it is not.

pingecho   pingecho (*host*[, *timeout*])

Provides backward compatibility with the previous version of Net::Ping. Uses the tcp protocol, with return values and parameters the same as described for ping.

Net::POP3

Implements a simple POP3 client in Perl (see Chapter 17). This module is part of the core Perl distribution starting with Perl 5.8.

Net::protoent

Returns information for an Internet protocol. Overrides the core getprotoent, getprotobyname, and getprotobynumber functions with object-oriented versions that return Net::protoent objects. The functions take a default second argument of tcp. The objects have methods that return the fields of the same name from the *protoent* structure in *netdb.h*:

Field	Description
aliases	List of aliases
name	Name of host
proto	Protocol

You can access the structure fields with the methods or by importing the fields into your namespace with the :FIELDS import tag and accessing them by prepending p_ to the field name:

    $proto_obj->name( )
    $p_name

getproto   getproto (*protocol*)

Frontend for getprotobynumber and getprotobyname. If *protocol* is numeric, calls getprotobynumber; otherwise, calls getprotobyname.

getprotobyname   getprotobyname (*addr*, *addrtype*)

Returns information about the host with address *addr* of type *addrtype*.

getprotobynumber

getprotobynumber (*hostname*)

Returns information about the host with name *hostname*.

getprotoent   getprotoent *(protocol)*

Frontend for getprotobynumber and getprotobyname. If *protocol* is numeric, calls getprotobynumber; otherwise, calls getprotobyname.

Net::servent

Returns information for an Internet service. Overrides the core getservent, getservbyname, and getservbyport functions, replacing them with versions that return Net::servent objects. The functions take a default second argument of tcp. The objects have methods that return the fields of the same name from the *servent* structure in *netdb.h*:

Field	Description
aliases	List of aliases
name	Name of service
port	Port
proto	Protocol to use

You can access the structure fields with the methods or by importing the fields into your namespace with the :FIELDS import tag and accessing them by prepending s_ to the field name:

```
$serv_obj->name( )
$s_name
```

getserv   getserv(*service*)

Frontend for getservbyport and getservbyname. If *service* is numeric, calls getservbyport; otherwise, calls getservbyname.

getservbyname   getservbyname(*name*)

Returns information for the Internet service with protocol name *name*.

getservbyport   getservbyport(*port*)

Returns information for the Internet service with port number *port*.

getservent   getservent

Returns entries from the database of Internet services.

Net::SMTP

Implements a simple SMTP client in Perl (see Chapter 16). This module is part of the core Perl distribution starting with Perl 5.8.

Net::Time

Provides subroutines that obtain the time on a remote machine. This module is part of the core Perl distribution starting with Perl 5.8.

Net::Time implements the following functions.

---

inet_daytime   inet_daytime([*host* [, *protocol* [, *timeout*]]])

Obtains the time on *host*, or a default host if *host* is not given. inet_daytime uses *protocol*, which can be either udp or tcp. Returns an ASCII string or undef on failure.

---

inet_time   inet_time([*host* [, *protocol* [, *timeout*]]])

Obtains the time on *host*, or a default host if *host* is not given. inet_time uses *protocol*, which can be either udp or tcp. Returns some units of time on success or undef on failure.

O

Generic interface to the Perl compiler backends. See also the B module.

```
perl -MO=backend[,options] perlscript
```

ODBM_File

Provides Perl programs with tied access to ODBM database files. See Perl's built-in tie function and the DB_File module.

Opcode

Permits defining an *operator mask* (opmask) so that any code containing a masked opcode will not compile or execute when Perl next compiles any code. Not usually used directly; for examples of Opcode's use, see the ops pragma and the Safe module.

Valid opcodes are listed in the array op_name in the file *opcode.h*. Many Opcode functions and methods take lists of operators, which are composed of elements. Each element can be a:

---

name (opname) or negated name

Name of operator, usually lowercase. Prefixing the name with an exclamation mark (!) removes it from the accumulated set of operations.

set (opset)

Operator set. Binary string holding a set of zero or more operators.

tag name (optag) or negated tag

Operator tag name; refers to groups (or sets) of operators. Begins with a colon (:). Negated by prefixing with an exclamation mark (!). Several *optags* are predefined, including the following. See the Opcode module's manpage for the opcodes included in each tag.

:base_core	:base_io	:base_loop
:base_math	:base_mem	:base_orig
:browse	:dangerous	:default
:filesys_open	:filesys_read	:filesys_write
:others	:ownprocess	:still_to_be_decided
:subprocess	:sys_db	

Functions

All the following functions can be exported.

---

define_optag   define_optag (*optag, opset*)

Defines *optag* as symbolic name for the set *opset*.

---

empty_opset   empty_opset

Returns an empty opset.

---

full_opset   full_opset

Returns an opset that includes all operators.

---

invert_opset   invert_opset (*opset*)

Returns an opset that is the inverse of *opset*.

---

opcodes   opcodes

In scalar context, returns the number of opcodes in this version of Perl.

---

opdesc   opdesc (*op, ...*)

Takes list of operator names and returns the corresponding list descriptions.

---

opdump	opdump ([*pat*])
	Writes two-column list of operator names and descriptions to STDOUT. If *pat* is specified, only lines matching the (case-insensitive) pattern are output.
opmask	opmask
	Returns an opset corresponding to the current opmask.
opmask_add	opmask_add (*opset*)
	Adds *opset* to the current opmask.
opset	opset (*op*, ...)
	Returns an opset containing the listed operators.
opset_to_hex	opset_to_hex (*opset*)
	Returns string representation of *opset*.
opset_to_ops	opset_to_ops (*opset*)
	Returns list of operator names corresponding to the operators in the set *opset*.
verify_opset	verify_opset (*opset*[, ...])
	Returns true if *opset* appears to be a valid opset, else returns false. croaks instead of returning false if optional second parameter is true.

ops

Pragma that disables unsafe opcodes during compilation. Can also be used to specify opcodes to be disabled. Generally used with the *–M* option on the command line:

```
perl -Mops=:default ...    # Allow only reasonably safe operations
perl -M-ops=system ...     # Disable system opcode
```

See the Opcode module for more information.

overload

Lets you substitute class methods or your own subroutines for standard Perl operators. For example, the code:

```
package Number;
use overload
    "+"  => \add,
    "*=" => "muas";
```

declares function add for addition and method muas in the Number class (or one of its base classes) for the assignment form *= of multiplication.

Arguments to use overload are key/value pairs, in which the key is the operation being overloaded, and the value is the function or method that is to be substituted. Legal values are values permitted inside a &{ ... } call, so a subroutine name, a subroutine reference, or an anonymous subroutine are all legal. Legal keys (overloadable operations) are:

Type	Operations
Arithmetic	+ - * / % ** << >> x .+= -= *= /= %= **= <<= >>= x= .=
Comparison	< <= > >= == != <=> lt le gt ge eq ne cmp
Bit and unary	% ^ | neg ! ~
Increment, decrement	++ -
Transcendental	atan2 cos sin exp abs log sqrt
Boolean, string, numeric conversion	bool "" 0+
Special	nomethod fallback =

The functions specified with the use overload directive are typically called with three arguments. If the corresponding operation is binary, then the first two arguments are the two arguments of the operation. However, the first argument should always be an object in the package, so in some cases, the order of the arguments will be interchanged before the method is called. The third argument provides information on the order and can have these values:

False (0)
> The order of arguments is as in the current operation.

True (1)
> The arguments are reversed.

Undefined (undef)
> The current operation is an assignment variant, but the usual function is called instead.

Unary operations are considered binary operations with the second argument undefined.

The special nomethod key should be followed by a reference to a function of four parameters and called when the overloading mechanism cannot find a method for an operation. The first three arguments are the arguments for the corresponding method if it was found; the fourth argument is the symbol corresponding to the missing method. If several methods are tried, the last one is used.

For example, 1-$a can be equivalent to:

```
&nomethodMethod($a, 1, 1, "-")
```

if the pair "nomethod" => "nomethodMethod" was specified in the use overload directive.

The special fallback key governs what to do if a method for a particular operation is not found. There are three possible cases, depending on the value associated with the fallback key:

Undefined
> Tries to use a substituted method. If that fails, it tries to call the method specified for nomethod; if that also fails, an exception is raised.

True
> The same as undefined, but no exception is raised. Instead, Perl silently reverts to non-overloaded operation.

Defined, but false
> Tries to call the method specified for nomethod; if that fails, an exception is raised.

The overload module provides the following public functions.

Method	overload::Method(*obj, op*)
	Returns the undefined value or a reference to the method that implements *op*.

Overloaded	overload::Overloaded(*arg*)
	Returns true if *arg* is subject to overloading of some operations.

StrVal	overload::StrVal(*arg*)
	Gives string value of *arg* if stringify overloading is absent.

PerlIO

An on-demand loader for PerlIO layers and the root of the PerlIO namespace. PerlIO allows you to expand the functionality of open(). For example:

```
use PerlIO 'special';
```

The code in *PerlIO.pm* then attempts to find 'special':

```
require PerlIO::special;
```

PerlIO currently defines the following layers:

unix
>   Low-level layer that calls read, write, lseek, etc.

stdio
>   Calls fread, fwrite, fseek, ftell, etc. stdio will use your operating system's I/O via the C library. That is, you cannot place any layers beneath stdio.

perlio
>   A reimplementation of a stdio-like buffering written as a PerlIO layer. As such, it will call whatever layer is below it for its operations.

crlf
>   Does CRLF translation depending on distinguishing text, and binary files a la MS-DOS.

utf8
>   Declares that the stream accepts Perl's internal encoding of characters (which is really UTF-8 on ASCII machines and UTF-EBCDIC on EBCDIC machines). This allows any character Perl can represent to be read from or written to the stream. The UTF-*X* encoding is chosen to render simple text parts (i.e., nonaccented letters, digits, and common punctuation) human-readable in the encoded file.

raw
>   A pseudo-layer that performs two functions. It forces the filehandle to be considered binary at that point in the layer stack, and it prevents the I/O system from searching before it in the layer specification. For example:
>
>    ```
>    open($fh,":raw:perlio",...);
>    ```
>
>   raw forces the use of the perlio layer even if the platform default or the use open default is something else (such as :encoding(iso-8859-7)).

PerlIO::Scalar

Supports in-memory I/O. It exists so it can use XSLoader to load C code that supports treating a scalar as an "in-memory" file. PerlIO::Scalar allows all normal file operations to be performed on the handle. Returns undef.

For example:

```
#!/usr/local/bin/perl -w
use PerlIO::Scalar;
open($fh, "<...", \$some_scalar);
```

This module is part of the core Perl distribution starting with Perl 5.8.

PerlIO::Via

A helper class for PerlIO layers implemented in Perl. PerlIO::Via ships with the Perl 5.8 source kit.

For example, you can use PerlIO::Via to call `MIME::Base64::encode_base64()` via `open()`:

```
#!/usr/local/bin/perl -w;
use MIME::Base64;
open(my $fh, ">Via(MIME::Base64)", "encode_base64");
```

PerlIO::Via implements the following methods.

CLOSE   CLOSE(*fh*)

Returns 0 on success and -1 on error.

EOF   EOF(*fh*)

Returns end-of-file state. The default behavior is to return a value of FILL() or READ().

ERROR   ERROR(*fh*)

Returns error state.

FILENO   FILENO(*fh*)

Returns a numeric value that represents the Unix-like file descriptor, or -1 if no file descriptor exists.

FILL   FILL(*fh*)

Returns a string that will be placed in the buffer.

FLUSH   FLUSH(*fh*)

Flushes any buffered write data. Returns 0 on success and -1 on error.

POPPED   POPPED([*fh*])

Removes a layer from PerlIO::Via.

PUSHED $class->PUSHED([*mode* [,*fh*]])

Returns an object or the class, or -1 on failure. PUSHED takes optional arguments for file open mode—r, w, w+, etc.—and takes a mandatory filehandle for the PerlIO layer itself.

READ	READ(*buffer*, *len*, *fh*)
	Returns the number of octets in *buffer*, which must be less than or equal to *len*.

SEEK	SEEK(*posn*, *where*, *fh*)
	Returns 0 on success and -1 on error.

TELL	TELL(*fh*)
	Returns the file position, without an available default.

UNREAD	UNREAD(*buffer*, *fh*)
	Returns the number of octets from *buffer* that have been successfully saved.

WRITE	WRITE(*buffer*, *fh*)
	Returns the number of octets in buffer that have been written.

Pod::Functions

Used internally by Pod::Html for converting from pod to HTML.

Pod::Html

Converts files from pod to HTML format. Not generally used directly, but via the *pod2html* script (see Chapter 4), which is included in the standard distribution.

Pod::ParseLink

Parses an L<> formatting code in POD text. It implements a single function, parselink(), which takes the text of an L<> formatting code and parses it. parselink() returns the anchor text for the link, the anchor text possibly inferred from the name and section, the name or URL, and the section and the type of link. The link type will be url, pod, or man. For example:

```
#!/usr/local/bin/perl -w
use Pod::ParseLink;
my $link = 'L<http://www.some-site.com/indexes/index.html>';
my ($text, $inferred, $name, $section, $type) = parselink ($link);
```

Pod::Text

Converts files from pod format to formatted ASCII text. Not generally used directly, but via the *pod2text* script (see Chapter 4). Termcap is optionally supported for boldface and underlining and can be enabled with:

```
$Pod::Text::termcap=1
```

Otherwise, backspaces are used to simulate bold and underlined text. Exports one function.

---

pod2text   pod2text (*filename*[, *filehandle*])

Converts from pod to text format. Takes the following arguments:

filename
    File to convert, or <&STDIN to read from STDIN.

filehandle
    Optional. Filehandle glob to which output should be sent (*STDOUT to write to STDOUT).

POSIX

Provides access to standard POSIX 1003.1 identifiers: functions, classes, and constants. Can be used to import one or multiple symbols:

```
use POSIX;                    # Import all symbols
use POSIX qw(setsid);         # Import one symbol
use POSIX qw(:errno_h :fcntl_h); # Import sets of symbols
```

Functions listed as C-specific are not implemented.

Function	Description
_exit	Identical to C function _exit(2)
abort	Identical to C function abort(3)
abs	Identical to Perl's abs function
access	Determines accessibility of a file; returns undef on failure
acos	Identical to C function acos(3)
alarm	Identical to Perl's alarm function
asctime	Identical to C function asctime(3)
asin	Identical to C function asin(3)
assert	Similar to C macro assert(3)
atan	Identical to C function atan(3)
atan2	Identical to Perl's atan2 function
atexit	C-specific; use END {}
atof	C-specific
atoi	C-specific

Function	Description
atol	C-specific
bsearch	Not supplied
calloc	C-specific
ceil	Identical to C function `ceil(3)`
chdir	Identical to Perl's `chdir` function
chmod	Identical to Perl's `chmod` function
chown	Identical to Perl's `chown` function
clearerr	Uses method `FileHandle::clearerr`
clock	Identical to C function `clock(3)`
close	Closes a file; returns `undef` on failure
closedir	Identical to Perl's `closedir` function
cos	Identical to Perl's `cos` function
cosh	Identical to C function `cosh(3)`
creat	Creates a new file
ctermid	Generates pathname for the controlling terminal
ctime	Identical to C function `ctime(3)`
cuserid	Gets user's login name
difftime	Identical to C function `difftime(3)`
div	C-specific
dup	Similar to C function `dup(2)`; returns `undef` on failure
dup2	Similar to C function `dup2(2)`; returns `undef` on failure
errno	Returns the value of `errno`
execl	C-specific; use Perl's `exec`
execle	C-specific; use Perl's `exec`
execlp	C-specific; use Perl's `exec`
execv	C-specific; use Perl's `exec`
execve	C-specific; use Perl's `exec`
execvp	C-specific; use Perl's `exec`
exit	Identical to Perl's `exit` function
exp	Identical to Perl's `exp` function
fabs	Identical to Perl's `abs` function
fclose	Uses method `FileHandle::close`
fcntl	Identical to Perl's `fcntl` function
fdopen	Uses method `FileHandle::new_from_fd`
feof	Uses method `FileHandle::eof`
ferror	Uses method `FileHandle::error`
fflush	Uses method `FileHandle::flush`
fgetc	Uses method `FileHandle::getc`
fgetpos	Uses method `FileHandle::getpos`
fgets	Uses method `FileHandle::gets`
fileno	Uses method `FileHandle::fileno`
floor	Identical to C function `floor(3)`

Function	Description
fmod	Identical to C function fmod(3)
fopen	Uses method FileHandle::open
fork	Identical to Perl's fork function
fpathconf	Returns value of a configurable limit on a file or directory, or undef on failure
fprintf	C-specific; use Perl's printf function
fputc	C-specific; use Perl's print function
fputs	C-specific; use Perl's print function
fread	C-specific; use Perl's read function
free	C-specific
freopen	C-specific; use Perl's open function
frexp	Returns mantissa and exponent of a floating-point number
fscanf	C-specific; use <> and regular expressions
fseek	Uses method FileHandle::seek
fsetpos	Uses method FileHandle::setpos
fstat	Gets file status
ftell	Uses method FileHandle::tell
fwrite	C-specific; use Perl's print function
getc	Identical to Perl's etc function
getchar	Returns one character from STDIN
getcwd	Returns name of current working directory
getegid	Returns effective group ID (gid)
getenv	Returns value of the specified environment variable
geteuid	Returns the effective user ID (uid)
getgid	Returns the user's real group ID (gid)
getgrgid	Identical to Perl's getgrgid function
getgrnam	Identical to Perl's getgrnam function
getgroups	Returns IDs of the user's supplementary groups
getlogin	Identical to Perl's getlogin function
getpgrp	Identical to Perl's getpgrp function
getpid	Returns ID of the process (pid)
getppid	Identical to Perl's getppid function
getpwnam	Identical to Perl's getpwnam function
getpwuid	Identical to Perl's getpwuid function
gets	Returns one line from STDIN
getuid	Returns user's ID (uid)
gmtime	Identical to Perl's gmtime function
isalnum	Identical to C function, but can apply to one character or a whole string
isalpha	Identical to C function, but can apply to one character or a whole string
isatty	Returns Boolean indicating whether the specified filehandle is connected to a TTY
iscntrl	Identical to C function, but can apply to one character or a whole string
isdigit	Identical to C function, but can apply to one character or a whole string
isgraph	Identical to C function, but can apply to one character or a whole string

Function	Description
islower	Identical to C function, but can apply to one character or a whole string
isprint	Identical to C function, but can apply to one character or a whole string
ispunct	Identical to C function, but can apply to one character or a whole string
isspace	Identical to C function, but can apply to one character or a whole string
isupper	Identical to C function, but can apply to one character or a whole string
isxdigit	Identical to C function, but can apply to one character or a whole string
kill	Identical to Perl's kill function
labs	C-specific; use Perl's abs function
ldexp	Identical to C function ldexp(3)
ldiv	C-specific; use division operator (/) and Perl's int function
link	Identical to Perl's link function
localeconv	Gets numeric formatting information; returns reference to a hash containing the current locale formatting values
localtime	Identical to Perl's localtime function
log	Identical to Perl's log function
log10	Identical to C function log10(3)
longjmp	C-specific; use Perl's die function
lseek	Moves the read/write file pointer; returns undef on failure
malloc	C-specific
mblen	Identical to C function mblen(3)
mbstowcs	Identical to C function mbstowcs(3)
mbtowc	Identical to C function mbtowc(3)
memchr	C-specific; use Perl's index
memcmp	C-specific; use eq
memcpy	C-specific; use =
memmove	C-specific; use =
memset	C-specific; use x
mkdir	Identical to Perl's mkdir function
mkfifo	Similar to C function mkfifo(2); returns undef on failure
mktime	Converts date/time information to a calendar time; returns undef on failure
modf	Returns integral and fractional parts of a floating-point number
nice	Similar to C function nice(3); returns undef on failure
offsetof	C-specific
open	Opens file for reading or writing; returns undef on failure
opendir	Opens directory for reading; returns undef on failure
pathconf	Retrieves value of a configurable limit on a file or directory; returns undef on failure
pause	Similar to C function pause(3); returns undef on failure
perror	Identical to C function perror(3)
pipe	Creates an interprocess channel
pow	Computes $x raised to the power $exponent
printf	Prints specified arguments to STDOUT
putc	C-specific; use Perl's print function

Modules

Function	Description
putchar	C-specific; use Perl's `print` function
puts	C-specific; use Perl's `print` function
qsort	C-specific; use Perl's `sort` function
raise	Sends specified signal to current process
rand	Nonportable; use Perl's `rand` function
read	Reads from a file; returns `undef` on failure
readdir	Identical to Perl's `readdir` function
realloc	C-specific
remove	Identical to Perl's `unlink` function
rename	Identical to Perl's `rename` function
rewind	Seeks to beginning of file
rewinddir	Identical to Perl's `rewinddir` function
rmdir	Identical to Perl's `rmdir` function
scanf	C-specific; use `<>` and regular expressions
setgid	Sets real group ID for this process
setjmp	C-specific; use `eval {}`
setlocale	Modifies and queries program's locale
setpgid	Similar to C function `setpgid(2)`; returns `undef` on failure
setsid	Identical to C function `setsid(8)`
setuid	Sets real user ID for this process
sigaction	Detailed signal management; returns `undef` on failure
siglongjmp	C-specific; use Perl's `die` function
sigpending	Examines blocked, pending signals; returns `undef` on failure
sigprocmask	Changes and/or examines this process's signal mask; returns `undef` on failure
sigsetjmp	C-specific; use `eval {}`
sigsuspend	Installs signal mask and suspends process until signal arrives; returns `undef` on failure
sin	Identical to Perl's `sin` function
sinh	Identical to C function `sinh(3)`
sleep	Identical to Perl's `sleep` function
sprintf	Identical to Perl's `sprintf` function
sqrt	Identical to Perl's `sqrt` function
srand	Identical to Perl's `srand` function
sscanf	C-specific; use regular expressions
stat	Identical to Perl's `stat` function
strcat	C-specific; use `.=`
strchr	C-specific; use `index`
strcmp	C-specific; use `eq`
strcoll	Identical to C function `strcoll(3)`
strcpy	C-specific; use `=`
strcspn	C-specific; use regular expressions
strerror	Returns error string for the specified `errno`
strftime	Converts date and time to string and returns the string

Function	Description
strlen	C-specific; use length
strncat	C-specific; use .= and/or substr
strncmp	C-specific; use eq and/or substr
strncpy	C-specific; use = and/or substr
stroul	C-specific
strpbrk	C-specific
strrchr	C-specific; use rindex and/or substr
strspn	C-specific
strstr	Identical to Perl's index function
strtod	C-specific
strtok	C-specific
strtol	C-specific
strtoul	C-specific
strxfrm	String transformation; returns the transformed string
sysconf	Retrieves values of system configurable variables; returns undef on failure
system	Identical to Perl's system function
tan	Identical to C function tan(3)
tanh	Identical to C function tanh(3)
tcdrain	Similar to C function tcdrain(3); returns undef on failure
tcflow	Similar to C function tcflow(3); returns undef on failure
tcflush	Similar to C function tcflush(3); returns undef on failure
tcgetpgrp	Identical to C function tcgetpgrp(3)
tcsendbreak	Similar to C function tcsendbreak(3); returns undef on failure
tcsetpgrp	Similar to C function tcsetpgrp(3); returns undef on failure
time	Identical to Perl's time function
times	Returns, in clock ticks, elapsed realtime since a point in the past, user and system times for this process, and user and system times for child processes
tmpfile	Uses method FileHandle::new_tmpfile
tmpnam	Returns a name for a temporary file
tolower	Identical to Perl's lc function
toupper	Identical to Perl's uc function
ttyname	Identical to C function ttyname(3)
tzname	Retrieves time conversion information from the tzname variable
tzset	Identical to C function tzset(3)
umask	Identical to Perl's umask function
uname	Gets name of current operating system
ungetc	Uses method FileHandle::ungetc
unlink	Identical to Perl's unlink function
utime	Identical to Perl's utime function
vfprintf	C-specific
vprintf	C-specific
vsprintf	C-specific

Modules

Function	Description
wait	Identical to Perl's wait function
waitpid	Waits for child process to change state; identical to Perl's waitpid function
wcstombs	Identical to C function wcstombs(3)
wctomb	Identical to C function wctomb(3)
write	Writes to file; returns undef on failure

The following sections show the classes that are defined and their methods.

POSIX::SigAction

new
$sigaction = POSIX::SigAction->new(sigsub, sigset, flags)

Constructor. Creates a new POSIX::SigAction object. Takes the following arguments:

sigsub
> The fully qualified name of a signal-handler subroutine

sigset
> A POSIX::SigSet object

flags
> The sa_flags

POSIX::SigSet

new
$sigset = POSIX::SigSet->new[()]

Constructor. Creates new SigSet object. Optional arguments are used to initialize the set.

addset
$sigset->addset(sig)

Adds signal sig to SigSet object; returns undef on failure.

delset
$sigset->delset(sig)

Removes signal sig from SigSet object; returns undef on failure.

emptyset
$sigset->emptyset()

Initializes SigSet object to empty; returns undef on failure.

fillset	`$sigset->fillset()`
	Initializes SigSet object to include all signals; returns undef on failure.

ismember	`$sigset->ismember(sig)`
	Tests SigSet object for a specific signal *sig*.

POSIX::Termios

new	`$termios = POSIX::Termios->new`
	Constructor. Creates new Termios object.

getattr	`$termios->getattr([fd])`
	Gets terminal control attributes for a given *fd* (default is 0 for STDIN); returns undef on failure.

getcc	`$c_cc[ind] = $termios->getcc(ind)`
	Retrieves value from the *c_cc* field of a Termios object. Takes index *ind* since @c_cc is an array.

getcflag	`$c_cflag = $termios->getcflag`
	Retrieves *c_cflag* field of a Termios object.

getiflag	`$c_iflag = $termios->getiflag`
	Retrieves *c_iflag* field of a Termios object.

getispeed	`$ispeed = $termios->getispeed`
	Retrieves input baud rate.

getlflag	`getlflag $c_lflag = $termios->getlflag`
	Retrieves *c_lflag* field of a Termios object.

getoflag	`$c_oflag = $termios->getoflag`
	Retrieves *c_oflag* field of a Termios object.
getospeed	`$ospeed = $termios->getospeed`
	Retrieves output baud rate.
setattr	`$termios->setattr(fd, option)`
	Sets terminal control attributes for a given *fd*; returns undef on failure. *option* tells when to set the attributes and is one of TCSADRAIN, TCSAFLUSH, or TCSANOW.
setcc	`$termios->setcc(ind, value)`
	Sets *value* in the *c_cc* field, indexed by *ind*, of a Termios object.
setcflag	`$termios->setcflag(flag)`
	Sets *flag* in the *c_cflag* field of a Termios object.
setiflag	`$termios->setiflag(flag)`
	Sets *flag* in the *c_iflag* field of a Termios object.
setispeed	`$termios->setispeed(value)`
	Sets input baud rate to *value*; returns undef on failure.
setlflag	`$termios->setlflag(flag)`
	Sets *flag* in the *c_lflag* field of a Termios object.
setoflag	`$termios->setoflag(flag)`
	Sets *flag* in the *c_oflag* field of a Termios object.
setospeed	`$termios->setospeed(value)`
	Sets the output baud rate to *value*; returns undef on failure.

Constants

The following constants are associated with the Termios class:

Baud rate values
```
B0   B75  B134 B200 B600  B1800 B4800 B19200
B50  B110 B150 B300 B1200 B2400 B9600 B38400
```

c_cc index values
```
VEOF VERASE VKILL VSUSP  VSTOP VTIME
VEOL VINTR  VQUIT VSTART VMIN  NCCS
```

c_cflag field values
```
CLOCAL CSIZE CS6 CS8    HUPCL  PARODD
CREAD  CS5   CS7 CSTOPS PARENB
```

c_iflag field values
```
BRKINT IGNBRK IGNPAR INPCK  IXOFF PARMRK
ICRNL  IGNCR  INLCR  ISTRIP IXON
```

c_lflag field values
```
ECHO   ECHONL ISIG
ECHOE  ICANON NOFLSH
ECHOK  IEXTEN TOSTOP
```

c_oflag field values
```
OPOST
```

Terminal interface values
```
TCSADRAIN TCIOFLUSH TCIFLUSH
TCSANOW   TCOFLUSH  TCSAFLUSH
TCOON     TCION     TCIOFF
```

The following are other constants defined in the POSIX module:

Pathname constants
```
_PC_CHOWN_RESTRICTED _PC_LINK_MAX   _PC_MAX_CANON
_PC_MAX_INPUT        _PC_NAME_MAX   _PC_NO_TRUNC
_PC_PATH_MAX         _PC_PIPE_BUF   _PC_VDISABLE
```

POSIX constants
```
_POSIX_ARG_MAX      _POSIX_CHILD_MAX   _POSIX_CHOWN_RESTRICTED
_POSIX_JOB_CONTROL  _POSIX_LINK_MAX    _POSIX_MAX_CANON
_POSIX_MAX_INPUT    _POSIX_NAME_MAX    _POSIX_NGROUPS_MAX
_POSIX_NO_TRUNC     _POSIX_OPEN_MAX    _POSIX_PATH_MAX
_POSIX_PIPE_BUF     _POSIX_SAVED_IDS   _POSIX_SSIZE_MAX
_POSIX_STREAM_MAX   _POSIX_TZNAME_MAX  _POSIX_VDISABLE
_POSIX_VERSION
```

System configuration
```
_SC_ARG_MAX      _SC_CHILD_MAX  _SC_CLK_TCK    _SC_JOB_CONTROL
_SC_NGROUPS_MAX  _SC_OPEN_MAX   _SC_SAVED_IDS  _SC_STREAM_MAX
_SC_TZNAME_MAX   _SC_VERSION
```

Error constants
```
E2BIG  EACCES  EAGAIN  EBADF  EBUSY        ECHILD EDEADLK
EDOM   EEXIST  EFAUL   EFBIG  EINTR        EINVAL
EIO    EISDIR  EMFILE  EMLINK ENAMETOOLONG ENFILE
ENODE  ENOENT  ENOEXEC ENOLCK ENOMEM       ENOSPC
```

```
ENOSYS    ENOTDIR ENOTEMPTY ENOTTY   ENXIO        EPERM
EPIPE     ERANGE  EROFS      ESPIPE   ESRCH        EXDEV
```

File control constants
```
FD_CLOEXEC  F_DUPFD    F_GETFD    F_GETFL  F_GETLK   F_OK
F_RDLCK     F_SETFD    F_SETFL    F_SETLK  F_SETLKW  F_UNLCK
F_WRLCK     O_ACCMODE  O_APPEND   O_CREAT  O_EXCL    O_NOCTTY
O_NONBLOCK  O_RDONLY   O_RDWR     O_TRUNC  O_WRONLY
```

Floating-point constants
```
DBL_DIG         DBL_EPSILON   DBL_MANT_DIG   DBL_MAX
DBL_MAX_10_EXP  DBL_MAX_EXP   DBL_MIN        DBL_MIN_10_EXP
DBL_MIN_EXP     FLT_DIG       FLT_EPSILON    FLT_MANT_DIG
FLT_MAX         FLT_MAX_10_EXP FLT_MAX_EXP   FLT_MIN
FLT_MIN_10_EXP  FLT_MIN_EXP   FLT_RADIX      FLT_ROUNDS
LDBL_DIG        LDBL_EPSILON  LDBL_MANT_DIG  LDBL_MAX
LDBL_MAX_10_EXP LDBL_MAX_EXP  LDBL_MIN       LDBL_MIN_10_EXP
LDBL_MIN_EXP
```

Limit constants
```
ARG_MAX     CHAR_BIT   CHAR_MAX    CHAR_MIN    CHILD_MAX
INT_MAX     INT_MIN    LINK_MAX    LONG_MAX    LONG_MIN
MAX_CANON   MAX_INPUT  MB_LEN_MAX  NAME_MAX    NGROUPS_MAX
OPEN_MAX    PATH_MAX   PIPE_BUF    SCHAR_MAX   SCHAR_MIN
SHRT_MAX    SHRT_MIN   SSIZE_MAX   STREAM_MAX  TZNAME_MAX
UCHAR_MAX   UINT_MAX   ULONG_MAX   USHRT_MAX
```

Locale constants
```
LC_ALL  LC_COLLATE  LC_CTYPE  LC_MONETARY  LC_NUMERIC  LC_TIME
```

Math constants
```
HUGE_VAL
```

Signal constants
```
SA_NOCLDSTOP SIGABRT    SIGALRM    SIGCHLD   SIGCONT   SIGFPE
SIGHUP       SIGILL     SIGINT     SIGKILL   SIGPIPE   SIGQUIT
SIGSEGV      SIGSTOP    SIGTERM    SIGTSTP   SIGTTIN   SIGTTOU
SIGUSR1      SIGUSR2    SIG_BLOCK  SIG_DFL   SIG_ERR   SIG_IGN
SIG_SETMASK  SIG_UNBLOCK
```

Stat constants
```
S_IRGRP  S_IROTH  S_IRUSR  S_IRWXG  S_IRWXO  S_IRWXU  S_ISGID
S_ISUID  S_IWGRP  S_IWOTH  S_IWUSR  S_IXGRP  S_IXOTH  S_IXUSR
```

Stat macros
```
S_ISBLK  S_ISCHR  S_ISDIR  S_ISFIFO  S_ISREG
```

Stdlib constants
```
EXIT_FAILURE  EXIT_SUCCESS  MB_CUR_MAX  RAND_MAX
```

Stdio constants
```
BUFSIZ  EOF  FILENAME_MAX  L_ctermid  L_cuserid  L_tmpname  TMP_MAX
```

Time constants
```
CLK_TCK  CLOCKS_PER_SEC
```

Unistd constants
```
R_OK    SEEK_CUR  SEEK_END     SEEK_SET  STDIN_FILENO
STDOUT_FILENO     STRERR_FILENO W_OK      X_OK
```

Wait constants
    WNOHANG WUNTRACED

Wait macros
    WIFEXITED WEXITSTATUS WIFSIGNALED WTERMSIG WIFSTOPPED WSTOPSIG

re

Pragma that lets you alter the behavior of regular expressions. Permits the following alterations:

use re 'debug'
> Causes Perl to produce debugging messages when compiling and at runtime when using regular expressions. See the *re* manpage and the section on "Debugging regular expressions" in the *perldebug* manpage for details.

use re 'eval'
> Permits a regular expression to contain (?{...}) zero-width assertion even if the regular expression contains variable interpolation, which normally isn't permitted for security reasons. The pragma is ignored if the regular expression comes from tainted data.

use re 'taint'
> When a tainted string is the target of a regular expression, causes the regular expression memories (or the values returned by the m// operator in list context) to be tainted.

Safe

Creates compartments for evaluating untrusted Perl code. Each compartment has an associated operator mask for excluding particular Perl operators from the compartment. (See the Opcode module for more information on operators and operator masks.) The default mask is applied during compilation to prevent all operations that give access to the system. Safe provides the following methods.

new	$cpt = new Safe [(namespace, mask)]

Constructor. Creates a new compartment. Takes the following arguments:

namespace
> Optional. Root namespace to use for the compartment. Default is Safe::Root0, which autoincrements for each new compartment.

mask
> Optional. Operator mask to use; defaults to a restrictive set.

mask	$cpt->mask ([mask])

Sets operator mask for the compartment if *mask* is specified; otherwise, it gets the current mask.

rdo	`$cpt->rdo (filename)`
	Evaluates the contents of file *filename* inside the compartment.

reval	`$cpt->reval (string)`
	Evaluates *string* as Perl code inside the compartment.

root	`$cpt->root ([namespace])`
	If *namespace* is specified, sets the root namespace for the compartment; otherwise, gets the current namespace.

share	`$cpt->share (varname[, ...])`
	Shares the variable(s) in the argument list with the compartment.

trap	`$cpt->trap (op[, ...])`
	For each operator specified in the argument list, sets the corresponding bit in the compartment's operator mask.

untrap	`$cpt->untrap (op[, ...])`
	For each operator specified in the argument list, resets the corresponding bit in the compartment's operator mask.

varglob	`$cpt->varglob (varname)`
	Returns a glob for the symbol table entry of *varname* in the compartment's package.

The following subroutines are available for export by Safe. The operator names can be found in the array op_name in the file *opcode.h* in the Perl distribution.

emptymask	`emptymask`
	Returns a mask with all operators unmasked.

fullmask	`fullmask`
	Returns a mask with all operators masked.

mask_to_ops	mask_to_ops (*mask*)
	Takes an operator mask *mask* and returns a list of the names of operators masked in *mask*.

MAXO	MAXO
	Returns the number of operators in a mask (and hence its length).

opcode	opcode (*op*[, ...])
	Takes a list of operator names and returns the corresponding list of opcodes.

op_mask	op_mask
	Returns the operator mask in effect at the time the invocation to the subroutine was compiled.

opname	opname (*op*[, ...])
	Takes a list of opcodes and returns the corresponding list of operator names.

ops_to_mask	ops_to_mask (*op*[, ...])
	Takes a list of operator names and returns an operator mask with those operators masked.

Scalar::Util

Implements a few useful scalar-related subroutines. Like List::Util, Scalar::Util is something useful that doesn't necessarily fit well as a keyword in the Perl core. By default, Scalar::Util does not export any subroutines. As of Perl 5.8, Scalar::Util is shipped with the source kit.

Scalar::Util implements the following methods.

blessed	blessed *expr*
	Evaluates whether *expr* is a blessed reference. If successful, blessed returns the name of the package. Otherwise, blessed returns undef.

```
use Scalar::Util qw(blessed);
use CGI;
```

```
                              my $cgi = CGI->new();
                              my $not_cgi = "IamNotCGI";

                              my $is_blessed = blessed($cgi);
                              if(defined($is_blessed) { print "$cgi\n;" } # Prints CGI

                              my $is_blessed2 = blessed($not_cgi);
                              if(defined($is_blessed2) { print "$not_cgi\n"; } # undef
```

---

dualvar

dualvar *number, string*

Returns a string that has the value *number* in a numeric context and
a value *string* in a string context. For example:

```
    my $context = dualvar(10, "Nathan");
    my $add_nums = $context + 1; # '11'
    my $str_add = $context . "Patwardhan"; # Nathan Patwardhan
```

---

isweak

isweak *expr*

Returns true if *expr* is a scalar, which is a weak reference:

```
    my $weak_ref = \$boo_hoo;
    my $i_am_weak = isweak($weak_ref); # false
    weaken($weak_ref);
    $i_am_weak = isweak($weak_ref); # true
```

---

openhandle

openhandle *fh*

Returns fh if *fh* is an open filehandle. *fh* may also be a tied filehandle. Returns undef on failure.

```
    my $fh = openhandle(*STDIN);
    $fh = openhandle("sumfin"); # undef, since sumfin isn't
                                # open
```

---

readonly

readonly *scalar*

Returns true if *scalar* is read-only.

---

reftype

reftype *expr*

Returns the reference type of *expr* if *expr* is a reference. Otherwise, returns undef.

```
    my $r_type = reftype "ORA"; # undef, not a reference
    my $r_type = reftype [];    # ARRAY
```

---

tainted

tainted *expr*

Returns true if the result of *expr* is tainted:

```
    my $is_tainted = tainted($ENV{PATH});
    # Returns true if -T is enabled
```

weaken	weaken *ref*
	Returns *ref* into a weak reference. When the reference count on an object reaches 0, *ref* will be set to undef.

SDBM_File

Provides Perl programs with tied access to SDBM database files. See Perl's built-in tie function and the DB_File module.

Search::Dict

Searches for a key in an ordered text file and sets the file position. Exports one function.

look	look **fh, key, dict, fold*
	Performs string search and sets the position in filehandle *fh* to the first line with a key equal to or greater than *key*. Returns the new file position, or -1 in case of error. Takes the following arguments:
	fh
	Filehandle of the dictionary file
	key
	Key to search for
	dict
	If true, searches in dictionary order, considering only word characters and whitespace
	fold
	If true, ignores case

SelectSaver

Provides a way to save and restore filehandles so you can temporarily use a different filehandle.

new	$*saver* = new SelectSaver[(*fh*)]
	Constructor. Creates a new SelectSaver object, $*saver*, which saves the current filehandle. The optional parameter *fh* is the filehandle that will temporarily replace the current filehandle. If *fh* is present, the current filehandle is saved in $*saver*, and the new one becomes

the current filehandle. With no parameter, the current filehandle is saved in the object $saver, and it remains current.

You can use the newly selected filehandle within the current block. When you exit the block, the previous filehandle is again made the current one, and the SelectSaver object in which it was stored is destroyed.

SelfLoader

Used when you want to include functions in your program but want to load them only if necessary. Functions that will be self-loaded are placed after the line:

```
__DATA__
```

in your program. When the code is compiled, compilation stops at the __DATA__ token. The SelfLoader exports the AUTOLOAD subroutine to the package; this subroutine loads the subroutines after __DATA__ when they are required.

Shell

Allows you to invoke Unix shell utilities as if they were Perl subroutines. Arguments (including switches) are passed to the utilities as strings:

```
use Shell qw(date cp ps);  # List shell commands you want to use

$date = date();   # Put the output of the date(1) command into $date
cp("-p" "/etc/passwd", "/tmp/passwd"); # Copy password file to a tmp file
print ps("-ww");  # Print the results of a "ps -ww" command
```

sigtrap

Pragma to enable simple signal handling. Provides two signal handlers that can be installed, or you can install your own handler; also provides options to specify which signals to trap. Ignores requests to trap signals not used in your system's architecture.

```
use sigtrap;                 # Initialize default signal handlers
use sigtrap qw(die normal-signals);
use sigtrap 'handler' => \handlername, 'normal-signals';
use sigtrap qw(handler handlername normal-signals
               stack-trace error-signals);
```

Signal Handler Options

Used to specify which handler will be installed for signals installed after the handler:

die
Installs handler that dies with a message indicating the signal that was trapped.

handler *handlername*
Installs your handler *handlername*.

stack-trace
Default signal handler. Outputs stack trace to STDERR and tries to dump core.

Signal List Options

You can specify your own list of options:

    use sigtrap qw(BUS SEGV PIPE ABRT);

or use one of the following built-in option lists:

error-signals
Signals that indicate a serious problem: ABRT, BUS, EMT, FPE, ILL, QUIT, SEGV, SYS, and TRAP.

normal-signals
Signals a program is most likely to encounter: HUP, INT, PIPE, and TERM.

old-interface-signals
Default. Signals trapped by default in older versions of sigtrap: ABRT, BUS, EMT, FPE, ILL, PIPE, QUIT, SEGV, SYS, TERM, and TRAP.

Other Options

any
Installs handlers only for subsequently listed signals that aren't already taken care of.

number
Requires that the version of sigtrap being used must be at least *number*.

signal
Installs a handler for any argument that looks like a signal name.

untrapped
Installs handlers only for subsequently listed signals not already trapped or ignored.

Socket

Translation of the C *socket.h* file that uses *h2xs* and your C compiler. See Chapter 13 for details.

sort

The sort pragma allows you to control sort() behavior. In Perl 5.6 and earlier, the default sort() behavior was written with quicksort. Perl 5.8, with which *sort. pm* is shipped in the source kit, implements mergesort. mergesort guarantees the worst-case behavior of O(N log N), where quicksort guarantees O(N ** 2).

Perl 5.8 and later shuffle large arrays before sorting. Note that *sort.pm* is global and not lexical in scope.

For example:

```
#!/usr/local/bin/perl -w
use sort '_quicksort'; # Or _qsort, if you'd like
sort(@something);
```

mergesort is better than quicksort for several reasons. First, mergesort is more stable and does fewer comparisons than quicksort, so it's better for more complicated sorting routines. In addition, mergesort takes preexisting order into account.

Storable

Storable.pm allows you to keep peristent state on your Perl data structures, which include objects of type SCALAR, ARRAY, HASH, and REF. In other words, Storable lets you deal with any Perl types that can be conveniently stored on disk and retrieved at a later time. At the heart of Storable is store, which takes a reference to the object that will be stored and the filename where the information should be written. And, while you're statefully keeping your Perl data on a filesystem, retrieve will open the file where the data is kept so you can work with it. As of Perl 5.8, Storable is shipped with the source kit.

For the cost of a slight header overhead, you can store to an already opened file descriptor using the store_fd routine and retrieve from a file via fd_retrieve. These names aren't imported by default, so you will have to do this explicitly if you need these routines. The file descriptor you supply must be opened for read if you're going to retrieve and for write if you wish to store. For example:

```
#!/usr/local/bin/perl -w
use Storable;

my $state_file = '/tmp/emp.cache';
my %empdata = (EmployeeNumber => 1, Person => 'Nathan Patwardhan');

store(\%empdata, $state_file);
my $h_ref = retrieve($state_file);
```

Storable implements the following methods.

---

lock_retrieve   lock_retrieve()

Gets an exclusive lock at the file before writing.

---

lock_store	lock_store()
	Same as store, except that it gets an exclusive lock at the file before writing.
nlock_store	nlock_store()
	Same as nstore(), except that it gets an exclusive lock at the file before writing.
nstore_fd	nstore_fd()
	Allows you to store data in network order so it can be shared across platforms. It also stores stringified double values to ensure portability. nstore_fd works the same as store_fd and behaves the same if errors are encountered.
retrieve	retrieve(*file*)
	Takes *file* as an option and recreates the objects in memory for you; a reference to the object is returned. retrieve returns undef if an I/O error is encountered.
store	store(*type, file*)
	Takes *type* (HASH, SCALAR, etc.) and writes it to *file*. store returns undef if an I/O error is encountered.
store_fd	store_fd(*type, fh*)
	Allows you to store *type* in an existing *fh* (filehandle). Similarly, you can retrieve data from *fh* using fd_retrieve. If *fh* isn't open, both store_fd and fd_retrieve will fail.

strict

Pragma for doing strict error checking within the current block. Can be turned off by prefixing with no:

```
use strict 'vars';
...
no strict 'vars';
```

Provides three kinds of restriction:

strict 'refs'

Generates runtime error if you use any symbolic references.

strict 'subs'

Generates compile-time error if you use a bareword identifier that's not a predeclared subroutine.

strict 'vars'

Generates compile-time error if you access a variable that wasn't declared via my, isn't fully qualified, or wasn't imported.

use strict by itself (with no import list) is the most restrictive, causing all possible restrictions to be imposed.

subs

Pragma that predeclares subroutines whose names are given in a list:

```
use subs qw(sub[, ...]);
sub $arg[, ...];
```

This lets you use the subroutines without parentheses even before they're defined and lets you override built-in functions.

Switch

Switch.pm implements a switch statement for Perl, which works something like the switch statement you'd find in C and other languages. *Switch.pm* is intended to supplement the standard Perl syntax with two control statements: switch and case. switch takes a single scalar argument of any type, specified in parentheses, that is then stored in a localized control variable. It is followed by any number of Perl statements (in a block) that are checked to meet various conditions, or cases, of the switch. case takes a single scalar argument, variable, or regular expression as an argument. If case finds a match, it will take the action that's specified between the braces on the right. *Switch.pm* is shipped with the Perl 5.8 source kit.

For example:

```
#!/usr/local/bin/perl -w
 use Switch;
 switch($some_value) {
     case 1          { print "number 1" }
     case "a"        { print "string a" }
     case [1..10,42] { print "number in list" }
     case (@array)   { print "number in list" }
     case /\w+/      { print "pattern" }
     case qr/\w+/    { print "pattern" }
     case (%hash)    { print "entry in hash" }
     case (\%hash)   { print "entry in hash" }
     case (\&sub)    { print "arg to subroutine" }
     else            { print "Get off my case." }
 }
```

Symbol

Provides functions for creating anonymous globs and qualifying variable names. Exports the following.

---

gensym   gensym

Creates an anonymous glob and returns a reference to it that can be used as a filehandle or directory handle.

---

qualify   qualify (*symname*[, *pkg*])

Turns unqualified symbol names into qualified variable names (e.g., turns myvar into MyPackage::myvar).

---

qualify_to_ref   qualify_to_ref (*symname*[, *pkg*])

Like qualify, but returns a glob reference that can be used even if use strict 'refs' is in effect.

---

ungensym   ungensym

For backward compatibility only; does nothing.

Sys::Hostname

Provides one function, hostname, which attempts to get the system hostname by doing checks appropriate to the operating system. Removes nulls, returns, and newlines from the result, which it then caches. croaks on failure.

```
use Sys::Hostname;
$host = hostname();
```

Sys::Syslog

Interfaces to Unix syslog(3) program. Requires the file *syslog.ph*, which must be created with *h2ph* by your system administrator. Provides the following four functions.

---

closelog   closelog

Closes the log file.

openlog
openlog *ident, logopt, facility*

Opens the log file. Takes the following arguments:

ident
> Prepended to every message

logopt
> Logging options, containing one or more of:
>
> cons
> > Writes messages to system console if they can't be sent to *syslogd*
>
> ndelay
> > Opens the connection immediately
>
> nowait
> > Doesn't wait for child processes before logging messages to the console
>
> pid
> > Logs process ID

facility
> Specifies the part of the system making the log entry

---

setlogmask
setlogmask *mask_priority*

Sets log mask to *mask_priority* and returns the old mask.

---

syslog
syslog *priority, mask, format, args*

If *priority* and *mask* permit, logs message formed as if by sprintf(*format, args*), with the addition that %m is replaced with the current error message from $!.

Term::Cap

Provides low-level functions to extract and use capabilities from a terminal capability (termcap) database. For general information about the use of this database, see the *termcap(5)* manpage. Provides the following functions.

Tgetent
$*terminal* = Tgetent Term::Cap { TERM => *termtype*, OSPEED=> *ospeed* }

Acts as the constructor for Term::Cap. Extracts the termcap entry for terminal type *termtype* and returns a reference to a terminal object. The termcap entry itself is $terminal->{TERMCAP}. Calls Carp::croak on failure. Takes the following arguments:

TERM => *termtype*
> Terminal type. Defaults to the value of the environment variable TERM if *termtype* is false or undefined.

OSPEED => *ospeed*
> The terminal output bit rate, specified as either a POSIX termios/SYSV termio speed or an old BSD-style speed. You can use the POSIX module to get your terminal's output speed (in *ospeed* here).

Tgoto	`$terminal->Tgoto('cm', col, row[, fh])`

Produces control string to move the cursor relative to the screen. Doesn't cache output strings, but does % expansion as needed on control string. Takes the following arguments:

`'cm'`
> Required first argument ("cursor move")

col, row
> Column and row to move cursor to

fh
> Filehandle that will receive the control string

Tpad	`$terminal->Tpad(string, count, fh)`

Specifies padding required to create delay needed by terminal. Takes the following arguments:

string
> The string to pad with

count
> The number of pad characters

fh
> The filehandle to pad

Tputs	`$terminal->Tputs('cap', count[, fh])`

Produces control string for capabilities other than cursor movement. Does not do % expansion, but does cache output strings if $count = 1. Takes the following arguments:

cap
> Capability to produce control string for

count
> Should be 1 unless padding is required (see Tpad); if greater than 1, specifies amount of padding

fh
> Filehandle to receive the control string

Trequire $terminal->Trequire(caps)

Checks to see whether the named capabilities, *caps*, are defined in the terminal's termcap entry. For example:

```
$terminal->Trequire(qw/ce ku kd/);
```

Any undefined capabilities are listed, and `Carp::croak` is called.

Term::Complete

Provides word completion on list of words in a specified array. Exports one function.

Complete   Complete ('*prompt_string*', *array*)

Sends string to the currently selected filehandle, reads the user's response, and returns the response. Takes the following arguments:

prompt_string
> The prompt for user input

array
> The array of words against which the user's input is matched

If any of the following characters are included in the user's response to *prompt_string*, they are treated as special characters:

Tab
> Does word completion, matching what the user has typed so far against the list of strings in *completion_list*. On a unique match, outputs the rest of the matched string and waits for the user to press Return. Otherwise, leaves partial input unchanged and sounds the bell.

Ctrl-D
> Prints all possible completions of the user's partial input, or the entire completion list if the partial input string is null, and reissues the prompt string and the partial input. Redefine by setting the variable $Term::Complete::complete.

Ctrl-U
> Erases any partial input. Redefine by setting the variable $Term::Complete::kill.

Del, BS
> Delete and backspace characters; both erase one character from the partial input string. Redefine by setting the variables $Term::Complete::erase1 and $Term::Complete::erase2.

Term::ReadLine

Frontend to other ReadLine packages. Currently interfaces to Term-ReadLine, which is available on CPAN. Defines the variables $IN and $OUT, which return the filehandles for input and output, respectively, or undef if Readline input and output cannot be used for Perl. Provides the following methods.

---

new
$*term* = new Term::ReadLine '*name*'

Constructor. Returns the handle for subsequent calls to other ReadLine methods. Argument *name* is the name of the application. Optionally can be followed by two arguments that are globs specifying input and output filehandles.

---

addhistory
$*term*->addhistory(*line*)

Adds *line* to the input history.

Features
$*term*->Features

Returns a reference to a hash whose keys are features present in the current implementation and whose values are assigned to each feature. Several optional features are used in the minimal interface:

appname
Should be present if the first argument to new is recognized

minline
Should be present if MinLine method is not a dummy

autohistory
Should be present if lines are put into history automatically (maybe subject to *MinLine*)

addhistory
Should be present if the addhistory method is not a dummy

---

findConsole
$*term*->findConsole

Returns array of two strings containing the most appropriate names for input and output files, using the conventions <$in and >$out.

MinLine
$*term*->MinLine([*size*])

With *size* argument, serves as a recommendation on minimal size of line to be added to history. Without an argument, does not add anything to the history. Returns the old value.

ReadLine	`$term->ReadLine`
	Returns the actual package that executes the commands. Some possible values are Term::ReadLine::Gnu, Term::ReadLine::Perl, or Term::ReadLine::Stub.

readline	`$term->readline(prompt)`
	Prompts for input line and gets the result. Removes trailing newline and returns undef at end-of-file.

Test

Provides a framework for writing test scripts so you don't need to know the particular output that Test::Harness expects to see. Useful if you are writing modules and writing tests for those modules. Provides the following test types:

Normal
: Tests that are expected to succeed.

Skip
: Tests that need a platform-specific feature. They work like normal tests except that the first argument should evaluate to true if the required feature is not present.

Todo
: Tests designed for maintaining an executable todo list; the tests aren't expected to succeed.

Test also provides an *onfail* hook that can trigger additional diagnostics for failures at the end of the test run. To use *onfail*, pass it an array reference of hash references in which each hash contains at least the package, repetition, and result fields, as well as any expected value or diagnostic string.

See the *Test* manpage for details and examples.

Test::Builder

A backend for building test libraries under Perl. Note that Test::Builder is in the early stages of development and that things may become more (or less) stable, or may change completely. Test::Builder is more flexible than other testing modules such as Test::Simple and Test::More.

Test::Builder implements the following methods.

new	new()
	Returns a Test::Builder object representing the current state of the test. There's no need to create more than one Test::Builder object, since you run only one test per program.
BAILOUT	BAILOUT(*reason*)
	Terminates all tests and exits immediately.
expected_tests	expected_tests()
	Gets and sets the tests that will run and prints out the correct headers.
exported_to	exported_to(*package*)
	Specifies the package you exported your functions to.
is_eq	is_eq(*got_from_test*, *expected_from_test*, *name_of_test*)
	Checks if *got_from_test* eq *expected_from_test*.
isnt_eq	isnt_eq(*got_from_test*, *did_not_expect*, *name_of_test*)
	Checks if *got_from_test* ne *did_not_expect*.
isnt_num	isnt_num(*got_from_test*, *did_not_expect*, *name_of_test*)
	Checks if *got_from_test* != *did_not_expect*.
is_num	is_num(*got_from_test*, *expected_from_test*, *name_of_test*)
	Checks if *got_from_test* == *expected_from_test*.
like	like(*string*, '/regex/', *name_of_test*)
	Checks if *string* matches the specified regular expression.
no_plan	no_plan()
	Declares that there may be an infinite number of tests.
ok	ok(*test*, *name*)
	Reports if *test* by *name* is true.

plan	`plan()`
	Sets up the tests for you, prints appropriate headers, and takes appropriate actions. plan can be used in lieu of any of the subsequent methods.
skip	`skip([reason])`
	Skips the current test, citing *reason*.
skip_all	`skip_all(reason)`

	Shamelessly skips all the tests, citing the given *reason*. Exits with 0.
	`my $reason = "I didn't feel like it today.";`
	`$Test->skip_all($reason);`

unlike	`unlike(string, '/regex/', name_of_test)`
	Checks if *string* does not match the specified regular expession.

Test::Harness

Used by MakeMaker; runs Perl test scripts and prints some statistics. You can use the Test module to write test scripts without knowing the exact output Test::Harness expects. Exports one function.

runtests	`runtests (tests)`
	Runs all test scripts named in *tests* and checks standard output for the expected ok*n* strings. Prints performance statistics after all tests have been run.

Test::More

Yet another framework for writing test scripts. Its more flexible successor is Test::Builder.

Test::Simple

Provides basic utilities for writing tests. It is shipped with the Perl source kit as of 5.8. For example:

```
my $name = 'Inigo Montoya';
my $quote = 'Prepare to die';
ok($name eq $quote, 'name is quote');
```

The ok function is given an expression to evaluate. ok() prints out 'ok' or 'not ok' along with the number of the test.

Here's another example that tests if you can use CGI.pm:

```
#!/usr/local/bin/perl -w
use Test::Simple tests => 2;
use CGI; # Test this

my $cgi = CGI->new();

# Test #1 -- this will be ok
ok(defined($cgi) and ref $cgi eq 'CGI', 'I have your CGI right here!');

my $header = $cgi->header(-type => 'text/plain');

# Test #2 -- this will not be ok
ok($header eq "Content-Type: text/mex");
```

Text::Abbrev

Given a list of strings, creates a hash of unambiguous abbreviations. Exports one function.

abbrev	abbrev (\%*hashref*, *list*)

Takes each string in *list* and constructs the hash referenced by \%*hashref*. Each key is an unambiguous truncation of one of the strings, and the value is the full string (in which unambiguous means that there is only one possible expansion that matches one of the strings in the list). For example, if *list* contains "file" and "find", then the key/value pairs created include:

```
fil  => file
file => file
fin  => find
find => find
```

Both "f" and "fi" are ambiguous, since they start both words, and therefore, they don't appear as keys.

Text::Balanced

Extracts delimited text sequences from strings. It implements various extract_-named subroutines to capture the delimited string.

In a list context, all Text::Balanced methods return a list that contains the extracted string with delimiters, the remainder of the string, and the parts of the string that were skipped. Text::Balanced is shipped with the Perl source kit as of 5.8.

Text::Balanced implements the following methods.

extract_bracketed

extract_bracketed(*text*, *delimiter*)

Extracts the initial substring of *text* that is bracketed with delimiters specified by *delimiter*. Note that *delimiter* should contain one of (), {}, [], or <>.

extract_codeblock

extract_codeblock(*text*, *delimiter*)

Extracts the initial substring of *text* that represents a block of Perl code. This code is specified by *delimiter*, which contains one of (), {}, [], or <>.

extract_delimited

extract_delimited(*text*, *delimiter*)

Extracts the initial substring of *text* that is delimited by two instances of *delimiter*.

extract_multiple

extract_multple(*text* ...)

Extracts the initial substrings of *text* that would be extracted by one or more sequential applications of the specified functions.

extract_quotelike

extract_quotelike(*text*)

Extracts the quoted portion of *text*.

extract_tagged

extract_tagged(*text*, "*TAG1*", "*TAG2*", undef, *nesting_allowed*)

Extracts the initial substring of *text* that is bounded by an HTML or XML tag:

```
# Extract HTML tags but don't allow <HTML> to be embedded
($extracted, $left) =
```

```
                    extract_tagged($text,"<HTML>","</HTML>",
                                   undef,{bad=>["<HTML>"]});
              extract_multiple($text, ...)
```

gen_delimited_pat

gen_delimited_pat(q{*pattern*})

Creates a string that represents the optimized pattern that matches a substring delimited by q{ *pattern* }.

Text::ParseWords

Parses lines of text and returns an array of words. Provides three functions.

Modules

old_shellwords   old_shellwords (*lines*)

Splits an array of lines into words. Exported on request. Same as the pre-Perl 5 program *shellwords.pl*.

quotewords   quotewords (*delim, keep, lines*)

Accepts delimiter and list of lines and breaks the lines into a list of words at occurrences of the delimiter. Exported by default. Takes the following arguments:

delim
　　Delimiter, which can be a regular expression. Occurrences inside quotes are ignored.

keep
　　Boolean. If false, quotes and single backslashes are removed from the list of words returned, and a double backslash is returned as a single backslash. If true, quotes and backslashes are retained.

lines
　　The list of lines to be parsed.

shellwords   shellwords (*lines*)

Works like old_shellwords, but does not default to using $_ if there is no argument. Exported by default.

Text::Soundex

Implements the soundex algorithm, which hashes a word (in particular, a surname) into a compressed form that approximates the sound of the word when spoken by an English speaker:

```
use Text::Soundex;

$code = soundex $string;  # Get soundex code for a string
@codes = soundex @list;   # Get list of codes for list of strings
```

Returns the value of the variable $soundex_nocode if there is no soundex code representation for a string. $soundex_nocode is initially set to undef, but can be reset to another value. For example:

```
$soundex_nocode = 'Z000';
```

Text::Tabs

Provides subroutines that expand tabs into spaces and compress ("unexpand") spaces into tabs. The appearance of the text is unchanged. Defines the tabstop variable, which defines the number of spaces equivalent to a tab. Default is 8. Exports the following functions.

---

expand   expand (*text*)

Given an array of strings (*text*) containing tabs, replaces each tab character with the equivalent number of spaces.

---

unexpand   unexpand (*text*)

Given an array of strings (*text*) that may or may not contain tabs, replaces each $tabstop consecutive spaces with a tab character.

Text::Wrap

Wraps text into a paragraph. Defines the $columns variable, which specifies the output line length. Default is 76. Exported on request. Provides the following function.

---

wrap   wrap (*init_str, other_str, text*)

Breaks lines of array *text* at the word boundary closest to the size of a line. Prepends *init_str* to the first output line and *other_str* to subsequent lines, for indentation. Exported by default.

Thread

Provides Perl multithreading support. Distributed as a beta feature with Perl 5.005 and runs only on versions of Perl that were built with thread support. Has the following functions and methods.

new

`$t = new Thread \&sub[, params]`

Constructor. Starts a new thread in the referenced subroutine, \sub, returning a thread object that represents the new thread. The optional parameter list is passed to the subroutine. Execution continues in both the new thread and the code.

async

`$t = async {block};`

Creates a new thread to execute the block that follows it. The block is treated as an anonymous subroutine (and therefore has a semi-colon after the closing bracket). Returns a thread object. async isn't exported by default, so you can specify use Thread qw(async); or fully qualify the name (Thread::async).

cond_broadcast

`cond_broadcast var`

Like cond_wait, but unblocks all threads blocked in a cond_wait on the locked variable, not just one thread.

cond_signal

`cond_signal var`

Takes the locked variable *var* and unblocks one thread that's cond_waiting on that variable. If multiple threads are so blocked, the one that will be unblocked can't be determined.

cond_wait

`cond_wait var`

Takes the locked variable *var*, unlocks it, and blocks until another thread does a cond_signal or cond_broadcast for that variable. The variable is relocked after the cond_wait has been satisfied. If multiple threads are cond_waiting, all but one will reblock waiting to reacquire the lock.

eval

`eval {$t->join}`

Wraps an eval around a join. Waits for a thread to exit and passes any return values from the thread, putting errors into $@.

Modules

join $t->join

Waits for a thread to end. When it does, returns any exit values from the thread. Blocks until the thread has ended, unless the thread has already terminated.

list   Thread->list

Returns list of thread objects for all running and finished, but not joined, threads.

lock   lock var

                            lock sub

Locks a variable or a subroutine. A lock on a variable is maintained until the lock goes out of scope. If the variable is already locked by another thread, the lock call blocks until the variable is available. You can recursively lock the variable, which stays locked until the outermost lock goes out of scope.

Note that locks on variables affect only other lock calls; they don't prevent normal access to a variable. Also, locking a container object (e.g., an array) doesn't lock each element of the container.

Locking a subroutine blocks any calls to the subroutine until the lock goes out of scope; no other thread can access the subroutine while the lock is in effect.

self   Thread->self

Returns an object representing the thread that made the call.

tid $id = $t->tid

Returns an object representing the tid (thread ID) of a thread. The ID is simply an integer that is incremented each time a new thread is created, starting with zero for the main thread of a program.

Thread::Queue

Provides a thread-safe queue. Any number of threads can add elements to the end of the queue or remove elements from the head.

new $q = new Thread::Queue

Creates a new empty queue. Returns an object representing the queue.

dequeue $q->dequeue

Removes and returns a scalar from the head of the queue. If the queue is empty, dequeue blocks the thread until another thread enqueues a scalar on the queue.

dequeue_nb $q->dequeue_nb

Like dequeue, but returns undef if the queue is empty instead of blocking.

enqueue $q->enqueue *list*

Adds the list of scalars, *list*, to the end of the queue.

pending $q->pending

Returns the number of items remaining in the queue.

Thread::Semaphore

Provides a mechanism to regulate access to resources. Semaphores are more general than locks because they aren't tied to a particular scalar. They can have values other than 0 or 1 and can be incremented or decremented by a specified number.

new $sem = new Thread::Semaphore([*val*])

Constructor. Creates a new semaphore object, with an optional initial count of *val*, or 1 if *val* isn't specified.

down   down [*number*]

Decrements the semaphore's count by the specified number, which defaults to 1. If the resulting count would be negative, blocks until the semaphore's count has been increased to be equal to or larger than the amount you want to decrease it.

up   up [*number*]

Increments the semaphore's count by the specified number, which defaults to 1. If a thread is blocked waiting to decrement the count, and the increment brings the count high enough, the blocked thread is unblocked.

Thread::Signal

Starts a special signal handler thread to reliably run signal handlers. All signals are handed to this thread, which runs the associated $SIG{*signal*} handlers for them.

```
use Thread::Signal;

$SIG{HUP} = handler;
```

Thread::Specific

Provides thread-specific keys.

---

key_create $k = key_create Thread::Specific

Constructor. Creates a Thread::Specific key object.

Tie::Array, Tie::StdArray

Provides methods for array-tying classes. (See the *perltie* manpage for the functions needed for tying an array to a package.) The basic Tie::Array package provides stub DELETE and EXTEND methods and implements PUSH, POP, SHIFT, UNSHIFT, SPLICE, and CLEAR in terms of basic FETCH, STORE, FETCHSIZE, and STORESIZE.

Tie::StdArray inherits from Tie::Array and provides the methods needed for tied arrays implemented as blessed references to an "inner" Perl array. It causes tied arrays to behave like standard arrays, allowing for selective method overloading.

See the *perltie* manpage for more detailed information and for examples. To write your own tied arrays, use the following required methods.

TIEARRAY   TIEARRAY *classname, list*

Constructor. This method is invoked by the command tie *@array*, *classname*. Associates an array instance with the specified class. *list* represents additional arguments needed to complete the association. Should return an object of a class that provides the remaining methods.

CLEAR

CLEAR *this*

Clears all values from the tied array associated with object *this*.

DESTROY

DESTROY *this*

Normal object destructor.

EXTEND

EXTEND *this, count*

Doesn't need to do anything. Provides information that the array will likely grow to have *count* entries.

FETCH

FETCH *this, index*

Retrieves the data item in *index* for the tied array associated with object *this*.

FETCHSIZE

FETCHSIZE *this*

Returns the number of items in the tied array associated with object *this*.

POP

POP *this*

Removes the last element from the array and returns it.

PUSH

PUSH *this, list*

Appends elements of *list* to the array.

SHIFT

SHIFT *this*

Removes and returns the first element of the array, shifting the remaining elements down.

SPLICE

SPLICE *this, offset, length, list*

Performs the equivalent of a *splice* on the array. Returns a list of the original *length* elements at the specified offset. The arguments are:

offset
Optional. Defaults to 0; if negative, counts back from the end of the array.

length
Optional. Defaults to the rest of the array.

list
May be empty.

STORE   STORE *this, index, value*

Stores value of a data item into *index* for the tied array associated with object *this*. If the resulting array is larger than the class's mapping for the array, undef should be returned for new positions.

STORESIZE   STORESIZE *this, count*

Sets the total number of items in the tied array associated with object *this* to *count*. If this makes the array larger than the class's mapping for the array, then undef should be returned for new positions. If it makes the array smaller than the mapping, then entries beyond *count* should be deleted.

UNSHIFT   UNSHIFT *this, list*

Inserts *list* elements at the beginning of the array, moving existing elements up to make room.

Tie::File

Represents a regular text file as a Perl array, such that each element in the array corresponds to a record in the file. The first line of the file is element 0 of the array, the second line is element 1, and so on. When you add a new item to the array, this change will be noted in the file immediately. Note that the file isn't loaded into memory, so the files can be very large if needed. Tie::File is shipped with the Perl 5.8 source kit.

Let's say that we have a file that contains:

```
One
Two
Three
Four
Five
Six
```

You can use Tie::File to report about the contents of the file as follows:

```
#!/usr/local/bin/perl -w

use Tile::File;

my $infile = 'mynotes.db.txt';
my @lines;

tie(@lines, 'Tie::File', $infile)
die("can't open $infile: $!");
```

```perl
my $n_recs = @lines;
print "$infile has [$n_recs]\n";
```

Now, set the second line of the file to 3:

```perl
$lines[2] = 3;
```

and lowercase everything that's in the file:

```perl
foreach my $line (@lines) {
    lc($line);
}
```

Add one line to the file:

```perl
push(@lines, "Here's one more for you");
```

Now we're done:

```perl
untie @lines;
```

Tie::File supports the following options:

recsep

> Changes $/ to what you'll use to separate the records (or lines) in your file.
> recsep may not be undefined.

```perl
my $file = 'datafile';
my $recsep = "\cA"; # Break records on ^A

tie @lines, 'Tie::File', $file, recsep => $recsep;
```

> Given the line:

```
this^Athat^Athe^Aother^Athing\n
```

> Tie::File would see the records like so:

```
0: this
1: that
2: the
3: other
4: thing
```

> If you do not specify a recsep, Tie::File will default to \n. Thus, the following
> are equivalent:

```perl
$lines[5] = "Sixty6";
$lines[5] = "Sixty6\n";
```

autochomp

> If specified, and if \n is your default recsep, \n will be removed as the record
> separator. Default is 0.

mode

> Sets if the file will be set for read, write, or read/write access. Options include
> O_RDWR and O_CREAT:

```perl
use Fcntl 'O_RDWR', 'O_CREAT';

# Open file RDWR, or CREAT if $file doesn't exist
tie @lines, 'Tie::File', $file, mode => O_RDWR | O_CREAT;
```

memory

Sets the upper limit on the amount of memory that Tie::File will consume.

dw_size

Specifies that data should be written into a deferred write buffer of a given size instead of in the file itself.

See the documentation for Tie for a description of the additional tie() methods.

Tie::Handle

Provides skeletal methods for handle-tying classes. Tie::Handle provides a new method as backup in case a class has no TIEHANDLE method. (See the *perltie* manpage for more detailed information and for examples.) To write your own tied-handle classes, use the following methods.

TIEHANDLE	TIEHANDLE *classname, list*
	Constructor. This method is invoked by the command tie **glob, classname*. Associates new glob instance with class *classname*. *list* represents any additional arguments needed to complete the association.
DESTROY	DESTROY *this*
	Frees storage associated with the tied handle *this*. Permits class to take some action when an instance is destroyed. Rarely needed.
GETC	GETC *this*
	Gets one character from tied handle *this*.
PRINT	PRINT *this, list*
	Prints the values in *list*.
PRINTF	PRINTF *this, format, list*
	Prints the values in *list* using *format*.
READ	READ *this, scalar, length, offset*
	Reads *length* bytes from *scalar* starting at *offset*.
READLINE	READLINE *this*
	Reads one line from *this*.

WRITE	WRITE *this*, *scalar*, *length*, *offset*
	Writes *length* bytes of data from *scalar* starting at *offset*.

Tie::Hash

Provides skeletal methods for hash-tying classes. Tie::Hash provides a new method, as well as the methods TIEHASH, EXISTS, and CLEAR. The new method is provided as backup in case a class has no TIEHASH method.

To write your own tied hashes, the methods listed here are required. See the *perltie* manpage for more detailed information and for examples.

TIEHASH	TIEHASH *ClassName*, *list*
	Constructor. Associates a new hash instance with class *ClassName*. *list* is a list of additional arguments needed to complete the association.
	tie %hash, *ClassName*, *list*

CLEAR	CLEAR *this*
	Clears all values from tied hash *this*.

DELETE	DELETE *this*, *key*
	Deletes *key* from tied hash *this*.

EXISTS	EXISTS *this*, *key*
	Verifies that *key* exists for tied hash *this*.

FETCH	FETCH *this*, *key*
	Retrieves value associated with *key* for tied hash *this*.

FIRSTKEY	FIRSTKEY *this*
	Returns key/value pair for the first key in tied hash *this*.

NEXTKEY	NEXTKEY *this*, *lastkey*
	Returns next key/value pair after *lastkey* for tied hash *this*.

STORE	STORE *this*, *key*, *value*
	Stores *value* into tied hash *this* with key *key*.

Tie::Memoize

Adds data to the hash when needed. That is, Tie::Memoize allows a tied hash to autoload all its values on first access and to use the cached value on subsequent accesses. Read accesses will result in one of the Tie::Memoize functions being called. Write accesses will act as if you're operating on a normal hash. For example:

```
#!/usr/local/bin/perl -w
require Tie::Memoize;
tie %hash, 'Tie::Memoize', \&fetch, $DATA, \&exists,
    {%ini_value}, {%ini_existence};
sub fetch { ... }
sub exists { ... }
```

Tie::RefHash

Provides the ability to use references as hash keys after you've tied a hash variable to the module:

```
use Tie::RefHash;

tie hashvariable, 'Tie::RefHash', list;
untie hashvariable;
```

Uses the TIEHASH interface and provides the same methods.

Tie::Scalar

The basic Tie::Scalar package provides a new method, as well as methods TIESCALAR, FETCH, and STORE. The new method is provided as backup in case a class has no TIESCALAR method.

To write your own tied hashes, the methods listed here are required. See the *perltie* manpage for more detailed information and for examples.

TIESCALAR	TIESCALAR *classname*, *list*
	Constructor. Associates new scalar instance with class *classname*. *list* represents any additional arguments needed to complete the association.
	`tie $scalar, classname, list`

DESTROY	DESTROY *this*

Frees storage associated with the tied scalar referenced by *this*. Permits a class to perform specific actions when an instance is destroyed. Rarely needed.

FETCH	FETCH *this*

Retrieves value of the tied scalar referenced by *this*.

STORE	STORE *this, value*

Stores *value* in the tied scalar referenced by *this*.

Tie::SubstrHash

Provides a hash table–like interface to a fixed-sized array that has a constant key size and record size:

```
require Tie::SubstrHash;
tie %myhash, "Tie::SubstrHash", key_len, value_len, table_size;
```

To tie a new hash to this package, specify the following:

key_len
  Length of each key

value_len
  Length of each value

table_size
  Size of the table given as the number of key/value pairs

An attempt to store a key/value pair in which either the key or the value is the wrong length, or in which the resulting table would be greater than *table_size*, results in a fatal error.

Time::gmtime

Replaces Perl's core gmtime function with a version that returns Time::tm objects. Exports two functions.

gmctime	*$gmc* = gmctime( )

Overrides the core gmtime function in scalar context; returns a string with the date and time:

```
use Time::gmtime;
$gmc = gmctime( );
print $gmc;
```

Then the output of the print command looks like:

```
Thu Apr 9 18:15:06 1998
```

gmtime

```
$gm = gmtime( )
```

Overrides the core gmtime function. The Time::tm object returned has methods with the same names as the structure fields they return. That is, to return the field mon, use the mon method:

```
use Time::gmtime;
$gm = gmtime( );
print $gm->mon;
```

The field names (and therefore the method names) are the same as the names of the fields in the *tm* structure in the C file *time.h*: sec, min, hour, mday, mon, year, wday, yday, and isdst. You can access the fields either with the methods or by importing the fields into your namespace with the :FIELDS import tag and prepending tm_ to the method name (for example, $tm_mon).

Time::HiRes

Provides "high-resolution" functionality for alarm, sleep, gettimeofday, and interval timers. Ordinarily, Perl deals in seconds when you use something like sleep() or alarm(), with which only positive integers are allowed. Time::HiRes allows you to use more granular times for functions such as sleep() and alarm(). For example:

```
#!/usr/local/bin/perl -w
use Time::HiRes qw(usleep);
my $ms = 349_000; # That's 349,000 microseconds
usleep($ms);

print "I'm awake now.\n";
```

Time::HiRes implements a Perl interface to usleep(), ualarm(), gettimeofday(), setitimer(), and getitimer().

Time::Local

Provides routines that take the time and return the number of seconds elapsed between January 1, 1970 and the specified time. The arguments are defined like the corresponding arguments returned by Perl's gmtime and localtime functions and the results agree with the results of those functions. Exports two functions; both return -1 if the integer limit is hit. On most machines, this applies to dates after January 1, 2038.

timegm	`$time = timegm(sec, min, hours, mday, mon, year)`
	Converts from Greenwich time.
timelocal	`$time = timelocal(sec, min, hours, mday, mon, year)`
	Converts from local time.

Time::localtime

Replaces Perl's core `localtime` function with a version that returns Time::tm objects. Exports two functions.

ctime	`$ct = ctime( )`
	Overrides the core `localtime` function in scalar context; returns a string with the date and time:

```
use Time::gmtime;
$ct = ctime( );
print $ct
```

Then the output of the `print` command looks like:

```
Thu Apr  9 16:50:10 1998
```

localtime	`$lt = localtime( )`
	Overrides the core `localtime` function. The Time::tm object returned has methods with the same names as the structure fields they return. That is, to return the field *mon*, use the mon method:

```
use Time::localtime;
$lt = localtime( );
print $lt->mon;
```

The field names (and therefore the method names) are the same as the names of the fields in the *tm* structure in the C file *time.h*: sec, min, hour, mday, mon, year, wday, yday, and isdst. You can access the fields with the methods or by importing the fields into your namespace with the :FIELDS import tag and prepending tm_ to the method name (for example, $tm_mon).

Time::tm

Used internally by Time::localtime and Time::gmtime. Don't use it directly. Creates addressable Time::tm struct object.

UNIVERSAL

Base class; all blessed references inherit from it:

```
$sub = $obj->can('print');

$yes = UNIVERSAL::isa($ref, "HASH");
```

Provides the following methods.

---

can $sub = $obj->can(method)

Checks if object $obj has a method method. If so, returns a reference to the subroutine; otherwise, returns undef. Can be called as a static or object method call, or as a subroutine:

```
$ref = UNIVERSAL::can(val, method)
```

Returns a reference to the subroutine if val is a blessed reference with a method method, and undef if val is not blessed or does not have method.

---

isa $io = $fd->isa(type)

Returns true if the reference is blessed into package type or inherits from that package. Can be called as a static or object method call, or as a subroutine:

```
UNIVERSAL::isa(val, type)
```

Returns true if the first argument is a reference and either of the following is true:

- val is a blessed reference and is blessed into package type or inherits from package type.
- val is a reference to a type of Perl variable (e.g., 'HASH').

VERSION VERSION([require])

Returns the value of the variable $VERSION in the package the object is blessed into. With require specified, VERSION dies if the version of the package is not equal to or greater than the version specified in require. Can be called as either a static or object method call.

User::grent

Overrides core getgrent, getgruid, and getgrnam functions with versions that return User::grent objects. The object returned has methods with the same names

---

as the structure fields they return. That is, to return the field *name*, use the name method:

```
use User::grent;
$gr = getgrgid(0) or die "No group zero";
if ( $gr->name eq 'wheel' && @{$gr->members} > 1 ) {
    print "gid zero name wheel, with other members";
}
```

The field names (and therefore the method names) are the same as the names of the fields in the *group* structure from the C file *grp.h*: *name*, *passwd*, *gid*, and *members* (not *mem*). The first three return scalars, the last an array reference. You can access the fields with the methods or by importing the fields into your namespace with the :FIELDS import tag and prepending gr_ to the method name (for example, gr_name). Exports four functions.

getgr	$*gr*->getgr(*arg*)
	Frontend that forwards a numeric *arg* to getgrid and other *arg*s to getgrname.
getgrent	$*gr* = getgrent( )
	Successive calls to getgrent return objects representing successive entries from the group file.
getgrgid	$*gr* = getgrgid(*gid*)
	Accesses the group file by group ID *gid*.
getgrnam	$*gr* = getgrnam(*gname*)
	Accesses the group file by group name *gname*.

User::pwent

Overrides core getpwent, getpwuid, and getpwnam functions with versions that return User::pwent objects. The object returned has methods with the same names as the structure fields they return. That is, to return the field *name*, use the name method:

```
use User::pwent;
$pw = getpwnam('daemon') or die "No daemon user";
if ( $pw->uid == 1 && $pw->dir =~ m#^/(bin|tmp)?$# ) {
    print "gid 1 on root dir";
}
```

The field names (and therefore the method names) are the same as the names of the fields in the *passwd* structure from the C file *pwd.h*: *name, passwd, uid, gid, quota, comment, gecos, dir,* and *shell*. You can access the fields with the methods or by importing the fields into your namespace with the :FIELDS import tag and prepending pw_ to the method name (for example, pw_name). Exports four functions.

getpw	$pw->getpw(*arg*) Frontend that forwards a numeric *arg* to getpwuid and other *args* to getpwnam.
getpwent	$pw->getpwent( ) Successive calls to getpwent return objects representing successive entries from the password table.
getpwnam	$pw->getpwnam(*name*) Accesses the password table by user's *name*.
getpwuid	$pw->getpwuid(*uid*) Accesses the password table by user's ID number, *uid*.

utf8

While Perl's implementation of Unicode support is incomplete, the use utf8 pragma tells the Perl parser to allow UTF-8 in the program text in its current lexical scope. no utf8 tells Perl to switch back to treating text as literal bytes in the current lexical scope. You'll probably use use utf8 only for compatibility, since future versions of Perl will standardize on the UTF-8 encoding for source text.

use utf8 has the following effects: bytes with their high-bit set (identifiers, string constants, constant regular expressions, package names) will be treated as literal UTF-8 characters and regular expressions within the scope of the utf8 pragma and will default to using character semantics instead of byte semantics. For example:

```
@bytes_or_chars = split //, $data;   # May split to bytes if data
                                     # $data isn't UTF-8
        {
            use utf8;                        # Forces char semantics
            @chars = split //, $data;        # Splits characters
        }
```

vars

Pragma that, given a list of variable names, predeclares all variables in the list, making sure they are available to routines with delayed loading (e.g., routines loaded by the AutoLoader or SelfLoader). This allows you to use the variables under use strict. The vars pragma also disables warnings about typographical errors.

```
use vars qw($var1 @var2 %var3);
```

vmsish

Controls VMS-specific language features. Currently, there are four VMS-specific features available: status ($?), exit, time, and hushed. If you're not using VMS, then this module won't have any affect.

vmsish is shipped with the Perl 5.8 source kit.

For example, without vmsish, you can't execute a hushed version of exit:

```
$ perl -e"exit 44;" Non-hushed error exit
%SYSTEM-F-ABORT, abort DCL message $ show sym $STATUS $STATUS ==
"%X0000002C"
```

When you use vmsish, you get... nothing!

```
$ perl -e"use vmsish qw(hushed); exit 44;"
```

vmsish implements the following options.

status

Causes $? and system to return the native VMS exit status instead of emulating the POSIX exit status.

exit

Causes exit 1 to produce a successful exit (with status SS$_NORMAL) instead of emulating Unix exit(), which considers exit 1 as an indication of an error. As with the CRTL's exit() function, exit 0 is also mapped to an exit status of SS$_NORMAL, and any other argument to exit() is used directly as Perl's exit status.

time

Makes all times relative to the local time zone instead of the default Universal Time (a.k.a. Greenwich Mean Time, or GMT).

hushed

Suppresses printing of VMS status messages to SYS$OUTPUT and SYS$ERROR if Perl terminates with an error status and allows programs that are expecting Unix-style Perl to avoid parsing VMS error messages. It does not supress any messages from Perl itself, just the messages generated by DCL after Perl exits. The DCL symbol $STATUS will still have the termination status, but with a high-order bit set.

XS::Typemap

Tests XS typemaps distributed with Perl. XS::Typemap implements a function that's available for each and every typemap that's in Perl. Generally, you should never use XS::Typemap directly. This module ships with the Perl 5.8 source kit.

IV

CGI

9

CGI Overview

Perl is the most commonly used language for CGI programming on the World Wide Web. The Common Gateway Interface (CGI) is an essential tool for creating and managing comprehensive web sites. With CGI, you can write scripts that create interactive, user-driven applications.

CGI allows the web server to communicate with other programs that are running on the same machine. For example, with CGI, the web server can invoke an external program, while passing user-specific data to the program (such as what host the user is connecting from, or input the user has supplied through an HTML form). The program then processes that data, and the server passes the program's response back to the web browser.

Rather than limiting the Web to documents written ahead of time, CGI enables web pages to be created on the fly, based upon the input of users. You can use CGI scripts to create a wide range of applications, from surveys to search tools, from Internet service gateways to quizzes and games. You can increment the number of users who access a document or let them sign an electronic guestbook. You can provide users with all types of information, collect their comments, and respond to them.

For Perl programmers, there are two approaches you can take to CGI. They are:

- Programs that handle all CGI interaction directly, without the use of a module such as CGI.pm. While often frowned upon by Perl programmers because it's more likely to introduce bugs, bypassing the modules has the advantage of avoiding the overhead of CGI.pm for quick, dirty tasks. This chapter explains the concepts of CGI necessary if you intend to write CGI programs from scratch.

- CGI.pm is a Perl module designed to facilitate CGI programming. For non-trivial CGI programs, especially ones that need to maintain state over multiple transactions, CGI.pm is indispensable, and is included in the standard Perl distribution as of Perl 5.004. Rather than discuss it in Chapter 8, with the rest of the standard libraries, however, its complexity and importance made it a candidate for its own chapter, Chapter 10.

One performance hit for CGI programs is that the Perl interpreter needs to be started up each and every time a CGI script is called. For improving performance on Apache systems, the *mod_perl* Apache module embeds the Perl interpreter directly into the server, avoiding the startup overhead. Chapter 11, talks about installing and using *mod_perl*.

A Typical CGI Interaction

For an example of a CGI application, suppose you create a guestbook for your website. The guestbook page asks users to submit their first name and last name using a fill-in form composed of two input text fields. Figure 9-1 shows the form you might see in your browser window.

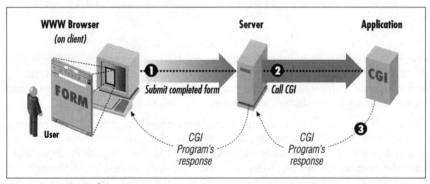

Figure 9-1. HTML form

The HTML that produces this form might read as follows:

```
<HTML><HEAD><TITLE>Guestbook</TITLE></HEAD>
<BODY>
<H1>Fill in my guestbook!</H1>
<FORM METHOD="GET" ACTION="/cgi-bin/guestbook.pl">
<PRE>
First Name:    <INPUT TYPE="TEXT" NAME="firstname">
Last Name:     <INPUT TYPE="TEXT" NAME="lastname">

<INPUT TYPE="SUBMIT">    <INPUT TYPE="RESET">
</FORM>
```

The form is written using special "form" tags, as follows:

- The <form> tag defines the method used for the form (either GET or POST) and the action to take when the form is submitted—that is, the URL of the CGI program to pass the parameters to.

- The <input> tag can be used in many different ways. In its first two invocations, it creates a text input field and defines the variable name to associate with the field's contents when the form is submitted. The first field is given the variable name firstname and the second field is given the name lastname.

- In its last two invocations, the <input> tag creates a "submit" button and a "reset" button.
- The </form> tag indicates the end of the form.

When the user presses the "submit" button, data entered into the <input> text fields is passed to the CGI program specified by the action attribute of the <form> tag (in this case, the *cgi-bin/guestbook.pl* program).

Transferring the Form Data

Parameters to a CGI program are transferred either in the URL or in the body text of the request. The method used to pass parameters is determined by the method attribute to the <form> tag. The GET method says to transfer the data within the URL itself; for example, under the GET method, the browser might initiate the HTTP transaction as follows:

```
GET /cgi-bin/guestbook.pl?firstname=Joe&lastname=Schmoe HTTP/1.0
```

The POST method says to use the body portion of the HTTP request to pass parameters. The same transaction with the POST method would read as follows:

```
POST /cgi-bin/guestbook.pl HTTP/1.0
    ... [More headers here]

firstname=Joe&lastname=Schmoe
```

In both of these examples, you should recognize the firstname and lastname variable names that were defined in the HTML form, coupled with the values entered by the user. An ampersand (&) is used to separate the variable=value pairs.

The server now passes the variable=value pairs to the CGI program. It does this either through Unix environment variables or in standard input (STDIN). If the CGI program is called with the GET method, then parameters are expected to be embedded into the URL of the request, and the server transfers them to the program by assigning them to theQUERY_STRING environment variable. The CGI program can then retrieve the parameters from QUERY_STRING as it would read any environment variable (for example, from the %ENV hash in Perl). If the CGI program is called with the POST method, parameters are expected to be embedded into the body of the request, and the server passes the body text to the program as standard input (STDIN).

Other environment variables defined by the server for CGI store such information as the format and length of the input, the remote host, the user, and various client information. They also store the server name, the communication protocol, and the name of the software running the server. (We provide a list of the most common CGI environment variables later in this chapter.)

The CGI program needs to retrieve the information as appropriate and then process it. The sky's the limit on what the CGI program actually does with the information it retrieves. It might return an anagram of the user's name, or tell her how many times her name uses the letter "t," or it might just compile the name into a list that the programmer regularly sells to telemarketers. Only the programmer knows for sure.

Creating Virtual Documents

Regardless of what the CGI program does with its input, it's responsible for giving the browser something to display when it's done. It must either create a new document to be served to the browser or point to an existing document. On Unix, programs send their output to standard output (STDOUT) as a data stream that consists of two parts. The first part is either a full or partial HTTP header that (at minimum) describes the format of the returned data (e.g., HTML, ASCII text, GIF, etc.). A blank line signifies the end of the header section. The second part is the body of the output, which contains the data conforming to the format type reflected in the header. For example:

```
Content-type: text/html
<HTML>
<HEAD><TITLE>Thanks!</TITLE></HEAD>
<BODY><H1>Thanks for signing my guest book!</H1>
    ...
</BODY></HTML>
```

In this case, the only header line generated is Content-type, which gives the media format of the output as HTML (text/html). This line is essential for every CGI program, since it tells the browser what kind of format to expect. The blank line separates the header from the body text (which, in this case, is in HTML format as advertised).

The server transfers the results of the CGI program back to the browser. The body text is not modified or interpreted by the server in any way, but the server generally supplies additional headers with information such as the date, the name and version of the server, etc.

CGI programs can also supply a complete HTTP header itself, in which case the server does not add any additional headers but instead transfers the response verbatim as returned by the CGI program. The server needs to be configured to allow this behavior; see your server documentation on NPH (no-parsed headers) scripts for more information.

Here is the sample output of a program generating an HTML virtual document, with a complete HTTP header:

```
HTTP/1.0 200 OK
Date:  Thursday, 28-June-96 11:12:21 GMT
Server: NCSA/1.4.2
Content-type: text/html
Content-length: 2041

<HTML>
<HEAD><TITLE>Thanks!</TITLE></HEAD>
<BODY>
<H1>Thanks for signing my guestbook!</H1>
    ...
```

```
</BODY>
</HTML>
```

The header contains the communication protocol, the date and time of the response, and the server name and version. (200 OK is a status code generated by the HTTP protocol to communicate the status of a request, in this case successful.) Most importantly, the header also contains the content type and the number of characters (equivalent to the number of bytes) of the enclosed data.

The result is that after users click the "submit" button, they see the message contained in the HTML section of the response thanking them for signing the guestbook.

URL Encoding

Before data supplied on a form can be sent to a CGI program, each form element's name (specified by the name attribute) is equated with the value entered by the user to create a key/value pair. For example, if the user entered "30" when asked for his or her age, the key/value pair would be "age=30". In the transferred data, key/value pairs are separated by the ampersand (&) character.

Since under the GET method the form information is sent as part of the URL, form information can't include any spaces or other special characters that are not allowed in URLs, and also can't include characters that have other meanings in URLs, like slashes (/). (For the sake of consistency, this constraint also exists when the POST method is being used.) Therefore, the web browser performs some special encoding on user-supplied information.

Encoding involves replacing spaces and other special characters in the query strings with their hexadecimal equivalents. (Thus, URL encoding is also sometimes called *hexadecimal encoding*.) Suppose a user fills out and submits a form containing his or her birthday in the syntax mm/dd/yy (e.g., 11/05/73). The forward slashes in the birthday are among the special characters that can't appear in the client's request for the CGI program. Thus, when the browser issues the request, it encodes the data. The following sample request shows the resulting encoding:

```
POST /cgi-bin/birthday.pl HTTP/1.0
Content-length: 21

birthday=11%2F05%2F73
```

The sequence %2F is actually the hexadecimal equivalent of the slash character.

CGI scripts have to provide some way to "decode" the form data that the client has encoded. The best way to do this is to use CGI.pm (covered in Chapter 10) and let someone else do the work for you.

Extra Path Information

In addition to passing query strings, you can pass additional data, known as *extra path information*, as part of the URL. The server gauges where the CGI program name ends; anything following is deemed "extra" and is stored in the environment variable PATH_INFO. The following line calls a script with extra path information:

```
http://some.machine/cgi-bin/display.pl/cgi/cgi_doc.txt
```

In this example, we use a script with a *.pl* suffix to make it clear where the CGI program's path ends and the extra path information begins. Everything after *display.pl* is the extra pathand is placed in the PATH_INFO environment variable. The PATH_TRANSLATED variable is also set, mapping the PATH_INFO to the DOCUMENT_ROOT directory (e.g., */usr/local/etc/httpd/public/cgi/cgi_doc.txt*).

CGI Environment Variables

Most of the information needed by CGI programs is made available via Unix environment variables. Programs can access this information as they would any environment variable (via the %ENV hash in Perl). The table below lists environment variables commonly available through CGI. However, since servers occasionally vary on the names of environment variables they assign, check with your own server documentation for more information.

Environment variable	Content returned
AUTH_TYPE	The authentication method used to validate a user. See REMOTE_IDENT and REMOTE_USER.
CONTENT_LENGTH	The length of the query data (in bytes or the number of characters)passed to the CGI program through standard input.
CONTENT_TYPE	The media type of the query data, such as text/html.
DOCUMENT_ROOT	The directory from which web documents are served.
GATEWAY_INTERFACE	The revision of the Common Gateway Interface that the server uses.
HTTP_ACCEPT	A list of the media types that the client can accept.
HTTP_COOKIE	A list of cookies defined for that URL.
HTTP_FROM	The email address of the user making the query (many browsers do not support this variable).
HTTP_REFERER	The URL of the document the client read before accessing the CGI program.
HTTP_USER_AGENT	The browser the client is using to issue the request.
PATH_INFO	Extra path information passed to a CGI program.
PATH_TRANSLATED	The translated version of the path given by the variable PATH_INFO.
QUERY_STRING	The query information passed to the program. It is appended to the URL following a question mark (?).
REMOTE_ADDR	The remote IP address from which the user is making the request.
REMOTE_HOST	The remote hostname from which the user is making the request.
REMOTE_IDENT	The user making the request.
REMOTE_USER	The authenticated name of the user making the query.
REQUEST_METHOD	The method with which the information request was issued (e.g., GET, POST, HEAD).
SCRIPT_NAME	The virtual path (e.g., */cgi-bin/program.pl*) of the script being executed.
SERVER_NAME	The server's hostname or IP address.
SERVER_PORT	The port number of the host on which the server is running.

Environment variable	Content returned
SERVER_PROTOCOL	The name and revision number of the server protocol.
SERVER_SOFTWARE	The name and version of the server software that is answering the client request.

Here's a simple Perl CGI script that uses environment variables to display various information about the server:

```perl
#!/usr/local/bin/perl

print << EOF
Content-type: text/html

<HTML>
<HEAD><TITLE>About this Server</TITLE></HEAD>
<BODY><H1>About this Server</H1>
<HR><PRE>
Server Name:        $ENV{'SERVER_NAME'}<BR>
Running on Port:    $ENV{'SERVER_PORT'}<BR>
Server Software:    $ENV{'SERVER_SOFTWARE'}<BR>
Server Protocol:    $ENV{'SERVER_PROTOCOL'}<BR>
CGI Revision:       $ENV{'GATEWAY_INTERFACE'}<BR>
<HR></PRE>
</BODY></HTML>
```

The preceding program outputs five environments as an HTML document. In Perl, you can access the environment variables with the %ENV hash. Here's typical output of the program:

```
<HTML>
<HEAD><TITLE>About this Server</TITLE></HEAD>
<BODY><H1>About this Server</H1>
<HR><PRE>
Server Name:        www.whatever.com
Running on Port:    80
Server Software:    NCSA/1.4.2
Server Protocol:    HTTP/1.0
CGI Revision:       CGI/1.1
<HR></PRE>
</BODY></HTML>
```

10

The CGI.pm Module

CGI.pm is a Perl module for creating and parsing CGI forms. It has been distributed with the Perl source kit since 5.004, but you can upgrade your existing CGI.pm installation from CPAN. As of the writing of this edition, the current version of CGI.pm is 2.81.

CGI is an object-oriented module. Don't let the object-oriented nature scare you off, though; CGI.pm is very easy to use, as evidenced by its overwhelming popularity among all levels of Perl programmers. To give you an idea of how easy it is to use CGI.pm, let's take a scenario in which a user fills out and submits a form containing her birthday. Without CGI.pm, the script would have to translate the URL-encoded input by hand (probably using a series of regular expressions) and assign it to a variable. For example, you might try an antiquated parsing method like this:

```perl
#!/usr/local/bin/perl
# CGI script without CGI.pm

$size_of_form_info = $ENV{'CONTENT_LENGTH'};
read ($STDIN, $form_info, $size_of_form_info);

# Split up each pair of key/value pairs
foreach $pair (split (/&/, $form_info)) {

    # For each pair, split into $key and $value variables
    ($key, $value) = split (/=/, $pair);

    # Get rid of the pesky %xx encodings
    $key =~ s/%([\dA-Fa-f][\dA-Fa-f])/pack ("C", hex ($1))/eg;
    $value =~ s/%([\dA-Fa-f][\dA-Fa-f])/pack ("C", hex ($1))/eg;

    # Use $key as index for $parameters hash, $value as value
    $parameters{$key} = $value;
}
```

```
# Print out the obligatory content type line
print "Content-type: text/plain\n\n";

# Tell the user what they said
print "Your birthday is on " . $parameters{birthday} . ".\n";
```

Regardless of whether this code actually works, you must admit it's ugly, and completely ignores important details such as dealing with tainted input. With CGI.pm, the script could be written as:

```
#!/usr/local/bin/perl -w
# CGI script with CGI.pm

use CGI;

my $query = CGI->new( );

my $bday = $query->param("birthday");

print $query->header(-type => 'text/plain');
print $query->p("Your birthday is $bday.");
```

Even for this tiny program, you can see that CGI.pm can alleviate many of the headaches associated with CGI programming.

As with any Perl module, the first thing you do is call the module with use. You then call the constructor (new( )), creating a new CGI object called $query. Next, get the value of the birthday parameter from the CGI program using the param method. Note that CGI.pm does all the work of determining whether the CGI program is called by the GET or POST methods, and it does all the URL decoding for you. To generate output, use the header method to return the content type header and the p method to generate a paragraph marker <P> tag.

However, this is only the tip of the iceberg as far as what CGI.pm can do for you. There are three basic categories of CGI.pm methods: CGI handling, creating forms, and retrieving environment variables. (A fourth category is creating HTML tags, but we don't cover those in detail.) Table 10-1 lists most of these methods. They are also covered in more detail later in this chapter.

Table 10-1. CGI.pm methods

Method	Description
CGI handling	
keywords	Gets keywords from an <ISINDEX> search
param	Gets (or sets) the value of parameters
append	Appends to a parameter
import_names	Imports variables into a namespace
delete	Deletes a parameter
delete_all	Deletes all parameters
save	Saves all parameters to a file
self_url	Creates self-referencing URL
url	Gets URL of current script without query information

Table 10-1. CGI.pm methods (continued)

Method	Description
header	Creates HTTP header
redirect	Creates redirection header
cookie	Gets (or sets) a cookie
nph	Declares this to be a NPH script
dump	Prints all name/value pairs
Form generation	
start_html	Generates an `<HTML>` tag
end_html	Generates an `</HTML>` tag
autoEscape	Sets whether to use automatic escaping
isindex	Generates an `<ISINDEX>` tag
startform	Generates a `<FORM>` tag
start_multipart_form	Generates a `<FORM>` tag for multipart/form-data encoding
textfield	Generates an `<INPUT TYPE=TEXT>` tag
textarea	Generates an `<TEXTAREA>` tag
password_field	Generates an `<INPUT TYPE=PASSWORD>` tag
filefield	Generates an `<INPUT TYPE=FILE>` tag
popup_menu	Generates a pop-up menu via `<SELECT SIZE=1>` and `<OPTION>` tags
scrolling_list	Generates a scrolling list via `<SELECT>` and `<OPTION>` tags
checkbox_group	Generates a group of checkboxes via multiple `<INPUT TYPE=CHECKBOX>` tags
checkbox	Generates a single checkbox via an `<INPUT TYPE=CHECKBOX>` tag
radio_group	Generates a group of radio buttons via `<INPUT TYPE=RADIO>` tags
submit	Generates a `<SUBMIT>` tag
reset	Generates a `<RESET>` tag
defaults	Generates a `<DEFAULTS>` tag
hidden	Generates an `<INPUT TYPE=HIDDEN>` tag
image_button	Generates a clickable image button via a `<SELECT>` tag
button	Generates a JavaScript button
Handling environment variables	
accept	Gets accept types from ACCEPT header
user_agent	Gets value of USER_AGENT header
path_info	Gets value of EXTRA_PATH_INFO header
path_translated	Gets value of PATH_TRANSLATED header
remote_host	Gets value of REMOTE_HOST header
raw_cookie	Gets value of HTTP_COOKIE header
script_name	Gets value of SCRIPT_NAME header
referer	Gets value of REFERER header
auth_type	Gets value of AUTH_TYPE header
remote_user	Gets value of REMOTE_USER header
user_name	Gets user name (not via headers)
request_method	Gets value of REQUEST_METHOD header

HTML Tag Generation

In addition to the form-generation methods, CGI.pm includes a group of methods for creating HTML tags. The names of the HTML tag methods generally follow the HTML tag name (e.g., p for <P>) and take named parameters that are assumed to be valid attributes for the tag (e.g., img(src=>'camel.gif') becomes <IMG SRC="camel.gif">). We do not list all tags in this book; see the CGI.pm manpage for more information, or the book *Official Guide to Programming with CGI.pm* by Lincoln Stein (John Wiley & Sons, 1998).

Importing Method Groups

The syntax for calling CGI methods can be unwieldy. However, if you choose not to use the object form of CGI.pm, you can import individual methods instead. The "birthday" example shown earlier could be written even more simply as:

```
#!/usr/local/bin/perl -w

use CGI qw(param header p);

my $bday = param("birthday");

print header('text/plain');
print "Your birthday is $bday.";
```

By importing the param, header, and p methods into your namespace, you no longer have to use the new constructor (since it is called automatically now), and you don't need to specify a CGI object with every method call.

CGI.pm also lets you import groups of methods, which can make your programs much simpler and more elegant. For example, to import all form-creation methods and all CGI-handling methods:

```
use CGI qw/:form :cgi/;
```

The method groups supported by CGI.pm are:

:cgi
  All CGI-handling methods

:cgi-lib
  All methods supplied for backward compatibility with *cgi-lib*

:form
  All form-generation methods

:html
  All HTML methods

:html2
  All HTML 2.0 methods

:html3
  All HTML 3.0 methods

:netscape
> All methods generating Netscape extensions

:ssl
> All SSL methods

:standard
> All HTML 2.0, form-generation, and CGI methods

:all
> All available methods

You can also define new methods for HTML tag generation by simply listing them on the import line and letting CGI.pm make some educated guesses. For example:

```
use CGI shortcuts,smell;
```

```
print smell {type=>'garlic',
            intensity=>'strong'}, "Scratch here!";
```

This will cause the following tag to be generated:

```
<SMELL TYPE="garlic" INTENSITY="strong">Scratch here!</SMELL>
```

Maintaining State

One of the first complications for any nontrivial CGI script is how to "maintain state." Since HTTP is a stateless protocol, there's no built-in mechanism for keeping track of requests from the server end. A CGI transaction involving multiple forms, therefore, needs to find a way to remember information supplied on previous forms. One way to deal with this issue is to use *cookies*, which allow the CGI program to save information on the browser's end; but not all browsers support cookies, and some users are uncomfortable with the perceived privacy infringement associated with cookies.

CGI.pm simplifies maintaining state without cookies. When a CGI.pm script is called multiple times, the input fields are given default values from the previous invocation.

Named Parameters

For most CGI.pm methods, there are two syntax styles. In the "standard" style, the position of the parameters determines how they will be interpreted—for example, parameter 1 is the name that the script should assign, parameter 2 is the initial value, etc. For example:

```
print $query=textfield('username', 'anonymous');
```

In the "named parameters" style, the parameters can be assigned like a hash, and the order doesn't matter. For example:

```
print $query->textfield(-name=>'name',
                        -default=>'value');
```

If you want to use named parameters, just call the use_named_parameters method early in the script.

Which syntax style should you use? It depends on how lazy you are and how much control you need. Generally, standard syntax is faster to type. However, it is also harder to read, and there are many features that are simply not available using standard syntax (such as JavaScript support). In general, we recommend using the named parameters syntax for all but the most trivial scripts.

Using JavaScript Features

CGI.pm supports JavaScript scripting by allowing you to embed a JavaScript script into the HTML form within <SCRIPT> tags and then calling the script using the -script parameter to the start_html method. You can then call the appropriate JavaScript functions to the form elements.

Debugging

A complication of writing CGI scripts is that when debugging the script, you have to wrestle with the web server environment. CGI.pm provides support for debugging the script on the command line.

If you run the script on the command line without arguments, you will be placed into an "offline" mode, in which name/value pairs can be entered one-by-one. When you press Ctrl-D, the script runs. For example:

```
% birthday
(offline mode: enter name=value pairs on standard input)
birthday=6/4/65
^D
Content-type: text/html

<P>Your birthday is 6/4/65.</P>
```

You can also supply the name/value parameters directly on the command line. For example:

```
% test birthday=6/4/65
Content-type: text/html

<P>Your birthday is 6/4/65.</P>
```

Multiple values can be separated by spaces (as separate arguments on the command line) or by ampersands (as in URL-encoded syntax). In fact, you can use URL-encoded syntax on the command line. This makes it easy to supply raw CGI input to the script for testing purposes. Just remember to protect the ampersand from the shell.

```
% test 'birthday=6%2f4%2f65&name=Fred%20Flintstone'
Content-type: text/html

<P>Fred Flintstone, your birthday is 6/4/65.</P>
```

CGI.pm Reference

The following methods are supported by CGI.pm.

accept $query->accept(['content_type'])

Returns a list of media types that the browser accepts.

content_type
    If specified, returns instead the browser's preference for the specified content type, between 0.0 and 1.0

---

append $query->append(-name=>'name',-values=>'value')

Appends a value or list of values to the named parameter.

-name=>'name'
    The parameter to append.

-values=>'value'
    The value to append. Multiple values can be specified as a reference to an anonymous array.

---

auth_type   auth_type( )

Returns the authorization method.

---

autoEscape $query->autoEscape(undef)

Turns off autoescaping of form elements.

---

button   print $query->button('name','function')

Generates a JavaScript button.

name
    The name of the button.

function
    The function to execute when the button is clicked. Using named parameters, the syntax is:

```
print $query->button(-name=>'name',
                     -value=>'label',
                     -onClick=>"function");
```

-value=>'label'
    The label to display for the button

---

checkbox   print $query->checkbox('name' [,'checked','value','label'])

Generates a single checkbox.

name
    The name to assign the input to (required).

checked
    Checkbox should be checked initially.

value
> The value to return when checked (default is on).

label
> The label to use for the checkbox (default is the name of the checkbox). Using named parameters, the syntax is:
>
> ```
> print $query->checkbox(-name=>'name',
>                        -checked=>'checked',
>                        -value=>'value',
>                        -label=>'label',
>                        -onClick=>function);
> ```

-onClick=>*function*
> Browser should execute *function* when the user clicks on any checkbox in the group

---

checkbox_group

```
print $query->checkbox_group('name', \@list
[, selected,'true',\%labelhash ])
```

Generates a list of checkbox elements.

name
> The name to assign the input to (required).

\@*list*
> An array reference with the list items. You can also use an anonymous array reference.

selected
> The menu item(s) to be initially selected (default is that nothing is selected). This can be a single value or a reference to an array of values.

'true'
> Insert newlines between the checkboxes.

\%*labelhash*
> A hash reference listing labels for each list item. Default is the list text itself. See popup_menu for an example. Using named parameters, the syntax is:
>
> ```
> print $query->checkbox_group(-name=>'name',
>                              -values=>\@list,
>                              -default=>selected,
>                              -linebreak=>'true',
>                              -labels=>\%labelhash,
>                              -columns=>n,
>                              -columnheader=>'string',
>                              -rows=>m,
>                              -rowheader=>'string',
>                              -onClick=>function);
> ```

-columns=>*n*
> The number of columns to use.

-columnheader=>'*string*'
> A header for the column.

-rows=*m*
> The number of rows to use. If omitted, and -columns is specified, the rows will be calculated for you.

-rowheader=>'*string*'
> A header for the row.

-onClick=>*function*
> Browser should execute *function* when the user clicks on any checkbox in the group.

---

cookie
$cookie=$query->cookie('*name*')

Defines or retrieves a cookie. See also header.

name
> Name of the cookie (required). Using named parameters, the syntax is:
>
> ```
> $cookie = $query->cookie(-name=>'name',
>                          -value=>'value',
>                          -expires=>'expcode',
>                          -path=>'partial_url',
>                          -domain=>'domain_name',
>                          -secure=>1);
> print $query->header(-cookie=>$cookie);
> ```

-value=>'*value*'
> A value to assign to the cookie. You can supply a scalar value, or a reference to an array or hash. If omitted, a cookie will be retrieved rather than defined.

-expires=>*expcode*
> Specifies an expiration timestamp (such as +3d for three days). Values for *expcode* are:
>
> *n*s
> > *n* seconds
>
> *n*m
> > *n* minutes
>
> *n*h
> > *n* hours
>
> *n*d
> > *n* days
>
> *n*M
> > *n* months
>
> *n*y
> > *n* years
>
> *day_of_week, dd-MMM-YY hh:mm:ss* GMT
> > At the specified time.
>
> now
> > Expires immediately.

-path=>'*partial_url*'
                The partial URL for which the cookie is valid.
                Default is the current URL.
        -domain=>'*domain_name*'
                The domain for which the cookie is valid.
        -secure=>1
                Use this cookie only for a secure session.

---

defaults   ```
print $query->defaults('label')
```

Generates a button that resets the form to its defaults. See also reset.

'*label*'
   The label to use for the button. If omitted, the label is Defaults.

---

**delete**    ```
$query->delete('parameter')
```

Deletes a parameter.

'*parameter*'
   The parameter to delete

---

delete_all   ```
$query->delete_all()
```

Deletes the entire CGI object.

---

**dump**    ```
print $query->dump([true])
```

Dumps all name/value pairs as an HTML list.

true
   If specified, prints as plain text

---

end_html   ```
print $query->end_html()
```

Ends an HTML document.

---

**filefield**    ```
print $query->filefield('name' [,'default',size,maxlength ])
```

Generates a file upload field for Netscape browsers.

name
   The filename to assign the supplied file contents to (required)

default
   The initial value (filename) to place in the text field

size
   The size of the text field (in characters)

maxlength

The maximum length of the text field (in characters)

Using named parameters, the syntax is:

```
print $query->textfield(-name=>'name',
                        -default=>'value',
                        -size=>size,
                        -maxlength=>maxlength,
                        -override=>1,
                        -onChange=>function,
                        -onFocus=>function,
                        -onBlur=>function,
                        -onSelect=>function);
```

-override=>1

Text field should not inherit its value from a previous invocation of the script

-onChange=>*function*

Browser should execute *function* when the user changes the text field

-onFocus=>*function*

Browser should execute *function* when the focus is on the text field

-onBlur=>*function*

Browser should execute *function* when the focus leaves the text field

-onSelect=>*function*

Browser should execute *function* when the user changes a selected portion of the text field

---

header

```
print $query->header([content_type ,status ,headers])
```

Generates the HTTP header for the document.

content_type

The content type to return. Default is text/html.

status

The HTTP status code and description to return. Default is 200 OK.

headers

Additional headers to include, such as Content-Length: 123. Using named parameters, the syntax is:

```
print $query->header(-type=>'content_type',
                     -nph=>1,
                     -status=>'status_code',
                     -expires=>'expcode',
                     -cookie=>'cookie',
                     -target=>'frame',
                     -header=>'value');
```

-type=>*content_type*
> Specifies the content type.

-nph=>1
> Uses headers for a no-parse-header script.

-status=>*status_code*
> Specifies the status code.

-expires=>*expcode*
> Specifies an expiration timestamp (such as +3d for three days). Values for *expcode* are:
>
> *n*s
> > *n* seconds
>
> *n*m
> > *n* minutes
>
> *n*h
> > *n* hours
>
> *n*d
> > *n* days
>
> *n*M
> > *n* months
>
> *n*y
> > *n* years
>
> *day_of_week, dd-MMM-YY hh:mm:ss* GMT
> > At the specified time
>
> now
> > Expires immediately

-cookie=>*cookie*
> Specifies a cookie. The cookie may be a scalar value or an array reference.

-header=>*value*
> Specifies any HTTP header.

-target=>*frame*
> Writes to specified frame.

---

hidden

```
print $query->hidden('name', 'value' [,'value'... ])
```

Generates a hidden text field.

name
> The name to give the value (required).

value
> The value to assign to *name*. Multiple values can be specified. Using named parameters, the syntax is:
>
> ```
> print $query->hidden(-name=>'name',
>                      -default=>'value');
> ```

With named parameters, the value can also be represented as
a reference to an array, such as:

```
print $query->hidden(-name=>'name',
                     -default=>['value1', 'value2',
... ]);
```

---

image_button   `print $query->image_button('name','url' [,'align'])`

Generates a clickable image map.

name
> The name to use. When clicked, the *x,y* position is returned as
> *name.x* and *name.y*, respectively.

url
> The URL of the image for the image map.

align
> The alignment type. May be TOP, BOTTOM, or MIDDLE. Using
> named parameters, the syntax is:
>
> ```
> print $query->image_button(-name=>'name',
>                            -src=>'url',
>                            -align=>'align',
>                            -onClick=>function);
> ```

> -onClick=>*function*
> > Browser should execute *function* when the user clicks on
> > the image

---

import_names   `$query->import_names('package')`

Creates variables in the specified package. Called import in older
versions of CGI.pm.

package
> The package to import names into

---

isindex   `print $query->isindex([action])`

Generates an <ISINDEX> tag.

action
> The URL of the index script. Default is the current URL.
> Using named parameters, the syntax is:
>
> ```
> print $query->isindex(-action=>$action);
> ```

---

keywords   `@keyarray = $query->keywords()`

Retrieves keywords from an <ISINDEX> search.

@keyarray
> The array that will contain the retrieved keywords

nph   nph(1)

Treats a CGI script as a no-parsed-header (NPH) script.

---

param   @name = $query->param([*parameter* [*newvalue1, newvalue2, ...*]])

Gets or sets parameter names.

@name
    The array that will contain the parameter names.

parameter
    An optional single parameter to fetch. When used with no arguments, param returns a list of all known parameter names.

newvalue1, newvalue2, ...
    The optional new values to assign to the parameter. Using named parameters, the syntax is:

```
$query->param(-name=>'parameter',
              -value=>'newvalue');
```

or:

```
$query->param(-name=>'parameter',
              -values=>'newvalue1', 'newvalue2', ...);
```

---

password_field   print $query->password_field('*name*' [,'*value*',*size*,*maxlength*])

Generates a password input field.

name
    The name to assign the input to (required).

value
    The default password to place in the password field.

size
    The size of the password field (in characters).

maxlength
    The maximum length of the password field (in characters). Using named parameters, the syntax is:

```
print $query->password_field(-name=>'name',
                             -default=>'value',
                             -size=>size,
                             -maxlength=>maxlength,
                             -override=>1,
                             -onChange=>function,
                             -onFocus=>function,
                             -onBlur=>function,
                             -onSelect=>function);
```

-override=>1
    Text field should not inherit its value from a previous invocation of the script

-onChange=>*function*
    Browser should execute *function* when the user changes the text field

-onFocus=>*function*
>Browser should execute *function* when the focus is on the text field

-onBlur=>*function*
>Browser should execute *function* when the focus leaves the text field

-onSelect=>*function*
>Browser should execute *function* when the user changes a selected portion of the text field

---

path_info   path_info( )

Returns extra path information.

---

path_translated   path_translated( )

Returns translated extra path information.

---

popup_menu   print $*query*->popup_menu('*name*', \@*array* [,'*selected*', \%*labelhash*])

Generates a popup menu.

name
>The name to assign the input to (required).

\@*array*
>An array reference listing the menu items. You can also use an anonymous array reference (see example below).

selected
>The menu item to be initially selected (default is first menu item or the item selected in previous queries).

\%*labelhash*
>A hash reference listing labels for each menu item. Default is menu item text. For example:

```
%labels = ('UPS'=>'United Parcel Service (UPS)',
          'FedExO'=>'Federal Express Overnight - 10AM
delivery',
          'FedExS'=>'Federal Express Standard - 2PM
delivery',
          'FedEx2'=>'Federal Express 2nd Day
Delivery');

print $query->popup_menu('delivery_method',
                        ['UPS', 'FedExO', 'FedExS',
'FedEx2'],
                        'FedExO',
                        \%labels);
```

>Using named parameters, the syntax is:

```
print $query->popup_menu(-name=>'name',
                        -values=>\@array,
```

```
                                      -default=>'selected',
                                      -labels=>\%labelhash,
                                      -onChange=>function,
                                      -onFocus=>function,
                                      -onBlur=>function);
```

-onChange=>*function*
> Browser should execute *function* when the user changes
> the text field

-onFocus=>*function*
> Browser should execute *function* when the focus is on on
> the text field

-onBlur=>*function*
> Browser should execute *function* when the focus leaves
> the text field

---

radio_group

print $*query*->radio_group('*name*', \@*list* [, *selected*, 'true',
\%*label*])

Generates a set of radio buttons.

name
> The name to assign the input to (required).

\@*list*
> An array reference with the list items. You can also use an
> anonymous array reference.

selected
> The menu item to be initially selected.

'true'
> Inserts newlines between radio buttons.

\%*label*
> A hash reference listing labels for each list item. Default is the
> list text itself. (See popup_menu for an example.) Using named
> parameters, the syntax is:
>
> ```
>      print $query->radio_group(-name=>'name',
>                                -values=>\@list,
>                                -default=>'selected',
>                                -linebreak=>'true',
>                                -labels=>\%labelhash,
>                                -columns=>n,
>                                -columnheader=>'string',
>                                -rows=>m,
>                                -rowheader=>'string');
> ```

-columns=>*n*
> The number of columns to use.

-columnheader=>'*string*'
> A header for the column.

-rows=*m*
> The number of rows to use. If omitted, and -columns is specified, the rows will be calculated for you.

-rowheader=>'*string*'
> A header for the row.

---

raw_cookie   raw_cookie( )

Returns the value of the HTTP_COOKIE header.

ReadParse   ReadParse( )

Creates a hash named %in containing query information. Used for backwards compatibility with the Perl4 *cgi-lib.pl*.

---

redirect   print $*query*->redirect('*url*')

Generates a header for redirecting the browser.

url
> The absolute URL to redirect to. Using named parameters, the syntax is:

```
print $query->redirect(-uri=>'url',
                       -nph=>1);
```

---

referer   referer( )

Returns the referring URL.

---

remote_host   remote_host( )

Returns the remote hostname or IP address, depending on the configuration of the server.

---

remote_user   remote_user( )

Returns the username supplied for authorization.

---

request_method   request_method( )

Returns the request method.

---

reset   print $*query*->reset

Generates a button that resets the form to its initial values. See also defaults.

---

save $query->save(*filehandle*)

Saves the form to the specified filehandle, to be read back with the new constructor.

filehandle
  The filehandle to save the file to

---

script_name   script_name( )

Returns the current partial URL.

---

scrolling_list   print

$query->scrolling_list('*name*',\@*list*[,*selected*,*size*,'true', \%*labelhash*]);

Generates a scrolling list.

name
  The name to assign the input to (required).

\@*list*
  An array reference with the list items. You can also use an anonymous array reference.

selected
  The menu item(s) to be initially selected (default is that nothing is selected). This can be a single value or a reference to a list of values.

size
  The number of elements to display in the list box.

'true'
  Allows multiple selections.

\%*labelhash*
  A hash reference listing labels for each list item. Default is the list text itself. (See popup_menu for an example.) Using named parameters, the syntax is:

```
print $query->scrolling_list(-name=>'name',
                             -values=>\@listarray,
                             -default=>selected,
                             -size=>size,
                             -multiple=>'true',
                             -labels=>\%labelhash,
                             -onChange=>function,
                             -onFocus=>function,
                             -onBlur=>function);
```

-onChange=>*function*
  Browser should execute *function* when the user changes the text field

-onFocus=>*function*
>   Browser should execute *function* when the focus is on on
>   the text field

-onBlur=>*function*
>   Browser should execute *function* when the focus leaves
>   the text field

---

self_url $*url* = $*query*->self_url

Returns the URL of the current script with all its state information
intact.

---

start_html   print $*query*->start_html(['*title*', '*email*', '*base*',
attribute='*value*'])

Generates <HTML> and <BODY> tags.

title
>   The title of the page.

email
>   The author's email address.

base
>   Whether to use a <BASE> tag in the header.

attribute='*value*'
>   Specifies an attribute to the <BODY> tag. Using named parame-
>   ters, the syntax is:
>
>   print $query->start_html(-title=>'*title*',
>   -author=>'*email_address*',
>   -base=>'true',
>   -xbase=>'*url*',
>   -meta=>{'*metatag1*'=>'*value1*',
>   '*metatag2*'=>
>   '*value2*'},
>   -script=>'$*script*',
>   -onLoad=>'$*function*',
>   -onUnload=>'$*function*',
>   -*attribute*=>'*value*');

-title=>'*title*'
>   Specifies the title of the page.

-author=>'*email_address*'
>   Specifies the author's email address.

-xbase=>'*url*'
>   Provides an HREF for the <BASE> tag. Default is the
>   current location.

-meta=>{'*metatag1*'=>'*value1*', ... }
>   Adds arbitrary meta information to the header as a refer-
>   ence to a hash. Valid tags are:

---

keywords
> Keywords for this document

copyright
> Copyright for this document description

description
> Description for this document

attribute=>'*value*'
> Specifies an attribute to the <BODY> tag

-script=>'$*script*'
> Specifies a JavaScript script to be embedded within a <SCRIPT> block.

-onLoad=>'$*function*'
> Browser should execute specified function upon entering page.

-onUnload=>'$*function*'
> Browser should execute specified function upon leaving page.

---

startform

print $*query*->startform([*method, action, encoding*])

Generates a <FORM> tag.

method
> The request method for the form. Values are:
>
> POST
> > Use the POST method (default).
>
> GET
> > Use the GET method.

action
> The URL of the CGI script. Default is the current URL.

encoding
> The encoding scheme. Possible values are application/x-www-form-urlencoded and multipart/form-data. Using named parameters, the syntax is:
>
> ```
> print $query->startform(-method=>$method,
>                         -action=>$action,
>                         -encoding=>$encoding,
>                         -name=>$name,
>                         -target=>frame,
>                         -onSubmit=>function);
> ```

-name=>*name*
> Names the form for identification by JavaScript functions

-target=>*frame*
> Writes to the specified frame

-onSubmit=>*function*
> A JavaScript function that the browser should execute upon submitting the form

start_multipart_form

```
print $query->start_multipart_form([method, action])
```

Generates <HTML> and <BODY> tags. Same as startform, but assumes
multipart/form-data encoding as the default.

submit

```
print $query->submit([ 'label','value' ])
```

Generates a Submit button.

label
> The label to use for the button.

value
> The value to return when the form is submitted. Using named
> parameters, the syntax is:
> ```
> print $query->submit(-name=>'name',
>                      -value=>'value',
>                      -onClick=>function);
> ```

> -onClick=>*function*
>> Browser should execute *function* when the user clicks on
>> the image

textarea

```
print $query->textarea('name' [,'value',rows,columns ])
```

Generates a large multiline text input box.

name
> The name to assign the input to (required).

value
> The initial value to place into the text input box.

rows
> The number of rows to display.

columns
> The number of columns to display. Using named parameters,
> the syntax is:
> ```
> print $query->textarea(-name=>'name',
>                        -default=>'value',
>                        -rows=>rows,
>                        -columns=>columns,
>                        -override=>1,
>                        -onChange=>function,
>                        -onFocus=>function,
>                        -onBlur=>function,
>                        -onSelect=>function);
> ```

> -override=>1
>> Text field should not inherit its value from a previous
>> invocation of the script

-onChange=>*function*
> Browser should execute *function* when the user changes the text field

-onFocus=>*function*
> Browser should execute *function* when the focus is on the text field

-onBlur=>*function*
> Browser should execute *function* when the focus leaves the text field

-onSelect=>*function*
> Browser should execute *function* when the user changes a selected portion of the text field

---

textfield

```
print $query->textfield('name' [,'value', size, maxlength])
```

Generates a text input field.

name
> The name to assign the input to (required).

value
> The initial value to place in the text field.

size
> The size of the text field (in characters).

maxlength
> The maximum length of the text field (in characters). Using named parameters, the syntax is:
>
> ```
> print $query->textfield(-name=>'name',
>                         -default=>'value',
>                         -size=>size,
>                         -maxlength=>maxlength,
>                         -override=>1,
>                         -onChange=>function,
>                         -onFocus=>function,
>                         -onBlur=>function,
>                         -onSelect=>function);
> ```

-override=>1
> Text field should not inherit its value from a previous invocation of the script

-onChange=>*function*
> Browser should execute *function* when the user changes the text field

-onFocus=>*function*
> Browser should execute *function* when the focus is on the text field

-onBlur=>*function*
> Browser should execute *function* when the focus leaves the text field

-onSelect=>*function*
> Browser should execute *function* when the user changes a selected portion of the text field

---

url $url = $query->url

Returns a URL of the current script without query information.

---

use_named_parameters

use_named_parameters( )

Specifies that functions should take named parameters.

---

user_agent $query->user_agent([*string*])

Returns the value of the HTTP_USER_AGENT header.

string
> If specified, returns only headers matching the specified string

---

user_name user_name( )

Returns the remote user's login name; unreliable.

11

Web Server Programming with mod_perl

A common criticism of CGI is that it requires forking extra processes each time a script is executed. If you have only a few hits an hour, or even a few hits a minute, this isn't a big deal. But for a high-traffic site, lots of repeatedly spawning CGI scripts can have an unfortunate effect on the machine running the web server. The CGI scripts will be slow, the web server will be slow, and other processes on the machine will slow to a crawl.

The solution to this problem is *mod_perl*. *mod_perl*, written by Doug MacEachern and distributed under CPAN, embeds the Perl interpreter directly into the web server. The effect is that your CGI scripts are precompiled by the server and executed without forking, thus running much more quickly and efficiently. Furthermore, CGI efficiency is only one facet of *mod_perl*. Since *mod_perl* is a complete Apache/Perl hybrid, other benefits to *mod_perl* include:

- Writing server-side includes in Perl
- Embedding Perl code into the Apache configuration files
- Writing complete Apache modules in Perl

Design of mod_perl

mod_perl is a Perl runtime library linked into the Apache server. With *mod_perl*, the Perl programmer has access to Apache's C language API through an object-oriented Perl interface. This means that you can write Apache modules and extensions entirely in Perl and embed Perl code and custom directives in your Apache configuration files. Furthermore, the embedded Perl interpreter removes the overhead that you'd experience if you'd merely written a Perl CGI program and put it in Apache's *cgi-bin*.

Aside from the framework mentioned above, another major benefit of *mod_perl* is the Apache::Registry module. Apache::Registry implements the CGI environment under the *mod_perl* framework, which means that you can reuse most of your existing Perl CGI programs to realize the benefits of *mod_perl*. Apache::Registry caches compiled scripts on the first execution of a script and updates scripts that have changed on disk.

Finally, *mod_perl* gives the Perl programmer the ability to interact with all stages of an HTTP request, many of which aren't available through CGI. These include the Apache handler phase, the HTTP header parser, URI translation, authentication, authorization, access (permissions), type checking, fixup, and logger stages.

Now that you've been subjected to two rather optimistic paragraphs, we'll take a few moments to appease the cynics. It might occur to you that sticking a large program into another large program makes a very, very large program. *mod_perl* certainly makes *httpd* significantly bigger. If you have limited memory capacity, *mod_perl* may not be for you. There are several ways to minimize the size of Apache with *mod_perl* (which you can find in the *mod_perl* manpage or the FAQs), ranging from fiddling with Apache configuration directives to building Perl with reduced memory consumption.

Installing mod_perl

If you already have Apache installed on your machine, you will have to rebuild it with *mod_perl*. If you prefer, you can install the *mod_perl*-enabled Apache installation somewhere else, which we'll also detail in this section. You can get the source for both Apache and *mod_perl* from *http://www.apache.org/dist/httpd/*. You can get *mod_perl* alone from CPAN or from *http://perl.apache.org/dist/*. The *mod_perl* build process is quite configurable, and after you've met some Perl module dependencies, you should be well on your way to building and getting your *mod_perl*-enabled Apache installation online.

First, you should take a look at your existing Apache installation (or installations) and make sure that you don't unintentionally interfere with a working Apache installation. If you're running Apache-1.3.X, it's likely that your Apache installation lives under */usr/local/apache*, or *C:\apache* if you're on a Win32 platform. Second, make sure that you're running a current version of Perl and that you've installed the LWP Bundle of modules. If you haven't installed the LWP modules bundle, *mod_perl* might not build correctly and will not run its tests correctly.

Once you've met the requirements listed above, you should unpack the Apache and *mod_perl* distributions and run:

```
% perl Makefile.PL EVERYTHING=1 APACHE_PREFIX=[target directory]
```

Next, run *make*, *make test*, and assuming all goes well, *make install* to install the *mod_perl*-enabled Apache:

```
% make
% make test
% make install
```

The EVERYTHING=1 option says to build *mod_perl* with all of the supported features. If this isn't what you were looking for or if you'd like to learn more about making a custom Apache build with *mod_perl*, you should read the *INSTALL* file that ships with *mod_perl*.

At the time of this writing, both Apache and *mod_perl* have been ported to Win32. However, you might have the best results with *mod_perl* under Win32 if you run ActiveState's Perl distribution and its precompiled version of *mod_perl*. For further information about building *mod_perl* under Win32, see *INSTALL. win32*.

mod_perl Handlers

To understand *mod_perl*, you should understand how the Apache server works. When Apache receives a request, it processes it in several stages. First, it translates the URL to the associated resource (i.e., filename, CGI script, etc.) on the server machine. Then it checks to see if the user is authorized to access that resource, perhaps by requesting and checking an ID and password or hostname and IP address. Once the user has passed inspection, the server figures out the kind of data it's sending back (e.g., it decides a file ending in *.html* is probably a text/html file), creates some headers, and sends those headers back to the client with the resource itself. When all is said and done, the server makes a log entry.

At each stage of this process, Apache looks for routines to "handle" the request. That is, if Apache doesn't find handlers you've told it to use, it knows to use its own. For example, if you've enabled CGI programs in *httpd.conf*, Apache knows to execute programs that live in *cgi-bin* if it encounters the cgi-script directive:

```
<Location /cgi-bin>
...
SetHandler cgi-script
...
</Location>
```

mod_perl allows you to write your own handlers in Perl by embedding the Perl runtime library directly into the Apache *httpd* server executable. To use *mod_perl* for CGI (which is all that most people want to do with it), assign the SetHandler directive to perl-script, and the *mod_perl*-specific PerlHandler directive to a special Perl module called Apache::Registry:

```
SetHandler perl-script
PerlHandler Apache::Registry
```

PerlHandler is the *mod_perl* handler for the content retrieval stage of the transaction.

To use other handlers, you don't need to reassign SetHandler. For example, to identify a handler for the logging stage of the request:

```
<Location /snoop/>
PerlLogHandler Apache::DumpHeaders
</Location>
```

For this to work, *mod_perl* must have been built with the logging hooks enabled (as described in the previous section), and the Apache::DumpHeaders module must have been installed. *mod_perl* looks in Apache::DumpHeaders for a routine called handler( ) and executes it as the logging handler for that resource.

The following is a list of each of the handler directives that can be enabled by
mod_perl and the stages that each is used for. Only PerlHandler is enabled by
default.

Handler	Purpose
PerlAccessHandler	Access stage
PerlAuthenHandler	Authentication stage
PerlAuthzHandler	Authorization stage
PerlChildInitHandler	Child initialization stage
PerlChildExitHandler	Child termination stage
PerlCleanupHandler	Cleanup stage
PerlFixupHandler	Fixup stage
PerlHandler	Response stage
PerlHeaderParserHandler	Header-parsing stage
PerlInitHandler	Initialization
PerlLogHandler	Logging stage
PerlPostReadRequestHandler	Post-request stage
PerlTransHandler	Translation stage
PerlTypeHandler	Type-handling stage

You can write your own handlers for each of these stages. But there are also
dozens of modules that you can download from CPAN, some of which are listed
at the end of this chapter.

Running CGI Scripts with mod_perl

What most people want to do with *mod_perl* is improve CGI performance. The
mod_perl installation assumes this request by enabling the PerlHandler callback
hook by default and by installing the Apache::Registry module. PerlHandler is the
handler used for the content retrieval stage of the server transaction.
Apache::Registry is the Perl module that emulates the CGI environment so you
can use "standard" Perl CGI scripts with *mod_perl* without having to rewrite them
(much). This is by far the cheapest way to get improved CGI performance.

With Apache::Registry, each individual CGI program is compiled and cached the
first time it is called (or whenever it is changed) and remains available for all
subsequent instances of that CGI script. This process avoids the costs of startup
time.

Whereas most CGI scripts are kept in *cgi-bin*, scripts that use Apache::Registry are
placed in a separate directory, e.g., *perl-bin*. The *access.conf* Apache configuration
file needs to point to this directory by setting an alias and defining a handler for
this new location:

```
Alias /perl-bin/ /usr/local/apache/perl-bin/

<Location /perl-bin>
SetHandler perl-script
```

```
PerlHandler Apache::Registry
PerlSendHeader On
Options ExecCGI
</Location>
```

Instead of using the `cgi-script` handler, we use the `perl-script` handler to give control to *mod_perl*. Next, the `PerlHandler` directive tells *mod_perl* that the Apache::Registry module should be used for serving all files in that directory. `PerlSendHeader` is another *mod_perl*-specific directive; in this case, it tells *mod_perl* to send response lines and common headers—by default, none are sent. (For NPH scripts, you'll want to turn this feature off again.) `Options ExecCGI` is a standard Apache header that is needed to tell Apache to treat the script as a CGI script.

If you want to load Perl modules in addition to Apache::Registry, you can use the PerlModule directive:

```
PerlModule CGI
```

If you include this line, you shouldn't need to explicitly use `CGI` in each Perl CGI script anymore, since CGI.pm will be loaded directly from the Apache server. Up to ten modules can be listed with the `PerlModule` directive.

CGI scripts in the new directory should work now. However, if you have problems, the *mod_perl* manpage offers some words of wisdom:

- Always use use `strict`. Standard CGI scripts start with a clean slate every time. When switching to *mod_perl*, CGI programmers are often surprised to learn how often they take advantage of this fact. use `strict` tells you when your variables haven't been properly declared and might inherit values from previous invocations of the script.

- Don't call exit( ). Calling exit( ) at the end of every program is a habit of many programmers. While often totally unnecessary, it usually doesn't hurt… except with *mod_perl*. If you're using *mod_perl* without Apache::Registry, exit( ) kills the server process. If exit( ) is the last function call, you can just remove it. If the structure of your program is such that it is called from the middle of the script, you can just put a label at the end of the script and use goto( ). There's also an Apache->exit( ) call you can use if you're really attached to exit( )s.

  If you're using Apache::Registry, you don't have to worry about this problem. Apache::Registry is smart enough to override all exit( ) calls with Apache->exit( ).

In addition, it is recommended that you should use recent versions of Perl and CGI.pm. You should scan the *mod_perl* documentation for the latest compatibility news.

Server-Side Includes with mod_perl

Server-side includes (SSIs) are tags embedded directly into an HTML file that perform special functions. They are most commonly used for running CGI scripts and displaying the result; most web page counters are performed using SSIs.

If you use *mod_perl* with *mod_include* (another Apache server module), you can embed Perl subroutines into SSI directives. For example:

```
<!--#perl sub="sub {print ++Count}" -->
```

The Apache::Include module lets you include entire Apache::Registry scripts:

```
<!--#perl sub="Apache::Include" arg="/perl-bin/counter.pl"-->
```

You could have used standard SSIs to include a CGI script for the same purpose, but this way is faster. To use *mod_include* with *mod_perl*, you need to configure *mod_perl* to do so at compile time.

<Perl> Sections

With *mod_perl*, you can use Perl in Apache configuration files. What this means is that you can make your Apache configuration much more flexible by using conditionals.

Any Perl code in Apache configuration files should be placed between <Perl> and </Perl> directives. This code can define variables and lists used by *mod_perl* to assign the associated Apache configuration directives; for example, assigning the $ServerAdmin variable will redefine the ServerAdmin Apache configuration directive.

Suppose you share the same Apache configuration files across multiple servers, and you want to allow personal directories on only one of them. You can use Perl directives like this:

```
<Perl>
if ('hostname' =~ /public/) {
        $UserDir = "public.html";
} else {
        $UserDir = "DISABLED";
}
1;
</Perl>
```

Directive blocks (such as <Location>...</Location>) can be represented as a hash. For example:

```
<Perl>
$Location{"/design_dept/"} = {
        DefaultType   => 'image/gif',
        FancyIndexing => 'On'
}
</Perl>
```

Apache:: Modules

Apache::Registry is the most commonly used *mod_perl* module. But there are many more, all available on CPAN. The following table lists the Apache::* modules and the handler they're designed to be used with, but you should also check the *apache-modlist.html* file on CPAN for the latest listing.

Module	Description
PerlHandler	
Apache::CallHandler	Maps filenames to subroutine calls
Apache::Dir	Controls directory indexing
Apache::Embperl	Embeds Perl code in HTML files
Apache::ePerl	Embedded Perl (ePerl) emulation
Apache::FTP	Emulates an FTP proxy
Apache::GzipChain	Compresses output from another handler
Apache::JavaScript	Generates JavaScript code
Apache::OutputChain	Chains multiple handlers via "filter" modules
Apache::PassFile	Sends files via OutputChain
Apache::Registry	Runs unaltered CGI scripts
Apache::RobotRules	Enforces *robots.txt* rules
Apache::Sandwich	Adds per-directory headers and footers
Apache::VhostSandwich	Adds headers and footers for virtual hosts
Apache::SSI	Implements server-side includes in Perl
Apache::Stage	Manages a document staging directory
Apache::WDB	Queries databases via DBI
PerlHeaderParserHandler	
Apache::AgentDeny	Denies abusive clients
PerlAuthenHandler	
Apache::Authen	Authenticates users
Apache::AuthCookie	Authenticates and authorizes users via cookies
Apache::AuthenDBI	Authenticates via Perl's DBI
Apache::AuthExpire	Expires authentication credentials
Apache::AuthenGSS	Authenticates users with Generic Security Service
Apache::AuthenLDAP	Authenticates users with LDAP
Apache::AuthNIS	Authenticates users with NIS
Apache::BasicCookieAuth	Accepts cookie or basic authentication credentials
Apache::DBILogin	Authenticates using a backend database
Apache::DCELogin	Authenticates within a DCE login context
Apache::AuthAny	Authenticates with any username/password
PerlAuthzHandler	
Apache::AuthCookie	Authenticates and authorizes via cookies
Apache::AuthzAge	Authorizes based on age
Apache::AuthzDCE	Authorizes based on DFS/DCE ACL
Apache::AuthzDBI	Authorizes groups via DBI
Apache::AuthNIS	Authenticates and authorizes via NIS
Apache::RoleAuthz	Role-based authorization
PerlAccessHandler	
Apache::AccessLimitNum	Limits user access by the number of requests
Apache::DayLimit	Limits access based on the day of the week
Apache::RobotLimit	Limits access of robots

CGI

Module	Description
PerlTypeHandler	
Apache::AcceptLanguage	Sends file types based on user's language preference
PerlTransHandler	
Apache::DynaRPC	Translates URIs into RPCs
Apache::Junction	Mounts remote web server namespace
Apache::LowerCaseGETs	Translates to lowercase URIs as needed
Apache::MsqlProxy	Translates URIs into mSQL queries
Apache::ProxyPassThru	Skeleton for vanilla proxy
Apache::ProxyCache	Caching proxy
PerlFixupHandler	
Apache::HttpEquiv	Converts HTML HTTP-EQUIV tags to HTTP headers
Apache::Timeit	Benchmarks Perl handlers
PerlLogHandler	
Apache::DumpHeaders	Displays HTTP transaction headers
Apache::Traffic	Logs the number of bytes transferred on a per-user basis
Apache::WatchDog	Looks for problematic URIs
PerlChildInitHandler	
Apache::Resource	Limits resources used by *httpd* children
Server configuration	
Apache::ConfigLDAP	Configures server via LDAP and <Perl> sections
Apache::ConfigDBI	Configures server via DBI and <Perl> sections
Apache::ModuleConfig	Interfaces to configuration API
Apache::PerlSections	Utilities for <Perl> sections
Apache::httpd_conf	Methods to configure and run an *httpd*
Apache::src	Methods for finding and reading bits of source
Database	
Apache::DBI	Manages persistent DBI connections
Apache::Sybase	Manages persistent DBlib connections
Apache::Mysql	Manages persistent mysql connections
Interfaces and integration with various Apache C modules	
Apache::Constants	Constants defined in *httpd.h*
Apache::Include	Enables use of Apache::Registry scripts within SSI with *mod_include*
Apache::Global	Gives access to server global variables
Apache::LogError	Gives an interface to *aplog_error*
Apache::LogFile	Gives an interface to Apache's piped logs, etc.
Apache::Mime	Gives an interface to *mod_mime* functionality
Apache::Module	Gives an interface to Apache C module structures
Apache::Options	Imports Apache::Constants "options"
Apache::Scoreboard	Gives an interface to scoreboard API
Apache::Servlet	Gives an interface to the Java Servlet engine
Apache::Sfio	Gives an interface to r->connection->client->sf*

Module	Description
Development and debug tools	
Apache::Debug	Provides debugging utilities to *mod_perl*
Apache::DProf	Hooks Devel::DProf into *mod_perl*
Apache::FakeRequest	Implements Apache methods offline
Apache::Peek	Emulates Devel::Peek for *mod_perl*
Apache::SawAmpersand	Makes sure no one is using $&, $ ´, or $ '
Apache::StatINC	Reloads files that are used or required files when updated
Apache::Status	Gets information about loaded modules
Apache::Symbol	Supports symbols
Apache::test	Defines handy routines for *make test* scripts
Miscellaneous	
Apache::Byterun	Runs Perl bytecode modules
Apache::Mmap	Shares data via Mmap module
Apache::Persistent	Stores data via IPC::, DBI, or disk
Apache::PUT	Handler for the HTTP PUT method
Apache::RegistryLoader	Apache::Registry startup script loader
Apache::Safe	Adaptation of *safecgiperl*
Apache::Session	Maintains client <-> *httpd* session/state
Apache::SIG	Signal handlers for *mod_perl*
Apache::State	Powerful state engine

CGI

V

Databases

12

Databases and Perl

Since one of Perl's greatest strengths is working with text, a genuine concern is how to store data. Flat files are one possibility, but they don't scale very well for large amounts of data. When working with lots of data, you'll likely need database software to satisfy your capacity and performance requirements.

There are two general solutions to using databases with Perl. For simple database purposes, Database Management (DBM) will serve your needs. DBM is a library supported by many (if not all) Unix systems and many non-Unix systems as well. DBM is more efficient than flat text files because of how it packs records into the database files and the (large) size of data it can store and retrieve efficiently. Perl's interface to your system's DBM is based on a hash, so you can add, store, and delete data by key.

When you need to store a larger variety of data and need other goodies such as searchability on multiple records, you'll probably need to use a database that supports SQL. To this end, you can buy a prepackaged database product such as Oracle or Sybase, or a shareware equivalent such as MySQL or PostgreSQL. For these larger database projects, you should use DBI and DBD. DBI is a module that provides a consistent interface for database solutions. DBD is a database-specific driver that translates DBI calls as needed for that database.

In this chapter, we'll cover DBM and talk at length about DBI/DBD.

DBM Databases and DBM Hashes

DBM is a simple database management facility for Unix systems. It allows programs to store a collection of key/value pairs in binary form, thus providing rudimentary database support for Perl. Practically all Unix systems ship with built-in DBM support, some with a separate libdb and others with DBM calls built into libc. In the absence of DBM support on your system, you can use gdbm from GNU, which is an extension to vanilla DBM or BerkeleyDB-3.x from *http://www.sleepycat.com/db*.

To use DBM databases in Perl, you can associate a hash with a DBM database through the AnyDBM module that uses tie( ). This hash (called a DBM array) is then used to access and modify the DBM database. Previously, you could use dbmopen( ) to open, read, write, and delete a database, but while dbmopen( ) remains available, you should use the AnyDBM module that's always suited to your underlying DBM implementation.[*] For example, with AnyDBM:

```
#!/usr/local/bin/perl -w

    use AnyDBM_File;
    use Fcntl; # needed for O_ thingies

    my %h;
    my $db_name = 'perl_in_a_nutshell2.dbmx';

    # tie %h. will fail if $db_name can't be created and $db_name can't be
    # written
    tie(%h, 'AnyDBM_File', $db_name, O_RDWR|O_CREAT, 0640)
        or die("can't create \%h: $!");

    # Populate %h
    foreach my $letter ('a' .. 'z') {
        $h{$letter} = uc($letter);
    }

    while(my($key, $value) = each(%h)) {
        print "$key -> $value\n";
    }

    untie(%h);
```

The %ARRAYNAME parameter is a Perl hash. (If it already has values, the values are discarded under DBM_File modules, although you can have multiple keys under BerkeleyDB-2.x and newer.) %ARRAYNAME is tied to a DBM database called $db_name. This database may be stored on disk as a single file, or as two files called *$db_name.dir* and *$db_name.pag*, depending on the DBM implementation.

The $mode parameter is a number that controls the permissions of the pair of files if the files need to be created. The number is in octal, so make sure that you use permissions such as 0640 instead of 640, which are different numbers in octal. If the files already exist, $mode has no effect. For example:

```
    tie(%BOOKS, "bookdb", O_RDWR|O_CREAT, 0666); # Open %BOOKS onto bookdb
```

This invocation associates the hash %BOOKS with the disk files *bookdb.dir* and *bookdb.pag* in the current directory. If the files don't already exist, they are created with a mode of 0666, modified by the current *umask*.

---

[*] If you're using BerkeleyDB-2.x or newer, you should not use AnyDBM_File, but should instead install and use the BerkeleyDB module.

`tie( )` returns undef upon any failure in opening the $db_name and sets $!.

Once the database is opened, anything you do to the DBM hash is immediately written to the database. See Chapter 4 for more information on hashes.

```
tie(%BOOKS, "bookdb", O_RDWR|O_CREAT, 0666)
    or die("can't open bookdb: $!"); # Open %BOOKS onto bookdb
$BOOKS{"1-56592-286-7"} = "Perl in a Nutshell";
```

The DBM array stays open throughout the program. When the program terminates, the association is terminated. You can also break the association in a manner similar to closing a filehandle by using `untie( )`. See Chapter 5 for more information on `tie`.

Design of DBI

If DBM is too primitive for your database requirements, you'll have to use a more sophisticated database package. Options include the commercial products Oracle, Sybase, and Informix, and the freely available *MySQL* and *Postgres*.

Prior to Perl Version 5 and DBI, the problem was that with all the database packages to choose from, there was no way to universalize database support for Perl. You'd have to rebuild the Perl executable itself against libraries that included subroutines for direct access to the database package. For example, *sybperl* and *oraperl* are both packages for building Perl Version 4 with Sybase and Oracle calls embedded, respectively. An application written for *sybperl* would not be portable to Oracle, or vice versa. However, since current versions of Perl support binary extension loading at runtime, database support can now be added at runtime, which simplifies adding database interfaces to Perl programs while keeping the size of the Perl binary to a minimum.

Support for binary extensions doesn't mean that database access has been standardized. There are still many database extensions to Perl, each with a different API. However, their underlying support for SQL (or ability to be manipulated into a form that mimics the behavior of SQL through a DBD) has made it possible to develop a standard set of methods to work with any database. DBI defines a set of functions, variables, and conventions that provide a consistent database programming interface for Perl.

Database Drivers (DBDs)

The success of DBI is that it is only half of the story. The other half is a DBD, or a database driver. DBI provides the interface and framework for the drivers, but it's the database drivers that do the real work. Drivers implement the DBI methods for the private interface functions of the corresponding database engine.

Unless you're developing a sophisticated database application, you probably don't care about the drivers except that you want to install the correct one. Table 12-1 lists database servers, where you can find them, and the DBD driver designed for it. (The freeware or shareware database servers are available for download, and some of the commercial servers offer evaluation copies for download.)

Table 12-1. *Database servers*

Server	URL	DBD
DB2	http://www.software.ibm.com/data/db2/	DBD::DB2
Empress	http://www.empress.com/	DBD::Empress
Fulcrum	http://www.fulcrum.com	DBD::Fulcrum
Informix	http://www.informix.com/	DBD::Informix
Ingres	http://www.cai.com/products/ingres.htm	DBD::Ingres
	http://epoch.cs.berkeley.edu:8000/postgres/index.html	
miniSQL	http://www.hughes.com.au/	DBD::mSQL
MySQL	http://www.tcx.se/	DBD::mysql
Oracle	http://www.oracle.com/	DBD::Oracle
PostgreSQL	http://www.postgresql.com/	DBD::Pg
QuickBase	http://www.openbase.com/	DBD::QBase
Solid	http://www.solidtech.com/	DBD::Solid
Sybase	http://www.sybase.com/	DBD::Sybase

Creating a Database

Before you can open a connection to a database with DBI, you must create the
database. DBI can't do this step for you, although your DBD might allow you to.
For example, DBD::MySQL implements a _CreateDB function. Your DBD might
also support the func method, which is used to call private (and often nonportable) methods in the driver. You could use a one-liner like this to create the
database from the command line:

```
perl -MDBI -e '$db_name = q[database_name_here]; \
    $result = DBD::mysql::dr->func($db_name, '_CreateDB');'
```

If your DBD allows to you to create databases via the API, it's likely that it will
allow you to drop them, too:

```
perl -MDBI -e '$db_name = q[database_name_here]; \
    $result = DBD::mysql::dr->func($db_name, '_DropDB');'
```

Database Handles and Statement Handles

DBI methods work on two different types of handles: database handles and statement handles. A database handle is like a filehandle; connect is a DBI class
method that opens a connection to a database and returns a database handle
object:

```
$db_handle = DBI->connect(dbi:mSQL:bookdb, undef, undef)
    || die("Connect error: $DBI::errstr");
```

Statement handles are another thing entirely. DBI makes a distinction between the
preparation of SQL statements and their execution by allowing you to preformat a
statement into a statement handle. You can prepare a statement with the prepare
method, which returns a statement handle. You can then assign a SQL statement
to the statement handle via various statement handle methods and execute it with

the execute method when you're done. (You can also prepare and execute in the same command with the do method.)

Changes to the database are written to the database automatically if the Auto-Commit attribute is turned on. If AutoCommit is off, use the commit method when you're ready to write the changes to the database.

AutoCommit is only one of many attributes that can be set for both database and statement handles. For example, if $st_handle is a statement handle, you can set $st_handle->{NULLABLE} to determine if the fields can contain null characters. Table 12-2 is a listing of all the attributes supported by database handles, statement handles, or both.

Table 12-2. Attributes for database and statement handles

Attribute	Description
Attribute for database handles	
AutoCommit	Commits any changes to the database immediately, instead of waiting for an explicit call to commit. Default is true.
Attributes for statement handles	
CursorName	The name of the cursor associated with the statement handle.
NAME	A reference to an array of field names.
NULLABLE	A reference to an array describing whether each field can contain a null character.
NUM_OF_FIELDS	Number of fields the prepared statement will return.
NUM_OF_PARAMS	Number of placeholders in the prepared statement.
Attributes common to all handles	
Warn	Enables warnings.
CompatMode	Enables compatible behavior for a specific driver.
InactiveDestroy	Destroying a handle does not close prepared statements or disconnect from the database.
PrintError	Errors generate warnings.
RaiseError	Errors raise exceptions.
ChopBlanks	Truncates trailing space characters in fixed-width character fields.
LongReadLen	Controls the maximum length of long data.
LongTruncOk	Controls whether fetching long data that has been truncated should fail.

Placeholders and Statement Handles

Many database drivers allow you to use question marks as placeholders in SQL statements and then bind values to the placeholders before executing them. This enables you to prepare a single statement with placeholders and reuse it for each row of the database. For example, the prepare statement might read:

```
$st_handle = $db_handle->prepare(q{
        insert into books (isbn, title) values (?, ?)
})  || die db_handle->errstr;
```

And a subsequent execute statement might read:

```
$st_handle->execute("1-56592-286-7", "Perl in a Nutshell")
        || die $db_handle->errstr;
```

DBI Methods

The following methods are available under DBI.

---

available_drivers

> @*drivers* = DBI->available_drivers([*nowarn*])

Returns a list of available drivers by searching @INC for the presence of DBD::* modules.

nowarn
> A Boolean value specifying whether to suppress warnings if some drivers are hidden by others of the same name in earlier directories. Default is false (don't suppress).

---

bind_col

> $*result* = $*st_handle*->bind_col(*col*, *variable* [, \%*attr*])

Binds a field of a select statement to a variable, to be updated whenever the row is fetched.

col
> The column number to bind

variable
> A reference to the variable to bind

\%*attr*
> Attributes to set for the statement handle

---

bind_columns

> $*result* = $*st_handle*->bind_columns(\%*attr*, @*reflist*)

Runs bind_col on each column of the statement.

\%*attr*
> Attributes to set for the statement handle

@*reflist*
> A list of references to the variables to bind

---

bind_param

> $*result* = $*st_handle*->bind_param(*n*, *value* [, *type*])

Binds a value with a placeholder in a prepared statement.

n
> The parameter number to bind.

value
> The value to associate with parameter *n*.

type
> The data type for the placeholder. The type can also be specified as an anonymous list ({TYPE => *type*}).

commit $result = $db_handle->commit

Commits the most recent changes. See also the AutoCommit attribute.

connect $db_handle = DBI->connect(*data_source, user, passwd*, [\%*attr*])

Connects to the specified database, returning a database handle object. The connect method automatically installs the driver if it has not already been installed.

data_source
> A string identifying the driver to connect to, and any other additional driver-specific information needed to identify the driver (e.g., a port number). The driver name is written in the form dbi:*driver_name*, e.g., dbi:mysql. (Default value is taken from the DBI_DSN environment variable.) For example, a connection string for the MySQL driver always starts with dbi:mysql:. The second colon should be followed by any information required by the driver to make the database connection. In the case of MySQL, you must supply a database name (bookdb in the following example), a hostname (localhost), and the port number of the database server (1114):

```
DBI:$driver:database=$database;host=$hostname;port=
$port
```

user
> The username for the database connection. (Default value is taken from the DBI_USER environment variable.)

passwd
> The password for the database connection. (Default value is taken from the DBI_PASS environment variable. Set this value at your own risk.)

\%*attr*
> A hash reference defining attributes for the database handle.

data_sources   @*drivers* = DBI->data_sources(*driver*)

Returns a list of all databases available for the named driver. (The database server must be running for data_sources to return any results.)

driver
> The driver to list. If unspecified, the value of DBI_DRIVER is used.

disconnect $result = $db_handle->disconnect

Disconnects the database.

do	$rows = $db_handle->do(statement [, \%attr, @bind_values])

Prepares and executes a statement, returning the number of rows affected.

statement
> The statement to execute

\%attr
> Attributes to set for the new statement

@bind_values
> Bind values for placeholder substitution

dump_results	$rows = DBI::dump_results(st_handle, maxlen, ldelim, fdelim, fileh)

Runs DBI::neat( ) on all the rows of a statement handle and prints them for testing purposes.

st_handle
> The statement handle to retrieve.

maxlen
> The length at which to truncate with "...". Default is 35.

ldelim
> The delimiter between rows. Default is \n.

fdelim
> The delimiter between individual fields. Default is , .

fileh
> The filehandle to print to. Default is STDOUT.

err	$handle->err

Returns the error code from the last driver function called.

errstr	$handle->errstr

Returns the error message from the last driver function called.

execute	$result = $st_handle->execute([@bind_values])

Executes a prepared statement.

@bind_values
> Binds values for placeholder substitution

fetch	$arrayref = $st_handle->fetch

Fetches the next row of data, returning an array reference with the field values.

fetchall_arrayref

$arrayref = $st_handle->fetchall_arrayref

Fetches all data from a prepared statement and returns a reference to an array of references.

fetchrow_array

$array = $st_handle->fetchrow_array

Fetches the next row of data, returning an array with the field values.

fetchrow_arrayref

$arrayref = $st_handle->fetchrow_arrayref

Fetches the next row of data, returning an array reference with the field values. Synonym for fetch.

fetchrow_hashref

$hashref = $st_handle->fetchrow_hashref

Fetches the next row of data, returning a hash reference containing the field values. The keys of the hash are the same as $st_handle->{NAME}.

finish

$result = $st_handle->finish

Disables further fetching from a statement.

func

$handle->func(@arguments, function)

Calls a private nonportable method on the specific handle.

@arguments
   The arguments to the function.

function
The function name. Note that the function name is specified last.

neat

$newstring = DBI::neat(string, maxlength)

Converts a string to one with quoted strings, null values shown as undef, and unprintable characters shown as ".".

string
   The string to convert

maxlength
   The length at which to truncate the string with "..."

neat_list $newstring$ = DBI::neat_list(\@$list$, $maxlength$, $delim$)

Converts each element of a list with DBI::neat and returns it as a string.

\@$list$
    A reference to the list to convert.

$maxlength$
    The length at which to truncate the string with "...".

$delim$
    The delimiter to use between list elements in the new string. Default is , .

---

ping $result$ = db_handle->ping

Determines if the database is still connected.

---

prepare st_handle = db_handle->prepare($statement$ [, \%$attr$])

Prepares a statement for execution and returns a reference to a statement handle object.

$statement$
    The statement to prepare

\%$attr$
    Attributes to set for the assigned statement handle

---

quote sql = db_handle->quote($string$)

Escapes special characters in a string for use in a SQL statement.

$string$
    The string to convert

---

rollback $result$ = db_handle->rollback

Undoes the most recent database changes if not yet committed.

---

rows $rows$ = st_handle->rows

Returns the number of rows affected by the last change to the database.

---

state $handle$->state

Returns an error code in a five-character format.

| **trace** | DBI->trace(*n*, *filename*) |

Traces the execution of DBI.

n
> An integer indicating the level of trace/debugging informa-
> tion, as follows:
>
> 0   Disable the trace.
>
> 1   Trace the execution of the DBI.
>
> 2   Output detailed call trace information including parame-
> ters and return values.

filename
> The file to append trace information to

| **trace** | $handle->trace(*n*, *filename*) |

Same as the class method DBI->trace, but for a specific database,
statement, or driver handle.

DBI Environment Variables

The following environment variables are defined for use with DBI:

DBI_DSN
> The data source value to use if none is specified with the connect method.

DBI_DRIVER
> The driver to use if none is specified with the connect method.

DBI_USER
> The username to use if none is specified with the connect method.

DBI_PASS
> The password to use if none is specified with the connect method. (For secu-
> rity purposes, this environment variable should not be set except for testing.)

DBI_TRACE
> Enables tracing behavior as with the trace method. DBI_TRACE can be set
> to any of the following values:

0   Disables the trace

1   Traces the execution of the DBI

2   Outputs detailed call trace information including parameters and return
     values

filename
> Appends trace information to the specified file; the trace level is set to 2.

VI

XML and SOAP

13

XML and Perl

The Extensible Markup Language (XML) is a metalanguage for providing complete, configurable information for documents and other types of data. XML is based loosely on SGML, but has divorced itself of much of the complexity that made SGML unsuitable for everyday use. Without opening a can of worms about the differences between SGML and XML, suffice it to say that SGML is the predecessor to XML, and XML is a subset of SGML, with extensions.

With XML, you aren't bound by a fixed format, but can mark up a document to make it easily adaptable to whatever final format you later decide to apply it to. In fact, this book is written in XML, to be produced later not only in a print format but in an online format as well.

XML is often associated with web content, but it is much more flexible than that. Lately, XML's application to web services such as SOAP and XML-RPC has given it a chance to flex its muscles and show what it's capable of. XML gives you the structure to hold any content you'd like, whether it be the pages of this book in their rawest form, a list of your favorite recipes, or the ledger from your checkbook. XML is structured so that you can represent any kind of data in XML. XML's openness means that you can implement an XML-based application on any platform.

This chapter is focused on parsing, checking and delivering XML content. Chapter 14 covers SOAP programming in XML.

XML Parsing and Validation

The two most common tasks that you'll perform on your XML content are likely to be parsing and validating. If you've ever combed around on CPAN for XML-related modules, you probably already know that there's no shortage of resources when it comes to Perl and XML. On the contrary, the sheer volume of modules available for Perl and XML is rather daunting, so you might be looking for a place to start.

This chapter covers two Perl/XML modules in particular: XML::Simple and XML::Parser. These modules were selected because they allow you to parse and manipulate most XML. While these modules themselves don't validate XML, we'll resort to a little bit of trickery to show you how you can do exactly that.

XML::Simple provides an easy API that allows you to read and write XML. It is built on top of XML::Parser, which will be covered shortly. As its name suggests, XML::Simple implements only two methods: XMLin( ) and XMLout( ). But don't let its apparent lack of methods fool you; XML::Simple lets you do great things simply, such as parsing XML-written configuration files.

Let's say that your company keeps a log of its Sun Microsystems servers and their respective operation-system versions, IP addresses, and current patch levels. While you could keep this information in your home directory as a delimited file (which you can parse and analyze when you need to, or import into a database, such as PostGresSQL or MySQL), why not just write it in XML? You'll find that by writing this information in an XML document, you'll be able to operate on this information just as flexibly as you can with one of the aforementioned strategies. In addition, your information would reside in a structure in which the relationships between items and their meanings are clear.

Let's say that your flat text log file looks like this:

```
# sunhosts - patches and levels
atlas|solaris|2.8|192.168.0.2|Generic_108528-10|5.6.1
carrie|solaris|2.8|192.168.1.10|Generic_108527-12|5.6.0
not4sun|solaris|2.8|192.168.0.25|Generic_108482-06|5.005_03
```

While you could parse this configuration file easily, and generate some kind of report from it, your configuration file doesn't really tell you anything about the data that it represents. You can represent the same data in XML like so:

```
<config servertype="sunhosts" reporttype="patches and levels">
    <server name="atlas" osname="solaris" osversion="2.8">
        <address>192.168.0.2</address>
        <patchlevel>Generic_108528-10</patchlevel>
        <perlversion>5.6.1</perlversion>
    </server>

    <server name="carrie" osname="solaris" osversion="2.8">
        <address>192.168.1.10</address>
        <patchlevel>Generic_108527-12</patchlevel>
        <perlversion>5.6.0</perlversion>
    </server>

    <server name="not4sun" osname="solaris" osversion="2.8">
        <address>192.168.0.25</address>
        <patchlevel>Generic_108482-06</patchlevel>
        <perlversion>5.005_03</perlversion>
    </server>
</config>
```

In the above XML, all of the entries will be keyed on server so that for each entry in your XML that's called server, you'll be able to view its information for address, patchlevel, and perlversion. The following XML::Simple code does just that:

```perl
#!/usr/local/bin/perl -w

use XML::Simple;

my $config = XMLin('./myconfig.xml');

# Simply show us the IP address of each server in our table
foreach my $server (keys %{$config->{server}}) {
    print "$server -> $config->{server}{$server}{address}\n";
}
```

Now that you've parsed your configuration file, let's say you want to write XML back to your configuration. To do this, you should use XMLout( ), which is covered in the XML::Simple documentation.

While XML::Simple doesn't provide a thorough method for validating XML, it does insist that a document is compliant XML. This means that if you present XML::Simple with a document that's not syntatically correct, XML::Simple will stop parsing the XML document and store the error message in $@. For example:

```xml
<config servertype="sunhosts" reporttype="patches and levels">
  <server name="atlas" osname="solaris" osversion="2.8">
    <address>192.168.0.2</address>
    <patchlevel>Generic_108528-10</patchlevel>
    <perlversion>5.6.1</perlversion>
</config>
```

The following code would find the error in your XML and exit upon finding it:

```perl
#!/usr/local/bin/perl -w

use XML::Simple;

my $config = eval { XMLin('./mybadconfig.xml') };
print("I found an error in your XML: $@") if $@;

foreach my $server (keys %{$config->{server}}) {
    print "$server -> $config->{server}{$server}\n";
}
```

This gives you:

```
I found an error in your XML:
mismatched tag at line 6, column 2, byte 241 at
/usr/local/lib/perl5/site_perl/5.6.1/sun4-solaris/XML/Parser.pm line 185
```

Two components are very useful for parsing XML with Perl: Expat and XML::Parser. Although there are several XML parsing options for Perl, such as GNOME's *libxml* and offerings from the PerlSAX2 project, we stick to Expat and XML::Parser in this chapter.

Expat is a nonvalidating (that is, it does not check XML for correctness) XML parser that was written by James Clark. XML::Parser, a Perl wrapper around Expat, was originally written by Larry Wall and later developed by Clark Cooper. If you're using the ActivePerl, you should be able to install XML::Parser with *ppm*. Otherwise, you'll have to build Expat first, then link XML::Parser against it.

Each call to one of the XML::Parser parsing methods creates a new instance of XML::Parser::Expat, which is then used to parse the document. Expat options may be provided when the XML::Parser object is created. These options are then passed on to the Expat object on each parse call. They can also be given as extra arguments to the parse methods, in which case they override options given at XML::Parser creation time.

The XML parser takes your XML document and turns it into a data structure that you can operate on. XML::Parser gives you low-level control (and precision) over the data structure that it created, from which you can build parsers on top of it. XML::Simple is an example of this.

The behavior of the parser is controlled either by Style and/or Handlers options or by the setHandlers method. These all provide mechanisms that XML::Parser can use to set the handlers needed by XML::Parser::Expat. If neither Style nor Handlers are specified, then parsing just checks if the document is well-formed.

When underlying handlers get called, they receive as their first parameter the Expat object, not the Parser object.

You can show the relationships between entries in a configuration file with XML::Parser as well. For example:

```
#!/usr/local/bin/perl -w

use XML::Parser;
use Data::Dumper;

# Simply dump all of the entries and their relationships
my $p1 = XML::Parser->new(Style => 'Tree');
my $tree = $p1->parsefile('myconfig.xml');

print Dumper($tree);
```

XML::Parser Methods

The following methods are defined by XML::Parser.

---

new   new(%*option*)

Constructor. Options are passed as keyword/value pairs. Recognized options are:

Style
> Sets the type of parser. The built-in styles are Debug, Subs, Tree, Objects, and Stream. Custom styles can be provided by giving a fully qualified package name containing at least one "::".

This package must have subroutines defined for each parser type.

Handlers

An anonymous hash containing the handler types as the keys with their associated values, which are references to subroutines for handling that type of event.

Pkg

Some styles will refer to subroutines defined in the specified package.

ErrorContext

The number of lines to show surrounding the line in which an error occurred.

ProtocolEncoding

Sets the protocol-encoding name (default is none). The built-in encodings are UTF-8, ISO-8859-1, UTF-16, and US-ASCII. You may introduce additional encodings by adding directories to @Encoding_Path.

Namespaces

If true, then namespace processing is done during the parse.

NoExpand

Normally, the parser will try to expand references to entities defined internally. If this option is true and a default handler is also set, then the default handler will be called when an entity reference is encountered.

Stream_Delimiter

A string for XML::Parser to interpret as end-of-file if found alone on a line. Useful when working with MIME multipart documents. The string should not contain a trailing newline.

ParseParamEnt

Unless standalone is set to yes in the XML declaration, setting this to true allows the external DTD to be read, and parameter entities to be parsed and expanded.

NoLWP

If true, forces the use of a file-based external entity handler.

Non-Expat-Options

An anonymous hash whose keys are options that shouldn't be passed to Expat. This should be a concern only for those subclassing XML::Parser.

---

parse

parse(*source* [, *opt* => *opt_value* [...]])

Parses the document. The *source* parameter should be either a string containing the entire XML document or an open IO::Handle. Options given as keyword/value pairs may follow the *source* parameter and will override any options or attributes passed from the XML::Parser instance.

parse exits with die if a parse error occurs or returns 1 with success.

parsefile	parsefile(*file* [, *opt* => *opt_value* [...]])

Opens *file* for reading, then calls parse with the open handle. The file is closed no matter what parse returns. Returns what parse returns.

parse_start	parse_start([*opt* => *opt_value* [...]])

Creates and returns a new instance of XML::Parser::ExpatNB. If an init handler is specified, it is called before returning the ExpatNB object. Documents are parsed with incremental calls to the parse_more. A single call to the parse_done method of this object indicates that the document is finished. The parse_done method returns whatever is returned by the final handler.

parsestring	parsestring

An alias for parse, for backwards compatibility.

setHandlers	setHandlers(*type*, *handler* [, *type*, *handler* [...]])

Registers handlers for various parser events. setHandlers overrides any previous handlers set in Style or Handler options or through earlier calls to setHandlers. Returns a list of type and handler pairs.

Expat Handlers

Expat is an event-based parser that recognizes parts of the document (such as the start or end tag for an XML element) and calls any handlers registered for that type of an event. All handlers receive an instance of XML::Parser::Expat as their first argument.

Init (Expat)
Called before parsing starts.

Final (Expat)
Called after parsing has finished, but only if no errors occurred.

Start (Expat, Element [, Attr, Val [,...]])
Generated when an XML start tag is encountered. *Element* is the name of the XML element type. *Attr* and *Val* pairs are generated for each attribute in the start tag of the element.

End (Expat, Element)
> Generated when an XML end tag or empty tag (<foo/>) is encountered.

Char (Expat, String)
> Generated when non-markup is recognized, with the non-markup sequence of characters in *String* given to the handler in UTF-8.

Proc (Expat, Target, Data)
> Generated when a processing instruction is recognized.

Comment (Expat, Data)
> Generated when a comment is recognized.

CdataStart (Expat)
> Called at the start of a CDATA section.

CdataEnd (Expat)
> Called at the end of a CDATA section.

Default (Expat, String)
> Called for any characters that aren't tied to a registered handler, including markup declarations. Whatever the encoding in the original document, the string is returned to the handler in UTF-8.

Unparsed (Expat, Entity, Base, Sysid, Pubid, Notation)
> Called for a declaration of an unparsed entity. *Entity* is the name of the entity. *Base* is the base to be used for resolving a relative URI. *Sysid* is the system ID. *Pubid* is the public ID. *Notation* is the notation name. *Base* and *Pubid* can be undefined.

Notation (Expat, Notation, Base, Sysid, Pubid)
> Called for a declaration of notation. *Notation* is the notation name. *Base* is the base to be used for resolving a relative URI. *Sysid* is the system ID. *Pubid* is the public ID. *Base*, *Sysid*, and *Pubid* can all be undefined.

ExternEnt (Expat, Base, Sysid, Pubid)
> Called when an external entity is referenced. *Base* is the base to be used for resolving a relative URI. *Sysid* is the system ID. *Pubid* is the public ID. *Base* and *Pubid* may be undefined. This handler should either return a string or an open filehandle that represents the contents of the external entity. A return value of undef indicates that the external entity couldn't be found.
>
> If an open filehandle is returned, it must be returned as either a glob or as a reference to a glob (e.g., an instance of IO::Handle). The default handler installed for this event is XML::Parser::lwp_ext_ent_handler unless NoLWP option is true, in which case XML::Parser::file_ext_ent_handler is the default handler for external entities.

ExternEntFin (Expat)
> Called after parsing an external entity unless no ExternEnt handler is set.

Entity (Expat, Name, Val, Sysid, Pubid, Ndata, IsParam)
> Called when an entity is declared. For internal entities, Val will contain the value, and the remaining three parameters will be undefined. For external

entities, *Val* will be undefined, and the *Sysid*, *Pubid*, and the *Ndata* parameters will be populated. The *IsParam* parameter is set to true if this is a parameter entity declaration.

If both this handler and the Unparsed handler are set, then this handler will not be called for unparsed entities.

Element (Expat, Name, Model)
> Called when an element declaration is found. *Name* is the element name, and *Model* is the content model as an XML::Parser::Content object.

Attlist (Expat, Elname, Attname, Type, Default, Fixed)
> Called for each attribute in an ATTLIST declaration. An ATTLIST with multiple attributes will generate multiple calls to Attlist. *Elname* is the name of the element with which the attribute is being associated. *Attname* is the name of the attribute. *Type* is the attribute type, given as a string. *Default* is the default value, which will be #REQUIRED, #IMPLIED, or a quoted string (i.e., the returned string will begin and end with a quote character). If *Fixed* is true, then this is a fixed attribute.

Doctype (Expat, Name, Sysid, Pubid, Internal)
> Called for DOCTYPE declarations. *Name* is the document type name. *Sysid* is the system ID of the document type, if it was provided; otherwise, it's undefined. *Pubid* is the public ID of the document type, which will be undefined if no public id was given. *Internal* is the internal subset, given as a string.

DoctypeFin (Parser)
> Called after parsing of the DOCTYPE declaration has finished, including any internal or external DTD declarations.

XMLDecl (Expat, Version, Encoding, Standalone)
> Called for XML declarations. *Version* is a string containing the version. *Encoding* is either undefined or contains an encoding string. *Standalone* is either true or false.

XML::Parser Styles

Debug
> Prints out the document in outline form.

Subs

> Allows you to define a subroutine so that when an element is encountered, the subroutine by that name is called, using the same parameters that the Start handler is called with. When an element ends, a subroutine with that name appended with an underscore ("_") is called with the same parameters that the End handler is called with.

Tree

> Returns a parse tree for the document. Each node in the tree takes the form of a tag/content pair. Text nodes use a pseudo-tag of "0" and the string that is their content. Elements represent their content in an array reference, in which the first item in the array is a hash reference containing attributes (if any).

The remainder of the array is a sequence of tag/content pairs representing the content of the element.

Objects

Similar to Tree, except that a hash object is created for each element.

Stream

Prints a copy of the document without comments or declarations if none of the following routines are found:

StartDocument

Called at the start of the parse.

StartTag

Called for every start tag with a second parameter of the element type. The $_ variable contains a copy of the tag, and the %_ variable contains attribute values supplied for that element.

EndTag

Called for every end tag with a second parameter of the element type. The $_ variable will contain a copy of the end tag.

Text

Called just before start or end tags with accumulated non-markup text in the $_ variable.

PI

Called for processing instructions. The $_ variable will contain a copy of the PI, and the target and data are sent as second and third parameters, respectively.

EndDocument

Called at conclusion of the parse.

Expat Encodings

XML documents may be encoded in character sets other than Unicode as long as they can be mapped into the Unicode character set. Expat has further restrictions on encodings. Read the *xmlparse.h* header file in the expat distribution to see details on these restrictions.

Expat has built-in encodings for: UTF-8, ISO-8859-1, UTF-16, and US-ASCII. Encodings are set through either the XML declaration encoding attribute or the ProtocolEncoding option to XML::Parser or XML::Parser::Expat.

For encodings other than the built-ins, Expat calls the function load_encoding in the Expat package with the encoding name. This function looks for a file in the path list @XML::Parser::Expat::Encoding_Path that matches the lowercased name with a *.enc* extension. The first one it finds, it loads.

If you wish to build your own encoding maps, check out the XML::Encoding module from CPAN.

XML::Parser::ContentModel Methods

The element declaration handlers are passed objects of this class as the content model of the element declaration. They also represent content particles, which are components of a content model.

When referred to as a string, these objects are automatically converted to a string representation of the model (or content particle):

isempty
>   Returns true if the object is EMPTY, false otherwise.

isany
>   Returns true if the object is ANY, false otherwise.

ismixed
>   Returns true if the object is (#PCDATA) or (#PCDATA|...)*, false otherwise.

isname
>   Returns true if the object is an element name.

ischoice
>   Returns true if the object is a choice of content particles.

isseq
>   Returns true if the object is a sequence of content particles.

quant
>   Returns undef or a string representing the quantifier (?, *, +) associated with the model or particle.

children
>   Returns undef or (for mixed, choice, and sequence types) an array of component content particles. There will always be at least one component for choices and sequences, but for a mixed content model of pure PCDATA, (#PCDATA), then undef is returned.

14

SOAP

XML's openness allows it to be implemented on any platform. Between the clear nature of XML and the ease at which you can deliver content over the Web, you can easily use XML to distribute content to a wide audience.

Imagine an order-entry system for a company with a heterogenous computing environment in locations all over the world. While you could write client software for every platform that you support, a preferable solution might be to deliver XML content over the Web and have an order-entry client that parses the XML, displays the results, and posts any changes back to the server via XML.

If you think that such an idea might be a workable one, but fear writing such a thing for yourself from scratch, you might consider trying SOAP or Frontier (XML-RPC2).

What Is SOAP?

SOAP (Simple Object Access Protocol) is a protocol that allows you to invoke methods on remote objects. SOAP was originally drafted in 1998 by Dave Winer, Microsoft, and DevelopMentor.

SOAP is not tied to any specific programming language. You can find similar SOAP implementations under Perl, Python, C, and Java. It is merely a protocol, one that is simple enough to function under HTTP.

SOAP implements its own XML vocabulary that represents methods, return values, and exceptions. By implementing its own set of HTTP headers, SOAP also allows you to handle SOAP packets at your firewall/proxy server.

There are two components to SOAP: RPC and EDI. RPC, or remote procedure call, is what you'd use to get a data response (in pairs) from another host, such as a set of items and prices from an order-entry system. EDI is the interface component of SOAP, returning content such as an order entry form, but leaving the actual data processing to RPC.

SOAP::Lite

You can try an implementation of SOAP with Perl called SOAP::Lite, written by Paul Kulchenko. SOAP::Lite is a collection of Perl modules that provide a simple and lightweight interface for both the client and server side. This version of SOAP::Lite supports the SOAP 1.1 specification (*http://www.w3.org/TR/SOAP*) and works with many SOAP implementions, including Apache SOAP, Frontier, Microsoft SOAP, Microsoft .NET, DevelopMentor, XMethods, 4s4c, Phalanx, Kafka, SQLData, Lucin (in Java), Perl, C++, Python, VB, COM, and XSLT.

Here's an example that uses SOAP::Lite. The following code creates a SOAP::Lite object and uses it, but what's special about the SOAP::Lite object is that it's based on code that lives on *www.soaplite.com*. In other words, the code that lives on the remote end of the connection might not be Perl at all—but by using SOAP::Lite, you can execute the f2c( ) function as if you were calling f2c( ) from your own Perl program.

Also note the uri and proxy options. The uri option is the URI for SOAP methods. Basically, uri tells SOAP::Lite where SOAP-related content lives. In Perl terms, uri can represent the class in which you'll find the function to execute. For example, let's say you have the following SOAP server that uses HTTP as its transport mechanism:

```
#!/usr/local/bin/perl -w

use SOAP::Transport::HTTP;

SOAP::Transport::HTTP::CGI
    -> dispatch_to('Hello::(?:hello)')
    -> handle
    ;
```

This example has two key parts: it will look for a module named "Hello" and will execute Hello::hello( ) when called. Note that you don't have to explicitly "require" *Hello.pm*; SOAP::Lite does this for you. Now, let's look at the client:

```
#!/usr/local/bin/perl -w

use SOAP::Lite;

# If you want to see why something isn't working, enable +trace after
# use SOAP::Lite, as shown below

#use SOAP::Lite +trace;

my $proxy = 'http://www.some.server/cgi-bin/hello';

print SOAP::Lite
    -> uri('urn:Hello')
    -> proxy($proxy)
    -> hello()
    -> result . "\n\n"
    ;
```

It's essential that uri, as used above, matches the module in which the hello( ) function lives. If it doesn't, you won't see any returned results, since SOAP::Lite won't be able to find the module in @INC (using the +trace option makes it clear that an unavailable module was not found in @INC). Now that we have some context, let's take a look at the proxy option. In the above example, proxy is the URL where the SOAP server lives. When SOAP::Lite sees the proxy option, it loads the appropriate module based on what you request.

SOAP::Lite Methods

All methods that SOAP::Lite provides can be used for setting and retrieving values. If you provide no parameters, you will get the current value, and if parameters are provided, a new value will be assigned to the object, and the method in question will return the current object (if not stated otherwise). This is suitable for stacking these calls. For example:

```
$lite = SOAP::Lite
  -> uri('http://simon.fell.com/calc')
  -> proxy('http://soap.4s4c.com/ssss4c/soap.asp')
;
```

The order is insignificant. You may call the new( ) method first, but if you don't, SOAP::Lite will do it for you. Calling the new( ) method explicitly gives you additional syntax:

```
$lite = SOAP::Lite->new(
  uri => 'http://simon.fell.com/calc',
  proxy => 'http://soap.4s4c.com/ssss4c/soap.asp'
);
```

The SOAP::Lite methods are:

new( )
> Accepts a hash with method names as keys. It will call the appropriate methods together with the passed values..

transport( )
> Provides access to the *SOAP/Transport* object. You probably shouldn't play with transport( ), since the object will be created for you.

serializer( )
> Provides access to the *SOAP/Serialization* object. You probably shouldn't play with serializer( ), since the object will be created for you.

endpoint( )
> Lets you specify an endpoint without changing/loading the protocol module. This is useful for switching endpoints without switching protocols. You should call proxy( ) first. No checks for protocol equivalence will be made.

outputxml( )
> If true, all methods will return raw XML code, which you can then parse with XML::Parser or a similar module.

autotype( )
: Specifies whether the serializer will try to enable autotyping. Default is true.

readable( )
: Specifies the format for the generated XML code, adding carriage returns and indentation for readability.

namespace( )
: Specifies the default namespace for generated envelopes (SOAP-ENV by default).

encodingspace( )
: Specifies the default encoding namespace for generated envelopes (SOAP-ENC by default).

encoding( )
: Specifies the encoding for generated envelopes (UTF-8 by default).

typelookup( )
: Gives you access to the typelookup table used for autotyping.

multirefinplace( )
: Determines whether the serializer should put values for multireferences in the first occurrence of the reference. Default is false.

on_action( )
: Specifies a handler (either globally or locally) to be triggered for an on_action event. The default handler is uri#method.

on_fault( )
: Specifies a handler (either globally or locally) to be triggered for an on_fault event. The default behavior will die on a transport error and do nothing on other error conditions.

on_debug( )
: Globally specifies a handler to be triggered for an on_debug event. Default behavior is to do nothing, since moving the +trace/+debug options is preferred.

on_nonserialized( )
: Specifies a handler to be triggered for an on_nonserialized event. The default behavior is to produce a warning, if warnings are enabled for these events.

call( )
: Provides an alternative interface for remote method calls, with additional options:

    Prefixed method
    : If you want to specify a prefix for generated method's element, try:

        ```
        call('myprefix:method' => @parameters)
        ```

    Access to any method
    : To access remote procedures that have the same names as methods of the SOAP::Lite object:

        ```
        call(new => @parameters)
        ```

Implementation of OO interface

To use the object-oriented interface:

```
# You should specify uri()
my $soap = SOAP::Lite
  -> uri('http://my.own.site/CLASS')
  # ..... other parameters
;

my $obj = $soap->call(new => @parameters)->result;
print $soap->call(method => $obj)->result;
```

Ability to set method's attributes

To specify attributes for a method element:

```
call(SOAP::Data->name('method')->attr({xmlns => 'mynamespace'})
    => @parameters)
```

self( )

Returns the object reference to *global* default object specified with the use
SOAP::Lite ... interface. For example:

```
my $proxy = 'http://www.some.server';
my $soap - SOAP::Lite->proxy($proxy);
print $soap->self->proxy;
```

This prints *http://www.some.server*.

dispatch_from( )

The same as autodispatch, but doesn't install the UNIVERSAL::AUTOLOAD
handler. It installs only the AUTOLOAD handlers in specified classes.

SOAP::Data

The SOAP::Data class allows you specify a value, name, type, URI, or other
attributes for SOAP elements. For example, you can serialize the name/value pair
of "Nate/31" with the following code:

```
SOAP::Data->name('Nate')->value(31);
```

This becomes <Nate>31</Nate>.

You can also import SOAP::Data methods with import( ). To import 'name':

```
SOAP::Data->import('name');
```

Once imported, 'name' can be used as follows:

```
name(Nate => 31);
```

SOAP::Data also provides an interface to get or set specific attributes, including
actor( ), mustUnderstand( ), encodingStyle( ), and root( ). For example:

```
SOAP::Data
    ->name(Nate => 31)
    ->encodingStyle('http://www.some.site/soap/showmetheliteral');
```

This is serialized as follows:

```
<Nate SOAP-ENV:encodingStyle="http://www.some.site/soap/showmetheliteral"
    xsi:type="xsd:int">31</Nate>
```

SOAP::Serializer

SOAP::Serializer does not need to be used directly except when autotyping is enabled. It allows you to specify types for your data.

You can specify a type with SOAP::Data, with code similar to the following:

```
SOAP::Data->type(something => [ ... ])
```

When serialization is reached, SOAP::Lite will attempt to serialize your data with the as_something method, if such a method exists. If you don't create an as_something method, no serialization will occur. You can create as_something with the following:

```
sub SOAP::Serializer::as_something {
    my $self = shift;
    my($key, $val) = @_;
    ...
    return [$key, {'xsi:type' => 'xsd:something', %attr}, $val];
}
```

SOAP::Fault

This class gives you access to a fault generated on the server side. To create a fault message, you can simply die on the server side, and the SOAP processor will wrap your message as a faultstring element and transfer the fault on the client side. But in some cases, you need to have more control over this process, and the SOAP::Fault class gives it to you. To use it, simply die with the SOAP::Fault object as a parameter:

```
die SOAP::Fault->faultcode('Server.Custom') # Will be qualified
                ->faultstring('Died in server method')
                ->faultdetail(bless {code => 1} => 'BadError')
                ->faultactor('http://www.soaplite.com/custom');
```

The faultdetail( ) and faultactor( ) methods are optional, and since faultcode and faultstring are required to represent a fault message, SOAP::Lite will use default values ("Server" and "Application error") if not specified.

VII

Network Programming

15

Sockets

Why build networking functionality into your Perl scripts? You might want to access your email remotely, or write a simple script that updates files on an FTP site. You might want to check up on your employees with a program that searches for Usenet postings that came from your site. You might want to check a web site for any recent changes, or even write your own home-grown web server. The network is the computer these days, and Perl makes network applications easy.

Perl programmers have their choice of modules for doing common tasks with network protocols; Chapters 14 through 17 cover the modules for writing email, news, FTP, and web applications in Perl. If you can do what you want with the available modules, you're encouraged to jump to those chapters and skip this one. However, there will be times when you'll have to wrestle with sockets directly, and that's when this chapter comes in.

Sockets are the underlying mechanism for networking on the Internet. With sockets, one application (a *server*) sits on a port waiting for connections. Another application (the *client*) connects to that port and says hello; then the client and server have a chat. Their actual conversation is done with whatever protocol they choose—for example, a web client and server would use HTTP, an email server would use POP3 and SMTP, etc. But at the most basic level, you might say that all network programming comes down to opening a socket, reading and writing data, and closing the socket.

You can work with sockets in Perl at various levels. At the lowest level, Perl's built-in functions include socket routines similar to the system calls in C of the same name. To make these routines easier to use, the Socket module in the standard library imports common definitions and constants specific to your system's networking capabilities. Finally, the IO::Socket module provides an object interface to the socket functions through a standard set of methods and options for constructing both client and server communications programs.

Sockets provide a connection between systems or applications. They can be set up to handle streaming data or discrete data packets. Streaming data continually comes and goes over a connection. A transport protocol such as TCP (Transmission Control Protocol) is used to process streaming data so that all of the data is properly received and ordered. Packet-oriented communication sends data across the network in discrete chunks. The message-oriented protocol UDP (User Datagram Protocol) works on this type of connection. Although streaming sockets using TCP are widely used for applications, UDP sockets also have their uses.

Sockets exist in one of two address domains: the Internet domain and the Unix domain. Sockets used for Internet connections require the careful binding and assignment of the proper type of address dictated by the Internet Protocol (IP). These sockets are referred to as Internet-domain sockets.

Sockets in the Unix domain create connections between applications either on the same machine or within a LAN. The addressing scheme is less complicated, often just providing the name of the target process.

In Perl, sockets are attached to a filehandle after they have been created. Communication over the connection is then handled by standard Perl I/O functions.

Built-in Socket Functions

Perl provides built-in support for sockets. The following functions are defined specifically for socket programming. For full descriptions and syntax, see Chapter 5.

socket
> Initializes a socket and assigns a filehandle to it.

bind
> For servers, associates a socket with a port and address. For clients, associates a socket with a specific source address.

listen
> (Server only.) Waits for incoming connection with a client.

accept
> (Server only.) Accepts incoming connection with a client.

connect
> (Client only.) Establishes a network connection on a socket.

recv
> Reads data from a socket filehandle.

send
> Writes data to a filehandle.

shutdown (or close)
> Terminates a network connection.

Regular functions that read and write filehandles can also be used for sockets, e.g., write, print, printf, and the diamond input operator, <>.

The socket functions tend to use hardcoded values for some parameters, which severely hurts portability. Perl solves this problem with a module called Socket, included in the standard library. Use this module for any socket applications that you build with the built-in functions (e.g., use Socket). The module loads the *socket.h* header file, which enables the built-in functions to use the constants and names specific to your system's network programming, as well as additional functions for dealing with address and protocol names.

The next few sections describe Perl socket programming using a combination of the built-in functions together with the Socket module. After that, we describe the use of the IO::Socket module.

Initializing a Socket

Both client and server use the socket call to create a socket and associate it with a filehandle. The socket function takes several arguments: the name of the filehandle, the network domain, an indication of whether the socket is stream-oriented or record-oriented, and the network protocol to be used. For example, HTTP (web) transactions require stream-oriented connections running TCP. The following lines create a socket for this case and associates it with the filehandle SH:

```
use Socket;
socket(SH, PF_INET, SOCK_STREAM, getprotobyname('tcp')) || die $!;
```

The PF_INET argument indicates that the socket will connect to addresses in the Internet domain (i.e., IP addresses). Sockets with a Unix domain address use PF_UNIX.

Because this is a streaming connection using TCP, we specify SOCK_STREAM for the second argument. The alternative would be to specify SOCK_DGRAM for a packet-based UDP connection.

The third argument indicates the protocol used for the connection. Each protocol has a number assigned to it by the system; that number is passed to socket as the third argument. In the scalar context, getprotobyname returns the protocol number.

Finally, if the socket call fails, the program will die, printing the error message found in $!.

Client Connections

On the client side, the next step is to connect with a server at a particular port and host. To do this, the client uses the connect call. connect requires the socket filehandle as its first argument. The second argument is a data structure containing the port and hostname that together specify the address. The Socket package provides the sockaddr_in function to create this structure for Internet addresses and the sockaddr_un function for Unix domain addresses.

The sockaddr_in function takes a port number for its first argument and a 32-bit IP address for the second argument. The 32-bit address is formed from the inet_aton function found in the Socket package. This function takes either a hostname (e.g., *www.oreilly.com*) or a dotted-decimal string (e.g., 207.54.2.25) and returns the corresponding 32-bit structure.

Continuing with the previous example, a call to connect could look like this:

```
my $dest = sockaddr_in (80, inet_aton('www.oreilly.com'));
connect (SH, $dest) || die $!;
```

This call attempts to establish a network connection to the specified server and port. If successful, it returns true. Otherwise, it returns false and dies with the error in $!.

Assuming that the connect call has completed successfully and a connection has been established, there are a number of functions we can use to write to and read from the filehandle. For example, the send function sends data to a socket:

```
$data = "Hello";
send (FH, $data);
```

The print function allows a wider variety of expressions for sending data to a filehandle:

```
select (FH);
print "$data";
```

To read incoming data from a socket, use either the recv function or the diamond input operator regularly used on filehandles. For example:

```
recv (FH, $buffer);
$input = <FH>;
```

After the conversation with the server is finished, use close or shutdown to close the connection and destroy the socket.

Server Connections

After creating a socket with the socket function as you did previously, a server application must go through the following steps to receive network connections:

1. Bind a port number and machine address to the socket
2. Listen for incoming connections from clients on the port
3. Accept a client request and assign the connection to a specific filehandle

We start out by creating a socket for the server:

```
my $proto = getprotobyname('tcp');
socket(FH, PF_INET, SOCK_STREAM, $proto) || die $!;
```

The filehandle $FH is the generic filehandle for the socket. This filehandle only receives requests from clients; each specific connection is passed to a different file-handle by accept, where the rest of the communication occurs.

A server-side socket must be bound to a port on the local machine by passing a port and an address data structure to the bind function via sockaddr_in. The Socket module provides identifiers for common local addresses, such as localhost and the broadcast address. Here we use INADDR_ANY, which allows the system to pick the appropriate address for the machine:

```
my $sin = sockaddr_in (80, INADDR_ANY);
bind (FH, $sin) || die $!;
```

The listen function tells the operating system that the server is ready to accept incoming network connections on the port. The first argument is the socket filehandle. The second argument gives a queue length, in case multiple clients are connecting to the port at the same time. This number indicates how many clients can wait for an accept at one time.

```
listen (FH, $length);
```

The accept function completes a connection after a client requests and assigns a new filehandle specific to that connection. The new filehandle is given as the first argument to accept, and the generic socket filehandle is given as the second:

```
accept (NEW, FH) || die $!;
```

Now the server can read and write to the filehandle NEW for its communication with the client.

Socket Module Functions

The following functions are imported from the Socket module for use in socket applications.

---

inet_aton   inet_aton (*hostname*)

Translates a hostname such as *www.oreilly.com* or 18.181.0.24 into a data structure (a four-byte string) used for socket addresses. If the hostname cannot be resolved, the function returns the undefined value.

---

inet_ntoa   inet_ntoa (*addr_string*)

Translates a four-byte address string (as returned by inet_aton) into a string with the dotted-quad form of IP address.

---

sockaddr_in   sockaddr_in (*port, addr_string*)

pack_sockaddr_in (*port, addr_string*)

Takes a port number and a four-byte *addr_string* (as returned by inet_aton) and returns the socket address structure including those arguments packed with the AF_INET argument. This structure is normally what you need for the arguments in bind, connect, and send, and is also returned by getpeername, getsockname, and recv.

---

sockaddr_un   sockaddr_un (*pathname*)

pack_sockaddr_un (*pathname*)

Takes one argument, a pathname, and returns the Unix domain socket address structure (the path packed in with AF_UNIX filled in). For Unix domain sockets, this structure is normally what you need for the arguments in bind, connect, and send, and is also returned by getpeername, getsockname, and recv.

---

unpack_sockaddr_in

> unpack_sockaddr_in (*sockaddr*)
>
> sockaddr_in (*sockaddr*)
>
> Takes a socket address structure and returns an array of two elements (in list context): the port number and the four-byte IP address.

---

unpack_sockaddr_un

> unpack_sockaddr_un (*sockaddr_un*)
>
> sockaddr_un (*sockaddr_un*)
>
> Takes a Unix domain socket address structure (as returned by sockaddr_un) and returns the pathname.
>
> The following constants are defined in the Socket module:
>
> INADDR_ANY
>> The four-byte packed string for the wildcard IP address that specifies any of the host's addresses (if the host has multiple addresses). This is equivalent to inet_aton('0.0.0.0').
>
> INADDR_BROADCAST
>> The four-byte packed string for the broadcast address. This is equivalent to inet_aton('255.255.255.255').
>
> INADDR_LOOPBACK
>> The four-byte packed string for the loopback address. This is equivalent to inet_aton('localhost').
>
> INADDR_NONE
>> The four-byte packed string for the "invalid" IP address (bitmask). Equivalent to inet_aton('255.255.255.255').

The IO::Socket Module

The IO::Socket module included in the core Perl distribution provides an object-oriented approach to socket programming. This module provides a convenient way to handle the large number of options you have to deal with, and it handles the laborious task of forming addresses. IO::Socket is built upon the Socket module provided in the standard library. It inherits from IO::Handle, which supports a class of filehandle objects for much of the IO library. The following IO::Socket functions are simply frontends for the corresponding built-in functions and use the same syntax:

```
socket
socketpair
bind
listen
send
recv
peername (same as getpeername)
sockname (same as getsockname)
```

The accept function in IO::Socket is slightly different from the equivalent function, however, and is described later in the chapter.

IO:Socket contains two subclasses: INET and UNIX. The INET subclass is used to create and manipulate Internet-domain sockets, such as those used in the examples. The UNIX subclass creates Unix domain sockets.

Client-Side Sockets

IO::Socket greatly simplifies the implementation of a socket for client communications. The following example creates an Internet-domain socket (using the INET subclass) and attempts to connect to the specified server:

```
use IO::Socket;
$sock = new IO::Socket::INET (PeerAddr => 'www.ora.com',
                              PeerPort => 80,
                              Proto    => 'tcp');
die "$!" unless $sock;
```

IO::Socket::INET::new creates an object containing a socket filehandle and connects it to the host and port specified in PeerAddr and PeerPort. The object $sock can then be written to and read from like other socket filehandles.

Server-Side Sockets

On the server side, IO::Socket provides a nice wrapper for creating server sockets. The wrapper encompasses the socket, bind, and listen procedures, while creating a new IO::Socket object. For example, we can create an Internet-domain socket with IO::Socket::INET:

```
use IO::Socket;
$sock = new IO::Socket::INET (LocalAddr => 'maude.ora.com',
                              LocalPort => 8888,
                              Proto     => 'tcp',
                              Listen    => 5);
die "$!" unless $sock;
```

The parameters for the new socket object determine whether it is a server or a client socket. Because we're creating a server socket, LocalAddr and LocalPort provide the address and port to bind to the socket. The Listen parameter gives the queue size for the number of client requests that can wait for an accept at any one time.

When the server receives a client request, it calls the accept method on the socket object. This creates a new socket object on which the rest of the communication can take place:

```
$new_sock = $sock->accept( );
```

When communication is finished on both client and server sockets, they should be destroyed with close. If a socket is not properly closed, the next time you attempt to use a socket with the same name, the system will complain that the socket is already in use.

IO::Socket Methods

The following methods are defined in IO::Socket and can be used on socket objects of either the INET or UNIX class.

accept	accept ([*pkg*])
	Performs the accept system call on a socket and returns a new object. The new object is created in the same class as the listen socket, unless *pkg* is specified. The object can be used to communicate with the client that tried to connect. In a scalar context, the new socket is returned, or undef is returned on failure. In an array context, a two-element array is returned containing the new socket and the peer address, or an empty list is returned on failure.
protocol	protocol
	Returns the protocol number for the protocol being used on the socket, if known. If the protocol is unknown, as with an AF_UNIX socket, returns 0
sockdomain	sockdomain
	Returns the number representing the socket address domain. For example, an AF_INET socket has the value &AF_INET.
sockopt	sockopt (*opt*, [*val*])
	Sets and retrieves socket option *opt* in the SOL_SOCKET level. The value *val* is set for the option, if given. If no value is provided, the function returns the current setting for the option.
socktype	socktype
	Returns the number representing the socket type. For example, a SOCK_STREAM socket has the value &SOCK_STREAM.

timeout	timeout ([*val*])

Sets or retrieves the timeout value associated with a socket. Without an argument, the current value is returned. If a timeout of *val* is given, the setting is changed to *val*, and the previous value is returned.

IO::Socket::INET Reference

An Internet-domain socket is created with the new method from the IO::Socket::INET subclass. The constructor can take the following options:

PeerAddr => *hostname*[:*port*]
Specifies the remote host and optional port number for a client connection. *hostname* can be either a name, such as *www.oreilly.com*, or an IP number of the form 207.44.21.2.

PeerPort => *port*
Specifies the port number on the remote host for a client connection. The name of the service (such as http or nntp) may be used for the argument if the port number is not known.

LocalAddr => *hostname*[:*port*]
Specifies the local address (and optional port number) to bind to a server-side socket.

LocalPort => *port*
Specifies the local port number (or service name) to bind to a server-side socket.

Proto => *name*
Specifies the protocol to be run on the socket, i.e., tcp or udp.

Type => SOCK_STREAM | SOCK_DGRAM
Specifies the type of socket. SOCK_STREAM indicates a stream-based socket connection, and SOCK_DGRAM indicates a message-based (datagram) connection.

Listen => *n*
Sets the listen-queue size to *n* number of client requests.

Reuse => 1
Given a nonzero number, this option allows the local bind address to be reused should the socket need to be reopened after an error.

Timeout => *n*
Sets the timeout.

Whether a server (receiving) or client (requesting) socket is created depends on the parameters provided to the constructor. If Listen is defined, a server socket is automatically created. If no protocol is specified, it is derived from the service on the given port number. If no port number is given, tcp is used by default.

IO::Socket::INET methods

The following methods can be used on socket filehandle objects created by
IO::Socket::INET.

peeraddr	peeraddr
	Returns the address part (packed string) of the socket-address data structure for the remote host to which a socket connects.
peerhost	peerhost
	Returns the remote host address in the dotted-quad string form, e.g., 207.44.27.2.
peerport	peerport
	Returns the port number for the remote host to which a socket connects.
sockaddr	sockaddr
	Returns the address part (as a packed string) of the socket-address data structure for the socket.
sockhost	sockhost
	Returns the address part of the socket-address data structure in the dotted-quad string form, e.g., 207.44.27.2.
sockport	sockport
	Returns the local port number for the socket.

IO::Socket::UNIX Reference

The IO::Socket::UNIX subclass creates a Unix-domain socket. Unix-domain
sockets are local to the current host and are used internally to implement pipes,
thus providing communication between unrelated processes. Using sockets
provides finer control than using named pipes, also called FIFO (first-in, first-out)
buffers. This is because receiving sockets can distinguish between different client
connections, which can then be assigned to different sessions with the accept call.

The IO::Socket::UNIX constructor (new( )) creates the socket and returns an
object containing a filehandle. The constructor can take the following options:

Type => SOCK_STREAM | SOCK_DGRAM
> Indicates the type of socket: SOCK_STREAM for streaming, SOCK_DGRAM for packets or datagrams.

Local => *pathname*
> Provides the pathname of the FIFO buffer to bind to the socket.

Peer => *pathname*
> Provides the pathname to the destination FIFO buffer.

Listen => *n*
> Creates a listen socket and sets the queue size to *n*.

The following methods can be used on an object created with IO::Socket::UNIX.

---

hostpath   hostpath

Returns the pathname to the local FIFO buffer.

---

peerpath   peerpath

Returns the pathname to the destination or peer FIFO.

16

Email Connectivity

Electronic mail is arguably the most essential Internet application. In fact, for many people, it's their introduction to the Internet. Thus, the Perl modules that deal with email are among the most useful modules. There are two major groups of modules that provide email capabilities. The first group is Graham Barr's *libnet* collection, which contains packages for developing client-side applications over the Internet in Perl. Table 16-1 lists some of the protocols implemented by the *libnet* modules.

Table 16-1. Protocols implemented by the libnet modules

Protocol	Module	Description
POP3	Net::POP3	Post Office Protocol, for reading email
SMTP	Net::SMTP	Simple Mail Transfer Protocol, for sending email
FTP	Net::FTP	File Transfer Protocol, for transferring files between hosts
NNTP	Net::NNTP	Network News Transfer Protocol, for reading Usenet news

In this chapter, we discuss Net::SMTP and Net::POP3. Chapter 17 talks about Net::NNTP, Chapter 18 discusses Net::FTP, and Chapter 19 covers Net::LDAP. Other *libnet* modules, such as Net::SNPP and Net::Time, are not described in this book, but you can get information about them from CPAN or with the *perldoc* command if *libnet* is installed on your system.

The second group of mail-related modules are the Mail modules, which can be found on CPAN as the MailTools collection. Other interesting mail-related modules include Mail::Folder and its subclasses, Mail::RBL, Mail::Audit, and Unix::AliasFile. This chapter describes the following subset of the Mail modules:

Mail::Send
> Built on top of Mail::Mailer, providing better control of mail headers

Mail::Mailer
> Interacts with external mail programs to send mail

Mail::Folder
> Provides a base class and subclasses to work with mail folders

Mail::Internet
> Provides functions to manipulate a mail message

Mail::Address
> Extracts and manipulates RFC 822-compliant mail addresses

Mail::RBL
> Provides domain lookups to the Real-time Blackhole List (RBL)

Mail::Audit
> Provides an easy interface for creating mail filters

Unix::AliasFile
> Perl interface to */etc/aliases* format files

The rest of this chapter describes the Net modules and the Mail modules.

The Net Modules

Net::SMTP and Net::POP3 are the modules for sending and receiving email via the SMTP and POP3 protocols. When you use these modules, you are working at the socket level; they directly implement the Internet protocols for sending and receiving mail as defined in the relevant RFCs: RFC 821 for SMTP and RFC 1081 for POP3.

Send Email with Net::SMTP

The Simple Mail Transfer Protocol, or SMTP, is responsible for clients negotiating RCPT ("to") and FROM ("from") requests with an SMTP server, sending data to the SMTP server, and then sending an end-of-data indicator. Net::SMTP is a subclass of Net::Cmd and IO::Socket::INET that implements an interface to the SMTP and ESMTP protocols. These protocols send mail by talking to an SMTP server through a socket, as described in RFC 821.

When would you want to use Net::SMTP instead of sending mail with an external program? Since socket communications don't involve spawning an external program, your programs won't suffer from the overhead associated with running an extra process. Talking to SMTP is convenient for sending a volume of mail messages. Naturally, your server must have an SMTP server running, or a remote mailhost must allow you to talk to it; otherwise, you won't be able to use this module. That's when you can turn to Mail::Mailer or Mail::Send and let them provide an interface to an external mail program for you. This is the case, for example, with home computers, which don't generally run their own SMTP server.

The SMTP Protocol and the SMTP Session

The SMTP protocol defines the set of commands a client sends to an SMTP server, which is generally bound to port 25 of a mailhost. Requests and responses are negotiated between client and server.

When a client negotiates an SMTP session with a server, the server tells the client that it's listening. Once you're connected, you introduce yourself to the server by issuing a HELO command. The HELO command accepts one parameter—your hostname—and defaults to your remote hostname if you don't specify one. If the command is successful, the server sends a 250 response, as follows:

```
HELO
250 mail.somename.com Hello some-remote-host.com [127.0.0.1], pleased to
meet
you
```

After you've been greeted by the server, send the MAIL command to tell the server who the message is from. The MAIL command takes the string From: user@hostname as an argument, and the server responds with a 250 message to indicate success:

```
MAIL From: <realuser@realhost.com>
250 realuser@realhost.com ... Sender ok
```

Then send the RCPT command to tell the server who the recipient is:

```
RCPT To: <nospam@rid-spam-now.com>
250 nospam@rid-spam-now.com ... Recipient ok
```

Now you're ready to send the body of your message to the server. The DATA command tells the server that all data until a . on a line by itself should be treated as the body of the mail message:

```
DATA
354 Enter mail, end with "." on a line by itself
Subject: Hi, just thought you'd be interested ...

Hi, this is the text of my mail message that I'm going to
send with Net::SMTP to show you how it works.
.
250 VAA09505 Message accepted for delivery
```

Once again, you get a 250 response, indicating that the message has been accepted for delivery. At that point, you can exit the SMTP session with the QUIT command, which returns 221 on success:

```
QUIT
221 mail.somename.com closing connection
Connection closed by foreign host.
```

Net::SMTP methods

The following methods are defined by Net:SMTP.

---

new $smtp = Net::SMTP->new(host[, options])

Constructor. Takes the hostname of the remote mail server, *host*, and possibly some options, and creates a new SMTP object. Any options are passed to new as a hash, in which the option is the key. The possible options are:

Debug
Enables debug mode if set to 1. Provides information about your connection, requests, and responses.

Hello
Sends a HELO command to the SMTP server. Takes a string that represents your domain; if not specified, Hello guesses your domain.

Timeout
Time (in seconds) after which the client stops trying to establish a connection with the SMTP server. Defaults to 120 seconds. If the connection cannot be established, the constructor returns undef.

---

banner $smtp->data([banner])

Returns the banner message with which the server replied when the initial connection was made. For example:

```
my $banner = $smtp->banner();
print "$banner\n";
```

---

data $smtp->data([bodydata])

Starts sending the body of the current message to the server. If specified, *bodydata* can be a list or a reference to a list; the contents of the list and the termination string .\r\n are sent to the server. Returns true if accepted.

If *bodydata* is not specified, then a true result means that the server is ready to receive data, which must be sent with the datasend and dataend methods (inherited from Net::Cmd).

---

dataend $smtp->dataend()

Net::Cmd method issued after datasend to end the sending of data. Sends .\r\n to the server telling it that there's no more data coming and that it should send the message.

Here's an example that uses datasend and dataend:

```
@list_data = (1..10);
$smtp->data();
$smtp->datasend(@list_data);
$smtp->dataend();
```

datasend
$smtp->datasend("*data*")

Net::Cmd method that sends the body of the message to the remote server if the body wasn't specified with the data method.

domain
$smtp->domain( )

Returns the domain of the remote SMTP server, or undef.

expand
$smtp->expand(*address*)

Requests the server to expand *address*. Returns an array containing the text from the server.

hello
$smtp->hello(*domain*)

Identifies your domain to the mail server. Executes automatically when you create a Net::SMTP object, so you shouldn't have to do it manually.

help
$help_text = $smtp->help([*subject*])

Returns help text from the server, or undef on failure. If *subject* is specified, returns help for that topic.

mail
$smtp->mail(*address*[, *options*])

$smtp->send(*address*)

send_or_mail(*address*)

send_and_mail(*address*)

Takes the sender's address and sends the appropriate command (MAIL, SEND, SOML, or SAML) to the server to initiate the message-sending process.

mail can take some ESMTP options, passed as key/value pairs. See the Net::SMTP documentation for the details.

quit
$smtp->quit

This method sends the QUIT command to the remote SMTP server and closes the socket connection.

recipient
$smtp->recipient(*addr*[, *addr*[, ...]])

Tells the server to send the current message to all specified recipients. As defined in the RFC, each address is sent as a separate command to the server. If the sending of any address fails, the process aborts and returns false; you can then call reset to reset the server.

reset

$smtp->reset( )

Resets the server's status. Useful for canceling a message after it has been initiated but before any data has been sent.

to

$smtp->to(address[, address[, ...]])

Interchangeable with recipient.

verify

$smtp->verify(address)

Verifies that the specified mail address is valid. However, many servers ignore verify, so it frequently doesn't work.

Retrieving Email with Net::POP3

You can use SMTP to send mail, but not to retrieve it. For retrieving messages, use the Post Office Protocol Version 3 (POP3), described in RFC 1081. One way to do this is to use the Net::POP3 module. POP3 provides commands for interacting with the POP server, typically bound to port 110. Net::POP3 automates the transfer of email from a remote server to the local machine.

The POP server retrieves messages from a specified spooling directory on the remote system. The messages are stored in a file named for the username; anonymous logins are not permitted. Authentication is based on username and password and is done by sending the USER and PASS commands to the POP server. For example, identification of user foo with password bar looks like this:

```
USER foo
PASS bar
```

Net::POP3 has user and pass methods but may also authenticate users with login, which takes both username and password arguments. If authentication fails, the user cannot retrieve, delete, or alter any messages from the mail server. login returns the number of messages on the POP server for the user, or undef if authentication fails.

Authenticated users can retrieve information about their mailboxes and can get specific messages by message number.

A POP session to retrieve a mail message is negotiated with the server through the following steps:

1. Connect to the POP server (the default port is 110).
2. Send USER command.

3. Send PASS command.

4. If authenticated, receive number of messages.

5. Send RETR *<message number>* command to retrieve a specific message.

6. Send QUIT command to end session.

The following methods are defined by Net:POP3.

---

new $pop = Net::POP3->new([*host*,] [*options*])

Constructor. Creates a new Net::POP3 object. *host* is the name of the remote host to which a POP3 connection will be made. If *host* is not specified, then the POP3_Host specified in Net::Config is used.

options are passed as key/value pairs, in which the option is the key. The possible options are:

ResvPort

Optional. If given, then the socket for the Net::POP3 object will be bound to the given local port using bind when the socket is created.

Debug

Enables debugging information

Timeout

Maximum time, in seconds, to wait for a response from the POP3 server. Default is 120 seconds.

---

apop $pop->apop(*user, pass*)

Authenticates *user* with password *pass* with the server. The password is not sent in clear text. Requires the MD5 package; otherwise, returns undef.

---

delete $pop->delete(*msgnum*)

Marks message *msgnum* for deletion from the remote mailbox. All messages marked for deletion are removed when the connection to the server is closed.

---

get $pop->get(*msgnum*)

Gets message *msgnum* from remote mailbox. Returns a reference to an array containing lines of text read from the server.

---

last $pop->last( )

Returns the highest message number.

---

list $pop->list([*msgnum*])

If called with an argument, returns the size of message *msgnum*. If called without an argument, returns a hash reference, in which the keys are the message numbers of all undeleted messages, and each corresponding value is the size of the message.

login $pop->login([*user*[, *pass*]])

Sends both USER and PASS commands. If the password, *pass*, is not given, then Net::Netrc is used to look up the password based on the host and the username, *user*. If *user* is not specified, the current username is used. Returns the count of messages in the mailbox, or undef if the server can't authenticate the user.

pass $pop->pass(*pass*)

Sends the PASS command with the password. Returns the number of messages in the mailbox.

popstat $pop->popstat( )

Returns a list with two elements: the number of undeleted elements and the size of the mailbox.

quit $pop->quit( )

Quits, closing the connection to the remote POP3 server and deleting all messages marked for deletion.

Note that if a Net::POP3 object goes out of scope before quit has been called, reset is called before the connection is closed, and any messages marked for deletion are not deleted.

reset $pop->reset( )

Resets status of the remote POP3 server. Clears the delete status on all messages that were marked for deletion.

top $pop->top(*msgnum*[, *numlines*])

Gets the header and the first *numlines* lines of body for message *msgnum*. Returns a reference to an array containing lines of text read from the server.

uidl	`$pop->uidl([msgnum])`
	Returns a unique identifier for *msgnum* if specified. If *msgnum* is not specified, returns a reference to a hash in which the keys are the message numbers, and the values are the unique identifiers.
user	`$pop->user(user)`
	Sends the USER command, identifying the user.

The Mail Modules

The Mail modules operate at a higher level than the Net modules, interacting with external mail packages such as *mail*, *mailx*, *sendmail*, or a POP3 server in the case of Net::POP3. This section describes some of the MailTools modules, Mail::Folder, and the other mail-related modules that were mentioned at the beginning of this chapter.

Send Email with Mail::Mailer

The Mail::Mailer module interacts with external mail programs. When you use Mail::Mailer or create a new Mail::Mailer object, you can specify which mail program you want your program to talk to:

```
use Mail::Mailer qw(mail);
```

Another way to specify the mailer is:

```
use Mail::Mailer;
$type = 'sendmail';
$mailprog = Mail::Mailer->new($type);
```

in which $type is the mail program. Once you've created a new object, use the open function to send the message headers to the mail program as a hash of key/value pairs, in which each key represents a header type, and the value is the value of that header:

```
# Mail headers to use in the message
%headers = (
    'To' => 'you@mail.somename.com',
    'From' => 'me@mail.somename.com',
    'Subject' => 'working?'
);
```

This code represents headers in which the recipient of the mail message is *you@mail.somename.com*, the mail was sent from *me@mail.somename.com*, and the subject of the mail message is *working?*.

Once %headers has been defined, it is passed to open:

```
$mailprog->open(\%headers);
```

You then send the body of the message to the mail program:

```
print $mailprog "This is the message body.\n";
```

Close the program when the message is finished:

```
$mailprog->close;
```

A practical example of using Mail::Mailer might be a command line–driven application that works much like the Unix *mail* program, either reading STDIN until end-of-file or mailing a file specified on the command line.

Mail::Mailer uses the environment variable PERL_MAILERS to augment or modify the built-in mailer selection. PERL_MAILERS is specified in the following format:

```
"type1:mailbinary1;mailbinary2;...:type2:mailbinaryX;...:..."
```

The possible types are listed for the new method below.

The following methods are defined in Mail::Mailer.

---

new $mailer = new Mail::Mailer [type, command]

Constructor. Creates a new Mailer object representing the message to be sent. If the optional arguments are specified, the value of *command* depends on *type*, which can be one of:

mail
> Uses the Unix *mail* program. *command* is the path to *mail*. The module searches for *mailx*, *Mail*, and *mail*, in that order.

sendmail
> Uses the *sendmail* program. *command* is the path to *sendmail*.

test
> Used for debugging. Calls */bin/echo* to display the data, but doesn't actually send any mail. *command* is ignored, if specified.

If no arguments are specified, the Mailer object searches for executables in the above order and uses the first one found as the default mailer.

---

close $mailer->close

Closes the mail program.

---

open $mailer->open(\%hashref)

Sends message headers to the *mail* program. The headers are passed via a reference to a hash, in which each key is the name of a header, and the value is the contents of the header field. The value can be either a scalar or a reference to an array of scalars.

Better Header Control with Mail::Send

Mail::Send is built on top of Mail::Mailer, which means that you can also choose the mail program that sends the mail. Mail::Send has implemented the methods to, cc, bcc, and subject to replace the %headers hash used in Mail::Mailer.

Mail::Send uses the open method to open the mail program for output; it is built on Mail::Mailer's new method, so that:

```
# Start mailer and output headers
$fh = $msg->open('sendmail');
```

serves the same purpose as:

```
# Use sendmail for mailing
$mailer = Mail::Mailer->new('sendmail)';
```

This code tells Mail::Send to use *sendmail* as the mail program.

Mail::Send also provides the set and add functions, which assign a value to a header tag and append a value to a header tag, respectively. The set function takes two arguments—a header tag and a value—and is used like this:

```
$msg->set($scalar, @array);
```

Therefore, to address a message to *you@mail.somename.com*:

```
$msg->set('To', 'you@mail.somename.com');
```

The above sets the To header to *you@mail.somename.com*; however, the following sets the To header to *postmaster@mail.somename.com* and *you@mail.somename. com* because they represent an array of values:

```
$msg->set('To', ('you@mail.somename.com', 'postmaster@mail.somename.com'));
```

You might think that you could use the set function as follows to add multiple values to a header value:

```
$msg->set('To', 'you@mail.somename.com');
$msg->set('To', 'someone@their.mailaddress.com');
```

However, set doesn't append information from one call to another, and the above example would send the mail only to *someone@their.mailaddress.com*. To append a name to the To header, use the add method. For example:

```
$msg->add('To', 'you@mail.somename.com');
$msg->add('To', 'someone@their.mailaddress.com');
```

The following methods are defined for Mail::Send.

---

new $msg = new Mail::Send [*header*=>'*value*'[, ...]]

Constructor. Creates a new Mail::Send object that is the mail message you want to send. You can include values for headers when you create the object, or include them later by calling the appropriate methods.

---

add

$msg->add(*header*, *values*)

Adds a header to the message. *header* is the header to be added, and *values* is a list of values to be appended to that header.

bcc

$msg->bcc(*values*)

Adds a Bcc header containing the mail addresses specified in the list of *values* to the message. If there already is a Bcc, the new values replace any old values.

cancel

$msg->cancel

Not implemented yet, but will cancel the message.

cc

$msg->cc(*values*)

Adds a Cc header containing the mail addresses in the list of *values* to the message. If there already is a Cc, the new values replace any old values.

close

$fh->close

Closes the filehandle $fh (which was returned by open) and sends the message.

delete

$msg->delete(*header*)

Deletes the header *header* from the message.

open

$fh = $msg->open

Opens a filehandle for the message object. The filehandle is a Mail::Mailer object.

set

$msg->set(*header*, *values*)

Sets the header *header* to the contents of the array *values*.

subject

$msg->subject('*What this message is about*')

Sets the value of the Subject field.

to	$msg->to(values)
	Sets the To field to the list of recipients in *values*.

Handle Folders with Mail::Folder

Once you've begun downloading and reading your mail from a POP server, you might want to save or categorize your messages into folders, which allow you to add, delete, save, and move messages easily. You can do this with Mail::Folder, which was written by Kevin Johnson as an object-oriented, folder-independent interface to mail folders. Mail::Folder supports a number of mailbox formats with the following interfaces:

Mail::Folder::Emaul
A folder interface somewhat similar to MH.

Mail::Folder::Maildir
An interface to *maildir* folders.

Mail::Folder::Mbox
Standard Unix mailbox format.

Mail::Folder::NNTP
The beginnings of an interface to NNTP. Not all the methods are implemented yet.

If you are interested in writing a folder interface, see the documentation for the module. The documentation explains the concepts and issues involved and describes some of the methods you may need to override.

The following methods are defined for Mail::Folder.

new	$folder = new(ftype[, foldername][, options])
	Creates a new Mail::Folder object of the specified type. Arguments are:
	ftype
	The type of folder. Possible values are mbox, maildir, emaul, or NNTP.
	foldername
	The name of the folder. If present, the open method is called with *foldername* as the argument.
	options
	A hash in which the following options may be the keys:
	Content-Length
	Content-length header is created or updated by append_message and update_message.
	Create
	If set, the folder is created if it doesn't already exist.

DefaultFolderType

> Autodetects folder type if create option is set and AUTODETECT has been set.

DotLock

> Uses *.lock*-style folder locking with the proper folder interface (currently used only with the *mbox* interface).

Flock

> Uses flock-style folder locking with the proper folder interface (currently used only with the *mbox* interface).

NFSLock

> Deals with NFS-style file locking with the proper folder interface and the NFS server in question.

notMUA

> If set, makes updates but doesn't save message labels or the current message indicator. If not set (the default), saves labels and the current message indicator as appropriate for the folder interface.

Timeout

> Overrides the default timeout value. Specified in seconds. Particularly useful for folder interfaces that involve network communications.

---

add_label $*folder*->add_label(*msg_num*, *label*)

Associates the label *label* with the message *msg_num*. Returns 1 on success or 0 if the label has a length of 0. Possible values of *label* are:

deleted

> Used by delete_message and sync to process message deletion.

edited

> Added by update_message to indicate that the message has been edited.

filed, forwarded, printed, replied

> Not acted on.

seen

> Message has been viewed by the user. Set by get_message for any message it has retrieved.

---

append_message

$*folder*->append_message(\$*mi_ref*)

Adds message to a folder. Argument is a reference to a Mail::Internet object.

clear_label $folder->clear_label(*label*)

Deletes the association with *label* for all messages in the folder. Returns the number of messages for which there was an association.

close $folder->close

Does any necessary housekeeping and closes the folder.

current_message

$folder->current_message([*msg_num*])

With no argument, returns the message number of the current message in the folder. With an argument, sets the current message number for the folder to *msg_num*.

debug $folder->debug([*value*])

Sets the level of debugging information for the object to *value*. With no argument, returns the current debugging level.

debug_print $folder->debug_print(*text*)

Prints *text*, plus some additional information, to STDERR.

delete_label $folder->delete_label(*msg_num, label*)

Deletes the association of *label* with *msg_num*. Returns 1 on success and 0 if there was no association.

delete_message $folder->delete_message(*msgs*)

Takes a list of messages, *msgs*, to be marked for deletion. The messages aren't actually deleted until sync is called.

dup $folder->dup(*msg_num*, \$folder_ref)

Copies the message specified by *msg_num* to the folder referenced by \$folder_ref. Like refile, but doesn't delete the original message. Generates a fatal error if no folder is currently open or if the folder doesn't contain message *msg_num*.

first_labeled_message

$folder->first_labeled_message(label)

Returns the message number of the first message in the folder that has label associated with it, or 0 if there are none.

first_message

$folder->first_message

Returns the message number of the first message in the folder.

foldername

$folder->foldername

Returns the name of the folder that the object has opened.

get_fields

$folder->get_fields(msg_num, fields)

Retrieves the fields specified in the list fields for message msg_num. If called in list context, returns a list; in scalar context, returns a reference to a list of the fields. Returns the fields in the same order as they were specified.

get_header

$folder->get_header(msg_num)

Extracts a message header; takes one argument: the message number. Returns a reference to a Mail::Header object.

get_message

$folder->get_message(msg_num)

Takes a message number as argument and returns a Mail::Internet object reference to that message, or 0 on failure.

get_message_file

$folder->get_message_file(msg_num)

Like get_message, but returns a filename instead of a Mail::Internet object reference.

get_mime_header

$folder->get_mime_header(msg_num)

Works much like get_header, but returns a reference to a MIME::Head object instead. Takes one argument, the message number.

get_mime_message

$*folder*->get_mime_message (*msg_num*[, *parserobject*][, *options*])

Returns a MIME::Entity object for the specified message. Calls get_message_file to get a message to parse, creates a MIME::Parser object, and uses that to create the MIME::Entity object. The arguments are:

msg_num
The number of the message.

parserobject
If specified, used instead of internally creating a parser object.

options
Maps onto the equivalent MIME::Parser methods. Specified as key/value pairs, with possible values of: output_dir, output_prefix, output_to_core. See the MIME::Parser documentation for details.

get_option

$*folder*->get_option(*option*)

Returns the setting for the specified option, or undef if the option doesn't exist.

inverse_select

$*folder*->inverse_select(\$*func_ref*)

Returns a list, in no specific order, of message numbers that do not match a set of criteria. The argument, \$*func_ref*, is a reference to a function used to determine the criteria. The function is passed a reference to a Mail::Internet object containing only a header.

is_readonly

$*folder*->is_readonly

Returns 1 if the folder has the readonly attribute set; otherwise, returns 0.

label_exists

$*folder*->label_exists(*msg_num*, *label*)

Returns 1 if *label* is associated with message *msg_num*; otherwise, returns 0.

last_labeled_message

$*folder*->last_labeled_message(*label*)

Returns the message number of the last message in the folder with the label *label* associated with it, or 0 if there is no such message number.

last_message $folder->last_message

Returns the message number of the last message in the folder.

list_all_labels $folder->list_all_labels

Returns a list, in no specific order, of all labels associated with messages in the folder. If called in scalar context, returns the number of labels associated with the messages.

list_labels $folder->list_labels(*msg_num*)

Returns a list, in no specific order, of all labels associated with *msg_num*. If called in scalar context, returns the number of labels associated with the message.

message_exists $folder->message_exists(*msg_num*)

Returns 1 if a message with the number *msg_num* exists in the folder; otherwise, returns 0.

message_list $folder->message_list

Returns a list of the message numbers in the folder, in no specific order. The syntax is:

```
print $folder->message_list."\n"
```

next_labeled_message

$folder->next_labeled_message(*msg_num, label*)

Returns the message number of the next message in the folder relative to *msg_number* that has the label *label* associated with it, or 0 if there is no such message.

next_message $folder->next_message([*msg_num*])

Returns the number of the next message in the folder relative to *msg_num* if it is specified; otherwise, relative to the current message. Returns 0 if at end of folder.

open $folder->open(*foldername*)

If you didn't specify a folder name in the constructor, you need to call the open method, which takes the folder name as an argument and opens the folder. Also sets readonly if the folder is determined to be read-only.

pack $folder->pack

For formats that allow message number sequences to have gaps, renames the files in the folders to eliminate any such gaps. May result in renumbering some messages.

---

prev_labeled_message

$folder->prev_labeled_message(*msg_num*, *label*)

Returns the message number of the previous message in the folder relative to *msg_num* that has the label *label* associated with it, or 0 if there is no such message.

---

prev_message $folder->prev_message([*msg_num*])

Returns the number of the previous message in the folder relative to *msg_num* if it is specified; otherwise, relative to the current message. Returns 0 if at the beginning of the folder.

---

qty $folder->qty

Returns the number of messages in the folder. The syntax is:

```
print "There are ".$folder->qty." messages in your
folder\n";
```

---

refile $folder->refile(*msg_num*, \$*fldr_ref*)

Moves messages between folders. Takes a message number and folder reference as arguments.

---

select $folder->select(\$*func_ref*)

Returns a list of messages that meet a set of criteria. The argument, \$*func_ref*, is a reference to a function used to determine the criteria. The function is passed a reference to a Mail::Internet object containing only a header. The list is returned in no specific order.

---

select_label $folder->select_label(*label*)

Returns a list of messages with the label *label*. If called in scalar context, returns the number of messages that have the label.

---

set_option $folder->set_option(*option*, *value*)

Sets the specified option to *value*.

---

set_readonly　　$folder->set_readonly

Sets the readonly attribute for the folder. Once readonly has been set, sync won't perform any updates to the actual folder.

sort　　$folder->sort(\$func_ref)

Returns a sorted list of messages. \$func_ref is a reference to a function that is passed two Mail::Header message references and returns an integer less than, equal to, or greater than 0 to indicate the sort order.

sync　　$folder->sync

Synchronizes the folder with internal data structures and reads in any new messages since the last open or sync. Does not perform any updates if the readonly attribute has been set.

undelete_message

$folder->undelete_message(msgs)

Unmarks a list of messages, msgs, that have been marked for deletion.

update_message

$folder->update_message(msg_num, \$mref)

Replaces the message specified by msg_num with the contents of the message given by \$mref, which is a reference to a Mail::Internet object.

Handle Messages with Mail::Internet

Mail::Internet implements a number of helpful functions for manipulating a mail message. These include body, print_header, and head. Mail::Internet is built on top of Mail::Header, which parses the header of an email message, and it inherits the Mail::Header constructor style that requires that a file descriptor or reference to an array be used. For example:

```
@lines = <STDIN>;
$mi_obj = new Mail::Internet([@lines]);
```

reads a mail message from STDIN (using a reference to an array). The following example reads a mail message from a filehandle, FILE:

```
open(FILE, "/home/nvp/Mail/nvp");
$mi_obj = new Mail::Internet(\*FILE);
close(FILE);
```

The print_header function outputs the header of a message to a file descriptor; the default is STDOUT:

```
open(FILE, "/home/nvp/Mail/nvp");
$mi_obj = new Mail::Internet(\*FILE);
close(FILE);
$mi_obj->print_header(\*STDOUT);
```

The above example might output:

```
From nvp Mon Jun  9 00:11:10 1997
Received: (from nvp@localhost) by mail.somename.com (8.8/8.8) id
    AAA03248 for nvp; Mon, 9 Jun 1997 00:11:09 -0500 (EST)
Date: Mon, 9 Jun 1997 00:11:09 -0500 (EST)
From: "Nathan V. Patwardhan" <nvp>
Message-Id: <199706090511.AAA03248@mail.somename.com>
To: nvp
Subject: pop test
X-Status:
X-Uid: 1
Status: RO
```

in which print_body also takes a file descriptor as an argument, but outputs only the body of the message, whereas the print function outputs an entire message.

Mail::Internet Reference

---

new $mail = new Mail::Internet ([arg], [options])

Creates a new Mail::Internet object. arg is optional and may be either a file descriptor (a reference to a glob) or a reference to an array. If present, the new object is initialized with headers either from the array or read from the file descriptor. options is a list of options in the form of key/value pairs. Possible options are:

Header
    Mail::Internet should not attempt to read a mail header from arg, if it was specified. Value is a Mail::Header object.

Body
    Mail::Internet should attempt to read the body from arg, if it was specified. Value is a reference to an array that contains the lines of the message body.

Modify
    Reformats the headers if true. Mail::Header option.

MailFrom
>Specifies behavior for headers in the form "From ".
Mail::Header option. Possible values are:

IGNORE
>Ignores and discards the headers

ERROR
>Calls die

COERCE
>Renames headers to Mail-From

KEEP
>Keeps headers as they are

FoldLength
>Value is default line length for folding headers. Mail::Header
option.

---

add_signature $mail->add_signature([file])

Appends a signature to the message. file is a file that contains the
signature; if not specified, the file $ENV{HOME}/.signature is
checked for a signature.

---

body $mail->body( )

Returns the body of the message as a reference to an array. Each
entry in the array represents one line of the message.

---

escape_from $mail->escape_from( )

Inserts a leading > on any line that starts with "From " to avoid the
problems that some applications have if a message contains a line
starting with "From ".

---

head $headobj = $mail->head( )

Returns the Mail::Header object that holds the headers for the
current message.

---

nntppost $mail->nntppost([options])

Posts an article via NNTP; requires Net::NNTP. Options are
passed as key/value pairs. Available options are:

Debug
>Debug value to pass to Net::NNTP

Host
>Name of NNTP server to connect to

Port
>Port number to connect to on remote host

print_header	`$mail->print_header([\*fd])`
	`$mail->print_body([\*fd])`
	`$mail->print([\*fd])`

Prints the header, body, or whole message to file descriptor *fd, which should be a reference to a glob. If the file descriptor is not given, the output is sent to STDOUT:

```
$mail->print(\*STDOUT);  # Print message to STDOUT
```

remove_sig	`$mail->remove_sig([nlines])`

Removes a user's signature from the body of a message. Looks for a line equal to "-- " within the last *nlines* lines of the message and removes that line and all lines after it. *nlines* defaults to 10.

reply	`$reply = $mail->reply( )`

Creates a new object with headers initialized for a reply to the current object and with a body that is an indented copy of the current message.

smtpsend	`$mail->smtpsend( )`

Sends the Mail::Internet message via SMTP to all addresses on the To, Cc, and Bcc lines. Finds the SMTP host by trying to connect first to hosts specified in $ENV{SMTPHOSTS}, then to mailhost, and then to localhost.

In a future release of Mail::Internet, smtpsend will be able to take the hostname as a parameter, as nntppost does.

tidy_body	`$mail->tidy_body( )`

Removes all leading and trailing lines that contain only whitespace from the message body.

unescape_from	`$mail->unescape_from( )`

Removes the escaping added by escape_from.

Parse Email Addresses with Mail::Address

Mail::Address parses RFC 822–compliant mail addresses of the form:

```
"Full Name or Phrase" <username@host> (Comment Area)
```

For example, under RFC 822, an address might be represented as:

```
"Nathan V. Patwardhan" <nvp@mail.somename.com> (No Comment)
```

or:

```
"Nathan V. Patwardhan" <nvp@mail.somename.com>
```

The Mail::Address constructor parses an email address into three parts based on the categories shown above:

```
$addr = Mail::Address->new("Full Name or Phrase",
                           "username@host",
                           "(Comment Area)");
```

Mail::Address also outputs portions of the mail address with the functions phrase, address, comment, format, name, host, and user. The phrase, address, and comment functions represent the first, second, and third entities that were passed to the Mail::Address constructor, in which the phrase function:

```
print $addr->phrase( );
```

outputs:

```
Nathan V. Patwardhan
```

the address function:

```
print $addr->address( );
```

outputs:

```
nvp@mail.somename.com
```

and the comment function:

```
print $addr->comment( );
```

outputs:

```
No Comment
```

A real mail address can be "unmangled," or parsed from its *user@somehost.com* format, with the user and host functions. The user function removes everything starting with the @ to the end of the address, and host removes everything up to and including the @. Using the previous example of *nvp@mail.somename.com*, the following line:

```
print $addr->user;
```

outputs:

```
nvp
```

And the following line using the host function:

```
print $addr->host;
```

outputs:

```
nvp@mail.somename.com
```

Mail::Address Reference

new $addr = Mail::Address->new(*phrase, address*[, *comment*])

Constructor. Creates new Mail::Address object representing an address with the specified elements. In a message, these three elements show up as:

    phrase <address> (comment)
    address (comment)

parse Mail::Address->parse(*line*)

Constructor. Parses the specified line, usually a To, Cc, or Bcc line, and returns a list of extracted Mail::Address objects.

address $addr->address( )

Returns the address part of the object.

canon $addr->canon( )

Unimplemented, but should return the UUCP canon for the message.

comment $addr->comment( )

Returns the comment part of the object.

format $addr->format( )

Returns a string representing the address in a form suitable for the To, Cc, or Bcc line of a message

host $addr->host( )

Returns the host portion of the address.

name $addr->name( )

Takes information contained in the object and uses various heuristics to try to identify the name of the person or group.

path $addr->path( )

Unimplemented, but should return the UUCP path for the message.

phrase	`$addr->phrase( )`
	Returns the phrase part of the object.

user	`$addr->user( )`
	Returns the user ID portion of the address.

Checking Blacklisted Hosts with Mail::RBL

Mail::RBL eases the task of checking if a given host is in the real-time blackhole list. Mail::RBL does this by speaking directly to the RBL server and searching for a specified host. Ordinarily, you build this functionality into your MTA (sendmail, qmail, Exim, etc.), but if your system administrator hasn't built RBL support into your MTA, you might consider integrating Mail::RBL into your own mail filter.

new(*suffix*)
> Creates a list handle. *suffix* is required because it denotes the host from which you'll check hostnames.

check($*host*)
> Performs the lookup against the RBL. $*host* can be a hostname or IP address, without trailing netmasks (represented by a / followed by an octet).

> For example:

```
use Mail::RBL;

my $host = q[some-spammer.domain.here];
my $rbl = Mail::RBL->new('list.org');

if($rbl->check($host)) {
    print "$host is in the RBL, and I won't deliver the mail."
} else {
    # Do something to deliver the email
}
```

Mail Filtering with Mail::Audit

Mail::Audit is a mail-filtering system for those who want to write good filter rules but choose not to use procmail. It was written to provide flexibility while realizing the strengths of Perl's regular expression engine. Inspired by Tom Christiansen's *audit_mail* and *deliverdb* programs, Mail::Audit allows an email message to be logged, examined, routed to another folder or INBOX, resent, or rejected. You should be able to write a simple ruleset or rulesets and put references to it in your *.forward* file. For example:

```
use Mail::Audit;

my $m_au = Mail::Audit->new( );
```

```
$m_au->reject("Let me call YOU at home!")
    if $m_au =~ /(spammer\@spammer.com|spammer2\@spammer2.com|spammer3\
@spammer3.com)/;

$m_au->accept("Majordomo") if $mail->from =~ /Majordomo\@/;

$m_au->accept( );
```

Mail::Audit implements the following methods.

---

new   new(*%options*)

Constructor. Reads a mail message from STDIN (or, if the data
option is set, from an array reference) and creates a Mail::Audit
object from it. Options include:

log=>*logfile*
    Writes a debugging log.

loglevel=>*n*
    Sets verbosity of the log on a scale of 1 to 4.

noexit=>1
    Do not exit after delivering mail.

If you specify a log level without a log file, logging will be written to
/tmp/username-audit.log, where *username* is replaced by your
username.

---

body   body( )

Returns a reference to an array of lines in the body of the email.

---

get   get(*header*)

Retrieves the named header from the mail message.

---

header   header( )

Returns the header as a single string.

---

ignore   ignore( )

Ignores an email message completely, dumping it into the bit
bucket.

---

pipe   pipe(*program*)

Opens a pipe to an external program and feeds the message to it.

---

put	put(*header, value*)
	Inserts a new header into the mail message with the given value.

reject	reject(*message*)
	Rejects an email message, then notifies the sender that the message is undeliverable with *message* as the reason given.

resend	resend(*address*)
	Bounces the email in its entirety to another address.

tidy	tidy( )
	Tidies up the email as per the Mail::Internet manpage.

xaccept	xaccept(*filename*)
	Writes the incoming (and filtered) mail into a mailbox at *filename*. If *filename* is undefined, mail is written to */var/spool/mail/$USER*. If you use Maildir instead of *mbox*-formatted mail, it will deliver the mail in Maildir style.

Alias Manipulation with Unix::AliasFile

While not a member of the Mail umbrella, Unix::AliasFile is an important module since it implements a complete interface to the Unix aliases text file that allows you to query, add, update, and delete aliases. In addition, it has a cleaner interface than Mail::Alias. Unix::AliasFile automatically handles file locking, comma and colon placement, and any other detail that's related to manipulating your Unix mail alias file. For example:

```
use Unix::AliasFile;

my $aliasfile = '/etc/mail/aliases';
my $uaf = Unix::AliasFile->new($aliasfile);

foreach my $alias $uaf->aliases( ) {
    chomp($alias);

    if($uaf->alias($alias) ne "$alias\@yourpopserver.your.domain") {
        # Doesn't exist, so add alias of the form:
        # alias: alias@yourpopserver.your.domain

        $uaf->alias($alias, ("$alias\@yourpopserver.your.domain"));
    } else {
```

```
            print "I already have $alias that way.\n";
        }
    }

    $uaf->commit();
    undef $uaf;
```

Unix::AliasFile implements the following methods.

---

new   new(*filename*)

Constructor. Creates a new Unix::AliasFile object.

---

add_user   add_user(*alias*, *@users*)

Adds *@users* to *alias*. If a user in *@users* already exists in *alias*, duplicates will be ignored. If *alias* is set to *, *@users* will be added to every alias.

---

alias   alias(*alias*, *@users*)

Adds, modifies, or returns information about an alias. When only *alias* is suppled, alias() returns a list of all members of an alias, or undef if *alias* does not exist. If you supply *@users*, *alias* will be modified or created if it doesn't already exist.

---

aliases   aliases()

Returns an alphabetized list of all existing aliases. In scalar context, this method returns the total number of aliases.

---

comment   comment(*alias*, *comment*)

Inserts a comment line before *alias*. *comment* must begin with #, but a newline will be appended to it. Returns 1 on success and 0 on failure.

---

commit   commit()

Writes the alias file.

---

delempty   delempty()

Deletes all existing aliases that have no members, returning a count of the number of aliases deleted.

---

delete   delete(*alias*)

Deletes *alias*.

---

remove_user   remove_user(*alias*, *@users*)

Removes the list of users from an existing alias. If a user in *@users* isn't a member of *alias*, the removal attempt will be silently ignored. remove_user( ) returns 1 on success and 0 on failure.

rename_user   rename_user(*oldname*, *newname*)

Changes one username to another in every alias. Returns the number of aliases affected.

uncomment   uncomment(*comment*)

Removes the comment from the file that is exactly matched to the supplied text. Returns 1 on success and 0 on failure.

17

Usenet News

Usenet is a collection of bulletin board–like newsgroups on the Internet, covering thousands of topics. Whatever your interest, chances are you'll find a newsgroup in which it is discussed.

Usenet has been around since late 1979. The current implementation is based on the Network NewsTransfer Protocol (NNTP), defined in RFC 977 and released in March 1986. Information is propagated through Usenet by a system of newsfeeds in which one site requests a newsfeed from another site, and a third site requests a newsfeed from the second site, etc. There is no central Usenet authority—like Perl, it runs on the spirit of cooperation and sharing. When you run a news reader, such as *tin* or the news reader in a web browser, your client software talks to the NNTP server on the news host. When you post a message to a newsgroup, this posting is received by your NNTP server and passed on to other servers throughout the distribution area you specified for the posting. Each server periodically receives updated newsgroup information and newly posted news articles.

This chapter explores NNTP commands and responses. It introduces Net::NNTP, which implements NNTP commands and simplifies the process of writing a Perl-based NNTP news client. It also describes News::Newsrc, a module that provides methods for managing a *.newsrc* file.

There are two kinds of NNTP commands: the official set of commands as defined in RFC 977 and a number of extensions that have been added since the RFC was written. The extensions are described in an IETF Internet Draft document, "Common NNTP Extensions" by Stan Barber, which can be found at *ftp://ftp. academ.com/pub/nntp/ietf/nntpext.txt*.

The NNTP Protocol

Before you write your own news client, you should have some idea of how the NNTP protocol works. Like other servers, an NNTP server is bound to a port (usually port 119). It listens for incoming connections, takes the appropriate action, and returns a response to the client. When a news client connects with an NNTP server, or to the port on which the NNTP server is running, a message such as the following is produced:

```
Trying 0.0.0.0...
Connected to hostname.mydomain.com.
Escape character is '^]'.
200 newshost.mydomain.com InterNetNews NNRP server INN 1.5.1 17-Dec-1996
ready
(posting ok).
```

Many NNTP servers understand the *help* (or *HELP*) command. When a client issues a *help* command, many NNTP servers respond with a list of all available commands. For example:

```
200 news.mydomain.com InterNetNews NNRP server INN 1.5.1 17-Dec-1996 ready
(posting ok).
HELP
100 Legal commands
  authinfo user Name|pass Password|generic <prog> <args>
  article [MessageID|Number]
  body [MessageID|Number]
  date
  group newsgroup
  head [MessageID|Number]
  help
  ihave
  last
  list [active|active.times|newsgroups|distributions|distrib.pats|
overview.fmt|subscriptions]
  listgroup newsgroup
  mode reader
  newgroups yymmdd hhmmss ["GMT"] [<distributions>]
  newnews newsgroups yymmdd hhmmss ["GMT"] [<distributions>]
  next
  post
  slave
  stat [MessageID|Number]
  xgtitle [group_pattern]
  xhdr header [range|MessageID]
  xover [range]
  xpat header range|MessageID pat [morepat...]
  xpath MessageID
Report problems to <usenet@news.mydomain.com>
```

After connecting to the NNTP server, you can get a list of available newsgroups with the *list active* command, and you can then select a newsgroup. If you were to connect directly to *news.mydomain.com* and use the *group* command to select the newsgroup *local.test*, your session might look like this:

```
200 news.mydomain.com InterNetNews NNRP server INN 1.5.1 17-Dec-1996 ready
(posting ok).
```

```
group local.test
211 4 1 4 local.test
QUIT
205 .
```

The four numbers (in this example, 211 4 1 4) preceding the group name (*local.
test*) represent the success code, total number of articles, and the first and last
article numbers, respectively. So in this example, 211 is the success code. There
are four articles in the *local.test* group, starting with article number 1 and ending
with number 4.

Every article in a newsgroup has two identifiers associated with it. The first is the
message number, and the second is a message ID. The message number is the
number of that article on the server to which you are connecting. The message ID
is an identifier that is always associated with the article on every server that
receives the article. An article that has the message number 4 on your server might
be number 83 on someone else's server. The message ID, however, will be the
same on both. So, for example, if you want to post an article that refers to another
article, use the message ID.

Once the *group* command has successfully identified a newsgroup, the client can
request a particular article by sending an *article* request to the server. The *article*
command takes either a message ID or a message number as an argument. For
example:

```
article 4
Path: newshost.mydomain.com!news-w.ans.net!newsfeeds.ans.net!philabs ...
From: user@mydomain.com (User Name)
Newsgroups: local.test
Subject: Is anybody there?
Date: 21 Apr 1997
...
```

If the *article* command is successful, the server returns the selected message.

The *xhdr* command returns the selected headers ("X-headers") from articles in a
certain newsgroup. The X-headers contain all the information about the news
article, including the poster's email address, the subject of the message, the date
and time the message was posted, the newsgroup(s) the message appears in, and
the message ID. For example, if you want to see the subjects of the articles in the
local.test newsgroup, you can run xhdr subject 1-4, as follows:

```
xhdr subject 1-4
221 subject fields follow
1   Is anybody there?
2   Re: Is anybody there?
3   Re: Is anybody there?
4   Get a life!
```

The 221 status code indicates that the *xhdr* completed successfully and returned
the requested headers. A Usenet client might display these headers to the user,
who can then select the articles to read based on the subject lines.

A command similar to *xhdr* is *xpat*, which matches X-headers against a pattern string you give it. For example, executing xpat subject 1-9 *anybody* for *local.test* might look like this:

```
xpat subject 1-9 *anybody*
221 subject matches follow.
1    Is anybody there?
2    Re: Is anybody there?
3    Re: Is anybody there?
```

You can also post news articles with NNTP. When you issue the *post* command, the server returns a code of 340 if posting is permitted. If you get an error, such as 501, you cannot post articles with this command. Most servers require that you include Newsgroups, Subject, and From headers. You will receive a 240 reply if your message has been successfully posted. Here's an example of posting to *local.test* using NNTP:

```
200 news.mydomain.com InterNetNews NNRP server INN 1.5.1 17-Dec-1996 ready
(posting ok).
post
340 Ok
Newsgroups: local.test
Subject: talking NNTP
From: user@mydomain.com
This is a test posting.
.
240 Article posted
QUIT
205 .
```

The server returns a code of 205 upon disconnecting. When the article arrives in *local.test*, it looks like this:

```
From news.mydomain.com!not-for-mail Sun Mar  9 19:18:37 1997
Path: news.mydomain.com!not-for-mail
From: user@mydomain.com
Newsgroups: local.test
Subject: talking NNTP
Date: 10 Mar 1997 00:09:33 GMT
Organization: Perl in a Nutshell
Lines: 2
Distribution: local
Message-ID: <5fvjft$k3$2@news.mydomain.com>
NNTP-Posting-Host: newshost.mydomain.com
Xref: newshost.mydomain.com local.test:6

This is a test posting.
```

Net::NNTP

Net::NNTP is one of the *libnet* modules. It provides methods for programming a news client to interface with an NNTP server. Net::NNTP implements the NNTP protocol as defined in RFC 977, as well as a number of extensions defined in the IETF Internet Draft document mentioned earlier.

For example, the following code:

```
$nntp->post(@message);
```

is equivalent to issuing the *post* command and associated X-headers directly to an NNTP server on port 119.

Initializing the NNTP Client

To use Net::NNTP, create a new Net::NNTP object:

```
use Net::NNTP;
$nntp = Net::NNTP->new;    # Use default port and options
```

Once you've created the object, you can use any of the Net::NNTP methods on that object. The Net::NNTP methods generally parallel the functionality of the raw NNTP commands. Your news client can be written to perform many functions, including:

- Authenticating a user to the server
- Listing available newsgroups
- Retrieving news headers and articles
- Extracting headers
- Checking for new articles
- Posting articles
- Listing information such as active messages in a newsgroup, new newsgroups, valid distribution areas, or message IDs of newly arrived messages

Net::NNTP Reference

Net::NNTP includes methods that implement many of the extensions to RFC 977; the description indicates if a method is an extension. Extensions that are not supported by Net::NNTP are AUTHINFO, GENERIC, XINDEX, XSEARCH, and XTHREAD. In addition, some extensions supported by Net::NNTP may not be supported by a particular server.

Unless otherwise stated, all the methods return either true or false to indicate success or failure. If a method returns a value instead, then it returns undef or an empty list to indicate failure.

In this list, *message-spec* refers to a single message ID, a single message number, or a reference to a list of two message numbers. It can also be passed as a list of two message numbers, but this is for compatibility only and is now deprecated.

Where pattern-matching is indicated, the matching is done according to the NNTP specification. See the Net::NNTP documentation for details.

new $nntp$ = Net::NNTP->new([host[, options]])

Constructor. Creates a new Net::NNTP object. Arguments are:

host
>   The name of the remote host to which an NNTP connection is required. If not specified, the constructor checks the environment variables NNTPSERVER and NEWSHOST, in that order, then Net::Config. Defaults to news if nothing is found.

options
>   Options. Passed as key/value pairs. Possible options are:

>   Timeout
>>   Maximum time, in seconds, to wait for a response from the NNTP server. Default is 120 seconds. A value of 0 causes all I/O operations to block.

>   Debug
>>   Enables printing of debugging information to STDERR.

---

active $nntp$->active([*pattern*])

Similar to list, but returns only active groups that match the pattern (an extension).

---

active_times $nntp$->active_times()

Returns a reference to a hash in which the keys are the group names, and the values are references to arrays containing the time the group was created and an identifier, possibly an email address, for the creator (an extension).

---

article $nntp$->article([*msgid*|*msgnum*])

Retrieves the header, a blank line, then the body (text) of the article, specified as either a message ID or a message number. With no arguments, returns the current article in the current newsgroup as a reference to an array containing the article.

---

authinfo $nntp$->authinfo(*user, pass*)

Authenticates the user to the server, passing the user's username and password.

---

body $nntp$->body([*msgid*|*msgnum*])

Retrieves the body (text) of the article specified by either a message ID or a message number. Takes the same arguments as article. Returns a reference to an array containing the body of the article.

date $nntp$->date( )

Returns the date on the remote server, in Unix time format (seconds since 1970).

distributions $nntp$->distributions( )

Returns a reference to a hash in which the keys are the valid distribution names, and the values are the distribution descriptions (an extension).

group $nntp$->group([$group$])

Sets and/or gets the current group. With no argument, returns information about the current group; otherwise, sets the current group to $group$.

In a scalar context, group returns the group name. In an array context, it returns a list containing the number of articles in the group, the first article number, the last article number, and the group name.

head $nntp$->head([$msgid|msgnum$])

Retrieves the header of the article specified by $msgid$ or $msgnum$. Takes the same arguments as article and returns a reference to an array containing the article's header.

ihave $nntp$->ihave($msgid$[, $message$])

Informs the server that the client has an article whose ID is $msgid$. The optional argument $message$ can be either an array of lines or a reference to an array. If $message$ is specified, and the server wants a copy, it is sent, returning true on successful completion.

If $message$ is not specified, then the message must be sent using the Net::Cmd datasend and dataend methods.

last $nntp$->last( )

Sets the current article pointer to the previous article in the current newsgroup. Returns the article's message ID.

list $nntp$->list( )

Returns information about all active newsgroups. The result is a reference to a hash in which the key is a newsgroup name, and each value is a reference to an array. The elements in the array are the first article number in the group, the last article number in the group, and any information flags.

listgroup   `$nntp->listgroup([group])`

Returns a reference to a list of all active messages in newsgroup *group*, or the current newsgroup if *group* is not specified (an extension).

newgroups   `$nntp->newgroups(since[, distributions])`

Like list, but returns groups created after a certain time and optionally in one of a set of distribution areas. Arguments are:

since
> Time value; only groups created after this time should be returned.

distributions
> Optional distribution pattern or reference to a list of distribution patterns. If present, only groups matching a specified distribution area should be returned.

newnews   `$nntp->newnews(since[, groups[, distributions]])`

Returns a reference to a list containing the message IDs of all news posted after *since* that are in newsgroups matching *groups*, with a distribution that matches *distributions*. Arguments are:

since
> Time value; only groups created after this time should be returned.

groups
> Optional group pattern or reference to a list of group patterns indicating which groups should be checked for new messages.

distributions
> Optional distribution pattern or reference to a list of distribution patterns. If present, only groups matching a specified distribution area should be returned.

newsgroups   `$nntp->newsgroups([pattern])`

Returns a reference to a hash in which the keys are all newsgroup names that match *pattern*, or all newsgroups if no pattern is specified, and each value contains the description text for the group (an extension).

next   `$nntp->next( )`

Sets the current article pointer to the next article in the current newsgroup. Returns the message ID of the article.

nntpstat $nntp$->nntpstat([$msgid$|$msgnum$])

Similar to article, except that no text is returned. When selecting
by message number within a newsgroup, sets the current article
pointer without sending text. Selecting by message ID is valid, but
doesn't alter the current article pointer and therefore is of little use.
Returns the message ID of the current article.

overview_fmt $nntp$->overview_fmt( )

Returns a reference to an array containing the names of the fields
returned by xover (an extension).

post $nntp$->post([$message$])

Posts a new article to the news server. If $message$ is specified and
posting is allowed, then the message is sent. If $message$ is not specified, the message must be sent using the Net::Cmd datasend and
dataend methods. $message$ can be either an array of lines or a reference to an array.

postok $nntp$->postok( )

Returns true if the server's initial response indicated that it allows
posting.

quit $nntp$->quit( )

Quits the remote server and closes the socket connection.

reader $nntp$->reader( )

Tells the server that you are a reader and not another server;
required by some servers (an extension).

slave $nntp$->slave( )

Tells the remote server that this is not a user client, but is probably
another news server.

subscriptions $nntp$->subscriptions( )

Returns a reference to a default list of newsgroups recommended
for new users to subscribe to (an extension).

xgtitle	`$nntp->xgtitle(pattern)`
	Returns a reference to a hash in which the keys are all the newsgroup names that match *pattern*, and each value is the text of the newsgroup's description (an extension).
xhdr	`$nntp->xhdr(header, message-spec)`
	Gets the header field *header* for all the messages specified in *message-spec*. Returns a reference to a hash in which the keys are the message numbers, and each value contains the text of the requested header for that message (an extension).
xover	`$nntp->xover(message-spec)`
	Returns a reference to a hash in which the keys are the message numbers, and each value contains a reference to an array of the overview fields for that message (an extension).
	The names of the fields can be obtained by calling `overview_fmt`.
xpat	`$nntp->xpat(header, pattern, message-spec)`
	Like xhdr, but returns only headers in which the text of the header matches *pattern* (an extension).
xpath	`$nntp->xpath(message-id)`
	Returns the path to the file on the server that contains the specified message (an extension).
xrover	`$nntp->xrover(message-spec)`
	Returns reference information for the article(s) specified. Returns a reference to a hash in which the keys are the message numbers, and the values are the References: lines from the articles (an extension).

The News::Newsrc Module

Most Unix-based newsreaders parse and extract your newsgroup information from a *.newsrc* file. This file contains an entry for each newsgroup, with the name of the group and a comma-separated list of article numbers from 1 to the current article. The first entry in the list shows articles that have been read; the remaining entries list unread articles. Each entry also has a colon (:) following the name if you are subscribed to that newsgroup, or an exclamation point (!) if you are currently unsubscribed.

To read a newsgroup, your newsreader needs to be connected to an NNTP server. The newsreader then checks the *.newsrc* entry for that newsgroup to determine which articles you haven't read, and displays the first unread article. You can then read the articles sequentially or select which articles you want to read. When you "catch-up" a newsgroup by marking all the articles as "read", or when you exit from the newsreader program, your *.newsrc* file is updated to reflect your activity during that session.

The News::Newsrc module provides methods for managing your *.newsrc* file. Some of the functions it provides include letting you add, remove, or reorder newsgroups; subscribe to or unsubscribe from newsgroups; and mark articles as read or unmark them. Unless you tell it to rearrange the order of the newsgroups in *.newsrc*, News::Newsrc leaves the order unchanged.

News::Newsrc Reference

---

new

$newsrc = new News::Newsrc

Constructor. Creates a new News::Newsrc object that contains no newsgroups.

---

add_group

$newsrc->add_group(groupname[, options])

Adds newsgroup to *.newsrc*, as a subscribed group. Defaults to adding at the end. The arguments are:

groupname
Name of the newsgroup to add.

options
Hash with one entry, indicating where to put the newsgroup. Key is where, and possible values are:

after => group
Put immediately after newsgroup group, or last if group is not there.

alpha
Put in alphabetical order.

before => group
Put immediately before newsgroup group.

first
Put as first newsgroup.

last
Put as last newsgroup.

number => n
Put at position n, where the first position is 0. If position is negative, count from the end of the list backwards n positions.

---

del_group $newsrc->del_group(*groupname*)

Removes specified newsgroup *groupname* from *.newsrc*.

---

exists $newsrc->exists(*groupname*)

Returns true if newsgroup *groupname* is in *.newsrc*.

---

groups $newsrc->groups( )

Returns list of newsgroups in *.newsrc*. In scalar context, returns an array reference.

---

load $newsrc->load([*filename*])

Loads newsgroups in *filename* into $newsrc, replacing any newsgroups that are already there. Defaults to $HOME/.newsrc.

---

mark $newsrc->mark(*groupname, article_number*[, *options*])

Adds an article to the list for a specified newsgroup. Arguments are:

groupname
    Newsgroup to add an article to.

article_number
    Article number of the article to add.

options
    Hash. See description under add_group.

---

marked $newsrc->marked(*groupname, article_number*)

Returns true if the newsgroup exists and contains the specified article. Arguments are:

groupname
    Group to report on

article_number
    Number of the article to verify

---

marked_articles $newsrc->marked_articles(*groupname*)

Returns the list of articles in group *groupname*. In scalar context, returns an array reference.

mark_list $newsrc->mark_list(groupname, \@article_list[, options])

Adds articles to the list for a specified group. Arguments are:

groupname
    Group to add articles to.

\@article_list
    Reference to list of articles to add.

options
    Hash. See description under add_group.

mark_range $newsrc->mark_range(groupname, n, m[, options])

Adds articles in the specified range to the list. Arguments are:

groupname
    Newsgroup to add articles to.

n
    Number of the first article in the range.

m
    Number of the last article in the range.

options
    Hash. See description under add_group.

save $newsrc->save( )

Saves changes to *.newsrc* file.

save_as $newsrc->save_as(filename)

Saves changes to specified file *filename*, rather than to *.newsrc* file.

sub_groups $newsrc->sub_groups( )

Returns list of subscribed groups in *.newsrc*.

subscribe $newsrc->subscribe(groupname)

Subscribes to newsgroup *groupname*. If the group is not in *.newsrc*, it is added; its location may be given in *options*, as specified for add_group.

subscribed $newsrc->subscribed(groupname)

Returns true if the group *groupname* exists and is subscribed to.

unmark

$newsrc->unmark(*groupname, article_number*[, *options*])

Removes specified article from the group list. Arguments are:

groupname
Newsgroup to remove articles from.

article_number
Article to remove.

options
Hash. See description under add_group.

unmarked_articles

$newsrc->unmarked_articles(*groupname, n, m*[, *options*])

Returns the list of articles from *n* to *m*, inclusive, that are not in the article list for the newsgroup. Arguments are:

groupname
Group to return articles from.

n
Number of the first article in the range.

m
Number of the last article in the range.

options
Hash. See description under add_group.

unmark_list

$newsrc->unmark_list(*groupname,* \@*article_list*[, *options*])

Removes specified list of articles from the group list. Arguments are:

groupname
Group to remove articles from.

\@*article_list*
Reference to list of articles to remove.

options
Hash. See description under add_group.

unmark_range

$newsrc->unmark_range(*groupname, n, m*[, *options*])

Removes a range of articles from *n* to *m* from *.newsrc*. Arguments are:

groupname
Group to remove articles from.

n
Number of the first article in the range.

m
> Number of the last article in the range.

options
> Hash. See description under add_group.

---

unsub_groups   `$newsrc->unsub_groups( )`

Returns list of unsubscribed groups in *.newsrc*. In scalar context, returns an array reference.

---

unsubscribe   `$newsrc->unsubscribe(groupname[, options])`

Unsubscribes from newsgroup in *.newsrc*. If the group is not in *.newsrc*, it is added. Arguments are:

groupname
> Group to unsubscribe from.

options
> Hash. See description under add_group.

18

FTP

The File Transfer Protocol (FTP) is a popular means of transferring files between computers. FTP communication follows the client/server model: the client initiates a conversation by sending commands, and the server responds with messages and status codes, as well as by sending or receiving files. This chapter discusses two FTP-related modules included in the *libnet* distribution: Net::FTP, which provides a number of wrapper functions for implementing the client side of FTP, and Net::Netrc, which provides an interface for getting information from a *.netrc* file.

The FTP protocol permits two-way file transactions, in which files can be sent to or taken from an FTP server. These transactions involve the local filesystem (on the client side) and the remote filesystem (on the server side). When a file is transferred between the local and remote systems, its filename on the destination system is the same as on the source system, unless you specify a new filename.

The FTP protocol also lists the types of files that can be transferred. These types define (among many other things) how end-of-line characters are handled for different types of files.

The FTP Protocol

When a server accepts FTP requests, it opens a port (generally port 21) for incoming connections and authenticates clients based on account or anonymous privileges. A user may log in with a legitimate account on that machine, provide her own password, and access any file she normally has access to under the Unix shell. Many servers also allow "anonymous" FTP, in which users log in with the name "anonymous" and use their email address as the password. They are then granted restricted access to a limited portion of the filesystem.

The FTP commands defined in RFC 959 are listed in the following table:

Command	Meaning
ABOR	Abort previous FTP command.
ACCT	Specify the user's account.
ALLO	Tell server to allocate additional storage for new file.
APPE	Tell server to append to an existing file.
CDUP	Change to parent directory.
CWD	Change directory.
DELE	Delete a file.
HELP	Get help.
LIST	List files for display.
MKD	Make a directory.
MODE	Specify the data transfer mode.
NLST	List files for additional processing.
NOOP	No-op.
PASS	Specify the user's password.
PASV	Tell server to go into "passive" mode.
PORT	Specify data port for connection.
PWD	Print working directory.
QUIT	Close connection.
REIN	Reinitialize connection.
REST	Restart a file transfer.
RETR	Retrieve a file.
RMD	Remove a directory.
RNFR	Specify pathname of file to be renamed.
RNTO	Specify new name of file being renamed.
SITE	Provide additional site-specific services.
SMNT	Mount a different filesystem.
STAT	Get status.
STOR	Tell server to accept a file for storage.
STOU	Tell server to create unique name for new file.
STRU	Specify the file structure.
SYST	Tell server to declare its operating system.
TYPE	Specify the data representation type.
USER	Specify the username.

Exactly which FTP commands are available depends on the server; some servers implement a subset, or possibly a superset, of the commands defined in the RFC. Net::FTP, which we'll discuss in this chapter, provides methods that implement all the commands except the following:

> ALLO
> HELP

MODE
REIN
SITE
SMNT
STAT
STRU
SYST

Net::FTP

Net::FTP is used to transfer files from remote hosts. With Net::FTP, you can write simple FTP clients that transfer files from remote servers based on information passed on the command line or from hardcoded variables. Here is an example of a client that connects to a remote FTP server and gets a file from the server:

```
#!/usr/local/bin/perl -w

use Net::FTP;

$hostname = 'remotehost.com';
$username = 'anonymous';
$password = 'myname@mydomain.com';

# Hardcode the directory and filename to get
$home = '/pub';
$filename = 'TESTFILE';

# Open the connection to the host
$ftp = Net::FTP->new($hostname);          # Construct object
$ftp->login($username, $password);        # Log in

$ftp->cwd($home),"\n";                    # Change directory
print $ftp->ls($home),"\n";

# Now get the file and leave
$ftp->get($filename);
$ftp->quit;
```

FTP clients have also been integrated with most World Wide Web browsers, using *ftp://* in place of *http://*. When the URL points to a directory, the browser displays a listing of the directory, in which each filename is a link to that file. When the URL points directly to a file, the remote file is downloaded.

Here's an example that uses Net::FTP to list files from a remote FTP server on a web page, with a link from each file to the URL of the file on the remote site:

```
#!/usr/local/bin/perl -w

use Net::FTP;

$hostname = 'remotehost.com';        # FTP host
$username = 'anonymous';             # Username
$password = 'myname@mydomain.com';   # Password
```

```
$home = '/pub';

$ftp = Net::FTP->new($hostname);      # Net::FTP constructor
$ftp->login($username, $password);    # Log in w/username and password

$pwd = $ftp->pwd;                     # Get current directory

print <<HTML;                         # Output HTML page
Content-type: text/html
<HTML>

  <HEAD>
    <TITLE>Download Files</TITLE>
  </HEAD>
  <BODY>

      <B>Current working directory:</B> $pwd<BR>
      Files to download: <P>
HTML

    @entries = $ftp->ls($home);     # Slurp all entries into an array
    foreach (@entries) { # Output links for all files in the ftp area
                         # as links
        print "<INPUT TYPE=hidden NAME=\"files\" VALUE=\"$_\">\n";
        print "<A HREF=\"ftp://$hostname$_\">",
        "<IMG SRC=\"http://www/icons/f.gif\" border=0>\n";
        print " $_</A><BR>\n";
    }
    print <<HTML;
  </BODY>
</HTML>
HTML
$ftp->quit;               # end FTP session
```

The Net::FTP module implements a subset (as shown earlier in this chapter) of the FTP protocol as defined in RFC 959. In addition to providing the methods shown below, the module inherits from Net::Cmd. Some of the Net::FTP methods return an object derived from the *dataconn* class (which is in turn derived from the IO::Socket::INET class), as noted in the entries for those methods.

The following methods are defined by Net::FTP.

---

new $*ftp* = Net::FTP->new(*host*[, *options*])

Constructs a new Net::FTP object. Arguments are:

host
> The name of the remote host

options
> A hash specifying any of the following information:

Firewall
> Name of an FTP firewall.

Port
> Port number to use for the FTP connection. Defaults to 21.

Timeout
> Timeout value. Defaults to 120 seconds.

Debug
> Debug level.

Passive
> True or false, specifying whether to perform transfers in passive mode.

---

abort

$ftp->abort( )

Aborts the current transaction.

---

appe

$ftp->appe(file)

Appends data to the end of the remote file *file*, which is created if it doesn't exist. If the user calls either pasv or port, returns true or false. Otherwise, returns a reference to a Net::FTP::dataconn object.

---

append

$ftp->append(local[, remote])

Appends the contents of a local file to an existing file on the remote system. Arguments are:

local
> Either the name of the file on the local system to transfer or a filehandle.

remote
> The name of the file on the remote system. If *local* is a filehandle, *remote* must be specified.

---

ascii

$ftp->ascii([args])

Changes the type of data transfer to ascii. Like type, without the need to specify the first argument.

---

authorize

$ftp->authorize([auth[, resp]])

Authorizes the user to send data outside the firewall, for use with FTP proxies. If authorization *auth* and response *resp* are not specified, authorize uses Net::Netrc to do a lookup.

Called with no arguments by login if the connection is through a firewall.

binary ftp->binary([$args$])

Changes the type of data transfer to binary. Like type, without the need to specify the first argument.

byte ftp->byte([$args$])

Changes the data transfer type to byte. Not supported. If specified, defaults to binary. Like type, without the need to specify the first argument.

cdup ftp->cdup( )

Goes up one level in the directory hierarchy.

cwd ftp->cwd([dir])

Changes the working directory to dir. With no argument, changes the directory to root.

delete ftp->delete([$filename$])

Deletes the specified file from the server.

dir ftp->dir([dir])

Lists the specified server directory in long format. Returns a reference to the list. dir defaults to the current working directory.

ebcdic ftp->ebcdic([$args$])

Changes the data transfer type to ebcdic. Not supported. If specified, defaults to binary. Like type, without the need to specify the first argument.

get ftp->get($remote$[, $local$])

Retrieves a file from the server. If specified, $local$ is the name to give the file on the local system; otherwise, the name stays the same. Arguments are:

$remote$
    Name of the file to retrieve from the remote system.

$local$
    Either the new filename on the local system or a filehandle. If omitted, the same filename is used.

list

$ftp->list([dir])

Lists a directory, *dir*, for display. If the user calls either pasv or port, returns true or false. Otherwise, returns a reference to a Net::FTP::dataconn object. If directory is omitted, defaults to the current directory.

login

$ftp->([login[, passwd[, account]]])

Logs user into an FTP server. Arguments are:

login
> Login name. If not specified, defaults to anonymous or to the value in *$HOME/.netrc*.

passwd
> Password. If not specified, defaults to the user's email address or to the value in *$HOME/.netrc*.

account
> Additional account information for files on the FTP server that have special access restrictions.

ls

$ftp->ls([dir])

Lists directory, *dir*, returning a reference to the list. Defaults to the current working directory.

mdtm

$ftp->mdtm(file)

Returns the modification time of remote file *file*.

mkdir

$ftp->mkdir(dir[, recursive])

Makes a new directory. Arguments are:

dir
> The new directory name

recursive
> If true, creates all directories in the path as needed

nlst

$ftp->nlst([dir])

Lists a directory, *dir*, for further processing. With no argument, defaults to the current directory. If the user calls either pasv or port, returns true or false. Otherwise, returns a reference to a Net::FTP::dataconn object.

Network
Programming

pasv $ftp->pasv( )$

                            Puts server in passive mode.

pasv_wait $ftp->pasv_wait(server)$

                            Waits for a transfer to complete between a passive and a nonpas-
                            sive server, in which *server* is the Net::FTP object for the
                            nonpassive server.

pasv_xfer $ftp->pasv_xfer(file1, server, [file2])$

                            Transfers a file between two remote servers. Arguments are:

                            file1
                                The file to transfer from the server represented by the
                                Net::FTP object.

                            server
                                Destination server.

                            file2
                                New name of the file on the destination server. If omitted, the
                                original name is used.

pasv_xfer_unique

                            $ftp->pasv_xfer_unique(file1, server[, file2])$

                            Like pasv_xfer, but stores the file on the remote server with a new
                            (unique) name.

port $ftp->port([port])$

                            Sends a PORT command telling the server to use port *port*. With
                            no argument, a socket is created, and its information is sent.

put $ftp->put(local[, remote])$

                            Puts a file onto the server. Arguments are:

                            local
                                The name of the file to transfer from the local system, or a
                                filehandle.

                            remote
                                The new filename on the remote system. If omitted, the same
                                filename is used. If *local* is a filehandle, the remote filename
                                must be specified.

put_unique	$ftp->put_unique(*local*[, *remote*])

Puts a file with a unique name onto the server. Arguments are:

local
> The name of the file to transfer from the local system, or a filehandle.

remote
> The new filename on the remote system. If a file exists by that name, a new unique filename is created.

pwd	$ftp->pwd( )

Returns the current directory path.

quit	$ftp->quit( )

Closes the connection.

quot	$ftp->quot(*cmd*[, *args*])

Sends a literal FTP protocol command to the server and waits for a response. Returns the most significant digit of the response code.

rename	$ftp->rename(*file1*, *file2*)

Renames a file on the server. Arguments are:

file1
> The old name of the file

file2
> The new name of the file

retr	$ftp->retr(*file*)

Retrieves file *file* from the remote server. If the user calls either pasv or port, returns true or false. Otherwise, returns a reference to a Net::FTP::dataconn object.

rmdir	$ftp->rmdir(*dir*)

Removes directory *dir*.

size	$ftp->size(*file*)

Returns the size of file *file* in bytes.

stor	`$ftp->stor(file)`
	Tells the server to store a new file under the name *file*. If the user calls either pasv or port, returns true or false. Otherwise, returns a reference to a Net::FTP::dataconn object.
stou	`$ftp->stou(file)`
	Like stor, but stores file on the remote server with a unique name, *file*. If the user calls either pasv or port, returns true or false. Otherwise, returns a reference to a Net::FTP::dataconn object.
supported	`$ftp->supported(cmd)`
	Returns true if the server supports the command *cmd*.
type	`$ftp->type(type[, args])`
	Changes the type of data transfer. Possible types are ascii, ebcdic, byte, and binary. The value of *args* depends on the type.
unique_name	`$ftp->unique_name( )`
	Returns the name of the last file stored with a unique name.

FTP Configuration with Net::Netrc

Unix-based FTP clients use a file called *.netrc*, which you can configure to automate FTP access to sites you frequently visit. With a properly defined *.netrc* file, you can simply execute the FTP command to a favorite FTP host and be automatically logged in to the FTP server. Your *.netrc* file contains one line for each connection you want to make. The following tokens can be specified for each entry:

machine *name*
> Specifies a remote machine to which you want to autologin:
>
>   machine remotehost.com
>
> Instead of machine *name*, you can specify the single word default to match any machine name. This is usually used for anonymous logins to machines not listed in *.netrc*.

login *name*
> If present, identifies the user who logs in to the remote machine, in which *name* is the login name.

password *passwd*

> If present, gives the password for the user. The autologin process uses the specified password if the remote server requires one.

account *acctpw*

> If present, gives an additional password for the user. The autologin process uses this password if the remote server requires one.

macdef *name*

> If present, defines a macro with the specified name. Net::Netrc simply parses this field, to maintain compatibility with FTP.

Here's an example of a typical *.netrc* entry:

```
machine remotehost.com login username password userpasswd
```

Entering your username and password for remote sites in unencrypted form has serious security implications. Many sites consider *.netrc* files a violation of security policy and do not allow them. In addition, most FTP clients require that the *.netrc* file be owned by you and readable by only you, with permissions set to 0400 or 0600. If the permissions aren't correctly set, the autologin process aborts. Net::Netrc follows this security convention—if the permissions and ownership are not correct, the *.netrc* file isn't read, and a warning message is issued.

Net::Netrc implements a simple interface to the *.netrc* file, telling you which hosts you can automatically connect to. It doesn't actually connect to any remote hosts; it's simply used to query your configuration file and return the value of the tokens.

The following methods are supplied by Net::Netrc.

---

lookup   `$machine = Net::Netrc->lookup(host[, login])`

Constructor. Looks up and returns a reference to the entry for the specified host machine *host*. Without the optional *login* argument, lookup returns the first entry in the *.netrc* file for the machine.

If there is no matching entry, lookup returns a reference to the default entry.

---

account   `$machine->account`

Returns account information specified by the *.netrc* account entry, if there is any.

---

login   `$machine->login`

Returns the username (login ID) specified by the *.netrc* login token.

lpa   (@*login_pass_account*) = $*machine*->lpa

Returns a list of login, password, and account information specified by the *.netrc* tokens.

password $*machine*->password

Returns the password specified by the *.netrc* password token.

19

Lightweight Directory Access with Net::LDAP

LDAP was designed as a client/server protocol to provide quick and simple access to entries that live in a directory. Initially, LDAP was designed to provide a better interface to X.500 directory services, but its ease of implementation and IETF-based change control means that LDAP has carved its own niche as a directory service.

What is a directory service? In short, the directory is where you store an entry. Each entry implements information about an object. Entries have attributes with a type and at least one value. These attributes have a strict syntax that determines the types of values allowed for the attributes. Such attribute syntaxes include strings, JPEG photographs, and URLs.

If you've ever tried to solve a complex problem in a heterogenous computing environment, such as syncing user accounts between different computing platforms, managing a company-wide address book, or building a public-key infrastructure, you might be interested in what LDAP has to offer.

While the IETF governs changes to the LDAP spec, you are not limited to a single source for the availability of an LDAP server. Companies such as iPlanet, Novell, and Microsoft sell commercial LDAP implementations, and you'll also find a good, free LDAP implemenation in OpenLDAP (*http://www.openldap.org*).

Net::LDAP implements the LDAP API for Perl programs. You can use Net::LDAP to search or modify the contents of your LDAP directory. In other words, Net::LDAP does everything that you need it to.

This chapter covers Net::LDAP and how to operate on data in an LDAP directory, but it is not an LDAP tutorial. If you're unfamiliar with LDAP, it is strongly encouraged that you refer to your LDAP server documentation before attempting to make any changes to your directory.

How Data Is Stored in LDAP

LDAP stores data in a structure as described in RFC 1617, which also offers guidelines as to how your naming style might look. While there are many ways to implement a data hierarchy in LADP, you can implement your directory structure so that all entries live under a single root that represents your organization. For example, you can import all your Unix account data for *your.domain* into a directory server with the following:

```
object: your.domain
Organizational Unit: People
Type for login name: uid
```

Your Unix account information would be stored in LDAP like so:

```
uid=youruser,ou=People,o=your.domain
```

At the simplest level, data as imported into LDAP by way of the LDAP Directory Interchange Format (LDIF). LDIF is a standard data format that specifies all the information about a record that you will insert into the directory. Take, for instance, a Unix account that lives in */etc/passwd*:

```
nvp:-password-:1000:1000:Nathan V. Patwardhan:/home/nvp:/usr/bin/bash
```

When you break the password entry down, the following fields exist:

```
login          nvp
password       -password-
uid            1000
gid            1000
gecos          Nathan V. Patwardhan
home directory /users/nvp
shell          /usr/bin/bash
```

The Unix */etc/passwd* entries correspond to entries that you've created in LDAP, with the following naming differences:

```
UNIX           LDAP equivalent
login          uid
password       userPassword
uid            uidNumber
gid            gidNumber
gecos          cn, gecos
home directory homeDirectory
shell          loginShell
```

Every LDIF begins with a DN, or distinguished name, which describes where the entry will live in the directory. Without the distinguished name, the LDIF is invalid. Unix accounts might live under ou=People, while addressbook entries might live under ou=Addresses. The LDIF also contains all of the attributes for a given entry and their corresponding values. For the Unix password entry shown above, the LDIF would look like:

```
dn: uid=nvp,ou=People,o=your.domain
uid: nvp
cn: Nathan Patwardhan
```

```
givenname: Nathan
sn: Patwardhan
objectClass: person
objectClass: organizationalPerson
objectClass: account
objectClass: shadowAccount
objectClass: top
userPassword:    {crypt}/-password-
loginShell:      /usr/bin/bash
uidNumber:       1000
gidNumber:       1000
homeDirectory:   /users/nvp
```

Net::LDAP can output an LDIF file for the data that you give it (from which you can use a tool such as *ldapadd* to add it to the directory) or add the record to the directory.

Searching an LDAP Directory with Net::LDAP

One of the most common actions you'll perform against LDAP is searching. If you're using LDAP as a repository for your mail aliases, you'll search the directory each time mail is sent to a given address. If you're using LDAP as a repository for user accounts, you'll search the directory every time a user logs into your system, or when a user performs a task on the system that requires information that resides only in LDAP.

Under LDAP, searching consists of three parts:

1. Binding to a directory server by name (or by other credentials, such as Kerberos tokens) and port. You can provide a login and password for the authentication or bind anonymously if you have permissions to search or write a part of the directory.

2. Passing your search request to the directory server.

3. Unbinding from the directory server, thus closing the connection.

Let's say that you want to find a user called nvp in the directory server that's living on *ldap.your.server*. With Net::LDAP, do the following:

```
use Net::LDAP;

my $lsvr = 'ldap.your.domain';
my $ldap = Net::LDAP->new($lsvr)
    or die "error connecting to $lsvr: $@";

$ldap->bind;   # Bind anonymously, that is, no login and pass

my $results = $ldap->search (  # Perform a search for 'nvp'
    filter => "(&(uid=nvp) (o=your.domain))"
    );

if($results->code) {
    die "received LDAP error: @{[$results->error]}";
```

```
}

foreach my $entry ($results->all_entries) {
    $entry->dump;
}

$ldap->unbind;    # Unbind and close connection
```

Adding an Entry to the Directory with Net::LDAP

Now that you've searched the directory with Net::LDAP, let's add an item. In the previous example, you bound to the directory anonymously, but when writing changes to the directory (that is, adding or deleting entries), you'll probably have to bind as an administrator or another user delegated with similar privileges. In this example, we'll use "Directory Manager" as the directory administrator.

Adding to a directory with Net::LDAP is a two-phase process:

1. Bind to the directory as a user who has privileges to write to the directory. In this instance, we'll use "Directory Manager".

2. Use Net::LDAP::add( ) to add the entry. add( ) takes the parts of the record that you will add to the directory as arguments.

This example, based on the following LDIF, uses add( ) to add an account for 'nvp' to the directory:

```
dn: uid=nvp,ou=People,o=your.domain
uid: nvp
cn: Nathan Patwardhan
givenname: Nathan
sn: Patwardhan
objectClass: person
objectClass: organizationalPerson
objectClass: account
objectClass: shadowAccount
objectClass: top
userPassword: {crypt}/-password-
loginShell: /usr/bin/bash
uidNumber: 1000
gidNumber: 1000
homeDirectory: /users/nvp
```

Here's the code:

```
my $admin = q[cn=Directory Manager];
my $ad_pw = q[adminpass];
my $lsvr  = q[ldap.my.domain];
my $org   = q[o=my.domain];
my $o_ou  = q[ou=People];
my $o_act = q[uid=nvp];

my $ldap = Net::LDAP->new($lsvr);

# Bind to a directory with DN and password
```

```
$ldap->bind($admin, password => $ad_pw);

my $l_rec = qq[$o_act, $o_ou, $org];
$result = $ldap->add($l_rec,
                attr => [ 'cn'   => ['Nathan Patwardhan'],
                          'sn'   => 'Patwardhan',
                          'mail' => 'nvp@my.domain',
                          'objectclass' => ['top', 'person',
'organizationalPerson', 'inetOrgPerson'],
                          'gecos' => ['Nathan Patwardhan'],
                          'loginShell' => '/usr/bin/bash',
                          'uidNumber'  => 1000,
                          'gidNumber'  => 1000,
                          'shadowPass' => 'XXXXXXXXX'
                        ]
        );

if($result->code) {
    warn "failed to add entry: @{[$result->error]}";
}

$ldap->unbind;
```

Net::LDAP Methods

Net::LDAP implements the following methods:

new (*host* [, *%options*])
> new( ) creates a new Net::LDAP object and opens a connection to *host*. *%options* include:

port
> Port to connect to on the remote server.

timeout
> The maximum time that Net::LDAP will take to connect to a host. The default is 120 seconds.

debug
> Shows details of the conversion between Net::LDAP and the directory server.

async
> Performs asynchronous entry retrieval so that search results are returned to the client as they are identified:
>
> ```
> $ldap = Net::LDAP->new('ldap.my.domain', async => 1);
> ```

onerror
> If set to true, and if async is also true, then Net::LDAP will check for errors on all methods. If an error exists in the resulting data, then one of the following actions will be taken: die( ), warn( ), undef.

CODEREF

> Calls the given coderef in a scalar context with the result message as the argument.

version( )

> Sets the version of the LDAP protocol to use. Values are LDAPv2 (default) and LDAPv3.

bind(*dn* [, *%options*])

> Binds to the server that's contained in the connection handle. *dn* is the DN to bind as. You'll end up binding anonymously if you call bind( ) without any arguments.
>
> As for *%options*, you should give no more than one of the following:

noauth

> Do not attempt to authenticate at all.

anonymous

> Binds without any password; the value passed with this option is ignored. This is the default if no arguments are given.

password

> Binds with the given password.

sasl

> Binds using an SASL mechanism. The argument given should be a subclass of Authen::SASL.
>
> ```
> my $dn = 'cn=Directory Manager';
> my $password = 'adminpass';
> my $sasl = Authn::SASL::stuff::here;
> $ldap->bind($dn, sasl => $sasl, version => 3);
> ```

unbind

> Does not take any parameters and unbinds the connection from the server. You will probably need to call bind( ) again if you wish to reconnect to the LDAP server.
>
> ```
> $ldap->unbind;
> ```

add (*dn* [, *%options*])

> Adds an entry to the directory. *dn* can be either a Net::LDAP::Entry object or a string that represents the DN.

attrs

> A reference to a list of attribute/value pairs. These attribute/value pairs correspond to the attributes of an entry in the directory. Each attribute can have multiple values. attrs is not used if *dn* is an existing Net::LDAP::Entry object. For example:
>
> ```
> $ldap->add($dn,
>         attrs => [
>             'uid'       => 'nvp',
>             'cn'        => ['Nathan Patwardhan', 'Enrico
> Pallazo'],
>             'gecos'     => 'Nathan Patwardhan',
>             'loginShell' => '/usr/bin/bash'
> ```

```
                         ]
              );
```
delete(*dn* [, *%options*])

> Deletes *dn* from the server. *dn* may be a string that represents the DN or a Net::LDAP::Entry object. For example:
>
> ```
> my $dn = q[uid=nvp,ou=People,o=my.domain];
> $ldap->delete($dn);
> ```

moddn(*dn*, *%options*)

> Modifies *dn*. *dn* may be a string or a Net::LDAP::Entry object.
>
> newrdn
>
> > A new RDN to assign to *dn*.
>
> deleteoldrdn
>
> > True if the existing RDN will be deleted.
>
> newsuperior
>
> > If given, this value should be the *dn* of the new superior for *dn*.
> >
> > ```
> > $ldap->moddn($dn, newrdn => 'cn=Nate Patwardhan');
> > ```

modify(*dn*, *%options*)

> Modifies the contents of *dn*. *dn* may be a string or a Net::LDAP::Entry object.
>
> add
>
> > Should be a reference to a HASH. HASH is comprised of the attributes to add, and the values may be a string or a reference to a list of values.
>
> delete
>
> > A reference to ARRAY that contains attributes to delete, or a reference to a HASH, if only specific values should be deleted. If the values for any attribute in HASH are references to an empty ARRAY, then all instances of the attribute will be deleted.
>
> replace
>
> > Works like add, but will replace any of the existing attributes.
>
> changes
>
> > An alternative to add, delete, and replace, in which the whole operation can be given in a single argument. The argument should be a reference to an ARRAY.
> >
> > Values in the ARRAY are used in pairs; the first is the operation add, delete, or replace, and the second is a reference to an ARRAY of attribute values.
> >
> > The attribute value list is also used in pairs. The first value in each pair is the attribute name, and the second is a reference to a list of values.
> >
> > Use this form if you want to control the order in which the operations will be performed:
> >
> > ```
> > my $dn = q[uid=nvp,ou=People,o=my.domain];
> >
> > $ldap->modify($dn, add => { sn => 'Patwardhan' });
> > $ldap->modify($dn, delete => { 'weight' => '175' });
> > $ldap->modify($dn, replace => { 'loginShell' => '/usr/bin/tcsh' });
> > ```

```
$ldap->modify( $dn,
    changes => [
        add     => [ sn => 'Patwardhan' ],
        delete  => [ faxNumber => []],
        delete  => [ weight => ['175']],
        replace => [ loginShell => '/usr/bin/tcsh']
    ]
);
```

search(@*options*)

Requests that an LDAP server perform a search and can read attributes from a single entry, entries immediately below a particular entry, or a whole subtree of entries. The result is an object of the class Net::LDAP::Search.

base

The DN that is the base object entry relative to the search that will be performed.

scope

By default, the search is performed on the whole tree below the specified base object. This may be changed by specifying a scope parameter with one of the following values:

base

Searches only the base object.

one

Searches the entries immediately below the base object.

sub

Searches the whole tree below the base object. This is the default.

deref

By default, aliases are dereferenced to locate the base object for the search, but not when searching subordinates of the base object. This may be changed by specifying a deref parameter with one of the following values:

never

Do not dereference aliases in searching or in locating the base object of the search.

search

Dereferences aliases in subordinates of the base object in searching, but not in locating the base object of the search.

find

Dereferences aliases in locating the base object of the search, but not when searching subordinates of the base object. This is the default.

always

Dereferences aliases both in searching and in locating the base object of the search.

sizelimit
:   Restricts the maximum number of entries to be returned as a result of the search. A value of 0, which is the default, means that no restriction is requested. Servers may enforce a maximum number of entries to return.

timelimit
:   Restricts the maximum time (in seconds) allowed for a search. A value of 0, which is the default, means that no timelimit will be requested.

typesonly
:   Indicates whether search results should contain both attribute types and values, or just attribute types. Setting this parameter to true causes only attribute types (no values) to be returned. Setting this field to false causes both attribute types and values to be returned. This is the default.

filter
:   Defines the conditions an entry in the directory must meet in order for it to be returned by the search. This may be a string or a *Net* object. See the Net::LDAP::Filter manpage for a further description of the filter format.

attrs
:   A reference to a list of attributes to be returned for each entry that matches the search filter.

    If not specified, then the server will return the attributes that are specified as accessible by default given your bind credentials.

    Certain additional attributes, such as createtimestamp, and other operational attributes may also be available for the asking:

    ```
    $ldap->search( ... , attrs => ['createtimestamp'] , ... );
    ```

    To retrieve the default attributes and additional ones, use "*":

    ```
    my $base_dn = q[o=my.domain];
    $mesg = $ldap->search(
      base   => $base_dn,
      scope  => 'sub',
      filter => '(|(objectclass=rfc822mailgroup)(sn=Patwardhan))'
    );

    Net::LDAP::LDIF->new(\*STDOUT,"w")->write($mesg->entries);
    ```

abandon(*id* [, *%options*])
:   Requires that a server abandons a request. *id* may be passed first, or as part of *%options*, and may be a number or a Net::LDAP::Message object that's returned from a previous method call.

    ```
    $mesg = $ldap->search(@search_args);
    $ldap->abandon($mesg); # This could be written as $mesg->abandon
    ```

compare(*dn*, *%options*)
:   Performs a comparison on the server. *dn* is the DN on which the comparison will be performed. *dn* may be a string or Net::LDAP::Entry object.

attr
> The name of the attribute to compare.

value
> The value to compare with.
>
> ```
> my $dn = q[uid=nvp,ou=People,o=my.domain];
> $ldap->compare($dn,
>     attr  => 'cn',
>     value => 'Nathan Patwardhan'
> );
> ```

start_tls([%options])
> Converts the connection to use Transport Layer Security (TLS), which provides an encrypted connection, if available. Bear in mind that TLS is supported only under LDAPv3. %options is a set of key/value pairs that describe how to configure the security of the connection:

verify
> Indicates how to verify the server's certificate. Its values can be none (the server may provide a certificate, but it will not be checked—this may mean you are connected to the wrong server), optional (verifies if the server offers a certificate), or require (the server must provide a certificate, and it must be valid). If you set verify to optional or require, you must also set either cafile or capath. The most secure option is require.

sslversion
> Defines the version of the SSL/TLS protocol to use. Defaults to tlsv1; other possible values are sslv2, sslv3, and sslv2/3.

ciphers
> Specifies which subset of cipher suites is permissible for this connection, using the standard OpenSSL string format. The default value for ciphers is ALL, which permits all ciphers, even those that don't encrypt!

clientcert
clientkey
> If you want to use the client to offer a certificate to the server for SSL authentication (which is not the same as for the LDAP Bind operation), then set clientcert to the user's certificate file and clientkey to the user's private key file. These files must be in PEM format.

capath
cafile
> When verifying the server's certificate, set either capath to the pathname of the directory containing CA certificates or cafile to the filename containing the certificate of the CA who signed the server's certificate. These certificates must all be in PEM format.
>
> The directory in capath must contain certificates named using the hash value of themselves. To generate these names, use OpenSSL in Unix, as follows:
>
> ```
> ln -s cacert.pem 'openssl x509 -hash -noout < cacert.pem'.0
> ```
>
> (assuming that the certificate of the CA is in cacert.pem).

cipher
> Returns the cipher mode being used by the connection in the string format used by OpenSSL.

certificate
> Returns an X509_Certificate object containing the server's certificate. For example, to get the subject name (in a peculiar OpenSSL-specific format, different from RFC 1779 and RFC 2253) from the server's certificate, do the following:
>
> ```
> print "Subject DN: " . $ldaps->certificate->subject_name . "\n";
> ```

version
> Returns the version of the LDAP protocol that is being used.

VIII

LWP

20

The LWP Library

The library for web access in Perl (LWP), is a bundle of modules that provide a consistent, object-oriented approach to creating web applications. The library, downloaded as the single file named *libwww-perl*, contains the following classes:

File
> Parses directory listings.

Font
> Handles Adobe Font Metrics.

HTML
> Parses HTML files and converts them to printable or other forms.

HTTP
> Provides client requests, server responses, and protocol implementation.

LWP
> The core of all web client programs. It creates network connections and manages the communication and transactions between client and server.

URI
> Creates, parses, and translates URLs.

WWW
> Implements standards used for robots (automatic client programs).

Each module in LWP provides different building blocks that allow you to do basically anything you can do in a Web browser—from connection, to request, to response and returned data. These parts are then encapsulated by an object to give a standard interface to every web program you write.

This chapter covers all the modules in the LWP distribution. While some modules are more useful than others, everything you need to know about LWP is included here. To begin with, the following section gives an overview of how LWP works to create a web client.

LWP Overview

Any web transaction requires an application that can establish a TCP/IP network connection and send and receive messages using the appropriate protocol (usually HTTP). TCP/IP connections are established using sockets, and messages are exchanged via socket filehandles. (See Chapter 15 for information on how to manually create socket applications.) LWP provides an object for this application with LWP::UserAgent for clients; HTTP::Daemon provides a server object. The UserAgent object acts as the browser: it connects to a server, sends requests, receives responses, and manages the received data. This is how you create a User-Agent object:

```
use LWP::UserAgent;
$ua = LWP::UserAgent->new( );
```

The UserAgent now needs to send a message to a server requesting a Universal Resource Locator (URL) using the request method. request forms an HTTP request from the object given as its argument. This request object is created by HTTP::Request.

An HTTP request message contains three elements. The first line of a message always contains an HTTP command called a *method*; a Universal Resource Identifier (URI), which identifies the file or resource the client is querying; and the HTTP version number. The following lines of a client request contain header information, which provides information about the client and any data it is sending the server. The third part of a client request is the entity body, which is data sent to the server (for the POST method). The following is a sample HTTP request:

```
GET /index.html HTTP/1.0
User-Agent: Mozilla/1.1N (Macintosh; I; 68K)
Accept: */*
Accept: image/gif
Accept: image/jpeg
```

LWP::UserAgent->request forms this message from an HTTP::Request object. A request object requires a method for the first argument. The GET method asks for a file, while the POST method supplies information such as form data to a server application. There are other methods, but these two are most commonly used.

The second argument is the URL for the request. The URL must contain the server name because this is how the UserAgent knows where to connect. The URL argument can be represented as a string or as a URI::URL object, which allows more complex URLs to be formed and managed. Optional parameters for an HTTP::Request include your own headers, in the form of an HTTP::Headers object, and any POST data for the message. The following example creates a request object:

```
use HTTP::Request;

$req = HTTP::Request->new(GET, $url, $hdrs);
```

The URL object is created like this:

```
use URI::URL;

$url = URI::URL->new('www.ora.com/index.html');
```

And a header object can be created like this:

```
use HTTP::Headers;

$hdrs = HTTP::Headers->new(Accept => 'text/plain',
                           User-Agent => 'MegaBrowser/1.0');
```

Then you can put them all together to make a request:

```
use LWP::UserAgent;  # This will cover all of them!

$hdrs = HTTP::Headers->new(Accept => 'text/plain',
                           User-Agent => 'MegaBrowser/1.0');

$url = URI::URL->new('www.ora.com/index.html');
$req = HTTP::Request->new(GET, $url, $hdrs);
$ua = LWP::UserAgent->new();
$resp = $ua->request($req);
if ($resp->is_success) {
        print $resp->content;}
else {
        print $resp->message;}
```

Once the request has been made by the user agent, the response from the server is returned as another object, described by HTTP::Response. This object contains the status code of the request, returned headers, and the content you requested, if successful. In the example, is_success checks to see if the request was fulfilled without problems, thus outputting the content. If unsuccessful, a message describing the server's response code is printed.

There are other modules and classes that create useful objects for web clients in LWP, but the above examples show the most basic ones. For server applications, many of the objects used above become pieces of a server transaction, which you either create yourself (such as response objects) or receive from a client (such as request objects).

Additional functionality for both client and server applications is provided by the HTML module. This module provides many classes for both the creation and interpretation of HTML documents.

The rest of this chapter provides information for the LWP, HTTP, HTML, and URI modules.

The LWP Modules

The LWP modules provide the core of functionality for web programming in Perl. It contains the foundations for networking applications, protocol implementations, media type definitions, and debugging ability.

The modules LWP::Simple and LWP::UserAgent define client applications that implement network connections, send requests, and receive response data from servers. LWP::RobotUA is another client application used to build automated web searchers following a specified set of guidelines.

LWP::UserAgent is the primary module used in applications built with LWP. With it, you can build your own robust web client. It is also the base class for the Simple and RobotUA modules. These two modules provide a specialized set of functions for creating clients.

Additional LWP modules provide the building blocks required for web communications, but you often don't need to use them directly in your applications. LWP::Protocol implements the actual socket connections with the appropriate protocol. The most common protocol is HTTP, but mail protocols (such as SMTP), FTP for file transfers, and others can be used across networks.

LWP::MediaTypes implements the MIME definitions for media type identification and mapping to file extensions. The LWP::Debug module provides functions to help you debug your LWP applications.

The following sections describe the RobotUA, Simple, and UserAgent modules of LWP.

LWP::RobotUA Sections

The Robot User Agent (LWP::RobotUA) is a subclass of LWP::UserAgent and is used to create robot client applications. A robot application requests resources in an automated fashion. Robots perform such activities as searching, mirroring, and surveying. Some robots collect statistics, while others wander the Web and summarize their findings for a search engine.

The LWP::RobotUA module defines methods to help program robot applications and observes the Robot Exclusion Standards, which web server administrators can define on their web site to keep robots away from certain (or all) areas of the site.

The constructor for an LWP::RobotUA object looks like this:

```
$rob = LWP::RobotUA->new(agent_name, email, [$rules]);
```

The first parameter, *agent_name*, is the user agent identifier used for the value of the User-Agent header in the request. The second parameter is the email address of the person using the robot, and the optional third parameter is a reference to a WWW::RobotRules object, which is used to store the robot rules for a server. If you omit the third parameter, the LWP::RobotUA module requests the *robots.txt* file from every server it contacts and generates its own WWW::RobotRules object.

Since LWP::RobotUA is a subclass of LWP::UserAgent, the LWP::UserAgent methods are used to perform the basic client activities. The following methods are defined by LWP::RobotUA for robot-related functionality.

as_string	`$rob->as_string( )`
	Returns a human-readable string that describes the robot's status.
delay	`$rob->delay ([time])`
	Sets or returns the specified *time* (in minutes) to wait between requests. The default value is 1.
host_wait	`$rob->host_wait(netloc)`
	Returns the number of seconds the robot must wait before it can request another resource from the server identified by *netloc*.
no_visits	`$rob->no_visits(netloc)`
	Returns the number of visits to a given server. *netloc* is of the form *user:password@host:port*. The user, password, and port are optional.
rules	`$rob->rules([$rules])`
	Sets or returns the WWW:RobotRules object *$rules*, which is used when determining if the module is allowed access to a particular resource.
use_sleep	`$rob->use_sleep ([boolean])`
	Determines whether the user agent should sleep( ) if requests arrive too fast. The default is true. If set to false, an internal SERVICE_UNAVAILABLE response is generated, with a Retry-After header indicating when it is permissable to send another request to this server. With no arguments, returns the current value of this flag.

LWP::Simple

LWP::Simple provides an easy-to-use interface for creating a web client, although it is only capable of performing basic retrieving functions. An object constructor is not used for this class; it defines functions for retrieving information from a specified URL and interpreting the status codes from the requests.

This module isn't named Simple for nothing. The following shows how to use it to get a web page and save it to a file:

```
use LWP::Simple;

$homepage = 'oreilly_com.html';
$status = getstore('http:www.oreilly.com/', $homepage);
print("hooray") if is_success($status);
```

The retrieving functions get and head return the URL's contents and header contents, respectively. The other retrieving functions return the HTTP status code of the request. The status codes are returned as the constants from the HTTP::Status module, which is also where the is_success and is_failure methods are obtained. See the section "HTTP::Status" for a listing of the response codes.

The user agent identifier produced by LWP::Simple is LWP::Simple/*n.nn*, in which *n.nn* is the version number of LWP being used.

The following are the functions exported by LWP::Simple.

---

get   get (*url*)

Returns the contents of the specified *url*. Upon failure, get returns undef. Other than returning undef, there is no way of accessing the HTTP status code or headers returned by the server.

---

getprint   getprint (*url*)

Prints the contents of *url* on standard output and returns the HTTP status code given by the server.

---

getstore   getstore (*url*, *file*)

Stores the contents of the specified *url* into *file* and returns the HTTP status code given by the server.

---

head   head (*url*)

Returns header information about the specified *url* in the form of: ($content_type, $document_length, $modified_time, $expires, $server). Upon failure, head returns an empty list.

---

is_error   is_error (*code*)

Given a status *code* from getprint, getstore, or mirror, returns true if the request was not successful.

---

is_success	is_success (*code*)
	Given a status *code* from getprint, getstore, or mirror, returns true if the request was successful.

mirror	mirror (*url*, *file*)
	Copies the contents of the specified *url* into *file*, when the modification time or length of the online version is different from that of the named file.

LWP::UserAgent

Requests over the network are performed with LWP::UserAgent objects. To create an LWP::UserAgent object, use:

```
$ua = LWP::UserAgent->new( );
```

You give the object a request, which it uses to contact the server, and the information you requested is returned. The most often used method in this module is request, which contacts a server and returns the result of your query. Other methods in this module change the way request behaves. You can change the timeout value, customize the value of the User-Agent header, or use a proxy server.

The following methods are supplied by LWP::UserAgent.

new	$ua->new(%options)
	Constructs a new LWP::UserAgent object and returns a reference to it. Key/value arguments may be provided to set up the initial state of the user agent. new accepts several options that correspond to the following attribute methods:

Key	Default
agent	"libwww-perl/#.##"
from	undef
timeout	180
use_eval	1
parse_head	1
max_size	undef
cookie_jar	undef
conn_cache	undef
protocols_allowed	undef
protocols_forbidden	undef
requests_redirectable	["GET", "HEAD"]

LWP

The options are:

env_proxy
> If set to true, proxy settings are read from environment variables.

keep_alive
> A number that will be passed on as the total_capacity for the connection. A LWP::ConnCache is set up (see the conn_cache method), and the HTTP/1.1 protocol module is enabled.

---

agent $ua->agent([string])

When invoked with no arguments, this method returns the current value of the identifier used in the User-Agent HTTP header. If invoked with an argument, the User-Agent header will use string as its identifier in the future.

_agent $ua->_agent( )

Returns the default agent identifier. This is a string of the form "libwww-perl/#.##", in which #.## is substituted with the version number of this library.

---

clone $ua->clone( )

Returns a copy of the LWP::UserAgent object.

---

conn_cache $ua->conn_cache([$cache_object])

Defines the LWP::ConnCache object to use. With no arguments, returns the current LWP::ConnCache object.

---

cookie_jar $ua->cookie_jar([$cjar])

Specifies the "cookie jar" object to use with the UserAgent object, or returns it if invoked with no argument. $cjar is a reference to an HTTP::Cookies object that contains client cookie data. See the HTTP::Cookies section for more information.

---

credentials $ua->credentials(netloc, realm, uname, pass)

Uses the given username and password for authentication at the given network location and realm. This method sets the parameters for either the WWW-Authenticate or Proxy-Authenticate headers in a request. The get_basic_credentials method is called by request to retrieve the username and passwords, if they exist. The arguments are:

---

netloc
> The network location (usually a URL string) to which the username and password apply.

realm
> The name of the server-defined range of URLs that this data applies to.

uname
> The username for authentication.

pass
> The password for authentication. By default, the password will be transmitted with MIME base-64 encoding.

---

env_proxy
    $ua->env_proxy( )

Defines a scheme/proxy URL mapping by looking at environment variables. For example, to define the HTTP proxy, one would define the HTTP_PROXY environment variable with the proxy's URL. To define a domain to avoid the proxy, one would define the NO_PROXY environment variable with the domain that doesn't need a proxy.

---

from
    $ua->from([*email*])

When invoked with no arguments, this method returns the current value of the email address used in the From header. If invoked with an argument, the From header will use that email address in the future. (The From header tells the web server the email address of the person running the client software.)

---

get
    $ua->get($url, [*Header* => *Value*])

Shortcut for $ua->request(HTTP::Request::Common::GET($url, Header => Value,...)).

---

get_basic_credentials

    $ua->get_basic_credentials(*realm, url*)

Returns the list containing the username and password for the given *realm* and *url* when authentication is required by the server. This function is usually called internally by request. This method becomes useful when creating a subclass of LWP::UserAgent with its own version of get_basic_credentials. From there, you can rewrite get_basic_credentials to do more flexible things, such as asking the user for the account information, or referring to authentication information in a file. All you need to do is return a list in which the first element is a username and the second element is a password.

| **head** | $ua->head($url, [Header => Value])

Shortcut for $ua->request(HTTP::Request::Common::HEAD($url, Header => Value,...)). |

is_protocol_supported

$ua->is_protocol_supported(proto)

Given a scheme, this method returns a true or false (nonzero or zero) value. A true value means that LWP knows how to handle a URL with the specified protocol. If it returns a false value, LWP does not know how to handle the URL.

| **max_size** | $ua->max_size([size])

Sets or returns the maximum size (in bytes) for response content. The default is undef, which means that there is no limit. If the returned content is partial because the size limit was exceeded, then an X-Content-Range header will be added to the response. |

| **mirror** | $ua->mirror(url, file)

Given a URL and file path, this method copies the contents of url into the file when the length or modification date headers are different from any previous retrieval. If the file does not exist, it is created. This method returns an HTTP::Response object, in which the response code indicates what happened. |

| **no_proxy** | $ua->no_proxy(domains)

Does not use a proxy server for the specified domains. |

| **parse_head** | $ua->parse_head([boolean])

Sets or returns a true or false value indicating whether response headers from the <head> sections of HTML documents are initialized. The default is true. |

| **post** | $ua->post($url, \%formref, [Header => Value])

Shortcut for $ua->request(HTTP::Request::Common::POST($url, \%formref, Header => Value,...)). The form reference is optional and can be either a hashref or an arrayref. |

protocols_allowed

$ua->protocols_allowed([\@protocols])

Assigns the list of protocols that $ua->request and $ua->simple_ request will exclusively allow. With no arguments, returns a list of the protocols currently allowed. Assigning to a value of undef deletes the list.

protocols_forbidden

$ua->protocols_forbidden([\@protocols])

Assigns the list of procotols that $ua->request and $ua->simple_ request will not allow. With no arguments, returns a list of the protocols currently prohibited. Assigning to a value of undef deletes the list.

proxy

$ua->proxy(prot, proxy_url)

Defines a URL (proxy_url) to use with the specified protocols, prot. The first parameter can be a reference to a list of protocol names or a scalar that contains a single protocol. The second argument defines a proxy URL to use with the protocol.

put

$ua->put($url, [Header => Value])

$ua-->gt;put($url, Header ==>gt; Value,...)

Shortcut for $ua->request(HTTP::Request::Common::PUT($url, Header => Value,...)).

redirect_ok

$ua->redirect_ok($this_request)

This method is called by request before it tries to follow a redirection to the request in $this_request. This should return a true value if this redirection is permissible.

request

$ua->request($request, [file | $sub, size])

Performs a request for the resource specified by $request, which is an HTTP::Request object. Returns the information received from the server as an HTTP::Response object. Normally, doing a $ua-> request($request) is enough. You can also specify a subroutine to process the data as it comes in or provide a filename in which to store the entity body of the response. The arguments are:

$request
An HTTP::Request object. The object must contain the method and URL of the site to be queried. This object must exist before request is called.

file

Name of the file in which to store the response's entity body. When this option is used on request, the entity body of the returned response object will be empty.

$sub

A reference to a subroutine that will process the data of the response. If you use the optional third argument, *size*, the subroutine will be called any time that number of bytes is received as response data. The subroutine should expect each chunk of the entity body data as a scalar in the first argument, an HTTP::Response object as the second argument, and an LWP::Protocol object as the third argument.

size

Optional argument specifying the number of bytes of the entity body received before the *sub* callback is called to process response data.

requests_redirectable

$*ua*->requests_redirectable([\@*requests*])

Assigns the list of request names that $ua->redirect_ok will allow to be redirected. With no arguments, returns the current list of request names. By default, GET and HEAD requests are allowed; to include POST requests, enter:

```
push @{ $ua->requests_redirectable }, 'POST';
```

timeout

$*ua*->timeout([*secs*])

When invoked with no arguments, timeout returns the timeout value of a request. By default, this value is three minutes. Therefore, if the client software doesn't hear back from the server within three minutes, it will stop the transaction and indicate that a timeout occurred in the HTTP response code. If invoked with an argument, the timeout value is redefined to be that value.

use_alarm

$*ua*->use_alarm([*boolean*])

Retrieves or defines the ability to use alarm for timeouts. By default, timeouts with alarm are enabled. If you plan on using alarm for your own purposes, or it isn't supported on your system, it is recommended that you disable alarm by calling this method with a value of 0.

The HTTP Modules

The HTTP modules implement an interface to the HTTP messaging protocol used in web transactions. Its most useful modules are HTTP::Request and HTTP::Response, which create objects for client requests and server responses. Other modules provide means for manipulating headers, interpreting server response codes, managing cookies, converting date formats, and creating basic server applications.

Client applications created with LWP::UserAgent use HTTP::Request objects to create and send requests to servers. The information returned from a server is saved as an HTTP::Response object. Both of these objects are subclasses of HTTP::Message, which provides general methods of creating and modifying HTTP messages. The header information included in HTTP messages can be represented by objects of the HTTP::Headers class.

HTTP::Status includes functions to classify response codes into the categories of informational, successful, redirection, error, client error, or server error. It also exports symbolic aliases of HTTP response codes; one could refer to the status code of 200 as RC_OK and refer to 404 as RC_NOT_FOUND.

The HTTP::Date module converts date strings from and to machine time. The HTTP::Daemon module can be used to create web server applications, utilizing the functionality of the rest of the LWP modules to communicate with clients.

HTTP::Request

This module summarizes a web client's request. For a simple GET request, you define an object with the GET method and assign a URL to apply it to. Basic headers would be filled in automatically by LWP. For a POST or PUT request, you might want to specify a custom HTTP::Headers object for the request, or use the contents of a file for an entity body. Since HTTP::Request inherits everything in HTTP::Message, you can use the header and entity body manipulation methods from HTTP::Message in HTTP::Request objects.

The constructor for HTTP::Request looks like this:

```
$req = http::Request->new (method, url, [$header, [content]]);
```

The method and URL values for the request are required parameters. The header and content arguments are not required, nor even necessary for all requests. The parameters are defined as follows:

method
> A string specifying the HTTP request method. GET, HEAD, and POST are the most commonly used. Other methods defined in the HTTP specification such as PUT and DELETE are not supported by most servers.

url
> The address and resource name of the information you are requesting. This argument may be either a string containing an absolute URL (the hostname is required), or a URI::URL object that stores all the information about the URL.

$header
> A reference to an HTTP::Headers object.

content
> A scalar that specifies the entity body of the request. If omitted, the entity body is empty.

The following methods can be used on HTTP::Request objects.

---

as_string

> `$req->as_string`
>
> Returns a text version of the request object as a string with \n placed after each line. Information about the object reference is also included in the first line. The returned string looks like this:
>
> ```
> -- HTTP::Request=HASH(0x68148) --
> PUT http:www.ora.com/example/hi.text
> Content-Length: 2
> Content-Type: text/plain
> hi
> -------------------
> ```

---

method

> `$req->method ([method])`
>
> Sets or retrieves the HTTP method for an HTTP::Request object. Without an argument, method returns the object's current method.

---

url

> `$req->url ([url])`
>
> Sets or retrieves the URL for the request object. Without an argument, this method retrieves the current URL for the object. *url* is a string containing the new URL to set for the request or a URI::URL object.

HTTP::Response

Responses from a web server are described by HTTP::Response objects. An HTTP response message contains a status line, headers, and any content data that was requested by the client (such as an HTML file). The status line is the minimum requirement for a response. It contains the version of HTTP that the server is running, a status code indicating the success, failure, or other condition the request received from the server, and a short message describing the status code.

If LWP has problems fulfilling your request, it internally generates an HTTP::Response object and fills in an appropriate response code. In the context of web client programming, you'll usually get an HTTP::Response object from LWP::UserAgent and LWP::RobotUA.

If you plan to write extensions to LWP or to a web server or proxy server, you might use HTTP::Response to generate your own responses.

The constructor for HTTP::Response looks like this:

```
$resp = HTTP::Response->new (rc, [msg, [header, [content]]]);
```

In its simplest form, an HTTP::Response object can contain just a response code. If you would like to specify a more detailed message than "OK" or "Not found," you can specify a text description of the response code as the second parameter. As a third parameter, you can pass a reference to an HTTP::Headers object to specify the response headers. Finally, you can also include an entity body in the fourth parameter as a scalar.

For client applications, it is unlikely that you will build your own response object with the constructor for this class. You receive a client object when you use the request method on an LWP::UserAgent object. For example:

```
$ua = LWP::UserAgent->new;
$req = HTTP::Request->new(GET, $url)
$resp = $ua->request($req);
```

The server's response is contained in the object $resp. When you have this object, you can use the HTTP::Response methods to get the information about the response. Since HTTP::Response is a subclass of HTTP::Message, you can also use methods from that class on response objects. See the section "HTTP::Message" for a description of its methods.

The following methods can be used on objects created by HTTP::Response.

---

as_string $resp->as_string( )

Returns a string version of the response with lines separated by \n. For example, this method would return a response string that looks like this:

```
-- HTTP::Response=HASH(0xc8548) --
RC: 200 (OK)
Message: all is fine

Content-Length: 2
Content-Type: text/plain

hi
------------------
```

---

base $resp->base( )

Returns the base URL of the response. If the response was hypertext, any links from the hypertext should be relative to the location returned by this method. LWP looks for the BASE tag in HTML and Content-Base/Content-Location HTTP headers for a base specification. If a base was not explicitly defined by the server, LWP uses the requesting URL as the base.

---

code	$resp->code ([code])

When invoked without any parameters, this method returns the object's response code. Sets the status code of the object when invoked with an argument.

current_age	$resp->current_age( )

Returns the number of seconds since the response was generated by the original server.

error_as_HTML	$resp->error_as_HTML( )

When is_error is true, this method returns an HTML explanation of what happened.

freshness_lifetime

$resp->freshness_lifetime( )

Returns the number of seconds until the response expires. If expiration was not specified by the server, LWP will make an informed guess based on the Last-Modified header of the response.

fresh_until	$resp->fresh_until( )

Returns the time when the response expires. The time is based on the number of seconds since January 1, 1970, UTC.

is_error	$resp->is_error( )

Returns true when the response code is 400 through 599. When an error occurs, you might want to use error_as_HTML to generate an HTML explanation of the error.

is_fresh	$resp->is_fresh( )

Returns true if the response has not yet expired.

is_info	$resp->is_info( )

Returns true when the response code is 100 through 199.

is_redirect	$resp->is_redirect( )

Returns true when the response code is 300 through 399.

is_success $resp->is_success()

Returns true when the response code is 200 through 299.

message $resp->message ([msg])

When invoked without any parameters, message returns the object's status code message (the short string describing the response code). When invoked with a scalar *msg* argument, this method defines the object's message.

status_line $resp->status_line()

Returns a string with the HTTP status code and message. If the message attribute is unspecified, the official message associated with code is used.

HTTP::Headers

This module deals with HTTP header definition and manipulation. You can use these methods on HTTP::Request and HTTP::Response objects to retrieve headers they contain, or to set new headers and values for new objects you are building.

The constructor for an HTTP::Headers object looks like this:

```
$h = HTTP::Headers->new([name => val],...);
```

This code creates a new headers object. You can set headers in the constructor by providing a header name and its value. Multiple *name=>val* pairs can be used to set multiple headers.

The following methods can be used by objects in the HTTP::Headers class. These methods can also be used on objects from HTTP::Request and HTTP::Response, since they inherit from HTTP::Headers. In fact, most header manipulation will occur on the request and response objects in LWP applications.

clone $h->clone()

Creates a copy of the current object, $h, and returns a reference to it.

header $h->header(*field* [=> $val],...)

When called with just an HTTP header as a parameter, this method returns the current value for the header. For example, $myobject->('content-type') would return the value for the object's Content-Type header. To define a new header value, invoke header with a hash of header=>value pairs, in which the value is a scalar or reference to an array. For example, to define the Content-Type header, you would do this:

```
$h->header('content-type' => 'text/plain');
```

init_header $h->init_header($field, $value)

Sets the specified header to the given value, but only if no previous value for that field is set. The header field name is not case-sensitive, and _ can be used as a replacement for -. The $value argument may be a scalar or a reference to a list of scalars. Previous values of the field are not removed.

push_header $h->push_header(field => val)

Adds a new header field and value to the object. Previous values of the field are not removed.

```
$h->push_header(Accept => 'image/jpeg');
```

remove_header $h->remove_header(field,...)

Removes the header specified in the parameter(s) and the header's associated value.

scan $h->scan($sub)

Invokes the subroutine referenced by $sub for each header field in the object. The subroutine is passed the name of the header and its value as a pair of arguments. For header fields with more than one value, the subroutine will be called once for each value.

The HTTP::Headers class allows you to use a number of convenience methods on header objects to set (or read) common field values. If you supply a value for an argument, that value will be set for the field. The previous value for the header is always returned. The following methods are available:

```
date
expires
if_modified_since
if_unmodified_since
last_modified
content_type
content_encoding
content_length
content_language
title
user_agent
server
from
referrer
www_authenticate
```

```
proxy_authenticate
authorization
proxy_authorization
authorization_basic
proxy_authorization_basic
```

HTTP::Status

This module provides methods to determine the type of a response code. It also exports a list of mnemonics that can be used by the programmer to refer to a status code.

The following methods are used on response objects:

is_info
> Returns true when the response code is 100–199.

is_success
> Returns true when the response code is 200–299.

is_redirect
> Returns true when the response code is 300–399.

is_client_error
> Returns true when the response code is 400–499.

is_server_error
> Returns true when the response code is 500–599.

is_error
> Returns true when the response code is 400–599. When an error occurs, you might want to use error_as_HTML to generate an HTML explanation of the error.

HTTP::Status exports the following constant functions to use as mnemonic substitutes for status codes. For example, you could do something like:

```
if ($rc = RC_OK) {....}
```

Here are the mnemonics, followed by the status codes they represent:

```
RC_CONTINUE (100)
RC_SWITCHING_PROTOCOLS (101)
RC_OK (200)
RC_CREATED (201)
RC_ACCEPTED (202)
RC_NON_AUTHORITATIVE_INFORMATION (203)
RC_NO_CONTENT (204)
RC_RESET_CONTENT (205)
RC_PARTIAL_CONTENT (206)
RC_MULTIPLE_CHOICES (300)
RC_MOVED_PERMANENTLY (301)
RC_MOVED_TEMPORARILY (302)
RC_SEE_OTHER (303)
```

LWP

```
RC_NOT_MODIFIED (304)
RC_USE_PROXY (305)
RC_BAD_REQUEST (400)
RC_UNAUTHORIZED (401)
RC_PAYMENT_REQUIRED (402)
RC_FORBIDDEN (403)
RC_NOT_FOUND (404)
RC_METHOD_NOT_ALLOWED (405)
RC_NOT_ACCEPTABLE (406)
RC_PROXY_AUTHENTICATION_REQUIRED (407)
RC_REQUEST_TIMEOUT (408)
RC_CONFLICT (409)
RC_GONE (410)
RC_LENGTH_REQUIRED (411)
RC_PRECONDITION_FAILED (412)
RC_REQUEST_ENTITY_TOO_LARGE (413)
RC_REQUEST_URI_TOO_LARGE (414)
RC_UNSUPPORTED_MEDIA_TYPE (415)
RC_REQUEST_RANGE_NOT_SATISFIABLE (416)
RC_INTERNAL_SERVER_ERROR (500)
RC_NOT_IMPLEMENTED (501)
RC_BAD_GATEWAY (502)
RC_SERVICE_UNAVAILABLE (503)
RC_GATEWAY_TIMEOUT (504)
RC_HTTP_VERSION_NOT_SUPPORTED (505)
```

HTTP::Date

The HTTP::Date module is useful when you want to process a date string. It exports two functions that convert date strings to and from standard time formats.

---

parse_date   parse_date($str)

Parses a date string and returns it as a list of numerical values followed by a time zone specification. If the date is unrecognized, then the empty list is returned.

---

str2time   str2time(str [, zone])

Converts the time specified as a string in the first parameter into the number of seconds since epoch. This function recognizes a wide variety of formats, including RFC 1123 (standard HTTP), RFC 850, ANSI C asctime, common log file format, Unix *ls –l*, and Windows *dir*, among others. When a time zone is not implicit in the first parameter, this function will use an optional time zone specified as the second parameter, such as –0800, +0500, or GMT. If the second parameter is omitted, and the time zone is ambiguous, the local time zone is used.

time2iso	`time2iso([$time])`
	Same as `time2str()`, but returns a "YYYY-MM-DD hh:mm:ss"–formatted string representing time in the local time zone.

time2isoz	`time2isoz([$time])`
	Same as `time2str()`, but returns a "YYYY-MM-DD hh:mm:ssZ"–formatted string representing Universal Time.

time2str	`time2str([time])`
	Given the number of seconds since machine epoch, this function generates the equivalent time as specified in RFC 1123, which is the recommended time format used in HTTP. When invoked with no parameter, the current time is used.

HTTP::Cookies

HTTP cookies provide a mechanism for preserving information about a client or user across several different visits to a site or page. The "cookie" is a name/value pair sent to the client on its initial visit to a page. This cookie is stored by the client and sent back in the request upon revisit to the same page.

A server initializes a cookie with the Set-Cookie header. Set-Cookie sets the name and value of a cookie, as well as other parameters such as how long the cookie is valid and the range of URLs to which the cookie applies. Each cookie (a single name/value pair) is sent in its own Set-Cookie header, so if there is more than one cookie sent to a client, multiple Set-Cookie headers are sent in the response. Two Set-Cookie headers may be used in server responses: Set-Cookie is defined in the original Netscape cookie specification, and Set-Cookie2 is the latest, IETF-defined header. Both header styles are supported by HTTP::Cookies. The latest browsers also support both styles.

If a client visits a page for which it has a valid cookie stored, the client sends the cookie in the request with the Cookie header. This header's value contains any name/value pairs that apply to the URL. Multiple cookies are separated by semi-colons in the header.

The HTTP::Cookies module is used to retrieve, return, and manage the cookies used by an LWP::UserAgent client application. Setting cookies from an LWP-created server requires only the coding of the proper response headers sent by an HTTP::Daemon server application. HTTP::Cookies is not designed to be used in setting cookies on the server side, although you may find use for it in managing sent cookies.

The new constructor for HTTP::Cookies creates an object called a cookie jar, which represents a collection of saved cookies usually read from a file. Methods on the cookie jar object allow you to add new cookies or send cookie information in a client request to a specific URL. The constructor may take optional parameters, as shown in the following example:

```
$cjar = HTTP::Cookies->new( file => 'cookies.txt',
                            autosave => 1,
                            ignore_discard => 0 );
```

The cookie jar object $cjar created here contains any cookie information stored in the file *cookies.txt*. The autosave parameter takes a Boolean value that determines if the state of the cookie jar is saved to the file upon destruction of the object. ignore_discard also takes a Boolean value to determine if cookies marked to be discarded are still saved to the file.

Cookies received by a client are added to the cookie jar with the extract_cookies method. This method searches an HTTP::Response object for Set-Cookie and Set-Cookie2 headers and adds them to the cookie jar. Cookies are sent in a client request using the add-cookie-header method. This method takes an HTTP::Request object with the URL component already set, and if the URL matches any entries in the cookie jar, adds the appropriate Cookie headers to the request.

These methods can be used on a cookie jar object created by HTTP::Cookies.

---

add_cookie_header

$cjar->add_cookie_header($request)

Adds appropriate Cookie headers to an HTTP::Request object $request. $request must already be created with a valid URL address. This method will search the cookie jar for any cookies matching the request URL. If the cookies are valid (i.e., have not expired), they are used to create Cookie headers and are added to the request.

---

as_string

$cjar->as_string([discard])

Returns the current contents of the cookie jar as a string. Each cookie is output as a Set-Cookie3 header line followed by "0". If *discard* is given and is true, cookies marked to be discarded will not be output. Set-Cookie3 is a special LWP format used to store cookie information in the save file.

---

clear

$cjar->clear([domain, [path, [key]]])

Without arguments, this method clears the entire contents of the cookie jar. Given arguments, cookies belonging to a specific *domain*, *path*, or with a name, *key*, will be cleared. The arguments are ordered for increasing specificity. If only one argument is given, all cookies for that domain will be deleted. A second argument specifies a distinct *path* within the *domain*. To remove a cookie by keyname, you must use all three arguments.

---

extract_cookies $cjar->extract_cookies($response)

Searches an HTTP::Response object $response for any Set-Cookie and Set-Cookie2 headers and stores the cookie information in the cookie jar.

---

load $cjar->load([file])

Loads cookie information into the cookie jar from the file specified during construction (default) or from the named *file*. The file must be in the format produced by the save method.

---

revert $cjar->revert

Restores the cookie jar to its state before the last save.

---

save $cjar->save([file])

Saves the state of the cookie jar to the file specified during construction (by default) or to the named *file*. The cookies are saved in a special LWP format as Set-Cookie3 header lines. This format is not compatible with the standard Set-Cookie and Set-Cookie2 headers, but you are not likely to use this file to set new cookies in response headers.

---

set_cookie $cjar->set_cookie(version, key, val, path, domain, port, path_spec, secure, maxages, discard, \%misc)

Sets a cookie in the cookie jar with the information given in the arguments. The number and order of arguments represent the structure of elements in the Set-Cookie3 header lines used to save the cookies in a file.

version
A string containing the cookie-spec version number.

key
The name of the cookie.

val
The value of the cookie.

path
The pathname of the URL for which the cookie is set.

domain
The domain name for which the cookie is set.

port
The port number of the URL for which the cookie is set.

path_spec

> A Boolean value indicating if the cookie is valid for the specific URL path or all the URLs in the domain. The path is used if true; otherwise, the cookie is valid for the entire domain.

secure

> A Boolean value indicating that the cookie should only be sent over a secure connection for true, or over any connection for false.

maxage

> The number of seconds that the cookie will be valid from the time it was received. Adding the *maxage* to the current time will yield a value that can be used for an expiration date.

discard

> A Boolean value indicating that the cookie should not be sent in any future requests and should be discarded upon saving the cookie jar, unless the `ignore_discard` parameter was set to true in the constructor.

%misc

> The final argument is a reference to a hash, *%misc*, that contains any additional parameters from the Set-Cookie headers such as Comment and URLComment, in key/value pairs.

---

scan   `$cjar->scan( \&callback )`

Invokes the *callback* subroutine for each cookie in the cookie jar. The subroutine is called with the same arguments given to the save method, described above. Any undefined arguments will be given the value `undef`.

HTTP::Cookies::Netscape

The HTTP::Cookies class contains one subclass that supports Netscape-style cookies within a cookie jar object. Netscape-style cookies were defined in the original cookie specification for Navigator 1.1, which outlined the syntax for the Cookie and Set-Cookie HTTP headers. Netscape cookie headers are different from the newer Set-Cookie2–style cookies in that they don't support as many additional parameters when a cookie is set. The Cookie header also does not use a version-number attribute. Many browsers and servers still use the original Netscape cookies, and the Netscape subclass of HTTP::Cookies can be used to support this style.

The new constructor for this subclass creates a Netscape-compatible cookie jar object like this:

```
$njar = HTTP::Cookies::Netscape->new(
            File    => "$ENV{HOME}/.netscape/cookies",
            AutoSave => 1 );
```

The methods described above can be used on this object, although many of the parameters used in Set-Cookie2 headers will simply be lost when cookies are saved to the cookie jar.

HTTP::Daemon

The HTTP::Daemon module creates HTTP server applications. The module provides objects based on the IO::Socket::INET class that can listen on a socket for client requests and send server responses. The objects implemented by the module are HTTP 1.1 servers. Client requests are stored as HTTP::Request objects, and all the methods for that class can be used to obtain information about the request. HTTP::Response objects can be used to send information back to the client.

An HTTP::Daemon object is created by using the new constructor. Since the base class for this object is IO::Socket::INET, the parameters used in that class's constructor are the same here. For example:

```
$d = HTTP::Daemon->new ( LocalAddr => 'maude.oreilly.com',
                         LocalPort => 8888,
                         Listen => 5 );
```

The HTTP::Daemon object is a server socket that automatically listens for requests on the specified port (or on the default port if none is given). When a client request is received, the object uses the accept method to create a connection with the client on the network.

```
$d = HTTP::Daemon->new;
while ( $c = $d->accept ) {
    $req = $c->get_request;
    # Process request and send response here
    }
$c = undef;   # Don't forget to close the socket
```

The accept method returns a reference to a new object of the HTTP::Daemon::ClientConn class. This class is also based on IO::Socket::INET and is used to extract the request message and send the response and any requested file content.

The sockets created by both HTTP::Daemon and HTTP::Daemon::ClientConn work the same way as those in IO::Socket::INET. The methods are also the same except for some slight variations in usage. The methods for the HTTP::Daemon classes are listed in the sections below and include the adjusted IO::Socket::INET methods. For more detailed information about sockets and the IO::Socket classes and methods, see Chapter 13.

The following methods can be used on HTTP::Daemon objects.

---

accept $d->accept ([*pkg*])

Accepts a client request on a socket object and creates a connection with the client. This method is the same as IO::Socket->accept, except it will return a reference to a new

---

HTTP::Daemon::ClientConn object. If an argument is given, the connection object will be created in the package named by *pkg*. If no connection is made before a specified timeout, the method will return undef.

product_tokens `$d->product_tokens`

Returns the string that the server uses to identify itself in the Server response header.

url `$d->url`

Returns the URL string that gives access to the server root.

HTTP::Daemon::ClientConn methods

The following methods can be used on HTTP::Daemon::ClientConn objects.

antique_client `$c->antique_client`

Returns true if the client uses the HTTP/0.9 protocol (i.e., no status code or headers should be returned).

crlf `$c->crlf( )`

Sends the CRLF sequence to the client.

daemon `$c->daemon`

Returns a reference to the HTTP::Daemon object from which the current ClientConn object was generated.

force_last_request

`$c->force_last_request( )`

Ensures that $c->get_request will not try to read more requests off this connection. If you generate a response that is not self-delimiting, then you should signal this fact by calling this method. This attribute is turned on automatically if the client announces protocol HTTP/1.0 or worse and does not include a Connection: Keep-Alive header. It is also turned on automatically when HTTP/1.1 or better clients send the Connection: Close request header

get_request $c->get_request

Reads information from the client request and returns a reference to an HTTP::Request object. Returns undef if the request failed.

proto_ge $c->proto_ge ([$new_value])

Returns true if the client announced a protocol with version number greater or equal to the given argument. The $proto argument can be a string such as "HTTP/1.1", or just "1.1".

read_buffer $c->read_buffer ([$new_value])

Bytes read, but not used, by $c->get_request are placed in the read buffer. The next time $c->get_request is called, it will consume the bytes in this buffer before reading more data from the network connection itself.

reason $c->reason( )

Returns a short string describing what happened if $c->get_request returns undef.

send_basic_header

$c->send_basic_header ([code, [msg, [proto]]])

Sends status line composed of the specified parameters and the Date and Server headers to the client. If no arguments are given, the default status line HTTP/1.1 200 OK is used.

send_error $c->send_error ([code, [msg]])

Returns an error response to the client. code can contain one of the error response codes; the default is 400 Bad Request. msg is a string describing the error displayed in the HTML entity body.

send_file $c->send_file (filename)

Copies contents of the file filename to the client as the response. filename can be a string that is interpreted as a filename, or a reference to a glob.

send_file_response

$c->send_file_response (filename)

Sends a response with the file filename as content. If filename is a directory, an index listing will be generated and sent as HTML.

LWP

send_redirect $c->send_redirect (*url*, [*code*, [*entity_body*]])

Sends a redirect response to the client, with the location *url*, an absolute or a relative URL. The optional *code* argument should be one of the redirect status codes; the default is 301 Moved Permanently. An *entity_body* string can be sent as HTML that informs the user of the redirection.

send_response $c->send_response ([$resp | @resplist])

Sends a response to the client created from the HTTP::Response object, $resp, or the list of parameters, @resplist. The *resplist* parameters are the same as those used in the constructor for HTTP::Response and must at least contain a status code. If no argument is given, the default OK response is sent.

send_status_line

$c->send_status_line ([*code*, [*msg*, [*proto*]]])

Sends the status line composed of the given arguments back to the client. If the arguments are given, the default status line is sent as HTTP/1.1 200 OK. The arguments are:

code
> The numeric code indicating the status of the request, e.g., 200 for an OK request or 404 for a request for a resource that doesn't exist

msg
> A short string describing the status code

proto
> A string indicating the protocol and version number used by the server, e.g., HTTP/1.1.

HTTP::Message

HTTP::Message is the generic base class for HTTP::Request and HTTP::Response. It provides a couple of methods used on both classes. The constructor for this class is used internally by the Request and Response classes, so you will probably not need to use it. Methods defined by the HTTP::Headers class will also work on Message objects.

add_content $r->add_content(*data*)

Appends *data* to the end of the object's current entity body.

clone

`$r->clone( )`

Creates a copy of the current object, `$r`, and returns a reference to it.

---

content

`$r->content ([content])`

Without an argument, content returns the entity body of the object. With a scalar argument, the entity body will be set to *content*.

---

content_ref

`$r->content_ref( )`

Returns a reference to the string containing the content body. This reference can be used to manage large content data.

---

headers

`$r->headers( )`

Returns the embedded HTTP::Headers object from the message object.

---

protocol

`$r->protocol([string])`

Sets or retrieves the HTTP protocol *string* for the message object. This string looks like HTTP/1.1.

The HTML Modules

HTML modules provide an interface to parse HTML documents. After you parse the document, you can print or display it according to the markup tags or extract specific information such as hyperlinks.

The HTML::parser module provides methods for, literally, parsing HTML. It can handle HTML text from a string or file and can separate out the syntactic structures and data. You shouldn't use HTML::Parser directly, however, since its interface hasn't been designed to make your life easy when you parse HTML. It's merely a base class from which you can build your own parser to deal with HTML in any way you want. And if you don't want to roll your own HTML parser or parser class, then there's always HTML::TokeParser and HTML::TreeBuilder, both of which are covered in this chapter.

HTML::TreeBuilder is a class that parses HTML into a syntax tree. In a syntax tree, each element of the HTML, such as container elements with beginning and end tags, is stored relative to other elements. This preserves the nested structure and behavior of HTML and its hierarchy.

A syntax tree of the TreeBuilder class is formed of connected nodes that represent each element of the HTML document. These nodes are saved as objects from the HTML::Element class. An HTML::Element object stores all the information from an HTML tag: the start tag, end tag, attributes, plain text, and pointers to any nested elements.

The remaining classes of the HTML modules use the syntax trees and its nodes of element objects to output useful information from the HTML documents. The format classes, such as HTML::FormatText and HTML::FormatPS, allow you to produce text and PostScript from HTML. The HTML::LinkExtor class extracts all of the links from a document. Additional modules provide means for replacing HTML character entities and implementing HTML tags as subroutines.

HTML::Parser

This module implements the base class for the other HTML modules. A parser object is created with the new constructor:

```
$p = HTML::Parser->new( );
```

The constructor takes no arguments.

The parser object takes methods that read in HTML from a string or a file. The string-reading method can take data in several smaller chunks if the HTML is too big. Each chunk of HTML will be appended to the object, and the eof method indicates the end of the document. These basic methods are described below.

---

eof $p->eof( )

Indicates the end of a document and flushes any buffered text. Returns the parser object.

---

parse $p->parse(*string*)

Reads HTML into the parser object from a given *string*. Performance problems occur if the string is too large, so the HTML can be broken up into smaller pieces, which will be appended to the data already contained in the object. The parse can be terminated with a call to the eof method.

---

parse_file $p->parse_file(*file*)

Reads HTML into the parser object from the given *file*, which can be a filename or an open filehandle.

When the parse or parse_file method is called, it parses the incoming HTML with a few internal methods. In HTML::Parser, these methods are defined, but empty. Additional HTML parsing classes (included in the HTML modules or ones you write yourself) override these methods for their own purposes. For example:

```
package HTML::MyParser;
require HTML::Parser;
@ISA=qw(HTML::MyParser);

sub start {
    your subroutine defined here
    }
```

The following list shows the internal methods contained in HTML::Parser.

---

comment   comment(*comment*)

Invoked on comments from HTML (text between <!- and ->). The text of the comment (without the tags) is given to the method as the string *comment*.

---

end   end(*tag, origtext*)

Invoked on end tags (those with the </tag> form). The first argument, *tag*, is the tag name in lowercase, and the second argument, *origtext*, is the original HTML text of the tag.

---

start   start(*tag, $attr, attrseq, origtext*)

Invoked on start tags. The first argument, *tag*, is the name of the tag in lowercase. The second argument is a reference to a hash, *attr*. This hash contains all the attributes and their values in key/value pairs. The keys are the names of the attributes in lowercase. The third argument, *attrseq*, is a reference to an array that contains the names of all the attributes in the order they appeared in the tag. The fourth argument, *origtext*, is a string that contains the original text of the tag.

---

text   text(*text*)

Invoked on plain text in the document. The text is passed unmodified and may contain newlines. Character entities in the text are not expanded.

---

xml_mode   xml_mode(*bool*)

Enabling this attribute changes the parser to allow some XML constructs such as empty element tags and XML processing instructions. It also disables forcing tag and attribute names to lowercase when they are reported by the `tagname` and `attr` arguments, and suppresses special treatment of elements parsed as CDATA for HTML.

HTML::TokeParser

As we said, you should use a subclassed HTML parser if you want a better interface to HTML parsing features than what HTML::Parser gives you. HTML::TokeParser by Gisle Aas is one such example. While HTML::TokeParser is actually a subclass of HTML::PullParser, it can help you do many useful things, such as link extraction and HTML checking.

In short, HTML::TokeParser breaks an HTML document into tokens, attributes, and content, in which the HTML `<a href="http://url">link</a>` would break down as:

```
token: a
    attrib: href
content: http://url
content: link
token /a
```

For example, you can use HTML::TokeParser to extract links from a string that contains HTML:

```
#!/usr/local/bin/perl -w

require HTML::TokeParser;

# Our string that turns out to be HTML!
my $html = '<p>Some text. <a href="http://blah"My name is Nate!</a></p>';
my $parser = HTML::TokeParser->new(\$html);

get_tag() tells TokeParser to match a tag by name
while (my $token = $parser->get_tag("a")) {
    my $url = $token->[1]{href} || "-";
    my $text = $parser->get_trimmed_text("/a");
    print "URL is: $url.\nURL text is: $text.\n";
}
```

HTML::TokeParser methods

---

new
new( )

Constructor. Takes a filename, filehandle, or reference to a scalar as arguments. Each argument represents the content that will be parsed. If a scalar is present, new looks for a filename $scalar. If a reference to a scalar is present, new looks for HTML in \$scalar. new will read filehandles until end-of-file. Returns undef on failure.

---

get_tag

get_tag( )

Returns the next start or end tag in a document. If there are no remaining start or end tags, get_tag returns undef. get_tag is useful because it skips unwanted tokens and matches only the tag that you want—if it exists. When a tag is found, it is returned as an array reference, like so: [$tag, $attr, $attrseq, $text]. If an end tag is found, is is returned—e.g., "/$tag".

get_text

get_text( )

Returns all text found at the current position. If the next token is not text, get_text returns a zero-length string. You can pass an "$end_tag" option to get_text to return all of the text before "end_tag".

get_token

get_token( )

Returns the next token found in the HTML document, or undef if no next token exists. Each token is returned as an array reference. The array reference's first and last items refer to start and end tags concurrently. The rest of the items in the array include text, comments, declarations, and process instructions. get_token uses the following labels for the tokens:

S   Start tag

E   End tag

T   Text

C   Comment

D   Declaration

PI Process instructions

Consider the following code:

```
#!/usr/local/bin/perl -w

require HTML::TokeParser;

my $html = '<a href="http://blah">My name is
Nate!</a></p>';
my $p = HTML::TokeParser->new(\$html);

while (my $token = $p->get_token) {
    my $i = 0;
    foreach my $tk (@{$token}) {
        print "token[$i]: $tk\n";
                    $i++;
    }
}
```

The items in each token (in the HTML) are displayed as follows:

```
token[0]: S
token[1]: a
```

```
token[2]: HASH(0x8146d3c)
token[3]: ARRAY(0x814a380)
token[4]: <a href="http://blah">
token[0]: T
token[1]: My name is Nate!
token[2]:
token[0]: E
token[1]: a
token[2]: </a>
token[0]: E
token[1]: p
token[2]: </p>
```

get_trimmed_text

> get_trimmed_text( )
>
> Works the same as get_text, but reduces all instances of multiple spaces to a single space and removes leading and trailing whitespace.

unget_token   unget_token( )

> Useful for pushing tokens back to the parser so they can be reused the next time you call get_token.

HTML::Element

The HTML::Element module provides methods for dealing with nodes in an HTML syntax tree. You can get or set the contents of each node, traverse the tree, and delete a node.

HTML::Element objects are used to represent elements of HTML. These elements include start and end tags, attributes, contained plain text, and other nested elements.

The constructor for this class requires the name of the tag for its first argument. You may optionally specify initial attributes and values as hash elements in the constructor. For example:

```
$h = HTML::Element->new('a', 'href' => 'http:www.oreilly.com');
```

The new element is created for the anchor tag, <a>, which links to the URL through its href attribute.

The following methods are provided for objects of the HTML::Element class.

as_HTML $h->as_HTML( )

Returns the HTML string that represents the element and its children.

---

attr $h->attr(*name* [,*value*])

Sets or retrieves the value of attribute *name* in the current element.

---

content $h->content( )

Returns the content contained in this element as a reference to an array that contains plain-text segments and references to nested element objects.

---

delete $h->delete( )

Deletes the current element and all of its child elements.

---

delete_content $h->delete_content( )

Removes the content from the current element.

---

dump $h->dump( )

Prints the tag name of the element and all its children to STDOUT. Useful for debugging. The structure of the document is shown by indentation.

---

endtag $h->endtag( )

Returns the original text of the end tag, including the </ and >.

---

extract_links $h->extract_links([*types*])

Retrieves the links contained within an element and all of its child elements. This method returns a reference to an array in which each element is a reference to an array with two values: the value of the link and a reference to the element in which it was found. You may specify the tags from which you want to extract links by providing their names in a list of *types*.

---

implicit $h->implicit([*boolean*])

Indicates whether the element was contained in the original document (false) or whether it was assumed to be implicit (true) by the parser. Implicit tags are elements that the parser included to conform to proper HTML structure, such as an ending paragraph tag (</p>). You may also set this attribute by providing a *boolean* argument.

insert_element $h->insert_element($element, implicit)

Inserts the object $element at the current position relative to the root object $h and updates the position (indicated by pos) to the inserted element. Returns the new $element. The *implicit* argument is a Boolean indicating whether the element is an implicit tag (true) or the original HTML (false).

is_empty $h->is_empty( )

Returns true if the current object has no content.

is_inside $h->is_inside(tag1 [,tag2, ...])

Returns true if the tag for this element is contained inside one of the tags listed as arguments.

parent $h->parent([$new])

Without an argument, returns the parent object for this element. If given a reference to another element object, this element is set as the new parent object and is returned.

pos $h->pos([$element])

Sets or retrieves the current position in the syntax tree of the current object. The returned value is a reference to the element object that holds the current position. The "position" object is an element contained within the tree that has the current object ($h) at its root.

push_content $h->push_content(content)

Inserts the specified content into the current element. *content* can be either a scalar containing plain text or a reference to another element. Multiple arguments can be supplied.

starttag $h->starttag( )

Returns the original text of the start tag for the element. This includes the < and > and all attributes.

tag	$h->tag([name])
	Sets or retrieves the tag *name* for the element. Tag names are always converted to lowercase.

traverse	$h->traverse(sub, [ignoretext])
	Traverses the current element and all of its children, invoking the callback routine *sub* for each element. The callback routine is called with a reference to the current element (the node), a startflag, and the depth as arguments. The start flag is 1 when entering a node and 0 when leaving (returning to a parent element). If the *ignoretext* parameter is true (the default), then the callback routine will not be invoked for text content. If the callback routine returns false, the method will not traverse any child elements of that node.

HTML::TreeBuilder

The HTML::TreeBuilder class provides a parser that creates an HTML syntax tree. Each node of the tree is an HTML::Element object. This class inherits both HTML::Parser and HTML::Elements, so methods from both of those classes can be used on its objects.

The methods provided by HTML::TreeBuilder control how the parsing is performed. Values for these methods are set by providing a Boolean value for their arguments.

ignore_text	$p->ignore_text(boolean)
	If set to true, text content of elements will not be included in elements of the parse tree. The default it false.

ignore_unknown	
	$p->ignore_unknown(boolean)
	If set to true, unknown tags in the HTML will be represented as elements in the parse tree.

implicit_tags	$p->implicit_tags(boolean)
	If set to true, the parser will try to deduce implicit tags such as missing elements or end tags that are required to conform to proper HTML structure. If false, the parse tree will reflect the HTML as is.

LWP

warn p->warn(*boolean*)

If set to true, the parser will make calls to warn with messages describing syntax errors when they occur. Error messages are off by default.

HTML::FormatPS

The HTML::FormatPS module converts an HTML parse tree into PostScript. The formatter object is created with the new constructor, which can take parameters that assign PostScript attributes. For example:

```
$formatter = HTML::FormatPS->new('papersize' => 'Letter');
```

You can now give parsed HTML to the formatter and produce PostScript output for printing. HTML::FormatPS does not handle table or form elements at this time.

The method for this class is format. format takes a reference to an HTML Tree-Builder object, representing a parsed HTML document. It returns a scalar containing the document formatted in PostScript. The following example shows how to use this module to print a file in PostScript:

```
use HTML::FormatPS;

$html = HTML::TreeBuilder->parse_file(somefile);
$formatter = HTML::FormatPS->new();
print $formatter->format($html);
```

The following list describes the attributes that can be set in the constructor:

PaperSize
Possible values are 3, A4, A5, B4, B5, Letter, Legal, Executive, Tabloid, Statement, Folio, 10x14, and Quarto. The default is A4.

PaperWidth
Width of the paper in points.

PaperHeight
Height of the paper in points.

LeftMargin
Left margin in points.

RightMargin
Right margin in points.

HorizontalMargin
Left and right margin. Default is 4 cm.

TopMargin
Top margin in points.

BottomMargin
> Bottom margin in points.

VerticalMargin
> Top and bottom margin. Default is 2 cm.

PageNo
> Boolean value to display page numbers. Default is 0 (off).

FontFamily
> Font family to use on the page. Possible values are Courier, Helvetica, and Times. Default is Times.

FontScale
> Scale factor for the font.

Leading
> Space between lines, as a factor of the font size. Default is 0.1.

HTML::FormatText

The HTML::FormatText module takes a parsed HTML file and outputs a plain-text version of it. None of the character attributes will be usable, i.e., bold or italic fonts, font sizes, etc.

This module is similar to FormatPS in that the constructor takes attributes for formatting, and the format method produces the output. A formatter object can be constructed like this:

```
$formatter = HTML::FormatText->new(leftmargin => 10, rightmargin => 80);
```

The constructor can take two parameters: leftmargin and rightmargin. The value for the margins is given in column numbers. The aliases lm and rm can also be used.

The format method takes an HTML::TreeBuilder object and returns a scalar containing the formatted text. You can print it with:

```
print $formatter->format($html);
```

The URI Module

The URI module contains functions and modules to specify and convert URIs. (URLs are a type of URI.) In addition to the URL module itself, there are also: URI::URL, URI::Escape, and URI::Heuristic. Of primary importance to many LWP applications is the URI::URL class, which creates the objects used by LWP::UserAgent to determine protocols, server locations, and resource names.

The URI::Escape module replaces unsafe characters in URL strings with their appropriate escape sequences. URI::Heuristic provides convenience methods for creating proper URLs out of short strings and incomplete addresses.

LWP

URI

The URI module is a successor to URI::URL and was written by Gisle Aas. While not clearly stated in the LWP documentation, you should use the URI module whenever possible, since URI.pm has essentially deprecated URI::URL.

The URI module implements the URI class. Objects created from the URI class represent Uniform Resource Identifiers (URIs). With the URI module, you can identify the key parts of a URI: scheme, scheme-specific parts, and fragment identifiers, which may be referred to respectfully as authority, path, and query components. For example, as shown in the URI module documentation:

```
<scheme>:<scheme-specific-part>#<fragment>
<scheme>://<authority><path>?<query>#<fragment>
<path>?<query>#<fragment>
```

You can break down *http://www.oreilly.com/somefile.html* as:

```
scheme: http
authority: www.oreilly.com
path: /somefile.html
```

In the case of relative URIs, you can use the URI module to deal with only the query component of a URI. With the URI module, you can parse the above URI as follows:

```perl
#!/usr/local/bin/perl -w

use URI;

my $url = 'http://www.oreilly.com/somefile.html';
my $u1 = URI->new($url);

print "scheme: ", $u1->scheme, "\n";
print "authority: ", $u1->authority, "\n";
print "path: ", $u1->path, "\n";
```

URI methods

The following methods give you access to components of a URI. These methods will return a string, unless the URI component is invalid, in which case undef is returned. Bear in mind that an empty string ("") is not equivalent to an undefined value.

---

new   new($*uri*, [$*scheme*])

Constructor. $*uri* is given as an argument with the optional $*scheme*. new removes additional whitespace, double quotes, and arrows from the URL. $*scheme* is used only when $*str* is a relative URI; it is a simple string that denotes the scheme or an absolute URI object. $*str* will be treated like a generic URI if $*scheme* isn't defined.

---

new	URI::file->new($*file*, [$*os*])
	Constructs a new file URI from a filename.
new_abs	URI::file->new_abs($*file*, [$*os*])
	Constructs a new absolute file URI from a filename.
abs	abs($*base_uri*)
	Returns an absolute URI reference. If $*uri* is already absolute, then a reference to $*uri* is returned. abs returns a new absolute URI that contains $*uri* and $*base_uri* if $*uri* is relative.
as_string	as_string
	Returns a URI object as a plain string.
authority	authority([$*auth*])
	Sets and gets the authority component of the $*uri*. This component will be escaped.
canonical	canonical
	Returns a normalized version of the URI. This includes lower-casing the scheme and hostname components, as well as removing an explicit port specification (if it mtaches the default port). canonical will return the original $*uri* if $*uri* was already in the correct form.
clone	clone
	Returns a copy of the URI.
cwd	URI::file->cwd
	Returns the current working directory as a file URI.
default_port	default_port()
	Returns the default port of the URI scheme that $*uri* belongs to. You cannot change the default port for a scheme.
eq	eq()
	Compares two URIs.

eq | 565

fragment
    fragment([$new_frag])

    Returns the fragment identifier of a URI reference as an escaped string.

host
    host([$new_host])

    Sets and gets the unescaped hostname. To specify a different port:
        $new_host = "hostname:port_number"

host_port
    host_port([$new_host_port])

    Sets and gets the host and port as a single unit. Hostname and port are colon-separated.

new_abs
    new_abs($str, $base_uri)

    Creates a new absolute URI object. $str represents the absolute URI, and $base_uri represents the relative URI.

opaque
    opaque([$new_opaque_value])

    Sets and gets the scheme-specific part of $uri.

path
    path([$path])

    Sets and gets the escaped path component of $uri. Returns empty string ("") if there is no path.

path
    path([$new_path])

    Gets and sets the same value as opaque, unless the URI supports the generic syntax for heirarchical namespaces. path returns the part of the URI between the hostname and the fragment.

path_query
    path_query([$path_here])

    Sets and gets the escapted path and query components.

path_segments
    path_segments([$seg])

    Sets and gets the path. In a scalar content, path_segments is equivalent to path. In a list contents, path_segments returns the unescaped path segments that make up the path.

port	port([$new_port])
	Sets and gets the port, which is an integer. If $new_port is not defined, then the default port of the URI scheme will be returned.

query	query([$q])
	Sets and gets the escaped query component of $uri.

query_form	query_form([$key => $val])
	Sets and gets query components that use the urlencoded format.

query_keywords

      query_keywords([$keywords])

      Sets and gets query components that use keywords separated by a +.

rel	rel($base_uri)
	Returns a relative URI reference, if one exists. Otherwise, $uri is returned.

scheme	scheme([$some_scheme])
	Sets and gets the scheme part of the URI. Such values include: data, file, ftp, gopher, http, https, ldap, mailto, news, nntp, pop, rlogin, rsync, snews, telnet, and ssh. In the case of relative URIs, scheme will return undef; otherwise, scheme will return the scheme in lowercase. With $some_scheme, scheme will set the scheme of the current URI. scheme will die if the scheme isn't supported, or if it contains non–US-ASCII characters.

userinfo	userinfo([$new_userinfo])
	Sets and gets the escaped "userinfo" part of the authority component (of the URI). Often, the userinfo will appear as a username and password separated by a colon. Bear in mind that sending a password in the clear is a bad idea.

URI::Escape

This module escapes or unescapes "unsafe" characters within a URL string. Unsafe characters in URLs are described by RFC 1738. Before you form URI::URL objects and use that class's methods, you should make sure your strings are properly escaped. This module does not create its own objects; it exports the following functions:

---

uri_escape   uri_escape *uri*, [*regexp*]

Given a URI as the first parameter, returns the equivalent URI with certain characters replaced with % followed by two hexadecimal digits. The first parameter can be a text string, such as "http:www.oreilly.com", or an object of type URI::URL. When invoked without a second parameter, uri_escape escapes characters specified by RFC 1738. Otherwise, you can pass in a regular expression (in the context of [ ]) of characters to escape as the second parameter. For example:

```
$escaped_uri = uri_escape($uri, 'aeiou')
```

This code escapes all lowercase vowels in $uri and returns the escaped version.

---

uri_unescape   uri_unescape *uri*

Substitutes any instance of % followed by two hexadecimal digits back into its original form and returns the entire URI in unescaped form.

URI::URL

This module creates URL objects that store all the elements of a URL. These objects are used by the request method of LWP::UserAgent for server addresses, port numbers, filenames, protocol, and many other elements that can be loaded into a URL.

The new constructor is used to make a URI::URL object:

```
$url = URI::URL->new($url_string [, $base_url])
```

This method creates a new URI::URL object with the URL given as the first parameter. An optional base URL can be specified as the second parameter and is useful for generating an absolute URL from a relative URL.

The following methods are for the URI::URL class.

---

abs $*url*->abs([*base*, [*scheme*]])

Returns the absolute URL, given a base. If invoked with no parameters, any previous definition of the base is used. The second parameter is a Boolean that modifies abs's behavior. When the second parameter is nonzero, abs will accept a relative URL with a scheme but no host, such as http:index.html.

---

as_string $url->as_string( )

Returns the URL as a scalar string. All defined components of the URL are included in the string.

base $url->base([base])

Gets or sets the base URL associated with the URL in this URI::URL object. The base URL is useful for converting a relative URL into an absolute URL.

crack $url->crack( )

Returns an array with the following data: (scheme, user, password, host, port, epath, eparams, equery, frag).

default_port $url->default_port([port])

When invoked with no parameters, this method returns the default port for the URL defined in the object. The default port is based on the scheme used. Even if the port for the URL is explicitly changed by the user with the port method, the default port is always the same.

eparams $url->eparams([param])

When invoked with no arguments, this method returns the escaped parameter of the URL defined in the object. When invoked with an argument, the object's escaped parameter is assigned to that value.

epath $url->epath( )

When invoked with no parameters, this method returns the escaped path of the URL defined in the object. When invoked with a parameter, the object's escaped path is assigned to that value.

eq $url->eq(other_url)

Returns true when the object's URL is equal to the URL specified.

equery $url->equery([string])

When invoked with no arguments, this method returns the escaped query string of the URL defined in the object. When invoked with an argument, the object's escaped query string is assigned to that value.

frag

$url->frag([*frag*])

When invoked with no arguments, this method returns the fragment of the URL defined in the object. When invoked with an argument, the object's fragment is assigned to that value.

full_path

$url->full_path( )

Returns a string consisting of the escaped path, escaped parameters, and escaped query string.

host

$url->host([*hostname*])

When invoked with no parameters, this method returns the hostname in the URL defined in the object. When invoked with a parameter, the object's hostname is assigned to that value.

netloc

$url->netloc([*netloc*])

When invoked with no parameters, this method returns the network location for the URL defined in the object. The network location is a string composed of "user:password@host:port", in which the user, password, and port may be omitted when not defined. When netloc is invoked with a parameter, the object's network location is defined to that value. Changes to the network location are reflected in the user, password, host, and port methods.

params

$url->params([*param*])

Same as eparams, except that the parameter that is set/returned is not escaped.

password

$url->password([*passwd*])

When invoked with no parameters, this method returns the password in the URL defined in the object. When invoked with a parameter, the object's password is assigned to that value.

path

$url->path([*pathname*])

Same as epath, except that the path that is set/returned is not escaped.

port

$url->port([*port*])

When invoked with no parameters, this method returns the port for the URL defined in the object. If a port wasn't explicitly defined in the URL, a default port is assumed. When invoked with a parameter, the object's port is assigned to that value.

query	`$url->query([param])`
	Same as equery, except that the parameter that is set/returned is not escaped.
rel	`$url->rel(base)`
	Given a base as a first parameter or a previous definition of the base, returns the current object's URL relative to the base URL.
scheme	`$url->scheme([scheme])`
	When invoked with no parameters, this method returns the scheme in the URL defined in the object. When invoked with a parameter, the object's scheme is assigned to that value.
strict	`URI::URL::strict(bool)`
	When set, the URI::URL module calls croak upon encountering an error. When disabled, the URI::URL module may behave more gracefully. The function returns the previous value of strict. This function is not exported explicitly by the module.
user	`$url->user([username])`
	When invoked with no parameters, this method returns the user for the URL defined in the object. When invoked with a parameter, the object's user is assigned to that value.

LWP

IX

Perl/Tk

21

Perl/Tk

Perl/Tk is an extension for writing Perl programs with a graphical user interface (GUI) on both Unix and Windows 95/NT. Tk was originally developed as an extension to the Tcl language, for use with the X Window System on Unix. With its port to Perl, Tk gives Perl programmers the same control over the graphical desktop that Tcl programmers have taken for granted.

The Tk extension makes it easy to draw a window, put widgets into it (such as buttons, checkboxes, entry fields, menus, etc.), and have them perform certain actions based on user input. A simple "Hello World" program would look like this:

```
#!/usr/bin/perl -w
use Tk;
my $mw = MainWindow->new;
$mw->Button(-text => "Hello World!", -command =>sub{exit})->pack;
MainLoop;
```

When you run it, it would look like Figure 21-1.

Figure 21-1. A simple Perl/Tk program

Clicking on the Hello World button exits the program, and your window disappears.

Let's walk through these few lines of code. After calling the Perl interpreter, the program calls the Tk module. It then proceeds to build a generic, standard window (MainWindow) to act as a parent for any other widgets you create. Line 4 of the program creates a button and displays it using the pack geometry manager. It also gives the button something to do when pushed (in this case, exit the program).

The last line tells the program to "go do it." MainLoop starts the event handler for the graphical interface, and the program draws windows until it reaches the MainLoop statement. Everything up to that point is preparation; until you reach the MainLoop statement, the program simply prepares its windows and defines what to do when certain events happen (such as a mouse click on the Hello World! button). Nothing is drawn until the MainLoop statement is reached.

Widgets

Widgets in Perl/Tk are created with *widget creation commands*, which include Button, Canvas, CheckButton, Entry, Frame, Label, Listbox, Menu, Menubutton, Message, Radiobutton, Scale, Scrollbar, Text, and Toplevel, among many, many others.

Positioning widgets is done with *geometry managers*. In the "Hello World" example shown earlier, the pack command is the geometry manager. Geometry managers determine where in the window (or frame) the widget will sit. We'll talk more about the Perl/Tk geometry managers later in this chapter.

Widget Methods

Widgets can be configured, queried, or manipulated via various *widget methods*. For example, all widgets support the configure widget method for changing widget properties after the widget is created. In addition, most widgets have specialized methods associated with them for manipulating the widget as needed throughout the program. For example, widgets that scroll support the xview and yview methods for determining the viewable portion of the content when the scrollbar is moved. The Entry and Text widgets have methods for inserting and deleting values. The Canvas widget has a whole series of methods for drawing shapes and inserting text into the canvas. And so on.

Widget methods are listed in the discussion of each widget later in this chapter. However, since all widgets support the configure and cget methods, we will cover them now.

The configure method

The configure method can be used to set and retrieve widget configuration values. For example, to change the width of a button:

```
$button->configure(-width => 100);
```

To get the value for a current widget, just supply it without a value:

```
$button->configure(-width);
```

The result is an array of scalars; the important values are the last two, which represent the default value and its current value, respectively.

You can also call configure without any options at all, which will give you a listing of all options and their values.

The cget method

For simply retrieving the value of an option, `configure` returns more information than you generally want. The `cget` method returns just the current value.

Scrollbars

Many widgets have scrollbars associated with them. Scrollbars can be added to a widget in two ways: with an independent Scrollbar widget or with the `Scrolled` method when creating a widget. For simple scrollbars, the `Scrolled` method is much easier and therefore preferable.

Using the Scrolled method

Use the `Scrolled` method to create both the widget and the scrollbar in a single command. For example:

```
$mainwindow->Scrolled('Entry', -scrollbars => 'os'
        -textvariable => \$address)->pack;
```

This creates an Entry widget with an "optional" scrollbar on the bottom. The first argument to `Scrolled` is the type of widget (in this case, an Entry widget). Then use the `-scrollbars` option to list the location of the scrollbar ("s" for the south, or bottom, edge of the widget). Here, we specify an "optional" scrollbar with "o", meaning that the scrollbar will appear only if needed.

Any additional options to the `Scrolled` method are taken as options to the widget itself. In this case, we're setting the `-textvariable` option to the Entry widget.

The Scrollbar widget

For more flexibility with a scrollbar, you can use the Scrollbar widget. To do so, you need to create the target widget to scroll. Set the `-xscrollcommand` or `-yscrollcommand` option as appropriate, configure the scrollbar to talk to the widget, and position the scrollbar and target widget next to one another. For example:

```
$scrollbar = $mainwindow->Scrollbar(-orient => 'vertical');
$listbox = $mainwindow->Entry(-yscrollcommand => ['set' => $scrollbar]);
$scrollbar->configure(-command => ['yview' => $listbox]);
$scrollbar->pack(-side => 'right', -fill => 'y');
$listbox->pack(-side => 'left', -fill => 'both');
```

First, we create the scrollbar with vertical orientation (which is actually the default). Next, we create the Listbox widget with the `-yscrollcommand` option to define a callback when the widget is scrolled vertically. The scrollbar is then configured with a callback that says to inform the Listbox widget when it is clicked vertically. Finally, the Scrollbar and Listbox widgets are packed side-by-side. See further discussion of the Scrollbar widget later in this chapter for more information.

Callbacks

Many widgets allow you to define a *callback*, which is a command to execute when the widget is selected. For example, when you press an exit button, the callback might be to a routine that cleans up and quits the program. When you click on a radio button, you might want to change the window to reflect the new preferences.

Widgets that support callbacks have a -command option to provide the callback function. In the "Hello World" example shown previously, the callback is to sub {exit}. In that example, the callback is called as an anonymous subroutine. You could also use a reference to a subroutine (e.g., \&routine). If you want to provide arguments to a subroutine, you can call it as an anonymous list (e.g., [\&routine, $arg, $arg, ...]).

Colors and Fonts

Tk was originally created for the X Window System and is still primarily used in that environment. For this reason, it has inherited the font and color scheme used for the X Window System.

Colors that can be used with Tk widgets are identified either by an RGB value or by a name that has been associated with an RGB value. In general, it is easier to use a color name than an explicit RGB value. For a listing of the color names that are supported, see the *rgb.txt* file in your X distribution or use the *showrgb* command. (Most common color names are supported, so you can say things such as "red," "pink," "green," and even "chartreuse" with confidence.)

Fonts are another matter. Under the X Window System, fonts are named things such as *-adobe-helvetica-medium-o-normal--12-120-75-75-p-67-iso8859-1*. Wildcards can make the fonts easier to use, but they're still a mouthful. For a listing of fonts available for a particular X server, use the *xlsfonts* command. There are a few font "aliases" that have been defined for your convenience (such as fixed, 6x10, 9x15, etc.), and you might prefer to just stick to those.

Geometry Managers

Creating widgets and determining how to display them are done with separate commands. You can create a widget with one of the widget creation methods (such as Button, Canvas, etc.), but you display them using a geometry manager. The three geometry managers are pack, grid, place, and form. pack is by far the most commonly used.

You can either pack a widget as you create it or create the widget object and pack it separately. For example, the previous "Hello World" example might have read:

```
#!/usr/bin/perl -w
use Tk;
my $mw = MainWindow->new;
$button = $mw->Button(-text => "Hello World!", -command =>sub{exit});
$button->pack;
MainLoop;
```

The pack Geometry Manager

With the pack geometry manager, widgets cannot overlap or cover each other, either partially or completely. Once a widget is packed into a window, the next widget is packed in the remaining space around it. pack sets up an "allocation rectangle" for each widget, determined by the dimensions of the parent window and the positioning of the widgets already packed into it. This means that the order in which you pack your widgets is very important.

By default, pack places widgets at the top center of the allocation rectangle. However, you can use options to pack to control where a widget is placed and how much padding is placed around it. Options for pack are:

-side => *side*
> Puts the widget against the specified side of the window. Values for *side* are left, right, top, and bottom. The default is top.

-fill => *direction*
> Causes the widget to fill the allocation rectangle in the specified direction. Values for *direction* are none, x, y, and both. The default is none.

-expand => *boolean*
> Causes the allocation rectangle to fill the remaining space available in the window. Values are yes, no, 1, and 0. The default is 0 (no).

-anchor => *position*
> Anchors the widget inside the allocation rectangle. Values for *position* are n, ne, e, se, s, sw, w, nw, and center. The default is center.

-after => *$widget*
> Puts the widget after another widget in packing order.

-before => *$widget*
> Puts the widget before another widget in packing order.

-in => *$window*
> Packs the widget inside another window rather than inside its parent.

-ipadx => *amount*
> Increases the size of the widget horizontally by *amount* × 2. *amount* can be represented as a number followed by c (centimeters), i (inches), m (millimeters), and p (printer points). Pixels are the default units.

-ipady => *amount*
> Increases the size of the widget vertically by *amount* × 2. amount can be represented as a number followed by c (centimeters), i (inches), m (millimeters), and p (printer points). Pixels are the default units.

-padx => *amount*
> Places padding on the left and right of the widget. *amount* can be represented as a number followed by c (centimeters), i (inches), m (millimeters), and p (printer points). Pixels are the default units.

-pady *amount*
> Places padding on the top and bottom of the widget. *amount* can be represented as a number followed by c (centimeters), i (inches), m (millimeters), and p (printer points). Pixels are the default units.

pack methods

The following methods are associated with widgets managed with pack:

packForget
> Causes a widget to be removed from view:
>
> ```
> $widget->packForget;
> ```
>
> The widget is not destroyed, but it is no longer managed by pack. The widget is removed from the packing order, so if it was repacked later, it would appear at the end of the packing order.

packInfo
> Returns a list containing all pack information about that widget:
>
> ```
> $info = $widget->packInfo;
> ```

packPropagate
> Enables or suppresses automatic resizing of a Toplevel or Frame widget to accommodate items packed inside of it. Automatic resizing is on by default; the following line turns off automatic resizing:
>
> ```
> $widget->packPropagate(0);
> ```

packSlaves
> Returns an ordered list of all the widgets packed into the parent widget:
>
> ```
> $children = $widget->packSlaves;
> ```

The grid Geometry Manager

The grid geometry manager divides the window into a grid composed of columns and rows starting at 0,0 in the upper lefthand corner. The resulting grid resembles a spreadsheet, with each widget assigned a cell according to the options to grid. To create a grid, create a frame packed inside the parent window and then grid the widgets within the frame.

You can specify explicit rows and columns using options to grid. However, if several widgets are meant to appear in the same row, you can use a single grid command with a list of widgets rather than calling grid for each one. The first widget invokes the grid command, and all other widgets for that column are specified as options to grid. Any subsequent grid commands increment the row by one and start again.

You can use special characters as placeholders:

- *(minus sign)*
> The previous widget should span this column as well. May not follow ^ or x.

x

> Leaves a blank space.

^

> The widget above this one (same column, previous row) should span this row.

Options to grid are:

`-column => n`
> The column in which to place the widget. *n* is any integer >= 0.

`-row => m`
> The row in which to place the widget. *m* is any integer >= 0.

`-columnspan => n`
> The number of columns for the widget to span, beginning with the column specified with -column. *n* is any integer > 0.

`-rowspan => m`
> The number of rows for the widget to span, beginning with the row specified with -row. *m* is any integer > 0.

`-sticky => sides`
> Sticks widget to specified side(s). *sides* contains characters n, s, e, or w.

`-in => $window`
> Grids widget inside another window instead of its parent.

`-ipadx => amount`
> Increases the size of the widget horizontally by *amount* × 2. *amount* can be represented as a number followed by c (centimeters), i (inches), m (millimeters), and p (printer points). Pixels are the default units.

`-ipady => amount`
> Increases the size of the widget vertically by *amount* × 2. *amount* can be represented as a number followed by c (centimeters), i (inches), m (millimeters), and p (printer points). Pixels are the default units.

`-padx => amount`
> Places padding on the left and right of the widget. *amount* can be represented as a number followed by c (centimeters), i (inches), m (millimeters), and p (printer points). Pixels are the default units.

`-pady amount`
> Places padding on the top and bottom of the widget. *amount* can be represented as a number followed by c (centimeters), i (inches), m (millimeters), and p (printer points). Pixels are the default units.

grid methods

The following methods are associated with widgets managed by grid:

`gridColumnconfigure`
> Configures the column specified by the first argument using -weight and -minsize arguments. The -weight argument determines the amount of space to allocate to that column, and the -minsize argument sets the minimum size in pixels. For example:
>
> ```
> $widget->gridColumnconfigure(3, -weight => 1);
> ```

`gridRowconfigure`
> Configures the row specified by the first argument using -weight and -minsize arguments. The -weight argument determines the amount of space to allocate

to that row, and the -minsize argument sets the minimum size in pixels. For example:

```
$widget->gridRowconfigure(3, -weight => 1);
```

gridRemove

Removes each of the $slaves from grid for its master and unmaps their windows. The slaves will no longer be managed by the grid geometry manager. gridRemove remembers the previous configuration options for the window. So, if $slave is managed once more by the grid geometry manager, the previous values will be retained.

gridBbox

Returns the bounding box in pixels for the space occupied by the specified grid position (in the order of column, row). For example:

```
$widget->gridBbox(3,2);
```

gridForget

Causes the widget(s) to be removed from view. Additional widgets can be specified as arguments.

```
$widget1->gridForget($widget2, widget3, ...);
```

gridInfo

Returns information about the widget in list format:

```
$widget->gridInfo;
```

gridLocation

Returns the column and row of the widget nearest the specified x,y coordinates (in pixels):

```
$widget->gridLocation(120, 32);
```

gridPropagate

Turns off automatic resizing of the widget:

```
$widget->gridPropagate;
```

gridSize

Returns the size of the grid, i.e., the number of columns and rows:

```
$widget->gridSize;
```

gridSlaves

Returns a list of all widgets contained within a master widget. Optional -row and -column arguments restrict the response to the widget(s) within that row or column:

```
@children = $widget->gridSlaves(-row => 2);
```

The place Geometry Manager

The place geometry manager lets you position a window at explicit x,y coordinates. With place, you can overlap widgets, which isn't allowed with grid or pack. For example, to position a button widget at the upper-left corner of a window:

```
$button->place(-x => 0, -y => 0);
```

Options to place are:

-anchor => *position*

    The position in the widget that will be placed at the coordinates specified. Values for *position* are n, ne, e, se, s, sw, w, nw, and center. Default is nw.

-bordermode => *location*

    Determines whether the border portion of the widget is included in the coordinate system. Values for *location* are inside, outside, and ignore.

-height => *amount*

    Absolute height of the widget. *amount* can be represented as a number followed by c (centimeters), i (inches), m (millimeters), and p (printer points). Pixels are the default units.

-in => *$window*

    The child widget will be packed inside the specified window instead of the parent that created it. Any relative coordinates or sizes will still refer to the parent.

-relheight => *ratio*

    The height of the widget relates to the parent widget's height by the specified ratio.

-relwidth => *ratio*

    The width of the widget relates to the parent widget's width by the specified ratio.

-relx => *xratio*

    The widget will be placed relative to its parent by the specified ratio. *xratio* is a floating point number from 0.0 to 1.0, with 0.0 representing the left side of the parent widget and 1.0 representing the right side.

-rely => *yratio*

    The widget will be placed relative to its parent by the specified ratio. *yratio* is a floating point number from 0.0 to 1.0, with 0.0 representing the top of the parent widget and 1.0 representing the bottom.

-width => *amount*

    The width of the widget will be the specified amount. *amount* can be represented as a number followed by c (centimeters), i (inches), m (millimeters), and p (printer points). Pixels are the default units.

-x => *xcoord*

    The widget will be placed at the specified x coordinate.

-y => *ycoord*

    The widget will be placed at the specified y coordinate.

The following methods are associated with widgets managed by place:

placeForget

    Causes the widget to be removed from view.

placeInfo

    Returns information about the widget.

placeSlaves

    Returns a list of widgets managed by the specified parent widget.

The form Geometry Manager

The form geometry manager arranges the geometry of children in the parent window according to attachment rules. In addition, form can be used as a replacement for the existing Tk pack and place geometry managers. For example, to position a widget $top_w on top of $bot_w, you'd do this:

```
$bot_w->form(-top=>[$topw_w, 0]);
```

Options to form are:

-b => *attachment*
  Abbreviation for the -bottom option.

-bottom => *attachment*
  Specifies an attachment for the bottom edge of the slave window.

-bottomspring => *attachment*
  Specifies the weight of the spring at the bottom edge of the slave window.

-bp => *value*
  Abbrevation for the -padbottom option.

-bs => *weight*
  Abbrevation for the -bottomspring option.

-fill => *style*
  Specifies the fillings when springs are used for this widget. The value must be x, y, both, or none.

-in => *$master*
  Places the slave window into the specified $master window. If the slave was originally in $another_master, all attachment values with respect to $original_ master are discarded. The attachment values will need to be specified again. If you use -in, it must be used first in the options list.

-l => *attachment*
  Abbreviation for the -left option.

-left => *attachment*
  Specifies an attachment for the left edge of slave window, $slave.

-leftspring => *weight*
  Specifies the weight of the spring at the edge of the slave window, $slave.

-lp => *value*
  Abbreviation for the -padleft option.

-ls => *weight*
  Abbreviation for the -leftspring option.

-padbottom => *value*
  Specifies the amount of external padding to leave on the bottom side of the slave.

-padleft => *value*
  Specifies the amount of external padding to leave on the left side of the slave.

-padright => *value*

Specifies the amount of external padding to leave on the right side of the slave.

-padtop => *value*

Specifies the amount of external padding to leave on the top side of the slave.

-padx => *value*

Specifies the amount of external padding to leave on both the left and right sides of the slave.

-pady => *value*

Specifies the amount of external padding to leave on both the top and bottom sides of the slave.

-r => *attachment*

Abbreviation for the -right option.

-right => *attachment*

Specifies an attachment for the right edge of the slave window.

-rightspring => *weight*

Specifies the weight of the spring at the right edge of the slave window.

-rp => *value*

Abbreviation for the -padright option.

-rs => *weight*

Abbreviation for the -rightspring option.

-t => *attachment*

Abbreviation for the -top option.

-top => *attachment*

Specifies an attachment for the top edge of the slave window.

-topspring => *weight*

Specifies the weight of the spring at the top edge of the slave window.

-tp => *value*

Abbreviation for the -padtop option.

-ts => *weight*

Abbreviation for the -topspring option.

The following methods are associated with widgets managed by form:

formCheck

Checks whether this is a circular dependancy between the master's slaves. It returns true if the dependancy exists and false otherwise.

formForget

Removes the slave from its master and unmaps its window. The slave will no longer be managed by form. All attachment values with respect to $master are discarded.

```
formGrid($size_x, $size_y)
```
Returns the number of grids to $master as integers in the form $size_x, $size_y. You may change the number of grids on the master window by passing $size_x and $size_y to formGrid.

```
formInfo(-option)
```
Queries the attachment options of a slave window. -option can be any of the options accepted by form. With no options, formInfo returns the current configuration values.

```
formSlaves
```
Returns a list of all the slaves for the master window.

Common Widget Configuration Options

In the remainder of this chapter, we'll discuss each widget, the commands used to create each widget, the options used to configure them, and the methods for manipulating them.

You'll find that there are many, many configuration options shared by multiple widgets. We could list them individually for each widget, but in the interest of saving a tree or two, we will instead list the shared options up front rather than repeating them over and over. That way, we can concentrate on the options that are crucial to the behavior of each particular widget and save the reader from being lost in a sea of options.

The following options are supported by the widgets noted:

```
-activebackground => color
```
Sets the background color when the mouse cursor is over the widget. Applicable widgets: Button, Checkbutton, Menu, Menubutton, Optionmenu, Radiobutton, Scale, Scrollbar.

```
-activeborderwidth => borderwidth
```
Sets a 3-D border around active elements. Applicable widgets: Menu, Menubutton, Optionmenu.

```
-activeforeground => color
```
Sets the text color when the mouse cursor is over the widget. Applicable widgets: Button, Checkbutton, Menu, Menubutton, Optionmenu, Radiobutton.

```
-anchor => position
```
Causes the text to stick to that position in the widget. Values for position are n, ne, e, se, s, sw, w, nw, and center. Applicable widgets: Button, Checkbutton, Label, Menubutton, Optionmenu, Radiobutton.

```
-background => color
-bg => color
```
Sets the background of the widget to the specified color. Applicable widgets: Button, Canvas, Checkbutton, Entry, Frame, Label, Listbox, Menu, Menubutton, Optionmenu, Radiobutton, Scale, Scrollbar, Text, Toplevel.

`-bitmap => 'bitmapname'`

Uses a bitmap instead of text in the widget. You can specify either a default bitmap or the location of a bitmap file (with @ in front of the path). Applicable widgets: Button, Checkbutton, Label, Menubutton, Optionmenu, Radiobutton.

`-borderwidth => amount`
`-bd => amount`

Changes the width of the edge drawn around the widget. Applicable widgets: Button, Canvas, Checkbutton, Entry, Frame, Label, Listbox, Menu, Menubutton, Optionmenu, Radiobutton, Scale, Scrollbar, Text, Toplevel.

`-cursor => 'cursorname'`

Mouse cursor will change to specified cursor when over the widget. Applicable widgets: Button, Canvas, Checkbutton, Entry, Frame, Label, Listbox, Menu, Menubutton, Optionmenu, Radiobutton, Scale, Scrollbar, Text, Toplevel.

`-disabledforeground => color`

Sets the color of the text when the widget is disabled. Applicable widgets: Button, Checkbutton, Menu, Menubutton, Optionmenu, Radiobutton.

`-exportselection => boolean`

Determines whether selected text is exported to the window system's clipboard. (For a listbox, the default of `-exportselection => 1` means two listboxes cannot have selections at the same time.) Applicable widgets: Entry, Listbox, Text.

`-font => 'fontname'`

Changes the font of all the text on the widget to *fontname*. Applicable widgets: Button, Checkbutton, Entry, Label, Listbox, Menu, Menubutton, Optionmenu, Radiobutton, Scale, Text.

`-foreground => color`
`-fg => color`

Changes the text color to *color*. Applicable widgets: Button, Checkbutton, Entry, Label, Listbox, Menu, Menubutton, Optionmenu, Radiobutton, Scale, Text.

`-height => amount`

Specifies the height of the widget. *amount* represents a number of characters if text is displayed, or a screen distance if an image or bitmap is displayed. Applicable widgets: Button, Canvas, Checkbutton, Frame, Label, Listbox, Menubutton, Optionmenu, Radiobutton, Text, Toplevel.

`-highlightbackground => color`

Sets the color of a non-focus rectangle. Applicable widgets: Button, Canvas, Checkbutton, Entry, Frame, Label, Listbox, Menubutton, Optionmenu, Radiobutton, Scale, Scrollbar, Text, Toplevel.

`-highlightcolor => color`

Sets the color of the focus rectangle. Applicable widgets: Button, Canvas, Checkbutton, Entry, Frame, Label, Listbox, Menubutton, Optionmenu, Radiobutton, Scale, Scrollbar, Text, Toplevel.

-highlightthickness => *amount*
> Sets the thickness of the black box around the widget that indicates focus. Applicable widgets: Button, Canvas, Checkbutton, Entry, Frame, Label, Listbox, Menubutton, Optionmenu, Radiobutton, Scale, Scrollbar, Text, Toplevel.

-image => *$imgptr*
> Uses an image instead of text. *$imgptr* is a pointer to a Photo or Image object made using a GIF or PPM file. For example:

```
$arrow = $mainwindow->Photo(-file => "image.gif");
$mainwindow->Button(-image => $arrow,
                    -command => sub {exit})->pack;
```

> Applicable widgets: Button, Checkbutton, Label, Menubutton, Optionmenu, Radiobutton.

-insertbackground => *color*
> Sets the color of the insert cursor. Applicable widgets: Canvas, Entry, Text.

-insertborderwidth => *amount*
> Sets the width of the insert cursor's border. Applicable widgets: Canvas, Entry, Text.

-insertofftime => *milliseconds*
> Defines the amount of time the insert cursor is "off." Applicable widgets: Canvas, Entry, Text.

-insertontime => *milliseconds*
> Defines the amount of time the insert cursor is "on." Applicable widgets: Canvas, Entry, Text.

-insertwidth => *amount*
> The width of the insert corner (default = 2 pixels). Applicable widgets: Canvas, Entry, Text.

-justify => *side*
> Justifies text against the specified side. *side* can be left, right, or center. Applicable widgets: Button, Checkbutton, Entry, Label, Menubutton, Optionmenu, Radiobutton.

-padx => *amount*
> Adds extra space to left and right of the widget inside the widget edge. Applicable widgets: Button, Checkbutton, Label, Menubutton, Optionmenu, Radiobutton, Text.

-pady => *amount*
> Adds extra space to top and bottom of the widget inside the widget edge. Applicable widgets: Button, Checkbutton, Label, Menubutton, Optionmenu, Radiobutton, Text.

-relief => *type*
> Changes the type of edges drawn around the widget. Values for *type* are flat, groove, raised, ridge, and sunken. Applicable widgets: Button, Canvas, Checkbutton, Entry, Frame, Label, Listbox, Menu, Menubutton, Optionmenu, Radiobutton, Scale, Scrollbar, Text, Toplevel.

`-selectbackground => `*`color`*
> Determines the background color of selected text in the entry widget. Applicable widgets: Canvas, Entry, Listbox, Text.

`-selectborderwidth => `*`amount`*
> Determines the width of the selection highlight's border. Applicable widgets: Canvas, Entry, Listbox, Text.

`-selectforeground => `*`color`*
> Determines the text color of selected text in the entry widget. Applicable widgets: Canvas, Entry, Listbox, Text.

`-state => `*`state`*
> Sets the state of responsiveness of the widget. Values for *state* are normal, disabled, and active. (disabled makes it not respond.) Applicable widgets: Button, Checkbutton, Entry, Menubutton, Optionmenu, Scale, Text.

`-takefocus => `*`focus`*
> Determines whether the widget gets focus. Values for *focus* are 0 (the widget will never get the focus), 1 (the widget always gets the focus), and the null string ("") (which lets the application decide). Applicable widgets: Button, Canvas, Checkbutton, Entry, Frame, Label, Listbox, Menu, Menubutton, Optionmenu, Scale, Scrollbar, Text, Toplevel.

`-underline => `*`n`*
> Underlines the *n*th character in the text string. Allows keyboard input via that character when the widget has the focus. Applicable widgets: Button, Checkbutton, Label, Menubutton, Optionmenu, Radiobutton.

`-width => `*`amount`*
> Width of the widget, represented in characters if text is displayed, or as a screen distance if an image or bitmap is displayed. Applicable widgets: Button, Canvas, Checkbutton, Frame, Label, Listbox, Menubutton, Optionmenu, Radiobutton, Scale, Scrollbar, Text, Toplevel.

`-wraplength => `*`amount`*
> Defines the maximum amount of text to be displayed on one line. Applicable widgets: Button, Checkbutton, Label, Menubutton, Optionmenu, Radiobutton.

`-xscrollcommand => `*`callback`*
> Assigns a callback to use when scrolling back and forth. Applicable widgets: Canvas, Entry, Listbox, Text.

`-yscrollcommand => `*`callback`*
> Determines a command to run when scrolled in the vertical direction. Applicable widgets: Canvas, Listbox, Text.

The Button Widget

Create a simple button with the Button method:

```
$parentwidget->Button (options)
```

The standard configuration options that apply to Button are: -activebackground, -activeforeground, -anchor, -background, -bg, -bitmap, -borderwidth, -bd, -cursor, -default, -disabledforeground, -font, -foreground, -fg, -height, -highlight-background, -highlightcolor, -highlightthickness, -image, -justify, -padx, -pady, -relief, -state, -takefocus, -underline, -width, and -wraplength.

Other options are:

-command => *callback*
> Pointer to a function that will be called when the button is pressed.

-text => '*text*'
> Defines the text string displayed on the button. See also -textvariable.

-textvariable => \$*variable*
> Points to the variable containing text to be displayed in the button. Button text will change as $*variable* does.

Button Methods

In addition to configure and cget, the following methods can be used for Button:

flash
> Causes the button to flash from the normal to active state colors.

invoke
> Invokes the callback command as if the button was clicked.

The Checkbutton Widget

Create a checkbutton with the Checkbutton command. A checkbutton has an indicator to the left of the label indicating whether the button is selected. The boolean status of the button (0, 1, or values as specified by the -onvalue and -offvalue options) is stored in the variable specified with the -variable option.

> $parentwidget->Checkbutton (*options*)

The standard configuration options that apply to Checkbutton are: -activeback-ground, -activeforeground, -anchor, -background, -bg, -bitmap, -borderwidth, -bd, -cursor, -disabledforeground, -font, -foreground, -fg, -height, -highlight-background, -highlightcolor, -highlightthickness, -image, -justify, -padx, -pady, -relief, -state, -takefocus, -underline, -width, and -wraplength.

Other options are:

-command => *callback*
> Pointer to a function that will be called when the checkbutton is pressed.

-indicatoron => *boolean*
> Determines whether to display the indicator. Default is on (1).

-offvalue => *newvalue*
> Specifies the value used when the checkbutton is off. Must be a scalar. Default is 0.

-onvalue => *newvalue*
> Specifies the value used when the checkbutton is on. Must be a scalar. Default is 1.

-selectcolor => *color*
> Color of the indicator when the checkbutton is on.

-selectimage => *imgptr*
> Defines the image to be displayed instead of text when the checkbutton is on. Ignored if -image is not used.

-text => '*text*'
> Defines the text string displayed in the checkbutton. See also -textvariable.

-textvariable => \$*variable*
> Points to the variable containing text to be displayed in the checkbutton. Button text will change as $*variable* does.

-variable => \$*variable*
> Associates the on/off value of the indicator with the specified variable.

Checkbutton Methods

In addition to configure and cget, the following methods are supported by Checkbutton:

deselect
> Sets the indicator to off.

select
> Sets the indicator to on.

flash
> Causes the button to flash from the normal to active state colors.

invoke
> Invokes the callback command as if the checkbuttons were clicked.

toggle
> Toggles the indicator from on to off, or from off to on.

The Radiobutton Widget

Create a radiobutton with the Radiobutton method. A radiobutton has an indicator to the left of the label indicating whether the button is selected. It differs from a checkbutton in that only one button may be selected at a time. Each button in a group of radiobuttons uses the same variable specified with the -variable option; when selected, the button assigns that variable the value specified by the -value option.

```
$parentwidget->Radiobutton (options)
```

The standard configuration options that apply to Radiobutton are: -activebackground, -activeforeground, -anchor, -background, -bg, -bitmap, -borderwidth, -bd,

-cursor, -disabledforeground, -font, -foreground, -fg, -height, -highlight-background, -highlightcolor, -highlightthickness, -image, -justify, -padx, -pady, -relief, -state, -underline, -width, and -wraplength.

Other options are:

-command => *callback*
    Pointer to a function that will be called when the radiobutton is pressed.

-indicatoron => *boolean*
    Determines whether to display the indicator. Default is on (1).

-selectcolor => *color*
    Color of the indicator when the radiobutton is on.

-selectimage => *imgptr*
    Defines the image to be displayed instead of text when the radiobutton is on. Ignored if -image is not used.

-text => '*text*'
    Defines the text string displayed in the radiobutton. See also -textvariable.

-textvariable => \$*variable*
    Points to the variable containing text to be displayed in the radiobutton. Button text will change as $*variable* does.

-value => *value*
    Sets $*variable* to the specified value when the radiobutton is selected. Default is 1.

-variable => \$*variable*
    Associates the on/off value of the indicator with the specified variable.

Radiobutton Methods

In addition to configure and cget, the following methods are supported by Radiobutton:

deselect
    Deselects the button and sets the variable to the empty string.

select
    Sets the radio button.

flash
    Causes the button to flash from the normal to active state colors.

invoke
    Selects the button and invokes the callback command as if the radiobutton was clicked.

The Label Widget

Create a noninteractive label with the Label command. A label is used to display text or an image.

```
$parentwidget->Label (options)
```

The standard configuration options that apply to Label are: -anchor, -background, -bg, -bitmap, -borderwidth, -bd, -cursor, -font, -foreground, -fg, -height, -highlightbackground, -highlightcolor, -highlightthickness, -image, -justify, -padx, -pady, -relief, -takefocus, -underline, -width, and -wraplength.

Other options are:

-text => 'text'
> Defines the text string displayed in the label. See also -textvariable.

-textvariable => \$variable
> Points to the variable containing text to be displayed in the label. Button text will change as $variable does.

The Entry Widget

Create an Entry widget with the Entry method. An entry widget is a space for the user to enter text. The value that the user has typed into the widget is stored in the variable pointed to by the -textvariable option.

> $parent->Entry (options)

The standard configuration options that apply to Entry are: -background, -bg, -borderwidth, -bd, -cursor, -exportselection, -font, -foreground, -fg, -highlightbackground, -highlightcolor, -highlightthickness, -insertbackground, -insertborderwidth, -insertofftime, -insertontime, -insertwidth, -justify, -relief, -selectbackground, -selectborderwidth, -selectforeground, -state, -takefocus, and -xscrollcommand.

Other options are:

-show => x
> Defines a character to be displayed in place of actual typed text (for use with passwords).

-textvariable => \$variable
> Points to the variable containing text to be displayed in the Entry widget. Button text will change as $variable does.

Text Indexes

In an Entry widget, several indexes are defined to identify positions in the entry text. These are used by the methods that retrieve and manipulate entry text.

n
> An integer representing a character position, with 0 as the first character in the string.

insert
> The character directly after the insert cursor.

sel.first
> The first character in the selection block.

sel.last
> The character after the last character in the selection block.

anchor
> The anchored position.

end
> The position just after the last character in the entry string.

@x
> The character containing the specified x coordinate.

Entry Methods

In addition to configure and cget, the following methods are supported for the Entry widget:

delete
> Deletes text from the widget. For example, to delete the selected text:
>
> ```
> $entry->delete('sel.first', 'sel.last');
> ```

get
> Gets the contents of the Entry widget. For example:
>
> ```
> $input = $entry->get;
> ```

icursor
> Places the cursor at the specified index. For example, to move the cursor to the end of the entry string:
>
> ```
> $entry->icursor('end');
> ```

index
> Converts a named index into a numeric one:
>
> ```
> $length = $entry->index('end');
> ```

insert
> Inserts text at the specified index. For example, to append the ".txt" string to the end of the entry string:
>
> ```
> $entry -> insert('end', '.txt');
> ```

selection
> Manipulates the selected block. The first argument can be any of:
>
> adjust
> > Extends selected text to the index specified in the second argument:
> >
> > ```
> > $entry->selection('adjust', 'end');
> > ```
>
> clear
> > Clears the selection block:
> >
> > ```
> > $entry->selection('clear');
> > ```
>
> from
> > Resets the anchor index to the index specified in the second argument:
> >
> > ```
> > $entry->selection('from',0);
> > ```

present
> Determines if any text is currently selected:
>
> ```
> if ($entry->selection('present')) {
>         $entry->delete('sel.first','sel.last');
> }
> ```

range
> Changes the selection range to the indexes specified in the second and third arguments. For example, to change the selection to include the entire entry string:
>
> ```
> $entry->selection('range',0,'end');
> ```

to
> Extends the selection from the current anchor position to the specified index:
>
> ```
> $entry->selection('to','insert');
> ```

xview

Manipulates the text in view. With no arguments, returns a list of two numbers between 0 and 1, defining the portion of the entry text that is currently hidden on the left and right sides, respectively. With arguments, the function of xview changes:

index
> If the first argument is an index, that position becomes the leftmost position in view. For example, to reset the visible portion to the beginning of the string:
>
> ```
> $entry->xview(0);
> ```

moveto
> Moves the specified fraction of the entry text to the left of the visible portion. For example, to hide the first 10% of the entry text:
>
> ```
> $entry->xview('moveto',0.1);
> ```

scroll
> Scrolls the text left or right by the specified number of units (characters, in this context) or pages. Used mainly as a callback to a scrollbar; pressing on an arrow moves by units (characters), and pressing on the trough moves by pages. The number is either 1 or -1, to move forwards or backwards, respectively. For example:
>
> ```
> $entry->xview('scroll',1,'units');
> ```

The Scrollbar Widget

Create a scrollbar with the Scrollbar method:

```
$parentwidget->Scrollbar (options)
```

The standard configuration options that apply to Scrollbar are: -activebackground, -background, -bg, -borderwidth, -bd, -cursor, -highlightbackground, -highlightcolor, -highlightthickness, -relief, -takefocus, and -width.

Other options are:

-activerelief => *type*
> Changes how active elements (arrow1, arrow2, and slider) in the scrollbar are drawn. Values for *type* are flat, groove, raised, ridge, and sunken. The default is raised.

-command => *callback*
> Pointer to a function that will be called when the scrollbar is clicked on.

-elementborderwidth => *amount*
> The width of the borders of the arrow1, arrow2, and slider elements.

-jump => *boolean*
> Determines whether the scrollbar will jump scroll. Default is 0 (jump scroll disabled).

-orient => *orientation*
> Determines the orientation of the scrollbar. Possible *orientation*s are horizontal and vertical (default).

-repeatdelay => *milliseconds*
> Determines the number of milliseconds to hold down an arrow before it will auto-repeat. Default is 300.

-repeatinterval => *milliseconds*
> Determines the number of milliseconds between auto-repeats once it is started. Default is 100.

-troughcolor => *color*
> Changes the color of the trough.

Scrollbar Methods

In addition to configure and cget, the following methods are supported by the Scrollbar widget:

set
> Changes the viewable portion of the data, with the two arguments being numbers between 0 and 1 representing the portions of the data that will be visible.
>
> ```
> $scrollbar->set(0.2,0.6);
> ```

get
> Returns the latest arguments to set.

activate
> With no arguments, returns the name of the current active element. With an argument of arrow1, arrow2, or slider, changes the color of the specified element to the active foreground color and relief type.

delta
> Given a number of pixels in the first argument, returns the fractional change needed to move the slider that amount.

fraction

Given an x,y coordinate as the first and second arguments, returns a number between 0 and 1 representing the fraction of the scrollbar that the coordinate would fall under.

identify

Given an x,y coordinate as the first and second arguments, returns the name of the element at those coordinates.

The Listbox Widget

Create a listbox with the Listbox method. You can then insert items into the listbox using the insert method.

> $parentwidget->Listbox (*options*)

The standard configuration options that apply to Listbox are: -background, -bg, -borderwidth, -bd, -cursor, -exportselection, -font, -foreground, -fg, -height, -highlightbackground, -highlightcolor, -highlightthickness, -relief, -select-background, -selectborderwidth, -selectforeground, -takefocus, -width, -xscroll-command, and -yscrollcommand.

Other options are:

-selectmode => *mode*

Determines the number of items that can be selected at once, as well as key/mouse bindings. *mode* can be any of:

> **single**
>
> Only one item can be selected at a time.
>
> **browse**
>
> Only one item can be selected at a time (default).
>
> **multiple**
>
> Multiple items can be selected at a time.
>
> **extended**
>
> Multiple items can be selected at a time.

-setgrid => *boolean*

Turns on gridding for the listbox. If the widget is resized, only complete lines and characters are displayed. Default is 0 (off).

Listbox Indexes

In a Listbox widget, several indexes are defined to identify positions in the listbox. These are used by the methods that retrieve and manipulate listbox entries.

n

An integer representing a position in the list, with 0 as the first item.

active

The item with the keyboard focus.

anchor
> The anchored position.

end
> The last element in the listbox.

@x,y
> The listbox item containing the specified x,y coordinate.

Listbox Methods

In addition to configure and cget, the following methods are supported by Listbox:

insert
> Adds items to a listbox at the specified index. For example, to insert items at the end of a list:
>
> ```
> $listbox->insert('end', "Puerto Rico", "Virgin Islands", "Guam");
> ```

delete
> Deletes items from a listbox. To delete all items:
>
> ```
> $listbox->delete(0,'end');
> ```

get
> Returns a list of elements within the specified range of indexes. For a list of all elements:
>
> ```
> @items = $listbox->get(0,'end');
> ```

curselection
> Returns a list of all currently selected elements in the listbox.

activate
> Sets the specified item to be the active element.

bbox
> Returns the location and dimensions of the bounding box surrounding the specified listbox element. The returned list contains four numbers representing (respectively) the x coordinate of the upper-left corner, the y coordinate of the upper-left corner, the width of the text in pixels, and the height of the text in pixels.

index
> Converts a named index into a numeric one.

nearest
> Gets the index of the listbox item nearest a given y coordinate.

see
> Pages the listbox up or down to display the specified item.

selection
> Manipulates the selected block of list items. The first argument can be any of:
>
> anchor
> > Sets the anchor index to the specified index.

clear

Clears any selected list items in the specified range. For example, to clear all selections:

```
$listbox->selection('clear', 0, 'end');
```

includes

Returns 0 or 1 depending on whether the specified item is already selected:

```
$listbox->selection('includes', 'end');
```

set

Selects a range of items in the listbox:

```
$listbox->selection('set', 0, 'end');
```

size

Returns the total number of items in the listbox.

xview

Manipulates the text in view. With no arguments, returns a list of two numbers between 0 and 1, defining the portion of the list text that is currently hidden on the left and right sides, respectively. With arguments, the function of xview changes:

index

If the first argument is an index, that position becomes the leftmost position in view.

moveto

Moves the specified fraction of the listbox to the left of the visible portion.

scroll

Scrolls the text left or right by the specified number of units (characters, in this context) or pages. Used primarily as a callback to a scrollbar; pressing on an arrow would move by units (characters), and pressing on the trough would move by pages. The number is either 1 or -1, to move forwards or backwards, respectively.

yview

Manipulates the text in view. With no arguments, returns a list of two numbers between 0 and 1, defining the portion of the list text that is currently hidden on the top and bottom, respectively. With arguments, the function of yview changes:

index

If the first argument is an index, that position becomes the topmost position in view.

moveto

Moves the specified fraction of the listbox to the top of the visible portion.

scroll

Scrolls the text up or down by the specified number of units (lines, in this context) or pages. Used primarily as a callback to a scrollbar;

pressing on an arrow would move by units (lines), and pressing on the trough would move by pages. The number is either 1 or -1, to move forwards or backwards, respectively.

The Text Widget

Create a Text widget with the Text method:

```
$parentwidget->Text ( options)
```

The standard configuration options that apply to Text are: -background, -bg, -borderwidth, -bd, -cursor, -exportselection, -font, -foreground, -fg, -height, -highlightbackground, -highlightcolor, -highlightthickness, -insertbackground, -insertborderwidth, -insertofftime, -insertontime, -insertwidth, -padx, -pady, -relief, -selectbackground, -selectborderwidth, -selectforeground, -state, -takefocus, -width, -xscrollcommand, and -yscrollcommand.

Other options are:

-setgrid => boolean
　　Turns on gridding for the Text widget. Default is 0 (off).

-spacing1 => amount
　　Defines the amount of space left on the top of a line of text that starts on its own line. Default is 0.

-spacing2 => amount
　　Defines the amount of space left on the top of a line of text after it has been automatically wrapped by the Text widget. Default is 0.

-spacing3 => amount
　　Defines the amount of space left after a line of text that has been ended by \n. Default is 0.

-tabs => list
　　Specifies a list of tab stops to use in the text widget. Default is undefined (no tab stops).

-wrap => mode
　　Sets the mode for determining automatic line wrapping. Values are none (no wrapping), char (wrap at any character), or word (wrap at a word boundary). Default is char.

Text Indexes and Modifiers

In a Text widget, several indexes are defined to identify positions in the text. These are used by the methods that retrieve and manipulate text.

n.m
　　Numbers representing character m on line n

@x,y
　　The character closest to the x,y coordinate

end
> The end of the text

insert
> The character after the insert cursor

current
> The position closest to the mouse cursor

mark
> Other marks defined for the widget (see discussion of text marks later in this section)

sel.first
> The first selected character

sel.last
> The character just after the last selected character

tag.first
> The first character in the widget of the specified tag type

tag.last
> The character just after the last character of the specified tag type

widget
> The location of an embedded widget

There are also several modifiers to use with text indexes. They are:

- *n* lines
+ *n* lines
> *n* lines before or after the index

- *n* chars
+ *n* chars
> *n* characters before or after the index

linestart
> The first character on the line

lineend
> The last character on the line (often a newline)

wordstart
> The first character in the word

wordend
> The character after the last character in the word

Text Methods

In addition to configure and cget, the following methods are defined for the Text widget:

bbox
> Returns the location and dimensions of the bounding box surrounding the character at the specified index. The returned list contains four numbers

representing (respectively) the x coordinate of the upper-left corner, the y coordinate of the upper-left corner, the width of the text in pixels, and the height of the text in pixels.

compare

Performs a comparison on two indexes. For example:

```
if ($text->compare('insert', '==', 'end') {
        # we're at the end of the text
}
```

The valid operators are <, <=, ==, >=, and !=.

debug

Given a Boolean, turns debugging on or off.

delete

Deletes text from the text widget. To delete everything:

```
$text->delete(0, 'end');
```

dlineinfo

Returns the location and dimensions of the bounding box surrounding the line at the specified index. The returned list contains five numbers representing (respectively) the x coordinate of the upper-left corner, the y coordinate of the upper-left corner, the width of the text in pixels, the height of the text in pixels, and the baseline position of the line.

get

Returns the text located in the given index range.

index

Given a named index, returns its numeric equivalent in the format *line.char*.

insert

Inserts text into the widget at the specified location. The second argument is the text to insert, and the third argument is either a single tag or a list reference containing the names of multiple tags to apply to the text. Subsequent arguments alternate between text and tags. For example:

```
$text->insert('end', 'You want to do ', 'normal',
                      'what?!', ['bold','red']);
```

search

Returns the index containing a particular string in the Text widget. For example, to search backwards for a case-insensitive hostname starting from the end of the text:

```
$hostindex = $text->search(-nocase, -backwards, $hostname, 'end');
```

The search method takes several switches to modify the search, each starting with -. The first argument that does not start with - is taken to be the search string. The switches are:

-forwards

Searches forwards starting at the specified index.

-backwards

Searches backwards starting at the specified index.

-exact

    Matches the string exactly (default).

-regexp

    Treat the pattern as a regular expression.

-nocase

    Ignores case.

-count => *$variable*

    Stores the number of matches into the specified variable.

--

    Interprets the next argument as the pattern. (Useful when the pattern starts with a -.)

see

    Scrolls the text so that the portion of the text containing the specified index is visible.

window

    Embeds widgets within the Text widget. The first argument can be any of: create, names, cget, and configure.

create

    Inserts an embedded widget at a specified index. Each widget occupies one character in the Text widget. The widget must have already been created as a child of the Text widget. For example:

```
$button = $text->Label(-text => "How ya doing?");
$text->window('create','end', -window => $button);
```

    Here, the -window option is used to identify the widget to embed. The list of options to window ('create') is:

-align

    Determines the positioning within the line of text. Values are baseline, bottom, top, or center (default).

-padx

    Adds padding in the x direction.

-pady

    Adds padding in the y direction.

-window

    Identifies the widget to embed.

names

    Returns a list of widget types embedded into the Text widget.

cget

    Returns information on the widget at the specified index:

```
$text->window('cget',0);
```

configure

    Configures widget at the specified index:

```
$text->window('configure',0,-background => "green");
```

xview

> Manipulates the text in view. With no arguments, returns a list of two numbers between 0 and 1, defining the portion of the text that is currently hidden on the left and right sides, respectively. With arguments, the function of xview changes:

> *index*
>> If the first argument is an index, that position becomes the leftmost position in view.

> moveto
>> Moves the specified fraction of the text to the left of the visible portion.

> scroll
>> Scrolls the text left or right by the specified number of units (characters, in this context) or pages. Used primarily as a callback to a scrollbar; pressing on an arrow would move by units (characters), and pressing on the trough would move by pages. The number is either 1 or -1, to move forwards or backwards, respectively.

yview

> Manipulates the text in view. With no arguments, returns a list of two numbers between 0 and 1, defining the portion of the text that is currently hidden on the top and bottom, respectively. With arguments, the function of yview changes:

> *index*
>> If the first argument is an index, that position becomes the topmost position in view.

> moveto
>> Moves the specified fraction of the text to the top of the visible portion.

> scroll
>> Scrolls the text up or down by the specified number of units (lines, in this context) or pages. Used primarily as a callback to a scrollbar; pressing on an arrow would move by units (lines), and pressing on the trough would move by pages. The number is either 1 or -1, to move forwards or backwards, respectively.

Tags

You can associate a distinct set of format properties to a portion of the text using *tags*. A tag is defined with the tagConfigure method, and text is associated with a tag via an option to the insert or tagAdd method. For example:

```
$text->Text->pack;
$text->tagConfigure('bold', -font =>
    '-*-Courier-Medium-B-Normal-*-120-*-*-*-*-*-*');
$text->insert('end', "Normal text\n");
$text->insert('end', "Bold text\n", 'bold');
```

There are several methods defined for manipulating text tags:

tagAdd

Adds a tag to the text within the specified index range. For example, to assign the bold tag defined above to the current selection:

```
$text->tagAdd('bold','sel.first','sel.last');
```

You can supply multiple ranges as arguments to tagAdd.

tagBind

Executes a callback when a specified event happens on the tagged text. For example:

```
$text->tagBind('goto_end', "<Button-1>", sub {shift->see('end');} );
```

tagConfigure

Creates or changes settings for a text tag. For example:

```
$text->tagConfigure('link', -foreground => 'red');
```

Options for configuring text tags are:

-background => *color*
> The color to use behind the text.

-bgstipple => *bitmap*
> A pattern to draw behind the text.

-borderwidth => *amount*
> The width of the edge drawn around the text.

-fgstipple => *bitmap*
> A pattern used to draw the text.

-font => *fontname*
> The font used for the text.

-foreground => *color*
> The color of the text.

-justify => *position*
> The justification of the text (any of left, right, and center). The default is left.

-lmargin1 => *amount*
> The indentation for the first line of a paragraph.

-lmargin2 => *amount*
> The indentation for subsequent lines of a paragraph (for hanging indents).

-offset => *amount*
> The amount the text is raised or lowered from the baseline (for subscripts and superscripts).

-overstrike => *boolean*
> Draws the text with a line through it.

-relief => *type*
> The types of edges drawn around the text. Values for *type* can be flat, groove, raised, ridge, and sunken. Default is flat.

-rmargin => *amount*
> The right margin.

-spacing1 => *amount*
> The amount of space left on the top of a line of text that starts on its own line.

-spacing2 => *amount*
> The amount of space left on the top of a line of text after it has been automatically wrapped by the Text widget.

-spacing3 => *amount*
> The amount of space left after a line of text ended by \n.

-tabs => *list*
> A list of tab stops to use in the Text widget.

-underline => *boolean*
> Whether to underline the text.

-wrap => *mode*
> Sets the mode for determining automatic line wrapping. Values are none (no wrapping), char (wrap at any character), or word (wrap at a word boundary).

tagCget
> Returns configuration settings for a tag.

tagDelete
> Deletes the specified tag(s).

tagRemove
> Removes the tags from the text in the specified index range. (The tag itself remains defined, but is no longer applied to that text.)

tagRaise
> Increases priority for a specified tag. With only one argument, the tag takes highest priority over all others; with a second argument of another tag, the tag's priority is just higher than the second tag. For example:

```
$text->tagRaise('bold','italic');
```

tagLower
> Decreases priority for a specified tag. With only one argument, the tag takes lowest priority to all others; with a second argument of another tag, the tag's priority is just lower than the second tag. For example:

```
$text->tagLower('italic','bold');
```

tagNames
> Returns the names of all tags applying to the specified index. With no index specified, returns all tags defined for the Text widget, regardless of whether they have been applied. For example:

```
@defined_tags = $text->tagNames;
```

tagRanges
> Returns a list of index ranges to which the specified tag is defined. The returned list contains pairs of starting and ending indexes for the ranges. For example:

```
@bold_indexes = $text->tagRanges('bold');
```

tagNextrange
> Given a tag name and an index, returns the next index range to which the specified tag is defined. For example:

```
@next_bold = $text->tagRanges('bold', 'insert');
```

Marks

A *mark* is a particular position between characters in a Text widget. Once you create a mark, you can use it as an index. The gravity of the mark affects to which side the text is inserted. Right gravity is the default, in which case the text is inserted to the right of the mark.

The two marks that are automatically set are insert and current. The insert mark refers to the position of the insert cursor. The current mark is the position closest to the mouse cursor.

The following methods are defined for marking:

markGravity
> Sets the gravity of a mark. For example:

```
$text->markGravity('insert', 'left');
```

markNames
> Returns a list of all marks defined for the Text widget.

markSet
> Creates a mark at a specified index:

```
$text->markSet('saved', 'insert');
```

markUnset
> Deletes mark(s) from the Text widget:

```
$text->markUnset('saved');
```

Note that you cannot delete the insert or current marks.

The Canvas Widget

Create a canvas for drawing with the Canvas method. The Canvas widget uses a coordinate system with the x coordinate increasing as you move right, and the y coordinate increasing as you move down (i.e., the y coordinate is mathematically upside-down). The x and y coordinates are specified in pixels by default.

```
$parentwidget->Canvas (options)
```

The standard configuration options that apply to Canvas are: -background, -borderwidth, -cursor, -height, -highlightbackground, -highlightcolor, -highlightthickness, -insertbackground, -insertborderwidth, -insertofftime, -insertontime, -insertwidth, -relief, -selectbackground, -selectborderwidth, -selectforeground, -state, -takefocus, -width, -xscrollcommand, and -yscrollcommand.

Other options are:

-closeenough => *amount*
> The distance considered "close enough" to an item to be judged to be within it. Default is 1 pixel.

-confine => *boolean*
> Whether to limit the canvas to the scroll region. Default is 1.

-scrollregion => [*x, y, w, h*]
> Sets the region that the user is allowed to scroll. The option is a list reference that conveniently corresponds to the return value of the bbox method.

-xscrollincrement => *amount*
> The distance to use for scrolling in the x direction.

-yscrollincrement => *amount*
> The distance to use for scrolling in the y direction.

Canvas Creation Methods

To place graphic elements in a canvas, there are several item creation methods:

createArc
> Creates an arc contained within the given bounding box. For example, to create an oval bounded by the box from (0,0) to (40,100):
>
> ```
> $canvas->createArc(0,0,40,100, -extent => 360);
> ```
>
> The -extent option gives a number between 0 and 360 defining the length of the arc. The default -extent is 90, or 1/4 of an oval; an extent of 360 gives you a full oval. The complete list of options to createArc is:
>
> -extent => *degrees*
> > Creates an arc of the specified extent. *degrees* can be any number between 0 and 360, as described above.
>
> -fill => *color*
> > Fills the arc with the specified color.
>
> -outline => *color*
> > Draws the arc with the specified color (default is black).
>
> -outlinestipple => *bitmap*
> > Draws the outline with the specified bitmap pattern.
>
> -start => *degrees*
> > Starts drawing the arc from the specified position, which is represented by a number from 0 to 360. The default is 0, which means to start drawing at the 3 o'clock position.

-stipple => *bitmap*
> Uses the specified bitmap to fill the arc (if -fill is also specified).

-style => *type*
> Draws the arc as specified. Values are:

> pieslice
>> Draws lines from the center to the ends of the arc (the default)

> chord
>> Draws a line connecting the two ends of the arc

> arc
>> Draws the arc with no other lines

-tags => *tagnames*
> Associates the arc with the specified tag(s). Multiple tag names can be supplied as an anonymous list.

-width => *amount*
> The width of the outline. Default is 1.

createBitmap
> Inserts a bitmap. For example, to place the calculator bitmap at the (0,0) coordinates:

> ```
> $canvas -> createBitmap(0, 0, -bitmap => 'calculator');
> ```

> Options are:

> **-anchor =>** *position*
>> Anchors the bitmap at the specified position. Values are center (default), n, e, s, w, ne, nw, se, and sw.

> **-background =>** *color*
>> Specifies the color to use for the 0 pixels in the bitmap (default is to be transparent).

> **-bitmap =>** *bitmap*
>> Specifies the bitmap name. For a built-in bitmap, just specify the name; for a local bitmap file, specify the name with an @ preceding it.

> **-foreground =>** *color*
>> Specifies the color to use for the 1 pixel in the bitmap (default is black).

> **-tags =>** *tagnames*
>> Associates the bitmap with the specified tag(s). Multiple tag names can be supplied as an anonymous list.

createImage
> Creates an image. For example, to place an image at (0,0):

> ```
> $canvas->createImage(0,0, -image => $imgptr);
> ```

> Options are:

> **-anchor =>** *position*
>> Anchors the image at the specified position. Values are center (default), n, e, s, w, ne, nw, se, and sw.

Perl/Tk

-image => *$imgptr*
> *$imgptr* is a pointer to a Photo or Image object made using a GIF or PPM file. For example:
>
> ```
> $imgptr = $mainwindow->Photo(-file => "doggie.gif");
> ```

-tags => *tagnames*
> Associate the image with the specified tag(s). Multiple tag names can be supplied as an anonymous list.

createLine
> Creates a line or several adjoining lines. For example, to create a line from (0,0) to (100,100) and then back to (100,0):
>
> ```
> $canvas->createLine (0,0,100,100,100,0);
> ```

The first four coordinates are required. Any additional coordinates are taken to represent a continuation of that line. Options are:

-arrow => *position*
> Specifies where to place arrowheads. Values are none (default), first, last, and both.

-arrowshape => [*head, length, flare*]
> Specifies the dimensions of the arrow as a three-element anonymous list, describing (in order) the distance from the base to the head of the arrow, the distance from the rear point(s) to the head of the arrow, and the distance from the rear point(s) to the line.

-capstyle => *type*
> Defines the type of arrowhead. Values are butt (the default), projecting, and round.

-fill => *color*
> The color to use to draw the line.

-joinstyle => *type*
> Defines how multiple lines are joined. Values are miter (default), bevel, and round.

-smooth => *boolean*
> Determines whether the lines are drawn with a Bezier spine. Default is 0.

-splinesteps => *n*
> Determines how smooth the Bezier curve is.

-stipple => *bitmap*
> Draws the line with the specified bitmap pattern.

-tags => *tagnames*
> Associates the line with the specified tag(s). Multiple tag names can be supplied as an anonymous list.

-width => *amount*
> The width of the line (default is 1 pixel).

createOval

Creates an oval. For example, to create a circle bounded by the box from (50,50) to (150,150):

```
$canvas->createOval(50,50,150,150);
```

Options are:

-fill => *color*
Fills the arc with the specified color.

-outline => *color*
Specifies the color for the outline (default is black).

-stipple => *bitmap*
Specifies a bitmap to fill the oval with.

-tags => *tagnames*
Associates the oval with the specified tag(s). Multiple tag names can be supplied as an anonymous list.

-width => *amount*
The width of the outline (default is 1 pixel).

createPolygon

Creates a polygon. At least three sets of coordinates are required; the first point is automatically connected to the last point to complete the polygon.

```
$canvas -> createPolygon(0,0,130, 20, 90, -35);
```

Options are:

-fill => *color*
The color to use to fill the polygon.

-outline => *color*
Specifies the color of the outline (default is black).

-smooth => *boolean*
Determines whether the outline is drawn with a Bezier spine. Default is 0.

-splinesteps => *n*
Determines how smooth the Bezier curve is.

-stipple => *bitmap*
Fills the polygon with the specified bitmap pattern.

-tags => *tagnames*
Associates the polygon with the specified tag(s). Multiple tag names can be supplied as an anonymous list.

-width => *amount*
The width of the outline (default is 1 pixel).

createRectangle

Creates a rectangle. For example, to create a square with one corner at (0,0) and another at (100,100):

```
$canvas->createRectangle(0,0,100,100);
```

Options are:

-fill => *color*
> The color to use to fill the rectangle.

-outline => *color*
> Specifies the color of the outline (default is black).

-stipple => *bitmap*
> Fills the rectangle with the specified bitmap pattern.

-tags => *tagnames*
> Associates the rectangle with the specified tag(s). Multiple tag names can be supplied as an anonymous list.

-width => *amount*
> The width of the outline (default is 1 pixel).

createText
> Places text in a canvas widget. For example, to write "Broadway" centered at the position (130,–40):
>
> ```
> $canvas->createText(130,-40, -text => "Broadway");
> ```
>
> Options are:
>
> -anchor => *position*
> > Anchors the text at the specified position. Values are center (default), n, e, s, w, ne, nw, se, and sw.
>
> -fill => *color*
> > The color to use for the text.
>
> -font => *fontname*
> > The font for the text.
>
> -justify => *position*
> > The justification of the text (either left, right, or center). The default is left.
>
> -stipple => *bitmap*
> > Fills the text with the specified bitmap pattern.
>
> -tags => *tagnames*
> > Associates the text with the specified tag(s). Multiple tag names can be supplied as an anonymous list.
>
> -text => *string*
> > Specifies the text to display.
>
> -width => *amount*
> > The maximum length of each line of text. Default is 0, which means that lines are broken only at explicit newline characters.
>
> There is a set of methods for manipulating text items within a Canvas widget. For each of these methods, the first argument is the tag name or tag ID, and subsequent arguments use text indexes as described for the Text widget.

dchars
>   Deletes characters from a text item, given the tag name or ID, and
>   indexes of the first and last characters to delete

icursor
>   Places the insert cursor at the specified index

index
>   Gets a numerical index from a named one

insert
>   Adds a string to the text item

createWindow
>   Embeds another widget inside of a canvas. The widget must have been
>   already created as a child of the canvas or of the canvas's parent. Options are:
>
>   -anchor => position
>>   Anchors the widget at the specified position. Values are center (default),
>>   n, e, s, w, ne, nw, se, and sw.
>
>   -height => amount
>>   Specifies the height of the widget.
>
>   -tags => tagnames
>>   Associates the widget with the specified tag(s). Multiple tag names can
>>   be supplied as an anonymous list.
>
>   -width => amount
>>   The width of the widget.
>
>   -window => $widget
>>   Specifies the widget to embed.

Item Tags and IDs

Each item in a Canvas widget is given a unique ID when it is created. This ID is
returned from the canvas creation command. In addition, each item can have a
tag associated with it, either when created or with the addtag method. You can use
either the ID or the tag to refer to an item in the canvas. Unlike IDs, tags do not
have to be unique, which makes it possible to configure several items as a group.

Two special tags are created automatically. The "all" tag refers to all items in the
canvas. The "current" tag refers to the item that the cursor is currently over, if
any.

Canvas Methods

In addition to configure and cget, the following methods are supported by the
Canvas widget:

addtag
>   Defines a tag for an already created canvas item. For example, to assign a tag
>   called "everything" to all items in a canvas:
>
>    ```
>    $canvas->addtag("everything", "all");
>    ```

Perl/Tk

To assign the tag origin to the item closest to the coordinates (0,0):

```
$canvas->addtag("origin", "closest", 0, 0);
```

The full list of identifiers is:

above
> Assigns the tag to the item above the specified item in the display list

all
> Assigns the tag to all items in the canvas

below
> Assigns the tag to the item below the specified item in the display list

closest
> Assigns the tag to the item closest to the specified x,y coordinate

enclosed
> Assigns the tag to all items that are completely enclosed within the specified bounding box

overlapping
> Assigns the tag to all items that are even partially inside the specified bounding box

withtag
> Assigns the tag to all items with the specified tag

bind
> Binds a callback to an item. (To bind a callback to the Canvas widget itself, you must specify Tk::bind.)

bbox
> Returns the bounding box of an item. For example, to get the bounding box for all items in the canvas:
>
> ```
> $canvas->bbox("all");
> ```

itemconfigure
> Configures one of the items within the canvas. Works just like the configure method for widgets, but the first argument is the tag name or ID for the canvas item.

itemcget
> Gets configuration information for one of the items within the canvas. Works just like the cget method for widgets, but the first argument is the tag name or ID for the canvas item.

move
> Moves an item on the canvas by adding the specified x and y distances to it:
>
> ```
> $canvas->move("circle1", 100, 100);
> ```

coords
> Gets the current x,y coordinates for an item, or moves an item to an explicit x,y coordinate.

lower

Sets the priority for the item in the display list to be lower than the item identified by the specified tag or ID.

raise

Sets the priority for the item in the display list to be higher than the item identified by the specified tag or ID.

delete

Removes an item from the canvas. You can specify as many tags or IDs in the argument list as you want.

find

Finds the specified items. The first argument can be any of:

above

Finds the item above the specified item in the display list

all

Finds all items in the canvas

below

Finds the item below the specified item in the display list

closest

Finds the item closest to the specified x,y coordinate

enclosed

Finds all items that are completely enclosed within the specified bounding box

overlapping

Finds all items that are even partially inside the specified bounding box

withtag

Finds all items with the specified tag

gettags

Retrieves a list of all tags associated with an item.

type

Determines the type of the specified item.

focus

Assigns the keyboard focus to the specified item.

postscript

Renders the canvas as PostScript. Options are:

-colormap => \@*colorcommand*

Specifies a PostScript command for setting color values.

-colormode => *mode*

Sets the mode to color (full color), gray (grayscale), or mono (black and white).

-file => *filename*

The name of the file to store the PostScript output.

-fontmap => \@*fontspec*
>   Specifies a font name and point size.

-height => *size*
>   The height of the area to print.

-pageanchor => *position*
>   The anchor position of the page. Values are center (default), n, e, s, and w.

-pageheight => *height*
>   The height of the printed page.

-pagewidth => *width*
>   The width of the printed page.

-pagex => *x*
>   The x positioning point.

-pagey => *y*
>   The y positioning point.

-rotate => *boolean*
>   Whether to rotate to landscape orientation. Default is 0.

-width => *size*
>   The width of the area to print.

-x => *x*
>   The left edge of the canvas.

-y => *y*
>   The top edge of the canvas.

scale
>   Changes the scaling of the canvas or any individual items. For example, to scale the entire canvas to half its dimensions:
>
>    ```
>    $canvas->scale("all", 0, 0, .5, .5);
>    ```

xview
>   Manipulates the canvas area in view. With no arguments, returns a list of two numbers between 0 and 1, defining the portion of the canvas that is currently hidden on the left and right sides, respectively. With arguments, the function of xview changes:
>
>   moveto
>   >   Moves the specified fraction of the text to the left of the visible portion.
>
>   scroll
>   >   Scrolls the canvas left or right by the specified number of units or pages. Used primarily as a callback to a scrollbar; pressing on an arrow would move by units (characters), and pressing on the trough would move by pages. The number is either 1 or -1, to move forwards or backwards, respectively.

yview
>   Manipulates the canvas in view. With no arguments, returns a list of two numbers between 0 and 1, defining that portion of the canvas that is

currently hidden on the top and bottom, respectively. With arguments, its function changes:

moveto
> Moves the specified fraction of the canvas area to the top of the visible portion.

scroll
> Scrolls the canvas up or down by the specified number of units or pages. Used primarily as a callback to a scrollbar; pressing on an arrow would move by units (lines), and pressing on the trough would move by pages. The number is either 1 or -1, to move forwards or backwards, respectively.

The Scale Widget

Create a "slider" widget representing a numeric value with the Scale method.

> $parent->Scale(*options*);

The standard configuration options that apply to Scale are: -activebackground, -background, -bg, -borderwidth, -bw, -cursor, -font, -foreground, -fg, -highlight-background, -highlightcolor, -highlightthickness, -relief, -state, -takefocus, and -width.

Other options are:

-bigincrement => *amount*
> The amount to change the slider when using large increments. Default is 0, which means 1/10 of the scale.

-command => *callback*
> Pointer to a function that will be called for every incremental change in the slider.

-digits => *amount*
> The number of digits to keep when converting from a number to a string.

-from => *n*
> Low end of the scale (default is 0).

-label => *string*
> The string to use as a label for the slider.

-length => *amount*
> The length of the scale.

-orient => *direction*
> The orientation of the slider. Values can be either vertical (default) or horizontal.

-repeatdelay => *milliseconds*
> Determines the number of milliseconds to hold down an arrow before it auto-repeats. Default is 300.

`-repeatinterval => milliseconds`
> Determines the number of milliseconds between auto-repeats once it is started. Default is 100.

`-resolution => value`
> The increments that the scale will change by (default is 1).

`-showvalue => boolean`
> Whether to show the current value of the slider (default is 1).

`-sliderlength => amount`
> The size of the slider. Default is 25 pixels.

`-tickinterval => n`
> The number of "ticks" to display for the slider (default is 0).

`-to => n`
> The top value of the scale (default is 100).

`-troughcolor => color`
> Changes the color of the trough.

`-variable => \$variable`
> Assigns the value of the slider to the specified variable.

Scale Methods

In addition to `configure` and `cget`, the following methods are defined for the Scale widget:

`get`
> Returns the current value if given no arguments. If given x and y coordinates as the first and second arguments, returns the value of the scale at that position.

`set`
> Assigns the value associated with the scale.

`coords`
> Returns the x and y coordinates associated with the value given in the first argument.

`identify`
> Returns "slider", "trough1", "trough2", or "", depending on which part of the scale corresponds to the given x, y coordinates.

The Menubutton Widget

Create a menubutton with the `Menubutton` method. For example:

```
$mainwindow->Menubutton(-text => "File",
        -menuitems => [ [ command => "New",
                            -command => \&newfile,
                        -underline => 0 ],
                        [ command => "Open",
                            -command => \&openfile,
```

```
                      -underline => 0 ],
            "-",
                  [ command => "Save",
                     -command => \&savefile,
                  -underline => 0 ],
                  [ command => "SaveAs",
                     -command => \&saveasfile,
                  -underline => 4 ] ] );
```

The -menuitems option takes a list of lists describing the menu items. For each menu item, an embedded anonymous list describes the type of menu item, the label to use, and the action to take when it is selected along with any other options desired to configure the menu item. In this example, each of the menu items is the command type, and we use the -command option for each item to point to the callback to execute when the menu item is selected. We also use the -underline option to enable the user to select a menu item using keystrokes. (\[quotedbl]-represents a separator between menu items.)

In addition to command, other types of menus are:

cascade

Embeds a cascade menu

checkbutton

Treats the menu item as a checkbutton

radiobutton

Treats the menu item as a radiobutton

You can configure both the menu itself and the individual menu items. The configuration options that apply to Menubutton are: -activebackground, -activeforeground, -anchor, -background, -bg, -bitmap, -borderwidth, -bw, -cursor, -disabledforeground, -font, -foreground, -fg, -height, -highlightbackground, -highlightcolor, -highlightthickness, -image, -justify, -padx, -pady, -relief, -state, -takefocus, -underline, -width, and -wraplength.

Other Menubutton options are:

-indicatoron => boolean

Determines whether to display an indicator.

-menu => $menu

Displays the menu associated with $menu.

-menuitems => list

Specifies items to create in the menu as a list of lists. See the description at the beginning of this section.

-tearoff => boolean

Whether to allow the menu to be "torn off." Default is 1.

-text => string

Specifies the text to display as a label for the button.

-textvariable => \$variable

Points to the variable containing text to be displayed in the menubutton. Button text will change as $variable does.

Menu Item Options

In addition to the menu itself, each individual menu item can be configured. The widget configuration options that apply to menu items are: -activebackground, -background, -bg, -bitmap, -font, -foreground, -fg, -image, -state, and -underline. Other options are:

-accelerator
> Displays an accelerator key sequence for the menu item. The key sequence must be independently defined with a bind.

-command => *callback*
> Pointer to a function that will be called when the menu item is selected.

-indicatoron => *boolean*
> Determines whether to display an indicator.

-label => *string*
> The string to use as a label for the menu item.

-menu => *$submenu*
> For a cascade menu, points to the menu to embed.

-offvalue => *newvalue*
> For a checkbutton, specifies the value used when the checkbutton is off.

-onvalue => *newvalue*
> For a checkbutton, specifies the value used when the checkbutton is on.

-selectcolor => *color*
> For a checkbutton or radiobutton, color of the indicator when on.

-selectimage => *imgptr*
> For a checkbutton or radiobutton, defines the image to be displayed instead of text when the radiobutton is on. Ignored if -image is not used.

-value => *value*
> For a radiobutton, sets *$variable* to the specified value when the radiobutton is selected (default is 1).

-variable => *$variable*
> Associates the value of the menu item to the specified variable.

Menubutton Methods

In addition to configure and cget, the following methods are defined for Menubutton widgets:

AddItems
> Adds menu items to the end of the menu. The arguments to AddItems are lists configuring each menu item, similar to the lists defined with the -menuitem option.

```
$menubutton->AddItems([command => "Print",
                                  -command => \&printscreen ],
```

```
                                    [command => "Exit",
                                     -command => \&exitclean ]);
```

command
> Adds a command item to the end of the menu. The above example could have read:

```
$menubutton->command(-label => "Print", -command => \&printscreen);
$menubutton->command(-label => "Exit", -command => \&exitclean);
```

checkbutton
> Adds a checkbutton item to the end of the menu:

```
$menubutton->checkbutton(-label => "Show Toolbar",
                -variable => \$toolbar);
```

radiobutton
> Adds a radiobutton item to the end of the menu:

```
$menubutton->radiobutton(-label => "Red", -variable => \$color);
$menubutton->radiobutton(-label => "Blue", -variable => \$color);
```

separator
> Adds a separator line to the end of a menu.

cascade
> Adds a cascade item to the end of the menu.

menu
> Returns a reference to the menu.

entrycget
> Gets information on a menu entry given an index and option to query.

entryconfigure
> Changes information on a specific menu item given an index.

The Menu Widget

Create a menu with the Menu method, to be displayed later with the post method.

```
$menu = $parent->Menu(options)
```

The standard configuration options that apply to Menu are: -activebackground, -activeforeground, -background, -bg, -borderwidth, -bw, -cursor, -disabledforeground, -font, -foreground, -fg, -relief, and -takefocus.

Other options are:

-activeborderwidth => amount
> Sets the width of the edges for the active menu item.

-menuitems => list
> Specifies items to create in the menu as a list of lists.

-postcommand => callback
> The command to invoke before the menu is posted. For example, to update the state of the menu items.

```
-tearoff => boolean
```
   Whether to allow the menu to be "torn off." Default is 1.

```
-selectcolor => color
```
   Color of the selection box for checkbuttons or radiobuttons.

Menu Indexes

Menus have indexes for manipulating individual menu items. They are:

n
   Menu item *n*, with 0 representing the first item

active
   The current menu item

end *or* last
   The last menu item

none
   No menu item

@n
   The menu item closest to the y coordinate specified by *n*

pattern
   The first menu item with text that matches the pattern

Menu Methods

In addition to `configure` and `cget`, the following methods are defined for the Menu widget:

add
   Adds items to the end of a menu. The first argument is the type of menu item to add, and additional arguments are options to the menu item. For example:

```
$menu = $mainwindow->Menu;
$menu->add( 'command', -label => "New", "-command" => \&newfile );
```

entrycget
   Gets information on a specific menu item given an index.

entryconfigure
   Changes information on a specific menu item given an index.

post
   Displays the menu widget.

unpost
   Removes the menu widget from display.

postcascade
   Unposts a submenu and posts the cascade menu associated with the menu item at the specified index.

delete

Removes menu items from the menu.

index

Given a named index, returns the numerical index for that menu item.

insert

Inserts a menu item at the specified index. Same as add, except that it takes an index as the first argument.

invoke

Invokes the menu item at the specified index as if it was selected.

type

Returns the type of menu item at the specified index.

yposition

Returns the y coordinate of the topmost pixel of the menu item.

The Optionmenu Widget

Use the Optionmenu method to create an option menu, in which the selected item is the value displayed. For example:

```
$mainwindow->OptionMenu(-textvariable => \$platform,
        -options => [ [ "UNIX", "unix" ],
                      [ "Windows NT", "winnt" ],
                      [ "Macintosh", "mac" ] ]) -> pack;
```

The -options argument takes a list of menu items. If the descriptions of the menu items displayed are different from those of the values stored, the menu items are themselves written as two-item lists.

The standard configuration options that apply to Optionmenu are: -activebackground, -activeforeground, -background, -bg, -bitmap, -borderwidth, -bw, -cursor, -disabledforeground, -font, -foreground, -fg, -highlightbackground, -highlightcolor, -highlightthickness, -image, -justify, -relief, -state, -takefocus, -underline, -width, and -wraplength.

Other options are:

-command => *callback*

The command to execute when a selection is made. Its arguments are the values of the -textvariable and -variable options.

-indicatoron => *boolean*

Determines whether to display an indicator.

-menu => *$menu*

Displays the menu associated with *$menu*.

-options => *list*

Lists the menu options, as described above.

`-tearoff => boolean`
> Whether to allow the menu to be "torn off." Default is 1.

`-text => string`
> Specifies the text to display as a label for the option menu.

`-textvariable => \$variable`
> Points to the variable containing text to be displayed in the option menu.

`-variable => \$variable`
> Points to a variable containing a stored value, distinct from the value shown in the option menu.

The Frame Widget

Create a frame for enclosing other widgets using the `Frame` method. For example:

```
$parent->Frame( options )
```

The standard configuration options that apply to `Frame` are: `-background`, `-bg`, `-borderwidth`, `-bw`, `-cursor`, `-height`, `-highlightbackground`, `-highlightcolor`, `-highlightthickness`, `-relief`, `-takefocus`, and `-width`.

Other options are:

`-class => name`
> The class associated with the frame.

`-colormap => \$window`
> Specifies another window to share the colormap with. You can point to another window or use the value new to specify a new colormap. Default is undef.

`-label => string`
> The string to use as a label for the frame.

`-labelPack`
> Specifies options for the pack command.

`-labelVariable => \$variable`
> Specifies a variable containing the text for the label.

`-visual => type n`
> For the X Window System, changes the depth of colors.

The Toplevel Widget

Create a toplevel widget, displayed independently from the main window with the same decoration as the window system, using the `Toplevel` method.

The standard configuration options that apply to `Toplevel` are: `-background`, `-bg`, `-borderwidth`, `-bw`, `-cursor`, `-height`, `-highlightbackground`, `-highlightcolor`, `-highlightthickness`, `-relief`, `-takefocus`, and `-width`.

Other options are:

-class => *name*
> The class associated with the Toplevel widget.

-colormap => \\$*window*
> Specifies another window to share the colormap with. You can point to another window or use the value new to specify a new colormap. Default is undef.

-screen => *screen*
> The screen to place the toplevel widget on.

-visual => *type n*
> For the X Window System, changes the depth of colors.

Toplevel Methods

In addition to cget and configure, the following methods are supported by the Toplevel widget. Note that since the MainWindow is a Toplevel widget, each of these methods applies to the MainWindow as well.

aspect
> Returns the constraints to the aspect of the window. The four-item list returned corresponds to the minimum width, the minimum height, the maximum width, and the maximum height.

client
> Assigns a name to the toplevel window.

colormapwindows
> For the X Window System, passes a list of windows to the window manager that have private colormaps. Controls the WM_COLORMAP_WINDOWS property.

command
> For the X Window System, returns the command used to start the application.

deiconify
> Displays an iconified window.

focusmodel
> Gives up the keyboard focus to another window.

frame
> Returns the ID of the parent widget as a hexadecimal string.

geometry
> For the X Window System, gets the geometry of the Toplevel widget.

grid
> Changes the size of the Toplevel's grid.

group
> Makes the widget the group leader of a set of related windows.

Perl/Tk

`iconbitmap`

Identifies a bitmap to use as an icon when the window is iconified.

`iconify`

Iconifies the window.

`iconmask`

Specifies a mask for the icon bitmap.

`iconname`

Assigns text to be associated with the icon.

`iconposition`

Specifies a position for the icon on the desktop.

`iconwindow`

Specifies a widget to use in place of an icon when iconified.

`maxsize`

Specifies the largest size for the window.

`minsize`

Specifies the smallest size for the window.

`overrideredirect`

Removes window decorations from the window.

`positionfrom`

Returns either `program` or `user` to tell you whether the user or window manager requested its current position.

`protocol`

Given one of the window managers WM_DELETE_WINDOW, WM_SAVE_YOURSELF, or WM_TAKE_FOCUS, allows you to define a callback to execute when an associated event is detected.

`resizable`

Takes Boolean values representing whether the window can be resized in width and height, respectively.

`sizefrom`

Returns either `program` or `user` to tell you whether the user or window manager requested its current size.

`state`

Returns `normal`, `iconic`, or `withdrawn`, indicating the current state of the window.

`title`

Changes the title at the top of the window.

`transient`

Indicates to the window manager that the window is transient.

`withdraw`

Makes the window nonvisible.

X

Win32

Win32 Modules and Extensions

If you use Perl on a Win32 system, a number of extension modules are available to provide Windows-specific functionality. Extension modules consist of a regular module written in Perl and a library written in C or C++ that can implement native Windows calls. The core of available modules is bundled together as *lib-win32* on CPAN, and with ActivePerl, Activestate's version of Perl for Win32. They provide such functionality as managing Windows processes, NT user administration, registry modification, and OLE automation.

The Win32 modules were originally written for Windows NT systems, so much of the functionality of the Win32 library is applicable only to Perl running on Windows NT. Many modules check to see which system they are on before installing. Many of the NT-specific modules such as NetAdmin and EventLog do not install at all on Windows 95. Modules such as Registry do their best to work on both systems, despite the differences in their registries.

This chapter covers most of the modules and extensions included in *lib-win32* and distributed with ActivePerl. Additional Windows modules are available at CPAN.

The following modules are described in this chapter:

Win32::Clipboard
Provides Windows clipboard interaction

Win32::Console
Provides Windows console interaction

Win32::ChangeNotify
Creates and uses ChangeNotify objects

Win32::EventLog
Reads from and writes to the Windows NT event log

Win32::File
Manages file attributes (read-only, system, hidden, etc.)

Win32::FileSecurity
:   Manages ACLs in Perl

Win32::Internet
:   Provides extensions for Internet services

Win32::IPC
:   Waits for objects (processes, mutexes, semaphores)

Win32::Mutex
:   Creates and uses mutexes

Win32::NetAdmin
:   Administers users and groups

Win32::NetResource
:   Manages resources (servers, file shares, printers)

Win32::PerfLib
:   Accesses the Windows NT Performance Counter

Win32::Pipe
:   Creates a named pipe under Win32

Win32::Process
:   Starts and stops Win32 processes

Win32::Registry
:   Reads and manages the Win32 Registry

Win32::Semaphore
:   Creates and uses semaphores

Win32::Service
:   Manages Windows NT services

Win32::Shortcut
:   Provides shell link interface

In addition to this chapter, Chapter 23 covers the Win32::OLE modules, and Chapter 24 covers the ODBC extension for Win32.

The reference material for the Clipboard, Console, Internet, and Shortcut modules was graciously provided by Aldo Capini, author and maintainer of many Win32 modules (*http://www.divinf.it/dada/perl/*).

Win32::Clipboard

The Win32::Clipboard module allows you to manipulate the Windows clipboard. You can use the clipboard as an object with the following syntax:

```
$clip = Win32::Clipboard( );
```

This functions as an implicit constructor. If you include a text string as an argument, that text will be placed on the clipboard. You can use the package-qualified method names instead of the object syntax, since the clipboard is a single entity:

```
$text = Win32::Clipboard::Get( );
Win32::Clipboard::Set("blah blah blah");
Win32::Clipboard::Empty( );
```

Alternatively, you can use the clipboard as an object with this syntax:

```
$Clip = Win32::Clipboard( );
$text = $Clip->Get( );
$Clip->Set("blah blah blah");
$Clip->Empty( );
```

Win32::Console

Win32::Console implements the Win32 console and character mode functions. They give you full control on the console input and output, including support of offscreen console buffers (e.g., multiple screen pages); reading and writing of characters, attributes, and whole portions of the screen; and complete processing of keyboard and mouse events.

The new constructor is used to create a console object. It can take two forms:

```
$con = Win32::Console->new(standard_handle);
$con = Win32::Console->new(accessmode, sharemode);
```

The first form creates a handle to a standard channel. standard_handle can be one of STD_OUTPUT_HANDLE, STD_ERROR_HANDLE, or STD_INPUT_HANDLE.

The second form creates a console screen buffer in memory, which you can access for reading and writing as a normal console, and then redirect on the standard output (the screen) with Display. In this case, you can specify accessmode to be GENERIC_READ, GENERIC_WRITE, or both, determining the permissions you will have on the created buffer.

sharemode affects how the console can be shared. It can be specified as either FILE_SHARE_READ, FILE_SHARE_WRITE, or both. If you don't specify any of those parameters, all four flags will be used.

The following methods are supported by the Win32::Console module.

Alloc $cons->Alloc

Allocates a new console for the process. Returns undef on error or a nonzero value on success. A process cannot be associated with more than one console, so this method will fail if there is already an allocated console. Use Free to detach the process from the console, and then call Alloc to create a new console.

Attr $cons->Attr([attr])

Gets or sets the current console attribute. This attribute is used by the Write method.

Cls

$cons->Cls([attr])

Clears the console with the specified *attr*, if given. Uses ATTR_NORMAL otherwise.

Cursor

$cons->Cursor([x, y, size, visible])

Gets or sets cursor position and appearance. Returns undef on error, or a four-element list containing x, y, size, and *visible*. x and y give the current cursor position.

Display

$cons->Display

Displays the specified console on the screen. Returns undef on error or a nonzero value on success.

FillAttr

$cons->FillAttr([value, number, col, row])

Fills the specified *number* of consecutive attributes, beginning at *col*, *row*, with the *value* specified. Returns the number of attributes filled, or undef on error.

FillChar

$cons->FillChar(char, number, col, row)

Fills the specified *number* of consecutive characters, beginning at *col*, *row*, with the character specified in *char*. Returns the number of characters filled, or undef on error.

Flush

$cons->Flush

Flushes the console input buffer. All the events in the buffer are discarded. Returns undef on error, a nonzero value on success.

Free

$cons->Free

Detaches the process from the console. Returns undef on error, a nonzero value on success.

GenerateCtrlEvent

$cons->GenerateCtrlEvent([type, processgroup])

Sends a break signal of the specified type to the specified process group. *type* can be one of CTRL_BREAK_EVENT or CTRL_C_EVENT, signaling, respectively, the pressing of Ctrl + Break and Ctrl-C. If not specified, *type* defaults to CTRL_C_EVENT. *processgroup* is the PID of a process sharing the same console. If omitted, it defaults to 0 (the current process), which is also the only meaningful value that you can pass to this function. Returns undef on error, a nonzero value on success.

GetEvents   `$cons->GetEvents`

Returns the number of unread input events in the console's input buffer, or undef on error.

Info   `$cons->Info`

Returns an array of information about the console, which contains:

- Number of columns (X size) of the console buffer
- Number of rows (Y size) of the console buffer
- Current column (X position) of the cursor
- Current row (Y position) of the cursor
- Current attribute used for `Write`
- Left column (X of the starting point) of the current console window
- Top row (Y of the starting point) of the current console window
- Right column (X of the final point) of the current console window
- Bottom row (Y of the final point) of the current console window
- Maximum number of columns for the console window, given the current buffer size, font, and screen size
- Maximum number of rows for the console window, given the current buffer size, font, and screen size

This example prints the cursor's current position:

```
@info = $CONSOLE->Info( );
print "Cursor at $info[3], $info[4].0";
```

Input   `$cons->Input`

Reads an event from the input buffer. Returns a list of values, determined by the type of event. A keyboard event will contain the following values, in order:

- Event type (1 for keyboard)
- Key state—true if the key is being pressed, false if the key is being released
- Repeat count—the number of times the key is held down
- Virtual keycode of the key
- Virtual scancode of the key
- ASCII code of the character (if the key is a character key, 0 otherwise)
- State of the control keys (Shifts, Ctrls, Alts, etc.)

A mouse event will return the following values, in order:

- Event type (2 for mouse)
- X coordinate (column) of the mouse location
- Y coordinate (row) of the mouse location
- Button state—the mouse button(s) that are pressed
- State of the control keys (Shifts, Ctrls, Alts, etc.)
- Event flags for the type of the mouse event

This method will return undef on error.

Note that the events returned depend on the input mode of the console; for example, mouse events are not intercepted unless ENABLE_MOUSE_INPUT is specified.

InputChar   `$cons->InputChar(number)`

Reads and returns number characters from the console input buffer, or returns undef on error.

InputCP   `$cons->InputCP([codepage])`

Gets or sets the input code page used by the console. Note that this doesn't apply to a console object, but to the standard input console. This attribute is used by the Write method.

MaxWindow   `$cons->MaxWindow`

Returns the size of the largest possible console window, based on the current font and the size of the display. The result is undef on error; otherwise, a two-element list containing the number of columns and rows is returned.

Mode   `$cons->Mode([flags])`

Gets or sets the input or output mode of a console. *flags* can be a combination of the following constants:

```
ENABLE_LINE_INPUT
ENABLE_ECHO_INPUT
ENABLE_PROCESSED_INPUT
ENABLE_WINDOW_INPUT
ENABLE_MOUSE_INPUT
ENABLE_PROCESSED_OUTPUT
ENABLE_WRAP_AT_EOL_OUTPUT
```

MouseButtons   `$cons->MouseButtons`

Returns the number of the buttons on your mouse, or undef on error.

OutputCP $cons->OutputCP([codepage])

Gets or sets the output code page used by the console. Note that this doesn't apply to a console object, but to the standard output console. You may want to use the noninstantiated form to avoid confusion:

```
$codepage = Win32::Console::OutputCP( );
Win32::Console::OutputCP(437);
```

PeekInput $cons->PeekInput

Does exactly the same as Input, except that the event read is not removed from the input buffer.

ReadAttr $cons->ReadAttr([number, col, row])

Reads the specified *number* of consecutive attributes from the console, beginning at *col*, *row*. Returns the attributes read (a variable containing one character for each attribute), or undef on error. You can then pass the returned variable to WriteAttr to restore the saved attributes on screen.

ReadChar $cons->ReadChar([number, col, row])

Reads the specified *number* of consecutive characters from the console, beginning at *col*, *row*. Returns a string containing the characters read, or undef on error. You can then pass the returned variable to WriteChar to restore the saved characters on screen.

ReadRect $cons->ReadRect(left, top, right, bottom)

Reads the content (characters and attributes) of the rectangle specified by *left*, *top*, *right*, and *bottom* from the console. Returns a string containing the rectangle read, or undef on error. You can then pass the returned variable to WriteRect to restore the saved rectangle on screen (or on another console).

Scroll $cons->Scroll(left, top, right, bottom, col, row, char, attr, [cleft, ctop, cright, cbottom])

Moves a block of data in a console buffer; the block is identified by the *left*, *top*, *right*, and *bottom* positions.

row and *col* identify the new location of the block. The cells left empty as a result of the move are filled with the character *char* and attribute *attr*.

Optionally, you can specify a clipping region with *cleft*, *ctop*, *cright*, and *cbottom* so that the contents of the console outside this rectangle are unchanged. Returns undef on error or a nonzero value on success.

```
# Scrolls the screen 10 lines down, filling with black
spaces
$CONSOLE->Scroll(0, 0, 80, 25, 0, 10, " ", $FG_BLACK |
$BG_BLACK);
```

Select

$cons->Select(*standard_handle*)

Redirects a standard handle to the specified console. *standard_handle* can have one of the following values:

```
STD_INPUT_HANDLE
STD_OUTPUT_HANDLE
STD_ERROR_HANDLE
```

Returns undef on error or a nonzero value on success.

Size

$cons->Size([*col*, *row*])

Gets or sets the console buffer size.

Title

$cons->Title([*title*])

Gets or sets the title bar string of the current console window.

Window

$cons->Window([*flag*, *left*, *top*, *right*, *bottom*])

Gets or sets the current console window size. If called without arguments, returns a four-element list containing the current window coordinates in the form of (*left*, *top*, *right*, *bottom*). To set the window size, you have to specify an additional flag parameter. If it is 0, coordinates are considered relative to the current coordinates; if it is nonzero, coordinates are absolute.

Write

$cons->Write(*string*)

Writes *string* on the console, using the current attribute, which you can set with Attr, and advances the cursor as needed. This isn't that different from Perl's print statement. Returns the number of characters written, or undef on error.

WriteAttr

$cons->WriteAttr(*attrs*, *col*, *row*)

Writes the attributes contained in the string attrs, beginning at *col*, *row*, without affecting the characters that are on screen. The string *attrs* can be the result of a ReadAttr function, or you can build your own attribute string; in this case, keep in mind that every attribute is treated as a character, not a number (see example). Returns the number of attributes written, or undef on error.

```
$CONSOLE->WriteAttr($attrs, 0, 0);
# note the use of chr()...
$attrs = chr($FG_BLACK | $BG_WHITE) x 80;
$CONSOLE->WriteAttr($attrs, 0, 0);
```

WriteChar $cons->WriteChar(chars, col, row)

Writes the characters in the string *attr*, beginning at *col*, *row*, without affecting the attributes that are onscreen. The string characters can be the result of a ReadChar function or a normal string. Returns the number of characters written, or undef on error.

WriteInput $cons->WriteInput(event)

Pushes data in the console input buffer. *event* is a list of values (for more information, see Input). The string characters can be the result of a ReadChar function or a normal string. Returns the number of characters written, or undef on error.

WriteRect $cons->WriteRect(rect, left, top, right, bottom)

Writes a rectangle of characters and attributes (contained in *rect*) on the console at the coordinates specified by *left*, *top*, *right*, and *bottom*. *rect* can be the result of a ReadRect function. Returns undef on error; otherwise, returns a four-element list containing the coordinates of the affected rectangle, in the format (*left*, *top*, *right*, *bottom*).

Constants

The following constants are exported in the main namespace of your script using Win32::Console:

```
BACKGROUND_BLUE                 BACKGROUND_GREEN
BACKGROUND_INTENSITY            BACKGROUND_RED
CAPSLOCK_ON                     CONSOLE_TEXTMODE_BUFFER
ENABLE_ECHO_INPUT               ENABLE_LINE_INPUT
ENABLE_MOUSE_INPUT              ENABLE_PROCESSED_INPUT
ENABLE_PROCESSED_OUTPUT         ENABLE_WINDOW_INPUT
ENABLE_WRAP_AT_EOL_OUTPUT       ENHANCED_KEY
FILE_SHARE_READ                 FILE_SHARE_WRITE
FOREGROUND_BLUE                 FOREGROUND_GREEN
FOREGROUND_INTENSITY            FOREGROUND_RED
LEFT_ALT_PRESSED                LEFT_CTRL_PRESSED
NUMLOCK_ON                      GENERIC_READ
GENERIC_WRITE                   RIGHT_ALT_PRESSED
```

```
RIGHT_CTRL_PRESSED          SCROLLLOCK_ON
SHIFT_PRESSED               STD_INPUT_HANDLE
STD_OUTPUT_HANDLE           STD_ERROR_HANDLE
```

Additionally, the following variables can be used:

```
$FG_BLACK                   $FG_BLUE
$FG_LIGHTBLUE               $FG_RED
$FG_LIGHTRED                $FG_GREEN
$FG_LIGHTGREEN              $FG_MAGENTA
$FG_LIGHTMAGENTA            $FG_CYAN
$FG_LIGHTCYAN               $FG_BROWN
$FG_YELLOW                  $FG_GRAY
$FG_WHITE                   $BG_BLACK
$BG_BLUE                    $BG_LIGHTBLUE
$BG_RED                     $BG_LIGHTRED
$BG_GREEN                   $BG_LIGHTGREEN
$BG_MAGENTA                 $BG_LIGHTMAGENTA
$BG_CYAN                    $BG_LIGHTCYAN
$BG_BROWN                   $BG_YELLOW
$BG_GRAY                    $BG_WHITE
$ATTR_NORMAL                $ATTR_INVERSE
```

ATTR_NORMAL is set to gray foreground on black background (DOS's standard colors).

Win32::ChangeNotify

This module provides access to Win32 change-notification objects, letting you monitor events relating to files and directory trees. The constructor for this class is new, which creates a ChangeNotify object for a specified path and indicates how it should be monitored:

```
$ntfy = Win32::ChangeNotify->new(path, subtree, events);
$ntfy->wait or warn "Something has failed: $!");
```

The function returns a reference to the object as $ntfy. *path* is the pathname of the directory to monitor. *subtree* is a Boolean value that, if true, forces the object to monitor all subdirectories of the object's path. The *events* parameter indicates the type of events that will trigger a notification. It can be one of the following string values:

Value	Description
ATTRIBUTES	Any attribute change
DIR_NAME	Any directory name change
FILE_NAME	Any filename change (creating/deleting/renaming)
LAST_WRITE	Any change to a file's last write time
SECURITY	Any security descriptor change
SIZE	Any change in a file's size

The following methods are used on notification objects created by new.

close $ntfy->close()

Stops the monitoring done by the notification object and destroys the object. This happens automatically when the program exits.

reset $ntfy->reset()

Resets the object to begin monitoring again after a change has occurred.

wait $ntfy->wait([timeout])

The wait method is inherited from the Win32::IPC package. It waits for the notification object to signal when it detects a change. timeout is the maximum time to wait (in milliseconds). If timeout is omitted, the method waits forever. If timeout is 0, the function returns immediately. The function returns the following values:

+1
> The object is signaled.

0
> Timed out.

undef
> An error occurred.

Use reset on the object after wait if you wish to continue monitoring.

Win32::Eventlog

This module makes the Windows NT event log accessible to your Perl programs. It allows you to create new records, read records, and create backup logfiles. The new constructor opens a server's event log as an object:

    $log = Win32::EventLog->new(source, [server]);

This function opens an event log and returns an object reference. source specifies the name of the source event, and server specifies the name of the server (local is assumed if no server name is given).

Many of the methods for this module require a reference to an empty variable as an argument. This is how the return value of the method will be placed, whether it is a hash or a scalar. The following methods can be used on event log objects.

Backup $log->Backup(filename)

Saves the current open event log to a file named by filename.

Clear

$log->Clear([*filename*])

Writes the current event log to the file *filename* (if supplied) and clears the event log.

GetNumber

$log->GetNumber(\$*number*)

Returns the number of events as the value of the scalar variable *number*.

GetOldest

$log->GetOldest(\$*record*)

Returns the record number of the oldest record in the event log to the scalar $*record*.

Read

$log->Read(*flags, offset, \%eventinfo*)

Reads an entry from the event log and returns the information in the *eventinfo* hash. *offset* specifies the record number you want to start at in the log. *flags* sets options for how you want to read the log, which can be any combination of the following:

EVENTLOG_FORWARDS_READ
   Eventlog is read in forward chronological order.

EVENTLOG_BACKWARDS_READ
   Eventlog is read in reverse chronological order.

EVENTLOG_SEEK_READ
   The read begins at the record specified by the $RecordOffset parameter. Must also specify EVENT_LOG_FORWARDS_READ or EVENTLOG_BACKWARDS_READ.

EVENTLOG_SEQUENTIAL_READ
   The read continues sequentially from the last read call.

The final argument is the output object for the event read. *eventinfo* is a reference to a hash that contains keys for each part of the event description. This same structure is used when you report new events to the event log using the Report method. The *eventinfo* hash looks like this:

```
%event = (
    EventID            => val,
    EventType          => val,
    Category           => val,
    ClosingRecordNumber => val,
    Source             => val,
    Computer           => val,
    Strings            => val,
    Data               => val,
);
```

Report

$log->Report(\%eventinfo)

Reports an event to the event log. The information for the event to be recorded is given in a hash, %eventinfo, which should contain values for at least the following keys:

EventType
> A string describing the type of event to be reported. The options for EventType are:

EVENTLOG_ERROR_TYPE	Error event
EVENTLOG_WARNING_TYPE	Warning event
EVENTLOG_INFORMATION_TYPE	Information event
EVENTLOG_AUDIT_SUCCESS_TYPE	Success Audit event
EVENTLOG_AUDIT_FAILURE_TYPE	Failure Audit event

Category
> An integer value for the category of the event, defined by the application.

EventID
> Source-specific ID for the event.

Data
> Raw binary data for the event.

Strings
> Any text strings to merge that provide a description of the event.

Win32::File

The Win32::File module allows you to view or set the attributes for files. There are two functions that allow you to do this, which must be explicitly imported to your namespace:

    use Win32::File qw/GetAttributes SetAttributes/;

The constant values for the attributes are exported by default.

GetAttributes

GetAttributes (*filename*, \$atts)

Returns the attribute settings for file *filename* and saves them as the variable referenced by $atts, which will contain an ORed combination of one or more of the following values:

> ARCHIVE
> DIRECTORY
> HIDDEN
> NORMAL
> READONLY
> SYSTEM

SetAttributes   SetAttributes *(filename, atts)*

> Sets the attributes for the file *filename* to the values contained in *atts*. The attributes are given as an ORed combination of one or more of the attribute values shown above.

Win32::FileSecurity

The Win32::FileSecurity module allows you to work with NT File System (NTFS) file permissions. File permissions are stored as Discretionary Access Control Lists (DACLs) for each file or directory. These lists contain a bitmask specifying the permission rights for users on the file or directory. This module implements a DACL as a *permissions* hash in which each key is a username, and the value is the bitmask for the permissions.

The FileSecurity module exports the following constants to describe user permissions:

```
ACCESS_SYSTEM_SECURITY      READ or R
CHANGE or C                 SPECIFIC_RIGHTS_ALL
DELETE                      STANDARD_RIGHTS_ALL
FULL or F                   STANDARD_RIGHTS_EXECUTE
GENERIC_ALL                 STANDARD_RIGHTS_READ
GENERIC_EXECUTE             STANDARD_RIGHTS_REQUIRED
GENERIC_READ                STANDARD_RIGHTS_WRITE
GENERIC_WRITE               SYNCHRONIZE
MAXIMUM_ALLOWED             WRITE_DAC
READ_CONTROL                WRITE_OWNER
```

Using the constant function on one of these constants gives its value, and bitmasks or multiple permissions settings can be made by supplying a list of these constants to the MakeMask function.

The following functions are exported by the Win32::FileSecurity module.

---

constant   constant *(name $val)*

> Takes the *name* of a permission constant and saves its value in the variable *val*.

EnumerateRights

> EnumerateRights *(mask, \@rights)*

> Takes a permissions bitmask (as returned by MakeMask or constant) and saves the corresponding list of string constants in *rights*.

Get   Get (*filename*, \%*permissions*)

Gets the access control list for *filename* (or directory) and saves in the specified *permissions* hash.

MakeMask   MakeMask (*stringlist*)

Takes a list of permission string constants and returns the bitmask.

Set   Set (*filename*, \%*permissions*)

Sets the access control list for the given *filename* (or directory) to the settings in the specified *permissions* hash.

Win32::Internet

The Win32::Internet extension implements the Win32 Internet APIs (found in *WININET.DLL*), providing support for HTTP, FTP, and Gopher connections.

All types of connections start as a basic Internet connection that must be opened with the following command:

```
use Win32::Internet;
$Connection = Win32::Internet->new( );
```

This creates an Internet object in Perl on which you use the functions provided in this module to create more specific connection objects. The objects and functions that create them are:

- Internet connections (the main object, with new)
- URLs (with OpenURL)
- FTP sessions (with FTP)
- HTTP sessions (with HTTP)
- HTTP requests (with OpenRequest)

This module provides different levels of implementation of the Win32 Internet functions. Some routines use several Win32 API functions to perform a complex task in a single call; they are simpler to use, but less powerful. Other functions implement nothing more and nothing less than the corresponding API function, so you can use all of their power, but with some additional programming steps.

For example, the function FetchURL fetches the contents of any HTTP, FTP, or Gopher URL with a simple command:

```
$inet = new Win32::Internet( );
$file = $inet->FetchURL("http://www.yahoo.com");
```

You can achieve the same result with this series of commands, which is what FetchURL actually does:

```
$inet = new Win32::Internet();
$url = $inet->OpenURL("http://www.yahoo.com");
$file = $url->ReadFile();
$url->Close();
```

General Internet Methods

The methods described in this section are used on Internet connection objects created with new:

```
$inet = Win32::Internet->new();
```

You can supply new with an optional list of arguments (or a reference to a hash containing them) that looks like this:

```
Win32::Internet->new [useragent, opentype, proxy, proxybypass, flags]
Win32::Internet->new [$hashref]
```

The parameters and their values are:

useragent
    The user agent string passed to HTTP requests. Default is Perl-Win32Internet/ version.

opentype
    How to access the Internet (e.g., directly or using a proxy). Default is INTERNET_OPEN_TYPE_DIRECT.

proxy
    Name of the proxy server (or servers) to use. Default is none.

proxybypass
    Optional list of hostnames or IP addresses that are known locally. Default is none.

flags
    Additional flags affecting the behavior of the function. Default is none.

If you pass a hash reference to the function, the following values are taken from the hash:

```
%hash=(
    "useragent"   => "useragent",
    "opentype"    => "opentype",
    "proxy"       => "proxy",
    "proxybypass" => "proxybypass",
    "flags"       => flags,
);
```

The following methods can be used on Internet connection objects.

CanonicalizeURL   *$inet*->CanonicalizeURL(*URL*, [*flags*])

    Converts a URL to a canonical format, which includes converting unsafe characters to escape sequences. Returns the canonicalized

---

URL, or undef on error. For the possible values of *flags*, refer to the Microsoft Win32 Internet Functions documentation.

Close

`$inet->Close([$obj])`

Closes an Internet connection. This can be applied to any Win32::Internet object. Note that it is not strictly required to close the connections you create, since the Win32::Internet objects are automatically closed when the program ends (or when such an object is destroyed by other means).

CombineURL

`$inet->CombineURL(baseURL, relativeURL, [flags])`

Combines a base and relative URL into a single URL. Returns the (canonicalized) combined URL, or undef on error. For the possible values of flags, refer to the Microsoft Win32 Internet Functions documentation.

ConnectBackoff

`$inet->ConnectBackoff([value])`

Reads or sets the delay value, in milliseconds, to wait between connection retries. If no value parameter is specified, the current value is returned; otherwise, the delay between retries is set.

ConnectionRetries

`$inet->ConnectRetries([value])`

Reads or sets the number of times a connection is retried before considering it failed. If no value parameter is specified, the current value is returned; otherwise, the number of retries is set. The default value is 5.

ConnectTimeout

`$inet->ConnectTimeout([value])`

Reads or sets the timeout value (in milliseconds) before a connection is considered failed. If no value parameter is specified, the current value is returned; otherwise, the timeout is set to *value*. The default value is infinity.

ControlReceiveTimeout

`$inet->ControlReceiveTimeout([value])`

Reads or sets the timeout value (in milliseconds) to use for non-data (control) receive requests before they are canceled. Currently, this value has meaning only for FTP sessions. If no value parameter is specified, the current value is returned; otherwise, the timeout is set. The default value is infinity.

ControlSendTimeout

$inet->ControlSendTimeout([value])

Reads or sets the timeout value (in milliseconds) to use for non-data (control) send requests before they are canceled. Currently, this value has meaning only for FTP sessions. If no value parameter is specified, the current value is returned; otherwise, the timeout is set. The default value is infinity.

CrackURL

$inet->CrackURL(URL, [flags])

Splits a URL into its component parts and returns them in an array. Returns undef on error. The array will contain the following values: (scheme, host, port, username, password, path, extrainfo). For example, the URL *http://www.divinf.it/index.html#top* can be split into:

```
http, www.divinf.it, 80, anonymous, dada@divinf.it, /
index.html, #top
```

If you don't specify a flags parameter, ICU_ESCAPE will be used by default; for the possible values of *flags*, refer to the Microsoft Win32 Internet Functions documentation.

CreateURL

$inet->CreateURL(scheme, hostname, port, username, password, path, extrainfo, [flags])

$inet->CreateURL($hashref, [flags])

Creates a URL from its component parts. Returns undef on error and the created URL if successful. If you pass a hash reference, the following values are taken from the array:

```
%hash=(
    "scheme"    => "scheme",
    "hostname"  => "hostname",
    "port"      => port,
    "username"  => "username",
    "password"  => "password",
    "path"      => "path",
    "extrainfo" => "extrainfo",
);
```

If you don't specify a flags parameter, ICU_ESCAPE will be used by default; for the other possible values of *flags*, refer to the Microsoft Win32 Internet Functions documentation.

DataReceiveTimeout

$inet->DataReceiveTimeout([value])

Reads or sets the timeout value (in milliseconds) to use for data receive requests before they are canceled. If no value parameter is specified, the current value is returned; otherwise, the timeout is set. The default value is infinity.

DataSendTimeout

$inet->DataSendTimeout([value])

Reads or sets the timeout value (in milliseconds) to use for data send requests before they are canceled. If no value parameter is specified, the current value is returned; otherwise, the timeout is set. The default value is infinity.

Error

$inet->Error()

Returns the last recorded error in the form of an array or string (depending on the context) containing the error number and an error description. Can be applied on any Win32::Internet object (FTP sessions, etc.). There are three types of errors you can encounter, recognizable by the error number returned:

−1
> A "trivial" error has occurred in the package. For example, you tried to use a method on the wrong type of object.

1–11,999
> A generic error has occurred, and the Win32::GetLastError error message is returned.

12,000 and higher
> An Internet error has occurred, and the extended Win32 Internet API error message is returned.

FetchURL

$inet->FetchURL(URL)

Fetches the content of an HTTP, FTP, or Gopher URL. Returns the contents of the file read (or undef if there was an error and nothing was read).

FTP

$inet->FTP($ftpobject, server, username, pwd, [port, pasv, context])

$inet->FTP($ftpobject, $hashref)

Opens an FTP connection to *server*, logging in with the given username and password. The new connection object is saved to *ftpobject*. The parameters and their values are:

server
> The server to connect to.

username
> The username used to log in to the server. Default is anonymous.

pwd

The password used to log in to the server. Default is none.

port

The port of the FTP service on the server. Default is 21.

pasv

If it is a value other than 0, use passive transfer mode. Otherwise, it is taken from the parent Internet connection object; you can set this value with the Pasv method.

context

A number to identify this operation if it is asynchronous. See SetStatusCallback and GetStatusCallback for more info on asynchronous operations.

If you pass a hash reference, the following values are taken from the hash:

```
%hash=(
    "server"   => "server",
    "username" => "username",
    "password" => "password",
    "port"     => port,
    "pasv"     => pasv,
    "context"  => context,
);
```

The FTP method returns undef if the connection failed, a number otherwise. You can then call any of the FTP functions as methods of the newly created FTP object.

GetResponse $*inet*->GetResponse( )

Returns the text sent by a remote server in response to the last function executed. It applies to any Win32::Internet object, particularly FTP sessions.

GetStatusCallback

$*inet*->GetStatusCallback(*context*)

Returns information about the progress of the asynchronous operation identified by context; this information consists of two values: a status code (one of the INTERNET_STATUS_* constants) and an additional value depending on the status code. For example, if the status code returned is INTERNET_STATUS_HANDLE_CREATED, the second value will hold the handle just created. For more information on these values, refer to the Microsoft Win32 Internet Functions documentation.

HTTP

$inet->HTTP(httpobject, server, username, password, [port, flags, context])

$inet->HTTP($httpobject, $hashref)

Opens an HTTP connection to *server*, logging in with the given username and password. The new connection object is saved as *httpobject*. The parameters and their values are:

server
> The server to connect to.

username
> The username used to log in to the server. Default is anonymous.

password
> The password used to log in to the server. Default is none.

port
> The port of the HTTP service on the server. Default is 80.

flags
> Additional flags affecting the behavior of the function.

context
> A number to identify this operation if it is asynchronous.

If you pass a hash reference, the following values are taken from the hash:

```
%hash=(
  "server"   => "server",
  "username" => "username",
  "password" => "password",
  "port"     => port,
  "flags"    => flags,
  "context"  => context,
);
```

The HTTP method returns undef if the connection failed, a number otherwise. You can then call any of the HTTP functions as methods of the newly created *httpobject*.

OpenURL

$inet->OpenURL(urlobject, URL)

Opens a connection to an HTTP, FTP, or Gopher URL. Returns undef on error, or a number if the connection was successful. You can then retrieve the URL content by applying the methods QueryDataAvailable and ReadFile on the newly created *urlobject*. See also FetchURL.

Password

$inet->Password([password])

Reads or sets the password used for an FTP or HTTP connection. If no password parameter is specified, the current value is returned.

QueryDataAvailable

$inet->QueryDataAvailable( )

Returns the number of bytes of data available to be read immediately by a subsequent call to ReadFile (or undef on error). Can be applied to URL or HTTP request objects.

QueryOption

$inet->QueryOption(option)

Queries an Internet option. For the possible values of option, refer to the Microsoft Win32 Internet Functions documentation.

ReadEntireFile

$inet->ReadEntireFile( )

Reads all the data available from an opened URL or HTTP request object. Returns what has been read, or undef on error.

ReadFile

$inet->ReadFile(bytes)

Reads and returns the specified number of bytes of data from an opened URL or HTTP request object. Returns undef on error. Be careful to keep bytes to an acceptable value.

SetOption

$inet->SetOption(option, value)

Sets an Internet option. For the possible values of option, refer to the Microsoft Win32 Internet Functions documentation.

SetStatusCallback

$inet->SetStatusCallback( )

Initializes the callback routine used to return data about the progress of an asynchronous operation. This is one of the steps required to perform asynchronous operations; the complete procedure is:

```
# Use the INTERNET_FLAG_ASYNC when initializing
$params{'flags'}=INTERNET_FLAG_ASYNC;
$inet = new Win32::Internet(params);

# Initialize the callback routine
$inet->SetStatusCallback();

# Specify the context parameter (the last 1 in this case)
$inet->HTTP($http, "www.yahoo.com", "anonymous", "dada\
@divinf.it",
            80, 0, 1);
```

At this point, control returns immediately to Perl, and $inet->
Error( ) will return 997, which means an asynchronous I/O operation is pending. Now, you can call:

```
$http->GetStatusCallback(1);
```

in a loop to verify what's happening; see also GetStatusCallback.

TimeConvert $inet->TimeConvert(time)

Takes an HTTP date/time string and returns the date/time
converted in the following array: (seconds, minutes, hours, day,
month, year, day_of_week).

UserAgent $inet->UserAgent([name])

Reads or sets the user agent name used for HTTP requests. If no
name is specified, the current value is returned.

Username $inet->Username([name])

Reads or sets the username used for an FTP or HTTP connection.
If no name parameter is specified, the current value is returned.

Version $inet->Version( )

Returns the version numbers for the Win32::Internet package and
the *WININET.DLL* version, as an array or string, depending on the
context. The string returned will contain *package_version/DLL_
version*, while the array will contain: *package_version, DLL_version*.
For example:

```
$version = $inet->Version( );
# Should return "0.06/4.70.1215"
@version = $inet->Version( );
# Should return ("0.06", "4.70.1215")
```

FTP Functions

The methods described in this section are used to control FTP sessions. They
apply to FTP session objects created by the FTP method on an Internet connection
object. FTP creates an open FTP session and assigns it to an object ($FTP):

```
use Win32::Internet;
$inet = new Win32::Internet( );
$inet->FTP($FTP, "hostname", "username", "password");
```

The following methods are used on FTP session objects.

Ascii

```
$FTP->Ascii( )

$FTP->Asc( )
```

Sets the ASCII transfer mode for this FTP session. It will be applied to subsequent Get functions.

Binary

```
$FTP->Binary( )

$FTP->Bin( )
```

Sets the binary transfer mode for this FTP session. It will be applied to subsequent Get functions.

Cd

```
$FTP->Cd(path)

$FTP->Cwd(path)

$FTP->Chdir(path)
```

Changes the current directory on the FTP remote host. Returns *path*, or undef on error.

Delete

```
$FTP->Delete(file)

$FTP->Del(file)
```

Deletes *file* on the FTP remote host. Returns undef on error.

Get

```
$FTP->Get(file, [local, overwrite, flags, context])
```

Gets the remote FTP *file* and saves it locally in *local*. If *local* is not specified, it will be the same name as *file*. Returns undef on error. The parameters and their values are:

file
> The name of the remote file on the FTP server.

local
> The name of the local file to create.

overwrite
> If 0, overwrites *local* if it exists. With any other value, the function fails if the local file already exists. Default is 0.

flags
> Additional flags affecting the behavior of the function. None by default.

context
> A number to identify this operation if it is asynchronous. (See SetStatusCallback and GetStatusCallback for more information on asynchronous operations.) None by default.

List

$FTP->List([pattern, listmode])

$FTP->Ls([pattern, listmode])

$FTP->Dir([pattern, listmode])

Returns a list containing the files found in the current directory, matching the given *pattern*, if specified. The content of the returned list depends on the *listmode* parameter, which can have the following values:

1 *(default)*
    The list contains the names of the files found.

2
    The list contains seven values for each file:

- The filename
- The DOS short filename, a.k.a. 8.3
- The size
- The attributes
- The creation time
- The last access time
- The last modified time

3
    The list contains a reference to a hash for each found file. Each hash contains the following key/value pairs:

```
name => filename
altname => DOS short filename, a.k.a. 8.3
size => size
attr => attributes
ctime => creation time
atime => last access time
mtime => last modified time
```

All times are reported as strings of the following format: second, hour, minute, day, month, year. For example:

```
$file->{'mtime'} == "0,10,58,9,12,1996"
# Stands for 09 Dec 1996 at 10:58:00
```

Mkdir

$FTP->Mkdir(name)

$FTP->Md(name)

Creates the directory *name* on the FTP remote host. Returns undef on error.

Mode

$FTP->Mode([mode])

If called with no arguments, returns the current transfer mode for this FTP session (asc for ASCII or bin for binary). The *mode* argument can be asc or bin, in which case the appropriate transfer mode is selected. Returns undef on error.

Pasv	$FTP->Pasv([mode])

If called with no arguments, returns 1 if the current FTP session has passive transfer mode enabled; 0 if not. You can call it with a *mode* parameter (0/1) only as a method of a Internet object, in which case it will set the default value for the next FTP object you create (i.e., set it before, because you can't change this value once you open the FTP session).

Put	$FTP->Put(file, [remote, context])

Uploads the local *file* to the FTP server, saving it under the name *remote*, which, if omitted, is the same name as *file*. Returns undef on error. *context* is a number to identify this operation if it is asynchronous. See SetStatusCallback and GetStatusCallback for more information on asynchronous operations.

Pwd	$FTP->Pwd( )

Returns the current directory on the FTP server, or undef on error.

Rename	$FTP->Rename(oldfile, newfile)
	$FTP->Ren(oldfile, newfile)

Renames a file on the FTP remote host. Returns undef on error.

Rmdir	$FTP->Rmdir(name)
	$FTP->Rd(name)

Removes the directory *name* on the FTP remote host. Returns undef on error.

HTTP Functions

The methods described in this section are used to create and control an HTTP session. Open an HTTP session using the HTTP method on an Internet connection object:

```
use Win32::Internet;
$inet = new Win32::Internet( );
$inet->HTTP($http, "hostname", "username", "password");
```

This opens the session and creates the HTTP session object $http. The following methods can be used on HTTP session objects.

AddHeader $request->AddHeader(header, [flags])

Adds HTTP request headers to an HTTP request object created with OpenRequest. For the possible values of *flags*, refer to the Microsoft Win32 Internet Functions documentation.

OpenRequest $http->OpenRequest(requestobject, [path, method, version, referer, accept, flags, context])

$http->OpenRequest($requestobject, hashref)

Opens an HTTP request and saves it as $*requestobject*. Returns undef on error, or a number if the connection was successful. You can then use one of the AddHeader, SendRequest, QueryInfo, QueryDataAvailable, and ReadFile methods on the newly created *requestobject*. The optional parameters and their values are:

path
> The object to request. This is generally a filename, an executable module, etc. The default is /.

method
> The method to use, which can be GET, POST, HEAD, or PUT. Default is GET.

version
> The HTTP version. Default is HTTP/1.0.

referer
> The URL of the document from which the URL in the request was obtained.

accept
> The content types accepted. They must be separated by a \0 (ASCII zero). Default types are text/* image/gif image/jpeg.

flags
> Additional flags affecting the behavior of the function.

context
> A number to identify this operation if it is asynchronous. See SetStatusCallback and GetStatusCallback for more information on asynchronous operations.

A reference to a hash containing the previous list of parameters can also be supplied to this method:

```
%hash=(
    "path"      => "path",
    "method"    => "method",
    "version"   => "version",
    "referer"   => "referer",
    "accept"    => "accept",
    "flags"     => flags,
    "context"   => context,
);
```

QueryInfo	$request->QueryInfo(header, [flags])
	Queries information about an HTTP request object ($request) created with OpenRequest. You can specify a header (for example, Content-type) and/or one or more flags. If you don't specify flags, HTTP_QUERY_CUSTOM will be used by default; this means that the header should contain a valid HTTP header name. For the possible values of flags, refer to the Microsoft Win32 Internet Functions documentation.

Request	$http->Request([path, method, version, referer, accept, flags])
	$http->Request(hashref)
	Performs an HTTP request and returns an array containing the status code, the headers, and the content of the file. It is a one-step procedure that executes OpenRequest, SendRequest, QueryInfo, ReadFile, and finally, Close. For a description of the parameters, see OpenRequest.

SendRequest	$request->SendRequest([postdata])
	Sends an HTTP request to the destination server. postdata contains any optional data to send immediately after the request header; this is generally used for POST or PUT requests. Your request object must contain the following content header for post data to be processed. You can add the header with AddHeader:

```
...
$request->AddHeader("Content-Type: application/x-www-form-
urlencoded");
$request->
SendRequest("key1=value1&key2=value2&key3=value3");
```

Win32::IPC

The Win32::IPC module provides synchronization for multiple objects created from the Semaphore, Mutex, Process, and ChangeNotify classes. The wait method of this class is inherited by objects of the preceding modules, as well as the functions wait_all and wait_any. You should not need to call Win32::IPC directly.

wait	$obj->wait([timeout])
	This method is used on any synchronization object. It waits for the object to become signaled. It returns 1 if the object is signaled, -1 if the object is an abandoned mutex, 0 if the call times out, and undef

on error. *timeout* is the time to wait (in milliseconds). If no *timeout* is specified, the method waits indefinitely.

Win32::IPC also defines the two functions wait_all and wait_any.

wait_all
wait_all(*@objects*, [*timeout*])

Waits for all the synchronization objects contained in *@objects* to be signaled. The optional *timeout* parameter is the same as described for wait. The return value will be an integer that identifies the last object to be signaled (the *n*th object in the list, starting from 1). A negative integer (*-n*) indicates that the *n*th object was an abandoned mutex. A return of 0 means that the function timed out; undef is returned on error.

wait_any
wait_any(*@objects*, [*timeout*])

Waits for at least one of the objects contained in *@objects* to be signaled. Return values are the same as for wait_all, above, indicating which object signaled.

Win32::Mutex

This module provides access to Win32 mutex objects, which control access to common resources. The new constructor creates the mutex and determines its initial availability. It has the following syntax:

```
$mut = Win32::Mutex->new(init, [name]);
```

The first argument determines the initial status of the mutex. If *init* is nonzero, the calling process has immediate ownership of the mutex object. A 0 value means that the mutex is available. The second argument assigns a name to the mutex that allows this object to be referenced by others via the open function.

Another object constructor for Win32::Mutex is open:

```
$mut = Win32::Mutex->open(name);
```

This call creates a new mutex object to access an existing mutex identified by *name*.

The following methods can be used on Win32::Mutex objects.

release
$*mut*->Release( )

Releases ownership of the mutex from the calling process, allowing anyone waiting on the mutex to take ownership.

wait $mut->wait([timeout])

The Win32::IPC method inherited by this module. Makes the calling process wait for ownership of the mutex object for the number of milliseconds specified by *timeout*. If the mutex doesn't become available before the timeout, the call returns 0.

Win32::NetAdmin

The Win32::NetAdmin module provides extensive functionality for administering users and groups on Windows NT servers. This module does not implement an object interface for administration; it exports several functions that execute administrative commands. (This module does not load on Windows 95 systems.)

The following functions are provided by the Win32::NetAdmin module. The *server* argument of each function is optional; however, a placeholder for the argument must be used if you don't supply a name. An empty string ("") will work, indicating that the local machine should be used.

GetDomainController

GetDomainController (*server*, *domain*, $name)

Returns the name of the domain controller for the specified *server* and *domain* to the variable $name.

GroupAddUsers

GroupAddUsers (*server*, *name*, *users*)

Adds users to group *name* on *server*. *users* can be a list of usernames or a list variable containing multiple usernames.

GroupCreate

GroupCreate (*server*, *name*, *comment*)

Creates a group with the specified *name* on *server*. *comment* is a string used to provide a description about the group.

GroupDelete

GroupDelete (*server*, *name*)

Deletes a group named *name* from *server*.

GroupDeleteUsers

GroupDeleteUsers (*server*, *name*, *users*)

Deletes a list of *users* from the group *name* on *server*.

GroupGetAttributes

GroupGetAttributes (*server, name, comment*)

Returns the comment for group *name* on *server* to the variable *comment*.

GroupGetMembers

GroupGetMembers (*server, name, $users*)

Returns the usernames that are members of group *name* on *server* to the array referenced by *users*.

GroupIsMember

GroupIsMember (*server, name, user*)

Queries group *name* on *server* to see if *user* is a member. Returns true if *user* is a member, false if not.

GroupSetAttributes

GroupSetAttributes (*server, name, comment*)

Sets the comment for group *name* on *server* to the string provided in *comment*.

LocalGroupAddUsers

LocalGroupAddUsers (*server, name, users*)

Adds users to local group *name* on *server*. *users* can be a list of usernames or a list variable containing multiple usernames.

LocalGroupCreate

LocalGroupCreate (*server, name, comment*)

Creates a local group with the specified *name* on *server*. *comment* is a string used to provide a description about the group.

LocalGroupDelete

LocalGroupDelete (*server, name*)

Deletes a local group named *name* from *server*.

LocalGroupDeleteUsers

LocalGroupDeleteUsers (*server, name, users*)

Deletes a list of *users* from the local group *name* on *server*.

LocalGroupGetAttributes

```
LocalGroupGetAttributes (server, name, $comment)
```

Returns the comment for local group *name* on *server* to the variable $comment.

LocalGroupGetMembers

```
LocalGroupGetMembers (server, name, \@users)
```

Returns the usernames that are members of local group *name* on *server* to the array referenced by *users*.

LocalGroupIsMember

```
LocalGroupIsMember (server, name, user)
```

Queries local group *name* on *server* to see if *user* is a member. Returns true if *user* is a member, false if not.

LocalGroupSetAttributes

```
LocalGroupSetAttributes (server, name, comment)
```

Sets the comment for local group *name* on *server* to the string provided in *comment*.

UserCreate

```
UserCreate (server, username, password, passwordage, privilege,
homedir, comment, flags, scriptpath)
```

Creates a new user with the specified settings:

server
: Name of the server

username
: Name of new user

password
: The user's password

passwordage
: Amount of time before password expires

privilege
: Privilege settings of the new user, which can be one of the following:

```
USER_PRIV_MASK
USER_PRIV_GUEST
USER_PRIV_USER
USER_PRIV_ADMIN
```

homedir
> Pathname of the user's home directory

comment
> A string containing a comment about the user

flag
> A flag containing user creation settings, which can be one of the following:

```
UF_TEMP_DUPLICATE_ACCOUNT
UF_NORMAL_ACCOUNT
UF_INTERDOMAIN_TRUST_ACCOUNT
UF_WORKSTATION_TRUST_ACCOUNT
UF_SERVER_TRUST_ACCOUNT
UF_MACHINE_ACCOUNT_MASK
UF_ACCOUNT_TYPE_MASK
UF_DONT_EXPIRE_PASSWD
UF_SETTABLE_BITS
UF_SCRIPT
UF_ACCOUNTDISABLE
UF_HOMEDIR_REQUIRED
UF_LOCKOUT
UF_PASSWD_NOTREQD
UF_PASSWD_CANT_CHANGE
```

scriptpath
> Pathname for the user's login script

UserDelete

UserDelete (*server*, *username*)

Deletes a user with *username* from *server*.

UserGetAttributes

UserGetAttributes (*server*, *username*, $password, $passwordage, $privilege, $homedir, $comment, $flags, $scriptpath)

Retrieves information from a user profile for the user identified by *username* on *server* and stores each piece in the corresponding variables you provide as arguments. The elements and order of user information are the same as described in the UserCreate function.

UserSetAttributes

UserSetAttributes (*server*, *username*, *password*, *passwordage*, *privilege*, *homedir*, *comment*, *flags*, *scriptpath*)

Sets attributes for user *username* on *server*. The attributes are those described for the UserCreate function.

Win32::NetResource

The Win32::NetResource module allows you to manage shared resources on a network, such as printers, disks, etc. Two data structures are used to provide or store information for many of the NetResource functions. The first is the share_info hash. This hash contains parameters for setting up a share, using the following structure:

```
%share_info = (
        netname       => "name of share",
        type          => "type of share",
        remark        => "a string comment",
        permissions   => "permissions value",
        maxusers      => "the max number of users",
        current-users => "the current number of users",
        path          => "the path of the share",
        passwd        => "password, if required"
);
```

A netresource data structure contains information about the shared resource or device. It has the following structure:

```
%netresource = (
        'Scope'       => "Scope of a resource connection (see list below for
                          values)",
        'Type'        => "The type of resource (see list below)",
        'DisplayType' => "How the resource should be displayed (see list
                          below)",
        'Usage'       => "How the resource should be used",
        'LocalName'   => "Name of the local device the resource is connected
                          to",
        'RemoteName'  => "Network name of the resource",
        'Comment'     => "Comment string",
        'Provider'    => "Provider of the resource"
);
```

The first three elements of the netresource hash contain values described in the following lists. The Scope value can be one of the following:

RESOURCE_CONNECTED
> Resource is already connected

RESOURCE_REMEMBERED
> Resource is reconnected each time the user logs on

RESOURCE_GLOBALNET
> Resource is available to the entire network

The Type element takes one of the following values:

RESOURCETYPE_ANY
> All resources

RESOURCETYPE_DISK
> Disk resources

RESOURCETYPE_PRINT
> Print resources

The Display element can be one of these values:

RESOURCEDISPLAYTYPE_DOMAIN
> Object is displayed as a domain

RESOURCEDISPLAYTYPE_SERVER
> Object is displayed as a server

RESOURCEDISPLAYTYPE_SHARE
> Object is displayed as a sharepoint

RESOURCEUSAGE_CONNECTABLE
> Resource can be connected to a local device

RESOURCEUSAGE_CONTAINER
> Resource contains more resources

The functions in Win32::NetResource use the share_info and netresource structures as input and output arguments. These arguments are used in the description of the functions below; you should name them whatever you want.

AddConnection   AddConnection (\%netresource, password, username, connection)

Connects to the resource described in %netresource, with the password and username of the user. The connection flag indicates whether the connection should be remembered for the user for all logins.

CancelConnection

CancelConnection (name, connection, force)

Cancels a connection to a resource connected to the local device specified by name. connection indicates the type of connection, with 1 being a persistent connection and 0 being nonpersistent. The force value is a Boolean indicating whether to force the connection.

GetError   GetError ($code)

Gets the last error caused by a Win32 network call and saves it in the variable named by code.

GetSharedResources

GetSharedResources (\@*resources*, *type*)

Gets a list of all network resources and saves the list as references to %*netresource* hashes in @*resources*. *type* is the type of enumeration.

GetUNCName

GetUNCName (\$*uncname*, *path*)

Gets the UNC name of the share connected to the local *path* and saves it to the variable specified by *uncname*.

NetShareAdd

NetShareAdd (\%*shareinfo*, \$*error*, [*server*])

Makes a disk resource described by *shareinfo* available for sharing on the network. *server* is the name of the server for the shared resource (local is assumed if not specified). Any error that occurs is saved in the variable named by *error*.

NetShareCheck

NetShareCheck (*device*, \$*type*, [*server*])

Returns true if a share on *device* is available for connection. The type of share is saved in the variable named by *type* (if the function returns true).

NetShareDel

NetShareDel (*name*, [*server*])

Removes the share named *name* on optional *server* from a machine's list of shares.

NetShareGetInfo

NetShareGetInfo (*name*, \%*shareinfo*, [*server*])

Gets the share information for the share *name* on optional *server* and saves it in the specified *shareinfo* variable.

NetShareSetInfo

NetShareSetInfo (*name*, \%*shareinfo*, \$*error*, [*server*])

Sets the information for the share *name* on *server* to the parameters given by *shareinfo*. The error status is saved to the variable named by *error*.

WNetGetLastError

WNetGetLastError (\$*code*, \$*description*, \$*name*)

Gets the extended network error and saves its information to the variables named by *code*, *description*, and *name*. An extended network error is given only when Win32::GetLastError returns ERROR_EXTENDED_ERROR.

Win32::PerfLib

The Win32::PerfLib module allows you to retrieve the performance counter of any computer running Windows NT in the network. All of the functions return false if they fail, unless otherwise noted. If the $server argument is undef, the local machine is assumed.

new $perflib->new($server)

Creates a connection to the performance counters of the given server.

Close $perflib->Close($hashref)

Closes the connection to the performance counters.

GetCounterHelp   GetCounterHelp($server, $hashref)

Retrieves the counter help strings and their indices from the registry and stores them in the hash reference.

GetCounterNames

GetCounterNames($server, $hashref)

Retrieves the counter names and their indices from the registry and stores them in the hash reference.

GetCounterType   GetCounterType(countertype)

Converts the counter type to a readable string.

GetObjectList $perflib->GetObjectList($objectid, $hashref)

Retrieves the object and counter list of the given performance object.

Win32::Pipe

This module gives Win32 Perl the ability to use named pipes. Under Windows NT, named pipes are used for processes to communicate with one another, and are not limited to the local machine.

Named pipes are created with new, which makes a new Win32::Pipe object and returns true on success. new has the following syntax:

```
my $named_pipe = Win32::Pipe->new($pipe_name);
```

Win32::Pipe Methods

The following methods are provided for objects of created by Win32::Pipe.

BufferSize   `$named_pipe->BufferSize( )`

Returns the size of the instance of the buffer of the named pipe.

Close   `$named_pipe->Close`

Closes the named pipe.

Connect   `$named_pipe->Connect`

Tells the named pipe to create an instance of the named pipe and wait until a client connects. Returns true on success, false on failure.

Disconnect   `$named_pipe->Disconnect`

Disconnects (and destroys) the instance of the named pipe from the client. Returns true on success, false on failure.

Error   `$named_pipe->Error`

Returns the last error messages pertaining to the named pipe, if used in context to the package. Returns a list containing ERROR_NUMBER and ERROR_TEXT.

Read   `$named_pipe->Read`

Reads from the named pipe. Returns data read from the pipe on success, undef on failure.

ResizeBuffer   `$named_pipe->ResizeBuffer(SIZE)`

Sets the size of the buffer of the instance of the named pipe to SIZE. Returns the size of the buffer on success, false on failure.

Write $named_pipe->Write(DATA)

Writes DATA to the named pipe. Returns true on success, false on failure.

Win32::Process

This module provides access to extended Win32 process creation and management abilities. Process objects are created with the Create method (the constructor). Additional methods can be used on objects to kill, suspend, resume, and set the priorities of processes.

The Create constructor has the following syntax:

```
Win32::Process->Create($Proc, app, cmnd, hndls, opts, dir)
```

The arguments to Create are as follows:

$Proc
    Name of the reference for the created process object.

app
    Full pathname of the executable.

cmnd
    Command line for executable.

hndls
    Determines handle inheritance. A value of 1 turns on inheritance; a 0 value turns it off.

opts
    Sets options to implement when the process is created. The available options for this argument are listed below.

dir
    The working directory for the executable.

The process is created by passing the command line in cmnd to the executable named in app. For example, a process object for a text file running in Notepad is created like this:

```
use Win32::Process;
Win32::Process->Create($proc, 'C:\\windows\\Notepad.exe',
                       "Notepad perlnut.txt", 1,
                       DETACHED_PROCESS, ".");
```

The process creation options given by the opts argument to Create are:

CREATE_DEFAULT_ERROR_MODE
    Gives the process the default error mode.

CREATE_NEW_CONSOLE
    Creates a new console for the process. Can't be used with DETACHED_PROCESS.

CREATE_NO_CONSOLE

Creates a new process, but without running the process in a new and visible window. That is, a new process will be created, but in the background.

CREATE_NEW_PROCESS_GROUP

Creates process as root of a new process group.

CREATE_SEPARATE_WOW_VDM

Runs process in its own Virtual DOS Machine (VDM). Only applicable to 16-bit applications.

CREATE_SUSPENDED

Starts process in a suspended state. The process can be started with the Resume method.

CREATE_UNICODE_ENVIRONMENT

Uses Unicode characters in the environment block of the new process.

DEBUG_PROCESS

Debugs the new process with the calling process.

DEBUG_ONLY_THIS_PROCESS

Doesn't debug the new process if calling process is being debugged.

DETACHED_PROCESS

Creates a process with no access to the console of the calling process.

Win32::Process Methods

The following methods are provided for objects of created by Win32::Process.

GetExitCode $proc->GetExitCode($ref)

Gets the exit code of a process and saves it to $ref.

GetPriorityClass $proc->GetPriorityClass($ref)

Gets the priority class of the process and stores it in $ref.

Kill $proc->Kill(exitcode)

Kills the process with the given exitcode, which is returned by the process.

Resume $proc->Resume

Resumes a suspended process. This method can also be used on processes created with the CREATE_SUSPENDED flag.

SetPriorityClass	`$proc->SetPriorityClass($priority)`

Sets the priority class of the object to $priority. The priority can be one of the following:

`IDLE_PRIORITY_CLASS`
> A process whith threads that run only when the system is idle

`NORMAL_PRIORITY_CLASS`
> A process with normal scheduling

`HIGH_PRIORITY_CLASS`
> A process that performs time-critical tasks that must be executed immediately

`REALTIME_PRIORITY_CLASS`
> The highest-priority process, even preempts operating-system threads

Suspend	`$proc->Suspend`

Suspends the process.

Wait	`$proc->Wait(n)`

Waits *n* milliseconds for the process to exit. If the process times out, the method returns false and sets `$!` to `WAIT_FAILED`. For no timeout, sets *n* to `INFINITE`.

Win32::Registry

This module provides access to the Windows Registry, the database that stores information about all parts of your system and software. Many operating-system and application behaviors are controlled by Registry data. The Win32::Registry module gives you a way to access and update registry information with Perl.

 Always be careful when making changes to the registry. If vital system information gets changed by mistake, your system could become inoperable. Always make certain you have a backup of your registry before you start making modifications.

The Registry module automatically creates objects for the top-level registry trees. These objects are created in the main:: namespace, and each key that you open or create is accessed via one of these root objects. The top-level objects are:

```
$HKEY_CLASSES_ROOT
$HKEY_CURRENT_USER
$HKEY_LOCAL_MACHINE
$HKEY_USERS
```

```
$HKEY_PERFORMANCE_DATA
$HKEY_CURRENT_CONFIG
$HKEY_DYN_DATA
```

If you are outside of the main (default) namespace, you should package declare the keys, e.g., $main::HKEY_USERS.

The Open method creates new key objects for subtrees or subkeys under another open key object. Initially, a new key is opened from one of the main key objects. For example:

```
use Win32::Registry;
$p = "SOFTWARE\Microsoft\Windows NT\CurrentVersion";
$HKEY_LOCAL_MACHINE->Open($p, $CurrVer) || die "Open $!";
```

This example creates a key object $CurrVer for the CurrentVersion key for Windows NT. This key contains several values for the current version of the operating system. With the new key open, you can read or change the values it contains (every key has at least one unnamed, default value), or open and create subkeys. The Open method can create key objects only for existing keys.

Registry values are represented in Win32::Registry functions by three elements: the name of the value, the data type of the value, and the value itself. There are several different data types for the values. Win32::Registry defines the following constants for these types:

REG_SZ
   String data

REG_DWORD
   Unsigned four-byte integer

REG_MULTI_SZ
   Multiple strings delimited with NULL

REG_EXPAND_SZ
   Strings that expand (e.g., based on environment variables)

REG_BINARY
   Binary data (no particular format is assumed)

Win32::Registry Methods

The following methods can be used on key objects, either on the preopened main keys or subkeys that you have already opened.

Create $key->Create($newkey, name)

Creates a new key identified by *name* and saves it as the object reference named by *$newkey*. If the key already exists, this function simply opens the key. New keys can only be created one level below the key on which Create is used.

DeleteKey   `$key->DeleteKey(subkey)`

Deletes a subkey of the current key. This function will delete all values in the subkey and the subkey itself. A key cannot be deleted if it contains any subkeys.

DeleteValue   `$key->DeleteValue(name)`

Deletes a value identified by *name* from the current key.

GetKeys   `$key->GetKeys($listref)`

Returns the names of the subkeys of the current key to the list referenced by *listref*.

GetValues   `$key->GetValues($hashref)`

Returns the values contained in the current key to the hash referenced by *hashref*. Each registry value name is a hash key, while the hash value is a reference to a three-element list containing the name of the value, the data type, and the value.

Load   `$key->Load(subkey, filename)`

Loads a registry file to the named *subkey* from file *filename*.

Open   `$parent->Open(keyname, $key)`

Opens a registry key named in *keyname* and saves it as the object reference named by *$key*. *keyname* is the name of a key relative to the object on which Open is used (*$parent*).

QueryKey   `$key->QueryKey($class, $subs, $vals)`

Retrieves information about the current key and returns it to the named scalar variables. The key class is saved in the *class* variable (it will be the null string "" on Win95 since it doesn't use key classes). The number of subkeys is saved in the *$subs* variable, and the number of values in the current key is saved in *$vals*.

QueryValue   `$key->QueryValue(name, $var)`

Returns the value of the registry value specified by *name* and saves it in the scalar variable *$var*.

Save	$key->Save(*filename*)
	Saves the registry tree root and the current key to a file, *filename*.

SetValue	$key->SetValue(*subkey*, *type*, *value*)
	Sets the default (unnamed) value for the specified subkey of the key object on which SetValue is used. The arguments are:
	subkey
	Name of the subkey
	type
	One of the type constants (listed above) describing the value
	value
	Value of the key

SetValueEx	$key->SetValueEx(*name*, *res*, *type*, *value*)
	Sets a value specified by *name* in the current key (or creates the value if it doesn't already exist). The arguments are:
	res
	A reserved argument for future use (use 0 as a placeholder)
	type
	The data type constant (listed above) describing the value
	value
	The value of the key

Win32::Semaphore

The Win32::Semaphore module implements semaphores, synchronizing access to shared resources. The constructor new creates a new semaphore object and sets the initial count and the maximum count of the semaphore. The constructor has the following syntax:

```
$sem = Win32::Semaphore->new(init, max, [name]);
```

The arguments are defined as follows:

init
> The initial count of the semaphore

max
> The maximum count of the semaphore

name
> A string containing a name of the semaphore

The open constructor opens an existing semaphore object specified by *name*:

```
$sem = Win32::Semaphore->open(name);
```

The following methods can be used on Win32::Semaphore objects.

---

release   `$sem->release(inc, [$var])`

Releases a semaphore and increments the count by the amount specified in *inc*. The last count (before the increment) is returned in the $*var* variable, if provided.

---

wait   `$sem->wait([timeout])`

The inherited Win32::IPC call. Waits for the semaphore's count to be nonzero, then decrements it. Optional *timeout* is given in milliseconds.

Win32::Service

The Win32::Service module provides a service control interface. It allows you to start, pause, resume, and stop Windows NT system services from Perl scripts.

The following functions are exported by this module. The *host* argument in each function gives the hostname of the machine a service is running (or will run) on. If you supply a null string (""), the local machine will be assumed.

GetServices   `GetServices (host, \%hash)`

Returns a list of services on *host* to the hash referenced by *hash*.

GetStatus   `GetStatus (host, service, \%status)`

Returns the status of *service* as a hash referenced by *status*. The keys for this hash are:

```
ServiceType
CurrentState
ControlsAccepted
Win32ExitCode
ServiceSpecificExitCode
CheckPoint
WaitHint
```

PauseService   `PauseService (host, service)`

Pauses the named *service* on machine *host* (only if the service is able to pause).

ResumeService	ResumeService (*host, service*)
	Resumes a paused *service* on *host*.

StartService	StartService (*host, service*)
	Starts the named *service* on the machine *host*. The specified service must be registered with the Service Control Manager.

StopService	StopService (*host, service*)
	Stops the named *service* on machine *host*.

Win32::Shortcut

This module allows you to create and manipulate Windows shortcut files (*.lnk* files) through Perl. The methods and properties of this module apply to shortcut objects created by new:

```
use Win32::Shortcut;
$link = Win32::Shortcut->new();
```

This creates the shortcut object $link, on which you can set properties and save into a file. If you supply a filename as an argument to new, the file will be loaded into the shortcut object.

The object can also be accessed as if it was a normal hash reference. The following properties (hash keys) are available:

```
$link->{'File'}
$link->{'Path'}
$link->{'ShortPath'}
$link->{'WorkingDirectory'}
$link->{'Arguments'}
$link->{'Description'}
$link->{'ShowCmd'}
$link->{'Hotkey'}
$link->{'IconLocation'}
$link->{'IconNumber'}
```

See the "Shortcut Properties" section for a description of each property.

The following example assumes you have a shortcut file named *test.lnk* in your current directory. This simple script will tell you where this shortcut points to:

```
use Win32::Shortcut;
$link=new Win32::Shortcut();
$link->Load("test.lnk");
```

```
print "Shortcut to: $link->{'Path'} $link->{'Arguments'} \n";
$link->Close();
```

But you can also modify its values:

```
use Win32::Shortcut;
$link=new Win32::Shortcut();
$link->Load("test.lnk");
$link->{'Path'}=~s/C:/D:/i;    # Move the target from C: to D:
$link->{'ShowCmd'}=SW_NORMAL; # Runs in a normal window
```

The methods provided by Win32::Shortcut are as follows.

---

new new Win32::Shortcut [*file*]

Creates a new shortcut object. If a filename is passed in *file*, automatically Loads this file also. Returns the object created, or undef on error.

Close $*link*->Close()

Closes a shortcut object. It is not strictly required to close the objects you created, since the Win32::Shortcut objects are automatically closed when the program ends (or when you otherwise destroy such an object).

Also note that a shortcut is not automatically saved when it is closed, even if you modified it. You have to call Save in order to apply modifications to a shortcut file.

Load $*link*->Load(*file*)

Loads the content of the shortcut file named *file* in a shortcut object and fills the properties of the object with its values. Returns undef on error, or true if everything was successful.

Resolve $*link*->Resolve([*flag*])

Attempts to automatically resolve a shortcut and returns the resolved path, or undef on error; if there is no resolution, the path is returned unchanged. Note that the path is automatically updated in the Path property of the shortcut.

By default, this method acts quietly, but if you pass a value of 0 in the *flag* parameter, it will eventually post a dialog box prompting the user for more information. For example:

```
# If the target doesn't exist...
if(! -f $link->Path) {

    # Save the actual target for comparison
    $oldpath = $link->Path;
```

```
                         # Try to resolve it (with dialog box)
                         $newpath = $link->Resolve(0);

                         die "Not resolved..." if $newpath == $oldpath;
                     }
```

Save $*link*->Save([*file*])

Saves the content of the shortcut object into the file named *file*. If
file is omitted, the filename is taken from the File property of the
object (which, if not changed, is the name of the last Loaded file).

If no file is loaded, and the File property doesn't contain a valid
filename, the method returns undef, which is also returned on
error. A true value is returned if everything was successful.

Set $*link*->Set(*path, arguments, workingdirectory, description,
                        showcmd, hotkey, iconlocation, iconnumber*)

Sets all the properties of the shortcut object with a single
command. This method is supplied for convenience only; you can
also set these values by changing the values of the properties. For
example:

```
                     $link->Set("C:\PERL5\BIN\PERL.EXE",
                                "-v",
                                "C:\PERL5\BIN",
                                "Prints out the version of Perl",
                                SW_SHOWMAXIMIZED,
                                hex('0x0337'),
                                "C:\WINDOWS\SYSTEM\COOL.DLL",
                                1);
```

This is the same as:

```
                     $link->Path("C:\PERL5\BIN\PERL.EXE");
                     $link->Arguments("-v");
                     $link->WorkingDirectory("C:\PERL5\BIN");
                     $link->Description("Prints out the version of Perl");
                     $link->ShowCmd(SW_SHOWMAXIMIZED);
                     $link->Hotkey(hex('0x0337'));
                     $link->IconLocation("C:\WINDOWS\SYSTEM\COOL.DLL");
                     $link->IconNumber(1);</PRE>
```

Shortcut Properties

The properties of a shortcut object can be accessed as:

```
    $link->{'property'}
```

For example, assuming that you have created a shortcut object with:

```
$link=new Win32::Shortcut();
```

you can see its description with:

```
print $link->{'Description'};
```

You can, of course, also set it like this:

```
$link->{'Description'}="This is a description";
```

The shortcut properties also have corresponding methods that can also set or read their values.

The properties of a shortcut reflect the content of the Shortcut Properties dialog box, which can be obtained by right-clicking on a shortcut file in the Windows 95 (or NT 4.0) Explorer and choosing "Properties." Shortcut properties are:

Arguments
> The arguments associated with the shell link object. They are passed to the targeted program (see *Path*) when it gets executed. In fact, joined with *Path*, this parameter forms the "Target" field of a Shortcut Properties dialog box.

Description
> An optional description given to the shortcut. Not implemented in Shortcut Properties dialog box.

File
> The filename of the shortcut file opened with Load and/or the filename under which the shortcut will be saved with Save (if the *file* argument is not specified).

Hotkey
> The hotkey associated with the shortcut, in the form of a two-byte number, of which the first byte identifies the modifiers (Ctrl, Alt, Shift, etc.), and the second is the ASCII code of the character key. Corresponds to the "Shortcut key" field of a Shortcut Properties dialog box.

IconLocation
> The file that contains the icon for the shortcut.

IconNumber
> The number of the icon for the shortcut in the file pointed to by *IconLocation*, in case more that one icon is contained in that file.

Path
> The target of the shortcut. This (joined with *Arguments*) is the content of the "Target" field in a Shortcut Properties dialog box.

ShortPath
> Same as *Path*, but expressed in a DOS-readable format (8.3-character filenames). It is available as read-only (well, you can change it, but it has no effect on the shortcut; change *Path* instead) once you Load a shortcut file.

ShowCmd

The condition of the window in which the program will be executed (can be Normal, Minimized, or Maximized). Corresponds to the "Run" field of a Shortcut Properties dialog box. Allowed values are:

Value	Meaning	Constant
1	Normal window	SW_SHOWNORMAL
3	Maximized	SW_SHOWMAXIMIZED
7	Minimized	SW_SHOWMINNOACTIVE

WorkingDirectory

The directory in which the targeted program will be executed. Corresponds to the "Start in" field of a Shortcut Properties dialog box.

Win32 Extensions

In addition to the modules listed previously, Perl for Win32 can use an additional set of functions from the Win32 extension. These functions provide useful tools for some Windows-specific tasks that don't require their own modules. They are exported from the Win32 package with:

```
use Win32;
```

Many of these functions do not take arguments and return the value (or values) of the requested information, unless otherwise noted.

Win32::CopyFile(*from, to, overwrite*)

Copies an existing file to a new file, while preserving all attributes of the original file, except the security information. If *to* exists, overwriting will take place only if *overwrite* is true. Read-only files will never be overwritten; they will need to be unlinked first.

Win32::FreeLibrary(*handle*)

Unloads a previously loaded DLL. *handle* is no longer valid after FreeLibrary() is called.

Win32::GetArchName()

Has been deprecated in favor of $ENV{PROCESSOR_ARCHITECTURE}.

Win32::GetChipName()

Returns the processor type of the machine under which the perl process is running. This string will be represented as 386, 486, 586, etc.

Win32::GetFullPathName(*filename*)

Combines *filename* with drive number and directory name. In a list context, GetFulllPathName() returns *path* and *file*.

Win32::GetLastError()

Returns the last error value generated by a call to a Win32 API function.

Win32::GetLongPathName(*pathname*)

Returns *pathname* as composed of longname components.

Win32::GetProcAddress(*instance, procname*)

 Returns the address of a function inside of a loaded library. Since GetProcAddress( ) is deprecated, you should use Win32::API instead.

Win32::LoadLibrary(*libname*)

 Loads a DLL into memory and returns its module handle. You can then use the returned module handle with Win32::GetProcAddress and Win32::FreeLibrary.

Win32::MsgBox(*message*, [, *flags*, [, *title*]])

 Creates a dialog box that contains *message*. *title* specifies an optional window title. FLAGS specifies the required icons according to the following:

```
0 = OK
1 = OK and Cancel
2 = Abort, Retry, and Ignore
3 = Yes, No and Cancel
4 = Yes and No
5 = Retry and Cancel
MB_ICONSTOP creates an "X" in a red circle
MB_ICONQUESTION creates a question mark in a bubble
MB_ICONEXCLAMATION creates an exclamation mark in a yellow triangle
MB_ICONINFORMATION creates an "i" in a bubble
```

MsgBox( ) returns the menu ID of the selected pushbutton:

```
0  Error
1  OK
2  Cancel
3  Abort
4  Retry
5  Ignore
6  Yes
7  No
```

Win32::OLELastError( )

 Returns the last error value generated by a call to a Win32 OLE API function.

Win32::BuildNumber( )

 Returns the build number of Perl for Win32.

Win32::LoginName( )

 Returns the username of the owner of the current Perl process.

Win32::NodeName( )

 Returns the Microsoft network node name of the current machine.

Win32::DomainName( )

 Returns the name of the Microsoft network domain that the owner of the current Perl process is logged into.

Win32::FsType( )

 Returns a string naming the filesystem type of the currently active drive.

Win32::GetCwd( )

 Returns the current active drive and directory. This function does not return a UNC path, since the functionality required for such a feature is not available under Windows 95.

`Win32::SetCwd(newdir)`

Sets the current active drive and directory to *newdir*. This function does not work with UNC paths, since the functionality required for such a feature is not available under Windows 95.

`Win32::SetLastError(error)`

Sets the value of the last error encountered to *error*. Does not work under Windows 95.

`Win32::GetOSVersion( )`

Returns a list of elements describing the version of the operating system. The elements of the list are an arbitrary descriptive string; the major version number of the operating system; the minor version number; the build number; and a digit indicating the actual operating system, which will be 0 for Win32s, 1 for Windows 95, and 2 for Windows NT. For example:

```
use Win32;
($string, $major, $minor, $build, $id) = Win32::GetOSVersion( );
```

`Win32::FormatMessage(error)`

Converts the Win32 error number supplied by *error* into a descriptive string. The error number can be retrieved using `Win32::GetLastError` or `Win32::OLELastError`.

`Win32::Spawn(command, args, $pid)`

Spawns a new process for the given *command*, passing the arguments in *args*. The ID of the new process is saved in the variable named by *pid*.

`Win32::LookupAccountName(sys, acct, $domain, $sid, $type)`

Returns the domain name, SID, and SID type to the specified variables for the account *acct* on system *sys*.

`Win32::LookupAccountSID(sys, sid, $acct, $domain, $type)`

Returns the account name, domain name, and SID type to the specified variables for the SID *sid* on system *sys*.

`Win32::InitiateSystemShutdown(machine, message, timeout, forceclose, reboot)`

Shuts down the specified *machine* in the specified *timeout* interval. *message* is broadcast to all users. If *forceclose* is true, all documents are closed (forcefully) without prompting the user. If *reboot* is true, the machine is rebooted.

`Win32::AbortSystemShutdown(machine)`

Aborts a shutdown on the specified *machine*.

`Win32::GetTickCount( )`

Returns the Win32 tick count.

`Win32::IsWinNT( )`

Returns true (nonzero) if the Win32 subsystem is Windows NT.

`Win32::IsWin95( )`

Returns true (nonzero) if the Win32 subsystem is Windows 95.

`Win32::ExpandEnvironmentStrings(envstring)`

Returns a string in which any environment variables in the given *envstring* are replaced with their values.

`Win32::GetShortPathName(`*`longpathname`*`)`
> Returns the short (8.3) pathname of *longpathname*.

`Win32::GetNextAvailDrive( )`
> Returns a string in the form of *d:*\, in which *d* is the first available drive letter.

`Win32::RegisterServer(`*`libraryname`*`)`
> Loads the DLL *libraryname* and calls the function `DllRegisterServer`.

`Win32::UnregisterServer(`*`libraryname`*`)`
> Loads the DLL *libraryname* and calls the function `DllUnregisterServer`.

`Win32::Sleep(`*`time`*`)`
> Pauses for the number of milliseconds specified by *time*.

23

OLE Automation

The Win32::OLE modules give Perl support for OLE automation. OLE automation is a Microsoft technology based on COM that allows objects created by another application to be used and manipulated by a program through a common interface.

The application (or DLL) that implements the automation interface is called the *automation server*. The application that creates and uses the interface is called the *automation controller* or *automation client*. Many popular applications expose their objects through automation. Microsoft Word, Excel, and other Office applications can be used as automation servers. Automation is widely used by Active Server Pages (ASP) and CGI scripts to access data repositories, perhaps via ActiveX Data Objects (ADO). You can even use automation to control many development environments and editors.

To create an automation object, the server needs to be *registered* on the system. This is typically done by the server's installation program, but can be done manually using a utility such as *regsvr32.exe*. This involves adding entries to the system registry to tell COM how to find the component, the types of interfaces it provides, the type of server it is, etc. You should be able to find the object model, available methods, and properties of the interface in the documentation provided by the application. This object model can be used via Perl's object syntax to create and control objects in your programs.

Four modules provide automation functionality to Perl:

Win32::OLE
> Provides the main interface for OLE automation. You can create or open automation objects, use their methods, and set their properties.

Win32::OLE::Enum
> Creates objects for collections and defines an interface for enumerating them.

Win32::OLE::Variant

Allows you to convert the Variant data type used in OLE.

Win32::OLE::Const

Imports constants from an automation object into your script.

Note that there are a few limitations to Win32::OLE. There is currently no support for OCXs or OLE events (notifications generated by the automation server). Win32::OLE implements the IDispatch interface only, and therefore cannot access a custom OLE interface.

Creating Objects

Automation objects are represented in Perl as instances of Win32::OLE objects. The module provides three constructors for creating objects from a registered automation server.

---

new

Win32::OLE->new(*progid, [destructor]*)

Creates a new automation object. This method always creates a new instance of the server, even if a previous instance of the server is running. If the object cannot be created, new returns undef.

progid, the program identifier (ProgID), is a string that uniquely identifies an automation object. *progid* is used to look up the object's class ID (CLSID), which is stored in the registry.

The second, optional argument to the new method describes a way to destroy the object in case the Perl program dies unexpectedly. *destructor* can be either a string with the name of the defined OLE destructor method, or a code reference that will destroy the object. You should use some form of *destructor* to close out all your objects, for they can be extremely expensive in terms of system resources. You can explicitly destroy an object using the undef function. If you don't explicitly destroy the object, Perl takes care of it for you when the last reference to the object goes away.

Here is what new would look like with the destructor arguments:

```
# Quit is the OLE-defined destructor method
$x1 = Win32::OLE->new("Excel.Application", 'Quit');

# The object reference is the first argument ($_[0])
passed to new
# The code reference will undef it to destroy the object
$x2 = Win32::OLE->new("Excel.Application", sub{undef $_
[0];})
```

Notice that we're supplying Excel.Application as the ProgID. Excel supports several different automation objects, including an Application object, WorkBook objects, and several more. You don't necessarily have to create the top-level object (Application, in this case) when dealing with automation objects (this is determined by the automation server). In Excel's case, we could have directly created a WorkSheet object (e.g., Excel.Sheet) or a Chart object, for example.

GetActiveObject	Win32::OLE->GetActiveObject(*progid*)

Creates an object for a currently active instance of a server, if one exists. If the server is registered, but no instance of it is running, the method returns undef. If the server is not registered, the method will croak.

You should probably call GetActiveObject inside an eval so that you can do exception handling in the event that the server is unregistered or is not currently running. If the method returns undef, you can just create a new instance of the server and the object with new.

GetObject	Win32::OLE->GetObject(*filename*)

Creates an automation object based on a document. *filename* is the full pathname of the document, which can be optionally followed by additional item subcomponents separated by exclamation marks (!). For example:

```
$doc = 'c:\test\test.xls';
$xl = Win32::OLE->GetObject($doc);
```

This code creates an Excel instance based on an Excel file. It is not always clear what type of object GetObject will return from a document since applications may register for more than one document type (e.g., worksheets, charts, macro files, etc. for Excel). You can use QueryObjectType on an object to get the class name of the object.

Automation Methods and Properties

Once you have created an automation object, you can use its methods or adjust its properties as you require. Automation methods are implemented as you'd expect with the Perl object syntax:

```
$obj->some_method(args);
```

Automation methods can often take a number of optional parameters. You can pass undef for any unwanted parameters in the arguments list. For example, you can save a WorkBook in Excel with SaveAs. Additional settings allow you to add the WorkBook to the MRU list and create a backup copy:

```
$xl->WorkBooks(1)->SaveAs($f, undef, undef, undef, undef, 1, undef, undef,
1);
```

For simplification, you can also use just the named parameters you want to set by passing a reference to a hash containing them. You can do this right in the argument list by creating an anonymous hash reference with {}. The previous example can therefore be written like this:

```
$xl->WorkBooks(1)->SaveAs($f, {AddtoMru => 1, CreateBackup => 1});
```

Properties of automation objects are accessed via hash reference notation on the object. For example:

```
$val = $obj->{"property"};        # Get a property value
$obj->{"property"} = $val;        # Set a property value
```

Be aware that properties may not be writable (or even readable). Many automation objects have read-only properties and will generate an exception if you try to write to them. You'll need to consult the documentation for the object to find out which properties you can safely set.

You can enumerate the properties of an automation object using the normal methods for enumerating hashes, which are keys and each. Here's how you can print the properties and values contained within an object:

```
$xl = Win32::OLE->new('Excel.Application', 'Quit');
while( ($key,$value) = each %$xl ) {
    print "$key=$value\n";
}
```

Win32::OLE Methods

Win32::OLE defines a couple of its own methods for dealing with the automation interface. These are not automation-defined methods, although they look the same. If a given method is not defined in Win32::OLE, the method call is dispatched to the automation object. If the method doesn't exist there, you will get an OLE error.

The following methods are defined by Win32::OLE.

Invoke $obj->Invoke(method, args)

This object method calls the given method for $obj with args as arguments. It is useful for invoking methods that would interfere with predefined names in Perl, or methods that contain characters that Perl can't recognize. You can also use Invoke to call an object's default method by using either undef or an empty string ("") as the first argument.

LastError Win32::OLE->LastError( )

This class method returns the last OLE error. In a numeric context, the error number is returned, while in a string context, the error message is returned.

QueryObjectType

> Win32::OLE->QueryObjectType($obj)

This class method returns the type of object queried ($obj). In list context, a two-element list of the type library name and the class name of the object is returned. In scalar context, just the class name is returned.

Win32::OLE Functions

The following functions are defined by Win32::OLE. They are not exported by default.

in

> in($coll)

Returns a list of all the members of a collection referenced by the collection object $coll. Same as Win32::OLE::Enum->All( ).

valof

> valof($obj)

Dereferences an automation object ($obj), calls the default method of the object, and returns the value.

with

> with($obj, property1 => value1, ...)

Sets the values of multiple properties on an object ($obj). The function calls $obj->{property}=value for each property/value pair.

Win32::OLE Class Variables

The Win32::OLE module defines certain class variables that set default behavior for automation usage:

$Win32::OLE::CP

Determines the codepage used by all translations between Perl strings and Unicode strings used by the OLE interface. The default value is CP_ACP, which is the default ANSI codepage. It can also be set to CP_OEMCP, which is the default OEM codepage. Both constants are not exported by default.

$Win32::OLE::LCID

Controls the locale identifier used for all OLE calls. It is set to LOCALE_NEUTRAL by default. Check the Win32 module for other locale-related information.

`$Win32::OLE::Warn`

Determines the behavior of the Win32::OLE module when an error happens. Valid values are:

0   Ignores error, returns `undef`.

1   Uses `Carp::carp` if `$^W` is set (*–w* option).

2   Always uses `Carp::carp`.

3   Uses `Carp::croak`.

The error number and message (without `Carp` line/module info) are also available through the `Win32::OLE->LastError` method.

Win32::OLE::Enum

The Win32::OLE::Enum module provides special support for collections. Collections are special automation data types that contain an array of objects or data. A collection supports enumeration; you can iterate through each item through a standard interface.

Collection objects should always provide a `Count` property (the number of items in the collection) and an `Item` method. The `Item` method is used to access a particular collection item using a subscript, which may be an integer or a string, depending on the server. Collection objects may also optionally contain an `Add` and a `Remove` method.

Collection objects also support a standard COM interface (IEnumVARIANT) that allows you to enumerate each item in a collection. It defines methods that let you advance the iteration to the next item, skip a given item, restart the enumeration, and create a new copy of the iterator. While all servers are supposed to provide this interface, some servers don't implement all of the methods (often `Reset` and `Clone` are not implemented).

Win32::OLE::Enum defines these methods for enumerating collections. The collection object should provide the `Count` and `Item` methods, which are often all you need to use on collections. For example:

```
$cnt = $coll->Count( );
if( $cnt) {
    $obj = $coll->Item(0);
    $obj->do_something( );
}
```

`Count` will tell you the number of items in the collection, and `Item` will return the desired item as a Win32::OLE object.

For the enumeration methods, you need to create an enumeration object for the collection object:

```
$coll = $obj->some_coll( );
$enum = Win32::OLE::Enum->new($coll);
```

Now you can use the enumeration methods on the object.

Win32::OLE::Enum Methods

The following methods are defined in Win32::OLE::Enum.

---

new   `Win32::OLE::Enum->new($obj)`

Creates a new Win32::OLE::Enum object. Provides it with a collection object or an existing Enum object, in which case it calls Clone.

All   `$Enum->All( )`

Returns a list of all objects in the collection. Note that to use All again, you need to first call Reset.

Clone   `$Enum->Clone( )`

Returns a copy of the current iterator. This method is supposed to maintain the same iteration position, if possible, but may be unimplemented.

Next   `$Enum->Next([count])`

Returns the next item in the collection. You can optionally provide Next with a count (which must be greater than zero), in which case it returns a list of the next count items. Note that if you provide a scalar context in conjunction with a count, you'll get only the last item in the list of returned items. Next returns undef if it is currently on the last item in the collection.

Reset   `$Enum->Reset( )`

Restarts the enumeration with the first item in the collection. Reset returns true if it succeeds, false if it fails. Note that this method may be unimplemented.

Skip   `$Enum->Skip([count])`

Skips the next *count* number of items of the enumeration (again, *count* must be positive and defaults to 1). Skip returns false if there are not at least *count* items left.

Win32::OLE::Variant

All automation data has to be coerced into a special type called a Variant. Most of the time, you don't need to worry about explicit type coercion. You just provide your scalar data, and the magic of automation takes care of the rest. However, there are times when you want to control the exact type of data you're sending to the automation server. The Win32::OLE::Variant module provides access to the Variant data type and lets you control exactly how the data is represented.

A Variant is an OLE data structure that contains a type field and a data field. The flags are implemented in Perl (as are many constants) as subroutines that return an integer value. The following table lists the Variant type flags, along with a brief description of each:

Type	Description
VT_EMPTY	No value specified. Incidentally, automation does not use VT_EMPTY for empty optional parameters. Rather, it uses VT_ERROR with a value of DISP_E_PARAMNOTFOUND (which isn't exported by Perl: the value in current Win32 SDK headers is 0x80020004).
VT_NULL	A propagating NULL value was specified (not to be confused with a null pointer). This is used for things like the NULL in SQL.
VT_I2	A two-byte integer value.
VT_I4	A four-byte integer value.
VT_R4	An IEEE four-byte real value.
VT_R8	An IEEE eight-byte real value.
VT_CY	An automation currency value.
VT_DATE	An automation date value.
VT_BSTR	A string value.
VT_DISPATCH	The value contains another automation object.
VT_ERROR	An error code was specified. The type of the error is determined by the actual value. As mentioned earlier, this is used to implement empty optional parameters.
VT_BOOL	A Boolean (true/false) value. If all bits are 1, it's true; if all bits are 0, it's false. Any other value is invalid.
VT_VARIANT	The value contains another Variant.
VT_UNKNOWN	The value contains an IUnknown pointer (the base class of COM objects).
VT_UI1	An unsigned one-byte character.
VT_BYREF	Can be combined with some fields to indicate that the data is being passed by reference, rather than by value.
VT_ARRAY	The value contains an OLE SAFEARRAY (this flag is not currently exported by Perl).

To convert data to a specific Variant type, create a variant object with either the new constructor method or the convenience function Variant:

```
$vnt = Win32::OLE::Variant->new(type, data);
$vnt = Variant(type, data);
```

For example, to force a string to be interpreted as a date, create a Variant object and set it to the VT_DATE type:

```
$dt = Variant(VT_DATE, "August 24, 1970");   # Create an explicit data type
$sheet->Cells(1,1)->{Value} = $dt;           # Set it to a spreadsheet cell
```

Win32::OLE::Variant Methods

The following methods are defined by Win32::OLE::Variant for working with Variant data types.

As	$vnt->As(type)
	Takes a *type* flag argument and converts the Variant object to the supplied type before converting it to a Perl value.

ChangeType	$vnt->ChangeType(type)
	Takes a *type* flag argument and converts the Variant object (in place) to the supplied type.

Type	$vnt->Type( )
	Returns the type of the variant $vnt.

Value	$vnt->Value( )
	Returns the value of the variant $vnt as a Perl value. The conversion is performed in the same manner as all return values of Win32::OLE method calls are converted.

Win32::OLE::Const

While browsing through the documentation for an automation object, you may have come across references to constant values. For example, if you're trying to save an Excel workbook to a different file format, you need to provide a file format constant. Since the server documentation typically provides symbolic constants (e.g., xlExcel5 or xlTemplate), we need a way to access those from Perl. This is the purpose of Win32::OLE::Const, which imports the constants from an automation object into your script.

You can either import the constants directly into your namespace as subs that return the constant value, or you can have them returned as a hash reference with the constant name as the key and its value as the value. Here's an example of the former:

```
use Win32::OLE::Const ("Microsoft Excel");
print "xlExcel5 = ", xlExcel5, "\n";
```

This produces something like:

```
xlExcel5 = 39
```

Here's an example using the Load method to return a hash reference populated with the constants and their values (this produces the same output as the previous example, of course):

```
use Win32::OLE::Const;

my $constants = Win32::OLE::Const->Load("Microsoft Excel");
print "xlExcel5 = $constants->{xlExcel5}\n";
```

Notice that, in both cases, we're supplying a regular expression for the name of the type library from which we want to import. Win32::OLE::Const searches the registry for matching type libraries and loads the one with the highest version number (you can override this by supplying the version you want). You can also specify the language you'd like. The parameters (for either Load or Win32::OLE::Const) are the typelib regular expression, the major version number, the minor version number, and the locale (LCID).

You can also provide the Load method with an automation object, which is then queried for its type library. Interestingly, the documentation notes that this seems to be slower than searching the Registry (though neither is really speedy with a large automation server like Excel). Here's an example of that:

```
use Win32::OLE;
use Win32::OLE::Const;

# Create an Excel application object
my $xl = Win32::OLE->new('Excel.Application', 'Quit') ||
    die "Can't create Excel: ", Win32::OLE->LastError;

# Import the constants from it
my $constants = Win32::OLE::Const->Load($xl);
```

Using Load (to get a hash reference for the constants) may be preferable to importing all of the constants into your namespace. Some automation servers provide a large number of constants (the current version of Excel has some 900+), so importing them into your namespace can clutter things considerably.

24

ODBC Extension for Win32

Win32::ODBC allows you to make a connection to a database that supports ODBC under both Win32 and Unix. Win32::ODBC allows you to support as many ODBC connections as are allowed by memory and ODBC.

Generally, you'll use Win32::ODBC to access databases such as those created under Microsoft Access, but there's also an ODBC driver available for MySQL if you want to connect to MySQL via ODBC and aren't able to use DBI and a DBD.

To get started, you'll need to use new( ) to create a new Win32::ODBC object. As arguments, new( ) takes a connection string (DSN) or an open ODBC object if one is given. new( ) returns a database handle on success and undef on failure. For example:

```
use Win32::ODBC;

my $dsn = "DSN=Name of Database;UID=Your UID Here;PWD=dbpasswd;"
my $DB  = Win32::ODBC->new($dsn);
```

ODBC Methods and Properties

Once you have created an ODBC object, you can use its methods or adjust its properties as you require. ODBC methods are implemented as you'd expect with the Perl object syntax.

The following methods are defined by Win32::ODBC.

Catalog $obj->Catalog(*qualifier, owner, name, type*)

Tells ODBC to create a data set that contains table information about the DSN. Use Fetch and Data or DataHash to retrieve the data. The returned format is:

[*qualifier*] [*owner*] [*name*] [*type*]

Returns true on error.

ColAttributes   Win32::ODBC->ColAttributes(*attributes*, [*field_names*])

Returns the attributes *attributes* on each of the fields in the list *field_names* in the current record set. If *field_names* is empty, then all fields are assumed. The attributes are returned as an associative array.

ConfigDSN   Win32::ODBC->ConfigDSN(*option*, *driver*, *attribute1* [, *attribute2*, *attribute3*, ...])

Configures a DSN. *option* takes on one of the following values:

ODBC_ADD_DSN
> Adds a new DSN

ODBC_MODIFY_DSN
> Modifies an existing DSN

ODBC_REMOVE_DSN
> Removes an existing DSN

ODBC_ADD_SYS_DSN
> Adds a new System DSN

ODBC_MODIFY_SYS_DSN
> Modifies an existing System DSN

ODBC_REMOVE_SYS_DSN
> Removes an existing System DSN

driver is a required argument. *attribute1* is the DSN, whose format is shown earlier. ConfigDSN( ) returns true on success and false on failure.

Connection   Win32::ODBC->Connection( )

Returns the connection number associated with the ODBC connection.

Close   Win32::ODBC->Close( )

Closes the ODBC connection. No return value.

Data   Win32::ODBC->Data([*field_name*])

Returns the contents of column name *field_name* or the current row (if nothing is specified).

DataHash   Win32::ODBC->DataHash([*field1, field2, ...*])

Returns the contents for *field1, field2, ...,* or the entire row (if nothing is specified) as an associative array consisting of:

    {Field Name} => Field Data

DataSources   Win32::ODBC->DataSources( )

Returns an associative array of data sources and ODBC remarks about them. They are returned in the form of:

    $ArrayName{'DSN'}=Driver

Debug   Win32::ODBC->Debug([0 | 1])

Sets the debug option to on or off. If nothing is specified, then nothing is changed. Returns the debugging value (1 or 0).

Drivers   Win32::ODBC->Drivers( )

Returns an associative array of ODBC Drivers and their attributes. They are returned in the form of:

    $ArrayName{'*driver*'}=*Attrib1;Attrib2;Attrib3;...*

in which *driver* is the ODBC driver name, and *AttribX* are the driver-defined attributes.

DropCursor   Win32::ODBC->DropCursor([*close_type*])

Drops the cursor associated with the ODBC object. This forces the cursor to be deallocated. This overrides SetStmtCloseType, but the ODBC object does not lose the StmtCloseType setting. *close_type* can be any valid SmtpCloseType and will perform a close on the statement using the specified close type. Returns true on success, false on failure.

DumpData   Win32::ODBC->DumpData( )

Dumps to the screen the fieldnames and all records of the current data set. Used primarily for debugging. No return value.

Error   Win32::ODBC->Error( )

Returns the last encountered error. The returned value is context-dependent.

If called in a scalar context, then a three-element array is returned:

    (*error_number, error_text, connection_number*)

If called in a string context, then a string is returned:

"[*error_number*] [*connection_number*] [*error_text*]"

If debugging is on, then two more variables are returned:

(..., *function*, *level*)

function is the name of the function in which the error occurred, and *level* represents extra information about the error (usually the location of the error).

FetchRow   Win32::ODBC->FetchRow(*row*, [*type*])

Retrieves the next record from the keyset. When *row* and/or *type* are specified, the call is made using SQLExtendedFetch instead of SQLFetch. Returns true when another record is available to read and false when there are no more records.

FieldNames   Win32::ODBC->FieldNames( )

Returns an array of fieldnames found in the current data set. The order isn't specified.

GetConnections   Win32::ODBC->GetConnections( )

Returns an array of connection numbers showing which connections are currently open.

GetConnectOption

Win32::ODBC->GetConnectOption(*option*)

Returns the value of the specified connect option *option*. (Refer to ODBC documentation for more information on the options and values.) Returns a string or scalar depending upon the option specified.

GetCursorName   Win32::ODBC->GetCursorName( )

Returns the name of the current cursor as a string or undef.

GetData   Win32::ODBC->GetData( )

Retrieves the current row from the dataset. This is not generally used by users; it is used internally. Returns an array of field data in which the first element is either false (if successful) or true (if not successful).

| **getDSN** | Win32::ODBC->getDSN([*dsn*]) |

Returns an associative array indicating the configuration for the specified *dsn*. If no *dsn* is specified, then the current connection is used. The returned associative array consists of:

```
keys=DSN keyword; values=Keyword value.
$Data{$Keyword}=Value
```

| **GetFunctions** | Win32::ODBC->GetFunctions([*function1, function2*]) |

Returns an associative array indicating the ability of the ODBC Driver to support the specified functions. If no functions are specified, then a 100-element associative array is returned containing all possible functions and their values. *function* must be in the form of an ODBC API constant such as SQL_API_SQLTRANSACT. The returned array will contain the results:

```
$Results{SQL_API_SQLTRANSACT}=Value
```

For example:

```
$Results = $0->GetFunctions(
    $0->SQL_API_SQLTRANSACT,
    SQL_API_SQLSETCONNECTOPTION
);
$ConnectOption = $Results{SQL_API_SQLSETCONNECTOPTION};
$Transact = $Results{SQL_API_SQLTRANSACT};
```

| **GetInfo** | Win32::ODBC->GetInfo([*option*]) |

Returns a string indicating the value of the particular option specified.

| **GetMaxBufSize** | Win32::ODBC->GetMaxBufSize( ) |

Returns the current allocated limit for MaxBufSize. For more info, see SetMaxBufSize.

| **GetSQLState** | Win32::ODBC->GetSQLState( ) |

Returns a string indicating the SQL state as reported by ODBC. The SQL state is a code that the ODBC Manager or ODBC Driver returns after the execution of a SQL function. This is helpful for debugging purposes.

GetStmtCloseType

Win32::ODBC->GetStmtCloseType([*connection*])

Returns a string indicating the type of closure that will be used every time the hstmt is freed. (See SetStmtCloseType for details.) By default, the connection of the current object will be used. If *connection* is a valid connection number, then it will be used.

GetStmtOption

`Win32::ODBC->GetStmtOption([option])`

Returns the value of the specified statement option *option*. (Refer to ODBC documentation for more information on the options and values.) Returns a string or scalar depending on the option specified.

MoreResults

`Win32::ODBC->MoreResults([connection])`

Reports whether there is data yet to be retrieved from the query. This can happen if the query was a multiple select:

```
"SELECT * FROM [foo] SELECT * FROM [bar]"
```

Returns 1 if there is more data, undef otherwise.

RowCount

`Win32::ODBC->RowCount([connection])`

For UPDATE, INSERT, and DELETE statements, the returned value is the number of rows affected by the request, or -1 if the number of affected rows is not available. Returns the number of affected rows, or -1 if not supported by the driver in the current context.

Run

`Win32::ODBC->Run(sql)`

Executes the SQL command *sql* and dumps to the screen info about it. Used primarily for debugging. No return value.

SetConnectOption

`Win32::ODBC->SetConnectOption(option)`

Sets the value of the specified connect option *option*. (Refer to ODBC documentation for more information on the options and values.) Returns true on success, false otherwise.

SetCursorName

`Win32::ODBC->SetCursorName(name)`

Sets the name of the current cursor. Returns true on success, false otherwise.

SetPos

`Win32::ODBC->SetPos(row, [option, lock])`

Moves the cursor to the row *row* within the current keyset (not the current data/result set). Returns true on success, false otherwise.

SetMaxBufSize   `Win32::ODBC->SetMaxBufSize(size)`

Sets the MaxBufSize for a particular connection. The amount of memory allocated to retrieve the field data of a record is dynamic and changes when it needs to be larger. Returns the maximum number of bytes.

SetStmtCloseType

`Win32::ODBC->SetStmtCloseType(type, [connection])`

Sets a particular hstmt close type for the connection. This is the same as `ODBCFreeStmt(hstmt, type)`. By default, the connection of the current object will be used. If *connection* is a valid connection number, then it will be used. *type* may be one of:

```
SQL_CLOSE
SQL_DROP
SQL_UNBIND
SQL_RESET_PARAMS
```

Returns a string indicating the newly set type.

SetStmtOption   `Win32::ODBC->SetStmtOption(option)`

Sets the value of the specified statement option *option*. (Refer to ODBC documentation for more information on the options and values.) Returns true on success, false otherwise.

Shutdown   `Win32::ODBC->Shutdown( )`

Closes the ODBC connection and dumps to the screen info about it. Used primarily for debugging. No return value.

Sql   `Win32::ODBC->Sql(SQL_STRING)`

Executes the SQL command *SQL_STRING* on the current connection. Returns ? on success, or an error number on failure.

TableList   `Win32::ODBC->TableList(qualifier, owner, name, type)`

Returns the catalog of tables available in the DSN. For an unknown parameter, just specify the empty string "". Returns an array of table names.

Transact   `Win32::ODBC->Transact(type)`

Forces the ODBC connection to perform a rollback or commit transaction. *type* may be one of:

```
SQL_COMMIT
SQL_ROLLBACK
```

Returns true on success, false otherwise.

Version

`Win32::ODBC->Version(`*packages*`)`

Returns an array of version numbers for the requested packages (*ODBC.pm* or *ODBC.PLL*). If the list *packages* is empty, then all version numbers are returned.

Index

We'd like to hear your suggestions for improving our indexes. Send email to *index@oreilly.com*.

defaults() (CGI.pm), 385
defined(), 99
deiconify() (Frame widget), 625
del() (DB_File module), 209
delay() (LWP::RobotUA), 529
Delete() (Win32::Internet module), 652
delete(), 99
    Canvas widget, 615
    CGI.pm module, 385
    Entry widget, 594
    HTML::Parser module, 559
    Listbox widget, 598
    Mail::Send module, 465
    Menu widget, 623
    Net::FTP module, 504
    Net::LDAP, 517
    Net::POP3 module, 460
    Text widget, 602
delete_all() (CGI.pm), 385
delete_content() (HTML::Parser), 559
DeleteKey() (Win32::Registry), 671
delete_label() (Mail::Folder), 468
delete_message() (Mail::Folder), 468
DeleteValue() (Win32::Registry), 671
del_group() (News::Newsrc), 495
delta() (Scrollbar), 596
Deparse backend (Perl compiler), 40
dereferencing, 76
deselect()
    Checkbutton widget, 591
    Radiobutton widget, 592
DESTROY method, 166
Devel::DProf module, 210
DevelopMentor, 435
Devel::PPPort module, 210
Devel::SelfStubber module, 211
diagnostics module, 211
diamond <...> operator, 78
die(), 78, 99
digest()
    Digest modules, 213
    Digest::MD5 module, 215
Digest modules, 212–215
Digest::MD5 module, 213–215
-digits option (Scale), 617
dir() (Net::FTP), 504
directories
    file-related functions, 93
    functions for, 93
directory service, 511
DirHandle module, 215

-disabledforeground option
    (widgets), 587
Disconnect() (Win32::Pipe), 666
disconnect() (DBI), 417
dispatch_from() (SOAP::Lite), 439
Display() (Win32::Console), 632
distinguished name (DN), 512
distributions() (Net::NNTP), 490
division (/) operator, 62
dlineinfo() (Text widget), 602
DN (distinguished name), 512
do(), 100
    DBI module, 418
do statement, conditional modifiers
    with, 52
Doctype handler (Expat), 432
DoctypeFin handler (Expat), 432
documentation, Perl, 25–26, 84–91
    = to signify in programs, 44
    utilities for, 88–91
dollar sign ($), 68
    dereferencing with, 76
    prototype symbol (scalar), 74
    signifying scalar variables, 48
    special variables, 68
domain() (Net::SMTP), 458
do_push() (CGI::Push module), 197
dot (.)
    .. (range) operator, 65
    ... (range) operator, 65
    .= (assignment) operator, 63
    concatenation operator, 65
    Perl debugger command, 148
    regular expression metacharacter, 68
downloading
    Perl language source code, 10
    Perl modules source code, 11, 16–25
dprofpp utility, 157
Drivers() (Win32::ODBC), 694
DropCursor() (Win32::ODBC), 694
Dump() (Data::Dumper), 206
dump(), 100
    CGI.pm module, 385
    HTML::Parser module, 559
DumpData() (Win32::ODBC), 694
Dumper() (Data::Dumper), 206
DumperX() (Data::Dumper), 206
dump_names function
    (ExtUtils::Constant
    module), 226
dump_results() (DBI), 418

S

\S (nonwhitespace) character class, 69
\s (whitespace) character class, 69
S command (Perl debugger), 154
s command (Perl debugger), 154
-S file test operator, 63
-s file test operator, 63
S<> interior sequence (pod), 87
-S option (perlbug), 160
-s option
    dprofpp, 158
    perlbug, 160
s/// (substitution) operator, 66
s pattern match modifier, 66, 73
Safe module, 327
-sav option (perlcc), 41
Save()
    Win32::Registry module, 672
    Win32::Shortcut module, 676
save()
    CGI.pm module, 393
    HTTP::Cookies module, 547
    News::Newsrc module, 496
save_as() (News::Newsrc), 496
scalar(), 50, 128
scalar context, 49
scalar prototype symbol ($), 75
scalars
    arrays of, 48
    functions for manipulating, 93
    lists of, 46, 47
    references, 76
Scalar::Util module, 329
scale() (Canvas), 616
Scale widget (Perl/Tk), 617
scan()
    HTTP::Cookies module, 548
    HTTP::Headers module, 542
scheme() (URI::URL), 571
scope, variable, 50, 74
    functions for, 93
-screen option (toplevel), 625
script_name() (CGI.pm), 393
scripts, Perl examples, obtaining, 13
Scroll() (Win32::Console), 635
Scrollbar widget (Perl/Tk), 577, 595
scrollbars, widget (Perl/Tk), 577
Scrolled() (Perl/Tk), 577
scrolling_list() (CGI.pm), 393
-scrollregion option (Canvas), 608
SDBM_File module, 331

Search::Dict module, 331
search()
    Net::LDAP, 518
    Text widget, 602
searching against LDAP, 513
see()
    Listbox widget, 598
    Text widget, 603
seek(), 128
seekdir(), 129
Seen() (Data::Dumper), 206
Select() (Win32::Console), 636
select(), 129
    Checkbutton widget, 591
    Mail::Folder module, 472
    Radiobutton widget, 592
-selectbackground option (widgets), 589
-selectborderwidth option (widgets), 589
-selectcolor option
    Checkbutton widget, 591
    Menu widget, 622
    Menubutton widget, 620
    Radiobutton widget, 592
-selectforeground option (widgets), 589
-selectimage option
    Checkbutton widget, 591
    Menubutton widget, 620
    Radiobutton widget, 592
selection()
    Entry widget, 594
    Listbox widget, 598
select_label() (Mail::Folder), 472
-selectmode option (Listbox), 597
SelectSaver module, 331
self() (SOAP::Lite), 439
self_and_super_path() (Class::ISA
        module), 198
self_and_super_versions() (Class::ISA
        module), 198
sel.first, sel.last indexes
    Entry widget, 593
    Text widget, 601
SelfLoader module, 332
self_url() (CGI.pm), 394
semaphores, implementing, 672–673
semctl(), 129
semget(), 130
semicolon (;)
    ending Perl statements, 43
    in prototype declarations, 75
semop(), 130

transport protocols, 444
traverse() (HTML::Parser), 561
Tree style (XML::Parser), 432
-troughcolor option
　　Scale widget, 618
　　Scrollbar widget, 596
truncate(), 141
-ts option (form geometry
　　　manager), 585
TTY option (PERLDB_OPTS), 156
Type() (Win32::OLE::Variant), 690
type()
　　Canvas widget, 615
　　Menu widget, 623
　　Net::FTP module, 508
Type option
　　IO::Socket::INET module, 451
　　IO::Socket::UNIX module, 453
typeglob prototype symbol (*), 75
typelookup() (SOAP::Lite), 438

U

\U (uppercase) characters, 70
u command (CPAN.pm), 25
-u file test operator, 63
-U option (dprofpp), 158
-u option (dprofpp), 158
uc(), 141
ucfirst(), 141
$UID ($<) variable, 55
uidl() (Net::POP3), 462
umask(), 142
unary operators, 61
unbind method (Net::LDAP), 516
uncompress command, 12
uncompressing Perl source code, 15
undef(), 142
undef value, 48
undelete_message() (Mail::Folder), 473
-underline option (widgets), 589
underscore (_)
　　filehandle, 58
　　improving number legibility, 45
unescape_from() (Mail::Internet), 476
unicode, 81
uniform resource locators (see URLs)
unique_name() (Net::FTP), 508
UNIVERSAL module, 362
universal resource identifiers (URIs), 526
Unix-domain sockets, 444

Unix systems
　　#! (shebang) line, 33
　　command processing, 34
　　installing Perl on, 12
unless modifier, 52
unless statement, 51
unlink(), 142
unmark() (News::Newsrc), 497
unmarked_articles()
　　　(News::Newsrc), 497
unmark_list() (News::Newsrc), 497
unmark_range() (News::Newsrc), 497
unpack(), 142
unpacking Perl source code, 15
unpack_sockaddr_in() (Socket), 448
unpack_sockaddr_un() (Socket), 448
Unparsed handler (Expat), 431
unpost() (Menu widget), 622
unshift(), 143
unsub_groups() (News::Newsrc), 498
unsubscribe() (News::Newsrc), 498
untie(), 143
until modifier, 52
until statement, 51
update_message() (Mail::Folder), 473
uri() (SOAP::Lite), 436
URI modules, 563–571
　　URI::Escape, 563–568
　　URI::Heuristic, 563
　　URI::URL, 526, 568–571
URIs (universal resource
　　　identifiers), 526
url()
　　CGI.pm module, 398
　　HTTP::Daemon module, 550
　　HTTP::Request module, 538
urllist parameter, CPAN configuration
　　　table, 203
URLs (uniform resource locators), 644
　　encoding, 373
　　extra path information, 373
　　URI::URL module, 526, 568–571
use directives, 163, 165
use_alarm() (LWP::UserAgent), 536
use_named_parameters()
　　　(CGI.pm), 398
Usenet news, 484–498
　　Net::News module, 487–493
　　News::Newsrc module, 493–498
Usenet newsgroups, Perl-related, 6
use(), 143

About the Authors

Nathan Patwardhan is a System Administrator with EDS, where he spends his time working with Solaris and Perl. In his spare time, Nathan is interested in recording his music with Cakewalk software, ogling perly.y, writing, cooking Indian food, baking bread, relaxing with friends, and hanging out with his pets.

Ellen Siever has been an editor, writer, production editor, and tools specialist for O'Reilly & Associates. Previously, she was a programmer for many years in the Boston area. In addition to computers, her interests include her family, travel (especially if it's in the Southwest), and photography.

Stephen Spainhour has contributed to many O'Reilly titles. He is an avid fan of professional tennis (and a terrible player), and when he's not checking for tennis scores on the Web, he enjoys cooking, electronic music, and watching lots of television.

Colophon

Our look is the result of reader comments, our own experimentation, and feedback from distribution channels. Distinctive covers complement our distinctive approach to technical topics, breathing personality and life into potentially dry subjects.

The animal on the cover of *Perl in a Nutshell*, Second Edition, is a camel (one-hump dromedary). Camels are large ruminant mammals, weighing between 1,000 and 1,600 pounds and standing 6 to 7 feet tall at the shoulders. They are well known for their use as draft and saddle animals in the desert regions, especially of Africa and Asia. Camels can go for days without water. If food is scarce, they will eat anything, even their owner's tent. Camels live up to 50 years.

Matt Hutchinson was the production editor and copyeditor for *Perl in a Nutshell*, Second Edition. Darren Kelly and Jeffrey Holcomb provided quality control. Seth Maislin and John Bickelhaupt wrote the index.

Edie Freedman designed the cover of this book. The cover image is a 19th-century engraving from the Dover Pictorial Archive. Emma Colby produced the cover layout with QuarkXPress 4.1 using Adobe's ITC Garamond font.

Melanie Wang designed the interior layout based on a series design by David Futato. Mike Sierra converted the files from XML to FrameMaker 5.5.6 using tools he created, as well as tools written in Perl by Erik Ray, Jason McIntosh, and Neil Walls. The text font is Linotype Birka; the heading font is Adobe Myriad Condensed; and the code font is LucasFont's TheSans Mono Condensed. The illustrations that appear in the book were produced by Robert Romano and Jessamyn Read using Macromedia FreeHand 9 and Adobe Photoshop 6. The tip and warning icons were drawn by Christopher Bing. This colophon was written by Michael Kalantarian.

Other Titles Available from O'Reilly

Perl

Learning Perl, 3rd Edition

By Randal Schwartz &
Tom Phoenix
3rd Edition July 2001
330 pages, ISBN 0-596-00132-0

Learning Perl is the quintessential tutorial for the Perl programming language. The third edition has not only been updated to Perl Version 5.6, but has also been rewritten from the ground up to reflect the needs of programmers learning Perl today. Other books may teach you to program in Perl, but this book will turn you into a Perl programmer.

Mastering Regular Expressions, 2nd Edition

By Jeffrey E. F. Friedl
2nd Edition July 2002 (est.)
456 pages (est.), ISBN 0-596-00289-0

Written by an expert in the topic, this book shows programmers not only how to use regular expressions, but how to think in regular expressions. Updated with a wealth of new material, the second edition explains how to use regular expressions to code complex and subtle text processing that you never imagined could be automated. Included are such key topics as avoiding common errors and optimizing expressions. The book covers many new features added to Perl—a language well endowed with regular expressions—as well as other languages such as Java, Python, and Visual Basic that include support for this powerful tool.

Embedded Perl in HTML with Mason

By Dave Rolsky & Ken Williams
1st Edition October 2002 (est.)
304 pages (est.), ISBN 0-596-00225-4

Mason, a Perl-based templating system, is becoming more and more popular as a tool for building web-sites and managing other dynamic collections. While using Mason is not difficult, creating Mason-based sites can be tricky, and this concise book helps you navigate around the obstacles. The book covers the most recent release of Mason, 1.10, which has many new features including line number reporting based on source files, sub-requests, and simplified use as a CGII. It also explores using Mason for dynamic generation of XML documents.

Perl & XML

By Erik T. Ray & Jason McIntosh
1st Edition April 2002
224 pages, ISBN 0-596-00205-X

Perl & XML is aimed at Perl programmers who need to work with XML documents and data. This book gives a complete, comprehensive tour of the landscape of Perl and XML, making sense of the myriad of modules, terminology, and techniques. The last two chapters of Perl and XML give complete examples of XML applications, pulling together all the tools at your disposal.

Mastering Perl/Tk

By Steve Lidie & Nancy Walsh
1st Edition January 2002
768 pages, ISBN 1-56592-716-8

Beginners and seasoned Perl/Tk programmers alike will find *Mastering Perl/Tk* to be the definitive book on creating graphical user interfaces with Perl/Tk. After a fast-moving tutorial, the book goes into detail on creating custom widgets, working with bindings and callbacks, IPC techniques, and examples using many of the non-standard add-on widgets for Perl/Tk (including Tix widgets). Every Perl/Tk programmer will need this book.

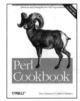

Perl Cookbook

By Tom Christiansen
& Nathan Torkington
1st Edition August 1998
794 pages, ISBN 1-56592-243-3

The *Perl Cookbook* is a comprehensive collection of problems, solutions, and practical examples for anyone programming in Perl. You'll find hundreds of rigorously reviewed Perl "recipes" for manipulating strings, numbers, dates, arrays, and hashes; pattern matching and text substitutions; references, data structures, objects, and classes; signals and exceptions; and much more.

O'REILLY®

To order: *800-998-9938* • *order@oreilly.com* • *www.oreilly.com*
Online editions of most O'Reilly titles are available by subscription at *safari.oreilly.com*
Also available at most retail and online bookstores.

Perl

Computer Science & Perl Programming: Best of The Perl Journal

Edited by Jon Orwant
1st Edition, November 2002 (est.)
600 pages (est.), ISBN 0-596-00310-2

The first of three volumes from the archives of *The Perl Journal* that O'Reilly has exclusive rights to distribute, this book is a compilation of the best from TPJ: 71 articles providing a comprehensive tour of how experts implement computer science concepts in the real world, with code walkthroughs, case studies, and explanations of difficult techniques that can't be found in any other book.

Perl & LWP

By Sean M. Burke
1st Edition, June 2002
464 pages, 0-596-00178-9

This comprehensive guide to LWP and its applications comes with many practical examples. Topics include programmatically fetching web pages, submitting forms, using various techniques for HTML parsing, handling cookies, and authentication. With the knowledge in Perl & LWP, you can automate any task on the Web, from checking the prices of items at online stores to bidding at auctions automatically.

Mastering Algorithms with Perl

By Jon Orwant, Jarkko Hietaniemi & John Macdonald
1st Edition August 1999
704 pages, ISBN 1-56592-398-7

There have been dozens of books on programming algorithms, but never before has there been one that uses Perl. Whether you are an amateur programmer or know a wide range of algorithms in other languages, this book will teach you how to carry out traditional programming tasks in a high-powered, efficient, easy-to-maintain manner with Perl. Topics range in complexity from sorting and searching to statistical algorithms, numerical analysis, and encryption.

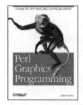

Perl Graphics Programming

By Shawn Wallace
1st Edition, December 2002 (est.)
504 pages (est.), 0-596-00219-X

This insightful volume focuses on scripting programs that enable programmers to manipulate graphics for the Web. The book also helps demystify the manipulation of graphics formats for web newcomers with a practical, resource-like approach. While most of the examples use Perl as a scripting language, the concepts are applicable to any programming language. The book documents ways to use several powerful Perl modules for generating graphics, including GD, PerlMagick, and GIMP.

Programming Web Services with Perl

By Randy J. Ray & Scott Guelich
1st Edition December 2002 (est.)
280 pages (est.), ISBN 0-596-00206-8

O'Reilly presents another Perl first: *Programming Web Services with Perl*. Like most O'Reilly books, it cuts through the hype on web services and concentrates on the useful and practical. It shows how to use Perl to create web services, introducing the major web service standards (XML-RPC, SOAP, WSDL, UDDI) and how to implement Perl servers and clients using these standards. Moving beyond the basics, the book offers solutions to the problems of security, authentication, and scalability.

Practical mod_perl

By Stas Bekman & Eric Cholet
1st Edition December 2002 (est.)
700 pages (est.), ISBN 0-596-00227-0

This is the only book that gives detailed instructions on how to use, optimize, and troubleshoot mod_perl. An excellent place for new mod_perl users to start, *Practical mod_perl* shows how to get this Apache module running quickly and easily. However, the bulk of this insightful volume shows how to take full advantage of the power of mod_perl through discussions on the Perl programming language, Apache's Perl API, and scripts that run under Apache::Registry. The authors provide tips and advice from their experience, as well as those from the mod_perl community at large.

Perl

Programming Perl, 3rd Edition

*Larry Wall, Tom Christiansen &
Jon Orwant*
3rd Edition July 2000
1104 pages, ISBN 0-596-00027-8

Programming Perl is not just a
book about Perl; it is also a
unique introduction to the language and its culture, as one might expect only
from its authors. This third edition has been
expanded to cover Version 5.6 of Perl. New topics
include threading, the compiler, Unicode, and other
features that have been added or improved since
the previous edition.

The Perl CD Bookshelf, Version 3.0

By O'Reilly & Associates, Inc.
Version 3.0 September 2002 (est.)
768 pages, Features CD-ROM
ISBN 0-596-00164-9

Version 3.0 of O'Reilly's *The Perl
CD Bookshelf* gives programmers
convenient online access to their
favorite Perl books, all from their
CD-ROM drive. We've updated this best-selling
product with electronic versions of 7 popular
books. Included are the second edition of *Perl in a
Nutshell*, the third editions of *Learning Perl* and
Programming Perl, the *Perl Cookbook*, and 3 new
titles: *Perl & XML*, *Perl & LWP*, and *Mastering
Perl/Tk*. A paperback version of *Perl in a Nutshell*
rounds out this incredible package.

Programming the Perl DBI

*By Alligator Descartes &
Tim Bunce*
1st Edition February 2000
362 pages, ISBN 1-56592-699-4

The primary interface for database
programming in Perl is DBI. *Programming the Perl DBI* is coauthored by Alligator Descartes, one of the most active
members of the DBI community, and by Tim Bunce,
the inventor of DBI. The book explains the architecture of DBI, shows you how to write DBI-based
programs and explains both DBI's nuances and the
peculiarities of each individual DBD. This is the
definitive book for database programming in Perl.

CGI Programming with Perl, 2nd Edition

By Shishir Gundavaram
2nd Edition July 2000
470 pages, ISBN 1-56592-419-3

Completely rewritten, this comprehensive explanation of CGI
for those who want to provide
their own Web servers features Perl 5 techniques
and shows how to use two popular Perl modules,
CGI.pm and CGI_lite. It also covers speed-up techniques, such as FastCGI and mod_perl, and new
material on searching and indexing, security, generating graphics through ImageMagick, database
access through DBI, Apache configuration, and
combining CGI with JavaScript.

Advanced Perl Programming

By Sriram Srinivasan
1st Edition August 1997
434 pages, ISBN 1-56592-220-4

This book covers complex techniques for managing production-ready Perl programs and explains
methods for manipulating data
and objects that may have looked like magic before.
It gives you necessary background for dealing with
networks, databases, and GUIs, and includes a discussion of internals to help you program more efficiently and embed Perl within C or C within Perl.

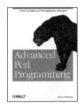

Perl Pocket Reference, 4th Edition

By Johan Vromans
4th Edition July 2002
96 pages, ISBN 0-596-00374-9

The fourth edition of our popular *Perl Pocket Reference* now covers the latest release—Perl
5.8—with a summary of Perl syntax rules, a complete list of operators, built-in functions, and
standard library modules. All with brief, easy-to-find descriptions. You'll find the newest Perl features, such as enhanced regular expressions,
multithreading, the Perl compiler, and Unicode
support. *Perl Pocket Reference* provides a complete
overview of Perl, packed into a convenient pocket-sized guide that's easy to take anywhere.

Perl

Perl for System Administration

By David N. Blank-Edelman
1st Edition July 2000
444 pages, ISBN 1-56592-609-9

Perl for System Administration is aimed at all levels of administrators on the Unix, Windows NT, or Mac OS platforms. Assuming only a little familiarity with Perl, it explores the pockets of administration where Perl can be most useful, including filesystem management, user administration, directory services, database administration, log files, and security and network monitoring. *Perl for System Administration* is for anyone who needs to use Perl for administrative tasks and needs to hit the ground running.

Perl in a Nutshell, 2nd Edition

By Ellen Siever, Stephen Spainhour & Nate Patwardhan
2nd Edition May 2002
768 pages, ISBN 0-59600-241-6

This complete guide to Perl includes the basics of the programming language itself, plus CGI programming, XML processing, network programming, database interaction, and graphical user interfaces. The expanded second edition features the latest version of Perl, and covers modules for recent technologies such as XML and SOAP. This book is for experienced and beginning programmers alike who want a single reference for all their needs.

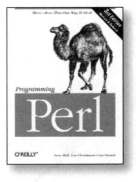

How to stay in touch with O'Reilly

1. Visit our award-winning web site

http://www.oreilly.com/

★ "Top 100 Sites on the Web"—PC Magazine
★ CIO Magazine's Web Business 50 Awards

Our web site contains a library of comprehensive product information (including book excerpts and tables of contents), downloadable software, background articles, interviews with technology leaders, links to relevant sites, book cover art, and more. File us in your bookmarks or favorites!

2. Join our email mailing lists

Sign up to get email announcements of new books and conferences, special offers, and O'Reilly Network technology newsletters at:

http://www.elists.oreilly.com

It's easy to customize your free elists subscription so you'll get exactly the O'Reilly news you want.

3. Get examples from our books

To find example files for a book, go to:

http://www.oreilly.com/catalog

select the book, and follow the "Examples" link.

4. Work with us

Check out our web site for current employment opportunites:

http://jobs.oreilly.com/

5. Register your book

Register your book at:

http://register.oreilly.com

6. Contact us

O'Reilly & Associates, Inc.
1005 Gravenstein Hwy North
Sebastopol, CA 95472 USA
TEL: 707-827-7000 or 800-998-9938
       (6am to 5pm PST)
FAX: 707-829-0104

order@oreilly.com
For answers to problems regarding your order or our products. To place a book order online visit:

http://www.oreilly.com/order_new/

catalog@oreilly.com
To request a copy of our latest catalog.

booktech@oreilly.com
For book content technical questions or corrections.

corporate@oreilly.com
For educational, library, and corporate sales.

proposals@oreilly.com
To submit new book proposals to our editors and product managers.

international@oreilly.com
For information about our international distributors or translation queries. For a list of our distributors outside of North America check out:

http://international.oreilly.com/distributors.html

O'REILLY®

To order: *800-998-9938* • *order@oreilly.com* • *www.oreilly.com*
Online editions of most O'Reilly titles are available by subscription at *safari.oreilly.com*
Also available at most retail and online bookstores.